THE CANADIAN YEARBOOK OF INTERNATIONAL LAW

2011

ANNUAIRE CANADIEN DE DROIT INTERNATIONAL

The Canadian Yearbook of International Law

VOLUME XLIX 2011 TOME XLIX

Annuaire canadien de droit international

Published under the auspices of

THE CANADIAN BRANCH, INTERNATIONAL LAW ASSOCIATION

AND

THE CANADIAN COUNCIL ON INTERNATIONAL LAW

Publié sous les auspices de

LA BRANCHE CANADIENNE DE L'ASSOCIATION DE DROIT INTERNATIONAL

ET

LE CONSEIL CANADIEN DE DROIT INTERNATIONAL

UBCPress

VANCOUVER, BC

Printed in Canada on FSC-certified ancient-forest-free paper that is processed chlorine- and acid-free.

ISBN 978-0-7748-2501-6
ISSN 0069-0058

Canadian Cataloguing in Publication Data

The National Library of Canada has catalogued this publication as follows:

The Canadian yearbook of international law — Annuaire canadien de droit international

Annual.
Text in English and French.
"Published under the auspices of the Canadian Branch, International Law Association and the Canadian Council on International Law."
ISSN 0069-0058

1. International Law — Periodicals.
I. International Law Association. Canadian Branch.
II. Canadian Council on International Law.
III. Title: The Canadian yearbook of international law.
JC 21.C3 341'.05 C75-34558-6E

Données de catalogage avant publication (Canada)

Annuaire canadien de droit international — The Canadian yearbook of international law

Annuel.
Textes en anglais et en français.
«Publié sous les auspices de la Branche canadienne de l'Association de droit international et le Conseil canadien de droit international.»
ISSN 0069-0058

1. Droit international — Périodiques.
I. Association de droit international. Branche canadienne.
II. Conseil canadien de droit international.
III. Titre: Annuaire canadien de droit international.
JC 21.C3 341'.05 C75-34558-6E

UBC Press
University of British Columbia
2029 West Mall
Vancouver, BC V6T 1Z2
www.ubcpress.ca

The Board of Editors, the Canadian Branch of the International Law Association, the Canadian Council on International Law, and the University of British Columbia are not in any way responsible for the views expressed by contributors, whether the contributions are signed or unsigned.

Les opinions émises dans le présent *Annuaire* par nos collaborateurs, qu'il s'agisse ou non d'articles signés, ne sauraient aucunement engager la responsabilité du Comité de rédaction, de la Branche canadienne de l'Association de droit international, du Conseil canadien de droit international ou de l'Université de la Colombie-Britannique.

Communications to the *Yearbook* should be addressed to:
Les communications destinées à *l'Annuaire* doivent être adressées à:

The Editor/Le directeur
The Canadian Yearbook of International Law/
Annuaire canadien de droit international
Faculty of Law, Common Law Section/
Faculté de droit, Section common law
University of/Université d'Ottawa
57 Louis Pasteur
Ottawa, Ontario K1N 6N5 Canada

Contents / Matière

Articles

KATIE SYKES 3 "Nations Like Unto Yourselves": An Inquiry into the Status of a General Principle of International Law on Animal Welfare

48 Sommaire et / and Summary

SARA L. SECK 51 Canadian Mining Internationally and the UN Guiding Principles for Business and Human Rights

115 Sommaire et / and Summary

ATHANASIOS YUPSANIS 117 The International Labour Organization and Its Contribution to the Protection of the Rights of Indigenous Peoples

175 Sommaire et / and Summary

ALBERTO ALVAREZ-JIMENEZ 177 Private Rights, the Use of Maps, State Responsibility, and Other Issues in the International Court of Justice's Boundary Jurisprudence: 2000-10

210 Sommaire et / and Summary

ASHLEY BARNES AND CHRISTOPHER WATERS 213 The Arctic Environment and International Humanitarian Law

240 Sommaire et / and Summary

Notes and Comments / Notes et commentaires

MATTHIEU ALDJIMA NAMOUNTOUGOU 243 Responsabilité pénale des agents ou fonctionnaires internationaux et immunité de juridiction

262 Summary and /et Sommaire

AVINASH SHARMA 265 The Entry into Force of the Lisbon Treaty: The European Union in Retrospect and Prospect

289 Sommaire et / and Summary

THE EDITORS 291 Leslie C. Green (1920-2011)

DONALD M. McRAE 293 Charles B. Bourne (1921-2012)

Chronique de droit international économique en 2010-11 / Digest of International Economic Law in 2010-11

RICHARD OUELLET ET HERVÉ A. PRINCE 295 Commerce

BERNARD COLAS 335 Le Canada et le système financier international en 2010-11

CÉLINE LÉVESQUE 353 Investissement

Canadian Practice in International Law / Pratique canadienne en matière de droit international

381 At the Department of Foreign Affairs and International Trade in 2010-11 / Au ministère des Affaires étrangères et du Commerce international en 2010-11, compiled by / préparé par Alan H. Kessel

419 Parliamentary Declarations in 2011 / Déclarations parlementaires en 2011, compiled by / préparé par Alexandra Logvin

497 Treaty Action Taken by Canada in 2010-11 / Mesures prises par le Canada en matière de traités en 2010-11, compiled by / préparé par Sylvie Cameron

Cases / Jurisprudence

519 Canadian Cases in Public International Law in 2010-11 / Jurisprudence canadienne en matière de droit international public en 2010-11, compiled by / préparé par Gib van Ert, Greg J. Allen, and Eileen Patel

559 Canadian Cases in Private International Law in 2011 / Jurisprudence canadienne en matière de droit international privé en 2011, compiled by / préparé par Joost Blom

599 *Book Reviews / Recensions de livres*

637 *Analytical Index / Index analytique*

645 *Index of Cases / Index de la jurisprudence*

Book Reviews / Recensions de livres

PAGE

Redirecting Human Rights: Facing the Challenge of Corporate Legal Humanity
By Anna Grear
PENELOPE SIMONS 599

The Islamic Law of War: Justifications and Regulations
By Ahmed Al-Dawoody
NATHAN REYES 604

Conflits de lois en droit maritime
Par Sergio M. Carbone
MAREL KATSIVELA 610

The Public International Law Regime Governing International Investment
By José E. Alvarez
OTABEK ISMAILOV 614

The Fog of Law: Pragmatism, Security, and International Law
By Michael J. Glennon
MARY DOMINICK 620

Making the Law of the Sea: A Study in the Development of International Law
Par James Harrison
YACOUBA CISSÉ 625

National Courts and the International Rule of Law
By André Nollkaemper
GIB VAN ERT 632

THE CANADIAN YEARBOOK OF INTERNATIONAL LAW

2011

ANNUAIRE CANADIEN DE DROIT INTERNATIONAL

"Nations Like Unto Yourselves": An Inquiry into the Status of a General Principle of International Law on Animal Welfare

KATIE SYKES

Introduction

An English member of parliament declares the use of wild animals in circuses a "barbaric activity" with "no place in a civilised society."[1] A Canadian self-styled pirate sea captain patrols the Antarctic to sabotage the operations of the Japanese whaling fleet, regarding himself and his crew as enforcers of international law.[2]

Katie Sykes, J.S.D. candidate, Schulich School of Law, Dalhousie University; J.D. (University of Toronto); LL.M. (Harvard University); LL.M. (Schulich School of Law, Dalhousie University). While writing this article, the author was supported by a Joseph-Armand Bombardier Canada Graduate Scholarship from the Social Sciences and Humanities Research Council of Canada and a John Peters Humphrey Fellowship from the Canadian Council on International Law, and benefited from an honourary Killam Scholarship. A previous version of this article was awarded the Ronald St. John Macdonald Young Scholars Award for best paper in the graduate student category (shared award) by the Canadian Council on International Law. The article is based in part on arguments and analysis set forth in the author's LL.M. thesis *The Beasts in the Jungle: Animal Welfare in International Law* (LL.M. thesis, Schulich School of Law, Dalhousie University, 2011) [unpublished]. Some of the ideas were presented at the 2011 Conference of the Canadian Council on International Law, in a joint presentation with Cynthia Westaway. The author is very grateful to Cynthia Westaway, Craig Forcese, and the members of the audience at that presentation for their perceptive questions and to Vaughan Black, Hugh Kindred, and David Vanderzwaag for their erudite and insightful comments on my thesis. The author is profoundly grateful to the editorial team of the *Canadian Yearbook of International Law* for their work on the manuscript, and in particular to the anonymous reviewer whose perspicacious comments pointed the way to significant improvements. All responsibility for the article's defects lies solely with the author.

1 United Kingdom, House of Commons, *Parliamentary Debates*, vol 528, col 499 (19 May 2011) (Bob Russell), online: <http://www.publications.parliament.uk/pa/cm201011/cmhansrd/cm110519/debtext/110519-0001.htm#11051950000005>.

2 For a profile of Paul Watson, leader of the environmental organization Sea Shepherd, see Raffi Katchadourian, "Neptune's Navy," *The New Yorker* (5 November 2007) at 58. Sea Shepherd's website has a page devoted to "Laws and

Environmentalists and (some) defenders of Chinese culture clash over the prospect of bans on the possession and sale of shark fins — used for making the traditional delicacy shark fin soup and controversial because the standard harvesting method is to cut off the fin and throw the shark, lethally wounded but still alive, back in the water.[3] These examples illustrate points where the treatment of animals touches on aspects of international law and policy. The field of animal law is gradually increasing in prominence, both in the academy and in practice (although it remains a specialized interest). However, the welfare of individual animals, as distinct from the conservation of species, is usually thought of as being within the purview of domestic, not international, law and policy.[4] And, yet, the examples cited earlier touch on some themes — the standards of behaviour of "civilized" nations, the confrontation of different cultural perceptions of the boundaries of acceptable behaviour, and the entanglement of animals with transnational issues such as trade or environmental protection — which suggest that the way human beings treat other animals indeed implicates international law.[5]

Charters," where it announces that "Sea Shepherd cooperates fully with all international law enforcement agencies and its enforcement activities complying [*sic*] with standard practices of law and policing enforcement." See Sea Shepherd, online <http://www.seashepherd.org/who-we-are/laws-and-charters.html>.

3 Jared Lindon, "Culture Clash Over Proposed Shark-Fin Ban," *National Post* (14 June 2011), online: <http://news.nationalpost.com/2011/06/14/culture-clash-over-proposed-shark-fin-ban/>.

4 See, eg, Peter L Fitzgerald, "'Morality' May Not Be Enough to Justify the EU Seal Products Ban: Animal Welfare Meets International Trade Law" (2011) 14:2 J Int'l Wildlife L & Pol'y 85 at 96, observing that "animal welfare measures are primarily the province of domestic law and typically reflect local values and customs rather than a broad international consensus."

5 It seems appropriate to acknowledge at the outset the difficulties of terminology in this area, in particular, with the centrally important word "animal." Some prefer to use "nonhuman animal," to stress the biological fact that we humans are animals too and to question the ideological view that sets us on a different plane from all of the rest of them. While I have some sympathy for this perspective, such encapsulations of argument in vocabulary tend to make the argument less persuasive to all but the already converted, and so I have retained the more common usage. A difficulty of imprecision is raised by the compendiousness of the word "animal," referring as it does to so many and such different creatures, from flea to elephant, from oyster to chimpanzee. Jacques Derrida has called attention to the dynamic of power and justice implicated by the naming of animals as a category, asserting that we do not have the right, confronted with the "heterogeneous multiplicity of the living," to name "animal in general." James Derrida, *The Animal That Therefore I Am*, edited by Marie-Louise Mallet, translated by David Wills (New York: Fordham University Press, 2008) at 31.

Douglas Johnston numbers the proponents of animal rights, along with humanists and pacifists, among the representatives of a "transnational ethical community" seeking a reflection of international morality in international law.[6] It has been argued that "the protection of animals from suffering and cruelty" is a "universal issue," one that should be addressed in international law.[7] There are two interwoven themes in this article. The first is an argument that international law on animal welfare both should and does exist. Although it is still very much in the process of emergence, it can be identified as an aspect both of positive law and of the idealistic conception of international law that Johnston calls "civic benevolence."[8] Michael Bowman, Peter Davies, and Catherine Redgwell have proposed that there is a general principle of law concerning animal welfare within the meaning of Article 38 of the Statute of the International Court of Justice (ICJ Statute).[9] This article is in significant part an exploration and evaluation of their proposition. Johnston's model, on the other hand, sees the international legal system as evolving to promote "civic enlightenment through transnational, cross-cultural policies of benevolence to all members of world society."[10] Animal protection fits into this conception of international law, if (and admittedly it is an important "if") it is accepted that animals are also members of world society. This article therefore also examines the status of animal welfare as an example of the kind of shared international morality, or civic benevolence, that Johnston alludes to — in other words, from the standpoint that international law shaped by universal ethical principles is possible and that "objectively justifiable norms of universal scope" exist.[11]

The second theme, which complicates the first, is the reality of the profound differences in cultural beliefs about human obligations

6 Douglas Johnston, *The Historical Foundations of World Order: The Tower and the Arena* (Leiden: Martinus Nijhoff, 2008) at 4.

7 Amy B Draeger, "More Than Property: An Argument for Adoption of the Universal Declaration of Animal Welfare" (2007) 12 Drake J Agric L 277 at 297.

8 Johnston, *supra* note 6 at 131.

9 Michael Bowman, Peter Davies, and Catherine Redgwell, *Lyster's International Wildlife Law*, 2nd edition (Cambridge: Cambridge University Press, 2010) at 680. Statute of the International Court of Justice, 26 June 1945, Can TS 1945 No 7 [ICJ Statute].

10 Johnston, *supra* note 6 at 131.

11 John Tasioulas, "International Law and the Limits of Fairness" (2002) 13 EJIL 993 at 1005.

towards animals. The way human beings use animals is deeply intertwined with some of our most meaningful cultural practices, including cuisine, clothing, spectacle, and hunting. Any claim that such activities are subject to moral or legal constraints imposed from the outside risks triggering nothing but resentment and resistance. In short, the treatment of animals is an instructive example of what Jutta Brunnée and Stephen Toope identify as "the greatest challenge facing international law," namely "to construct normative institutions while admitting and upholding the diversity of peoples in international society."[12]

The methodological approach employed here also combines two separate strands, which are in tension with each other — but productively so. First, much of the article is organized around the application of the interactional theory of international law that Brunnée and Toope have set forth in their recent book.[13] This theory is applied to the various manifestations of a commitment to animal welfare in legal sources, which Bowman, Davies, and Redgwell describe as addressing animal welfare problems in an "ad hoc and piecemeal fashion,"[14] to investigate whether a more generally applicable, consensually recognized principle, with a legal as well as an ethical character, can be extrapolated from this raw material.

The second strand proposes that animal welfare is one of those objectively defensible ethical universals referred to earlier. Brunnée and Toope, for their part, reject "universalizing discourses" about substantive values, and they also all but ignore the general principles of law as a category in their account of international law.[15] This approach makes the marriage of their model with an ethical approach to international law a challenge. However, the analytical tools provided by the interactional theory, which foreground the indispensability of a genuinely interactional and mutual engagement as a condition for creating consensual norms as well as delineating a rigorous distinction between principles that are ethical only and those that have the hallmarks of law, can be very usefully borrowed (even if the borrowing is not completely in the spirit of the original model) to evaluate a postulated universal, ethically grounded legal

12 Jutta Brunnée and Stephen Toope, *Legitimacy and Legality in International Law: An Interactional Account* (Cambridge: Cambridge University Press, 2010) at 21.

13 *Ibid.*

14 Bowman, Davies, and Redgwell, *supra* note 9 at 698.

15 Brunnée and Toope, *supra* note 12 at 79.

norm. In turn, the elements that are excluded from Brunnée and Toope's framework — in particular, general principles of law — indicate how this framework can be considered incomplete as an account of international law from an ethically based perspective (a perspective that, admittedly, differs somewhat from their own). In other words, the interactional framework and the ethical perspective complement each other's shortcomings. Brunnée and Toope's analytical tools and emphasis on interaction impose a salutary discipline on an ethical analysis, and an ethically grounded critique indicates what is lacking in their framework.

The third part of this article is a summary of Brunnée and Toope's model of interactional law. The fourth part considers the category of general principles of law, the perspective of ethical universalism, and the implications of the interactional model's rejection of both. The fifth part is a survey of evidence of a commitment to animal welfare in international legal instruments, and the sixth part evaluates this material using Brunnée and Toope's model. It is perhaps not giving away too much at the beginning to say that animal welfare fails Brunnée and Toope's test for binding international law, but the evaluation does not stop there. The final section of the article returns to the proposition that there is a general principle of international law concerning animal welfare and evaluates it in light of the insights that the interactional analysis yields. However, I begin with something of a detour, which nevertheless introduces some concepts that echo throughout the argument set out here — the idea of international law as a metaphor for the human-animal relationship.

Other Nations

The title of this article comes from a passage in the Koran translated by Raoutsi Hadj Eddine Sari Ali: "No creature is there crawling on the earth, no bird flying with its wings, but they are nations like unto yourselves. We have neglected nothing in the Book; then to their Lord they shall be gathered."[16] Ali notes that the Arabic word *umma,* meaning "nation," derives from "the essential (umm = essence) relationship among individuals, which necessitates awareness of others and responsibility towards them."[17] This description of other

16 Koran 6:38, cited in Raoutsi Hadj Eddine Sari Ali, "Islam," in Council of Europe, ed, *Ethical Eye: Animal Welfare* (Brussels, Belgium: Council of Europe Publishing, 2006) 145 at 145.

17 *Ibid.*

animals as "nations like us" brings to mind a passage from the most important work of the American naturalist Henry Beston, *The Outermost House*, which is an account of his year living and observing the natural world in an outpost on Cape Cod.[18] Reflecting on the flaws in human understanding of animals, Beston writes:

> Remote from universal nature, and living by complicated artifice, man in civilization surveys the creature through the glass of his knowledge and sees thereby a feather magnified and the whole image in distortion. We patronize them for their incompleteness, for their tragic fate of having taken form so far below ourselves. And therein we err, and greatly err. For the animal shall not be measured by man. In a world older and more complete than ours they move finished and complete, gifted with extensions of the senses we have lost or never attained, living by voices we shall never hear. They are not brethren, they are not underlings; *they are other nations,* caught with ourselves in the net of life and time, fellow prisoners of the splendour and travail of the earth.[19]

The juxtaposition of these two sources, invoking the same metaphor from very different cultural traditions and historical contexts, is not just an illustration of the way that diverse cultures reflect common ideas about our relationship with animals. The metaphor that appears in both sources, animals as nations, is powerful and suggestive. It evokes, tantalizingly, the possibility of transcending the "rights" versus "welfare" debate that divides animal law scholars and practitioners. In simplified terms, the argument over whether legal reform for animals should aim at improving the conditions of the lives of animals used for the benefit of human beings, or at reconceptualizing animals as legal persons, with certain inviolable legal rights (which would theoretically preclude their being used as a means to someone else's ends).[20]

Beston's call for "another and a wiser and perhaps a more mystical concept of animals" sheds new light on the difficulties of the rights/welfare dichotomy.[21] Both schools of thought do what Beston says

18 Henry Beston, *The Outermost House* (New York: Owl Books, 1992; first published 1928).

19 *Ibid* at 25 [emphasis added].

20 The literature on this debate is extensive. A useful recent overview is Gary L Francione and Robert Garner, *The Animal Rights Debate: Abolition or Regulation?* (New York: Columbia University Press, 2010).

21 Beston, *supra* note 18 at 24.

we must not do: they measure the animal by man. Rights theorists would make animals equivalent to human beings as bearers of rights — at least, some animals (often those who have characteristics similar to those of human beings, such as intelligence and strong social bonds). To some extent, "welfarists" seek to improve animal well-being, measured by an analogy to positive and negative human physical and mental states — inevitably, since this is what we understand — and traded off against human needs. Both approaches are laudable at least in that they condemn the most brutal forms of animal exploitation. However, Beston's admonition, and the Koranic command, give us cause to reflect on their limitations.

Animals are not versions of ourselves, with capabilities that resemble, but only approximate, ours. Their capabilities, their societies, and their experiences are to a significant extent beyond our knowledge — they are foreign. We live with animals, we are sometimes friends with them and sometimes in competition with them, we often dominate them and are sometimes vulnerable to them, and while we and they are sovereign in important senses our survival is also predicated on our interdependence. The coexistence of the human and animal nations is not entirely unlike the coexistence of nation states.[22]

These reflections suggest that international law may be an especially valuable framework for thinking about justice between human beings and other animals. Such metaphorical extemporizing should not of course be taken to suggest that animals have anything like the legal status of nation states in international law. Far from it — even individual human beings are accorded international legal personality only to a limited extent and in specific circumstances.[23] To the extent that international law deals with animal welfare, it is indeed "welfarist," indicating only outer limits to what can be done to animals for the benefit or pleasure of human beings. Yet even such limits are based on the recognition of animals as sentient

22 Sue Donaldson and Will Kymlicka, in their recent book *Zoopolis* (Oxford: Oxford University Press, 2011), apply the model of citizenship to human-animal relationships (and they too seek to overcome the shortcomings of the "rights versus welfare" dichotomy). Their approach has commonalities with the idea of animal nations, taking the nation as the equivalent of the citizen at the level of international law. It might be useful to think of human beings as having relationships both with individual animals, as "citizens," and with collectivities of animals, the animal nations — with issues of justice implicated in both cases.

23 Ian Brownlie, *Principles of Public International Law,* 7th edition (Oxford: Oxford University Press, 2008) at 57-58, 65, ch 25.

beings,[24] creatures whose well-being and suffering are morally significant (that is, who can meaningfully be described as being well or suffering), and such a conception of animals is not absolutely distinct from the notion of their having "rights." There is an emerging recognition in international law that animals have some significance in themselves and as individual beings, not merely as a means to human ends and not just as members of species.

Later in this article, I will discuss some of the manifestations of this view in international legal instruments and look at how these legal phenomena fit into Brunnée and Toope's interactional theory. Preliminary to that exercise, however, the following section summarizes the interactional framework.

Interactional International Law

Brunnée and Toope's approach is a normative account of international law, but it rejects the enlistment of international law to impose *a priori* normative propositions just because they are (or some think they are) good or desirable. Brunnée and Toope are mindful of how easily the imposition of cultural or political preferences by the powerful on the less powerful can be rationalized as the bringing of enlightenment, or the "civilizing mission" in Koskenniemi's phrase, of international law.[25] Their account combines constructivist ideas about international relations and international law with a theory of the distinctive character of law as a form of social ordering based on Lon Fuller's concept of law's "internal morality," which Fuller describes as a "procedural version of natural justice."[26] Importantly, for Brunnée and Toope, the morality that law reflects, and law itself, are not imposed in a top-down manner. Rather, they are created through a mutual, interactive process of construction. Moreover, law is characterized not so much by the substantive values it expresses as by its "distinctive internal qualities" *as* law — that is, generally, a reasoned, non-arbitrary, and transparent kind of social ordering, as distinguished from tyranny.[27]

Brunnée and Toope's theory is also rooted in the constructivist tradition of international legal and international relations scholarship.

[24] See discussion of the Amsterdam Protocol, *infra* note 159.

[25] Martti Koskenniemi, *The Gentle Civilizer of Nations* (Cambridge: Cambridge University Press, 2002) at 71.

[26] Lon Fuller, *The Morality of Law*, revised edition (New Haven, CT: Yale University Press, 1969) at 4, 96.

[27] Brunnée and Toope, *supra* note 12 at 56.

Constructivism views interaction and mutual constitution as central to the formation of practice, culture, and law.[28] Legal rules do not simply operate to tell social actors what to do, but the construction of law is also a reciprocal process in which legal norms play a role in shaping the mores, preferences, and priorities of individuals and states and are also shaped by them.[29] Paul Schiff Berman sums up this idea of reciprocity as follows: "We all take part in the construction of legal consciousness, even as we are also inevitably affected by the legal categories of the social structures around us."[30]

ELEMENTS OF INTERACTIONAL LAW

There are three elements of binding international law in the interactional account. First, law arises out of common social norms based on "shared understandings," which are only a necessary and not a sufficient condition for the formation of law.[31] What distinguishes commonly recognized social norms from legal ones is that law "arises only when shared understandings come to be intertwined with distinctive internal qualities of law and practices of legality."[32] The second prong of Brunnée and Toope's argument is that "to count as interactional law, norms must meet a set of criteria of legality," and those criteria are Fuller's.[33] The third is that "interactional norms are built, maintained, and sometimes destroyed through a continuing practice of legality."[34] This combination of a basis in shared understandings, adherence to the criteria of legality, and ongoing construction through practices of legality gives rise to legitimate and binding legal norms.[35]

Shared Understandings

The term "shared understandings" refers to a thin or modest version of normative consensus. Brunnée and Toope specifically reject

28 *Ibid* at 13.

29 *Ibid* at 7; Paul Schiff Berman, "Seeing beyond the Limits of International Law" (2006) 84 Tex L Rev 1265 at 1268-70, 1280-95.

30 Berman, *supra* note 29 at 1284.

31 Brunnée and Toope, *supra* note 12 at 43-44, 56.

32 *Ibid.*

33 *Ibid* at 130.

34 *Ibid.*

35 *Ibid.*

any notion of a global society or of universal fundamental values.[36] The prerequisite for engagement in the international process of law making can be as basic as a collective understanding on the part of those involved of "what they are doing and why."[37] However, the process can give rise to, and expand, "normative convergence" on concrete issues.[38] The concept has obvious parallels with John Rawls' concept of overlapping consensus, which is, similarly, distinct from strict consensus on substantive values.[39]

Brunnée and Toope draw on the notion of "norm cycles," which is advanced by Martha Finnemore and Kathryn Sikkink, to shed light on how shared understandings are built up. Finnemore and Sikkink describe three stages in the life cycle of a norm: norm emergence, in which "[n]orm entrepreneurs [who may include such actors as states, non-governmental organizations, and individuals] attempt to convince a critical mass of states (norm leaders) to embrace new norms,"[40] norm acceptance or a norm "cascade," and, finally, internalization, where the norm attains a "'taken-for-granted' quality."[41] The critical shift occurs in the change from emergence

36 *Ibid* at 79.

37 *Ibid* at 13.

38 *Ibid* at 43.

39 John Rawls, "The Idea of an Overlapping Consensus" (1987) 7 Oxford J Leg Legal Stud 1; John Rawls, *A Theory of Justice*, revised edition (Cambridge, MA: Belknap Press, 1999 (original edition published 1971). Rawls' theory of political justice focuses on the institutional framework (the "basic structure") of a polity — that is, on domestic, rather than international, ordering. However, Rawls was also interested in extending the principles he identified, or their analogues, to "the relations between states and the system of cooperation between them" ("Idea of an Overlapping Consensus" at 3, n 3), and he turned to international law in his last book, *The Law of Peoples* (Cambridge, MA: Harvard University Press, 1999). His account of international law based on an overlapping consensus between societies with different values and political structures avoids reducing it to either an unstable *modus vivendi* among states with competing selfish interests (as realism risks doing) or to "universalist claims of a 'community' of states" that, in Brunnée and Toope's words, *supra* note 12 at 79, "obfuscate the reality of deep cultural and social diversity." (It would be remiss to invoke Rawls in a discussion of animals and justice without mentioning the work of Mark Rowlands, who, in *Animals Like Us* (London: Verso, 2002), adapts Rawls' famous thought experiment, the "original position," by including non-human animals, at least those with a mental life — so that each agent choosing the principles of justice in the original position, from behind a "veil of ignorance," does not know whether he or she is a human being or a member of another species.)

40 Martha Finnemore and Kathryn Sikkink, "International Norm Dynamics and Political Change" (1998) 53 Int'l Organization 887 at 895.

41 *Ibid* at 904.

to acceptance, with a threshold or "tipping point" coming after the norm entrepreneurs "have persuaded a critical mass of states to become norm leaders and adopt new norms."[42] This adoption leads to a process of "socialization" whereby the states that have adopted the norm — the "norm leaders" — convince others to adhere to it as well, and more states adopt the norm: "What happens at the tipping point is that enough states and enough critical states endorse the new norm to redefine appropriate behavior for the identity called 'state' or some relevant subset of states (such as a 'liberal' state or a European state)."[43]

Another concept that is useful in the analysis of shared understandings is the idea of an "epistemic community."[44] Epistemic communities are "knowledge-based networks, most often focused on scientific, economic or technical matters," whose members "enjoy authority not merely due to their expertise, but also because of the perceived impartiality of their activities."[45] The recommendation of an epistemic community is often seen as "politically untainted and, therefore, more likely to 'work,' in the political sense that it will be embraced and followed by political authorities concerned about the need for appearing impartial."[46]

Brunnée and Toope see the work of norm entrepreneurs and epistemic communities as being insufficient in themselves to give rise to genuine shared understandings, as what they do can be characterized as "the unidirectional diffusion of norms, rather than as an interactional, mutual process."[47] The interactional and mutual development of norms takes place in the context of "communities of practice,"[48] a constructivist concept that does not take the aims of norm entrepreneurs or the knowledge of epistemic communities

42 *Ibid* at 901.

43 *Ibid* at 902.

44 Brunnée and Toope, *supra* note 12 at 59.

45 *Ibid*; see also Peter Haas, "Epistemic Communities," in Daniel Bodansky, Jutta Brunnée, and Ellen Hey, eds, *The Oxford Handbook of International Law* (Oxford: Oxford University Press, 2007) 792 at 793.

46 Haas, *supra* note 45.

47 Brunnée and Toope, *supra* note 12 at 62.

48 The concept of "communities of practice" was applied to the analysis of international relations by Emanuel Adler (Brunnée and Toope, *supra* note 12). International practices, for Adler (and co-author Vincent Pouliot) are "the dynamic material and ideational processes that enable structures to be stable or to evolve, and agents to reproduce or transform structures." Emanuel Adler and Vincent Pouliot, "International Practices: Introduction and Framework," in

as being pre-existing but, rather, sees them as being formed through engagement in the community: "People's understandings of the world, and of themselves, are produced and reproduced through continuous interactions and negotiations of meanings."[49] The diffusion of norms is not a one-way process of transmission but, rather, involves an "expansion of the community of practice to include a broader range of actors":

> [O]n the one hand, both norm entrepreneurs [and] experts draw on the background knowledge already existing within the various communities of practice to which they belong: on the other hand, it is only when new actors, be they states, international organizations or non-state actors, become actively engaged in a community of practice that its understandings come to be more widely shared (and, possibly, again re-shaped).[50]

Fuller's Criteria of Legality

Fuller believed that the law exhibits certain distinguishing characteristics that are implicit in what he termed the "internal morality of law."[51] The idea that a form of morality is inherent in the nature of law was the crux of Fuller's famous disagreement with Herbert Hart and the legal positivists, who insisted on the separation of law and morals, the distinction between "law as it is and law as it should be."[52] Fuller's parable of Rex, the imaginary king who attempts to promulgate a new system of law for his kingdom but repeatedly fails to do so because his rules lack the basic attributes of law (not publicly promulgated, when promulgated impossible to understand, when clarified they turn out to be contradictory, and so on), shows that Rex's attempts are not just bad law but not law at all.[53] Rex's subjects, by failing to comply with his rules, remain faithful to him as king but are not faithful to his law "because he never made any."[54]

Emanuel Adler and Vincent Pouliot, eds, *International Practices* (Cambridge: Cambridge University Press, 2011) 3.

49 Brunnée and Toope, *supra* note 12 at 62.

50 *Ibid* at 64.

51 Fuller, *supra* note 26 at 4.

52 HLA Hart, "Positivism and the Separation of Law and Morals" (1958) 71 Harv L Rev 593.

53 Fuller, *supra* note 26 at 33-38.

54 *Ibid* at 41.

For Brunnée and Toope, Fuller's legal theory is "a helpful lens through which to reflect on international law" and, in particular, on how obligations under international law, and fidelity to the system of international law, are formed.[55] It provides a response to assertions that international law is not really law because it is not hierarchical or promulgated by a central authority and that compliance is voluntary rather than enforced. Fuller's theory states that these characteristics of authority, command, and force are not what define domestic law, or any kind of law for that matter. (The edicts of King Rex might have exhibited all of those characteristics, but they still would not be law.) Thus, Fuller's account offers an opportunity to rehabilitate international law from its "poor cousin" status and to identify the defining features of legal norms "[w]ithin a conception of law that is non-hierarchical, not defined by the use of force, and mutually constructed by actors who may be both governors and governed (creators and subjects of law)."[56]

Fuller's criteria of legality are: generality (a requirement that "there must be rules" and that cases cannot be determined on an ad hoc basis);[57] promulgation, so that people know the rules they are supposed to observe;[58] the principle that rules should generally be prospective and not retroactive;[59] clarity;[60] avoidance of contradictions;[61] not requiring the impossible;[62] a relative constancy through time (or avoiding such frequent changes that people cannot arrange their behaviour to conform to the rules);[63] and congruence between official actions and declared rules.[64]

Fuller emphasizes the practical necessity that all of these criteria are not to be applied with the utmost stringency in all cases but, rather, must be tailored to circumstances, adjusted in light of what he calls the "external moralities" (or substantive aims) of law, and traded off against one another as appropriate.[65] The art

55 Brunnée and Toope, *supra* note 12 at 7.

56 *Ibid* at 7, 25.

57 Fuller, *supra* note 26 at 46-49.

58 *Ibid* at 49-51.

59 *Ibid* at 51-62.

60 *Ibid* at 63-65.

61 *Ibid* at 65-70.

62 *Ibid* at 70-79.

63 *Ibid* at 79-81.

64 *Ibid* at 81-91.

65 *Ibid* at 45.

of knowing "how, under what circumstances, and in what balance these things should be achieved is no less an undertaking than being a lawgiver."[66]

Brunnée and Toope describe Fuller's position as a "'weak' variety of natural law, in that it contains only a very limited range of substantive commitments"[67] and a "thin conception of the rule of law."[68] They find the agnosticism of Fuller's theory with respect to stronger normative goals well suited to analyzing international law, because it "is congenial to diversity, but permits and encourages the gradual building up of global interaction."[69] It is only through such interaction, they contend, that "ambitious social norms" (such as rights claims and environmental commitments) can become law, for "[t]here is no possibility of simply imposing significant social change by fiat in the absence of some degree of social consensus, expressed in practice."[70]

A Practice of Legality

The third "ingredient" for making international law in Brunnée and Toope's account is a practice of legality — the application of norms in a way that satisfies the criteria of legality.[71] It is through this ongoing practice that "legal norms are built, maintained, and sometimes destroyed."[72] The requirement of a practice of legality means that a good deal of significance is accorded to the actual behaviour of states, whether or not it manifests a commitment to a posited legal norm. Fuller's eighth criterion — congruence between rules and official action — also measures the validity of law in terms of state practice, although here the emphasis on practice is mitigated by the fact that congruence is only one criterion to be looked at in balance with the other seven.

FORMAL LAW AND THE INTERACTIONAL MODEL

Brunnée and Toope stress that what establishes interactional international law is not its inclusion in the formal categories of "sources of law" but, rather, the three elements of shared understandings,

66 *Ibid* at 94.

67 Brunnée and Toope, *supra* note 12 at 29.

68 *Ibid* at 42.

69 *Ibid.*

70 *Ibid* at 32.

71 *Ibid* at 6-7.

72 *Ibid* at 15.

the criteria of legality, and the practice of legality.[73] Formal categories are not irrelevant; they "provide useful indicia of the existence of binding rules and, of course, 'validity' on the terms of the system."[74] However, the fact that a rule is written down in a treaty or deemed to meet the traditional formulation of customary international law does not in itself show that it gives rise to "fidelity" or "any real sense of obligation."[75] For Brunnée and Toope, "it is crucial not to mistake the formal representation of law for successful lawmaking."[76] They seek to resolve the conceptual difficulties of customary international law, particularly the "mystical" element of *opinio juris*, by focusing on "practice rooted in the criteria of legality," which, they say, can be objectively ascertained (unlike the rather metaphysical notion of subjective belief on the part of a state that it is legally bound).[77]

General Principles of Law and Ethical Universalism

Brunnée and Toope examine the formal recognition of treaty and customary law in relation to their interactional framework, but they almost entirely neglect the third category of formal international law listed in the ICJ Statute — general principles of law. This omission is no doubt because they see the taint of the old colonialist "civilizing mission" in the statute's reference to "the general principles of law recognized by civilized nations."[78] This formulation implies that the legitimate sources of legal principles were "limited to Europe (and a handful of 'white' colonies or dominions), the United States of America, a few great Asian civilizations, and a scattering of independent South American states," excluding the laws and traditions of the rest — the "uncivilized."[79] To make matters worse, one of the leading pronouncements on the general principles

73 *Ibid* at 46-52.

74 *Ibid* at 46.

75 *Ibid* at 47.

76 *Ibid.*

77 In a more traditional doctrinal formulation, it might be said that practice of this kind constitutes evidence of *opinio juris* on the part of states. Brunnée and Toope would find this explanation unsatisfying. *Ibid.*

78 ICJ Statute, *supra* note 9, Article 38(1)(c).

79 *Ibid* at 78, here discussing the identical language in Article 38 of the Statute of the Permanent Court of International Justice, 16 December 1920, as amended 14 September 1929, reprinted in (1930) 16 Trans Grotius Soc 131, which was adopted in the ICJ Statute.

of law, the *International Status of South-West Africa* case,[80] involved the continuation of South Africa's colonial mandate over what would eventually (after much more international litigation and armed struggle) become the independent state of Namibia, confirming the association between the European-originated international legal system's "general principles" and the legacy of colonialism and imperialism.[81]

More recently, however, international jurists have conceived of general principles of law very differently, interpreting the text of the ICJ Statute in an evolutionary manner as an inclusive, rather than hegemonic, category of genuinely shared concepts of justice in a diverse world. Judge Christopher Weeramantry of the ICJ, in his separate opinion in the *Case Concerning the Gabčíkovo-Nagymaros Project (Hungary v Slovakia)*, used the concept of general principles of law to bring in examples from his native Sri Lanka[82] as well as from Tanzanian tribes,[83] Iran,[84] China,[85] and the Incan civilization[86] to contribute to the design of a modern legal principle of sustainable development that achieves a balance between economic development and environmental protection. Judge Antonio Cançado Trindade of the ICJ, in a separate opinion in the recent *Case Concerning Pulp Mills on the River Uruguay (Argentina v Uruguay)*, rehabilitates general principles as the moral foundation of international law, describing them as the "basic pillars of the international legal system (as of any legal system)" that "[reflect] the conscience of the international community."[87]

80 *International Status of South-West Africa*, Advisory Opinion, [1950] ICJ Rep 128, which applied the basic principles of the legal trust (common, in the court's view, to "[n]early every legal system" (at 149)) to elucidate the international legal nature and implications of the post-First World War mandate system.

81 Wang Tieya, "The Third World and International Law," in Ronald St John Macdonald and Douglas Johnston, eds, *The Structure and Process of International Law: Essays in Legal Philosophy, Doctrine and Theory* (Dordrecht: Martinus Nijhoff, 1983) 955 at 973.

82 *Case Concerning the Gabčíkovo-Nagymaros Project (Hungary v Slovakia)*, [1997] ICJ Rep 7 at 98-102 [*Gabčíkovo-Nagymaros* case].

83 *Ibid* at 104.

84 *Ibid* at 105.

85 *Ibid.*

86 *Ibid* at 106.

87 *Case Concerning Pulp Mills on the River Uruguay (Argentina v Uruguay)*, [2010] ICJ Rep 135 at para 39.

The disregard of general principles of law in Brunnée and Toope's account (although not unusual in Anglo-American analyses of international law) follows from one of the key premises of the interactional theory. It plays down the possibility of international law based on ethical norms that are genuinely shared in a diverse world, a possibility that is contemplated, even aspired to, in the analyses of Weeramantry and Cançado Trindade JJ. On Brunnée and Toope's own terms, this omission is not a shortcoming — their theory proclaims itself to be agnostic as to substantive principles of justice and suspicious of substantive universalist claims. Yet perhaps they are too ready to give up the possibility of objectively identifiable and consensually recognized ethical parameters for international law — more ready, indeed, than they are themselves apparently happy to be.[88]

The practice of international actors is important to all three of the parts of the formula for interactional law: shared understandings arise in communities of practice; the criteria of legality include congruence between law and practice; and a practice that upholds the legality of a norm is a *sine qua non* for its status as law. In contrast, general principles of law are the category of international law that is least dependent on state practice. The status of a customary norm is based on practice by states and a recognition of its legal character, but general principles of law acquire their status by reason of *recognition* of their intrinsically legal nature, without an overt requirement of consistent practice that adheres to the principle.[89]

The requirement of conforming practice leads Brunnée and Toope to conclude that the international norm prohibiting torture, which is widely considered to be *jus cogens*, may not qualify as international interactional law because contrary state practice is so widespread.[90] (*Jus cogens*, it should be noted, is considered by some scholars to be a subcategory of general principles of law, rather than of customary international law, deriving legal force from the fact that it is based on fundamental and especially compelling principles and not from state practice.[91]) They disagree with the standard arguments that the torture prohibition must have legal force because

88 As indicated in their discussion of their conclusions regarding torture. See discussion in text accompanying note 97.

89 Bin Cheng, *General Principles of International Law as Applied by International Courts and Tribunals* (Cambridge: Grotius Publications, 1987; first published 1953) at 24.

90 Brunnée and Toope, *supra* note 12 at 265-66.

91 See discussion in M Cherif Bassiouni, "A Functional Approach to 'General Principles of International Law'" (1990) 11:3 Mich J Int'l L 768 at 779-81.

states that violate the norm do so in secret or claim that what they are doing is not torture: "In our view, this type of argument has always been an unsatisfying attempt to gloss over weaknesses in the law. It has led to charges that international lawyers are naïve idealists."[92]

Perhaps not surprisingly, Brunnée and Toope are unhappy with the conclusion to which their analysis leads:

> The case of torture points to both the robustness of our interactional analysis of international law and to the hard-headed approach that the analysis demands. Quite frankly, we are not at all comfortable with the conclusion to which our analysis draws us in relation to the prohibition on torture, but we are firmly convinced that the analysis is nonetheless correct.[93]

Torture is surely a limiting case for an ethically defined international jurisprudence. If international law does not really prohibit torture, which must be among the clearest cases of ethically unacceptable conduct, then international law must be unconstrained by ethics. What price is paid for the hard-headedness and robustness that Brunnée and Toope prize in their theory? Practice compliant with norms that protect the powerless — such as torture victims and animals — is always going to be an unlikely occurrence, unless human beings change a great deal. Does this mean we must accept that only law that suits the preferences of the powerful can really become, and remain, binding international law? Brunnée and Toope's logic leads them to one of the puzzles that positivist theories of international law have also failed to solve: can it ever be said that states violate international law if practice that conforms to the law is an absolute requirement for its status as such? And if it is questionable whether international law can be violated, is the law anything more than what states choose to do?[94] The interactional

92 Brunnée and Toope, *supra* note 12 at 260.

93 *Ibid* at 268.

94 This is not to deny the importance of state practice, and indeed of realism, to an ethical view of international law. As Tasioulas, *supra* note 11 at 993, observes, "[t]he normativity of values and norms depends on their being suitably integrated with human capacities, both of individuals and groups. So the need for realism, for the avoidance of issuing utopian prescriptions that are normatively idle, is one that emerges from within the ethical point of view itself." This observation points to why borrowing the tools of the interactional framework is so useful even from an ethical universalist perspective that the framework itself would not support; it helps to ground the ethically oriented analysis and keep it honest.

theory expressly challenges realist models of international law and international relations (notably by bringing out the process of mutuality whereby states' interests and practices are shaped by, and shape, the law), but, fundamentally, its conclusions can depart from those of realism only to a limited degree.

A theory of international law that omits, even denies, the possibility of general principles of law based on what Cançado Trindade J calls the "conscience of the international community" sells short the potential of international law at its best, its promise of justice for the weak and the oppressed. When it comes to animal welfare, a theory in which state practice plays such a defining role is unlikely to have much room for recognizing legal principles that protect animals for their own sake. For human nations, rules of this type always require, at least to some extent, that self-interest yields to a perceived ethical imperative. The animal "other nations" do not have seats at the United Nations and do not get a say in the creation of our international laws (a fact that indicates the limits of the explanatory power of the metaphor).

And yet the interactional framework is an extremely valuable tool for analyzing the emergence of animal welfare as a subject matter of international law. It enables a disciplined, organized investigation of what the "ad hoc and piecemeal" elements of international law addressing animal welfare add up to, if anything, and of whether a genuine international consensus on foundational ethical principles, formed through interaction rather than imposed by the dominant on the recalcitrant, and with the character of a legal norm, really exists.[95]

Animal Welfare in International Law: Sources of Law

This section of the article surveys the evidence for a principle concerning animal welfare in what the Supreme Court of Canada has referred to as "international law and policy"[96] — both the "black

[95] Bowman, Davies, and Redgwell, *supra* note 9 at 698.

[96] *114957 Canada Ltée (Spraytech, Société d'arrosage) v Hudson (Ville)*, 2001 SCC 40, [2001] 2 SCR 241 at para 30 (noting that the regulation of pesticide use by a municipality was "consistent with principles of international law and policy," including the precautionary principle). This category of policy, values, or principles has been described by Mayo Moran as including "'influential authority' which is reducible neither to binding authority nor to what we might call the permissive extreme of persuasive authority," a type of authority whose "demands tend to take shape at the level of *values*." Mayo Moran, "Authority, Influence and Persuasion: *Baker*, *Charter* Values and the Puzzle of Method," in David Dyzenhaus,

letter" law of treaties and the wide range of statements, practices, and manifestations of intention by state and non-state actors in the international system. Both categories are important for the interactional theory, which holds that whether or not a norm is formally recognized by treaty does not end the inquiry as to its status as effective law. Formal indicators of legal force are "but reference points for efforts to understand, build or maintain" the potential of an international legal norm to bind.[97]

There is an abundance of international legal sources manifesting a commitment to animal welfare, but this commitment tends to be a supplemental concern in legal instruments focused primarily on other things, such as conservation or health. The "absence of reference to this matter [animal welfare] in standard and contemporary accounts of international law" has been remarked upon.[98] This very absence might indicate that the "ad hoc and piecemeal" instances of animal welfare protection in international law do not add up to a coherent whole.[99] However, there is evidence of both a widespread recognition of basic, limited obligations towards animals as a matter of legal principle and an increasingly sophisticated, sustained international discourse around the promotion and protection of animal welfare. The following sections summarize some of the most important examples.[100]

INTERNATIONAL WILDLIFE LAW

A sophisticated regime for the conservation, protection, and management of wildlife at the international level has developed since

---

ed, *The Unity of Public Law* (Oxford: Hart Publishing, 2004) 389 at 390-91 [emphasis in the original].

97 Brunnée and Toope, *supra* note 12 at 8. Brunnée and Toope do, however, consider the distinction between binding and non-binding law important and have accused the Supreme Court of Canada of diluting the obligatory nature of binding international law by blurring that distinction in its invocation of "law and policy." Jutta Brunnée and Stephen Toope, "A Hesitant Embrace: *Baker* and the Application of International Law by Canadian Courts," in Dyzenhaus, *supra* note 96, 357 at 358.

98 Bowman, Davies, and Redgwell, *supra* note 9 at 678.

99 *Ibid* at 698.

100 For further discussion of these and other examples, see Bowman, Davies, and Redgwell, *supra* note 9 at 672-99; Michael Bowman, "The Protection of Animals under International Law" (1989) 4 Conn J Int'l L 487; and Bruce A Wagman

the late nineteenth century.[101] Many wildlife conventions also have provisions or associated recommendations or guidelines (such as statements by bodies responsible for monitoring the treaty or regulating practices under it) that seek to promote the welfare and minimize the suffering of individual animals.[102] Since it is largely irrelevant to a species' survival whether individual animals experience well-being or suffering, the fact that attention and energy are expended on these matters is evidence of at least some level of commitment to an independent principle of animal welfare.

Perhaps the most prominent example is the Convention on International Trade in Endangered Species of Wild Fauna and Flora (CITES).[103] This treaty, which regulates international trade in wildlife specimens, has been described as being "replete with provisions relating to the welfare of individual living specimens," although in reality, unfortunately, these obligations "have been routinely disregarded in the practices of many of the parties."[104] CITES requires that living specimens in transit be cared for in such a way as to minimize the risk of injury, damage to health, or "cruel treatment."[105] CITES also provides that confiscated animals that were transported illegally may be placed in a rescue centre established to "look after

---

and Matthew Liebman, *A Worldview of Animal Law* (Durham, NC: Carolina Academic Press, 2011) at 279-335.

101 See generally Bowman, Davies, and Redgwell, *supra* note 9.

102 *Ibid* at 672-99.

103 Convention on International Trade in Endangered Species of Wild Fauna and Flora, 3 March 1973, 993 UNTS 243, Can TS 1975 No 32 (entered into force 1 July 1975) [CITES], reprinted in Mark Austen and Tamara Richards, eds, *Basic Legal Documents on International Animal Welfare and Wildlife Conservation* (London: Kluwer Law International, 2000) at 16.

104 Michael Bowman, "Conflict or Compatibility? The Trade, Conservation and Animal Welfare Dimensions of CITES" (1998) 1 J Int'l Wildlife L & Policy 9 at 10, 59. See also the discussion of the effectiveness and enforcement of CITES more generally in Thomas G Kelch, *Globalization and Animal Law* (Alphen aan den Rijn, The Netherlands: Kluwer Law International, 2011) at 231-37.

105 CITES, *supra* note 103, Article 8(3). Parallel requirements are found in Article 3(2)(c) (export of Appendix I species); Article 3(4)(b) (re-export of Appendix I species); Article 4(2)(c) (export of Appendix II species); Article 4(5)(b) (re-export of Appendix II species); Article 4(6)(b) (introduction from the sea of Appendix II species); Article 5(2)(b) (export of Appendix III species); and Article 7(7)(c) (waivers for travelling exhibitions). However, see Bowman, *supra* note 100 at 43-45, on whether an apparent drafting quirk renders this requirement inoperative.

the welfare of living specimens."[106] The Conference of the Parties (COP) has recommended that import from, and export or re-export to, states that are not members of CITES should only be authorized "in special cases where it benefits the conservation of the species or provides for the welfare of the specimens."[107]

Obviously, if an animal dies in transit or if it is injured or its health compromised to the extent that the risk of death is increased, the objective of the species' conservation is undermined. However, cruel treatment is another matter. An animal could be transported in a way that causes temporary pain, fear, or other forms of suffering, without any implications for the conservation of its species. The recognition under CITES of animal welfare and cruel treatment as subjects to be regulated internationally is an important indicator of global consensus, as CITES is one of the most widely ratified international conservation treaties, with 175 parties.[108]

The proceedings of the CITES COP also provide evidence of an independent concern about cruelty, extending even beyond the parameters of the treaty itself. At the 1983 COP, the Gambian delegation tabled a draft resolution stating that the requirement that animals be "prepared and shipped" in a manner that minimizes the risk of cruel treatment should be understood to cover the manner in which the animal was taken from the wild and, in particular, that export permits should be refused in those cases where specimens are captured using cruel and painful trapping devices. In the end, this measure was not adopted, as it was considered outside the scope of the convention.[109]

Other treaty regimes for wildlife protection also manifest a commitment to the humane treatment of individual animals. One example dates back several decades. The 1958 UN Conference on the Law of the Sea unanimously adopted a resolution requesting states "to prescribe, by all means available to them, those methods for the capture and killing of marine life, especially of whales and seals,

106 CITES, *supra* note 103, Articles 8(4) and 8(5).

107 "Trade with States Not Party to the Convention," Resolution Conf 9.5 (Rev COP14), CITES, COP-9, Fort Lauderdale, United States, 7-18 November 1994, online: <http://www.cites.org/eng/res/all/09/E09-05R14.pdf> [emphasis added].

108 CITES, "What Is CITES?" online: <http://www.cites.org/eng/disc/what.shtml>.

109 Stuart R Harrop, "The International Regulation of Animal Welfare and Conservation Issues through Standards Dealing with the Trapping of Wild Mammals" (2000) 12:3 J Envt'l L 333 at 337-38; Bowman, *supra* note 100 at 27-28.

which will spare them suffering to the greatest extent possible."[110] More recently, Annex II to the 1991 Protocol on Environmental Protection to the Antarctic Treaty provides that "[a]ll taking of native mammals and birds shall be done in the manner that involves the least degree of pain and suffering practicable."[111] The 2004 Addis Ababa Principles and Guidelines for the Sustainable Use of Biodiversity under the Convention on Biological Diversity, which was adopted at COP-7 and intended as a framework for advising various stakeholders on carrying out the objectives of the convention, call for parties to "[p]romote more efficient, *ethical and humane* use of components of biodiversity."[112]

An example that has been the focus of much international attention is the regime for the regulation of whaling under the International Convention for the Regulation of Whaling.[113] Since the 1970s, the International Whaling Commission has been actively involved in studying methods of killing whales, promoting the development of methods that reduce suffering and shorten the time to death, and recommending restrictions on the use of inhumane methods.[114]

INITIATIVES FOCUSING ON ANIMAL WELFARE

The auxiliary, but increasingly important, presence of animal welfare as an objective of international wildlife law has been one factor prompting steps towards the development of an international regime with animal welfare as its central focus. To date, there is still

110 Resolution 5 on the Humane Killing of Marine Life, United Nations Conference on the Law of the Sea, Official Records 144, Doc A/CONF.13/L56 (1958), Vol II, Annexes at 109, cited in Bowman, Davies, and Redgwell, *supra* note 9 at 679.

111 Protocol on Environmental Protection to the Antarctic Treaty, 4 October 1991, 30 ILM 1455, Article 3(6) (entered into force 14 January 1998), Annex II, reprinted in Austen and Richards, *supra* note 103 at 40.

112 Addis Ababa Principles and Guidelines for the Sustainable Use of Biodiversity, Secretariat of the Convention on Biological Diversity, Montreal, 2004, online: <http://www.cbd.int/doc/publications/addis-gdl-en.pdf> at 18 (operational guideline pursuant to Principle 11) [emphasis added]. Convention on Biological Diversity, 5 June 1992, 1760 UNTS 79, Can TS 1993 No 24 (entered into force 29 December 1993).

113 International Convention for the Regulation of Whaling, 2 December 1946, 161 UNTS 72 (entered into force 10 November 1948) [ICRW], reprinted in Austen and Richards, *supra* note 103 at 121.

114 Alexander Gillespie, "Humane Killing: A Recognition of Universal Common Sense in International Law" (2003) 6 J Int'l Wildlife L & Policy 1 at 6-7.

no multilateral animal welfare treaty. However, there have been efforts to develop an international legal instrument — either a treaty or a resolution of the United Nations General Assembly (UNGA) — addressing this issue at a global level. In the 1980s, the International Committee for a Convention for the Protection of Animals began working on a draft International Convention for the Protection of Animals (Protection Convention). This initiative originated in discussions among observer groups at the 1983 CITES COP.[115] The draft convention used a multi-level approach similar to the one commonly adopted for environmental treaties: "[A] series of broadly-stated substantive provisions and organizational and implementation arrangements; a series of related protocols addressing specific animal welfare issues in greater detail; and annexes or appendices itemizing particular care standards and proscribed devices."[116]

A more recent initiative, the Universal Declaration on Animal Welfare (UDAW), was initially proposed in June 2000 by the World Society for the Protection of Animals (WSPA). In contrast to the draft Protection Convention and its protocols, which set out detailed standards for specific situations, the UDAW is an open and general outline of broad guiding principles. This is fitting for a declaration that is proposed for endorsement as a non-binding resolution by the UNGA. If the UDAW is adopted, it is conceivable that it could eventually serve as a conceptual foundation for the adoption of prescriptive, and more detailed, treaty commitments along the lines of the draft Protection Convention.

The text of the draft UDAW has been revised twice and has still not been finalized.[117] The current draft states a commitment to certain basic principles:

- animals (all vertebrates and potentially some invertebrates) are sentient beings whose welfare should be respected;

115 Bowman, *supra* note 100 at 497.

116 *Ibid.* The draft texts of the International Convention for the Protection of Animals and four protocols (the Welfare Protocol of Companion Animals, the Protocol for the Care of Exhibited Wildlife, the Protocol for the Taking of Wild Animals, and the Protocol for the International Transportation of Animals) are available online: <http://www.animallaw.info/treaties/itconfprotanimal.htm>.

117 The provisional draft text of the proposed Universal Declaration on Animal Welfare as of 2011 is available online: <http://s3.amazonaws.com/media.animalsmatter.org/files/resource_files/original/Latest%20draft%20UDAW%20Text%20-%202011.pdf?1314177486>.

- the welfare of animals should be a common objective for states;
- there should be improved measures for animal welfare both nationally and internationally;
- animals should be cared for and treated in a humane and sustainable manner; and
- appropriate policies should be developed for specific situations such as farming and experimentation.

So far, about forty governments have announced their support for the adoption of the UDAW,[118] and the WSPA continues to work towards securing more endorsements (from individuals as well as from governments). On 6 November 2009, Canadian members of parliament voted unanimously in favour of a motion calling on the government to support in principle the development of the UDAW.[119]

WORLD ORGANISATION FOR ANIMAL HEALTH (OIE)

The World Organisation for Animal Health (which has preserved the acronym OIE, based on its former name, the Office International des Epizooties) warrants discussion as an important international institution engaged in the development of animal welfare standards. Its history also reflects the evolution of an international commitment to animal welfare over time. The OIE was created in 1924.[120] At that time, it had no mandate to deal with issues of animal welfare. It was set up as an international response to outbreaks of disease among livestock, which caused economic loss and, in many cases, led to the transmission of infections from animal to human populations.[121] A need was seen for international co-operation in addressing

118 The World Society for the Protection of Animals (WSPA) stated that forty governments have endorsed the UDAW in a news item posted on its website in 2010. WSPA, "Support Grows in Latin America for a UDAW," online: <http://news.animalsmatter.org/>.

119 *House of Commons Debates*, 40th Parl, 2nd Sess, No 109 (6 November 2009) at 1400; WSPA, "UDAW Campaign Reaches Critical Milestone," online: <http://news.animalsmatter.org/page/2>.

120 The constitutive instrument is the 1924 International Agreement for the Creation at Paris of an International Office for Epizootics, 25 January 1924, 57 UNTS 135.

121 Bowman, Davies, and Redgwell, *supra* note 9 at 698. The World Organisation for Animal Health (OIE) was formed following an outbreak of rinderpest ("cattle plague") in Belgium in 1920, originating from cattle in international transit via the Belgian port of Antwerp. OIE, "History," online: <http://www.oie.int/about-us/history/>.

these problems so that if an outbreak occurred in one country it would inform others, enabling them to take action to prevent its spread.[122] The creation of the OIE also meant that there was an internationally recognized organization to look to for scientifically based information on the best methods of combating animal diseases.[123] Today, the OIE is the World Trade Organization's reference organization for standards on animal health, and it publishes codes and manuals on terrestrial and aquatic animal health and sanitary standards.[124]

Since 2001, animal welfare has become an integral aspect of the OIE's responsibilities. This aspect of the OIE's mandate originated in its strategic plan for 2001-05, which identified animal welfare and food safety as two areas for OIE involvement. Both were adopted as strategic initiatives by the OIE World Assembly in 2001.[125] The OIE's animal welfare mandate was reaffirmed by the World Assembly in 2009.[126] The organization has a permanent Animal Welfare Working Group, which was inaugurated by the World Assembly in 2002.[127] Two OIE-sponsored Global Conferences on Animal Welfare have been held, the first in Paris in February 2004[128] and the second in Cairo in October 2008.[129]

122 Bernard Vallat, "Foreword," in *Proceedings of the Global Conference on Animal Welfare: An OIE Initiative, Paris, 2004* (Paris, Luxembourg: Office for Official Publications of the European Communities, 2004) vii at vii, online: <http://www.oie.int/fileadmin/Home/eng/Conferences_Events/docs/pdf/proceedings.pdf> [2004 Conference Proceedings].

123 *Ibid.*

124 OIE, "International Standards," online: <http://www.oie.int/international-standard-setting/overview/>.

125 AC David Bayvel, "The International Animal Welfare Role of the Office International des Epizooties: The World Organisation for Animal Health," in Jacky Turner and Joyce D'Silva, eds, *Animals, Ethics and Trade: The Challenge of Animal Sentience* (London: Earthscan, 2006) 248 at 248.

126 Resolution no 23 on Animal Welfare, 2009, OIE, adopted during the 77th General Session, 24-29 May 2009, Paris, online: <http://www.oie.int/doc/ged/D6124.PDF>.

127 OIE, "The OIE's Objectives and Achievements in Animal Welfare," online: <http://www.oie.int/animal-welfare/animal-welfare-key-themes/>.

128 2004 Conference Proceedings, *supra* note 122.

129 OIE, *Second Global Conference on Animal Welfare: Putting the OIE Standards to Work*, Cairo, Egypt, 20-22 October, 2008, online: <http://www.oie.int/fileadmin/Home/eng/Conferences_Events/sites/A_AW2008/home.htm>.

The OIE's Terrestrial Animal Health Code includes Guiding Principles on Animal Welfare,[130] which were adopted in 2004.[131] The Guiding Principles acknowledge that the use of animals by humans "makes a major contribution to the wellbeing of people" and state that such use "carries with it an ethical responsibility to ensure the welfare of such animals to the greatest extent practicable."[132] To date, the OIE has adopted seven animal welfare standards as part of the Terrestrial Animal Health Code and two welfare standards as part of the Aquatic Animal Health Code.[133]

More generally, the OIE considers its role to be significant to the evolution of the relationship between human beings and other animals. In the foreword to the 2004 conference proceedings, OIE Director-General Bernard Vallat states that "the OIE must also conduct a new mission that has not yet been undertaken at worldwide level, namely to convince all the decision-makers in its member countries of the need to take into account the human-animal relationship in favour of a greater respect for animals."[134]

The important work that the OIE does in harmonizing scientifically based welfare standards is a practical prerequisite to the development of a global approach to regulating animal welfare. Bowman, Davies, and Redgwell observe that "[i]n order to develop a more coherent and co-ordinated regime, certain reforms appear desirable, including the establishment of an acceptable global forum for the elaboration and harmonisation of appropriate welfare standards," and the achievement of this goal requires "as a minimum, the identification of a suitable inter-governmental institution to undertake responsibility for this task."[135] With its adoption of a mandate for animal welfare, the OIE is stepping into the role of such an institution.[136]

ANIMAL WELFARE IN GLOBAL DOMESTIC LAW

One of the clearest signs of an international commitment to animal welfare is the fact that almost every country in the world now has

130 Terrestrial Animal Health Code, 20th edition (OIE, 2011), Article 7.1.2, online: <http://www.oie.int/international-standard-setting/terrestrial-code/access-online/> [Terrestrial Code].

131 OIE, *supra* note 129.

132 Terrestrial Code, *supra* note 130, Articles 7.1.2(5) and 7.1.2(6).

133 Aquatic Animal Health Code, contained in OIE, *supra* note 127.

134 2004 Conference Proceedings, *supra* note 122 at viii.

135 Bowman, Davies and Redgwell, *supra* note 9 at 698.

136 *Ibid.*

some form of domestic law against animal cruelty.[137] A number of countries even have constitutional provisions recognizing the status of animals as sentient beings deserving legal protection. Some of them are European countries, which might be expected given the general perception that Europe prioritizes animal welfare. The German Basic Law provides that "the state shall protect the natural foundations of life and animals by legislation and, in accordance with law and justice, by executive and judicial action, all within the framework of the constitutional order."[138] The Swiss Constitution provides that the federal government shall legislate on the protection of animals and, in particular, on the keeping and care of animals, experiments on animals, the use of animals, imports of animals and animal products, trade in and transport of animals, and animal slaughter,[139] and it specifies that in legislating on the use of reproductive and genetic material from animals, plants, and other organisms the government "shall take account of the dignity of living beings as well as the safety of human beings, animals and the environment."[140]

137 This section is necessarily only a cursory treatment of an extensive field. A much more detailed treatment is found in Bruce Wagman and Matthew Liebman's recent book on comparative animal law, *supra* note 100. Another very useful summary of animal protection laws, organizations, and enforcement practices around the world is found in Neil Trent et al, "International Animal Law, with a Concentration on Latin America, Asia, and Africa," in Deborah J Salem and Andrew N Rowan, eds, *The State of the Animals III 2005* (Washington, DC: Humane Society Press, 2005) 65. The Animal Legal and Historical Center of the University of Michigan College of Law maintains a collection of laws from around the world (as well as some international materials). Animal Legal and Historical Center, online: <http://www.animallaw.info/nonus/index.htm>. See also discussion of the global growth of animal welfare law and of burgeoning public opinion around the world to the effect that animal welfare is an important issue, in Kate Cook and David Bowles, "Growing Pains: The Developing Relationship of Animal Welfare Standards and the World Trade Rules" (2010) Rev Eur Comm & Int'l Envt'l L 227 at 228-29.

138 *Basic Law for the Federal Republic of Germany* (23 May 1949, as amended through 21 July 2010), Article 20a, English version available online: <http://www.gesetze-im-internet.de/englisch_gg/index.html>. The reference to animals was inserted by an amendment in 2002. See discussion in Claudia E Haupt, "The Nature and Effects of Constitutional State Objectives: Assessing the German Basic Law's Animal Protection Clause" (2010) 16:2 Animal L 213.

139 Federal Constitution of the Swiss Confederation (18 April 1999, as amended through 1 January 2011), Article 80, English version available online: <http://www.admin.ch/ch/e/rs/1/101.en.pdf>.

140 *Ibid*, Article 120(2).

The Brazilian Constitution also provides that the government must "protect the fauna and the flora, with prohibition, in the manner prescribed by law, of all practices which represent a risk to their ecological function, cause the extinction of species, or subject animals to cruelty."[141] The first constitutional provision enshrining animal protection was Article 51(A) of the Constitution of India, enacted in 1949 (decades before the human-protecting rights provisions in the Canadian Charter of Rights and Freedoms), which provides that every citizen has a duty "to have compassion for living creatures."[142]

There is, generally speaking, unevenness in the level of protection provided for animals by both legislation and enforcement in different regions of the world, with Africa, East Asia (except Japan), and most of the former Soviet countries generally having the lowest level of legislative standards and enforcement and Europe having the highest.[143] However, even in the countries with lower levels of protection, animal welfare is, even if slowly and incrementally, establishing a place on the political agenda and in public opinion.[144]

China is an especially significant case in light of its stature in international relations and trade. Given China's prominence on the world stage, its position on any issue, including animal welfare, is inevitably influential. Conversely, international public opinion and standards are exerting a growing influence on some areas of Chinese domestic policy, and this effect seems to be happening, gradually, with animal welfare. China is associated with some extremely cruel practices towards animals, including a fur-farming industry in which animals are routinely skinned while alive and conscious[145] and live animal entertainments such as watching big predators tear live animals apart

141 Constitution of the Federative Republic of Brazil (5 October 1988, as amended through 1996), Article 225(I)(VIII), English version available online: <http://pdba.georgetown.edu/Constitutions/Brazil/english96.html>.

142 Constitution of India (26 January 1950, as amended through 23 September 2011), Article 51(A)(g), English version available online: <http://lawmin.nic.in/olwing/coi/coi-english/coi-indexenglish.htm>. *Canadian Charter of Rights and Freedoms,* Part 1 of the *Constitution Act, 1982,* being Schedule B to the *Canada Act 1982* (U.K.), 1982, c. 11.

143 Trent et al, *supra* note 137.

144 Kyle Ash, "The Rights of Nonhuman Animals and World Public Order: A Global Assessment" (1983-84) 38 NYL Sch L Rev 377 at 409.

145 Ros Clubb, "The Welfare of Animals Bred for Their Fur in China," in Turner and D'Silva, *supra* note 125, 180 at 186-89.

for food.[146] There is no general animal welfare law in China. However, the situation is changing. It was announced in 2011 that the horrific circuses and live animal entertainments at Chinese state-owned zoos had been banned.[147] A draft animal welfare law was reportedly considered in 2004[148] and again in 2009.[149] There is also ample evidence of growing consciousness of animal welfare issues and support for such legislation among the Chinese people.[150]

EUROPEAN ANIMAL WELFARE LAW

European law is a species of supranational law that differs from true international law in key ways. In the case of European Union (EU) law, EU member states are automatically bound by virtue of being part of the EU club, in contrast to states' freedom to opt into such international treaties as they choose.[151] Non-member states are, of course, out of the club altogether, and, for them, EU law is equivalent to the domestic law of another state — at most, of comparative interest. Treaties adopted under the aegis of the Council of Europe are more similar to general international treaties in that states can choose whether or not to sign on, but these conventions tend to be framed around concerns and values that are identified as particularly European. The emergence of an especially robust animal protection legal regime in Europe, then, is of limited relevance to the status of animal welfare in international law (and perhaps a sign of a kind of European exceptionalism in this area). Nevertheless, it is an interesting example of the development of animal welfare principles beyond the merely domestic level.

146 Malcolm Moore, "China Bans Animal Circuses," *Daily Telegraph* (18 January 2011), online: <http://www.telegraph.co.uk/news/worldnews/asia/china/8266563/China-bans-animal-circuses.html>, describing "attractions where live chickens, goats, cows and even horses are sold to visitors who can then watch them be torn apart by big cats."

147 *Ibid.*

148 Trent et al, *supra* note 137 at 73.

149 Cook and Bowles, *supra* note 137 at 228.

150 *Ibid* at 229; Song Wei, "Animal Welfare Legislation in China: Public Understanding and Education," in Turner and D'Silva, *supra* note 125, 101; Peter J Li, "The Evolving Animal Rights and Welfare Debate in China: Political and Social Impact Analysis," in Turner and D'Silva, *supra* note 125, 111.

151 And, arguably, to choose whether or not to be bound by customary international law (since states create custom through their practice and recognition of the law and also have the option of remaining unbound by being "persistent objectors"), although this is a more complicated issue.

A number of Council of Europe conventions deal with animal welfare issues. There are treaties on farm animal welfare,[152] the international transportation of animals,[153] animal slaughter,[154] laboratory animals,[155] and pets.[156] The impact of these conventions is subject to certain limitations in practice, both because member states are not obligated to enter into or ratify them and because those that have ratified them can choose to put their provisions into effect either through legislation or, alternatively, through codes of practice or educational programs.[157]

EU law also contains extensive provisions on animal welfare. There is an explicit basis in the constitutive treaties for legislation on this subject. In 1997, the Treaty of Amsterdam Amending the Treaty on European Union, the Treaties Establishing the European Communities and Certain Related Acts (Treaty of Amsterdam),[158] which amended the Consolidated Treaty on European Union,[159] adopted a Protocol on Protection and Welfare of Animals (Amsterdam Protocol),[160] which provides the following:

152 European Convention for the Protection of Animals Kept for Farming Purposes, 10 March 1976, 1976 Eur TS 87 (entered into force 10 September 1978), reprinted in Austen and Richards, *supra* note 103 at 327.

153 European Convention for the Protection of Animals during International Transport, 6 November 2003, CETS 193 (entered into force 14 March 2006).

154 European Convention for the Protection of Animals for Slaughter, 10 May 1979, Eur TS 102 (entered into force 11 June 1982), reprinted in Austen and Richards, *supra* note 103 at 334.

155 European Convention for the Protection of Vertebrate Animals Used for Experimental and Other Scientific Purposes, 18 March 1986, Eur TS 123 (entered into force 1 January 1991), reprinted in Austen and Richards, *supra* note 103 at 356; see also Protocol of Amendment to the European Convention for the Protection of Vertebrate Animals Used for Experimental and Other Scientific Purposes, 22 June 1998, Eur TS 170, reprinted in Austen and Richards, *supra* note 103 at 366.

156 European Convention for the Protection of Pet Animals, 13 November 1987, Eur TS 125 (entered into force 1 May 1994), reprinted in Austen and Richards, *supra* note 103 at 349.

157 David B Wilkins, "Outlawed in Europe: Animal Protection Progress in the European Union" in Turner and D'Silva, *supra* note 125, 219 at 220.

158 Treaty of Amsterdam Amending the Treaty on European Union, the Treaties Establishing the European Communities and Certain Related Acts, 2 October 1997, [1997] OJ C 340/1, 37 ILM 56 (entered into force 1 May 1999).

159 Treaty on European Union, [2010] OJ C 83/13.

160 Protocol on Protection and Welfare of Animals to the Treaty of Amsterdam Amending the Treaty on European Union, the Treaties Establishing the European Communities and Certain Related Acts, [1997] OJ C 340/110 [Amsterdam Protocol].

THE HIGH CONTRACTING PARTIES,
DESIRING to ensure improved protection and respect for the welfare of animals as sentient beings,
HAVE AGREED UPON the following provision which shall be annexed to the Treaty establishing the European Community,

In formulating and implementing the Community's agriculture, transport, internal market and research policies, the Community and the Member States shall pay full regard to the welfare requirements of animals, while respecting the legislative or administrative provisions and customs of the Member States relating in particular to religious rites, cultural traditions and regional heritage.

The Amsterdam Protocol creates an obligation, at least as a procedural matter,[161] to consider animal welfare in creating policy on the specified areas (agriculture, transport, internal market, and research policies). The mandate set out in the Amsterdam Protocol is now Article 13 of the Treaty on the Functioning of the European Union.[162]

Pursuant to this authority, the EU has enacted a number of directives that together make up one of the world's strongest legal regimes for animal protection.[163] Directives are binding on member states, but national authorities are free to choose the form and method used to implement them in domestic law.[164]

This strong legal framework for the protection of animals is seen as the reflection of shared European ideals. In 1961, the Council of Europe declared that "the humane treatment of animals is one of the hall-marks of Western civilisation."[165] For the English biologist

161 See Bowman, Davies, and Redgwell, *supra* note 9 at 680-81 (positing that animal protection may function in international law in general mainly as a procedural principle that requires due regard to be paid to welfare considerations when formulating or implementing policies) and discussion later in this article.

162 Treaty on the Functioning of the European Union, [2010] OJ C 83/47.

163 Critics have argued, however, that EU measures still do not go far enough in certain respects. See, eg, Peter Stevenson, *European Union Law on the Welfare of Farm Animals* (Petersfield, UK: Compassion in World Farming Trust, 2004) at 23-28, online: <http://www.ciwf.org.uk/includes/documents/cm_docs/2008/e/eu_law_2004.pdf>, arguing for the adoption of various reforms to enhance animal protection.

164 *Ibid* at 4.

165 Recommendation no. 287 on the International Transit of Animals, Council of Europe, 13th Sess (Second Part), Doc 1340 (1961). See discussion in Bowman, Davies, and Redgwell, *supra* note 9 at 679; and Egbert Ausems, "The Council of Europe and Animal Welfare" in Council of Europe, *supra* note 16, 233 at 233.

and writer Colin Tudge, the test of a shared European civilization is "our treatment of those who are vulnerable, and cannot fight back if we treat them badly: vulnerable people, and all non-human species."[166] From this point of view, European law protecting animals is not merely a matter of harmonizing rules to facilitate commerce or arming bureaucrats with new checklists but, rather, "to a significant extent ... [a] measure [of] the worth of the European ideal."[167]

Applying the Interactional Framework

This section considers the legal sources surveyed earlier in this article in relation to Brunnée and Toope's framework of interactional international law, with its three central concepts: shared understandings, the criteria of legality, and a practice of legality. It is clear that any general international law of animal welfare is still at an early stage of development, but is it anything more than a collection of "ad hoc and piecemeal" references scattered through disparate legal instruments?[168] This section is an investigation of whether an underlying principle with real legal force can be extrapolated from the source material structured around an evaluation of those sources against the standards of the interactional framework.

Shared Understandings

The question of shared understandings when it comes to animal welfare is a fraught one, given the accusations of ethnocentrism and cultural imperialism that are often levelled at advocates for animal rights. To take one prominent example, Japanese resistance to the prevailing international norm against whaling is often framed as a rejection of alien values. Many Japanese believe that whaling and whale eating are a "distinct and unique" aspect of their culture and that Western pressure to give up these practices is an expression of cultural imperialism and racism.[169]

The accusation of ethnocentrism against the proponents of animal protection is perhaps most eloquently set out by a fictional character, Thomas O'Hearn, the foil for the title character in J.M. Coetzee's

166 Colin Tudge, "Conclusion: Animal Welfare and the Ideal of Europe," in Council of Europe, *supra* note 16, 255 at 255.

167 *Ibid.*

168 Bowman, Davies, and Redgwell, *supra* note 9 at 698.

169 Keiko Hirata, "Why Japan Supports Whaling" (2005) 8 J Int'l Wildlife L & Pol'y 129 at 141-42.

novel *Elizabeth Costello* (who is herself an animal rights advocate, as is the author in real life).[170] In a public debate, O'Hearn expresses a view widely subscribed to among the non-fictional when he says:

> My first reservation about the animal-rights movement … is that by failing to recognize its historical nature, it runs the risk of becoming, like the human-rights movement, yet another Western crusade against the practices of the rest of the world, claiming universality for what are simply its own standards … [Other] cultures have their own norms for the treatment of animals and see no reason to adopt ours, particularly when ours are of such recent invention.[171]

To see animal welfare as an export imposed by "Western civilization" on the rest of the world is, however, to miss significant aspects of its genealogy as a legal norm. Around the late eighteenth to the early nineteenth centuries, England, which in 1822 adopted the first law against animal cruelty to be passed by a national legislature,[172] went through a remarkable transformation, from a nation notorious throughout Europe for appalling animal cruelty to a pioneer of legal protection for animals.[173] An indispensable factor in this sea change was the influence of Indian ideas about the value and moral significance of animals.

India has the oldest constitutional provision on animals. It is also likely that it had the very earliest animal welfare laws. The Indian emperor Ashoka (approximately 274-232 BCE) became a Buddhist convert after he led a violent war of conquest. Following his conversion, Ashoka turned away from violence to embrace mercy and kindness.[174] He embraced a philosophy of compassion and non-violence,

170 JM Coetzee, *Elizabeth Costello* (New York: Viking, 2003).

171 *Ibid* at 105. This passage is used by Maneesha Deckha as the entry point for a discussion of post-colonialism and animal justice in "Animal Justice, Cultural Justice: A Posthumanist Response to Cultural Rights in Animals" (2007) 2 J Animal L & Ethics 189.

172 An Act to Prevent the Cruel and Improper Treatment of Cattle, Geo IV, c 7 [Martin's Act]. The state of Maine adopted an animal cruelty statute one year earlier. See David Favre and Vivien Tsang, "The Development of Anti-Cruelty Laws during the 1800s" (1993) 1 Detroit College L Rev 1 at 8-9.

173 This sea change, and the early development of English animal welfare law, are recounted in Kathryn Shevelow, *For the Love of Animals: The Rise of the Animal Protection Movement* (New York: Henry Holt, 2008).

174 Richard McKeon, "Introduction," in NA Nikam and Richard McKeon (ed and trans), *The Edicts of Ashoka* (Chicago: University of Chicago Press, 1966) v at ix;

and in keeping with this commitment he "vociferously proclaimed" an ethic of animal protection, promulgating a number of edicts requiring that animals be treated "with kindness and consideration."[175] Ashoka's edicts were carved on rocks and pillars, a number of which survive. Among the edicts are a prohibition on the killing of various wild and domestic animals, including "she-goats, ewes and sows which have young or are in milk, and also their young less than six months old"; a rule against animal slaughter in Ashoka's capital city; prohibitions on the castration and branding of animals on certain days; and a rule that "cocks must not be made into capons" (that is, castrated).[176]

These early codes reflected deep religious and cultural traditions that valued compassion, respect, and fellow feeling for other animals and held human beings to be obligated to treat animals with respect and refrain from harming them. The most ancient indigenous Indian religion, Jainism, manifests "an unparalleled concern for life" of all kinds, recognizing a life force not only in animals and plants but also in natural features such as rocks, mountains, and water.[177] In keeping with the Jain doctrine of *ahimsa* — non-violence or refraining from doing harm — adherents follow strictures based on deep respect for other lives, including eating a restrictive vegetarian diet.[178] The doctrine of *ahimsa* is also fundamental in Hinduism, which considers action in accordance with this principle "as the best of all actions."[179]

"Rock Edict XIII" in Nikam and McKeon (at 27) (expressing "profound sorrow and regret because the conquest of a people previously unconquered involves slaughter, death and deportation"); Christopher Key Chapple, *Nonviolence to Animals, Earth and Self in Asian Traditions* (Albany, NY: State University of New York Press, 1993) at 26.

175 Rod Preece, *Sins of the Flesh: A History of Ethical Vegetarian Thought* (Vancouver: UBC Press, 2008) at 69.

176 "Rock Edict I," in Nikam and McKeon, *supra* note 174 at 55-57 (providing that "[n]o living creature shall be slaughtered here ... Many thousand living creatures were formerly slaughtered every day for curries in the kitchens of His Majesty. At present, when this edict on Dharma is prescribed, only three living creatures are killed daily, two peacocks and a deer ... In the future, not even these animals shall be slaughtered.")

177 Chapple, *supra* note 174 at 9-11.

178 *Ibid* at 11.

179 *Ibid* at 17.

Islamic tradition also includes ethical concern for animals.[180] Human use of animals, including meat eating and ritual sacrifice, are certainly permitted, but Islamic scriptural sources portray animals "as having feelings and interests of their own" and humans as owing them "compassionate consideration."[181] The great Mughal Emperor Akbar, who ruled over most of northern and central India in the sixteenth century, is reputed to have "passed laws requiring the protection of mice, oxen, leopards, hares, fish, serpents, horses, sheep, monkeys, roosters, dogs, and hogs, either banning or limiting their slaughter."[182]

The prominent American animal rights scholar Steven Wise has questioned whether the notion of dignity-based rights or equality for animals can find acceptance "in such societies as China, Japan and India, where equality is sometimes pejoratively characterized as a Western ideal."[183] In response, M. Varn Chandola points out that "it is only under Eastern philosophy that the principles of non-violence or *'ahimsa'* have been equally applied to humans and animals alike."[184] Chandola puts forward Indian examples of legal protection for animals that predate Western animal protection laws by centuries. He reports, for example, that some of the kings of the Indian state of Gujarat "were so profoundly influenced by Jainism that they not only prohibited the killing of animals but also set up special courts to prosecute [those who committed] cruelty to them."[185] (To this day, the array of legal protections for animals in India, at both the national and state levels, is extraordinarily comprehensive by the standards of most Western countries.)[186] Chandola sees Wise's statement as evidence of a missed opportunity

180 Ali, *supra* note 16 at 149 (noting that for Muslims "the rights of animals are part of an ethical system … embracing human rules of conduct vis-à-vis all creatures").

181 Richard C Foltz, *Animals in Islamic Tradition and Muslim Cultures* (Oxford: Oneworld Publications, 2006) at 27.

182 *Ibid.* The modifying phrase "very nearly" is, of course, significant.

183 Steven M Wise, "Hardly a Revolution: The Eligibility of Nonhuman Animals for Dignity-Rights in a Liberal Democracy" (1998) 22:4 Vt L Rev 793 at 890.

184 M Varn Chandola, "Dissecting American Animal Protection Law: Healing the Wounds with Animal Rights and Eastern Enlightenment" (2002) 8 Wis Envtl LJ 3 at 28, n 252.

185 *Ibid* at 25.

186 These statutes, as well as codes of practice and some key cases, are brought together in Maneka Gandhi, Ozair Husain, and Raj Panjwani, eds, *Animal Laws of India,* 3rd edition (New Delhi: Universal Law, 2006).

to explore concepts resembling the ideas of rights or equality for animals in Eastern traditions.

One side effect of the British colonial enterprise in India was exposure to Indian ideas about human obligations towards animals. These notions could make a powerful mixture with Enlightenment ideals of rights, equality, justice, and the sanctity of nature. A particularly romantic figure who epitomizes such a cultural meld is the Scottish poet and radical John Oswald. Oswald was an officer in the British army in India until he resigned his commission in protest of the British soldiers' treatment of the Indian people.[187] He travelled extensively in India before returning to England, learning and adopting Hindu customs, including vegetarianism.[188] (He eventually returned to Europe and was killed fighting against the counter-revolutionaries in France.) In 1791, Oswald published *The Cry of Nature*, a pro-vegetarian polemic in which he held up India as a model of humanity in contrast to the brutality of the West:

> [T]he humane mind … turning her eyes to Hindostan, dwells with heartfelt consolation on the happy spot, where mercy protects with her right hand the streams of life, and every animal is allowed to enjoy in peace the portion of bliss which nature prepared it to receive.[189]

Jeremy Bentham's famous presentation, in *Principles of Morals and Legislation*, of a case for legal protection of animals also invokes India as an example to emulate, noting that "[u]nder the Gentoo and Mahometan [Hindu and Muslim] religions, the interests of the rest of animal creation seem to have met with some attention."[190]

The contrast between respect for animal interests in "the happy spot" of India, on the one hand, and, on the other, the disregard for the interests of "the rest of animal creation" manifest in callous and brutal English pastimes such as cockfighting and bear-baiting presented (at least for some) a profound challenge to common assumptions about the moral superiority of the West. Tristram Stuart observes:

[187] Shevelow, *supra* note 173 at 75-80.

[188] *Ibid.*

[189] John Oswald, *The Cry of Nature; or, an Appeal to Mercy and to Justice, on Behalf of the Persecuted Animals*, reprinted in Aaron Garrett, ed, *Animal Rights and Souls in the Eighteenth Century*, volume 4 (Bristol, UK: Theommes Press, 2000) at 81.

[190] Jeremy Bentham, *Principles of Morals and Legislation* (New York: Hafner Publishing, 1961; first published 1789) at 310, n 1.

Attempts to sustain the idea that European Christians had the best society often crumbled in the face of evident virtue and integrity in other peoples. International vegetarianism, which plugged directly into European discourses on diet and the relationship between man and nature, proved a serious challenge to Western norms. As readers back home assimilated the information in the travelogues, Indian vegetarianism started to exert influence on the course of European culture.[191]

So the political and intellectual currents that eventually led to the passage of *An Act to Prevent the Cruel and Improper Treatment of Cattle* — and the transformation of England from a country notorious for brutality to animals to one renowned for soppiness about its pets and wildlife — were set in motion, in significant part, by the inspiration of Indian traditions and perhaps even by an element of moral competitiveness with them.[192] In other words, the first European animal protection law was a product of international interaction.

The near ubiquity of domestic laws protecting animal welfare, the deep roots of these legal provisions in a diversity of cultures and traditions, and the numerous manifestations of a commitment to animal welfare at the international level indicate that there is a convergence of global opinion at least on basic principles concerning animal welfare. One of the case studies that Brunnée and Toope consider, the international climate change regime, is characterized by robust shared understandings about core principles, including the need for an international regime to address climate change and its overall objectives, but is also characterized by considerable divergence on specific commitments.[193] Similarly, in the case of animal welfare, there is a high degree of consensus on foundational principles, including the very basic idea that individual animals have moral significance and that they are "sentient beings" capable of experiencing pleasure and pain, well-being, and suffering. There is also evidence of a shared understanding on a basic concept that informs animal welfare law at all levels — the idea that the way human beings treat animals should be regulated by a kind of proportionality test balancing human purposes against the severity of the

191 Tristram Stuart, *The Bloodless Revolution: A Cultural History of Vegetarianism from 1600 to Modern Times* (New York: WW Norton, 2007) at 59.

192 Martin's Act, *supra* note 172.

193 Brunnée and Toope, *supra* note 12 at 141-77.

suffering involved for the animals.[194] The idea of a proportionality or cost-benefit analysis that takes animal interests into account is captured in vocabulary proscribing the causing of "unnecessary" suffering, forbidding "cruelty" (a term that captures in a single word the idea of unnecessary or gratuitous infliction of pain), or requiring "humane" treatment. I will refer to this core cluster of basic, interrelated principles — animal sentience, animal moral significance, and the proportionality requirement — as the principle of the humane treatment of animals.

Although there is widespread consensus on the principle of humane treatment, there is disagreement about the specifics and especially about the outcome of the proportionality analysis in particular cases. Which human activities are important enough to be given greater weight in the balance (eating hamburgers or eating whales, testing new pharmaceuticals or obtaining ingredients for traditional medicines), and how do we know how much protection and consideration different species are entitled? Protests against the perceived heavy-handed imposition of "Western" standards of animal welfare are often framed as objections to hypocrisy about the application of animal welfare standards but not as a rejection of the idea that there should be such standards.[195]

THE CRITERIA OF LEGALITY

Does the international principle of humane treatment measure up to Fuller's criteria of legality? This section will consider all of the criteria except the last, congruence, which is discussed in the next section. There is a considerable overlap between the criterion of congruence between legal norms and the actions of officials and a

194 As articulated by Justice of Appeal Antonio Lamer (as he then was), interpreting in the domestic Canadian context the criminal offence of animal cruelty (then defined in the Canadian Criminal Code, RSC 1970, c C-34, s 402(1), as willfully causing "unnecessary pain, suffering or injury to an animal or a bird") in *R v Ménard* (1978), 43 CCC (2d) 458 (Que CA) at 465-66: "[T]he legality of a painful operation must be governed by the necessity for it, and even where a desirable and legitimate object is sought to be attained, the magnitude of the operation and the pain caused thereby must not so far outbalance the importance of the end as to make it clear to any reasonable person that the object should be abandoned rather than that *disproportionate suffering* should be inflicted" [emphasis added].

195 See, eg, Hirata, *supra* note 169 at 142, observing that "[t]o the Japanese, it is hypocritical that Westerners consider it morally wrong to kill certain mammals such as whales but consider it acceptable to kill others, such as kangaroos (in Australia) and cattle (in the United States)."

practice of legality — both inquiries look at whether there is in fact an established, ongoing practice of upholding a norm. Brunnée and Toope take the same "blended" approach in assessing the international prohibition on torture, in order to avoid repetition, since the absence of a practice of legality supporting a norm also indicates that the criterion of congruence is not met.[196]

The humane treatment principle is a general rule in that it purports to express an obligation that applies to human beings universally and is based on inherent characteristics of all animals (sentience and moral significance).[197] Cross-cultural controversies about "hypocrisy" in the promotion of animal welfare can be looked at as struggles over the status of the humane treatment principle as a generally applicable, even-handed rule. To some extent, these controversies reflect the difficulty inherent in applying an apparently simple principle to complex facts. While it may be accepted that there are differences in how much certain animals experience suffering and deserve protection relative to others (a fruit fly versus an elephant, for example), agreement on where to draw these lines in specific cases can be elusive.

Versions of the principle (standards requiring "humane" treatment, proscribing "cruelty," and/or outlawing the infliction of "unnecessary suffering") are widely promulgated, mainly in domestic law as well as in many international legal instruments. The principle does not purport to apply retroactively. With respect to clarity, the principle of humane treatment itself is straightforward enough — the complications, again, arise with its application in specific circumstances. There may be general agreement that animals should be treated humanely but not, for example, that this rule requires (or is even satisfied by) the EU directive outlawing "barren" battery cages for egg-laying hens.[198] Similar to the prohibition on torture discussed by Brunnée and Toope, the humane treatment principle has a core of clear meaning but "grey definitional edges."[199] Brunnée and Toope note that "virtually all legal norms contain such 'grey areas'; that is why we emphasize the importance of interpretation through continuing practice."[200]

196 Brunnée and Toope, *supra* note 12 at 259.

197 *Ibid* at 64.

198 EC Council Directive 1999/74 Laying Down Minimum Standards for the Protection of Laying Hens, [1999] OJ L 203/53.

199 Brunnée and Toope, *supra* note 12 at 256.

200 *Ibid.*

The humane treatment principle avoids contradictions in that there is no international norm that *requires* or, arguably at least, expressly *permits* cruelty as such to animals. The desirability of avoiding cruelty may be balanced against other international norms such as trade liberalization, cultural rights, or sovereignty over natural resources, but none of these considerations would actually mandate or authorize cruelty for its own sake. The principle of humane treatment does not demand the impossible. Indeed, the balancing of human purposes and needs against animal welfare requirements, which would preclude impossible demands, is built into its structure. Disagreements may arise about whether a particular regulation or welfare standard imposes too great a burden, but the underlying norm expressly permits the subjugation of animal interests to considerations of what is possible, practicable, or even preferable for human beings. It is not a very onerous standard. Finally, the expression of the humane treatment principle in law has been fairly constant over time since it first began to be encoded in the early nineteenth century (although, again, perceptions of what it requires in practice have tended to shift over time), and, as we have seen, its historical roots go much further back than that.

To sum up, the principle of humane treatment rests on a solid foundation of shared understandings, and it satisfies most of the criteria of legality. As discussed in the next section, however, its chief weakness arises from a widespread lack of commitment manifested in practice, and this weakness would preclude classifying it as a principle of binding law under the interactional framework.

CONGRUENCE AND A PRACTICE OF LEGALITY

As noted in the preceding section, congruence (the final criterion of legality in Fuller's list) and a practice of legality are considered together, as there is significant overlap between the two concepts. There are concrete signs in international law of emergence of a genuinely cross-cultural and interactional practice of legality concerning animal welfare and of some degree of international practice congruent with the principle of humane treatment. Progress does, however, remain limited.

The cause of animal welfare at the international level has been advanced by "norm entrepreneurs" (to use Finnemore and Sikkink's phrase[201]), including international animal-focused non-governmental

201 Finnemore and Sikkink, *supra* note 40.

organizations (NGOs) such as the International Fund for Animal Welfare and the WSPA, which has shepherded the development of the UDAW and persuaded national governments and other influential actors around the world to endorse it. An umbrella organization, the International Coalition for Farm Animal Welfare (ICFAW), was formed in 2001 to represent animal welfare NGOs from around the world at the OIE, providing the OIE with "an internationally based animal welfare body that it can consult during its decision-making process."[202] The efforts of these norm entrepreneurs are redefining the global ethical consensus on the moral significance of animal suffering and the rules that should be in place to mitigate it. Advances in animal protection at the domestic level in many countries (and at the regional level in Europe) also contribute to gradually moving the baseline of acceptable animal welfare practices.

The OIE itself plays a very important role in developing an authoritative and widely accepted discourse on animal welfare standards. Its leadership is based on scientific expertise, and its processes are designed to take account of the input of various stakeholders as well as the regional and cultural aspects of animal welfare issues. The guidelines and codes developed by the OIE, therefore, enjoy the credibility of the products of an "epistemic community," backed up by the impartiality and trustworthiness of an organization of experts.[203]

The increasingly sophisticated and widespread process of generating international law and internationally accepted standards on animal welfare in fora such as the CITES COP, the OIE, and the ICFAW indicates that a community of practice does exist in which international animal welfare norms are being formed, often as an incidental, but increasingly important, concern in an institutional setting established primarily to address something else — for example, conservation or health. Compared to more developed systems such as the international climate change regime that Brunnée and Toope examine, it is still limited and relatively rudimentary, but it does exist.

If a multilateral treaty on animal welfare is eventually created, then a more robust community of practice can be expected to grow

202 David B Wilkins, "Outlawed in Europe: Animal Protection Progress in the European Union" in Turner and D'Silva, *supra* note 125, 219 at 224; see also ICFAW, "Representing Global Animal Welfare Organisations at the OIE," online: <http://www.icfaw.org/index.html>.

203 As the term is used by Haas, *supra* note 45.

from the processes and structures associated with the treaty. Today, the status of animal welfare is perhaps more similar to that of environmentalism a generation or two ago, when the "green internationalism" movement generated the momentum that eventually led to sophisticated legal systems such as the international regulation of climate issues.[204] A burgeoning "international animal" movement is promoting legal initiatives such as drive to adopt the UDAW and is itself, in turn, being constituted through these efforts.

The emergence of laws (both domestic and international) protecting animal welfare over the last two centuries or so has been driven by "an expansion of the community of practice to include a broader range of actors," from the example of India that inspired thinkers such as Oswald and Bentham in the eighteenth century, to the evolution of a strong commitment to animal protection in European law since the 1960s (setting standards that can exert an influence on non-European countries), and continuing now with the progress of animal welfare law in China.[205] It would be inaccurate to see this process as a unidirectional transfer of "Western" values to the rest of the world, although this type of transmission has happened. Rather, the story overall has been, and continues to be, a far more complex one of engagement and negotiation involving the interaction of actors and norms in a context of cross-cultural dialogue, conflict, and accommodation.

There are, however — as might be expected — significant issues with animal welfare as a legal principle when it comes to Fuller's criterion of congruence between stated rules and official actions. The express animal welfare provisions of both international and national law are disregarded and under-enforced to a significant extent. For example, Bowman discusses the evidence of widespread failures to comply with CITES standards for the transportation of animals as well as the failure of states to maintain records as required under CITES on mistreatment and mortality during transportation so that any progress or lack thereof can be effectively monitored.[206] Neil Trent and his colleagues discuss the lack of enforcement of domestic animal welfare law in most, if not all, countries, particularly where resources for law enforcement are scarce.[207] There is strong

[204] Brunnée and Toope, *supra* note 12 at 131.

[205] *Ibid* at 64.

[206] Bowman, *supra* note 100 at 60-61.

[207] Trent et al, *supra* note 137.

evidence — indeed, it is a matter of common sense and common knowledge — that much verbal fealty is paid to the idea of animal welfare, while, in reality, animals are subjected to the most horrific abuses as a matter of course, and with impunity, in (it is probably safe to say) every country in the world.

A General Principle of Law Concerning Animal Welfare

This article now returns to the proposition with which it started — the argument of Bowman, Davies, and Redgwell that there has been "convergence on a general principle of law" protecting animal welfare.[208] The application of the interactional framework points to the conclusion that there is no international animal welfare norm with the character of binding, international law primarily because animal welfare is frequently disregarded in practice. Yet, the interactional framework does not directly address whether animal welfare may be the subject of a general principle of law because it has next to nothing to say about general principles as a category of international law.

The analytical tools that Brunnée and Toope's theory provides are, however, very useful for exploring and testing the suggestion put forward by Bowman, Davies, and Redgwell. General principles are said to be generated by "recognition" by the international community (or perhaps by "civilized nations"). Brunnée and Toope's concept of "shared understandings" unpacks this idea, emphasizing that purportedly consensual norms are only valid if they are based on genuine dialogue and interaction. As John Tasioulas observes, the very possibility of ethically defined international law in a world of diversity depends on such an exchange: "[P]art of the process of converging upon objectively justifiable norms of universal scope will be entering into dialogue with adherents of other traditions."[209] In addition, the criteria of legality distinguish between principles that are ethical desiderata only and those that are legal in nature.

Looked at in this light, the application of the interactional framework both supports the view that a general principle concerning animal welfare exists and also highlights the need for more robust, consistent practice in conformity with this principle. Bowman, Davies, and Redgwell see such a principle as primarily a procedural

208 Bowman, Davies, and Redgwell, *supra* note 9 at 680; see also the discussion in the first section of this article.

209 Tasioulas, *supra* note 11 at 1005.

one, "rendering national decisions amenable to some sort of international institutional review, while reserving ultimate discretion to governments in respect of concrete application," by analogy to the principle of sustainable development as it was applied in the *Gabčíkovo-Nagymaros* case.[210] They also suggest that animal welfare might function "as a 'meta-principle,' i.e., one relevant to the interpretation and amplification of norms established by other means."[211] Thus, the interpretation of international treaties and other instruments that touch on the way animals are treated — even if indirectly — may properly reflect a recognition of these basic principles organizing our relationship with animals. This view is in keeping with the widely recognized interpretive function of general principles of international law in the construction of "ambiguous or uncertain language" and the determination of basic, assumed rights and obligations of states in the context of conventional and customary law.[212] Through the ongoing process of creating international law, the consequences of such an interpretive practice might be far-reaching.

Conclusion

Commitment to animal welfare is a principle that can be credibly claimed to count among the shared values of humankind. It is profoundly intertwined with many of the world's cultures and belief systems, and cross-cultural normative convergence has played an important part in the development of legal protection for animals at both the national and international levels. Understanding animal welfare as a value that crosses (and travels between) different cultures provides important insight into the foundations of animal welfare in international law and a more informed basis for imagining how it is likely to develop in the future. The analysis set out in this article indicates that the principle of humane treatment of animals has already come a considerable way towards becoming established as part of international law and that the groundwork has been laid for this process to continue. In turn, the interactive process of generating international law has the potential to illuminate and enrich our understanding of our relationship with, and obligations towards, other animals — those nations like unto ourselves.

210 Bowman, Davies, and Redgwell, *supra* note 9 at 680.

211 *Ibid* at 681.

212 Bassiouni, *supra* note 91 at 776-77.

Sommaire

Cet article propose l'existence d'un principe général de droit international concernant le traitement sans cruauté des animaux. La préoccupation à l'égard des "droits des animaux" est souvent associée à l'impérialisme culturel occidental se faisant passer pour une éthique universelle. Le bien-être des animaux présente donc une étude de cas instructive de ce que Jutta Brunnée et Stephen Toope ont qualifié du défi principal du droit international, celui de la "[traduction libre] construction d'institutions normatives tout en admettant et en soutenant la diversité des peuples dans la société internationale." L'article emprunte donc l'analyse "interactionnelle " du droit international énoncée par Brunnée et Toope dans leur livre récent *Legitimacy and Legality in International Law,* tout en questionnant le poids qu'accorde cette analyse à la pratique ainsi que leur conclusion que des principes largement reconnus mais non-respectés par les États n'ont pas force de loi. L'article examine également l'émergence de lois interdisant la cruauté envers les animaux, retraçant leurs origines justement à des échanges culturels interactifs entre l'Est et l'Ouest, en particulier entre l'Angleterre et l'Inde. Il conclut que le cadre de Brunnée et Toope, même s'il ne traite pas en profondeur des principes généraux de droit (une source de droit international qui ne s'appuie pas principalement sur la pratique), est néanmoins un outil utile pour comprendre comment un principe contesté au niveau culturel s'inscrit dans le droit international; et soutient en fin de compte qu'il existe un principe général de droit international concernant la protection des animaux.

Summary

This article proposes that there is a general principle of international law concerning the humane treatment of animals. Preoccupation with "animal rights" has been associated with Western cultural imperialism masquerading as a universal ethic. Animal welfare is thus an instructive case study of what Jutta Brunnée and Stephen Toope have identified as the key challenge for international law, that of "construct[ing] normative institutions while admitting and upholding the diversity of peoples in international society." This article applies the framework of interactional international law set out in Brunnée and Toope's recent book *Legitimacy and Legality in International Law,* while raising questions about the weight that their analysis accords to practice and their willingness to conclude that widely recognized principles to which states fail to adhere in practice lack legal force. The article also examines how laws prohibiting cruelty to animals have emerged precisely from an interactive cultural exchange between East and West, in particular, between England and India. It concludes that Brunnée and Toope's framework, although it does not deal at any length with general principles of law (a source of international law in which practice plays a relatively minor role), is nevertheless a useful tool for understanding how a culturally contested principle fits into international law and ultimately supports the view that there is a general principle of international law concerning animal welfare.

Canadian Mining Internationally and the UN Guiding Principles for Business and Human Rights

SARA L. SECK

INTRODUCTION

Between 2005 and 2011, there was much debate both within Canada and at the United Nations (UN) over what role, if any, home states should play in regulating and adjudicating transnational corporate conduct to prevent and remedy associated human rights harms. In June 2005, the Canadian Parliament's Standing Committee on Foreign Affairs and International Trade (SCFAIT) adopted an all-party report of the Parliamentary Subcommittee on Human Rights and International Development entitled *Mining in Developing Countries* [*SCFAIT Report*].[1] The *SCFAIT Report* concludes that "mining activities in some developing countries have had adverse effects on local communities," and it expressed concern that "Canada does not yet have laws to ensure that the activities of Canadian mining companies in developing countries conform to human rights standards."[2] In October 2005, the Canadian government tabled a response rejecting many of the *SCFAIT Report*'s recommendations due in part to the view that the international community was "still in the early stages of defining and measuring" corporate social responsibility (CSR), "particularly with respect to human rights."[3]

Sara L. Seck, Faculty of Law, Western University. The author would like to thank Sheliza Pyarali, David Vaughan, and Aleesha Khan for their excellent research assistance and the Social Sciences and Humanities Research Council of Canada and the Law Foundation of Ontario for financial support.

1 House of Commons, Standing Committee on Foreign Affairs and International Trade (SCFAIT), *Fourteenth Report: Mining in Developing Countries*, 38th Parl, 1st Sess (June 2005) [*SCFAIT Report*].

2 *Ibid* at 1-2.

3 Canada, Department of Foreign Affairs and International Trade (DFAIT), *Mining in Developing Countries — Corporate Social Responsibility: The Government's Response*

Mining in Developing Countries — Corporate Social Responsibility: The Government's Response to the Report of the Standing Committee on Foreign Affairs and International Trade (*Government's Response*) did, however, commit Canada to working with other states to "enhance and clarify the international normative framework for CSR and accountability" and expressed support for the work of Harvard professor John G. Ruggie.[4]

Ruggie had been appointed Special Representative of the UN Secretary-General (SRSG) on the issue of human rights and transnational corporations and other business enterprises in July 2005 — a month after the release of the *SCFAIT Report* — pursuant to a resolution of the Commission on Human Rights (precursor to the UN Human Rights Council) co-sponsored by Canada.[5] Part of his mandate was to "elaborate on the role of States in effectively regulating and adjudicating" business activities relating to human rights.[6] In June 2008, the SRSG presented the *Protect, Respect and Remedy Framework for Business and Human Rights* to the Human Rights Council.[7] *Protect, Respect, and Remedy* rested upon three complementary principles: the state duty to protect against human rights abuses by non-state actors, including business; the corporate responsibility to respect rights; and the need for greater access by victims to effective remedies. It was unanimously welcomed by member states

---

to the Report of the Standing Committee on Foreign Affairs and International Trade (October 2005) at 2-3, 4 [*Government's Response*].

4 *Ibid* at 3-5.

5 UN Commission on Human Rights (CHR), *Human Rights and Transnational Corporations and Other Business Enterprises*, CHR Res 2005/69, UNCHR, 61st Sess, UN Doc E/CN.4/RES/2005/69 (2005). However, Canada is not identified as an ongoing co-sponsor of the mandate by the Special Representative of the UN Secretary-General (SRSG) in his final oral submission to the UN Human Council in May 2011, where he thanks Argentina, India, Nigeria, Norway, and the Russian Federation "for their steadfast leadership and support." See *Ruggie Statement to UN Human Rights Council May 30, 2011*, online: Business and Human Rights Resource Centre <http://www.business-humanrights.org/media/documents/ruggie-statement-to-un-human-rights-council-30-may-2011.pdf>.

6 *Promotion and Protection of Human Rights: Interim Report of the Special Representative of the Secretary-General on the Issue of Human Rights and Transnational Corporations and Other Business Enterprises*, UNCHR, 62nd Sess, UN Doc E/CH.4/2006/97 (22 February 2006) at 1 [*Interim Report*].

7 John Ruggie, *Promotion and Protection of All Human Rights, Civil, Political, Economic, Social and Cultural Rights, Including the Right to Development: Protect, Respect and Remedy: A Framework for Business and Human Rights*, UNHRC, 8th Sess, UN Doc A/HRC/8/5 (2008) [*Protect, Respect, and Remedy*].

in the Human Rights Council, and the SRSG was given a renewed three-year mandate to provide concrete and practical recommendations for its implementation.[8]

The Canadian government reiterated its support for the SRSG's mandate in a 26 March 2009 policy paper entitled *Building the Canadian Advantage: A Corporate Social Responsibility Strategy for the Canadian International Extractive Sector.*[9] Curiously, however, *Building the Canadian Advantage* gave remarkably little space to *Protect, Respect, and Remedy*, which was endorsed more than six months earlier.[10] In May 2011, the SRSG presented a final report to the Human Rights Council consisting primarily of *Guiding Principles on Business and Human Rights: Implementing the United Nations "Protect, Respect and Remedy" Framework* (*Guiding Principles*).[11] The *Guiding Principles* too

8 UN Human Rights Council (HRC), *Mandate of the Special Representative of the Secretary-General on the Issue of Human Rights and Transnational Corporations and Other Business Enterprises*, HRC Res 8/7, UNHRC, 8th Sess, UN Doc A/HRC/RES/8/7 (2008).

9 Canada, DFAIT, *Building the Canadian Advantage: A Corporate Social Responsibility Strategy for the Canadian Extractive Sector* (26 March 2009) at 8, online: <http://www.international.gc.ca/trade-agreements-accords-commerciaux/ds/csr-strategy-rse-stategie.aspx?view=d> [*Building the Canadian Advantage*].

10 *Ibid.* The reference to the SRSG's work is discussed in a single short paragraph within the fifteen-page document: "Obligations under international human rights conventions apply to states and do not directly create obligations for companies … [The UN framework contains] recommendations on the duties and responsibilities of both States and corporations with regard to human rights." Moreover, the list of international standards identified on the website of the Centre for Excellence in CSR, one of the outcomes of *Building the Canadian Advantage*, does not even list *Protect, Respect, and Remedy* among UN international standards. See listed resources under Centre for Excellence in CSR, *Policies and Regulations — United Nations*, online: Centre for Excellence in CSR, <http://web.cim.org/csr/MenuPage.cfm?sections=44&menu=45> (listing the UN Global Compact; the UN Development Programme; the UN Environment Programme; the UNEP Finance Initiative; and the UN Department of Economic and Social Affairs as well as three publications by the United Nations Conference on Trade and Development). The Human Rights Council is not listed nor are *Protect, Respect, and Remedy* or the *Guiding Principles*. See also the extensive list of additional CSR frameworks under *Tools and Resources: CSR Toolkits: Additional CSR Frameworks*, online: Centre for Excellence in CSR <http://web.cim.org/csr/MenuPage.cfm?sections=44,136&menu=138>).

11 John Ruggie, *Report of the Special Representative of the Secretary-General on the Issues of Human Rights and Transnational Corporations and Other Business Enterprises: Guiding Principles on Business and Human Rights: Implementing the United Nations "Protect, Respect and Remedy" Framework*, UNHRC, 17th Sess, UN Doc A/HRC/17/31 (2011) [*Guiding Principles*]. The *Guiding Principles* were accompanied by three

were unanimously endorsed by the Human Rights Council on 16 June 2011, establishing for the first time an international standard, or, in the words of the SRSG, a "global reference point," for business and human rights.[12]

This article begins with a more detailed overview of these as well as other developments in Canada between 2005 and 2011 relating to the regulation and adjudication of human rights concerns associated with global mining. This overview will document the challenges faced by legal reform proposals designed to prevent and remedy global mining harms. In particular, it will discuss the *SCFAIT Report*, the *Government's Response*, and a multi-stakeholder Advisory Group report completed in March 2007.[13] Following this discussion, an account will be given of the arguments put forward in favour of, and against, Bill C-300, An Act Respecting Corporate Accountability for the Activities of Mining, Oil or Gas in Developing Countries, which was defeated in October 2010.[14] An assessment will then be provided of the non-judicial dispute resolution process of the Office of the Extractive Industries CSR Counsellor, which opened the same year.

The article will then turn to a review of the work of the SRSG in relation to the home state duty to protect human rights, highlighting

---

addenda: *Addendum: Piloting Principles for Effective Company/Stakeholder Grievance Mechanisms: A Report of Lessons Learned*, UNHRC, 17th Sess, UN Doc A/HRC/17/3/Add.1 (2011); *Addendum: Human Rights and Corporate Law: Trends and Observations from a Cross-National Study Conducted by the Special Representative*, UNHRC, 17th Sess, UN Doc A/HRC/17/31/Add.2 (2011) [*Corporate Law Addendum*]; and *Addendum: Principles for Responsible Contracts: Integrating the Management of Human Rights Risks into State-Investor Contract Negotiations: Guidance for Negotiators*, UNHRC, 17th Sess, UN Doc A/HRC/17/31/Add.3 (2011).

12 See United Nations Human Rights Office of the High Commissioner, *New Guiding Principles on Business and Human Rights Endorsed by the Human Rights Council*, News Release (16 June 2011), online: Business and Human Rights Resource Centre <http://www.business-humanrights.org/media/documents/ruggie/ruggie-guiding-principles-endorsed-16-jun-2011.pdf>. See also UN Human Rights Commission, *Revised Draft Resolution, Human Rights and Transnational Corporations and Other Business Enterprises*, UNHRC, 17th Sess, UN Doc A/HRC/17/L.17/Rev.1 (2011) (sponsored by Argentina, Austria, Canada, Denmark, Guatemala, India, Nigeria, Norway, Peru, Russian Federation, Sweden, and Turkey).

13 National Roundtables on Corporate Social Responsibility (CSR) and the Canadian Extractive Industry in Developing Countries, *Advisory Group Report*, 29 March 2007, online: <http://www.mining.ca/www/media_lib/MAC_Documents/Publications/CSRENG.pdf> [*Advisory Group Report*].

14 Bill C-300, An Act Respecting Corporate Accountability for Mining, Oil and Gas Corporations in Developing Countries, 2nd Sess, 40th Parl (2009).

the conclusions reached in the *Guiding Principles.* Particular focus will be placed on the non-legally binding nature of many of the *Guiding Principles,* which are notable for their reluctance to recognize explicitly the existence of home state obligations under international human rights law. After a brief assessment of the extent to which Canadian developments may be consistent with the *Guiding Principles,* the article will reflect on the implications of industry and industry lawyer participation in the development of international norms relating to the existence, scope, and content of home state obligations. Specifically, the article will argue that, while engaging corporations and corporate lawyers in both domestic and international processes relating to business and human rights may be necessary for pragmatic reasons, the resulting outcomes appear to be oriented away from legally binding regulation and adjudication. The article will conclude by reflecting upon the implications of this phenomenon for our understanding of international law, justice, and ethics.

Canadian Mining Internationally: From the *SCFAIT Report* to the Advisory Group Report (2005-08)

The June 2005 *SCFAIT Report* arose out of concerns that had been brought before the Subcommittee on Human Rights and International Development over several years in relation to Canadian mining projects in Latin America, Africa, and Asia.[15] The report called upon the Canadian government to implement "stronger incentives" designed to "encourage" mining companies to act "in a socially and environmentally responsible manner and in conformity with international human rights standards" when operating outside of Canada.[16] Specifically identified was the need to make Canadian government export and project financing, as well as services provided at missions abroad, conditional upon compliance with corporate social responsibility and human rights standards, including human rights impact assessments.[17] Stronger monitoring and complaints mechanisms were called for to address claims of

15 *SCFAIT Report, supra* note 1 at 1. See also Sara L Seck, "Home State Responsibility and Local Communities: The Case of Global Mining" (2008) 11 Yale Human Rights & Dev LJ 177 at 177-80 (outlining some of the evidence presented at committee hearings in March and May 2005 by a range of participants, including affected communities, civil society, and mining companies).

16 *SCFAIT Report, supra* note 1 at 2.

17 *Ibid.*

"socially and environmentally irresponsible conduct and human rights violations," and the need to "clarify, formalize and strengthen the rules and the mandate" of Canada's National Contact Point (NCP) for the Organisation for Economic Co-operation and Development's (OECD) Guidelines for Multinational Enterprises (OECD Guidelines) was recognized.[18] Further, Canada was called upon to "[w]ork with like-minded countries" to strengthen the substance of the OECD Guidelines with respect to human rights and to make compliance mandatory.[19] Strikingly, the *SCFAIT Report* explicitly states that there is a need to establish "clear legal norms in Canada to ensure that Canadian companies and residents are held accountable" for environmental and human rights violations "associated with the activities of Canadian mining companies."[20]

The *Government's Response* identified a number of "practical policy challenges" in "translating" the recommendations of the *SCFAIT Report* into practice, including the underdeveloped nature of the "international CSR architecture"; the lack of consensus on "appropriate boundaries between governments, companies and other stakeholders," which leads to a "blurring of lines between public and private responsibilities"; and the need to "reconcile" the "primary responsibility of host governments" with the call for "global business standards and accountability mechanisms."[21] While conceding that more could be done to provide businesses with incentives to achieve positive environmental and social results in their operations abroad, the *Government's Response* took the position that "further developments" would be necessary in the definition and measurement of CSR with respect to human rights before government support could

18 *Ibid* at 2-3. See further OECD, *Guidelines for Multinational Enterprises* (Paris: OECD, 2000), online: OECD <http://www.oecd.org/dataoecd/56/36/1922428.pdf> [OECD Guidelines]; and DFAIT Canada, *Canada's National Contact Point for the OECD MNE Guidelines*, online: DFAIT <http://www.international.gc.ca/trade-agreements-accords-commerciaux/ncp-pcn/index.aspx?lang=eng&menu_id=1> [*Canada's NCP*].

19 *SCFAIT Report*, *supra* note 1 at 3.

20 *Ibid* at 3. Also identified was the importance of the rights of indigenous peoples (*ibid* at 2).

21 *Government's Response*, *supra* note 3 at 2. Furthermore: "[W]hile the Canadian government can influence companies that are headquartered in Canada but where officers are subject to domestic law, it has few mechanisms at its disposal with which to influence companies that are headquartered abroad and managed by non-residents but incorporated in Canada or listed on a Canadian stock exchange" (*ibid* at 3).

be made conditional on companies meeting human rights standards as recommended by the *SCFAIT Report*.[22] Accordingly, other important means of encouraging CSR should be recognized, including market-based incentives such as reporting on social and environmental performance through international reporting initiatives, for example, the Global Reporting Initiative (GRI).[23]

The *Government's Response* specifically disagreed with the *SCFAIT Report*'s recommendations regarding the OECD Guidelines and the NCP process. With respect to the process, the *Government's Response* stated categorically:

> It is clear that the drafters of the OECD Guidelines did not intend the NCP to play an investigative or quasi-judicial role in settling disputes. Rather, the intention was to ... facilitate a positive and constructive dialogue between multinational enterprises (MNEs) and those affected by their operations with a view to finding solutions to problems ... [T]he non-binding, voluntary nature of the Guidelines has significantly increased the ability of like-minded governments to build greater international support than would have been possible had the intention been to build an instrument that was binding.[24]

With regard to the substance of the OECD Guidelines relating to human rights, the *Government's Response* suggested that the OECD was not the most appropriate forum to clarify this issue, as OECD members were largely developed states.[25] In contrast, the UN Human Rights Commission was best positioned to address human rights standards, for its membership was "drawn from all geographic regions, including both developed and developing countries."[26]

22 *Ibid* at 4. However, Export Development Canada (EDC) had already taken steps to address human rights issues "such as involuntary resettlement, compensation, public consultation and Indigenous peoples" as part of "environmental reviews and political risk assessments" (*ibid* at 6). These commitments reflected changes to the Organisation for Economic Co-operation and Development (OECD)'s *Common Approaches on Environment and Officially Supported Export Credits*, which in turn draw upon the experience of development banks, including the World Bank Group. See OECD, *Recommendation on Common Approaches to Export Credits and Environment* (Paris: OECD, 2007), online: OECD <http://www.oecd.org/dataoecd/26/33/21684464.pdf> [*Common Approaches*].

23 *Government's Response, supra* note 3 at 6-7. See Global Reporting Initiative (GRI), online: GRI <https://www.globalreporting.org/Pages/default.aspx>.

24 *Government's Response, supra* note 3 at 7.

25 *Ibid* at 13.

26 *Ibid.*

Accordingly, the Canadian government was committed to working with other states to clarify a human rights framework, notably through support for John Ruggie's work at the UN, and to incorporate "emerging conclusions" into the work of the OECD's Investment Committee.[27]

Arguably, the most controversial recommendation in the *SCFAIT Report* was that Canada establish clear legal norms to ensure that Canadian companies are held accountable for rights violations outside of Canada.[28] This recommendation arose in light of the failed attempts by impacted communities to bring claims against Canadian companies in Canadian courts alleging environmental and human rights harms.[29] The "failure" of these claims was not with regard to their substance, which was never heard by the Canadian courts but, rather, with regard to their likely dismissal on the basis of the common law doctrine of *forum non conveniens*. While the assertion of adjudicative jurisdiction by courts over civil actions is clearly distinct from the exercise of prescriptive jurisdiction through legislation, these categories are not entirely without consequence for one another, as evidenced in the US context where civil actions for violations of the law of nations have been made possible due to the existence of legislation in the form of the Alien Tort Claims Act.[30]

The *Government's Response* asserted that "civil remedies *may* be available to ... foreign plaintiff[s] in Canadian courts" and, thus,

27 *Ibid* at 4-5, 13-14.

28 *SCFAIT Report, supra* note 1.

29 Sara L Seck, "Environmental Harm in Developing Countries Caused by Subsidiaries of Canadian Mining Corporations: The Interface of Public and Private International Law" (1999) 37 Can YB Int'l Law 139 at 154-68 (discussing *Recherches Internationales Québec v Cambior Inc,* [1998] QJ no 2554 (QL) (Qc Sup Ct)) and 168-74 (discussing the Mozambique doctrine); *Seck, supra* note 15 at 183-84 (discussing the Talisman litigation in US courts). See more generally Jennifer A Zerk, *Multinationals and Corporate Social Responsibility* (Cambridge: Cambridge University Press, 2006) at 124-27, 189-240; Craig Scott and Robert Wai, "Transnational Governance of Corporate Conduct through the Migration of Human Rights Norms: The Potential Contribution of Transnational 'Private' Litigation," in C Joerges, P Sand, and G Teubner, eds, *Transnational Governance and Constitutionalism* (Oxford: Hart, 2004) 287; Craig Scott, ed, *Torture as Tort: Comparative Perspectives on the Development of Transnational Tort Litigation* (Portland, OR: Hart Publishing, 2001).

30 Alien Tort Claims Act, 28 USC § 1350 (2000) (providing subject matter jurisdiction for civil actions brought before US federal courts in relation to a modest number of clearly defined norms recognized by the law of nations).

that "Canadian corporations or their directors and employees *may* be pursued in Canada for their wrongdoing in foreign countries."[31] However, the *Government's Response* also acknowledged that, due to the *forum non conveniens* doctrine, "Canadian judges may decide that they should not exercise jurisdiction over a particular claim if another court is better placed to hear the matter."[32] In terms of prescriptive jurisdiction, the *Government's Response* highlighted that "Canadian law does not generally provide for extraterritorial application" as this could raise problems including "conflict with the sovereignty of foreign states; conflicts where states have legislation that differs from that of Canada; and difficulties with Canadian officials taking enforcement action in foreign states."[33] However, where there was a "sufficient nexus" to Canada or "where the international community has agreed ... on the need for such jurisdiction," Canadian law might provide for extraterritorial application.[34]

One proposal in the *SCFAIT Report* that the *Government's Response* did embrace was to hold multi-stakeholder public consultations on problems arising from Canadian mining companies operating in developing countries, with the intention of providing the SCFAIT with recommendations not only for the Canadian government but also for "NGOs, labour organizations, businesses and industry associations."[35] National Roundtables on Corporate Social Responsibility and the Extractive Sector in Developing Countries were accordingly held in four Canadian cities from June to November 2006. An Advisory Group, composed of representatives of Canadian industry and civil society, working closely with an inter-governmental steering committee, issued a report in March 2007.[36] The Advisory Group's

31 *Government's Response, supra* note 3 at 10 [emphasis in original].

32 *Ibid.*

33 *Ibid* at 9.

34 *Ibid.* Criminal law examples provided included: where there is a factual link between Canada and the offence constituting a "real and substantial link" to Canada, although whether asserting jurisdiction would "offend international comity" must still be considered; and where the international community has determined that certain offences are so important that "a country will have jurisdiction to prosecute, regardless of where the acts took place, on the basis of criteria established by treaty (such as the nationality of the offender or victim)." However, there remains the question of whether "the relevant crimes can, as a matter of international law, be committed by corporations" (*ibid* at 9).

35 *Ibid* at 3 (embracing a proposal in the *SCFAIT Report, supra* note 1 at 2).

36 *Advisory Group Report, supra* note 13.

report consisted of extensive consensus-based recommendations, which notably did not include a recommendation that Canada should implement legislation to ensure that allegations of transnational corporate wrongdoing could be heard in Canadian courts.[37] Instead, the Advisory Group's report recommended that the government develop a CSR framework composed of standards that Canadian extractive sector companies operating abroad would be expected to meet, reinforced through "reporting, compliance and other mechanisms," including an independent ombudsman office and a tripartite compliance review committee.[38] The framework standards would initially comprise International Finance Corporation (IFC) standards,[39] supplemented by the Voluntary Principles on Security and Human Rights,[40] with a multi-stakeholder Canadian Extractive Sector Advisory Group advising the government on both the implementation and further development of the CSR framework.[41] The GRI was recommended as the standard to be endorsed for the reporting component of the Canadian CSR framework.[42]

Civil society participants in the Advisory Group had urged the Canadian government to adopt federal legislation to regulate the foreign operations of Canadian extractive companies in accordance with the CSR framework standards, which would be linked to a civil liability system of enforcement.[43] However, industry partici-

37 *Ibid* at 41-45. There was support for the Canadian government to "continue to work with relevant law enforcement authorities to identify and remedy legal and other barriers to the extraterritorial application of Canadian criminal law" and to "[a]mend the Corruption of Foreign Public Officials Act to clarify that it applies extraterritorially to Canadian nationals" (*ibid* at xii, 45).

38 *Ibid* at iii; for details, see 8-24.

39 *Ibid* at 11-14 (stating also that the application and interpretation of these standards "shall observe and enhance respect for principles of the Universal Declaration of Human Rights and other related instruments" and that "[s]pecific guidelines related to the application and interpretation of human rights principles will be developed"). See further International Finance Corporation (IFC) of the World Bank Group, *Sustainability Framework,* online: <http://www1.ifc.org/wps/wcm/connect/Topics_Ext_Content/IFC_External_Corporate_Site/IFC+Sustainability/Sustainability+Framework/>.

40 *Advisory Group Report, supra* note 13 at 11-14. See further Voluntary Principles on Security and Human Rights, online: <http://www.voluntaryprinciples.org/files/voluntary_principles_english.pdf> [Voluntary Principles].

41 *Advisory Group Report, supra* note 13 at iv-v, 58-60.

42 *Ibid* at 15-19. See further GRI, *supra* note 23.

43 *Advisory Group Report, supra* note 13 at 42-44.

pants argued that existing criminal and civil liability regimes under Canadian law, combined with voluntary guidelines, were sufficient.[44] Moreover, industry participants expressed concern that new regulation would "violate rules against extraterritorial legislation, interfere with Canada's foreign policy objectives and damage international trade and investment."[45] Instead, the independent ombudsman office would be "mandated to provide advisory, fact-finding and reporting functions," while the tripartite Compliance Review Committee would "determine the nature and degree of any company non-compliance with the CSR standards."[46] Consideration was also given to how access to government services could serve as a possible incentive mechanism, and a number of government institutions and initiatives that provide financing, insurance, or political services to extractive companies were identified.[47] It was further recommended that a CSR Centre of Excellence be created that could "provide CSR information and advice to Canadian missions, Canadian companies, NGOs, affected communities, host governments and indigenous communities," while also serving to "promote Canada as a country committed to CSR and to the sustainable economic and social development of the countries in which the Canadian extractive industry operates."[48]

The Advisory Group's report explicitly recommended that the Canadian government "exercis[e] influence" within "relevant regional and multinational fora to optimize the positive contribution of the extractive sector," including by supporting and promoting CSR capacity building and advancing the rights of indigenous

44 *Ibid* at 42-44.

45 *Ibid* at 42.

46 *Ibid* at 23-24. This could include referral to an external dispute resolution process (*ibid* at 21-23). The Advisory Group saw the OECD NCP as playing "an important mediation role, a function that could not be assigned to the ombudsman's office" (*ibid* at 23).

47 *Ibid* at 46. These include the EDC, the Canada Fund for Local Initiatives, the Canada Investment Fund for Africa, Canadian International Development Agency, and support provided through trade missions and Canadian embassies (*ibid* at 47-49).

48 *Ibid* at 30-31. On the competitive advantage of CSR, the Advisory Group concluded: "[T]he reputation of meeting or even exceeding CSR standards can offer extractive companies a competitive advantage and increase their overall economic success. The social and environmental performance of Canadian extractive companies can also reflect positively on the long-term success of Canadian business as a whole" (*ibid* at 7).

peoples.[49] It further recommended that Canada continue to support the ongoing work of the SRSG within the UN system.[50] Ultimately, the Advisory Group recommendations were passed along to an inter-governmental Steering Committee, which was to pick from the many recommendations a set of actionable ideas to present to Cabinet for inclusion in a report that was to be sent back to the SCFAIT. While the Advisory Group's report was presented in March 2007, it took until March 2009 for the government to respond officially, perhaps due to the disparate government departments involved as well as a federal election in October 2008.[51] Notably, the inter-departmental Steering Committee, chaired by the Department of Foreign Affairs and International Trade (DFAIT), included representatives from Natural Resources Canada (NRCan), Environment Canada, the Canadian International Development Agency (CIDA), Indian and Northern Affairs Canada, the Department of Justice, Export Development Canada (EDC), and the Privy Council Office.[52] While the wheels of government were slowly turning, the industry-civil society consensus behind the Advisory Group's report began to unravel.

Canadian Mining Internationally: From Bill C-300 to the Office of the CSR Counsellor (2009-11)

February 2009 marked the beginning of a very busy period for those interested in Canada's role in global mining. On 9 February 2009,

49 *Ibid* at 56. These include: the Intergovernmental Forum on Mining, Minerals, Metals and Sustainable Development; the World Mines Ministries Forum; the Mines Ministries of the Americas; the African Mining Partnership; and the Global Gas Flaring Reduction Partnership (*ibid* at 54).

50 *Ibid* at 56. Further recommendations included that Canada endorse the Voluntary Principles on Security and Human Rights by becoming a participant country, and formally participate in the Extractive Industries Transparency Initiative by becoming a supporting country while also encouraging Canadian extractive industries to participate (*ibid* at 56-57).

51 In the interim, Canada became a supporter of the Extractive Industries Transparency Initiative (EITI), online: <http://eiti.org/>. See Department of Finance Canada, *Canada's New Government Supports an International Initiative to Improve Governance in Resource-Rich Countries*, News Release (10 February 2007), online: <http://www.fin.gc.ca/n07/07-012-eng.asp>.

52 *Advisory Group Report*, *supra* note 13 at 2. The presence of representatives from Indian and Northern Affairs Canada on the Steering Committee suggests a keen awareness that the outcome of the roundtables process would not have implications only for Canadian companies engaged in mining internationally but also for mining within Canada on First Nations lands.

Bill C-300 was tabled in Parliament as a private member's bill by Liberal Member of Parliament (MP) John McKay.[53] Just over a month later, the government of Canada released *Building the Canadian Advantage*.[54] One notable proposal in *Building the Canadian Advantage* was to set up an Office of the Extractive Sector CSR Counsellor to "enable" the resolution of "CSR disputes related to the Canadian extractive sector active abroad in a timely and transparent manner."[55] Marketa Evans was appointed to the position in October 2009,[56] and she released the Rules of Procedure for the CSR Counsellor's review mechanism on 20 October 2010, just days before the vote on Bill C-300.[57]

Further proposed legislation aimed at least in part at the global activities of the Canadian mining industry was tabled in Parliament on 1 April 2009 by New Democratic Party MP Peter Julian, in the form of private member's Bill C-354, An Act to Amend the Federal Courts Act (International Promotion and Protection of Human Rights).[58] Unlike either Bill C-300 or the CSR Counsellor, the purpose of Bill C-354 was explicitly to address access to legally binding remedies by non-Canadian plaintiffs for violations of international law.[59] Possible claims that could be brought under Bill C-354

53 Bill C-300, *supra* note 14.

54 *Building the Canadian Advantage*, *supra* note 9.

55 *Ibid* at 10-11.

56 CSR Counsellor, *Background,* online: Department of Foreign Affairs and International Trade <http://www.international.gc.ca/csr_counsellor-conseiller_rse/Background-Contexte.aspx?lang=eng&menu_id=123&view=d>.

57 Canada, *Rules of Procedure for the Review Mechanism of the Office of the Extractive Sector Corporate Social Responsibility Counsellor* (20 October 2010), online: Department of Foreign Affairs and International Trade <http://www.international.gc.ca/csr_counsellor-conseiller_rse/assets/pdfs/rules_procedure-regles_procedure-eng.pdf

58 Bill C-354, An Act to Amend the Federal Courts Act (International Promotion and Protection of Human Rights), 2nd Sess, 40th Parl (2009) [Bill C-354]. Previously known as Bill C-492, it had originally been introduced in Parliament on 10 December 2007. Subsequently, following spring elections in 2011, Bill C-354 was reintroduced as Bill C-323 and received first reading in October 2011.

59 *Ibid.* Section 1 of Bill C-354 provided that section 25 of the Federal Courts Act, RSC 1985, c F-7, be amended to explicitly provide the Federal Court with "original jurisdiction in all cases that are civil in nature in which the claim for relief or remedy arises from a violation of international law or a treaty to which Canada is a party and commenced by a person who is not a Canadian citizen, if the act alleged occurred in a foreign state or territory or on board a ship or aircraft registered in a foreign state while the ship or aircraft is outside Canada."

included those arising from a consistent pattern of gross violations of internationally recognized human rights as well as violations of various international labour and environmental rules.[60] While Bill C-354 itself made no specific mention of business enterprises, Peter Julian explicitly linked it to increased corporate accountability in his introductory remarks.[61]

Meanwhile, foreign plaintiffs alleging violations of their human rights by mining companies linked to Canada were not waiting for Bill C-354 to bring legal actions in Canadian courts. The courts had not been enlisted to address these types of issues since the dismissal with costs, on the basis of *forum non conveniens*, of an action brought by local community plaintiffs in 1997 alleging severe environmental harm due to the collapse of a tailings dam at a mine owned by Cambior Incorporated in Guyana,[62] although similar cases against Canadian companies had already been argued in US courts.[63] This situation changed in March 2009 with the filing in the Ontario Superior Court of Justice of a statement of claim, against Copper

---

Curiously, the insistence that "the act" occur abroad arguably limited the relevance of this amendment in situations where a Canadian company is involved and the act may be characterized as relating to conduct by directors or officers on Canadian soil, although this was likely not the intent.

60 *Ibid* at s 1(2).

61 *House of Commons Debates*, 40th Parl, 2nd Sess, No 038 (1 April 2009) at 1520 (Hon Peter Julian): "The bill would ensure corporate accountability for Canadian firms operating abroad. It would broaden the mandate of the Federal Court so that it protects foreign citizens against rights violations committed by corporations operating outside of Canada."

62 See the authorities in notes 29 and 30 and accompanying text. See also Bill C-354, *supra* note 58, s 3, proposing amendments to section 50 of the Federal Courts Act, *supra* note 59, which would amend the common law doctrine of *forum non conveniens* by preventing federal courts from staying proceedings "unless the defendant clearly, cogently and convincingly establishes" that the Federal Court of Appeal or the Federal Court is not a suitable forum in which to decide the case, a more appropriate forum is available that will fairly and effectively provide a final and binding decision, the more appropriate forum will likely provide a final and binding decision in a timely and efficient manner, and the interests of justice adamantly require that a stay of proceedings be granted.

63 See, eg, *The Presbyterian Church of Sudan v Talisman Energy Inc*, 582 F 3d 244 (2nd Cir 2009) (upholding dismissal on summary judgment motion). Plaintiffs petitioned for writ of *certiorari* to the US Court of Appeals, 2nd Circuit, in October 2010, which was denied. See also *Provincial Gov't of Marinduque v Placer Dome Inc*, 582 F 3d 1083 (9th Cir 2009) (reversing dismissal on *forum non conveniens* and act of state doctrine).

Mesa Mining Corporation and the Toronto Stock Exchange, alleging that the defendants were responsible for violence inflicted by security personnel at a mine site upon the plaintiffs, who opposed the mine.[64] By the time the dismissal of this action was upheld by the Court of Appeal for Ontario in March 2011,[65] another three lawsuits alleging violations of human rights overseas had been brought in Canadian courts against Canadian mining companies.[66]

Host state communities concerned about the conduct of Canadian-based mining companies operating in their backyards were also increasingly making use of other Canadian mechanisms to draw attention to their concerns. For example, a number of complaints against Canadian mining companies were brought, from 2000 on, to the Canadian NCP for the OECD Guidelines.[67] These specific instances included submissions made between 2009 and 2011 in relation to mines in Guatemala, Mongolia, Papua New Guinea, and Zambia.[68] In addition, concerned company shareholders, sometimes supported by local communities from the host states, and sometimes

64 See *Piedra v Copper Mesa Mining Corp*, 2010 ONSC 2421 (Plaintiffs' Statement of Claim), online: <http://www.ramirezversuscoppermesa.com/statement-of-claim.pdf>. The allegations against the TSX focused upon the listing of the company in order to raise equity financing without any effort to prevent foreseeable harm to the plaintiffs, who were engaged in peaceful protests.

65 *Piedra v Copper Mesa Mining Corp*, 2010 ONSC 2421, aff'd 2011 ONCA 191, 332 DLR (4th) 118.

66 See details of three cases launched in Ontario against Hudbay Minerals Incorporated in relation to the actions of security forces at mine sites in Guatemala, as described on the website of counsel for the plaintiffs, online: Klippensteins, Barristers and Solicitors <http://www.chocversushudbay.com/>. See further *Choc v Hudbay Minerals Inc*, 2011 ONSC 4490. See also *Association canadienne contre l'impunité (ACCI) v Anvil Mining Ltd*, 2011 QCCA 1035 [*Anvil Mining*] (accepting jurisdiction to hear the case), but see *Anvil Mining v Association canadienne contre l'impunité (ACCI)*, 2012 QCCA 117 (determining that the case cannot be heard in Québec).

67 *Canada's NCP, supra* note 18; see also *Canada's National Contact Point (Specific Instances)*, online: Department of Foreign Affairs and International Trade Canada <http://www.international.gc.ca/trade-agreements-accords-commerciaux/ncp-pcn/specific-specifique.aspx?lang=eng&menu_id=7>.

68 Canada's National Contact Point (NCP), *Annual Report* (Ottawa: Department of Foreign Affairs and International Trade, 2010) at s 8; Canada's NCP, *Annual Report* (Ottawa: DFAIT, 2011) at s 7. See also brief summaries of the four specific instances considered by the NCP as of December 2008, all concerning mining companies, online: Department of Foreign Affairs and International Trade Canada <http://www.international.gc.ca/trade-agreements-accords-commerciaux/ncp-pcn/specific-specifique.aspx?lang=eng&menu_id=7&view=d>.

not, drew attention to local community concerns over global mining development through the use of shareholder proposals brought forward at company annual general meetings held in Canada.[69] Other complaints relating to CSR issues could have been filed, in theory, with the office of the Compliance Officer for Export Development Canada, which was created in 2002. However, few complaints that were deemed to fall within the Compliance Officer's mandate were received.[70]

It is beyond the scope of this article to describe fully the considerable developments briefly noted here. Instead, the following discussion will focus upon the debate surrounding the highly controversial Bill C-300 and contrast this debate with the initiatives that were implemented by the federal government pursuant to the policy paper *Building the Canadian Advantage*, most notably the creation of the Office of the CSR Counsellor. The debate surrounding Bill C-300 will illustrate the challenges facing even a mild law reform proposal in this area, whereas examination of the Office of the CSR Counsellor will demonstrate that even where home state non-judicial mechanisms are adopted, industry consent is deeply embedded within their structure.

BILL C-300

Bill C-300 was designed to ensure that extractive sector companies receiving support from the Canadian government act "in a manner consistent with international environmental best practices and with Canada's commitments to international human rights standards."[71]

69 See generally Aaron A Dhir, "The Politics of Knowledge Dissemination: Corporate Reporting, Shareholder Voice and Human Rights" (2009) 47 Osgoode Hall LJ 47; Johann A Klaassen, "Sustainability and Social Justice" (2011) 31 Issues in Business Ethics 179 at 182-83. For specific discussion of the use of the shareholder proposal mechanism in relation to Goldcorp's Marlin mine in Guatemala, see Shin Imai, Ladan Mehranvar, and Jennifer Sander, "Breaching Indigenous Law: Canadian Mining in Guatemala" (2007) 6 Indigenous LJ 101; Aaron A Dhir, "Shareholder Engagement in the Embedded Business Corporation: Investment Activism, Human Rights and TWAIL Discourse" (2012) 22 Business Ethics Quarterly 99.

70 See *Export Development Canada Compliance Officer*, online: EDC <http://www.edc.ca/english/compliance.htm>; EDC, *2009 Compliance Officer's Annual Report on Third Party Complaints*, online: EDC <http://www19.edc.ca/english/docs/compliance_officer_report_e.pdf> (noting that twenty-three complaints have been received from third parties of which six fell within the compliance officer's mandate).

71 Bill C-300, *supra* note 14 at s 3.

The bill would have applied only to "mining, oil or gas activities" located "in the territory of a developing country or on the high seas where such activities are controlled directly or indirectly by a Canadian corporation."[72] Within a year of the bill coming into force, the minister of foreign affairs and the minister of international trade were to issue guidelines articulating corporate accountability standards,[73] after consulting with government departments or agencies, industry representatives, and non-governmental organizations (NGOs), among others.[74] The corporate accountability standards were to incorporate social and environmental standards of the IFC[75] and the Voluntary Principles on Security and Human Rights,[76] which were both CSR standards proposed in the Advisory Group's report. They were also to incorporate "(c) human rights provisions that ensure corporations operate in a manner that is consistent with international human right standards; and (d) any other standards consistent with international human rights standards."[77] However, no specific reference was made to *Protect, Respect, and Remedy,* despite it having been adopted by the UN Human Rights Council more than six months earlier.[78]

Under Bill C-300, the ministers of foreign affairs and international trade would have been empowered to receive written complaints about Canadian companies or citizens in relation to mining, oil, or gas activities in developing countries, which they would then have been obligated (absent a determination that the complaint was frivolous or vexatious) to assess for compliance with the corporate

72 *Ibid,* s 2(1). "Developing countries" were defined as "countries and territories named in the list of countries and territories eligible for Canadian development assistance established by the Minister of International Cooperation." This definition proved problematic as there was no longer any such list. An amendment, defining developing countries as those "classified as low income, lower middle income or upper middle income in the World Bank list of economies, as defined from time to time," was subsequently proposed. Regarding proposed amendments, see *House of Common Debates,* 40th Parl, 3rd Sess, No 66 (20 September 2010), Motion no 4, online: House of Commons <http://www.parl.gc.ca/HousePublications/Publication.aspx?DocId=4656017&Language=E&Mode=1&Parl=40&Ses=3 - SOBQ-3267199> (Hon. John McKay).

73 Bill C-300, *supra* note 14, s 5.

74 *Ibid,* s 5(3).

75 *Ibid,* s 5(2)(a).

76 *Ibid,* s 5(2)(b).

77 *Ibid,* s 5(2)(c)-(d).

78 *Protect, Respect, and Remedy, supra* note 7.

accountability standards.[79] In doing so, the ministers would have been able to consider information from the corporation or the public, including witnesses from outside Canada, and results were to be published within eight months following receipt of the complaint.[80] If a corporation's activities were determined to be inconsistent with the standards, the ministers were to notify the EDC and the Canada Pension Plan Investment Board (CPPIB).[81] According to Bill C-300, continued compliance with the standards was to be a condition of any contract entered into by the EDC, and investment managers for CPPIB were to ensure that no assets were invested in companies that were not in compliance with these standards.[82] Moreover, the Department of Foreign Affairs and International Trade Act[83] was to be amended to ensure that, with the exception of ordinary consular services, no mining, oil, or gas activities that were not in compliance with the standards would receive support or promotion from the minister.[84] Bill C-300 also provided for amendments to the Special Economic Measures Act[85] to allow for orders and regulations to be made restricting or prohibiting mining, oil, or gas activities in cases of grave breaches of international peace and security or human rights.[86]

Many civil society groups and academics spoke out in support of Bill C-300. For example, Bill C-300 was compared favourably to proposals in the Advisory Group's report in a report written by McGill professor Richard Janda for the civil society coalition Canadian

[79] Bill C-300, *supra* note 14, s 4(1)-(3), (5). The ministers would also be able to examine a matter on their own initiative if they had reason to believe a company had contravened the guidelines (s 4(5)).

[80] *Ibid,* s 4(6). If a complaint was found to be frivolous or vexatious, reasons for this determination were also to be published (*ibid,* s 4(7)).

[81] *Ibid,* s 4(8).

[82] *Ibid,* ss 8, 10. However, proposed amendments would have greatly curtailed the role of the Canada Pension Plan Investment Board (CPPIB). See *House of Common Debates,* 40th Parl, 3rd Sess, No 66 (20 September 2010), Motion nos 11, 16, online: House of Commons <http://www.parl.gc.ca/HousePublications/Publication.aspx?DocId=4656017&Language=E&Mode=1&Parl=40&Ses=3%20-%20SOBQ-3267199> (Hon. John McKay).

[83] Department of Foreign Affairs and International Trade Act, RSC 1985, c E-22.

[84] Bill C-300, *supra* note 14, s 9 (amending s 10 of the Department of Foreign Affairs and International Trade Act, *supra* note 83).

[85] Special Economic Measures Act, SC 1992, c 17.

[86] Bill C-300, *supra* note 14, s 11.

Network on Corporate Accountability.[87] Supporters argued that Bill C-300 would provide Canadian companies with a competitive advantage over others by providing a forum to address complaints[88] and by requiring companies to respect human rights, thus reducing the chance of operations being disrupted by local communities experiencing unrest.[89] This would, in the words of Toby Heaps, provide a "maple leaf stamp of approval" as junior companies, encouraged to adhere to environmental and human rights standards, could subsequently sell their properties for higher values, while senior companies would experience fewer "headaches" as the junior properties they acquired would have fewer messes to clean up.[90] Moreover, if Bill C-300 led some of the worst performers to leave Canada, Janda and others queried why Canadians should care.[91]

Some supporters suggested that most companies were already adhering to the standards in Bill C-300, which were in effect pre-existing de facto international standards due to financing requirements implemented by export credit agencies and banks following the Equator Principles.[92] While there was clearly some truth to the

87 Richard Janda, *Bill C-300: Sound and Measured Reinforcement for CSR — A Report on the Legal and Policy Dimensions of Bill C-300 Prepared for the Canadian Network on Corporate Accountability* (September 2009), online: Canadian Network on Corporate Accountability <http://cnca-rcrce.ca/wp-content/uploads/Bill-C-300-Report-Janda.pdf>.

88 *Ibid* at 8-9; House of Commons, SCFAID , *Minutes of Proceedings and Evidence*, 40th Parl, 3rd Sess, No 21 (3 June 2010) (Penelope Simons), online: House of Commons <http://www.parl.gc.ca/HousePublications/Publication.aspx?DocId=4588646&Language=E&Mode=1&Parl=40&Ses=3#T1145> [*Evidence* (Simons)].

89 House of Commons, SCFAID, *Minutes of Proceedings and Evidence*, 40th Parl, 2nd Sess, No 35 (27 October 2009) (Alex Neve), online: House of Commons <http://www.parl.gc.ca/HousePublications/Publication.aspx?DocId=4178126&Language=E&Mode=1&Parl=40&Ses=2#T0920> [*Evidence* (Amnesty — Neve)].

90 House of Commons, SCFAID, *Minutes of Proceedings and Evidence*, 40th Parl, 2nd Sess, No 44 (3 December 2009) (Toby A.A. Heaps), online: House of Commons <http://www.parl.gc.ca/HousePublications/Publication.aspx?DocId=4292634&Language=E&Mode=1&Parl=40&Ses=2#T0945> [*Evidence* (Corporate Knights)].

91 House of Commons, SCFAID, *Minutes of Proceedings and Evidence*, 40th Parl, 2nd Sess, No 32 (8 October 2009) (Richard Janda), online: House of Commons <http://www.parl.gc.ca/HousePublications/Publication.aspx?DocId=4134547&Language=E&Mode=1&Parl=40&Ses=2#Int-2885901> [*Evidence* (Janda)]; *Evidence* (Simons), *supra* note 88.

92 *Evidence* (Simons), *supra* note 88; *Evidence* (Janda), *supra* note 91. However, others acknowledged that the standards list in Bill C-300 needed to include specific reference to human rights because of deficiencies in the standards of the IFC,

claim that the standards incorporated in Bill C-300 were already de facto requirements for mining internationally due to the requirements of project financing, the claim that international human rights standards apply to corporate actors was highly controversial.[93] Indeed, it was precisely because of the contested nature of this claim that John Ruggie was appointed to the position of SRSG in the first place.[94]

Many of the supporters of Bill C-300 were also aware of its limitations — notably, that it was best understood as a government accountability bill that would ensure government money did not go to support unworthy corporate actors. For those seeking to punish corporate offenders or remedy environmental harm or human rights violations, Bill C-300 was far too limited.[95] A few submissions

---

which serve as the baseline standards adopted by Equator Principles banks. See House of Commons, SCFAID, *Minutes of Proceedings and Evidence*, 40th Parl, 2nd Sess, No 32 (8 October 2009) (Catherine Coumans), online: House of Commons <http://www.parl.gc.ca/HousePublications/Publication.aspx?DocId=4134547&Language=E&Mode=1&Parl=40&Ses=2#Int-2885944> [*Evidence* (Mining Watch Canada)]; *Evidence* (Amnesty — Neve), *supra* note 89. See also Equator Principles Association, *Equator Principles* (June 2006), online: Equator Principles Association <http://www.equator-principles.com/resources/equator_principles.pdf> [Equator Principles].

93 Matthew DG DeBock, Roger R Taplin, and Adam D Wanke, *Mining Law Update: Bill C-300* (1 March 2010), online: McCarthy Tetrault, LLP <http://www.mccarthy.ca/article_detail.aspx?id=4889>; Prospectors and Developers Association of Canada (PDAC), *Bill C-300 Myths and Facts* (17 December 2009), online: PDAC <http://www.pdac.ca/pdac/publications/na/pdf/091217-bill-c-300-myths-facts.pdf> at 2; Canadian Foundation for the Americas (FOCAL), *FOCAL Views: A Corporate Accountability Bill of No Avail* (April 2010), online: FOCAL <http://www.focal.ca/publications/focalpoint/235-april-2010-focal-views>.

94 David Kinley, Justine Nolan, and Natalie Zerial, "The Politics of Corporate Social Responsibility: Reflections on the United Nations Human Rights Norms for Corporations" (2007) 25 Company & Securities L J 30 at 33-37; Nina Seppala, "Business and the International Human Rights Regime: A Comparison of UN Initiatives" (2009) 87 J Business Ethics 401 at 408; John Gerard Ruggie, "Current Developments, Business and Human Rights: The Evolving International Agenda" (2007) 101 AJIL 819 at 821.

95 Rights Action, "Bill C-300 Will Perpetuate Effective Immunity From Legal Recourse in Canada" (20 October 2009), online: Rights Action <http://www.rightsaction.org/articles/Analysis_Bill_C-300.htm>. See also House of Commons, SCFAID, *Minutes of Proceedings and Evidence*, 40th Parl, 3rd Sess, No 19 (25 May 2010) (Karin Lissakers), online: House of Commons <http://www.parl.gc.ca/HousePublications/Publication.aspx?DocId=4547693&Language=E&Mode=1&Parl=40&Ses=3#T1110> [*Evidence* (Revenue Watch)].

grounded their support for Bill C-300 with reference to *Protect, Respect, and Remedy*.[96] Yet, as noted earlier, *Protect, Respect, and Remedy* was not directly referenced by Bill C-300. Instead, Bill C-300 proposed a year-long consultation process to define the precise nature of the human rights standards to be applied,[97] a process that did not satisfy industry representatives[98] despite the ongoing engagement of global industry associations, such as the International Council on Mining and Metals (ICMM), with the problem of human rights and global mining.[99]

Opposition from the Canadian mining industry to Bill C-300 was fierce and premised on several key claims. First, some argued that there were structural issues with the bill that would create practical compliance difficulties or unfairness. For example, the Mining Association of Canada pointed out that the bill would create problems for companies that acquired properties that were out of compliance, as no grace period was built in to allow for these properties

96 See *Evidence* (MiningWatch Canada), *supra* note 92; House of Commons, SCFAID, *Minutes of Proceedings and Evidence*, 40th Parl, 3rd Sess, No 19 (25 May 2010) (Shanta Martin), online: House of Commons <http://www.parl.gc.ca/HousePublications/Publication.aspx?DocId=4547693&Language=E&Mode=1&Parl=40&Ses=3#Int-3174606> [*Evidence* (Amnesty — Martin)]; House of Commons, SCFAID, *Minutes of Proceedings and Evidence*, 40th Parl, 3rd Sess, No 22 (8 June 2010) (Audrey Macklin), online: House of Commons <http://www.parl.gc.ca/HousePublications/Publication.aspx?DocId=4598846&Language=E&Mode=1&Parl=40&Ses=3#Int-3213529>.

97 Bill C-300, *supra* note 14, s 5.

98 See, eg, House of Commons, SCFAID, *Minutes of Proceedings and Evidence*, 40th Parl, 2nd Sess, No 42 (26 November 2009) (Mac Penney), online: House of Commons <http://www.parl.gc.ca/HousePublications/Publication.aspx?DocId=4266713&Language=E&Mode=1&Parl=40&Ses=2#Int-2974648> [*Evidence* (Kinross Gold)]. See also House of Commons, SCFAID, *Minutes of Proceedings and Evidence*, 40th Parl, 3rd Sess, No 21 (3 June 2010) (Gary Nash), online: House of Commons http://www.parl.gc.ca/HousePublications/Publication.aspx?DocId=4588646&Language=E&Mode=1&Parl=40&Ses=3#T1120> (citing the length of time it was taking John Ruggie to finalize his recommendations as evidence that one year was too short a time).

99 See, eg, International Council on Mining and Metals (ICMM), *Projects: Business and Human Rights*, online: ICMM <http://www.icmm.com/page/225/our-work/projects/articles/business-and-human-rights> (outlining the work of the ICMM on mining and human rights, including links to submissions to the SRSG); see also ICMM, *Human Rights in the Mining and Metals Industry: Overview, Management Approach and Issues* (May 2009), online: ICMM <http://www.icmm.com/page/14809/human-rights-in-the-mining-and-metals-industry-overview-management-approach-and-issues>.

to be brought into compliance.[100] Second, it was claimed that the bill would create a competitive disadvantage for Canadian companies, resulting in projects in developing countries either being developed by foreign competitors or not being developed at all, as responsible companies would avoid projects that might constitute a legal risk.[101] Not only would Bill C-300 disadvantage Canadian companies, claimed some industry lawyers, but it would also cause

100 House of Commons, SCFAID, *Minutes of Proceedings and Evidence*, 40th Parl, 2nd Sess, No 32 (8 October 2009) (Gordon Peeling), online: House of Commons <http://www.parl.gc.ca/HousePublications/Publication.aspx?DocId=4134547&Language=E&Mode=1&Parl=40&Ses=2#T1005> [*Evidence* (Mining Association of Canada)]; see also House of Commons, SCFAID, *Minutes of Proceedings and Evidence*, 40th Parl, 2nd Sess, No 39 (17 November 2009) (Robert Wisner), online: House of Commons <http://www.parl.gc.ca/HousePublications/Publication.aspx?DocId=4231494&Language=E&Mode=1&Parl=40&Ses=2#Int-2948675> [*Evidence* (McMillan LLP)]. This issue was to have been addressed in the proposed amendments. See discussion in the text accompanying note 108.

101 *Evidence* (Kinross Gold), *supra* note 98; House of Commons, SCFAID, *Minutes of Proceedings and Evidence*, 40th Parl, 2nd Sess, No 40 (19 November 2009) (Perrin Beatty), online: House of Commons <http://www.parl.gc.ca/HousePublications/Publication.aspx?DocId=4237707&Language=E&Mode=1&Parl=40&Ses=2#T0910> [*Evidence* (Canadian Chamber of Commerce — Beatty)]; House of Commons, SCFAID, *Minutes of Proceedings and Evidence*, 40th Parl, 3rd Sess, No 19 (25 May 2010) (Shirley-Ann George), online: House of Commons <http://www.parl.gc.ca/HousePublications/Publication.aspx?DocId=4547693&Mode=1&Parl=40&Ses=3&Language=E#Int-3175148> [*Evidence* (Canadian Chamber of Commerce — George)]; House of Commons, SCFAID, *Minutes of Proceedings and Evidence*, 40th Parl, 3rd Sess, No 21 (3 June 2010) (David Stewart-Patterson), online: House of Commons <http://www.parl.gc.ca/HousePublications/Publication.aspx?DocId=4588646&Language=E&Mode=1&Parl=40&Ses=3#Int-3203121> [*Evidence* (Canadian Council of Chief Executives)]; House of Commons, SCFAID, *Minutes of Proceedings and Evidence*, 40th Parl, 2nd Sess, No 42 (26 November 2009) (Peter Sinclair), online: House of Commons <http://www.parl.gc.ca/HousePublications/Publication.aspx?DocId=4266713&Language=E&Mode=1&Parl=40&Ses=2#Int-2974680> [*Evidence* (Barrick Gold)]; House of Commons, SCFAID, *Minutes of Proceedings and Evidence*, 40th Parl, 3rd Sess, No 18 (13 May 2010) (Carlo Dade), online: House of Commons <http://www.parl.gc.ca/HousePublications/Publication.aspx?DocId=4533191&Language=E&Mode=2&Parl=40&Ses=3#T1215> [*Evidence* (FOCAL)]; House of Commons, SCFAID, *Minutes of Proceedings and Evidence*, 40th Parl, 2nd Sess, No 42 (3 December 2009) (Robert Blackburn), online: House of Commons <http://www.parl.gc.ca/HousePublications/Publication.aspx?Language=E&Mode=1&Parl=40&Ses=2&DocId=4292634&File=0#Int-2994434> [*Evidence* (SNC Lavalin)]; Tony Andrews, *Bill C-300 Position Statement* (PDAC, August 2009) at 4, online: PDAC <http://www.pdac.ca/pdac/publications/na/pdf/090812-bill-c-300-position-statement.pdf>.

"an exodus of companies from Canada" and thereby disadvantage Canada itself as a mining jurisdiction of choice.[102] Third, many submissions claimed that Bill C-300 would violate the sovereignty of host states, promoting a "West knows best" mentality.[103] Finally, the industry raised concerns that "anti-mining" groups who launched complaints would be subject to no penalty for reputational damage to companies.[104]

102 House of Commons, SCFAID, *Minutes of Proceedings and Evidence*, 40th Parl, 2nd Sess, No 42 (26 November 2009) (Michael Bourassa), online: House of Commons <http://www.parl.gc.ca/HousePublications/Publication.aspx?DocId=4266713&Language=E&Mode=1&Parl=40&Ses=2#Int-2974922> [*Evidence* (Fasken Martineau DuMoulin LLP — Bourassa)]; House of Commons, SCFAID, *Minutes of Proceedings and Evidence*, 40th Parl, 2nd Sess, No 42 (26 November 2009) (Hon. James Peterson), online: House of Commons <http://www.parl.gc.ca/HousePublications/Publication.aspx?DocId=4266713&Language=E&Mode=1&Parl=40&Ses=2#Int-2974821> [*Evidence* (Fasken Martineau DuMoulin LLP — Peterson)]; *Evidence* Canadian Chamber of Commerce — George), *supra* note 101; Michael Bourassa, "Bill C-300 Threatens Canada's International Extractive Sector," (2009) 4 CIM Magazine 53; Fasken Martineau DuMoulin LLP, *Sharp Criticism for Bill C-300: Lawyers Tell Parliamentary Committee Private Member's Bill Threatens Canada's Minerals Industry* (26 November 2009), online: Fasken Martineau DuMoulin LLP <http://www.fasken.com/firm-opposes-bill-c-300-in-ottawa>; Harvey Enchin, "Will Mining Suffer If Bill C-300 Becomes Law? YES: It's Biased and Overly Punitive," *Vancouver Sun* (27 May 2010); Peter Koven, "Mining Bill Needs to Be Defeated: Industry Reps," *Financial Post* (25 November 2009); Gary Nash, "Canada's Very Flawed Bill C-300 Anti-Mining Legislation Should be Withdrawn," *Republic of Mining* (10 June 2010), online: Republic of Mining <http://www.republicofmining.com/2010/06/10/canadas-very-flawed-bill-c- 300-anti-mining-legislation-should-be-withdrawn-by-gary-nash>.

103 House of Commons, SCFAID, *Minutes of Proceedings and Evidence*, 40th Parl, 3rd Sess, No 19 (25 May 2010) (Robert Anthony Hodge), online: House of Commons <http://www.parl.gc.ca/HousePublications/Publication.aspx?DocId=4547693&Language=E&Mode=1&Parl=40&Ses=3#Int-3175079> [*Evidence* (ICMM)]; PDAC, *The Prospectors and Developers Association of Canada Urges a House of Commons Standing Committee to Recognize the Ethically Responsible Nature of Canada's Mineral Industry and Reject Bill C-300*, News Release (19 November 2009), online: PDAC <http://www.pdac.ca/pdac/misc/pdf/091117-bill-c-300.pdf>; *Evidence* (Canadian Chamber of Commerce — Beatty), *supra* note 101; House of Commons, SCFAID, *Minutes of Proceedings and Evidence*, 40th Parl, 2nd Sess, No 42 (26 November 2009) (Raymond Chrétien), online: House of Commons <http://www.parl.gc.ca/HousePublications/Publication.aspx?DocId=4266713&Language=E&Mode=1&Parl=40&Ses=2#Int-2974947> [*Evidence* (Fasken Martineau DuMoulin, LLP — Chrétien)]; *Evidence* (Canadian Council of Chief Executives), *supra* note 101.

104 *Evidence* (Canadian Chamber of Commerce — Beatty), *supra* note 101; *Evidence* (Canadian Council of Chief Executives), *supra* note 101; *Evidence* (Canadian

Various federal government departments also weighed in against Bill C-300. For example, government bodies named in the bill complained that they had not been consulted and that confusion would be created as the "legislative" approach adopted in Bill C-300 would be inconsistent with the policy approach to CSR being adopted by government bodies — which might, for example, permit a body such as the EDC to give money to a company and then engage it in raising its CSR standards.[105] DFAIT, which would have been required to implement the legislation, complained that it would have to build capacity to investigate and adjudicate claims due to the quasi-judicial process contemplated by Bill C-300.[106] The EDC reiterated industry concerns that Bill C-300 would create competitive disadvantage for Canadian companies.[107]

The drafters of the bill were willing to acknowledge some of its deficiencies, and a number of the complaints raised in relation to

Chamber of Commerce — George), *supra* note 101; House of Commons, SCFAID, *Minutes of Proceedings and Evidence*, 40th Parl, 3rd Sess, No 22 (8 June 2010) (Thomas Shrake), online: House of Commons <http://www.parl.gc.ca/HousePublications/Publication.aspx?DocId=4598846&Language=E&Mode=1&Parl=40&Ses=3#Int-3213839> [*Evidence* (Pacific Rim Mining Corporation)].

105 House of Commons, SCFAID, *Minutes of Proceedings and Evidence*, 40th Parl, 2nd Sess, No 33 (20 October 2009) (Dr. Stephen Lucas, Minerals and Metals Sector, Department of Natural Resources), online: House of Commons <http://www.parl.gc.ca/HousePublications/Publication.aspx?DocId=4148257&Language=E&Mode=1&Parl=40&Ses=2#Int-2895130>; House of Commons, SCFAID, *Minutes of Proceedings and Evidence*, 40th Parl, 2nd Sess, No 35 (27 October 2009) (Jim McArdle, EDC), online: House of Commons <http://www.parl.gc.ca/HousePublications/Publication.aspx?DocId=4178126&Language=E&Mode=1&Parl=40&Ses=2%20-%20T1000> [*Evidence* (EDC)]; House of Commons, SCFAID, *Minutes of Proceedings and Evidence*, 40th Parl, 2nd Sess, No 39 (17 November 2009) (Donald Raymond, CPPIB), online: House of Commons <http://www.parl.gc.ca/HousePublications/Publication.aspx?DocId=4231494&Language=E&Mode=1&Parl=40&Ses=2%20-%20Int-2948327>; House of Commons, SCFAID, *Minutes of Proceedings and Evidence*, 40th Parl, 2nd Sess, No 39 (17 November 2009) (Ian Dale, CPPIB), online: House of Commons <http://www.parl.gc.ca/HousePublications/Publication.aspx?DocId=4231494&Language=E&Mode=1&Parl=40&Ses=2%20-%20Int-2948923>.

106 House of Commons, SCFAID, *Minutes of Proceedings and Evidence*, 40th Parl, 2nd Sess, No 43 (1 December 2009) (Grant Manuge, Trade Commissioner Service, DFAIT), online: House of Commons <http://www.parl.gc.ca/HousePublications/Publication.aspx?DocId=4281177&Language=E&Mode=1&Parl=40&Ses=2%20-%20Int-2984517>.

107 *Evidence* (EDC), *supra* note 105.

Bill C-300 were the subject of proposed amendments to the bill.[108] Yet, ultimately, on 27 October 2010, by a close vote of 138 to 134, Bill C-300 passed into history.[109]

BUILDING THE CANADIAN ADVANTAGE AND THE OFFICE OF THE CSR COUNSELLOR

The policy paper *Building the Canadian Advantage* describes itself as providing a "comprehensive strategy on corporate social responsibility for the extractive sector operating abroad," informed by the national roundtables and the *SCFAIT Report*.[110] In keeping with its name, *Building the Canadian Advantage* specifically claims that it will

> *improve the competitive advantage* of Canadian international extractive sector companies by *enhancing* their ability to manage social and environmental risks. It recognizes that, while most Canadian companies are committed to the highest ethical, environmental and social standards, those that lack the commitment can cause harm to communities abroad and undermine the competitive position of other Canadian companies.[111]

Accordingly, *Building the Canadian Advantage* first promises to support initiatives that enhance the capacities of developing countries to manage the development of minerals, oil, and gas so that they might benefit from these resources to reduce poverty.[112] Second,

108 *House of Common Debates*, 40th Parl, 3rd Sess, No 66 (20 September 2010), online: House of Commons <http://www.parl.gc.ca/HousePublications/Publication.aspx?DocId=4656017&Language=E&Mode=1&Parl=40&Ses=3%20-%20SOBQ-3267199> (Hon. John McKay).

109 The vote tally, organized by party, is available online: House of Commons <http://www2.parl.gc.ca/HouseChamberBusiness/ChamberVoteDetail.aspx?Language=E&Mode=1&Parl=40&Ses=3&Vote=125&GroupBy=party&FltrParl=40&FltrSes=3>. See also Jane Taber, "Ignatieff's Mixed Messages on Mining Leaves Liberal Heads Spinning," *Globe and Mail* (28 October 2010), online: Globe and Mail <http://www.theglobeandmail.com/news/politics/ottawa-notebook/ignatieffs-mixed-message-on-mining-leaves-liberal-heads-spinning/article1776539/>; Mining Watch Canada, *Bill C-300 a High Watermark for Mining and Government Accountability* (16 November 2010), online: Mining Watch Canada <http://www.miningwatch.ca/article/bill-c-300-high-water-mark-mining-and-government-accountability>.

110 *Building the Canadian Advantage, supra* note 9 at 4.

111 *Ibid* [emphasis added].

112 *Ibid* at 4-5. The report highlights the role that CIDA has played in "building and modernizing the governance regimes to ensure that natural resources are

DFAIT and NRCan commit to promoting three "widely recognized" international CSR performance guidelines — not surprisingly, those identified by the Advisory Group — with Canadian extractive companies operating abroad.[113] Third, the Office of the CSR Counsellor is to be set up.[114] Finally, a CSR Centre of Excellence is to be developed to encourage the Canadian international extractive sector to implement the voluntary performance guidelines by developing and disseminating high-quality CSR information, training, and tools.[115]

With respect to international CSR performance guidelines, the IFC Performance Standards on Social and Environmental Sustainability are described in *Building the Canadian Advantage* as "*de facto* performance benchmarks for projects in developing countries that require substantial financial investment,"[116] due to their adoption by financial institution signatories to the Equator Principles.[117] The Voluntary Principles on Security and Human Rights, developed through a partnership of states, corporations, and NGOs in 2000, are said to have been "designed specifically" to address the challenges

---

managed in a technically and environmentally sound manner," including through legal and judicial reform (*ibid* at 6.) Also highlighted is the role that NRCan has played, at times with CIDA, in technical assistance, policy development, and training at the domestic level, while providing support for multigovernmental mining organizations and the establishment of the Intergovernmental Forum on Mining, Minerals, Metals and Sustainable Development (*ibid* at 6-7). See further, on the Intergovernmental Forum, online: <http://www.globaldialogue.info/wn_e.htm> and note 263 in this article.

113 *Building the Canadian Advantage, supra* note 9 at 4-5.

114 *Ibid.*

115 *Ibid.* See further CSR Centre of Excellence, *supra* note 10.

116 *Building the Canadian Advantage, supra* note 9 at 8. The performance standards "set expectations of conduct in eight issue areas, including Social and Environmental Assessment and Management Systems; Labour and Working Conditions; Pollution Prevention and Abatement; Community Health, Safety and Security; Land Acquisition and Involuntary Resettlement; Biodiversity Conservation and Sustainable Natural Resource Management; Indigenous Peoples; and Cultural Heritage" (*ibid*).

117 *Ibid* at 8. Eighty percent of global financing for extractive sector projects is provided by these institutions, which agree to adopt lending practices consistent with the IFC performance standards (*ibid*); see also Equator Principles, *supra* note 92. However, the Equator Principles specify that a different review process applies to projects in high income OECD countries. See Equator Principles Association, *FAQs*, online: <http://www.equator-principles.com/index.php/about-ep/faqs/42-about/frequently-asked-questions/21>.

of "violence-related risk assessment," including security provider and extractive industry relations.[118] The Global Reporting Initiative (GRI), "developed ... via a multi-stakeholder process involving industry, investors, civil society and labour," is characterized as "broadly recognized as the *de facto* international reporting standard."[119]

Yet, in terms of human rights, *Building the Canadian Advantage* states:

> Obligations under international human rights conventions apply to states and do not directly create obligations for companies. While such obligations can serve to guide the development of CSR standards, the international legal environment is under pressure for change and adaptation.[120]

Building the Canadian Advantage highlights the UN Human Rights Council's unanimous endorsement in 2008 of *Protect, Respect, and Remedy*, yet makes no reference to any of its three pillars or to what these might mean for the Canadian government's own responsibility to address problems associated with Canadian companies engaged in global mining. Nor is there mention of the international human rights treaties to which Canada is a party. This appears to be a notable omission, given *Building the Canadian Advantage*'s explicit reference to Canada's anti-bribery obligations as a state party to numerous multilateral corruption conventions.[121] The clear implication is that, while Canada's international anti-bribery commitments require it

118 *Building the Canadian Advantage, supra* note 9 at 9; Voluntary Principles, *supra* note 40.

119 *Building the Canadian Advantage, supra* note 9 at 9. *Building the Canadian Advantage* also discusses the environmental disclosure requirements in place for issuers listing on Canadian stock exchanges and the role of provincial securities laws in relation to disclosure (*ibid* at 9-10). See also GRI, *supra* note 23; GRI, *Reporting Framework,* online: GRI <https://www.globalreporting.org/reporting/reporting-framework-overview/Pages/default.aspx>; GRI, *Mining and Metals Sector Supplement,* online: GRI <https://www.globalreporting.org/resourcelibrary/MMSS-Complete.pdf>.

120 *Building the Canadian Advantage, supra* note 9 at 8.

121 *Ibid* at 14, referring to the OECD's Convention on Combating Bribery of Foreign Public Officials in International Business Transactions, 21 November 1997, Can TS 1999 No 23 [Anti-Bribery Convention]; the Inter-American Convention against Corruption, 29 March 1996, Can TS 2000 No 21; the United Nations Convention against Transnational Organized Crime, 15 November 2000, 2225 UNTS 209; and the United Nations Convention against Corruption, 31 October 2003, 2349 UNTS 41.

to address corporate conduct, its international human rights commitments do not.

Interestingly, legal incentives are proposed in the anti-corruption context, with a commitment to "examine the possibility of extending the application of the offence of bribing a foreign public official" under the Corruption against Foreign Officials Act[122] "on the basis of the active nationality principle."[123] While traditional bases of jurisdiction that prevail in Canadian law are noted, there is no mention of the fact that Canada has been criticized for its reluctance to implement nationality-based jurisdiction in the bribery context as has been required for years under the OECD's Convention on Combating Bribery of Foreign Public Officials in International Business Transactions.[124] As a whole, the lack of reference to obligations under international human rights law and the limited understanding of jurisdiction expressed in *Building the Canadian Advantage* reflect a preoccupation with avoiding any exercise of either legislative (prescriptive) or judicial (adjudicative) jurisdiction that could be perceived as an infringement of host state sovereignty.[125]

Building the Canadian Advantage identifies steps to "ensure that government services align with high standards of corporate social responsibility."[126] For example, CIDA will ensure that CSR is practised within the Canada Investment Fund for Africa by "assess[ing] its procedures and guidelines related to projects involving Canadian private sector partners."[127] The EDC already uses the OECD's

122 Corruption against Foreign Officials Act, SC 1998, c 34.

123 *Building the Canadian Advantage, supra* note 9 at 14-15.

124 Anti-Bribery Convention, *supra* note 121. See, eg, OECD Working Group on Bribery in International Business Transactions, *Canada: Phase 2: Follow-up Report on the Implementation of the Phase 2 Recommendations on the Application of the Convention and the 1997 Recommendation on Combatting Bribery of Public Officials in International Business Transactions* (2006) at 5, online: OECD <http://www.oecd.org/dataoecd/5/6/36984779.pdf>. See also Julian Sher, "Canada Ranked Worst of G7 Nations in Fighting Bribery, Corruption," *Globe and Mail* (24 May 2011), online: Globe and Mail <http://www.theglobeandmail.com/news/politics/canada-ranked-worst-of-g7-nations-in-fighting-bribery-corruption/article592312/; Transparency International, "Progress Report 2011: Enforcement of the OECD Anti-Bribery Convention" (2011), online: Transparency International <http://www.transparency.org/whatwedo/pub/progress_report_2011_enforcement_of_the_oecd_anti_bribery_convention>.

125 See generally Seck, *supra* note 15.

126 *Building the Canadian Advantage, supra* note 9 at 11.

127 *Ibid* at 11-12. Canada Investment Fund for Africa (CIFA) is a public-private investment fund designed to stimulate growth in Africa, with approximately a quarter

Common Approaches on Environment and Officially Supported Export Credits when developing policy and practices for evaluating the environmental and social impacts of projects.[128] Moreover, the EDC is a signatory to the Equator Principles[129] and issued a statement on human rights in April 2008 committing to human rights due diligence for projects and countries determined to have a higher potential human rights risk.[130] *Building the Canadian Advantage* also notes the CPPIB's *Policy on Responsible Investing*, along with the CPPIB's role as a contributor and signatory to both the UN Principles for Responsible Investment and the Extractive Industries Transparency Initiative.[131]

Arguably, the most interesting proposal in *Building the Canadian Advantage* is the creation of the Office of the CSR Counsellor, which is justified on the basis that "[u]nresolved disputes directly affect business through expensive project delays, damaged reputations, high conflict management costs, investor uncertainty, and, in some cases, loss of investment capital."[132] Accordingly, a CSR Counsellor would enable CSR disputes related to extractive activity abroad to be resolved in a "timely and transparent manner."[133] The position was created by an Order in Council,[134] and, in October 2009,

---

of its investments in six extractive sector projects. Four of these are operated by Canadian or Canadian-listed companies. See CIFA, *Portfolio Summaries*, online: CIFA <http://www.cifafund.ca/en/portfolio.html>.

128 *Ibid* at 12-13. See *Common Approaches, supra* note 22. See also generally EDC's environmental commitments, online: EDC <http://www.edc.ca/EN/About-Us/Corporate-Social-Responsibility/Environment/Pages/default.aspx>.

129 *Building the Canadian Advantage, supra* note 9 at 13. IFC standards are also a benchmark standard under the *Common Approaches, supra* note 22. However, the EDC subjects G-7 countries to a streamlined approach, in keeping with the Equator Principles, *supra* note 92 and EDC, *Environmental and Social Review Directive*, para 29(c), online: EDC <http://www.edc.ca/EN/About-Us/Corporate-Social-Responsibility/Environment/Documents/environment-social-review-directive.pdf>.

130 *Building the Canadian Advantage, supra* note 9 at 13. See EDC, *Business Ethics: Human Rights*, online: <http://www.edc.ca/EN/About-Us/Corporate-Social-Responsibility/Documents/human-rights-statement.pdf>.

131 *Building the Canadian Advantage, supra* note 9 at 3-14. See also the *United Nations Principles of Responsible Investment (UNPRI)*, online: UNPRI <http://www.unpri.org/>; and note 51 on the Extractive Industries Transparency Initiative.

132 *Building the Canadian Advantage, supra* note 9 at 10.

133 *Ibid* at 11.

134 Order in Council, PC 2009-0422 (25 March 2009), online: <http://www.pco-bcp.gc.ca/OIC-DDC.asp?lang=eng&Page=&txtOICID=2009-0422&txtFromDate

Marketa Evans was appointed.[135] The CSR Counsellor "report[s] directly to and [is] accountable to" the minister of international trade.[136] The office officially opened in Toronto in March 2010.[137]

Before accepting complaints, the CSR Counsellor held public consultations regarding the rules of procedure that should govern her review process.[138] Notably, the consultations were held not only in Canada but also overseas and included stakeholders from "industry, civil society, host country governments and Canadian government officials."[139] The Rules of Procedure were released in October

---

=&txtToDate=&txtPrecis=&txtDepartment=&txtAct=&txtChapterNo=&txtChapterYear=&txtBillNo=&rdoComingIntoForce=&DoSearch=Search+%2F+List&viewattach=20393>.

135 CSR Counsellor, *supra* note 56.

136 Order in Council, *supra* note 134, s 7(1). This structure has raised concerns as to the ability of the CSR Counsellor to act impartially and at arm's length from DFAIT. See *Meeting Summary Report: Legal Experts Meeting on 'Identifying and Exploring the Key Legal Issues Associated with the Office of the Extractive Sector Corporate Social Responsibility Counsellor* (6 May 2010) at 6, online: DFAIT <http://www.international.gc.ca/csr_counsellor-conseiller_rse/assets/pdfs/Legal%20issues%20Workshop%201%20May%202010.pdf> [*CSR Experts Report*].

137 Office of the Extractive Sector Corporate Social Responsibility Counsellor, *Building a Review Process for the Canadian International Extractive Sector: A Backgrounder* (June 2010) at 2, online: DFAIT <http://www.international.gc.ca/csr_counsellor-conseiller_rse/assets/pdfs/building%20a%20review%20process%20backgrounder%20FINAL%20June%202010.pdf>.

138 See Office of the Extractive Sector Corporate Social Responsibility Counsellor, *Public Consultations Summary Report: Building a Review Process for the Canadian International Extractive Sector: A Summary of Public Consultations Held June-August 2010* (September 2010) at 4-5, online: DFAIT <http://www.international.gc.ca/csr_counsellor-conseiller_rse/assets/pdfs/Consultations%20Summary%20Report%20Sept%202010.pdf> [*CSR Consultations Summary*], describing the public consultations as consisting of "five separate but complementary activities: (1) a series of full day, professionally facilitated workshops in 5 cities across Canada; (2) a 90 minute interactive webinar; (3) formal and informal interviews and dialogue sessions with international stakeholders in Mexico, Mali, and Senegal; (4) an invitation to provide written feedback on the draft rules of procedure; and (5) three legal experts workshops."

139 *Ibid* at 2. See further individual consultation reports, online: DFAIT <http://www.international.gc.ca/csr_counsellor-conseiller_rse/publications-publications.aspx?lang=eng&view=d>. See also description of stakeholders in Office of the Extractive Sector Corporate Social Responsibility Counsellor, *Annual Report to Parliament October 2009 – October 2010* (February 2011) at 3, online: DFAIT <http://www.international.gc.ca/csr_counsellor-conseiller_rse/publications-publications.aspx?lang=eng&view=d>: "[T]he Counsellor has spent much of

2010,[140] and, in April 2011, a Review Process Participant Guide was unveiled, identifying six guiding principles: "accessible, effective, independent, transparent, responsive, predictable."[141]

As emphasized in the summary report of the public consultations, the content of the Rules of Procedure was limited by the mandate given to the CSR Counsellor in the Order in Council.[142] According to section 4 of the Order in Council, the CSR Counsellor is to both "review" the CSR practices of "Canadian extractive sector companies operating outside Canada" and "advise on the implementation of the performance guidelines."[143] Unlike Bill C-300, the possibility of review is not limited to companies operating in developing countries. However, a Canadian extractive sector company is defined as an "oil, gas or mining company that has been incorporated in Canada or that has its head office in Canada."[144] Thus, companies that list on Canadian stock exchanges, for example, are presumably excluded without further connecting factors, despite the fact that the GRI is included as a performance standard.[145]

---

the past year in conversations with the multitude of constituencies who have an interest in the issues ... These stakeholders include Canadian companies, host country authorities, project affected communities and individuals, joint venture partners, Canadian industry associations, overseas industry associations, professional associations, Canadian NGOs, non-Canadian civil society groups, Canadian parliamentarians, host country regulators, service providers including the legal and consulting communities, socially responsible investors, academics, international financial institutions, global initiatives, and others."

140 *CSR Rules of Procedure, supra* note 57; Office of the Extractive Sector CSR Counsellor, *Launch of the Review Process of Canada's Office of the Extractive Sector Corporate Social Responsibility Counsellor,* News Release (20 October 2010), online: Department of Foreign Affairs and International Trade <http://www.international.gc.ca/csr_counsellor-conseiller_rse/launch_Oct2010_lancement.aspx?view=d>.

141 Office of the Extractive Sector Corporate Social Responsibility Counsellor, *The Review Process Participant Guide* (April 2011), online: Department of Foreign Affairs and International Trade <http://www.international.gc.ca/csr_counsellor-conseiller_rse/assets/pdfs/Participant%20guide%20April%202011.pdf> [*Review Process Participant Guide*].

142 *CSR Consultations Summary, supra* note 138 at 4.

143 Order in Council, *supra* note 134, s 4.

144 *Ibid,* s 1. This definition is repeated in the *CSR Rules of Procedure, supra* note 57, s 1.

145 For a typology of Canadian mining companies, categorizing them according to their head office and government jurisdiction, among other factors, see DFAIT-Canada, *Discussion Paper, Prepared for the National Roundtables on Corporate Social Responsibility and the Extractive Sector in Developing Countries* (June 2006) at 26-27, Table 2.

More restrictively, the Order in Council provides that the CSR Counsellor requires the "express written consent of the parties involved" in order to undertake a review.[146] Furthermore, she is not permitted to make "binding recommendations" or "policy or legislative recommendations" or to "create new performance standards."[147] Nor may she apply any standards other than the designated performance guidelines (the IFC Performance Standards, the Voluntary Principles, and the GRI),[148] together with the OECD Guidelines.[149]

The CSR Counsellor may review a complaint if requested by "an individual, group or community" that "reasonably believes" it is, or may be, affected by activities of a Canadian extractive sector company that are inconsistent with the performance guidelines.[150] More strikingly, the CSR Counsellor may also review a complaint if approached by a Canadian extractive sector company that "believes it is the subject of unfounded allegations concerning its corporate conduct outside Canada in relation to the performance guidelines."[151] This provision was clearly designed to appease industry

146 Order in Council, *supra* note 134, s 6. The CSR Counsellor is also not to review any activity that occurred before the day on which the first Counsellor was appointed (*ibid,* s 5(1)), which is identified in the *CSR Rules of Procedure* as 19 October 2009. *CSR Rules of Procedure, supra* note 57, s 3(a).

147 Order in Council, *supra* note 134, s 5(5).

148 *Ibid.*

149 *Ibid,* s 1. However, the NCP for the OECD Guidelines is to remain the "primary authority" concerning these (*ibid,* s 5(2)-(4)). As the GRI is a voluntary guideline for sustainability reporting, it is unclear how it could be used. One possibility is that a community that believes it is being impacted by company conduct could complain to the CSR Counsellor if it believes the company is not accurately reporting CSR issues as required under the GRI. Another possibility is that a concerned investor group could approach the CSR Counsellor, although it is unclear whether an investor group would qualify as a "requestor."

150 Order in Council, *supra* note 134, s 6(1)(a). An "individual, group or community" may authorize an "individual or organization" to aid or assist them in the submission of a request for review, thus allowing for the possibility that Canadian civil society organizations could assist foreign complainants in accessing the review process. *CSR Rules of Procedure, supra* note 57, s 5(a). Anonymous requests may not be submitted, although submissions may be made that request confidentiality (*ibid,* s 3(c)).

151 Order in Council, *supra* note 134, s 6(1)(b). Such a request must "clearly name the Responding party." *CSR Rules of Procedure, supra* note 57, s 5(b). Presumably this responding party must then consent in writing to the review process under section 5(6) of the Order in Council.

concerns over "civil society" accountability, yet appears to be without precedent in any similar non-judicial CSR dispute resolution mechanism. Finally, the CSR Counsellor is not on her own initiative to review the activities of a Canadian extractive sector company, although she "may informally approach a company if ... she believes that early dialogue could prevent a dispute from arising or escalating."[152]

The aim of the five-stage review process is "to foster constructive collaboration and dialogue between stakeholders."[153] The CSR Counsellor does have the discretion to refuse to deal with a request for review,[154] yet she must consider listed factors when conducting a review, including whether the request was made in good faith.[155] While submissions must be made in either of Canada's official languages (French or English), the CSR Counsellor has hired Spanish interpreters to conduct field visits in relation to the first complaint received.[156] The participant guide identifies the need for the requester to ensure that they have "adequate resources and capacity" to continue the process through to its conclusion,[157] yet no resources are specifically designated to support a requestors' capacity to engage the process.

Once a review has been concluded, the CSR Counsellor is to issue a "written public statement"[158] and is also to submit an annual report that is to be tabled in Parliament by the minister of international

152 Order in Council, *supra* note 134, s 6(2).

153 *Ibid*, s 6(3). The five stages are: (1) initial assessment; (2) informal mediation; (3) fact finding; (4) access to formal mediation; and (5) reporting (*ibid*, s 6(4)).

154 *Ibid*, s 6(5)(a); see also generally s 6(5).

155 *Ibid*, s 6(6)(d); see also generally s 6(6).

156 *CSR Rules of Procedure*, *supra* note 57, s 9. See field visit reports concerning the complaint filed by Excellon Workers, National Mining Union, and Proyecto de Derechos Económicos, Sociales y Culturales A.C. in relation to Excellon Resources Incorporated, online: DFAIT <http://www.international.gc.ca/csr_counsellor-conseiller_rse/Registry-web-enregistrement.aspx?view=d> [Excellon Complaint].

157 *Review Process Participant Guide*, *supra* note 141 at 17.

158 Order in Council, *supra* note 134, s 6(8). Before issuing the public statement, the CSR Counsellor is to inform the parties of the result and share the statement with the ministers of international trade and natural resources as well as the minister of international co-operation if relevant. See section 6(9). According to section 6(10), the minister of international trade may direct the CSR Counsellor to study additional matters.

trade.[159] If an annual report "would reflect adversely on any person or organization," the CSR Counsellor is to give them an opportunity to comment and "shall include a fair and accurate summary" of their comments in the report.[160] Ultimately, if the CSR Counsellor finds that company operations are "inconsistent with the performance guidelines," the CSR Counsellor is to "make recommendations to assist the company in ensuring that its activities are consistent."[161] No sanction follows, beyond the presumed shaming inherent in the making of the written public statement.

The adoption of the Rules of Procedure and concomitant activation of the review mechanism was greeted with some enthusiasm by industry representatives in the week preceding the vote on Bill C-300, including the Prospectors and Developers Association of Canada (PDAC)[162] and the Mining Association of Canada (MAC).[163] Civil society supporters of Bill C-300 were less enthusiastic, however, noting that while the CSR Counsellor might be of some use in less serious cases, companies were unlikely to consent to the process in the case of more serious allegations, which represented the bulk of complaints received by civil society.[164] Moreover, it was argued that the CSR Counsellor's review process "lacks a transparent fact-finding function and will lead to neither recommendations to government

159 *Ibid*, s 7(2).

160 *Ibid*, s 7(4).

161 *Ibid*, s 8(2).

162 PDAC, *Canada's Exploration and Mining Companies Welcome Canada's Independent CSR Counsellor*, News Release (20 October 2010), online: PDAC <http://www.pdac.ca/pdac/misc/101020.html>.

163 Mining Association of Canada (MAC), *Mining Association of Canada Welcomes the Launch of the CSR Counsellor's Review Mechanism*, Press Release (20 October 2010), online: MAC <http://www.mining.ca/www/media_lib/MAC_News/2010/10_20_10_Press_Releaserev.pdf>.

164 Canadian Network on Corporate Accountability, *Civil Society Statement on CSR Counsellor: Government's New Toothless Review Mechanism Underlies Why Responsible Mining Bill C-300 Is Necessary*, Press Release (26 October 2010), online: Halifax Initiative <http://www.halifaxinitiative.org/content/civil-society-statement-csr-counsellor>. According to the civil society statement, the most common complaints received were "allegations of serious environmental pollution, collaboration with paramilitary networks and deliberate attempts to corrupt government and the judiciary of the host country where the Canadian company establishes its operations." Moreover, as the CSR Counsellor mechanism "lacks an investigative function to clarify disputed facts," it is unclear how she would be able to resolve disputes without establishing first "whether the allegations are well founded."

nor to sanctions."[165] As of December 2011, one review process begun in relation to a mine in Mexico[166] had concluded unsatisfactorily as the company subsequently withdrew from the process.[167] A second request for a review had also been received.[168]

PRELIMINARY CONCLUSIONS

The overview provided in the two preceding sections suggests that, while there is a consensus that the federal government has a role to play in preventing and remedying environmental and human rights harms occurring at mines outside Canada with links to Canadian companies, there is no consensus at this point as to the scope and structure of the relevant implementing mechanisms. For example, Bill C-300 would have applied only to mines in developing countries, yet the CSR Counsellor may in theory respond to problems at Canadian mining operations anywhere outside of Canada.[169] The CSR Counsellor's reach is inherently limited, however, by the requirement of all-party consent.[170] There is also disagreement over

165 *Ibid.* See further MiningWatch Canada, *The Government's New 'CSR Counsellor' for the Extractive Sector*, Newsletter 27 (5 January 2010), online: MiningWatch Canada <http://www.miningwatch.ca/government-s-new-csr-counsellor-extractive-sector>; JP Laplante and Catherine Nolin, "Snake Oil and the Myth of Corporate Social Responsibility" (25 January 2011) 45:1 Canadian Dimension, online: Canadian Dimension <http://canadiandimension.com/articles/3613/>.

166 See Excellon Complaint, *supra* note 156.

167 See Office of the Extractive Sector Corporate Social Responsibility Counsellor, *Closing Report, Request for Review File #2011-01-MEX* (October 2011), online: DFAIT <http://www.international.gc.ca/csr_counsellor-conseiller_rse/assets/pdfs/Closing_report_MEX.pdf>.

168 See complaint filed by Maître Ahmed Mohamed Lemine and others in relation to First Quantums Minerals Limited, online: DFAIT Trade <http://www.international.gc.ca/csr_counsellor-conseiller_rse/Registry-web-enregistrement.aspx?view=d>. This request has since been closed.

169 Complaints have been made about Canadian mining companies operating in developed countries such as the United States. See UN Committee on the Elimination of Racial Discrimination, *Consideration of Reports Submitted by States Parties Under Article 9 of the Convention: Concluding Observations of the Committee on Elimination of Racial Discrimination,* UN Doc CERD/C/CAN/CO/18 (5 March 2007) at para 17 (responding to Western Shoshone Defense Project, *Report on Effects of Canadian Transnational Corporate Activities on the Western Shoshone Peoples of the Western Shoshone Nation: Report Submitted to CERD in relation to Canada's 17th and 18th Periodic Reports of CERD 4 (2007)*).

170 The OECD's NCP process, by contrast, does not require company consent. See notes 67 and 68 in this article. However, OECD NCP complaints have withered

the content of the applicable standards and, in particular, whether or not human rights specifically may or should be invoked. Similarly, there are clear differences of opinion over the appropriate structure of any non-judicial dispute resolution mechanisms, such as whether they should have investigative or merely fact-finding powers, act in an independent ombudsperson capacity,[171] or, as with the CSR Counsellor, serve a mediating role.[172]

More profoundly, it remains contentious whether legal sanctions should be enforced against companies that are not prepared to comply with applicable standards or whether respect for CSR standards should be "voluntary."[173] Yet even mild sanctions, such as the removal of government support from non-compliant companies, is seen as a major threat by industry and industry legal counsel, who raise fears of an exodus of companies from Canada. Further, the need to ensure access to legal remedies for victims of environmental and human rights harms appears beyond contemplation once industry is at the table. And it is equally clear from the anti-bribery experience that, even in the face of a clear multilateral commitment to prohibit specified behaviour, the Canadian government is reluctant to implement legislative reform sanctioning transnational corporate conduct. Clearly, Canadian government regulation facilitating binding remedies or punishment for CSR breaches by recalcitrant companies will not readily be forthcoming. The result is that a non-judicial dispute resolution mechanism — one, moreover, that would permit industry complaints against civil society — has emerged as the government's sole remedial response — a response best seen as having the potential to prevent only minor harms and encourage

due to withdrawal by civil society and community groups frustrated by the process.

171 Jyll Hansen et al, *Canada's Extractive Industry Ombudsperson: Background and Recommendations for an Ombudsperson for Canadian Extractive Companies Operating Abroad: Brief Submitted to the Government of Canada Roundtables on Corporate Social Responsibility in the Extractive Sector* (November 2006), online: <http://halifaxinitiative.org/updir/OmbudspersonMemo.pdf>.

172 Of course, it may be that a layering of non-judicial mechanisms serving different roles would be the ideal solution.

173 The government of Canada frequently states that compliance with identified international standards is voluntary. However, the line between "voluntary" and "mandatory" is generally understood to be less clear than this would suggest. See, eg, Michael Kerr, Richard Janda, and Chip Pitts, *Corporate Social Responsibility: A Legal Analysis* (Markham, ON: LexisNexis, 2009) at 93-104 (examining the voluntary versus regulatory debate and concluding that the debate is unhelpful).

the equivalent of strategic litigation against public participation.[174] While the CSR Counsellor is to be commended for her efforts to achieve consensus on the functioning of the mechanism to which she was appointed, the power and influence of her position is, ultimately, inherently limited.

Finally, it is striking how competing claims relating to competitive advantage and disadvantage feature prominently in the discourse documented earlier. Civil society generally claims that Bill C-300 would provide Canadian companies with a competitive advantage, while industry opponents frame their critiques by asserting that Bill C-300 would create a competitive disadvantage. The contested and, at the same time, persuasive nature of competitive (dis)advantage claims is highlighted by the significantly titled *Building the Canadian Advantage.* Whether or not meaningful home state regulation of transnational corporate conduct is politically feasible appears to hinge greatly upon perceptions of the effects of such regulation on competitive advantage. This point was highlighted in 2008 by John Ruggie in *Protect, Respect, and Remedy,* to which we now turn.[175]

THE UN'S *PROTECT, RESPECT, AND REMEDY* FRAMEWORK AND THE *GUIDING PRINCIPLES*

INTRODUCTION: *PROTECT, RESPECT, AND REMEDY* AND THE RUGGIE PROCESS

Prior to the appointment of John Ruggie as SRSG, the UN Sub-Commission on the Promotion and Protection of Human Rights had produced a set of draft *Norms on the Responsibilities of Transnational Corporations and Other Business Enterprises with regard to Human Rights* (*Norms*).[176] The draft *Norms* were not adopted by the UN Human Rights Commission, which, in 2004, described them

174 See recent Ontario report calling for legislation against strategic litigation against public participation (SLAPP). Anti-SLAPP Advisory Panel, *Report to the Attorney General* (28 October 2010), online: Ministry of the Attorney General <http://www.attorneygeneral.jus.gov.on.ca/english/anti_slapp/anti_slapp_final_report_en.pdf>. See also Barrick Gold lawsuit against small publisher in Quebec (which has anti-SLAPP legislation), *Barrick Gold Corp. c Éditions écosociété inc,* 2011 QCCS 4232; and parallel lawsuit in Ontario, *Banro Corporation v Éditions Écosociété Inc,* 2009 CanLII 7168 (ONSC).

175 *Protect, Respect, and Remedy, supra* note 7 at para 14.

176 UN Sub-Commission on the Promotion and Protection of Human Rights, *Norms on the Responsibilities of Transnational Corporations and Other Business Enterprises*

as a draft proposal of no legal standing but that contained useful elements and ideas.[177] The SRSG's appointment was designed to "move beyond the stalemate" produced by the draft *Norms*, which, while widely endorsed by civil society groups, were opposed by business and governments.[178] Thus, when the SRSG was initially appointed, "there was little that counted as shared knowledge across different stakeholder groups in the business and human rights domain."[179] Accordingly, the SRSG "began an extensive programme of systematic research," resulting ultimately in "[s]everal thousand pages of documentation" available on the Internet and actively disseminated.[180] Among the research highlights of the first two phases of the SRSG's mandate were reports that provided a "scientific mapping" of the position taken by the UN human rights mechanisms with regard to the obligations of both states and corporations.[181]

---

with Regard to Human Rights, UN Doc E/CN.4/Sub.2/2003/12/Rev.2 (26 August 2003). See generally John Gerard Ruggie, "Current Developments: Business and Human Rights: The Evolving International Agenda" (2007) 101 AJIL 821.

177 *Interim Report, supra* note 6 at 55. See also David Weissbrodt and Muria Kruger, "Norms on the Responsibilities of Transnational Corporations and Other Business Enterprises with Regard to Human Rights" (2003) 97 AJIL 901; David Kinley and Junko Tadaki, "From Talk to Walk: The Emergence of Human Rights Responsibilities for Corporations at International Law" (2004) 44 Va J Int'l L 931.

178 *Interim Report, supra* note 6 at para 55. The 2005 mandate included the need to "identify and clarify standards of corporate responsibility and accountability for transnational corporations and other business enterprises with regard to human rights" and to "elaborate on the role of States in effectively regulating and adjudicating the role of transnational corporations and other business enterprises with regard to human rights, including through international cooperation" (*ibid* at para 1).

179 *Guiding Principles, supra* note 11 at para 4.

180 *Ibid* at para 4, referring to the SRSG's web portal, online: Business and Human Rights Resource Centre <http://www.business-humanrights.org/SpecialRepPortal/Home>.

181 John Ruggie, *Business and Human Rights: Mapping International Standards of Responsibility and Accountability for Corporate Acts*, UNHRC, 4th Sess, UN Doc A/HRC/4/35 (19 February 2007). Summary conclusions of this mapping included: explicit recognition of the existence of direct legal obligations for business under international criminal law, despite the lack of an international forum to hear claims (*ibid* at paras 21, 19-32); explicit recognition that international law does not (yet) recognize direct legal obligations for business for violations of less egregious international human rights law norms (*ibid* at paras 33, 33-44); the "uncontested nature" of the "firmly established" fact that "states have a duty to protect against nonstate human rights abuses within their

He also conducted several legal expert consultations [182] and numerous multi-stakeholder consultations,[183] touching upon various aspects of his mandate including the issues of whether corporations have direct obligations under international human rights law, the extent of the state duty to protect human rights, and the role of states in conflict-affected areas.

In 2008, *Protect, Respect, and Remedy* was unanimously welcomed by member states of the UN Human Rights Council.[184] It is aimed at all human rights[185] and is designed to "assist all social actors — governments, companies, and civil society — to reduce the adverse human rights consequences of [institutional] misalignments."[186] It identifies the "root cause" of the business and human rights problem

---

jurisdiction, and that this duty extends to protection against abuses by business entities" (*ibid* at para 10). See also John Ruggie, *Report of the Special Representative of the Secretary-General on the Issue of Human Rights and Transnational Corporations and Other Business Enterprises, Addendum: State Responsibilities to Regulate and Adjudicate Corporate Activities under the United Nations Core Human Rights Treaties: An Overview of Treaty Body Commentaries*, UNHRC, 4th Sess, UN Doc A/HRC/4/35/Add.1 (13 February 2007).

182 *Report of the Special Representative of the Secretary-General on the Issue of Human Rights and Transnational Corporations and Other Business Enterprises, Addendum: Corporate Responsibility under International Law and Issues in Extraterritorial Regulation: Summary of Legal Workshops*, UNHRC, 4th Sess, UN Doc A/HRC/4/35/Add.2 (15 February 2007). The author attended the New York legal experts' consultation.

183 SRSG, *Corporate Responsibility to Protect Human Rights: Summary Report on Consultation in Geneva (4-5 December 2007)*, online: Business and Human Rights Resource Centre <http://www.reports-and-materials.org/Ruggie-Geneva-4-5-Dec-2007.pdf>; SRSG, *The Role of States in Effectively Regulating and Adjudicating the Activities of Corporations With Respect to Human Rights: Summary Report on Meeting in Copenhagen (8-9 November 2007)*, online: Business and Human Rights Resource Centre <http://www.business-humanrights.org/Documents/Ruggie-Copenhagen-8-9-Nov-2007.pdf>; SRSG, *Business and Human Rights in Conflict Zones: The Role of Home States: Summary Report of Consultation Co-convened by SRSG and Global Witness in Berlin (5 November 2007)*, online: Business and Human Rights Resource Centre <http://www.reports-and-materials.org/Ruggie-Global-Witness-Berlin-report-5-Nov-2007.pdf>. The author attended the Copenhagen multi-stakeholder consultation. See also links to summary reports of all consultations, meetings, and workshops throughout the mandate, online: Business and Human Rights Resource Centre <http://www.business-humanrights.org/SpecialRepPortal/Home/Consultationsmeetingsworkshops>.

184 *Protect, Respect, and Remedy, supra* note 7; UNHRC, *supra* note 8.

185 *Protect, Respect, and Remedy, supra* note 7 at paras 24, 52.

186 *Ibid* at paras 7, 17.

today as "governance gaps created by globalization — between the scope and impact of economic forces and actors, and the capacity of societies to manage their adverse consequences."[187]

Protect, Respect, and Remedy consists of three "differentiated but complementary responsibilities": the state duty to protect against human rights abuses by business enterprises; the corporate responsibility to respect human rights; and the need for greater access by victims to effective remedies. While the state duty to protect is described by the SRSG as lying "at the very core of the international human rights regime," the corporate responsibility to respect is described as "the basic expectation society has of business in relation to human rights."[188] Access to remedies is also essential because "even the most concerted efforts cannot prevent all abuse."[189]

Protect, Respect, and Remedy notes that international human rights treaty bodies recommend that states take all necessary steps to protect against abuse by non-state actors, including prevention, investigation and punishment, and provision of access to redress.[190] The duty to protect has both legal and policy dimensions, and while states have discretion in terms of how to implement this duty, both regulation and adjudication are appropriate.[191] However, home states "may feel reluctant to regulate against overseas harms" either because the "permissible scope of national regulation with extraterritorial effect remains poorly understood" or "out of concern that those firms might lose investment opportunities or relocate their headquarters."[192] In terms of the jurisdictional scope of the duty, international law provides that states are required to protect against human rights abuses by businesses "affecting persons within their territory or jurisdiction."[193] Yet

> [e]xperts disagree on whether international law requires home States to help prevent human rights abuses abroad by corporations based within their territory. There is greater consensus that those States are not prohibited from doing so where a recognized basis of jurisdiction exists, and

187 *Ibid* at para 3.

188 *Ibid* at paras 9 and 55.

189 *Ibid* at para 82.

190 *Ibid* at para 18.

191 *Ibid.*

192 *Ibid* at para 14.

193 *Ibid* at para 18.

the actions of the home State meet an overall reasonableness test, which includes non-intervention in the internal affairs of other States. Indeed, there is increasing encouragement at the international level, including from the treaty bodies, for home States to take regulatory action to prevent abuse by their companies overseas.[194]

Notably, the elaboration of the state duty to protect in *Protect, Respect, and Remedy* focuses very much on the policy dimensions of the duty, encouraging rather than mandating that they do more and never chastising host states for their failures.[195]

The role of home states is also discussed under the access to remedies pillar. Here, *Protect, Respect, and Remedy* outlines the problems that complainants have encountered when seeking judicial remedies in home state courts, such as costs, lack of standing, and the common law doctrine of *forum non conveniens*.[196] The SRSG suggests that the "law is slowly evolving in response to some of these obstacles" and concludes that states "should strengthen judicial capacity to hear complaints and enforce remedies against all corporations operating or based in their territory, while also protecting against frivolous claims."[197] The discussion of non-judicial remedies also makes reference to home state mechanisms in the form of the OECD's NCPs and the OECD Guidelines.[198] While the NCPs have potential, *Protect, Respect, and Remedy* concludes that they fall short of the requirements for credible and effective non-judicial mechanisms due to potential conflicts of interest, lack of resources, uncertain time frames, and lack of transparent outcomes.[199] As with the state duty to protect, the elaboration of the access to remedies pillar

194 *Ibid* at para 19.

195 See Sara L Seck, "Collective Responsibility and Transnational Corporate Conduct," in Tracy Isaacs and Richard Vernon, eds, *Accountability for Collective Wrongdoing* (Cambridge: Cambridge University Press, 2011) 140 at 158 (noting *Protect, Respect, and Remedy*'s focus on policy recommendations for state implementation of the duty to protect rather than mandatory prescriptions coupled with sanctions against recalcitrant states).

196 *Protect, Respect, and Remedy, supra* note 7 at para 89.

197 *Ibid* at paras 90 and 91. Further, states should "address obstacles to access to justice, including for foreign plaintiffs — especially where alleged abuses reach the level of widespread and systemic human rights violations" (*ibid*).

198 *Ibid* at paras 98-99.

199 *Ibid* at paras 98, 92. However, some NCPs are taking innovative approaches that the OECD and adhering states "should consider" (*ibid* at para 99).

appears designed to encourage states to increase the availability of remedies, through both judicial and non-judicial mechanisms, rather than chastising states for not living up to their obligations under international human rights law. *Protect, Respect, and Remedy* concludes that the existing "patchwork of grievance mechanisms at different levels of the international system, with different constituencies and processes" leaves "considerable numbers of individuals whose human rights are impacted by corporations [without] access to [any] remedy."[200] While this situation is attributed in part to a "lack of information," the SRSG remarks, strikingly: "It also reflects *intended* and unintended limitations in the competence and coverage of existing mechanisms."[201]

The third phase of the SRSG's mandate consisted of an additional three-year period to "operationalize" *Protect, Respect, and Remedy* — "that is, to provide concrete and practical recommendations for its implementation."[202] The SRSG was asked to proceed "in the same research-based and consultative manner" as he had for *Protect, Respect, and Remedy.*[203] Of significance to the SRSG in embarking on this next phase of his work was the fact that *Protect, Respect, and Remedy* was "endorsed or employed" not only by individual governments but also by "business enterprises and associations, civil society and workers' organizations, national human rights institutions, and investors" as well as "such multilateral institutions as the International Organization for Standardization and the [OECD]" and other UN special procedures.[204] He attributed the "widespread positive reception" of *Protect, Respect, and Remedy* to both its "utility" and "the large number and inclusive character of stakeholder consultations convened by and for the mandate."[205] Indeed, by the time the draft *Guiding Principles* were being considered in January 2011, "the mandate had held 47 international consultations, on all continents," and the SRSG and his team "had made site visits to business operations and their local stakeholders in more than 20 countries."[206] The *Guiding Principles* were thus

200 *Ibid* at para 102.

201 *Ibid* at para 103 [emphasis added].

202 *Guiding Principles, supra* note 11 at para 9.

203 *Ibid* at para 10.

204 *Ibid* at para 7.

205 *Ibid* at para 8.

206 *Ibid.*

informed by extensive discussions with all stakeholder groups, including Governments, business enterprises and associations, individuals and communities directly affected by the activities of enterprises in various parts of the world, civil society, and experts in the many areas of law and policy that the Guiding Principles touch upon.[207]

In addition, some of the *Guiding Principles* were "road tested" and thus provide "guidance informed by actual practice."[208] For example, the *Guiding Principles* that address how governments should help companies avoid being drawn into human rights abuses in conflict-affected areas "emerged from off-the-record, scenario-based workshops with officials from a cross-section of States that had practical experience in dealing with these challenges."[209] Corporate lawyers were involved in the corporate law project, in which more than twenty leading corporate law firms from around the world assisted, on a pro bono basis, to "identify whether and how corporate and securities law in 39 jurisdictions currently encourages companies to respect human rights."[210]

The *Guiding Principles* themselves were "subject to extensive consultations," first in October 2010 at sessions held separately with Human Rights Council delegates, business enterprises and associations, and civil society groups, at which an annotated outline of the proposals was discussed.[211] In November 2010, a full draft of the *Guiding Principles* and related commentary was "sent to all Member States" and simultaneously "posted online for public comment" until the end of January 2011.[212]

207 *Ibid* at para 10.

208 *Ibid* at para 11.

209 *Ibid.* See John Ruggie, *Report of the Special Representative of the Secretary-General on the Issue of Human Rights and Transnational Corporations and other Business Enterprises: Business and Human Rights in Conflict-Affected Regions: Challenges and Options towards State Responses*, UNHRC 17th Sess, UN Doc A/HRC/17/32 (27 May 2011) [*Conflict-Affected Regions*]. Three workshops were convened involving participants from 12 countries representing a balance of "home and host states": Belgium, Brazil, Canada, China, Columbia, Guatemala, Nigeria, Norway, Sierra Leone, Switzerland, the United Kingdom, and the United States (*ibid* at para 2).

210 *Corporate Law Addendum, supra* note 11 at paras 6, 11.

211 *Guiding Principles, supra* note 11 at para 12.

212 *Ibid.* See John Ruggie, *Draft Report of the Special Representative of the Secretary-General on the Issue of Human Rights and Transnational Corporations and other Business Enterprises: Guiding Principles for the Implementation of the United Nations 'Protect, Respect and Remedy' Framework*, online: <http://www.reports-and-materials.org/

THE *GUIDING PRINCIPLES*

The *Guiding Principles* were presented to the UN Human Rights Council on 30 May 2011. The report highlights that endorsement of the *Guiding Principles* by the UN Human Rights Council would "mark the end of the beginning: by establishing a common global platform for action, on which cumulative progress can be built, step-by-step, without foreclosing any other promising longer-term developments."[213] Significantly, the normative contribution of the *Guiding Principles*

> lies not in the creation of new international law obligations but in elaborating the implications of existing standards and practices for States and businesses; integrating them within a single, logically coherent and comprehensive template; and identifying where the current regime falls short and how it should be improved.[214]

The *Guiding Principles* are structured in chapters following the template of *Protect, Respect, and Remedy*, with each pillar described as "an essential component in an inter-related and dynamic system of preventative and remedial measures."[215]

Two foundational principles underlie the state duty to protect. Principle 1 provides:

Ruggie-UN-draft-Guiding-Principles-22-Nov-2010.pdf> [*Draft Guiding Principles*]. The online consultation "attracted 3,576 unique visitors from 120 countries and territories," and "[s]ome 100 written submissions were sent directly to the Special Representative, including by Governments." The *Draft Guiding Principles* were further "discussed at an expert multi-stakeholder meeting, and then at a session with Council delegations, both held in January 2011." *Guiding Principles, supra* note 11 at para 12. For links to commentaries and submissions on the *Draft Guiding Principles*, see online: Business and Human Rights Resource Centre <http://www.business-humanrights.org/SpecialRepPortal/Home/Protect-Respect-Remedy-Framework/GuidingPrinciples/CommentariesonDraftGuidingPrinciples> and online: Business and Human Rights Resource Centre <http://www.business-humanrights.org/SpecialRepPortal/Home/Protect-Respect-Remedy-Framework/GuidingPrinciples/Submissions> [Submissions to Consultations on *Draft Guiding Principles*].

213 *Guiding Principles, supra* note 11 at para 13.

214 *Ibid* at para 14. Moreover, while the *Guiding Principles* are "universally applicable," "one size does not fit all," given the "fact that we live in a world of 192 United Nations Member States, 80,000 transnational enterprises, 10 times as many subsidiaries and countless millions of national firms, most of which are small and medium-sized enterprises" (*ibid* at para 15).

215 *Ibid* at para 6.

States must protect against human rights abuse within their territory and/ or jurisdiction by third parties, including business enterprises. This requires taking appropriate steps to prevent, investigate, punish and redress such abuse through effective policies, legislation, regulations and adjudication.[216]

According to Principle 2, "[s]tates should set out clearly the expectation that all business enterprises domiciled in their territory and/ or jurisdiction respect human rights throughout their operations."[217] The commentary to Principle 2 begins with a statement reminiscent of the uncertainty identified in *Protect, Respect, and Remedy* regarding the permissibility of home state regulation despite a lack of obligation under international human rights law.[218] However, the commentary also notes the existence of strong "policy reasons" for home states to clearly set out expectations, in particular, where the state is either involved in the business or supports it, in part so as to preserve the reputation of the home state itself.[219] Moreover, the commentary highlights that a range of approaches have been adopted by states to date including both "domestic measures with extraterritorial implications"[220] and "direct extraterritorial legislation

216 *Ibid* at 6, Principle 1. The chapter outlining the state duty to protect is described as focused upon preventative measures (*ibid* at 7). As the state duty to protect is a standard of conduct, states are not "per se responsible for human rights abuse by private actors" but, rather, "may breach their international human rights law obligations where such abuse can be attributed to them" or where they "fail to take appropriate steps to prevent, investigate, punish and redress private actors' abuse" (*ibid* at 7, Commentary to Principle 1).

217 *Ibid* at 7, Principle 2.

218 *Ibid* at 7, Commentary to Principle 2. See text accompanying note 194.

219 *Guiding Principles, supra* note 11 at 7, Commentary to Principle 2.

220 *Ibid.* These measures include "requirements on 'parent' companies to report on the global operations of the entire enterprise; multilateral soft-law instruments such as the [OECD] Guidelines; and performance standards required by institutions that support overseas investments." The distinction between measures with extraterritorial effect and direct extraterritorial measures was first introduced by the SRSG in a keynote address in Stockholm in November 2009 and elaborated upon in his 2010 report. See John G Ruggie, *Keynote Presentation at EU Presidency Conference on the 'Protect, Respect and Remedy' Framework*, Stockholm, 10-11 November 2009, online: <http://www.reports-and-materials.org/Ruggie-presentation-Stockholm-10-Nov-2009.pdf>; John Ruggie, *Report of the Special Representative of the Secretary-General on the Issue of Human Rights and Transnational Corporations and other Business Enterprises: Business and Human Rights: Further Steps toward the Operationalization of the "Protect, Respect and Remedy*, UNHRC, 14th Sess, UN Doc A/HRC/14/27 (9 April 2010) at para 48.

and enforcement."[221] The commentary concludes that a variety of factors "contribute to the perceived and actual reasonableness of States' actions," including whether they are "grounded in multi-lateral agreement."[222]

Following these foundational principles, the chapter outlining the state duty to protect presents a series of operational principles categorized within four overarching themes. The first theme on "general state regulatory and policy functions" highlights both Principle 3 on the importance of enforcement and periodic assessment of the adequacy of existing laws and the need to ensure that "laws and policies governing the creation and ongoing operation of business enterprises, such as corporate law, do not constrain but enable business respect for human rights."[223] The principle elaborates on the need for states to provide businesses with "effective guidance" on "how to respect human rights throughout their operations" and to "[e]ncourage or where appropriate require, business enterprises to communicate how they address their human rights impacts."[224]

The second theme on "the state-business nexus" encompasses Principles 4, 5, and 6.[225] According to Principle 4, states should "take additional steps" when business enterprises are "owned or controlled by the State" or "receive substantial support and services from State agencies," including export credit agencies and official investment insurance or guarantee agencies.[226] These additional steps may include "requiring human rights due diligence."[227] The third theme, "supporting business respect for human rights in conflict-affected areas," is addressed in Principle 7 and consists of four recommendations for states due to the heightened risk of gross human rights abuses in conflict zones.[228] These include: engaging with businesses

221 *Guiding Principles, supra* note 11 at 7, Commentary to Principle 2. This includes "criminal regimes that allow for prosecution based on the nationality of the perpetrator no matter where the offence occurs."

222 *Ibid.*

223 *Ibid* at 8, Principle 3.

224 *Ibid.*

225 *Ibid.* Principle 5 addresses privatization, while Principle 6 focuses on procurement activities.

226 *Ibid* at 9, Principle 4.

227 *Ibid.*

228 *Ibid* at 10, Principle 7.

to help them "identify, prevent and mitigate" human rights-related risks at the "earliest stage possible"; providing "adequate assistance to business enterprises to assess and address the heightened risks"; "denying access to public support and services" where a business enterprise involved in gross human rights abuses refuses to co-operate; and ensuring that the risks of business involvement in gross human rights abuses are effectively addressed by "current policies, legislation, regulations and enforcement measures."[229]

"Ensuring policy coherence," which is the fourth and final theme under the state duty to protect, is addressed in Principles 8 through 10. Most relevant to home states is Principle 8, according to which "governmental departments, agencies or State-based institutions that shape business practices" need to be "aware of and observe the State's human rights obligations" when fulfilling their mandates.[230] Finally, Principle 10 provides that, as members of multilateral institutions, states should promote business respect for human rights by helping other states meet their duty to protect through "technical assistance, capacity-building and awareness-raising" while also drawing upon the *Guiding Principles* to promote "shared understandings" and "advance international co-operation" on business and human rights.[231]

The role of home states is also considered in the final chapter of the *Guiding Principles,* "Access to Remedy." A single foundational principle, Principle 25, informs the chapter:

> As part of their duty to protect against business-related human rights abuse, States must take appropriate steps to ensure, through judicial, administrative, legislative or other appropriate means, that when such abuses occur within their territory and/or jurisdiction those affected have access to effective remedy.[232]

[229] *Ibid* at 10-11, Principle 7. See also *Conflict-Affected Regions, supra* note 209.

[230] *Guiding Principles, supra* note 11 at 11, Principle 8. Principle 9 highlights the need for states to maintain "adequate domestic policy space" and regulatory ability to meet their own human rights obligations, even when pursuing investment treaties or contracts with other States or business enterprises(*ibid* at 12, Principle 9).

[231] *Ibid* at 12, Principle 10. Principle 10 further provides that as members of multilateral institutions dealing with business-related issues, States should ensure that the institutions do not "restrain the ability of their member States to meet their duty to protect."

[232] *Ibid* at 22, Principle 25.

The commentary elaborates that access to effective remedies includes both "procedural and substantive aspects" and that remedies may include "apologies, restitution, rehabilitation, financial or non-financial compensation and punitive sanctions (whether criminal or administrative, such as fines), as well as the prevention of harm through, for example, injunctions or guarantees of non-repetition."[233] The term "grievance" is defined as "a perceived injustice evoking an individual's or a group's sense of entitlement," while "grievance mechanism" is used "to indicate any routinized, State-based or non-State-based, judicial or non-judicial process" through which grievances "can be raised and remedy can be sought."[234]

Five operational principles appear under the chapter "Access to Remedy." Principle 26 on "state-based judicial mechanisms," provides that states should "ensure the effectiveness of domestic judicial mechanisms" by considering how to reduce legal and other barriers that "could lead to a denial of access to remedy."[235] The commentary highlights the importance of states ensuring that they do not "erect barriers to prevent legitimate cases from being brought before the courts" and ensuring that the "legitimate and peaceful activities of human rights defenders are not obstructed."[236] Principle 27 on "state-based non-judicial grievance mechanisms," suggests that "alongside judicial mechanisms," states should "provide effective and appropriate non-judicial grievance mechanisms ... as part of a comprehensive State-based system for the remedy of business-related human rights abuse."[237] The commentary notes that a judicial remedy is not always required nor is it always the approach favoured by claimants "even where judicial systems are effective and well-resourced." Consequently, there is an essential role for administrative, legislative, and other non-judicial mechanisms as a complement and supplement to judicial mechanisms.[238]

233 *Ibid* at 22, Commentary to Principle 25.

234 *Ibid.* A grievance may be based on "law, contract, explicit or implicit promises, customary practice, or general notions of fairness of aggrieved communities."

235 *Ibid* at 23, Principle 26.

236 *Ibid* at 23, Commentary to Principle 26.

237 *Ibid* at 24, Principle 27.

238 *Ibid* at 24, Commentary to Principle 27.

Principles 28 to 30 address "non-state grievance mechanisms." Principle 28 highlights that states should play a role in facilitating access to effective non-state-based grievance mechanisms.[239] The commentary identifies two different categories of non-state-based grievance mechanisms: first, those "administered by a business enterprise alone or with stakeholders, by an industry association or a multi-stakeholder group"[240] and, second, "regional and international human rights bodies," which, while most often dealing with "alleged violations by States of their obligations to respect human rights," have also at times dealt with the "failure of a State to meet its duty to protect against human rights abuse by business enterprises."[241] This commentary is striking for several reasons. Positively, it highlights that access to remedies may include remedies against the state rather than against the business enterprise alone, as appears implicit in the rest of the "Access to Remedy" chapter.[242] However, by categorizing regional and international human rights mechanisms as non-state-based grievance mechanisms rather than enforcers of international law, the *Guiding Principles* curiously appear to equate such mechanisms with private company or industry grievance mechanisms.

Principle 31, the final principle under the "Access to Remedy" chapter, outlines "effectiveness criteria for non-judicial grievance mechanisms" and is applicable to both state-based and non-state-based mechanisms.[243] To be effective, grievance mechanisms should

239 *Ibid* at 24, Principle 28. Principle 29 then focuses upon the need for business enterprises to "establish or participate in effective operational-level grievance mechanisms for individuals and communities" in order to address and remediate grievances early on, while Principle 30 provides that "collaborative initiatives that are based on respect for human rights-related standards," whether industry or multi-stakeholder, should "ensure that effective grievance mechanisms are available" in order to achieve greater legitimacy (*ibid* at 25-26).

240 *Ibid* at 24, Commentary to Principle 28. According to the commentary, non-state-based grievance mechanisms administered by business enterprises offer potential benefits, including "transnational reach." The commentary also notes that non-state-based grievance mechanisms are "non-judicial, but may use adjudicative, dialogue-based or other culturally appropriate and rights-compatible processes."

241 *Ibid* at 25, Commentary to Principle 28.

242 Seck, *supra* note 195 at 158-59 (discussing with respect to *Protect, Respect, and Remedy*).

243 *Guiding Principles, supra* note 11 at 26, Principle 31.

be: (1) legitimate;[244] (2) accessible;[245] (3) predictable;[246] (4) equitable;[247] (5) transparent;[248] (6) rights-compatible;[249] and (7) a source of continuous learning.[250] Operational grievance mechanisms should also be "[b]ased on engagement and dialogue," including by "consulting stakeholder groups for whose use they are intended on their design and performance."[251]

PRELIMINARY CONCLUSIONS

In sum, the *Guiding Principles* do not definitively state that home states have binding obligations under international human rights law to regulate and adjudicate transnational corporations so as to prevent and remedy human rights harms. However, they do provide guidance as to the types of measures that all states should implement to prevent and remedy business harms and so can serve as a useful tool for evaluating the recent Canadian developments described earlier with regard to global mining. Further reflection on how the "Ruggie process" informed the substance of his conclusions on the existence and scope of home state obligations will be provided in the following section.

244 *Ibid.* Legitimate means "enabling trust from the stakeholder groups for whose use they are intended, and being accountable for the fair conduct of grievance processes."

245 *Ibid.* Accessible means "being known to all stakeholder groups for whose use they are intended, and providing adequate assistance for those who may face particular barriers to access."

246 *Ibid.* Predictable means "providing a clear and known procedure with an indicative timeframe for each stage, and clarity on the types of process and outcome available and means of monitoring implementation."

247 *Ibid.* Equitable means "seeking to ensure that aggrieved parties have reasonable access to sources of information, advice and expertise necessary to engage in a grievance process on fair, informed and respectful terms."

248 *Ibid.* Transparent means "keeping parties to a grievance informed about its progress, and providing sufficient information about the mechanism's performance to build confidence in its effectiveness and meet any public interest at stake."

249 *Ibid.* Rights-compatible means "ensuring that outcomes and remedies accord with internationally recognized human rights."

250 *Ibid.* Continuous learning is defined as "drawing on relevant measures to identify lessons for improving the mechanism and preventing future grievances and harms."

251 *Ibid.* Dialogue should be the means used to address and resolve grievances.

Discussion

CANADA, GLOBAL MINING, AND THE *GUIDING PRINCIPLES*

The *Guiding Principles* use permissive language in making several recommendations relating to the home state duty to protect rights. Thus, Principle 3(a) indicates that states "should" enforce laws requiring business enterprises to respect rights and review existing laws to identify and address any gaps. The Canadian roundtables process could qualify as a review of the adequacy of Canadian laws relating to global mining. Its multi-stakeholder approach, mirroring in some ways that of the SRSG's process, might even be viewed as commendable. Principle 3(b) identifies the need to ensure that corporate laws do not constrain business respect for human rights. Recent developments in Canadian corporate law suggest that some steps may have been taken to make director fiduciary duties more human rights friendly,[252] while shareholder proposals reflecting affected community concerns may now be brought to annual general meetings with greater ease than in the past.[253] However, there is no guarantee that these proposals will influence decision making.[254]

Principle 3(c)'s recommendation that states provide further guidance to businesses on "how to respect human rights throughout their operations" is met at least in part by the existence of the Centre of Excellence for CSR, although as noted earlier in this article, the list of CSR standards to which the centre refers companies does not include *Protect, Respect, and Remedy* or the *Guiding Principles.*[255]

252 See *BCE Inc v 1976 Debentureholders,* 2008 SCC 69, [2008] 3 SCR 560. For related commentary, see, eg, Mohamed F Khimji, "People v. Wise — Conflating Directors' Duties, Oppression, and Stakeholder Protection" (2006) 39 UBCL Rev 209; Anthony Vanduzer, "*BCE v 1976 Debentureholders*: The Supreme Court Hits and Misses in Its Most Important Corporate Law Decision since *Peoples*" (2010) 43 UBC L Rev 205. See also Stikeman Elliott LLP, *Corporate Law Tools Project* (September 2009), online: Business and Human Rights Resource Centre <http://www.business-humanrights.org/media/documents/ruggie/corp-law-tools-canada-stikeman-elliott-for-ruggie-sep-2009.pdf> [*Stikeman Elliott CLT Report*].

253 See *ibid* at 19; Aaron A Dhir, "Realigning the Corporate Building Blocks: Shareholder Proposals as a Vehicle for Achieving Corporate Social and Human Rights Accountability" (2006) 43 Am Bus LJ 365.

254 Dhir, "Shareholder Engagement," *supra* note 69.

255 See text accompanying note 10 in this article.

Principle 3(d) calls upon states to encourage or even require business enterprises to communicate how they address their human rights impacts. This recommendation may be partially met by the inclusion of the GRI as a performance standard for the CSR Counsellor,[256] although there have also been calls for increased social disclosure under securities laws in Ontario.[257]

The EDC's human rights and environmental policies may be in keeping with Principle 4's recommendation that human rights impact assessments be conducted when states provide substantial support or services to business ventures.[258] However, no similar requirement exists in relation to other government support such as that provided through Canadian missions abroad, despite such a proposal in Bill C-300. Moreover, unlike Bill C-300, the *Guiding Principles* do not suggest that this financing or support should be made conditional upon company compliance with human rights standards. The one exception is where enterprises engaged in gross human rights abuses in conflict-affected areas refuse to co-operate to address the situation.[259] Yet even in this seemingly extreme case, Canada has not adopted conditionality.

Other recommendations in Principle 7(a) and (b) concern engagement with, and assistance to, business enterprises that are at a heightened risk of committing abuses so that they might identify, prevent, and mitigate these risks. These recommendations may be partially addressed by the inclusion of the Voluntary Principles on Security and Human Rights in the CSR Counsellor's mandate.[260] Principle 7(d) also proposes that states ensure that their policies, legislation, regulations, and enforcement measures are effective in addressing these risks. The possibility of "civil, administrative or criminal liability for enterprises domiciled or operating in" a state's

256 See note 149 in this article.

257 See Ontario Securities Commission (OSC), *OSC Corporate Sustainability Reporting Initiative: Report to Minister of Finance* (18 December 2009) at 14, online: OSC <http://www.osc.gov.on.ca/documents/en/Securities-Category5/rule_20091218_51-717_mof-rpt.pdf>; Hennick Centre for Business and Law and Jantzi-Sustainalytics, *Corporate Social Reporting Initiative: Report to Minister of Finance* (June 2010) at 8, online: Hennick Centre <http://www.hennickcentre.ca/documents/FINALREPORT.pdf>. See also increased disclosure requirements in the OECD Guidelines, which are promoted by Canada's NCP. *OECD Guidelines, supra* note 18 at 15.

258 See notes 129-30 and accompanying text in this article.

259 *Guiding Principles, supra* note 11 at 10-11, Principle 7.

260 See Voluntary Principles, *supra* note 40.

territory and/or jurisdiction that contribute to gross human rights abuses is raised here, a possibility that may, or, more likely, may not be met in Canada.[261] Effective enforcement remains unlikely given Canada's historically poor enforcement record in the bribery context.

Principle 8's recommendation that government departments achieve policy coherence with state human rights commitments may be partially met by the existence of federal department CSR policies.[262] Finally, Principle 10's emphasis on multilateral engagement through multilateral institutions, including technical assistance, capacity building, and "awareness-raising" may be met by Canada's leadership role in the Intergovernmental Forum on Mining, Minerals, Metals and Sustainable Development.[263]

The role of the home state is also addressed in the *Guiding Principles* under "Access to Remedy" chapter. In terms of access to judicial remedies, as discussed earlier, there have been no recent legislative changes to facilitate this recourse,[264] although it remains to be seen whether courts will themselves begin to embrace this type of litigation, at least by not exercising their discretion to decline to hear such cases.[265] While increasing numbers of non-judicial mechanisms have been implemented, it appears unlikely

261 See James Yap, "Corporate Civil Liability for War Crimes in Canadian Courts: Lessons from *Bil'in (Village Council) v. Green Park International Ltd.*" (2010) 8 J Int'l Crim Justice 631; W. Cory Wanless, "Corporate Liability for International Crimes under Canada's Crimes against Humanity and War Crimes Act" (2009) 7 J Int'l Criminal Justice 201.

262 See, eg, the list of government departments with links to CSR policies on the website of the CSR Centre of Excellence, online: <http://web.cim.org/csr/MenuPage.cfm?sections=126&menu=131#block253>.

263 See further on the Intergovernmental Forum on Mining, Minerals, Metals and Sustainable Development, *supra* note 112. However, another view of the Intergovernmental Forum and other capacity-building exercises in developing countries would be that these are designed to facilitate the exploitation of host state natural resources to benefit Canadian companies. See, eg, critical commentary surrounding the support provided by CIDA to "development NGOs" for "CSR projects" of mining companies at mine sites overseas by Catherine Coumans, *Brief Prepared for the House of Commons Standing Committee on Foreign Affairs and International Development's Study on the Role of the Private Sector in Achieving Canada's International Development Interests* (MiningWatch Canada: January 2012), online: MiningWatch Canada <http://www.miningwatch.ca/sites/www.miningwatch.ca/files/Mining_and_Development_FAAE_2012.pdf>.

264 However, see Bill C-354, *supra* note 58.

265 See notes 64-66 in this article.

that any would meet the list of effectiveness criteria outlined in Principle 31.[266]

This review would not be complete without acknowledging the influence of the SRSG's contributions to other international standards referenced by Canadian government mechanisms. For example, the most recent version of the OECD Guidelines for Multinational Enterprises, released in May 2011, includes a new chapter on human rights designed to reflect the recommendations in *Protect, Respect, and Remedy* and the *Guiding Principles*.[267] Greater attention was also paid to the design of the NCP process in order to better reflect the recommendations of the SRSG.[268] There is pressure from human rights advocates for the OECD to take human rights into account in the current review of the OECD Recommendation on Export Credits and the Environment.[269] The most recent revisions to the IFC's Sustainability Framework and Policies and Procedures, dating from May 2011, also include increased references to human rights, although it may be debated whether they are sufficiently aligned with *Protect, Respect, and Remedy* and the *Guiding Principles* to satisfy the SRSG himself.[270] On 23 March 2011, the GRI

266 In this regard, it is interesting to compare the *Guiding Principles'* list of criteria, *supra* notes 243-51 with the list of claims made by the Office of the Extractive Sector CSR Counsellor, *supra* note 140.

267 See generally materials on the update process on the OECD website, online: OECD <http://www.oecd.org/document/33/0,3746,en_2649_34889_44086753_1_1_1_1,00.html>. See also new text OECD, *OECD Guidelines for Multinational Enterprises: Recommendations for Responsible Business Conduct in a Global Context* (25 May 2011), online: OECD <http://www.oecd.org/dataoecd/43/29/48004323.pdf >. As of 25 May 2011, adhering governments are all OECD members as well as Argentina, Brazil, Egypt, Latvia, Lithuania, Morocco, Peru, and Romania.

268 OECD, *OECD Guidelines for Multinational Enterprises: Recommendations for Responsible Business Conduct in a Global Context* (OECD Ministerial Meeting, 2011) at 32, online: OECD <http://www.oecd.org/dataoecd/43/29/48004323.pdf>.

269 See Amnesty International, *A Call for OECD's Export Credit Group to Protect the Rights of Those Affected by Business-Related Human Rights Abuses* (28 June 2011), online: Amnesty International <http://www.amnesty.org/fr/node/24942>; Amnesty International, *Review of the Revised Recommendation on Common Approaches on the Environment and Officially Supported Export Credits*, Submission of Amnesty International (20 February 2010) (March 2010), online: Amnesty International <http://www.amnesty.org/en/library/asset/POL30/002/2010/en/a1b48827-bdc9-4d8b-afd8-7cc25daed63a/pol300022010en.pdf>.

270 See letter to World Bank Group President from John Ruggie sent March 2011, online: Business and Human Rights Resource Centre <http://www.business-humanrights.org/media/documents/ruggie/ruggie-ltr-to-world-bank-president-zoellick-re-ifc-policies-standards-review-3-mar-2011.pdf>. The revised

released the latest revised and updated GRI reporting standards, the G3.1 Guidelines, which explicitly incorporate human rights reporting.[271] Thus, even without explicit reference to *Protect, Respect, and Remedy* or the *Guiding Principles*, Canada's promotion of other international standards will increasingly include a human rights component — although it appears unlikely to be in a legally binding form.

INTERNATIONAL LAW AND CORPORATE POWER

Protect, Respect, and Remedy has been described as a polycentric governance framework, an attempt to "build simultaneous public and private governance systems as well as coordinate, without integrating, their operations."[272] This article has sought to determine what role is envisioned within this framework for home states in regulating and adjudicating to prevent and remedy human rights harms, and how measures implemented by the Canadian government measure up to the *Guiding Principles*. As seen earlier, Canadian practice is clearly not fully consistent with the *Guiding Principles*. However, a bigger question is why the *Guiding Principles* themselves frame the home state duty to protect in suggestive terms rather than as a binding legal obligation under international human rights law.[273] From a legal perspective, the *Guiding Principles* are curious. While they have received a significant amount of support, many international human rights lawyers are critical of their substance.[274]

Sustainability Framework was released in May 2011 (online: IFC <http://www.ifc.org/ifcext/policyreview.nsf>) and includes revisions to the Policies and Performance Standards (online: IFC <http://www.ifc.org/ifcext/policyreview.nsf#SF>. See full text of revised Sustainability Framework, online: IFC <http://www.ifc.org/ifcext/policyreview.nsf/AttachmentsByTitle/Updated_IFC_SFCompounded_August1-2011/$FILE/Updated_IFC_SustainabilityFramework Compounded_August1-2011.pdf>.

271 For text see online: GRI <https://www.globalreporting.org/reporting/latest-guidelines/g3-1-guidelines/Pages/default.aspx>. See also Global Reporting Initiative, *G3.1 Guidelines: Human Rights — Current Project Status*, online: GRI <http://www.globalreporting.org/reportingframework/g31guidelines/guidelines.htm> (stating that revisions address Ruggie's work).

272 Larry Catá Backer, *On the Evolution of the United Nations' "Protect-Respect-Remedy" Project: The State, the Corporation and Human Rights in a Global Governance Context* (2011) 9 Santa Clara J Int'l L 37 at 43.

273 See discussion on this point in Seck, *supra* note 195 at 158-59.

274 See, eg, Business and Human Rights Resource Centre, "Commentaries Issued after UN Council Endorsement of Guiding Principles," online: Business and

It is worth reflecting on the substance of the *Guiding Principles* in light of the process used to formulate them. Rather than ignoring the reality of corporate power, the SRSG pragmatically chose to engage it. The idea that multi-stakeholder engagement is an essential tool of global governance is guided by Ruggie's contributions as a constructivist international relations scholar, notably in his recognition of a "newly emerging global public domain that is no longer coterminous with the system of states."[275] Defined as an "institutionalized arena of discourse, contestation and action organized around the production of global public goods," the global public domain is "constituted by interactions among non-state actors as well as states."[276] Ruggie suggests that the development of new non-territorial political spaces may create a more inclusive institutional arena in which the global public domain is equated not simply with states and the interstate realm but also includes non-state actors such as civil society organizations, transnational corporations, and international organizations.[277] This new global public domain does

Human Rights Resource Centre <http://www.business-humanrights.org/Documents/UNGuidingPrinciples/Commentaries>, in particular the critical commentary from the Child Rights Information Network (21 June 2011), International Federation for Human Rights (17 June 2011), and Human Rights Watch (16 June 2011). See also Penelope Simons, "International Law's Invisible Hand and the Future of Corporate Accountability for Violations of Human Rights" (2012) 3 J Human Rights & the Environment 5, online: Edward Elgar Publishing <http://e-elgar.metapress.com/content/uq8l855458700m334/fulltext.pdf>. See also David Bilchitz, "The Ruggie Framework: An Adequate Rubric for Corporate Human Rights Obligations?" (2010) 7 Sur Int'l J Human Rights 199; Robert McCorquodale, "Corporate Social Responsibility and International Human Rights Law" (2009) 87 J Business Ethics 385.

275 John Gerard Ruggie, "Reconstituting the Global Public Domain: Issues, Actors and Practices" (2004) 10 Eur J Int'l Relations 499 at 519. See also John G Ruggie, "Territoriality and Beyond: Problematizing Modernity in International Relations" (1993) 47 Int'l Org 139; John G Ruggie, "What Makes the World Hang Together? Neo-utilitarianism and the Social Constructivist Challenge" (1998) 52 Int'l Org 855. For a complete list of Ruggie's academic work, see online: Harvard University <http://www.hks.harvard.edu/m-rcbg/johnruggie/index.html>.

276 Ruggie, "Public Domain," *supra* note 275 at 519. See also Glen Whelan, Jeremy Moon, and Marck Orlitzky, "Human Rights, Transnational Corporations and Embedded Liberalism: What Chance Consensus?" (2009) 87 J of Business Ethics 367 at 373; Hevina S Dashwood, "Canadian Mining Companies and Corporate Social Responsibility: Weighing the Impact of Global Norms" (2007) 40 Can J Political Science 129 at 133.

277 Ruggie, "Public Domain," *supra* note 275 at 502.

not "replace states," but its effect is to "embed systems of governance in broader global frameworks of social capacity and agency."[278]

With this in mind, it is worth considering Principles 1 and 2 of the *Guiding Principles* anew and what they might mean for home state obligations in the human rights realm. While Principle 1 indicates that "States must protect against human rights abuse within their territory and/or jurisdiction by third parties," Principle 2 provides that "States should set out clearly the expectation that all business enterprises domiciled in their territory and/or jurisdiction respect human rights throughout their operations." The somewhat curious choice of language in the two principles differs slightly from the wording that appeared in the draft *Guiding Principles*.[279] Notably, Principle 2 of the draft *Guiding Principles* was extensively critiqued in submissions by industry, civil society, and academic commentators.[280] Generally speaking, civil society commentators, joined by many academics, were concerned that the use of "should encourage"

278 *Ibid* at 519. Ruggie describes the global public domain as "exist[ing] in transnational non-territorial spatial formations" and being "anchored in norms and expectations as well as institutional networks and circuits within, across and beyond states" (*ibid*). However, see Ronen Shamir, "Corporate Social Responsibility: Towards a New Market-Embedded Morality?" (2008) 9 Theor Inq L 371. Socio-legal scholars such as Shamir have described similar phenomena as leading "towards a new market-embedded morality," with the rationality of the market becoming the organizing principle for society as a whole while a "process of responsibilization" follows in which it is assumed that various social actors have "reflexive moral capacities" (*ibid* at 371, 374, 379).

279 While the text of Principle 1 is virtually unchanged, the revised commentary to Principle 1 no longer discusses the specific language of the UN human rights treaties. See *Guiding Principles: supra* note 11 at 6-7. It does, however, include a reference to the state duty to "protect and promote the rule of law, including by taking measures to ensure equality before the law, fairness in its application, and by providing adequate accountability, legal certainty, and procedural and legal transparency" (*ibid* at 7). Principle 2 was more substantially changed. In the draft *Guiding Principles*, it stated: "States should *encourage* business enterprises domiciled in their territory and/or jurisdiction to respect human rights throughout their *global* operations, *including those conducted by their subsidiaries and other related legal entities*." See *Draft Guiding Principles, supra* note 212 [emphasis added], reflecting words omitted from the final version). In the final text, "encourage" was replaced by "clearly set out the expectation." See *Guiding Principles, supra* note 11 at 7.

280 See Submissions to Consultation on *Draft Guiding Principles, supra* note 212. The problem of extraterritorial jurisdiction was also the subject of a legal experts' consultation in September 2010. John Ruggie, *Exploring Extraterritoriality in Business and Human Rights: Summary Note of Expert Meeting* (14 September 2010),

in draft Principle 2 was not strong enough given the importance of "extraterritorial" home state regulation as a tool to fill global governance gaps. Moreover, it did not accurately reflect the absence of jurisdictional limits in international human rights instruments such as the International Covenant on Economic, Social and Cultural Rights.[281] Industry submissions, on the other hand, including submissions from the PDAC and Talisman Energy, were concerned that any reference to a role for home states and the possibility of "extraterritorial" jurisdiction would create confusion.[282] Notably, the submission on behalf of Talisman Energy stated:

---

online: Business and Human Rights Resource Centre <http://www.business-humanrights.org/media/documents/ruggie-extraterritoriality-14-sep-2010.pdf>.

281 International Covenant on Economic, Social and Cultural Rights, 16 December 1966, 993 UNTS 3 (in force 3 January 1976) [ICESCR]. See Submissions to Consultation on *Draft Guiding Principles*, Document 3, *supra* note 212, in particular, the submissions by Emily Howie, The Human Rights Law Resource Centre (11 January 2011); Robert Grabosch (28 January 2011); John Knox (17 January 2011); Bernd Nilles, CIDSE (31 January 2011); Thomas Lazzeri (27 January 2011); Maplecroft (31 January 2011); Center for Human Rights and Environment (31 January 2011); Cathal Doyle (31 January 2011); Earth Rights International (January 31, 2011); Joint statement signed by twenty organizations including Amnesty International and the International Center for Economic & Social Rights (January 2011); OXFAM (31 January 2011); Chip Pitts (31 January 2011); Responsible Mineral Sector Initiative, Segal Graduate School of Business, Simon Fraser University (31 January 2011); SOMO (31 January 2011); Castan Centre for Human Rights Law, Monash University (January 2011, prepared by Sarah Joseph and Adam McBeth); Robert McCorquodale (January 2011); Sherpa (January 2011); Amnesty International, CIDSE, ESCR-Net, Human Rights Watch, International Commission of Jurists, International Federation for Human Rights (FIDH), Rights and Accountability in Development (RAID) (14 January 2011); European Centre for Constitutional and Human Rights (27 January 2011); and Peter Muchlinski (24 January 2011) (raising concern over the limitations of the term "domicile"). Submissions by various governments and state human rights commissions also supported an expanded understanding of extraterritorial jurisdiction. The Canadian government did not make a public submission.

282 See especially PDAC, *Submission* (January 2011), online: Business and Human Rights Resource Centre <http://www.business-humanrights.org/media/documents/ruggie/pdac-submission-re-guiding-principles-jan-2011.pdf> [*PDAC Submission*]; and Hogan Lovells LLP, *Talisman Energy's Comments to Draft Guiding Principles* (20 December 2010) at 5-6, online: Business and Human Rights Resource Centre <http://www.business-humanrights.org/media/documents/talisman-comments-on-guiding-principles-dec-2010.pdf> [*Talisman Energy*]. See also submissions by US Chamber of Commerce Institute for Legal Reform (31 January 2011), online: Business and Human Rights Resource Centre <http://

We believe that the Special Representative can make a significant contribution in the area of extraterritorial jurisdiction by making specific recommendations for the creation of a forum and a process to enable *States* to engage in multilateral deliberation with a view to developing a set of principles in relation to the assertion of extraterritorial jurisdiction to protect human rights.[283]

The suggestion that the scope of home state jurisdiction should be determined through a state-based process is in keeping with a positivist, state-centric analysis of international law. At first glance, this approach may appear commendable, raising the prospect that states will come together to agree formally to exercise extraterritorial jurisdiction in order to regulate and adjudicate transnational corporate harms. However, further thought raises the question of why Talisman's lawyers would have considered it appropriate to make such a submission in the first place. If corporate counsel believed that some things are best left to states, it was arguably inconsistent for them to make submissions on these issues in the first place. At the same time, submissions on other aspects of the *Guiding Principles* (those *not* best left to states) might be entirely appropriate.

The *Guiding Principles* contain two other principles that are relevant to the issue of home state jurisdiction: Principle 7 on conflict-affected areas[284] and Principle 25 on access to remedies.[285]

---

www.business-humanrights.org/media/documents/ruggie/us-chamber-of-commerce-inst-for-legal-reform-re-guiding-principles-31-jan-2011.pdf>; Commission on Multinational Enterprises of the Confederation of Netherlands' Industry and Employers VNO-NCW (31 January 2011), online: Business and Human Rights Resource Centre <http://www.business-humanrights.org/media/documents/ruggie/vno-ncw-comments-on-draft-guiding-principles-jan-2011.doc>.

283 *Talisman Energy, supra* note 282 at 6 [emphasis added].

284 *Guiding Principles, supra* note 11, Principle 7; *Draft Guiding Principles, supra* note 212, Principle 10. See, eg, submission by Michael Deas (31 January 2011) (expressing concern that there is little emphasis on the role of home states in conflict-affected areas), online: Business and Human Rights Resource Centre <http://www.business-humanrights.org/SpecialRepPortal/Home/Protect-Respect-Remedy-Framework/GuidingPrinciples/Submissions>.

285 *Guiding Principles, supra* note 11, Principle 25; *Draft Guiding Principles, supra* note 212, Principle 23. See the submission of Earth Rights International (31 January 2011), online: Business and Human Rights Resource Centre <http://www.business-humanrights.org/media/documents/ruggie/earthrights-comments-on-guiding-principles-31-jan-2011.pdf> (noting that Principle 23 (new Principle 25) is ambiguous with respect to remedies that home states may provide against

Principle 7 must be read in light of the SRSG's separate report on *Business and Human Rights in Conflict-Affected Regions* (*Conflict-Affected Regions*), a report that, notably, was "road-tested" in an exclusively state-based process.[286] While this report would have provided an excellent opportunity to highlight the necessity of home state action where businesses are operating in conflict-affected areas that are clearly beyond host state regulatory control, *Conflict-Affected Regions* is far more tentative. For example, "'home' States ... have a role to play in assisting both ... corporations and host States to ensure that businesses are not involved with human rights abuses," such as using "policies, laws and regulations" to warn business enterprises of the "heightened risk of being involved with gross abuses of human rights in conflict-affected areas" and "clearly communicat[ing] their expectations with regard to business respect for human rights, even in such challenging environments."[287] Unco-operative enterprises might be subject to an ombudsperson or national contact point mechanism as well as the "withdrawal of consular and/or business development support," among other measures.[288] In extreme situations where gross human rights abuses have been committed, "States should explore civil, administrative or criminal liability," among other measures.[289] Ultimately, however, in a striking echo of the Talisman submission and the Canadian experience with Bill C-300, *Conflict-Affected Regions* concludes with a recommendation that "multilateral standard-setting on this issue may be a necessary part of ensuring that states move forward in the fulfillment of the state duty to protect human rights" because "States are more inclined to adopt policies that set standards *that do not put their own businesses at an unfair disadvantage*."[290] Thus, as with *Protect, Respect, and Remedy*, the SRSG's conclusions on the role of home states, even in conflict-affected areas where egregious human rights violations are most likely to occur, are tempered by a dose of realism. Ultimately, home states will not regulate for fear of competitive disadvantage, even

business entities within their legal jurisdiction for acts that occur outside their territorial jurisdiction, with the ambiguity stemming from the phrase "territory and/or jurisdiction" as it is not clear if "jurisdiction" in this context is intended to include "extraterritorial jurisdiction").

286 *Conflict-Affected Regions, supra* note 209.

287 *Ibid* at paras 6 and 12.

288 *Ibid* at para 17.

289 *Ibid* at para 18.

290 *Ibid* at para 21 [emphasis added].

where host states clearly lack the capacity to protect rights and harms unquestionably amount to serious violations of universal human rights norms. It is left unclear, however, how in practice this multilateral standard-setting exercise is likely to reach consensus, given that states seem unlikely to agree to anything that might be perceived as harming the competitive advantage of home state businesses. Even if a text could be agreed, implementation would remain a challenge.

Interestingly, a slightly different analysis emerges if Principle 1 is read together with foundational Principle 25 on "access to remedy." Under Principle 25, states' duty to protect clearly includes an obligation to provide access to effective remedies where abuses occur "within their territory and/or jurisdiction." This formulation mirrors the language of Principle 1. Yet, a notable example of a state-based non-judicial mechanism included in the commentary to Principle 25 is that of the NCPs for the OECD Guidelines — a home state mechanism.[291] The OECD Guidelines are explicitly referred to under Principle 2 as an example of a multilateral soft law instrument that requires implementation of domestic measures with extraterritorial implications. This raises the question of how to understand the term "jurisdiction" in Principle 25 and, consequently, in foundational Principle 1. As both Principles 1 and 25 use mandatory language ("must"), there is clearly room to argue that, at least in some circumstances, home states already have obligations to exercise jurisdiction to protect against and remedy human rights abuses. There is some support for this analysis if Principle 2 is read in the context of many of the operational principles under "the State duty to protect human rights," which either implicitly or explicitly recommend either direct extraterritorial regulation or domestic measures with exterritorial implications.[292] As these are all written in permissive language, they are equally consistent with

291 *Guiding Principles, supra* note 11 at 22, Commentary to Principle 25. See also Commentary to Principle 26, which identifies legal barriers as including both the attribution of legal responsibility across members of corporate groups, and denial of justice due to lack of access to home State courts (*ibid* at 23).

292 See especially *ibid*, Principles 3, 4, 7 and 8. Further analysis of this issue is beyond the scope of this paper, but see further Sara L Seck, "Conceptualizing the Home State Duty to Protect Human Rights," in Karin Buhmann, Lynn Roseberry, and Mette Morsing, eds, *Corporate Social and Human Rights Responsibilities: Global Legal and Management Perspectives* (Hampshire, UK: Palgrave Macmillan, 2010) 1 (exploring this jurisdictional question from both a permissive and mandatory perspective).

Principle 2 and with an encouraging, rather than sanctioning, understanding of Principle 1.[293]

While this interpretation may have merit, the adoption of multi-stakeholder processes to inform substantive outcomes such as the Advisory Group's report and the *Guiding Principles*, and the space created for industry lawyer submissions in legislative deliberations such as those relating to Bill C-300, ultimately make it unlikely that traditional binding "command-and-control" regulation, or even the conditionality of support with legally binding sanctions, will be implemented in home state practice any time soon, at least in Canada. This unlikelihood can be attributed in part to beliefs about the impact of the relevant instruments on the competitive advantage of businesses. However, there are implications for legal theory, too, that are generally neither discussed nor reflected in the submissions of either civil society or industry contributors. Constructivist international relations scholarship, including Ruggie's work, has influenced international legal scholars such that they may be more likely to acknowledge that non-state actors are participants in the creation of international legal norms.[294] Yet many submissions by non-state actor participants in the processes described earlier seem to reflect a state-centric understanding of international law that is arguably inconsistent with their own participation. Thus, they may be more likely to promote narrow views of the principles of sovereign equality and non-interference in the internal affairs of other states[295] as well as views that strongly endorse the value of legal, over non-judicial, remedial mechanisms.[296]

Another related and extremely important aspect of multi-stakeholder discourse is recognition. For a multi-stakeholder process to work, participants must recognize each other as being legitimately at the table. Yet this requirement begs the question of what happens

293 See Seck, *supra* note 195.

294 See, eg, Jutta Brunnée and Stephen J Toope, "International Law and Constructivism: Elements of an Interactional Theory of International Law" (2000) 39 Colum J Transnat'l L 19; Julie Mertus, "Considering Nonstate Actors in the New Millenium: Toward Expanded Participation in Norm Generation and Norm Application" (2000) 32 NYUJ Int'l L & Pol 537.

295 PDAC Submission and *Talisman Energy*, *supra* note 282.

296 MiningWatch Canada, Comments on the Draft Guiding Principles (31January, 2011), online: Business and Human Rights Resource Centre <http://www.business-humanrights.org/SpecialRepPortal/Home/Protect-Respect-Remedy-Framework/GuidingPrinciples/Submissions>.

when some potential participants are not recognized by others (for example, affected, perhaps indigenous, communities; "anti-development" NGOs; or even "anti-community-consent" businesses) and are consequently deemed unworthy of participation. Similarly, what happens when relationships break down? A curious feature of Bill C-300 is that it was not all that different from a proposal contained in the industry-civil society Advisory Group's report. Yet industry and civil society relationships clearly deteriorated in the interim, producing a remarkable industry backlash that was wildly out of proportion to the mild proposals in the bill.

The Canadian initiatives aimed at addressing allegations of wrongdoing by Canadian mining companies operating internationally, reviewed earlier, are in marked contrast with the situation in 1999 when I reviewed in this Yearbook the public and private international law dimensions of environmental harm caused by Canadian mining companies overseas.[297] This increased Canadian activity could serve as evidence of state practice supporting the emergence of customary international legal rules confirming either the permissive or mandatory nature of home state jurisdiction to regulate and adjudicate transnational corporate conduct to prevent and remedy environmental and human rights harms. As Canada is known as "a particularly strong player in the global mining sector," the exercise of jurisdiction by Canada over transnational mining companies in order to prevent and remedy environmental and human rights harms would serve as a significant step in the development of customary international law.[298] As a consequence, the outcomes of processes such as the roundtables and Bill C-300 have implications not only for Canada but also for the international community more generally.[299] Yet the role of business and corporate counsel in influencing this state practice is easily overlooked in traditional international legal analysis.

Conclusions

This article has provided an overview of developments in Canada between 2005 and 2011 relating to the regulation and adjudication of human rights concerns associated with global mining, with the

297 Seck, *supra* note 29.

298 *Building the Canadian Advantage, supra* note 9 at 3.

299 See generally Sara L Seck, "Unilateral Home State Regulation: Imperialism or Tool for Subaltern Resistance?" (2008) 46 Osgoode Hall LJ 565 at 576-80.

aim of documenting the challenges faced by legal reform proposals designed to prevent or remedy global mining harms. The article has also described the work undertaken by the SRSG in relation to the home state duty to protect human rights, highlighting the conclusions reached in the *Guiding Principles* in relation to the existence and scope of home state obligations. In both contexts, industry, industry lawyers, and other non-state actors participated in processes designed to address these issues. And, in each context, the outcome of such participation is that traditional legal frameworks, whether domestic command and control, conditionality laws, or international human rights laws articulating firm home state obligations, will have a limited role to play. This result gives cause to reflect on the implications of non-state corporate actor participation in the development of international norms relating to the existence and scope of home state human rights obligations.

The implications are important not only for the specific question of the regulation of human rights concerns arising from global mining but also for related ones. For example, James Anaya, the UN special rapporteur on the rights of indigenous peoples, recently endorsed the SRSG's pragmatic approach in relation to an issue of great importance to both the global mining industry and indigenous peoples. Anaya's July 2011 report to the UN Human Rights Council proposes the need to develop a set of specific guidelines or principles "operationaliz[ing] the rights of indigenous peoples in the context of natural resource extraction and development projects affecting indigenous territories."[300] To do so, Anaya calls for "expert consultations and studies" so as to promote an "effective and practicable" understanding of indigenous rights.[301] According to Anaya, of "utmost importance" is the "bridging of divergent viewpoints of States, indigenous peoples and corporate actors" though a "process of wide consultations and dialogues with all actors."[302]

This article shows both the possibilities and the potential limitations for law reform of such an approach. The processes reviewed in this article suggest that engaging with industry and industry lawyers will lead to outcomes that may in theory reduce the number of corporate human rights abuses in the mining sector due to the

[300] James Anaya, *Report of the Special Rapporteur on the Rights of Indigenous Peoples: Extractive Industries Operating Within or Near Indigenous Territories*, UNHR 18th Sess, UN Doc A/HRC/18/35 (11 July 2011) at para 79.

[301] *Ibid.*

[302] *Ibid.*

proliferation of voluntary codes, host state local community capacity building, and the CSR education of junior mining companies. Yet even if this optimistic picture proves well founded, improved access to legal remedies for those that ultimately are harmed will not be forthcoming.

Importantly, it does not necessarily follow from these conclusions that businesses and their lawyers should not be allowed to participate in these processes. Indeed, it is inevitable that they will, whether directly in the process that creates the legal framework or after the fact by contesting an outcome that they did not participate in shaping. My conclusion, then, is the more modest claim that if the reality of industry and corporate legal power is recognized and accommodated, it should come as no surprise that legislated remedies or internationally binding rules prove unattainable. We must either come to terms with a new understanding of the limitations of both domestic and international law or seek new ways of harnessing corporate power, perhaps by exploring the ethical obligations of corporate lawyers as participants in international legal processes.[303]

Sommaire

Entre 2005 et 2011, les débats se multiplient, tant au Canada qu'au sein de l'Organisation des Nations Unies (ONU), sur le rôle des États d'origine dans la réglementation et la poursuite des violations des droits de la personne liées aux activités transnationales de sociétés. Au Canada, ce débat est axé sur des préoccupations liées à l'exploitation minière mondiale, et conduit à une série de rapports et de propositions de la part du gouvernement, des parties de l'opposition et d'autres intervenants. En résulte, en 2010, la nomination d'une conseillère du secteur des entreprises extractives sur la responsabilité sociale et la défaite du projet de loi C-300 (la Loi sur la responsabilisation des sociétés à l'égard de leurs activités minières, pétrolières ou gazières dans les pays en développement). Entretemps, le professeur John G. Ruggie est nommé Représentant spécial du Secrétaire général chargé de la question des droits de l'homme et des sociétés transnationales par la Commission (depuis: le Conseil) des droits de l'homme de l'ONU. Le travail de Ruggie

303 See, eg, Advocates for International Development, Lawyers Eradicating Poverty, *Law Firm's Implementation of the Guiding Principles on Business and Human Rights: Discussion Paper* (November 2011), online: Advocates for International Development <http://a4id.org/resource/report/guidingprinciples>.

conduit à l'élaboration, en 2008, du cadre de référence "*Protéger, respecter et réparer*" et, en 2011, des "*Principes directeurs relatifs aux entreprises et aux droits de l'homme.*" Bien que ces deux documents reconnaissent le devoir qui incombe aux États de protéger contre les violations des droits de l'homme par les entreprises et la nécessité d'accès à des recours par les victimes, le rôle des États d'origine à cet égard y est contesté. Cet article compare les développements au Canada entre 2005 et 2011 avec ceux de l'ONU en ce qui concerne les devoirs d'États d'origine pour la protection des droits de la personne dans le contexte d'exploitation transnationale par les sociétés. Il offre également des réflexions sur les enjeux de l'inévitabilité de la participation d'entreprises et de leurs avocats pour le développement d'obligations juridiques pour les états d'origine.

Summary

Between 2005 and 2011, there was much debate, both within Canada and at the United Nations (UN), over what role home states should play in the regulation and adjudication of human rights harms associated with transnational corporate conduct. In Canada, this debate focused upon concerns related to global mining that led to a series of government, opposition and multi-stakeholder reports and proposals. These culminated in 2010 with the appointment of an Extractive Sector Corporate Social Responsibility Counsellor and the defeat of Bill C-300, An Act Respecting Corporate Accountability for the Activities of Mining, Oil or Gas in Developing Countries. Meanwhile, at the UN Human Rights Commission/Council, John G. Ruggie was appointed Special Representative to the UN Secretary-General on Business and Human Rights (SRSG). Ruggie's work led to the 2008 *Protect, Respect and Remedy: A Framework for Business and Human Rights* and the 2011 *Guiding Principles for Business and Human Rights* (the latter designed to "operationalize" the former). While both documents highlight state duties to protect against human rights violations by businesses and the need for access to remedies by victims, the role of home states in this regard was contested. This article compares the developments in Canada between 2005 and 2011 with the work of the SRSG in relation to the home state duty to protect human rights in the transnational corporate context. It also offers reflections on the implications of the inevitability of industry and industry lawyer participation for the development of home state legal obligations.

The International Labour Organization and Its Contribution to the Protection of the Rights of Indigenous Peoples

ATHANASIOS YUPSANIS

Introduction: The International Labour Organization (ILO) and Its Structure

The ILO was created in 1919, as part of the Treaty of Versailles that ended the First World War, and was the only international institution of its time to survive the Second World War, becoming the first specialized agency of the United Nations (UN) system.[1] The ILO's mandate entails, *inter alia,* the improvement of those labour conditions that, because they involve such injustice, hardship, and privation for large numbers of people, produce unrest and thus imperil world peace and prosperity.[2] Under Article 2 of its Constitution, the ILO has three main organs: (1) the International Labour Conference, which is the principal policy-making and legislative body of the organization and in which every member state is represented; (2) the Governing Body, which decides the agenda of the International Labour Conference, adopts the draft program

---

Athanasios Yupsanis, LL.M., Ph.D. in public international law, Aristotle University of Thessaloniki; Adjunct Lecturer, Faculty of Law, Democritus University of Thrace, Komotini, Greece.

1 Lee Swepston, "ILO Standards and Globalization," in Roger Blanpain, ed, *Confronting Globalization: The Quest for a Social Agenda — Geneva Lectures* (The Hague: Kluwer Law International, 2005) 11 at 11. The original ILO Constitution was incorporated as Part XIII of the Treaty of Peace between the Allied and Associated Powers and Germany, 28 June 1919, Articles 387-427, online: <http://www.ilo.org/public/english/bureau/leg/download/pArticlexiii-treaty.pdf> [Treaty of Versailles].

2 See Monique Zarka-Martres and Monique Guichard-Kelly, "Decent Work, Standards and Indicators," in David Kucera, ed, *Qualitative Indicators of Labour Standards: Comparative Methods and Applications* (Dordrecht: Springer, 2007) 83 at 83.

and budget of the organization for submission to the conference, and elects the director-general; and (3) the International Labour Office, which is the permanent secretariat of the organization as well as a research and documentation centre.[3]

One particular feature of the ILO's structure is the tripartite composition of its organs, in which representatives of employers' and workers' associations participate alongside government delegates.[4] It is a system that to some degree breaks the state monopoly on the formation of international law.[5] Thus, by virtue of Article 3(1) of the ILO Constitution, the International Labour Conference is composed of four representatives from each of the member states, of whom two are government delegates and the other two representatives of the state's employers and labour force respectively.[6] Further, Article 7(1) provides for a Governing Body of fifty-six persons, twenty-eight representing governments, fourteen representing employers, and fourteen representing workers.[7]

The ILO and Indigenous Peoples: Historical Background

The ILO was the first international organization to turn its attention to the issue of indigenous peoples, within the framework of its mandate to improve labour rights and working conditions.[8] From the very beginning, the organization concerned itself with these peoples because of the widespread exploitation of their

[3] Constitution of the International Labour Organization, 1 April 1919, Article 2, online: <http://www.ilo.org/ilolex/english/constq.htm> [ILO Constitution]; see also International Labour Office, *International Labour Standards: A Workers' Educational Manual*, 4th edition (Geneva: ILO, 1998) at 11-14.

[4] Ebere Osieke, *Constitutional Law and Practice in the International Labour Organization* (Dordrecht: Martinus Nijhoff, 1985) at 52.

[5] See Nicolas Valticos, "The Role of the ILO: Present Action and Future Perspectives" in BG Ramcharan, ed, *Human Rights: Thirty Years after the Universal Declaration* (The Hague: Martinus Nijhoff, 1979) 211 at 218.

[6] ILO Constitution, *supra* note 3, Article 3(1); Lucie Lamarche, "The Right to Social Security in the International Covenant on Economic, Social and Cultural Rights" in Audrey Chapman and Sage Russell, eds, *Core Obligations: Building a Framework for Economic, Social and Cultural Rights* (Antwerp: Intersentia, 2002) 87 at 90.

[7] ILO Constitution, *supra* note 3, Article 7(1); Eve C Landau and Yves Beigbeder, *From ILO Standards to EU Law: The Case of Equality between Men and Women at Work* (Leiden: Martinus Nijhoff, 2008) at 13.

[8] Hurst Hannum, ed, *Documents on Autonomy and Minority Rights* (Dordrecht, Boston, London: Martinus Nijhoff, 1993) at 8.

workforces.[9] Thus, as early as 1921, it undertook a series of studies on indigenous workers,[10] while in 1926 it set up a Committee of Experts on Native Labour, whose recommendations led to the adoption of conventions and recommendations on such native labour issues as abusive labour practices, forced labour, and coercive recruitment.[11] It also developed and implemented, in concert with other international organizations (the UN, the UN Educational, Scientific and Cultural Organization (UNESCO), the UN International Children's Emergency Fund (UNICEF), the Food and Agriculture Organization (FAO), and the World Health Organization (WHO)), the Andean Indian Programme (1952-72). This program was an inter-agency, multidisciplinary development program initiated in Bolivia, Ecuador, and Peru and later expanded to Argentina, Chile, Colombia, and Venezuela, which aimed at integrating native Andean Indians into their national societies.[12]

The paternalistic attitude prevailing in the international community at the time, however, meant that indigenous peoples themselves were left entirely out of the planning and implementation of

9 Hans-Joachim Heintze, "The Protection of Indigenous Peoples under the ILO Convention" in Michael Bothe, Thomas Kurzidem, and Christian Schmidt, eds, *Amazonia and Siberia: Legal Aspects of the Preservation of the Environment and Development in the Last Open Spaces* (London: Graham and Trotman, 1993) 310 at 312.

10 Hurst Hannum, "New Developments in Indigenous Rights" (1988) 28 Va J Int'l L 649 at 652.

11 See Patrick Thornberry, *Indigenous Peoples and Human Rights* (Manchester, UK: Manchester University Press, 2002) at 320; Hurst Hannum, *Autonomy, Sovereignty and Self-Determination: The Accommodation of Conflicting Rights*, revised edition (Philadelphia, PA: University of Pennsylvania Press, 1990) at 77. See also ILO Convention no. 64 Concerning the Regulation of Written Contracts of Employment of Indigenous Workers, 27 June 1939, online: <http://www.ilo.org/dyn/no.rmlex/en/f?p=1000:12100:0::NO.::P12100_ILO_CODE:C064> [Convention no. 64]; Convention no. 65 Concerning Penal Sanctions for Breaches of Contracts of Employment by Indigenous Workers, 27 June 1939, online: <http://www.ilo.org/dyn/normlex/en/f?p=1000:12100:0::NO.::P12100_ILO_CODE:C065> [Convention no. 65]; Convention no. 86 Concerning the Maximum Length of Contracts of Employment of Indigenous Workers, 11 July 1947, online: <http://www.ilo.org/dyn/normlex/en/f?p=1000:12100:0::NO.::P12100_ILO_CODE:C086> [Convention no. 86]; Convention no. 104 Concerning the Abolition of Penal Sanctions for Breaches of Contracts of Employment by Indigenous Workers, 21 June 1955, online: <http://www.ilo.org/dyn/normlex/en/f?p=1000:12100:0::NO.::P12100_ILO_CODE:C104> [Convention no. 104].

12 See Chris Tennant, "Indigenous Peoples, International Institutions and the International Legal Literature from 1945-1993" (1994) 16 Hum Rts Q 1 at 27-28.

these programs.[13] This same paternalistic mentality also governed the organization's very important 1953 study, *Indigenous Peoples: Living and Working Conditions of Aboriginal Populations in Independent Countries.*[14]

ILO Convention no. 107 Concerning the Protection and Integration of Indigenous and Other Tribal and Semi-Tribal Populations in Independent Countries (Convention no. 107)

The Philosophy of the Convention

The ILO's concern for indigenous peoples culminated, initially, in the framing — jointly with the UN and other international organizations (the FAO, UNESCO, and the WHO) — and adoption of Convention no. 107.[15] The convention came into force on 2 June 1959 and, along with the accompanying Recommendation 104 of the same name,[16] was the first, and for thirty years the only, international legally binding instrument focusing specifically on the rights (individual for the most part) of indigenous peoples.[17] Its eight parts cover general policy (Articles 1-10), land rights (Articles 11-14), recruitment and conditions of employment (Article 15), vocational training, handicrafts, and rural industries (Articles 16-18), social security and health (Articles 19-20), education and means of

[13] See Ronald Niezen, "Recognizing Indigenism: Canadian Unity and the International Movement of Indigenous Peoples" (2000) 42 Comparative Studies in Society and History 119 at 127.

[14] International Labour Office (ILO), *Indigenous Peoples: Living and Working Conditions of Aboriginal Populations in Independent Countries* (Geneva: ILO, 1953). See Ravi de Costa, *A Higher Authority: Indigenous Transnationalism and Australia* (Sydney: University of New South Wales Press, 2006) at 70, noting that the study "was a development in international thinking on indigenous rights, but maintained a philosophy of uplifting those that did not yet 'fully share in the national economy and culture.'"

[15] Convention no. 107 Concerning the Protection and Integration of Indigenous and Other Tribal and Semi-Tribal Populations in Independent Countries, 26 June 1957, online: <http://www.ilo.org/dyn/normlex/en/f?p=1000:12100:0::NO.::P12100_ILO_CODE:C107> [Convention no. 107].

[16] See ILO, *Recommendation Concerning the Protection and Integration of Indigenous and Other Tribal and Semi-Tribal Populations in Independent Countries*, 26 June 1957, online: <http://www.ilo.org/dyn/normlex/en/f?p=1000:12100:0::NO.::P12100_ILO_CODE:R104> [Recommendation 104].

[17] Robert K Hitchcock, "International Human Rights, the Environment and Indigenous Peoples" (1994) 5 Colo J Int'l Envtl L and Pol'y 1 at 9.

communication (Articles 21-26) and administration (Article 27).[18] Its aim, as indicated by its title and proclaimed in its preamble and many of its provisions, is the protection and integration of indigenous populations into the body of national societies, a paternalistic approach that was a product of the ethnocentric view of those populations as being "less advanced."[19] The dual aim of protection and integration is entrusted chiefly to state agencies,[20] for Article 2(1) of the convention gives governments the primary responsibility for developing co-ordinated and systematic action for the protection of the populations concerned and their progressive integration into the life of their countries.[21] The same article also excludes measures tending towards the artificial assimilation of these populations[22] as well as the use of force or coercion as a means of achieving integration.[23] This framing generates questions, for although the

18 Convention no. 107, *supra* note 15, Articles 1-27. See Gudmundur Alfredsson, "International Law, International Organizations, and Indigenous Peoples" (1982) 36 J Int'l Affairs 113 at 120; Thornberry, *supra* note 11 at 327.

19 See Convention no. 107, *supra* note 15, Article 1(1)(a). See also Douglas Sanders, "The Re-emergence of Indigenous Questions in International Law" (1983) 1 Can Hum Rts YB 3 at 19; Thornberry, *supra* note 11 at 327.

20 The convention simply requires governments to "seek the collaboration" of the populations concerned and their representatives in applying its provisions, without clarifying what seeking collaboration entails. See Convention no. 107, *supra* note 15, Article 5(a). See also James W Colborn, "International Labour Organization Convention Number 169: Celebrate the Differences" (1994) 2 Willamette Bulletin Int'l L and Pol'y 1 at 4. However, while the convention makes no provision for the direct participation of indigenous populations in government decision-making procedures, it has been interpreted by the Committee of Experts on the Application of Conventions and Recommendations (which is charged with reviewing reports submitted by states on their compliance with the commitments they have assumed) as requiring consultation with the peoples concerned in planning and implementing development programs. See Russel Lawrence Barsh, "An Advocate's Guide to the Convention on Indigenous and Tribal Peoples" (1990) 15 Okla City UL Rev 209 at 212.

21 Convention no. 107, *supra* note 15, Article 2(1). See Gerhard Stuby, "Autochthonous Peoples and Their International Legal Protection — Sixteen Theses," in Manfred O Hinz and F Thomas Gatter, eds, *Global Responsibility — Local Agenda: The Legitimacy of Modern Self-Determination and African Traditional Authority* (Berlin: Lit Verlag, 2006) 203 at 209; Thornberry, *supra* note 11 at 328.

22 Convention no. 107, *supra* note 15, Article 2(2)(c). See NK Behura, "ILO Convention: Indigenous and Tribal Peoples — An Analysis," in Rabindra Nath Pati and Jagannatha Dash, eds, *Tribal and Indigenous People of India: Problems and Prospects* (New Delhi: APH Publishers, 2002) 29 at 30.

23 Convention no. 107, *supra* note 15, Article 2(4). See Natan Lerner, "The 1989 ILO Convention on Indigenous Populations: New Standards?" in Yoram Dinstein

convention does make an initial distinction between integration and assimilation, it does not lay down solid criteria for distinguishing satisfactorily between these two concepts and the corresponding related policies.[24]

In any case, the view that indigenous populations are less advanced, and the consequent emphasis in the convention on the need for their gradual and progressive integration into the national community as the sole, inevitable, and indisputable option,[25] had by the end of the 1970s become the target of attack by both scholars in the field and indigenous peoples themselves, who pointed out the unilateral, undesirable, and destructive nature of this approach.[26] On the other hand, it must be noted that this approach was only to be expected, since the prevailing mentality within the UN and the overwhelming majority of its member states at the time the text was adopted was generally ethnocentric and paternalistic.[27] When the ILO determined priorities for the future of indigenous peoples without consulting them, it was acting entirely in keeping with the ideas of the times.[28] One must also acknowledge the good

---

and Mala Tabory, eds, *The Protection of Minorities and Human Rights* (Dordrecht: Martinus Nijhoff, 1992) 213 at 223.

24 See Patrick Macklem, "Indigenous Recognition in International Law: Theoretical Observations" (2008) 30 Mich J Int'l L 177 at 194.

25 "Governments at the time thought that the best way to advance the health and well-being of indigenous peoples was through integration and assimilation into mainstream societies." Scott Simon, "Indigenous Peoples and Hunting Rights," in Errol P Mendes and Sakunthala Srighanthan, eds, *Confronting Discrimination and Inequality in China: Chinese and Canadian Perspectives* (Ottawa: University of Ottawa Press, 2009) 405 at 407. See also Jack Horner, *Seeking Racial Justice: An Insider's Memoir of the Movement for Aboriginal Advancement* (Canberra, Australia: Aboriginal Studies Press, 2004) at 55, noting that "the tone of the Convention was conservative throughout, for in Europe it was assumed that an enlightened and peaceful 'integration' into the national life was the best hope for Indigenous peoples."

26 Bernadette Kelly Roy and Gudmundur Alfredsson, "Indigenous Rights: The Literature Explosion" (1987) 13 Transnational Perspectives 19 at 19.

27 See Margaret E Galey, "Indigenous Peoples, International Consciousness Raising and the Development of International Law on Human Rights" (1975) 8 Revue des Droits de l'Homme 21 at 24.

28 "The agents who drafted Convention 107 represented governments and businesses, and included expert anthropologists, but not indigenous people. They debated how fast indigenous peoples would be integrated into national societies, but did not consider the possibility of their continued autonomy." John H Bodley, *The Power of Scale: A Global History Approach* (New York: ME Sharpe, 2003) at 260.

faith motives of those who drew up the convention, most of whom truly believed that integration (interpreted as assimilation by many state governments) was the most humane and effective way of addressing the problems these populations faced. Finally, it should be pointed out that no indigenous movement had yet arisen to make its objections heard and to promote its own positions.[29]

THE CONVENTION'S PROTECTION FRAMEWORK

Moving on to an analysis of some of the fundamental elements of the Convention no. 107, two types of state action are required. One is of a more permanent nature, consisting of preventing discrimination,[30] and one is of a more temporary nature, in particular, the taking of "special measures," wherever social, economic, and cultural conditions prevent indigenous populations from enjoying the benefits of the general laws of the nation, for the effective protection of their institutions, persons, property, and labour.[31] The latter, positive action is subject to the proviso that it need only continue for so long as there is a need for special protection and only to the extent that such protection is necessary, so as not to create or prolong a state of segregation between the various segments of the population.[32]

The imposition of an obligation on the state to adopt special measures was unquestionably a positive development, especially for the period. However, the temporary nature of these provisions, in the context of the overall philosophy of Convention no. 107 (that is, the final integration of indigenous populations), conflicts with the aspirations and claims of the peoples concerned, who reject assimilation and demand permanent protection of a sort that would enable them to determine their own priorities and preserve their identity.[33]

29 See Lee Swepston, "Indigenous and Tribal Populations: A Return to Centre Stage" (1987) 126 Int'l Labour Rev 447 at 450.

30 See, eg, Convention no. 107, *supra* note 15, Article 15(2).

31 *Ibid*, Articles 3(1), 15(1), 17(1).

32 *Ibid*, Articles 3(2)(a)-(b), 17(3). See Ian Brownlie, *Treaties and Indigenous Peoples*, edited by FM Brookfield (Oxford: Clarendon Press, 1992) at 64-65; Patrick Thornberry, *International Law and the Rights of Minorities* (Oxford: Clarendon Press, 1992) at 343-44; Russel Lawrence Barsh, "Indigenous North America and Contemporary International Law" (1983) 62 Or L Rev 73 at 82.

33 See Garth Nettheim, "'Peoples' and 'Populations' — Indigenous Peoples and the Rights of Peoples," in James Crawford, ed, *The Rights of Peoples* (Oxford: Clarendon Press, 1988) 107 at 125-26.

Another noteworthy element of the convention is found in Article 7(2), which allows indigenous populations "to retain their own customs and institutions where these are not incompatible with the national legal system or the objectives of integration programmes" — the latter proviso weakening the potential of the clause.[34] Significant also is the stipulation (albeit in a particularly weak formulation) in Article 8(b) that requires national authorities to "bear in mind" the customs of indigenous populations for dealing with crimes or offences committed by members of those groups.[35]

The most important contribution of Convention no. 107 lies, however, in the fact that it was the first international legally binding instrument to include provisions concerning the rights of indigenous peoples to their lands, even though it failed to deal with the equally crucial question of natural resources pertaining to such lands.[36] Concretely, Article 11 of the convention recognizes the right of individual or collective ownership, by the members of the populations concerned, of the lands they traditionally occupy,[37] while Article 12(1) deals with the particularly serious problem of the removal of indigenous populations from their habitual territories, expressly stating that this cannot take place without their free consent.[38] This provision, however, is undermined by a series of vague, general escape clauses entitling governments to relocate indigenous populations against their will when this is "in accordance with

[34] Convention no. 107, *supra* note 15, Article 7(2). See Abdullah Al Faruque and Najnin Begum, "Conceptualising 'Indigenous Peoples' Rights: An Emerging New Category of Third — Generation Rights" (2004) 2 Asia Pac JHR and L 1 at 15; Thornberry, *supra* note 11 at 331.

[35] Convention no. 107, *supra* note 15, Article 8(b). See generally Gordon E Bennet, "The I.L.O. Convention on Indigenous and Tribal Populations — The Resolution of a Problem of Vires" (1972-73) 46 Brit YB Int'l L 382 at 383.

[36] See Gordon Bennet, "The International Law of Aboriginal Rights" (1979) 22 Int'l Comm Jur Rev 37 at 44, noting in relation to rights over natural resources that Article 4 of Recommendation 104, *supra* note 16, provides simply that indigenous populations shall be treated in the same way as the rest of the national population. See also Lee Swepston and Roger Plant, "International Standards and the Protection of the Land Rights of Indigenous and Tribal Populations" (1985) 124 Int'l Labour Rev 91 at 97, 99.

[37] Convention no. 107, *supra* note 15, Article 11. See Lawrence B Landman, "International Protection for American Indian Land Rights?" (1987) 5 BU Int'l LJ 59 at 82; Thornberry, *supra* note 11 at 333.

[38] Convention no. 107, *supra* note 15, Article 12(1). See Nico Schrijver, *Sovereignty over Natural Resources: Balancing Rights and Duties* (Cambridge: Cambridge University Press, 1997) at 315.

national laws and regulations for reasons relating to national security, or in the interest of national economic development or of the health of the said populations."[39] This discretionary flexibility to remove indigenous populations is partially counterbalanced by the requirement that governments, in cases where removal of indigenous populations is deemed necessary as an exceptional measure, provide the groups concerned "with lands of quality at least equal to those previously occupied by them, suitable to provide for their present needs and future development."[40] The convention also provides for the possibility of compensation in money or in kind, if the populations concerned should so prefer, and for full compensation for any loss or injury resulting from such removal.[41] A last provision worth noting in this regard is that requiring respect for the customary procedures of indigenous peoples relating to the transmission of rights of ownership and use of land,[42] albeit within the framework of national laws and regulations and only to the extent such procedures meet the needs and do not hinder the economic and social development of such peoples.[43]

ASSESSING THE CONVENTION

As a general assessment of Convention no. 107 — which is now closed to new ratifications but remains in force for those countries that have ratified it and have not adhered to Convention no. 169 Concerning Indigenous and Tribal Peoples in Independent Countries[44] — one might say that its paternalistic orientation, which was

39 Convention no. 107, *supra* note 15, Article 12(1). See Marc Pallemaerts, "Development, Conservation, and Indigenous Rights in Brazil" (1986) 8 Hum Rts Q 374 at 395.

40 Convention no. 107, *supra* note 15, Article 12(2). See Michael Barutciski, "International Law and Development-Induced Displacement and Resettlement Projects" in Chris J De Wet, ed, *Development-Induced Displacement: Problems, Policies and People* (Oxford: Berghahn Books, 2006) 71 at 77-78.

41 Convention no. 107, *supra* note 15, Article 12(2)-(3). See Eric Lucas, "Towards an International Declaration on Land Rights" (1984) 33 Int'l Comm Jur Rev 61 at 65.

42 Lee P Breckenridge, "Protection of Biological and Cultural Diversity: Emerging Recognition of Local Community Rights in Ecosystems under International Environmental Law (1992) 59 Tenn L Rev 735 at 753-54.

43 Aman Gupta, *Human Rights of Indigenous Peoples, Volume 2: Comparative Analysis of Indigenous People* (New Delhi: Isha Books, 2005) at 37.

44 Convention no. 169 Concerning Indigenous and Tribal Peoples in Independent Countries, 27 June 1989, 28 ILM 1382, online: <http://www.ilo.org/dyn/

wholly compatible, as has been seen, with the general climate of the period in which it was adopted, was the focus of criticism in the late 1970s. In particular, its integrationist philosophy was said to serve as an open invitation to governments to indulge in "harsh" assimilation policies, which were catastrophic for the culture and identity of the peoples concerned.[45] In recent years, too, its assimilationist orientation has prevented some states, for example, Australia, from adhering to it.[46] In addition, indigenous peoples themselves have avoided invoking the provisions of the convention, some of which offer satisfactory protection, in order not to legitimize the policy of integration (interpreted as assimilation by several governments) that permeates it.[47] Rather, they have asked from the very beginning that it be revised or abolished.[48]

Moreover, the inevitable corollary of its integrationist viewpoint was — save for the provision of Article 11 concerning collective indigenous ownership of traditional lands — the avoidance of the recognition of collective rights (considered essential for the

---

normlex/en/f?p=1000:12100:0::NO.::P12100_ILO_CODE:C169> [Convention no. 169]. See Alessandro Fodella, "International Law and the Diversity of Indigenous Peoples" (2006) 30 Vt L Rev 565 at 585. Convention no. 107 was ratified by twenty-seven states and continues to be in force for seventeen of them (namely Angola, Bangladesh, Belgium, Cuba, the Dominican Republic, Egypt, El Salvador, Ghana, Guinea-Bissau, Haiti, India, Iraq, Malawi, Pakistan, Panama, Syria, and Tunisia). Of the remaining ten, nine (namely Argentina, Bolivia, Brazil, Colombia, Costa Rica, Ecuador, Mexico, Paraguay, and Peru) adhered to Convention no. 169 while Portugal denounced Convention no. 107 without subscribing (at the time of writing) to its successor. See ILO, "Ratifications of C107 – Indigenous and Tribal Populations Convention, 1957 (no. 107)," online: <http://www.ilo.org/dyn/normlex/en/f?p=NO.RMLEXPUB:11300:0::NO.:11300:P11300_INSTRUMENT_ID:312252:NO.>.

45 "Although directed integration of the kind contemplated by Convention 107 was viewed as progressive in the 1940s and 50s, in the context of indigenous peoples it is readily apparent that state programmes of this nature have had ethnocidal consequences." Howard R Berman, "The International Labour Organization and Indigenous Peoples: Revision of ILO Convention no. 107 at the 75th Session of the International Labour Conference, 1988" (1988) 41 Int'l Comm Jur Rev 48 at 49.

46 See Michael D Kirby, "Human Rights and Industrial Relations" (2002) 44 J Industrial Relations 562 at 566.

47 See Lee Swepston, "A New Step in the International Law on Indigenous and Tribal Peoples: ILO Convention no. 169 of 1989" (1990) 15 Okla City UL Rev 677 at 689.

48 See Henry Minde, "Sami Land Rights in Norway: A Test Case for Indigenous Peoples" (2001) 8 Int'l J Minority & Group Rights 107 at 117.

preservation of indigenous societies) and all forms of internal (let alone external) self-determination. In this context, the individualistic orientation of Convention no. 107, granting rights to *members* of indigenous populations but not to indigenous groups *per se*, is entirely compatible with the letter and spirit of the major international human rights instruments (including those protecting the rights of minorities).[49] In the same vein, the drafters of the convention deliberately chose to use the "neutral" term "populations"[50] to describe indigenous peoples — a term that, save in this convention, does not entail the recognition in international law of any collective rights,[51] in particular that of self-determination,[52] constituting thus an ideal way of precluding *a priori*, at least on paper, any link between indigenous peoples and this particularly thorny topic.[53] Finally, it should be noted once again that several of the convention's provisions are formulated in such a way as to give national governments considerable room to manoeuvre in regard to the implementation of their obligations.

These shortcomings in fact led some commentators to speculate about the ILO's real motives in adopting the convention, which in their view exceeded the limits of the organization's mandate.[54] On the other hand, it should be noted that despite their deficiencies,

[49] "Convention no. 107 was framed in terms of members of indigenous populations ... Indigenous peoples or groups as such were only secondarily, if at all, made beneficiaries of rights of protection." Anna Meijknecht, *Towards International Personality: The Position of Minorities and Indigenous Peoples in International Law* (Antwerp: Intersentia, 2001) at 149. See also CM Brölmann and MYA Zieck, "Indigenous Peoples," in C Brölmann, R Lefeber, and N Zieck, eds, *Peoples and Minorities in International Law* (Dordrecht: Martinus Nijhoff, 1993) 187 at 201.

[50] See MO Hinz, "Legal Pluralism in Jurisprudential Perspective," in Manfred O Hinz and Helgard K Patemann, eds, *The Shade of New Leaves — Governance in Traditional Authority: A South African Perspective* (Berlin: Lit Verlag, 2006) 29 at 37.

[51] Frank Hirtz, "It Takes Modern Means to Be Traditional: On Recognizing Indigenous Cultural Communities in the Philippines" (2003) 34 Development & Change 887 at 893.

[52] See Richard H Thompson, "Ethnic Minorities and the Case for Collective Rights" (1997) 99 Am. Anthropologist 786 at 792-93.

[53] See Gudmundur Alfredsson, "The Right of Self-Determination and Indigenous Peoples," in C Tomuschat, ed, *The Modern Law of Self-Determination* (Dordrecht: Martinus Nijhoff, 1993) 41 at 45-46; Russel Lawrence Barsh, "Indigenous Peoples: An Emerging Object of International Law" (1986) 80 AJIL 369 at 376.

[54] See Virginia A Leary, "Labor," in Christopher C Joyner, ed, *The United Nations and International Law* (Cambridge: Cambridge University Press, 1997) 208 at 213-14.

the convention's provisions, especially those relating to land rights, were valued by many international legal commentators as a positive contribution to the promotion of indigenous rights.[55] In this context, it has been said that the convention laid the foundation for further developments in the field of indigenous peoples' rights.[56] It remains true, however, that the ambivalences and inadequacies of its text, together with its small number of ratifications (only twenty-seven), gradually undermined whatever potential or practical value the convention had.[57] This fact, together with the mobilization of indigenous peoples, the resulting reversal (beginning in the 1970s) of attitudes regarding the necessity of assimilation, and the concomitant emergence of new views regarding the directions a legal regime for the protection of indigenous peoples ought to take, paved the way for its partial revision.[58]

ILO Convention no. 169

Convention no. 169: A Partial Revision of Convention no. 107

Indigenous peoples' disapproval of Convention no. 107, combined with a steady shift in attitude by the UN, some national governments, and several international law scholars from the 1970s on, spurred

55 See Hurst Hannum, "Minorities, Indigenous Peoples and Self-Determination," in Louis Henkin and John Lawrence Hargrove, eds, *Human Rights: An Agenda for the Next Century* (Washington, DC: American Society of International Law, 1994) 1 at 3-4, noting that "[d]espite its broadly assimilationist approach, Convention no. 107 recognized that special protection for indigenous peoples was necessary and recognized, *inter alia,* the right of collective indigenous land ownership, the relevance of indigenous customary laws, and the right to be compensated for land taken by the state."

56 See Glenn T Morris, "In Support of the Right of Self-Determination for Indigenous Peoples under International Law" (1986) 29 German YB Int'l L 277 at 311.

57 See Anthony Simpson, "The Role of Indigenous Nongovernment Organizations in Developing Human Rights Standards Applicable to Indigenous Peoples" (1987) 81 Am Society Int'l L Proceedings 282 at 284, commenting that the "unacceptable integrationist and paternalistic theme and tone, apart from its other deficiencies, have made it virtually a dead letter." See also Bennet, *supra* note 35 at 44-45, observing that "the practical impact of Convention 107 has probably been minimal." Heintze, *supra* note 9 at 313, noting that Convention no. 107's effects "were rather poor."

58 See Glenn T Morris, "International Law and Politics: Toward a Right to Self-Determination for Indigenous Peoples," in M Annette Jaimes, ed, *The State of Native America: Genocide, Colonization, and Resistance* (Boston: South End Press, 1992) 55 at 76.

the Governing Body of the ILO to organize in September 1986 a two-week meeting of fifteen experts to look into the possibility of revising the convention.[59] The experts unanimously agreed in their report that "the integrationist approach of the Convention was obsolete and its application was detrimental in the modern world,"[60] and they recommended that it be revised as early as possible in a way that would ensure that indigenous peoples had the greatest possible control over their economic, social, and cultural development.[61] These recommendations had a decisive impact within the ILO. The Governing Body placed the partial revision of Convention no. 107 on the agenda of the 1988 annual meeting of the International Labour Conference, setting in motion a series of processes that resulted in the adoption of Convention no. 169 on 27 June 1989.[62]

THE NEW APPROACH: FROM INTEGRATION/ASSIMILATION TO RESPECT FOR, PROTECTION, AND PRESERVATION OF THE CULTURAL IDENTITY OF INDIGENOUS PEOPLES

Structurally, the new convention is largely similar to its predecessor for it deals with matters of general policy,[63] rights to land and natural resources,[64] recruitment and conditions of employment,[65] vocational training, handicrafts, and rural industries,[66] social security and

59 See Lee Swepston, "Indigenous and Tribal Peoples and International Organizations: New Perspectives" (1987) 13 Transnational Perspectives 15 at 17; Gudmundur Alfredsson, "Fourth Session of the Working Group on Indigenous Populations" (1986) 55 Nordic J Int'l L 22 at 23.

60 See Patrick Thornberry, "Minority Rights," in Academy of European Law, ed, *Collected Courses of the Academy of European Law* (Dordrecht: Kluwer Law International, 1997) vol 6, bk 2, 307 at 374.

61 See Russel Lawrence Barsh, "Revision of ILO Convention no. 107" (1987) 81 AJIL 756 at 761.

62 Convention no. 169, *supra* note 44. The convention was adopted by the ILO Conference with 328 votes in favour, one vote against, and forty-nine abstentions. See S James Anaya, *Indigenous Peoples in International Law* (Oxford: Oxford University Press, 1996) at 52-53, 67, n 92, noting that the single negative vote came from the delegate of the employers' associations of the Netherlands and that ninety-two of the 328 votes in favour came from government delegates. See also Thornberry, *supra* note 11 at 340.

63 Convention no. 169, *supra* note 44, Articles 1-12.

64 *Ibid*, Articles 13-19.

65 *Ibid*, Article 20.

66 *Ibid*, Articles 21-23.

health,[67] education and means of communication,[68] contacts and co-operation across borders,[69] and administration.[70] However, it distances itself wholly — as is evident from the removal of the word "integration" from its title — from Convention no. 107 in regard to its general philosophy.[71]

Concretely, as stated in the fourth paragraph of the preamble, it was felt that, in light of developments that had taken place in international law and in the situation of indigenous peoples since 1957, it was appropriate "to adopt new international standards on the subject with a view to removing the assimilationist orientation of the earlier standards."[72] In this new context, the drafters of the convention recognized, in the fifth paragraph of the preamble, "the aspirations of these peoples to exercise control over their own institutions, ways of life and economic development and to maintain and develop their identities, languages and religions within the framework of the states in which they live."[73]

Convention no. 169 thus abandons the assimilationist approach of its predecessor and recognizes, *inter alia,* the right of indigenous peoples to their own distinct cultural identity.[74] In this light, it entrenches, in a series of provisions, the right of indigenous peoples to maintain and develop their societies, requiring governments, among other things, to develop, with the participation of the peoples concerned, co-ordinated and systematic action to protect their rights

67 *Ibid*, Articles 24-25.

68 *Ibid*, Articles 26-31.

69 *Ibid*, Article 32.

70 *Ibid*, Article 33.

71 See Siegfried Wiessner, "Rights and Status of Indigenous Peoples: A Global Comparative and International Legal Analysis" (1999) 12 Harv Hum Rts J 57 at 100.

72 Elizabeth A Pearce, "Self-Determination for Native Americans: Land Rights and the Utility of Domestic and International Law" (1991) 22 Colum HRL Rev 361 at 382; Thornberry, *supra* note 11 at 342.

73 See Lars Adam Rehof, "Human Rights and Self-Government for Indigenous Peoples" (1994) 61/62 Nordic J Int'l L 19 at 23.

74 See Siegfried Wiessner, "Indigenous Sovereignty: A Reassessment in Light of the UN Declaration on the Rights of Indigenous Peoples" (2008) 41 Vand J Transnat'l L 1141 at 1156, noting that "[t]he Convention has as its basic theme the right of indigenous people to live and develop as distinct communities by their own designs." Mattias Åhrén, "Protecting Peoples' Cultural Rights: A Question of Properly Understanding the Notion of States and Nations?" in Francesco Francioni and Martin Scheinin, eds, Cultural Human Rights (Boston: Martinus Nijhoff, 2008) 91 at 103.

and guarantee respect for their integrity;[75] to respect, in adopting measures to promote the full realization of the social, economic, and cultural rights of those peoples, "their social and cultural identity, customs, traditions and institutions";[76] to take specific measures — insofar as these are not contrary to the freely expressed will of the peoples concerned[77] — to safeguard the persons, institutions, property, labour, cultures, and environment of those peoples;[78] to recognize and protect their social, cultural, religious, and spiritual values and practices;[79] to respect the integrity of their values, practices, and institutions;[80] to establish means for the full development of their institutions and, in appropriate cases, provide the resources necessary for this purpose;[81] and to pay due regard, in applying national laws and regulations, to their customs or customary laws.[82]

75 Convention no. 169, *supra* note 44, Article 2(1). See Garth Nettheim, Gary D Meyers, and Donna Craig, *Indigenous Peoples and Governance Structures: A Comparative Analysis of Land and Resource Management Rights* (Canberra, Australia: Aboriginal Studies Press, 2002) at 18; see also Stephan Marquadt, "International Law and Indigenous Peoples" (1995) 3 Int'l J on Group Rights 47 at 56, who, being very critical of the convention generally, comments that Article 2(1) does not specify the type or degree of participation to which it refers.

76 Convention no. 169, *supra* note 44, Article 2(2)(b). See Federico Lenzerini, "Indigenous Peoples' Cultural Rights and the Controversy over Commercial Use of Their Traditional Knowledge" in Francioni and Scheinin, *supra* note 74, 119 at 127-28; Thornberry, *supra* note 11 at 358.

77 Convention no. 169, *supra* note 44, Article 4(2). See Erric Dannenmaier, "Beyond Indigenous Property Rights: Exploring the Emergence of a Distinctive Connection Doctrine" (2008) 86 Wash UL Rev 53 at 70.

78 Convention no. 169, *supra* note 44, Article 4(1). See Johannes van Aggelen, "The Shift in the Perception of Multiculturalism at the United Nations since 1945," in Sienho Yee and Jacques-Yvan Morin, eds, *Multiculturalism and International Law — Essays in Honour of Edward McWhinney* (Leiden: Martinus Nijhoff, 2009) 169 at 191.

79 Convention no. 169, *supra* note 44, Article 5(a). See Mattias Åhrén, "Culture and Natural Resources" (2008) 2 Gáldu Čála/Journal of Indigenous Peoples' Rights 79 at 86.

80 Convention no. 169, *supra* note 44, Article 5(b). See Catherine M Tucker, "Land, Tenure Systems, and Indigenous Intellectual Property Rights," in Mary Riley, ed, *Indigenous Intellectual Property Rights: Legal Obstacles and Innovative Solutions* (Walnut Creek, CA: AltaMira Press, 2004) 127 at 131.

81 Convention no. 169, *supra* note 44, Article 6(1)(c). See Annika Tahvanainen, "Commentary to Professor Guibernau: National Minorities and Indigenous People" (2004) 25 Mich J Int'l L 1283 at 1285.

82 Convention no. 169, *supra* note 44, Article 8(1). See Natan Lerner, "The 1989 ILO Convention on Indigenous Populations: New Standards?" (1990) 20 Israel YB Human Rights 223 at 237.

This last provision has been interpreted as seeming "to require that judges and administrators applying all forms of law to Aboriginal people must take into account to an extent appropriate in the circumstances, the customary law of that person, both in determining substantive liability, and in procedural matters."[83] More specifically, it provides that indigenous peoples have the right to maintain their customs and institutions insofar as these are not incompatible with the fundamental rights defined by the national legal system and with internationally recognized human rights.[84] The latter proviso, however, has been severely criticized by indigenous peoples, who view the requirement that their customs and institutions be compatible with national laws and internationally recognized rights as, in essence, an invitation to governments to press for further assimilation,[85] since "[t]he assumption underlying the language of article 8 is that the state legal system is intrinsically good and any possible alternative or contradiction to it is evil."[86] It has also been attacked by certain scholars who argue that the conditional recognition of indigenous customs and institutions is a "nullity" because it means that "indigenous rights only begin where majoritarian proscription ends."[87]

Similar is the approach of Article 9(1), requiring that the "methods customarily practised by the peoples concerned for dealing with offences committed by their members shall be respected," but only "[t]o the extent compatible with the national legal system and internationally recognised human rights."[88] Article 9(2) further

[83] Alison Humphry, "An Opportunity Lost for Aboriginal Self-Determination: Australia's Compliance with ILO 169" (1995) 2 Murdoch University Electronic J L, online: <http://www.murdoch.edu.au/elaw/issues/v2n1/humphry21.html>, noting further that "it is still up to the government or decision maker to determine the extent of this 'due regard.'"

[84] Convention no. 169, *supra* note 44, Article 8(2). See Curtis G Berkey, "International Law and Domestic Courts: Enhancing Self-Determination for Indigenous Peoples" (1992) 5 Harv Hum Rts J 65 at 85; Thornberry, *supra* note 11 at 359.

[85] See Andrée Lawrey, "Contemporary Efforts to Guarantee Indigenous Rights under International Law" (1990) 23 Vand J Transnat'l L 703 at 719-20.

[86] Sharon Venne, "The New Language of Assimilation: A Brief Analysis of ILO Convention 169" (1990) 2 Without Prejudice 53 at 61.

[87] Collin Miller, "Banishment from Within and Without: Analyzing Indigenous Sentencing under International Human Rights Standards" (2004) 80 NDL Rev 253 at 280.

[88] Convention no. 169, *supra* note 44, Article 9(1). See Megan Davis, "The Recognition of Aboriginal Customary Law and International Law Developments," in

provides that the "customs of these peoples in regard to penal matters shall be taken into consideration by the authorities and courts dealing with such cases,"[89] while Article 10 states that "in imposing penalties as laid down by general law on members of these peoples account shall be taken of their economic, social and cultural characteristics,"[90] and it provides that preference shall be given to methods of punishment other than imprisonment.[91]

The convention further provides that the procedures established by the peoples concerned for the transmission of land rights among their members shall be respected.[92] It also recognizes such traditional indigenous activities as hunting, fishing, trapping, and gathering as important factors in the maintenance of indigenous cultures and indigenous economic self-reliance and development and requires that governments ensure, with the participation of the peoples concerned and "where appropriate," that these activities are strengthened and promoted.[93] Regarding the cultural aspects of health issues, the convention provides that health services "shall be planned and administered in co-operation with the peoples concerned and take into account their economic, geographic, social and cultural conditions as well as their traditional preventive care,

---

Indigenous Peoples: Issues in International and Australian Law (Sydney: International Law Association (Australian Branch), 2007) 25 at 29.

89 Convention no. 169, *supra* note 44, Article 9(2). See Tiina Saaresranta, "Indigenous Law and the Protection of Indigenous Peoples' Rights in Ecuador" (2003) 9 Hum Rts Dev 127 at 142. See also Barsh, *supra* note 20 at 223, observing that: "[t]his encourages courts not to interfere in internal disputes and to read national law as broadly as possible to be consistent with indigenous customary law, but falls short of recognizing the right to establish autonomous indigenous legal systems."

90 Convention no. 169, *supra* note 44, Article 10(1).

91 *Ibid*, Article 10(2). See Rachel Sieder, "The Judiciary and Indigenous Rights in Guatemala" (2007) 5 Int'l J Constitutional L 211 at 221, n 38. See also Humphry, *supra* note 83, noting that "the high rate of Aboriginal deaths in custody has made it open to question whether imprisonment per se is less cruel and inhuman" than other forms of indigenous punishment which are considered as such by non-indigenous scholars, legislators, and so on.

92 Convention no. 169, *supra* note 44, Article 17(1). See Graeme Neate, "Looking after Country: Legal Recognition of Traditional Rights to and Responsibilities for Land" (1993) 16 UNSWLJ 161 at 168.

93 Convention no. 169, *supra* note 44, Article 23. See Marina Hadjioannou, "The International Human Right to Culture: Reclamation of the Cultural Identities of Indigenous Peoples under International Law" (2005) 8 Chapman L Rev 201 at 216.

healing practices and medicines."[94] In the linguistic field, the convention requires, *inter alia,* that measures be taken to preserve and promote the development and practice of indigenous languages.[95] Finally, the convention calls for the adoption of "measures appropriate to the traditions and cultures of the peoples concerned, to make known to them their rights and duties, especially in regard to labour, economic opportunities, education and health matters, social welfare and their rights deriving from this Convention."[96]

It is worth pointing out that, in the context of this pluralistic and multicultural approach, the convention emphasizes self-identification as a fundamental criterion for determining the groups to which its provisions apply,[97] thus meeting one of the central claims of the indigenous agenda.[98] Indeed, the Committee of Experts on the Application of Conventions and Recommendations focuses particularly on this issue, addressing "direct requests" to governments for information regarding the ways this right is implemented.[99] According to some scholars, the ILO has advocated "an unlimited right to 'self-identification' for indigenous peoples in order to counter possible actions of 'host' states who might deny indigenous claims within their borders."[100] In any case, the criterion of self-identification is

94 Convention no. 169, *supra* note 44, Article 25(2). See Chidi Oguamanam, "Between Reality and Rhetoric: The Epistemic Schism in the Recognition of Traditional Medicine in International Law" (2003) 16 St Thomas L Rev 59 at 72.

95 Convention no. 169, *supra* note 44, Article 28(3). See Lynda Frost, "Human Rights Education Programs for Indigenous Peoples: Teaching Whose Human Rights?" (1995) 7 St Thomas L Rev 699 at 707-8.

96 Convention no. 169, *supra* note 44, Article 30(1). See Cynthia Price Cohen, "Development of the Rights of the Indigenous Child under International Law" (1996) 9 St Thomas L Rev 231 at 233.

97 Convention no. 169, *supra* note 44, Article 1(2). See Willem Van Genugten and Camilo Perez-Bustillo, "The Emerging International Architecture of Indigenous Rights: The Interaction between Global, Regional, and National Dimensions" (2004) 11 Int'l J on Minority & Group Rights 379 at 388-89.

98 See Bengt G Karlsson, "Anthropology and the 'Indigenous Slot': Claims to and Debates about Indigenous Peoples' Status in India" (2003) 23 Critique of Anthropology 403 at 413.

99 See Tanja Joona, "International Norms and Domestic Practices in Regard to ILO Convention no. 169 — with Special Reference to Articles 1 and 13-19" (2010) 12 Int'l Community L Rev 213 at 236-44.

100 Jeff J Corntassel, "Who Is Indigenous? 'Peoplehood' and Ethnonationalist Approaches to Rearticulating Indigenous Identity" (2003) 9 Nationalism & Ethnic Politics 75 at 75; see also African Commission on Human and Peoples' Rights,

held to prevent government authorities from trying to determine indigeneity on the basis of parameters established by non-indigenous societies, while permitting indigenous peoples to maintain, develop, and transmit their identity and their cultural heritage.[101]

Based on these aforementioned provisions, a persuasive argument can be made that Convention no. 169 is anti-assimilationist in orientation and spirit,[102] embodying an approach governed by recognition of, and respect for, indigenous cultures and ways of life.[103] On the other hand, precisely the opposite position has also been taken, namely that "the ILO revision is meant to protect the non-indigenous peoples from the indigenous peoples" and that in this context "Convention 169 is still assimilationist and far more destructive than its predecessor" since the "colonists have become a little more sophisticated," changing the language of assimilation but retaining the same policies unabated.[104] Adherents of this view focus on a series of issues, such as the requirement that indigenous customs and institutions be compatible with internationally recognized human rights and the fundamental rights defined by national legal systems,[105] or other provisions[106] that are critiqued in order to argue that the new convention, "rather than taking a small step forward

Report of the African Commission's Working Group of Experts on Indigenous Populations/Communities (Banjul, Gambia, Copenhagen: ACHPR, IWGIA, 2005) at 78, where it is noted: "It could be argued that, irrespective of the fact that many African states do not recognize the existence of indigenous people within their territories ... Article 1.2 of ILO Convention 169 of 1989 grants rights and protection to people identifying themselves as indigenous in Africa."

101 Carlos Yescas Angeles Trujano, *Indigenous Routes: A Framework for Understanding Indigenous Migration* (Geneva: International Organization for Migration, 2008) at 19; see also Barsh, *supra* note 20 at 215, observing that: "Indigenous representatives have warned repeatedly ... that state power to classify groups as non-indigenous is power to extinguish their legal rights."

102 See Stephen May and Sheila Aikman, "Indigenous Education: Addressing Current Issues and Developments" (2003) 39 Comparative Education 139 at 140.

103 See Kealeboga N Bojosi, "Protecting Indigenous Peoples in Africa: An Analysis of the Approach of the African Commission on Human and Peoples' Rights" (2006) 6 African Human Rights L J 382 at 386.

104 Venne, *supra* note 86 at 53, 56, 66.

105 Convention no. 169, *supra* note 44, Article 8(2). See Venne, *supra* note 86 at 60, arguing that: "[i]f the bases for legal systems are rooted in two different needs and concerns there is very little compatibility."

106 Eg, Convention no. 169, *supra* note 44, Articles 1(3), 6(2), 7(1), 15, 16.

... appears to take a giant leap sideways," since it embodies a new language of assimilation.[107]

However, these reservations regarding Convention no. 169 and second thoughts as to its real or underlying philosophy expressed during the first decade after it came into force, while admittedly not baseless, seem to have been laid to rest by subsequent developments. In Latin America, at least, where most ratifications of the convention have occurred, it stands as a key reference point. On the one hand, it has inspired constitutional reforms and provisions for the recognition of indigenous rights, while, on the other, it has been applied in national courts and by the bodies of the inter-American human rights system (that is, the commission and court) in a manner supportive of indigenous perspectives, demands, and interests, thus making a substantial and fertile contribution to respect for, and protection of, indigenous cultural identity and rights.[108]

FROM "POPULATIONS" TO "PEOPLES"

One of the most important elements of the new convention is the replacement of the term "populations," used in Convention no. 107, by that of "peoples."[109] This change in terminology met a standing demand of the peoples concerned,[110] who insisted particularly on this point during the revision process, stressing their identity as peoples entitled to the right to self-determination like other peoples and asking to be referred to as such, rather than as populations, in the text of the revised convention.[111] Several governments, on the other hand, expressed their preference for the notion of "populations,"[112]

[107] Lisa Strelein, "The Price of Compromise: Should Australia Ratify ILO Convention 169?" in Creta Bird, Gary Martin, and Jennifer Nielsen, eds, *Majah: Indigenous Peoples and the Law* (Leichhardt: Federation Press, 1996) 63 at 85.

[108] See Christian Courtis, "Notes on the Implementation by Latin American Courts of the ILO Convention 169 on Indigenous Peoples" (2009) 6 Sur — Int'l J on Human Rights 53.

[109] Scott Forrest, "Indigenous Self-Determination in Finland: A Case Study in Normative Change" (2006) 42 Polar Record 229 at 229; Thornberry, *supra* note 11 at 342.

[110] See Sharon Hellen Venne, *Our Elders Understand Our Rights: Evolving International Law Regarding Indigenous Rights* (Penticton, BC: Theytus Books, 1998) at 90-92.

[111] Catherine J Iorns, "Indigenous Peoples and Self-Determination: Challenging State Sovereignty" (1992) 24 Case W Res J Int'l L 199 at 263.

[112] Mireya Maritza Peña Guzmán, "The Emerging System of International Protection of Indigenous Peoples' Rights" (1996) 9 St Thomas L Rev 251 at 257; Thornberry, *supra* note 11 at 342-43.

fearing that inclusion of the term "peoples" in the convention might pave the way towards secession.[113] These different approaches to the use of the term "peoples" almost brought the entire revision process to a standstill, threatening conclusion of the convention.[114] The matter was, and remains, one of primary importance, since by virtue of the provisions of relevant international legal instruments only "peoples" are recognized as having the right to self-determination,[115] while "populations" is a concept without a specific set of rights in international law (of course, other than in Convention no. 107).[116]

The solution to the impasse was a compromise: adoption of the term "peoples" but subject to the caveat crystallized in Article 1(3), which clarifies that the use of the term has no implications in regard to the rights attached to it in international law.[117] This formulation was considered, by indigenous peoples and their advocates, as a "half victory,"[118] since it appears to exclude the exercise of external self-determination.[119] While indigenous peoples had repeatedly stated that that was not what they were seeking,[120] they had also emphatically claimed that they ought not to be subjected as a matter of principle

113 Moana Jackson, "The Face behind the Law: The United Nations and the Rights of Indigenous Peoples" (2005) 8 YB of New Zealand Jurisprudence 10 at 19.

114 See Russel Lawrence Barsh, "Indigenous Peoples in the 1990s: From Object to Subject of International Law?" (1994) 7 Harv Hum Rts J 33 at 44.

115 *Michael Halewood*, "Indigenous and Local Knowledge in International Law: A Preface to Sui Generis Intellectual Property Protection" (1999) 44 McGill LJ 953 at 958.

116 Serv Wiemers, "The International Legal Status of North American Indians after 500 Years of Colonization" (1992) 5 Leiden J Int'l L 69 at 75.

117 Convention no. 169, *supra* note 44, Article 1(3). See Luis Rodríguez-Piñero, *Indigenous Peoples, Postcolonialism, and International Law: The ILO Regime (1919-1989)* (Oxford: Oxford University Press, 2005) at 307-8; Thornberry, *supra* note 11 at 343-44.

118 Asbjørn Eide, "Rights of Indigenous Peoples: Achievements in International Law during the Last Quarter of a Century" (2007) 4 Gáldu Čála/Journal of Indigenous Peoples' Rights 40 at 73.

119 See Gudmundur Alfredsson, "Human Rights Challenges in the Arctic," in Laisi Heininen and Kari Laine, eds, *The Borderless North* (Oulu: Thule Institute, University of Oulu, Northern Research Forum, 2008) 150 at 152; Geir Ulfstein, "Indigenous Peoples' Right to Land" (2004) 8 Max Planck YB of UN L 1 at 12.

120 See Ted Moses, "Renewal of the Nation," in Gudmundur Alfredsson and Maria Stavropoulou, eds, *Justice Pending: Indigenous Peoples and Other Good Causes — Essays in Honour of Erica-Irene A. Daes* (The Hague: Martinus Nijhoff, 2002) 57 at 63, noting that "very few indigenous peoples anywhere in the world are

to more restrictions on its enjoyment than other peoples — for that, as they reasonably argued, would constitute racial discrimination and establish a double standard.[121] The ILO, for its part, argued that the specific provision did not constitute a refusal to recognize the right of indigenous peoples to self-determination, taking the position rather that it was up to the UN, as the competent body, to rule on the matter.[122] This reasoning, albeit defensible from a strictly legal point of view, did not seem to persuade several indigenous peoples[123] and scholars, who directed criticism against the provision.[124]

---

secessionists." See also Andrew Huff, "Indigenous Land Rights and the New Self-Determination" (2005) 16 Colo J Int'l Envtl L and Pol'y 295 at 320, noting that the insistence of states on invoking chaotic consequences that could ensue on the international stage from the recognition of indigenous peoples' right to self-determination appears obtuse in view of those peoples' repeated declarations that secession is not their object. According to Huff, this argument was advanced to cover states' fears of losing control over natural resources (and their related benefits).

121 For an illustrative overview of the thesis of many indigenous peoples on the issue of self-determination, see the joint submission of a number of indigenous groups to the Working Group Established in Accordance with UN Commission on Human Rights Resolution 1995/32, "'General Provisions' of the Draft U.N. Declaration on the Rights of Indigenous Peoples," UN Doc E/CN.4/2005/WG.15/CRP.2 (24 November 2005).

122 "In the ILO Convention, a provision was added as paragraph 3 of Article 1 stating: 'The use of the term "peoples" in this Convention shall not be construed as having any implications regarding the rights which may attach to the term under international law.' This has been taken by some — in particular by some representatives of indigenous and tribal peoples — to mean that the ILO Convention denies that those covered by it have the right to self-determination. *This is clearly not the case, however; the International Labour Conference simply took the position that the question of self-determination was for the United Nations to resolve, not for the ILO.*" International Labour Office, "Comments on the Draft United Nations Declaration on the Rights of Indigenous Peoples," UN Doc E/CN.4/1995/119 (6 February 1995) at paras 14-15 [emphasis added]. See also Ronald Niezen, *The Origins of Indigenism: Human Rights and the Politics of Identity* (Berkeley, CA: University of California Press, 2003) at 162, noting that: "[i]n effect, the ILO, in the interests of realizing a convention that would meet the immediate needs of indigenous peoples, postponed the debate on indigenous self-determination by handing it over to its parent body, the United Nations."

123 See Patrick Cleveland, "Apposition of Recent U.S. Supreme Court Decisions Regarding Tribal Sovereignty and International Indigenous Rights Declarations" (2000) 12 Pace Int'l L Rev 397 at 409.

124 As has been noted: "It is interesting that an International Organization is telling over 350 million people that they don't exist as peoples. It raises the question of whose rights are protected: those of the indigenous peoples or the non

In any case, it has been argued that the contested wording in no way undermines the collective nature of the rights affirmed by the convention,[125] which are vested in indigenous peoples *per se*.[126] Furthermore, it should be noted that the ILO has stressed that there is nothing in the convention that would be incompatible with any international legal instrument that might establish or define indigenous peoples' right to self-determination.[127] One should also keep in mind that even the United Nations Declaration on the Rights of Indigenous Peoples (UNDRIP), which most indigenous peoples

---

indigenous peoples?" Tanja Joona, "ILO Convention no. 169 — A Solution for Land Disputes in the Nordic Countries?" in Heininen and Laine, *supra* note 119, 155 at 162; Venne, *supra* note 86 at 56, commenting sarcastically that "[p]erhaps the revised Convention should be called the Convention concerning nonindigenous Peoples in Indigenous Peoples' Territories and Their Right to Exist in Those Territories." Strelein, *supra* note 107 at 70, criticizing the ILO's thesis that the issue of self-determination is outside the scope of an ILO instrument as a reflection of its inappropriateness as a forum to accommodate indigenous peoples' concerns.

125 See James Anaya, "Indigenous Law and Its Contribution to Global Pluralism" (2007) 6 Indigenous LJ 3 at 6; see also Barsh, *supra* note 20 at 215, observing: "Indeed, the convention's use of the term "peoples," while deprived of its usual connotation under international law, was accepted as a way of affirming that indigenous peoples have 'an identity of their own' and comprise organized societies rather than 'mere groupings' of individuals sharing some racial or ethnic characteristics."

126 See S James Anaya, "Indian Givers: What Indigenous Peoples Have Contributed to International Human Rights Law" (2006) 22 Wash U JL & Pol'y 107 at 112. According to Thornberry, the convention's "commitment to collective rights is remarkable and thoroughgoing." Thornberry, *supra* note 11 at 366-67. Rodríguez-Piñero for his part argues that "[f]ramed by the recognition of indigenous peoples as 'peoples,' Convention no. 169 takes a decisive stand on the collective nature of indigenous rights, transforming what the earlier convention defined as an object of applied anthropological concern into a collective subject of rights." Rodríguez-Piñero, *supra* note 117 at 321. Compare with Donders, who notes that this collective approach does not take "the form of substantive collective rights adjudged to indigenous peoples as such, but instead reflects State obligations towards these peoples. Thus, indigenous peoples are not subjects of these provisions, but their beneficiaries. Yvonne Donders, "The UN Declaration on the Rights of Indigenous Peoples: A Victory for Cultural Autonomy?" in Ineke Boerefijn and Jenny Goldschmidt, eds, *Changing Perceptions of Sovereignty and Human Rights: Essays in Honour of Cees Flinterman* (Antwerp: Intersentia, 2008) 99 at 113.

127 See John B Henriksen, Martin Scheinin, and Mattias Åhrén, "The Saami People's Right to Self-Determination" (2007) 3 Gáldu Čála / Journal of Indigenous Peoples' Rights 52 at 59.

have relied upon for recognition of their right to self-determination, contains provisions that seem to restrict the right of self-determination of indigenous peoples exclusively to its internal dimension — that is, to forms of autonomy and self-government within existing states.[128] This is so notwithstanding the fact that the declaration is not a legally binding text (as is Convention no. 169) and that one might therefore have expected to meet with fewer state concerns regarding the extent of the right to self-determination of the peoples concerned recognized therein. And yet this right can in any case be deduced, via an admittedly broad interpretation, from Convention no. 169 itself.[129]

128 United Nations Declaration on the Rights of Indigenous Peoples, UNGA Res 61/295, UN Doc A/RES/61/295 (13 September 2007), Articles 4, 46(1) [UNDRIP]. See Timo Koivurova, "Sovereign States and Self-Determining Peoples: Carving Out a Place for Transnational Indigenous Peoples in a World of Sovereign States" (2010) 12 Int'l Comm L Rev 191 at 201-3.

129 "The Convention does, however, aim to create the conditions necessary for 'self-management' by indigenous peoples, defined with reference to the preamble's call for 'control over their own institutions,' which is apparently synonymous with at least some degree of 'self government.'" Christopher J Fromherz, "Indigenous Peoples' Courts: Egalitarian Juridical Pluralism, Self-Determination, and the United Nations Declaration on the Rights of Indigenous Peoples" (2008) 156 U Pa L Rev 1341 at 1366. Along the same lines, Alfredsson observes that "even if the ILO Convention does not employ the term 'autonomy,' it is in fact dealing with group control over functions which have traditionally been delegated to autonomous regimes and which are necessary for maintaining group identity and culture." Gudmundur Alfredsson, "Indigenous Peoples and Autonomy," in Markku Suksi, ed, *Autonomy: Applications and Implications* (The Hague: Kluwer Law International, 1998) 125 at 127. Thornberry holds that "[i]n as far as self-determination is increasingly understood to contain an internal aspect, it may be that certain aspects of self-determination can be read into Convention 169 — notably in the area of participation rights and self-government." Thornberry, *supra* note 11 at 344. According to Xanthaki, the convention "seems to contain the possibility of cultural autonomy." Alexandra Xanthaki, "Indigenous Cultural Rights in International Law" (2000) 2 Eur JL Ref 343 at 348. Barsh argues that "[a]lthough the new convention does not refer explicitly to a right to self-determination, self-government, or autonomy, it plainly achieves the same result indirectly. It guarantees respect for indigenous 'institutions' generally and refers to a wide variety of specific rights of collective action." Barsh, *supra* note 20 at 215. Ulfstein notes that "the Convention provides for extensive rights of participation in decision making, which is an important part of internal self-determination." Ulfstein, *supra* note 119 at 12. For a view holding that Convention no. 169 grants "no effective rights of autonomy," see Paul Keal, *European Conquest and the Rights of Indigenous Peoples: The Moral Backwardness of International Society* (Cambridge: Cambridge University Press, 2003) at 116.

CONSULTATION, CO-OPERATION, AND PARTICIPATION: THE KEYWORDS OF THE CONVENTION

The principles of consultation, co-operation, and participation constitute some of the central themes of Convention no. 169.[130] In fact, "almost every article in the Convention, which prescribes measures to be taken for the protection and promotion of the interests of indigenous and tribal peoples, including measures for land, education, health care, employment, *etc.*, requires the participation of, co-operation of, or consultation with, indigenous or tribal peoples."[131] In this context, the "key article of the whole Convention" is Article 6, which lays down the general normative framework for the right of indigenous peoples to be consulted.[132] First of all, it states that "[i]n applying the provisions of this Convention, governments shall: consult the peoples concerned, through appropriate procedures and in particular through their representative institutions, whenever consideration is being given to legislative or administrative measures which may affect them."[133] It should be noted that, in regard to the major issue of representativity, the ILO ad hoc tripartite committees examining "representations" alleging violations of the convention have emphasized that "it could be difficult in many circumstances to determine who represents any given community. However, if an appropriate consultation process is not developed with the indigenous and tribal institutions or organizations that are truly representative of the communities affected, the resulting consultations will not comply with the requirements of the Convention."[134]

130 See UN Secretariat of the Permanent Forum on Indigenous Issues, "Contribution of the ILO," International Workshop on Free, Prior and Informed Consent and Indigenous Peoples (New York, 17-19 January 2005), UN Doc PFII/2005/WS.2/4, para 2 [Contribution of the ILO].

131 Saeko Kawashima, "The Right to Effective Participation and the Ainu People" (2004) 11 Int'l J on Minority & Group Rights 21 at 28-29.

132 Alexandra Xanthaki, "Indigenous Rights in the Russian Federation: The Case of Numerically Small Peoples of the Russian North, Siberia, and Far East" (2004) 26 Hum Rts Q 26 74 at 85.

133 Convention no. 169, *supra* note 44, Article 6(1)(a). See Greg Marks, "Avoiding the International Spotlight: Australia, Indigenous Rights and the United Nations Treaty Bodies" (2002) 2 Hum Rts L Rev 19 at 50.

134 ILO, *Report of the Committee Set up to Examine the Representation Alleging non-Observance by Ecuador of the Indigenous and Tribal Peoples Convention, 1989 (no. 169), made under Article 24 of the ILO Constitution by the Confederación Ecuatoriana de Organizaciones Sindicales Libres (CEOSL)*, 14 November 2001, ILO Doc (GB.277/18/1):(GB.282/14/4) at para 44 [Ecuador Report].

Article 6 further provides that "[t]he consultations carried out in application of this Convention shall be undertaken, in good faith and in a form appropriate to the circumstances, with the objective of achieving agreement or consent to the proposed measures."[135] This provision, and more particularly its final phrase (which was the product of the fusion of diametrically differing views), has been interpreted by the Secretariat of the ILO as not requiring the agreement of the peoples concerned in order to comply with its substance. Rather, it merely "expresses an objective for the consultations."[136] The convention does not, in other words, recognize a right of veto to indigenous peoples.[137]

This development was intensely displeasing and disappointing to several indigenous peoples who sought nothing less than the recognition of a requirement of consent.[138] It also fuelled caustic criticism among some commentators.[139] However, despite these reactions, which were to be expected and to a certain degree justified, it has been argued that Article 6 is

135 Convention no. 169, *supra* note 44, Article 6(2). See Lee Swepston, "The ILO Indigenous and Tribal Peoples Convention (no. 169): Eight Years after Adoption," in Cynthia Price Cohen, ed, *Human Rights of Indigenous Peoples* (Ardsley, NY: Transnational Publishers, 1998) 17 at 23.

136 "The Committee recalls that in the discussion concerning the adoption of Article 6 of the Convention on prior consultation, a representative of the Secretary-General stated that in drafting the text the Office had not intended to suggest that the consultations referred to would have to result in the obtaining of agreement or consent of those being consulted, but rather to express an objective for the consultations." Ecuador Report, *supra* note 134 at para 39.

137 See Mauro Barelli, "Free, Prior and Informed Consent in the Aftermath of the UN Declaration on the Rights of Indigenous Peoples: Developments and Challenges Ahead" (2012) 16 Int'l JHR 1 at 6; Leena Heinämäki, "Protecting the Rights of Indigenous Peoples -Promoting the Sustainability of the Global Environment?" (2009) 11 Int'l Comm L Rev 3 at 36.

138 See Venne, *supra* note 86 at 58-59, arguing that "consultation" "is used as an alibi to say that they did ask us, but there is no requirement to implement our position" and further concluding that it is better "to ignore the consultation game and ... insist on consent as a prerequisite to any project that affects our life ... Anything short of this minimum will be rejected." See also Thornberry, *supra* note 11 at 349, noting that from the perspective of some indigenous peoples, the Convention "did not properly recognize the crucial requirement of indigenous consent."

139 See Strelein, *supra* note 107 at 77, criticizing the notion that the consent of indigenous peoples may not be required where decisions directly affect them as illustrative of "the paternal statist approach of Convention 169."

one of the new convention's most powerful tools, as it not only requires negotiations with indigenous representatives in advance of legislation, but subjects them to ILO supervision. Challenging the form or character of "consultations," indigenous organizations can argue, *inter alia*, that the procedures adopted are not "appropriate," not sufficiently "representative" (if, for example, the government selects indigenous spokesmen), or, not "in good faith with the objective of achieving agreement."[140]

In this context, it has also been noted that,

[w]hile no veto is available for indigenous peoples in the process of participation and consultation, the 1998 Guide to ILO Convention No. 169 provides that there must be: "actual consultation in which [indigenous and tribal] ... peoples have a right to *express their point of view* and a *right to influence the decision.* This means that the governments have to supply the enabling environment and conditions to permit indigenous and tribal peoples to make a meaningful contribution."[141]

This interpretation has also been adopted by the ILO ad hoc tripartite committees examining representations alleging violations of Convention no. 169. These committees have found that a series of government actions, such as dividing indigenous lands into individual lots (Peru), granting logging rights on indigenous lands to third parties (Bolivia), granting drilling concessions on traditional indigenous lands to an oil company (Ecuador, Colombia), and the construction of a hydroelectric dam near indigenous lands (Colombia), had taken place without prior consultation. In doing so, the committees have noted that the convention's requirement of prior consultation with indigenous peoples is not an obligation merely to

140 Barsh, *supra* note 20 at 219-20. See also Colborn, *supra* note 20 at 5.

141 Annika Tahvanainen, "The Treaty Making Capacity of Indigenous Peoples" (2005) 12 Int'l J Minority & Group Rights 397 at 414 [emphasis in original]. See also ILO, *Report of the Committee Set up to Examine the Representation Alleging Non-Observance by Colombia of the Indigenous and Tribal Peoples Convention, 1989 (no. 169), Made under Article 24 of the ILO Constitution by the Central Unitary Workers' Union (CUT) and the Colombian Medical Trade Union Association*, 14 November 2001, ILO Doc (GB.277/18/1):(GB.282/14/4) at para 61 [Colombia Report], noting that "[i]n the opinion of the Committee, while Article 6 does not require consensus to be obtained in the process of prior consultation, it does provide that the peoples concerned should have the possibility to participate freely at all levels in the formulation, implementation and evaluation of measures and programmes that affect them directly."

inform them of measures affecting them but also to give them the real possibility of influencing decisions affecting their interests.[142]

Next, the convention requires that governments "establish means by which these peoples can freely participate, to *at least the same extent* as other sectors of the population, at all levels of decision-making in elective institutions and administrative and other bodies responsible for policies and programmes which concern them,"[143] a provision that "does not, however, specify the participatory rights in more detail, and does not give special privileges to indigenous peoples."[144] This provision has also been criticized as expressing a particular liberal democratic notion of equal participation that intimates acceptance of non-indigenous decision-making processes, functioning therefore as a powerful tool of assimilation.[145] On the other hand, it has been noted that this provision was understood during its drafting as permitting specific forms of representation that are not available to non-indigenous citizens.[146]

142 See, eg, Colombia Report, *supra* note 141 at para 90, where "[t]he Committee considers that the concept of consultation with the indigenous communities that might be affected with a view to exploiting natural resources must encompass genuine dialogue between the parties, involving communication and understanding, mutual respect and good faith, and the sincere desire to reach a consensus. A meeting conducted merely for information purposes cannot be considered as being consistent with the terms of the Convention. Furthermore, according to Article 6, the consultation must be 'prior' consultation, which implies that the communities affected are involved as early on as possible in the process, including in environmental impact studies."

143 Convention no. 169, *supra* note 44, Article 6(1)(b) [emphasis added]. See Sarah Pritchard, "Native Title from the Perspective of International Standards" (1997) 18 Australian YB of Int'l L 127 at 162.

144 Ulfstein, *supra* note 119 at 15. See also Strelein, *supra* note 107 at 80, commenting that "[t]his kind of participation, which enshrines the 'majority rules' syndrome, fails to accommodate marginalised groups. Similarly, the argument that all individuals should be treated equally does not accept preferential rights that must be recognized in order to rectify historical and current marginalisation by the democratic majority."

145 See Venne, *supra* note 86 at 59, observing that "[i]n many instances, our people have become involved in the administrative framework of the government. The result has been that our own people become the tools of assimilation ... When an indigenous person is elected within the political framework of the non-indigenous system, an onus is placed on that person to follow 'the rules of the game', a game which has historically involved our dispossession ... This is not a solution for us. For to be included in their way is the ultimate goal of assimilation." See also Strelein, *supra* note 107 at 80.

146 See Barsh, *supra* note 20 at 220, n 46.

The other two fundamental principles of the convention are those of co-operation and participation, as enshrined in Article 7. Thus, "[g]overnments shall take measures, in co-operation with the peoples concerned, to protect and preserve the environment of the territories they inhabit,"[147] while "[t]he improvement of the conditions of life and work and levels of health and education of the peoples concerned, with their participation and co-operation, shall be a matter of priority in plans for the overall economic development of areas they inhabit."[148] The normative scope of indigenous peoples' rights of participation regarding development issues is specified more precisely in the first paragraph of Article 7, which provides that "[t]he peoples concerned shall have the right to decide their own priorities for the process of development as it affects their lives, beliefs, institutions and spiritual well-being and the lands they occupy or otherwise use, and to exercise control, to the extent possible, over their own economic, social and cultural development."[149] This paragraph also recognizes the right of indigenous peoples to "participate in the formulation, implementation and evaluation of plans and programmes for national and regional development which may affect them directly."[150]

Article 7(3) further provides, though in an admittedly weak formulation, that "[g]overnments shall ensure that, *whenever appropriate*, studies are carried out, in co-operation with the peoples concerned, to assess the social, spiritual, cultural and environmental impact on them of planned development activities."[151] Despite the loose wording, the ILO ad hoc tripartite committees have paid

147 Convention no. 169, *supra* note 44, Article 7(4). See Dinah Shelton, "Human Rights, Environmental Rights and the Right to Environment" (1991) 28 Stan J Int'l L 103 at 127.

148 Convention no. 169, *supra* note 44, Article 7(2). See Kristian Myntti, "The Right of Indigenous Peoples to Participate in Development Projects" (2002) 8 Human Rights & Development YB 225 at 245.

149 Convention no. 169, *supra* note 44, Article 7(1). See Patrick Thornberry, "Minority and Indigenous Rights at 'the End of History'" (2002) 2 Ethnicities 515 at 526; Gudmundur Alfredsson, "Minimum Requirements for a New Nordic Sami Convention" (1999) 68 Nordic J Int'l L 397 at 405.

150 Convention no. 169, *supra* note 44, Article 7(1). See Patrick Macklem, "Indigenous Rights and Multinational Corporations at International Law" (2001) 24 Hastings Int'l and Comp L Rev 475 at 479.

151 Convention no. 169, *supra* note 44, Article 7(3) [emphasis added]. See Cherie Metcalf, "Indigenous Rights and the Environment: Evolving International Law" (2003-04) 35 Ottawa L Rev 101 at 112.

attention to the matter, asking the Governing Body to request that governments "consider the possibility of establishing, in each particular case, especially in the case of large-scale exploitations such as those affecting large tracts of land, environmental, cultural, social and spiritual impact studies, jointly with the peoples concerned, before authorizing exploration and exploitation of natural resources in areas traditionally occupied by indigenous peoples."[152] The results of these studies will be considered fundamental criteria for the implementation of such activities.[153]

Article 7 has been criticized by certain indigenous groups and commentators, along with Article 6, as incorporating a "historic, paternalistic attitude" that implies that indigenous peoples are backward, underdeveloped, and incapable of taking care of themselves and deciding their own future.[154] Nonetheless, despite these criticisms — to a certain degree justified, particularly in relation to Article 6(2) — the convention's repeated use of the terms "consultation" and "participation" in several of its provisions, and the emphasis laid on them by the tripartite committees in their findings and recommendations, seem to justify the position that "the spirit of consultation and participation constitutes the cornerstone of Convention No 169 on which all its provisions are based."[155]

LAND AND RESOURCE RIGHTS: THE HEART OF THE CONVENTION

The whole second part of the convention (Articles 13-19) concerns the protection of indigenous land rights,[156] thus recognizing the

152 ILO, *Report of the Committee Set up to Examine the Representation Alleging non-Observance by Bolivia of the Indigenous and Tribal Peoples Convention, 1989 (no. 169), Made under Article 24 of the ILO Constitution by the Bolivian Central of Workers (COB)*, March 1999, ILO Doc (GB.272/8/1):(GB.274/16/7) at para 39 [Bolivia Report].

153 Convention no. 169, *supra* note 44, Article 7(3). See Helen Quane, "The Rights of Indigenous Peoples and the Development Process" (2005) 27 Hum Rts Q 652 at 669.

154 See Venne, *supra* note 86 at 60; Joona, *supra* note 124 at 162.

155 See UN Economic and Social Council, *Report of the Secretary-General on the Preliminary Review by the Coordinator of the International Decade of the World's Indigenous Peoples on the Activities of the United Nations System in Relation to the Decade*, 25 June 2004, UN Doc E/ 2004/CRP.12 at 39; Ecuador Report, *supra* note 134 at para 31; Contribution of the ILO, *supra* note 130 at para 2.

156 See Asbjørn Eide, "Good Governance, Human Rights, and the Rights of Minorities and Indigenous Peoples," in Hans-Otto Sano and Gudmundur Alfredsson,

vital importance,[157] and, indeed, the collective dimension,[158] of indigenous peoples' relationship with their ancestral lands for their physical, cultural, and economic survival.[159] In this context, the convention first requires governments to "respect the special importance for the cultures and spiritual values of the peoples concerned of their relationship with the lands or territories, or both as applicable, which they occupy or otherwise use, and in particular the collective aspects of this relationship"[160] and then provides for the recognition of indigenous peoples' rights of ownership and possession over the lands that they "traditionally occupy."[161] The

---

eds, *Human Rights and Good Governance: Building Bridges* (The Hague, London, New York: Martinus Nijhoff, 2002) 47 at 61.

157 See Viniyanka Prasad, "The UN Declaration on the Rights of Indigenous Peoples: A Flexible Approach to Addressing the Unique Needs of Varying Populations" (2010) 9 Chicago J Int'l L 297 at 312; Thornberry, *supra* note 11 at 351.

158 See ILO, *Report of the Committee Set up to Examine the Representation Alleging non-Observance by Peru of the Indigenous and Tribal Peoples' Convention, 1989 (no. 169), made under Article 24 of the ILO Constitution by the General Confederation of Workers of Peru (CGTP)*, 1998, ILO Doc (GB.270/16/4):(GB.273/14/4) at para 32 (b), where the committee makes the following recommendation to the Governing Body: "b) to remind the Government of the special importance for the cultures and spiritual values of the peoples concerned of their relationship with the lands or territories, or both as applicable, which they occupy or otherwise use, and *in particular the collective aspects of this relationship*, and that when communally owned indigenous lands are divided and assigned to individuals or third parties, this often weakens the exercise of their rights by the community or the indigenous peoples and in general they may end up losing all or most of the land, resulting in a general reduction of the resources that are available to indigenous peoples when they own their land communally" [emphasis added].

159 "The relation of an indigenous community with its land must be recognized and understood as the fundamental basis of its culture, spiritual life, integrity and economic survival. For such peoples their communal nexus with the ancestral territory is not merely a matter of possession and production, but rather consists in material and spiritual elements that must be fully integrated and enjoyed by the community, so that it may preserve its cultural legacy and pass it on to the future generation." *Case of the Moiwana Community (Suriname)* (2005), Inter-Am Ct HR (Ser C) no. 124 at para 131.

160 Convention no. 169, *supra* note 44, Article 13(1). See Cindy L Holder and Jeff J Corntassel, "Indigenous Peoples and Multicultural Citizenship: Bridging Collective and Individual Rights" (2002) 24 Hum Rts Q 126 at 148; Thornberry, *supra* note 11 at 351.

161 Convention no. 169, *supra* note 44, Article 14(1). See Doreen Lustig and Benedict Kingsbury, "Displacement and Relocation from Protected Areas: International Law Perspectives on Rights, Risks and Resistance" (2006) 4 Conservation and

use of the present, and not the past, tense limits the rights protected by the latter provision to the lands indigenous peoples occupy *in the present*,[162] since any proposals made during the preparatory works for the recognition of rights to lands "traditionally occupied" in the past were vehemently opposed[163] — a fact criticized by both indigenous peoples and international law commentators.[164] Certain safeguards were, however, included. For example, the convention requires that measures be taken "in appropriate cases to safeguard the right of the peoples concerned to use lands not exclusively occupied by them, but to which they have traditionally had access for their subsistence and traditional activities."[165] The same provision also urges that particular attention be paid to the situation of nomadic peoples and shifting cultivators,[166] a situation for which Convention no. 107 made no provision.[167]

Article 14(2) moves further towards real protection of land rights, for it requires that governments "take steps as necessary to identify the lands which the peoples concerned traditionally occupy"[168] — a

---

Society 404 at 409; Thornberry, *supra* note 11 at 352, noting that "[i]n the Convention perspective, land rights are not granted by the State, which must recognize them as a matter of international obligation arising from traditional occupation."

162 See Stephen Allen, "Looking beyond the Bancoult Cases: International Law and the Prospect of Resettling the Chagos Islands" (2007) 7 Hum Rts L Rev 441 at 476-77.

163 See Barsh, *supra* note 20 at 225.

164 See Venne, *supra* note 86 at 61; Joona, *supra* note 124 at 162.

165 Convention no. 169, *supra* note 44, Article 14(1). See Asbjørn Eide, "Legal and Normative Bases for Saami Claims to Land in the Nordic Countries" (2001) 8 Int'l J on Minority & Group Rights 127 at 143.

166 Convention no. 169, *supra* note 44, Article 14(1). See Peter Manus, "Sovereignty, Self-Determination, and Environment-Based Cultures: The Emerging Voice of Indigenous Peoples in International Law" (2005) 23 Wis Int'l LJ 553 at 595.

167 This issue was, however, addressed in Recommendation 104, *supra* note 16, albeit in the context of the integrationist approach of the late 1950s. See Jérémie Gilbert, "Nomadic Territories: A Human Rights Approach to Nomadic Peoples' Land Rights" (2007) 7 Hum Rts L Rev 681, noting that this reference to nomadic peoples is "a welcome development within international law" (at 695-96) and in this regard the convention "stands as the leading treaty on the issue" (at 697).

168 Convention no. 169, *supra* note 44, Article 14(2). See Alexandra Xanthaki, "Land Rights of Indigenous Peoples in South-East Asia" (2003) 4 Melbourne J Int'l L 467 at 477; Rodríguez-Piñero, *supra* note 117 at 324.

provision not found in the more recent UNDRIP[169] — and "to guarantee effective protection of their rights of ownership and possession."[170] In addition, governments must establish "adequate penalties for unauthorised intrusion upon, or use of, the lands of the peoples concerned, and to take measures to prevent such offences."[171] The framework of protection established by Article 14 is completed by a clause requiring states to ensure adequate mechanisms within national legal systems to resolve land claims by the peoples concerned,[172] a provision that entitles these peoples to claim recognition of land rights, compensation, and so on for lands of which they were unfairly deprived in the past.[173]

Another important provision for the protection of indigenous land rights is that requiring consultation "whenever consideration is being given to their capacity to alienate their lands or otherwise transmit their rights outside their own community."[174] In the same

169 UNDRIP, *supra* note 128. See Jérémie Gilbert, "Indigenous Rights in the Making: The United Nations Declaration on the Rights of Indigenous Peoples" (2007) 14 Int'l J on Minority & Group Rights 207 at 226, noting that "[t]he Declaration remains vague by affirming that 'states shall give legal recognition and protection to these lands, territories and resources' but does not provide for a clear obligation to demarcate indigenous lands."

170 Convention no. 169, *supra* note 44, Article 14(2). See Kelley C Yukich, "Aboriginal Rights in the Constitution and International Law" (1996) 30 UBCL Rev 235 at 253.

171 Convention no. 169, *supra* note 44, Article 18. See Emmanuel Spiry, "From 'Self-Determination' to a Right to 'Self-Development' for Indigenous Groups" (1995) 38 German YB Int'l L 129 at 149; Rodríguez-Piñero, *supra* note 117 at 324.

172 Convention no. 169, *supra* note 44, Article 14(3). See Timo Koivurova, "Jurisprudence of the European Court of Human Rights Regarding Indigenous Peoples: Retrospect and Prospects" (2011) 18 Int'l J on Minority & Group Rights 1 at 21.

173 See S James Anaya, "The Native Hawaiian People and International Human Rights Law: Toward a Remedy for Past and Continuing Wrongs" (1994) 28 Ga L Rev 309 at 348, observing that the use in Article 14(1) of the wording "traditionally occupy" in the present tense, and the deliberate rejection of the past tense, implies that there needs to be a link in the present time between the people concerned and their lands in order for the latter to be covered by this provision. In his view, it is possible for the mechanisms called for in Article 14(3) to be applied to traditionally occupied indigenous lands of which the traditional occupants were arbitrarily deprived in the past. See also Thornberry, *supra* note 11 at 358.

174 Convention no. 169, *supra* note 44, Article 17(2). See Karen Engle, *The Elusive Promise of Indigenous Development: Rights, Culture, Strategy* (Durham, NC: Duke University Press, 2010) at 178, noting sarcastically that one should read "if ever" instead of "whenever."

context, the convention further provides that "[p]ersons not belonging to these peoples shall be prevented from taking advantage of their customs or of lack of understanding of the laws on the part of their members to secure the ownership, possession or use of land belonging to them."[175]

The convention also focuses in Article 15 on the major issue of natural resources pertaining to indigenous lands, recognizing, in the spirit of Article 7, the right of indigenous peoples to participate in the use, management, and conservation of these resources.[176] More specifically, in cases where the state retains ownership of mineral or other sub-surface resources, or rights to other resources pertaining to lands, the convention provides that "governments shall establish or maintain procedures through which they shall consult these peoples, with a view to ascertaining whether and to what degree their interests would be prejudiced, before undertaking or permitting any programmes for the exploration or exploitation of such resources pertaining to their lands."[177] The same paragraph also provides that indigenous peoples "shall *wherever possible* participate in the benefits of such activities, and shall receive fair compensation for any damages which they may sustain as a result of such activities."[178] In other words, the convention "falls short of upholding rights to mineral or subsurface resources in cases in which the state generally retains ownership of these resources."[179]

175 Convention no. 169, *supra* note 44, Article 17(3). See Karen E Bravo, "Balancing Indigenous Rights to Land and the Demands of Economic Development: Lessons from the United States and Australia" (1997) 30 Col JL & Soc Probs 529 at 537-38.

176 Convention no. 169, *supra* note 44, Article 15(1). See Johanna Lindqvist, "Reindeer Herding: A Traditional Indigenous Livelihood" (2009) 6 Macq J Int'l & C Envtl L 83 at 100-1; Thornberry, *supra* note 11 at 356.

177 Convention no. 169, *supra* note 44, Article 15(2). See Gillian Triggs, "Australia's Indigenous Peoples and International Law: Validity of the Native Title Amendment Act 1998 (CTH)" (1999) 23 Melbourne UL Rev 372 at 389; Thornberry, *supra* note 11 at 356.

178 Convention no. 169, *supra* note 44, Article 15(2) [emphasis added]. See Michael L Ferch, "Indian Land Rights: An International Approach to Just Compensation" (1992) 2 Transnat'l L & Contemp Probs 301 at 323.

179 S James Anaya, "Indigenous Peoples' Participatory Rights in Relation to Decisions about Natural Resources Extraction: The More Fundamental Issue of What Rights Indigenous Peoples Have in Lands and Resources" (2005) 22 Ariz J Int'l & Comp L 7 at 10. See also Elsa Stamatopoulou, "Indigenous Peoples and the

This result has aroused the ire of indigenous peoples, some of whom have labelled the provision "truly shameful" because it does not recognize their right of ownership of the natural resources on their lands and makes their participation in the benefits of exploitation of these resources dependent on the discretion of the state.[180] Regarding the lack of recognition of indigenous ownership, one should bear in mind that "many states maintained that the government generally has ownership rights to natural resources and that there was no question of departing from this in respect of indigenous peoples."[181] Regarding benefit sharing, it should also be noted that this is not even mentioned in the UNDRIP.[182] In any case, it cannot be denied that "the Convention asserts that indigenous peoples are to have a say in any resource exploration or extraction on their lands and to benefit from those activities."[183]

The convention next deals with a question of major importance to indigenous peoples, that of their relocation. Article 16(1) provides that "the peoples concerned shall not be removed from the lands which they occupy."[184] This provision, however, is followed by a series of exceptions to, and departures from, the general rule, which are in turn subject to a series of provisos. Article 16(2) thus provides that, in cases where it is considered necessary, the relocation of indigenous peoples is essentially permitted as an exceptional measure, as long as it takes place with the free and informed consent of the people concerned.[185] If consent cannot be obtained, "such

---

United Nations: Human Rights as a Developing Dynamic" (1994) 16 Hum Rts Q 58 at 74; Huff, *supra* note 120 at 305, noting that "[w]hile Article 15 requires a framework of consultation and, if possible, participation and compensation, signatory States clearly retain ultimate authority over the disposition of resources within indigenous territories."

180 Venne, *supra* note 86 at 62.

181 Ulfstein, *supra* note 119 at 27; see also Swepston, *supra* note 47 at 704.

182 UNDRIP, *supra* note 128. See Enzamaria Tramontana, "The Contribution of the Inter-American Human Rights Bodies to Evolving International Law on Indigenous Rights over Lands and Natural Resources" (2010) 17 Int'l J on Minority & Group Rights 241 at 247.

183 S James Anaya, "International Human Rights and Indigenous Peoples: The Move toward the Multicultural State" (2004) 21 Ariz J Int'l & Comp L 13 at 39.

184 Convention no. 169, *supra* note 44, Article 16(1). See Natan Lerner, *Group Rights and Discrimination in International Law*, 2nd edition (The Hague: Martinus Nijhoff, 2003) at 120.

185 Convention no. 169, *supra* note 44, Article 16(2). See Lee Swepston and Manuela Tomei, "The International Labour Organization and Convention 169," in Lydia

relocation shall take place only following appropriate procedures established by national laws and regulations, including public inquiries *where appropriate*, which provide the opportunity for effective representation of the peoples concerned."[186]

The convention further provides that "*[w]henever possible*, these peoples shall have the right to return to their traditional lands, as soon as the grounds for relocation cease to exist."[187] It continues: "When such return is not possible, as determined by agreement or, in the absence of such agreement, through appropriate procedures, these peoples shall be provided in all possible cases with lands of quality and legal status at least equal to that of the lands previously occupied by them, suitable to provide for their present needs and future development."[188] Provision is also made for the possibility of compensation, in money or in kind, if those affected should prefer this option,[189] and for payment of full compensation for any loss or injury resulting from such relocation.[190]

These provisions have been severely criticized by some representatives of indigenous peoples and even sarcastically described as a "work of art."[191] It has been pointed out, for example, that the right

---

van de Fliert, ed, *Indigenous Peoples and International Organizations* (Nottingham, UK: Spokesman Books, 1994) 56 at 59. See also Swepston, *supra* note 47 at 705, 707, noting that the representatives of indigenous peoples during the negotiations asked that their consent constitute an absolute precondition for relocation away from their lands, a demand, however, that was rejected on the grounds that there were cases where relocation was imperative (eg, because of some natural disaster, epidemic, and so on) regardless of the will or consent of the people concerned.

186 Convention no. 169, *supra* note 44, Article 16(2) [emphasis added]. See Roberta Cohen and Francis M Deng, *Masses in Flight: The Global Crisis of Internal Displacement* (Washington, DC: Brookings Institution Press, 1998) at 91.

187 Convention no. 169, *supra* note 44, Article 16(3) [emphasis added]. See Joy K Asiema and Francis DP Situma, "Indigenous Peoples and the Environment: The Case of the Pastoral Maasai of Kenya" (1994) 5 Colo J Int'l Envtl L & Pol'y 149 at 152.

188 Convention no. 169, *supra* note 44, Article 16(4). See Leslie Sturgeon, "Constructive Sovereignty for Indigenous Peoples" (2005) 6 Chicago J Int'l L 455 at 457.

189 Convention no. 169, *supra* note 44, Article 16(4).

190 *Ibid*, Article 16(5). See David C Baluarte, "Balancing Indigenous Rights and a State's Right to Develop in Latin America: The Inter-American Rights Regime and ILO Convention 169" (2004) 4 Sustainable Development L & Pol'y 9 at 11.

191 Venne, *supra* note 86 at 63.

of relocation to lands of "equal quality" is meaningless since the relationship of indigenous peoples with land is with their *specific* ancestral lands (which have a unique significance for them) and not with the land in general.[192] It has also been observed that the right to compensation raises the pragmatic, and by no means rhetorical, question: "How much compensation can be paid to a people for the loss of their way of life?"[193] On the other hand, some commentators have noted as positive the fact that, unlike its predecessor, Convention no. 169 "establishes procedural barriers to relocation for *any reason*."[194] The fact that Article 16 refers (other than in the first paragraph) to *relocation* rather than *removal*— a choice of words that appears to imply that in all cases where indigenous peoples lose their lands they must be given new lands — has also been hailed as a significant development.[195]

Closing this section on the convention's provisions with respect to land rights, it is noteworthy that diametrically opposing opinions as to their content and potential have been expressed. On the one hand, for example, it has been argued that "it is pretty clear that the land rights provided for by Part II of the Convention amount, rather than to sovereign states, to a mere right of ownership that is generally recognized by most States in favor of any citizen (despite that in the case of indigenous peoples such right is of collective character), a right that may be expropriated when it is required by public needs, subject only to the granting of fair compensation in favor of the expropriated person(s)."[196] On the other hand, there are those who think that "[t]he text provides for a legal regime for these peoples which may be separate from that applied to others in each country within existing structures, while allowing for development in the future. Some very fundamental positive rights are created, but above all procedural rights are laid down."[197] Although a strictly grammatical reading of the convention seems to support the first of these views, the "evolutionary" interpretation given to the right to property enshrined in the American Convention on Human Rights

192 *Ibid.*

193 *Ibid.*

194 Barsh, *supra* note 20 at 227.

195 Swepston, *supra* note 47 at 706.

196 Federico Lenzerini, "Sovereignty Revisited: International Law and Parallel Sovereignty of Indigenous Peoples" (2006) 42 Tex Int'l LJ 155 at 179.

197 Swepston, *supra* note 47 at 697-98.

(ACHR),[198] on the basis, *inter alia,* of Convention no. 169's land rights provisions and, indeed, the broad interpretation generally given to the latter provisions by bodies of the inter-American system of human rights protection in the past ten years, seem to confirm the second.[199] Such interpretations, which appear to be both particularly positive for indigenous peoples and compatible with their ways of thinking, likely justify Barsh's views expressed over twenty years ago that international standards often begin weak but may grow stronger over time and that Convention no.169 would prove effective if used frequently and aggressively by indigenous peoples and interpreted progressively by advocates for indigenous rights.[200]

EDUCATIONAL AND LINGUISTIC RIGHTS

Another issue emphasized in the convention is that of education, which is usually one of the key factors in the preservation of a group's language and identity.[201] Article 26 thus requires that governments take steps "to ensure that members of the peoples concerned have the opportunity to acquire education at all levels *on at least an equal footing* with the rest of the national community."[202] This requirement is followed by the provisions of Article 27(1), which, in the spirit of Article 7, states that the "[e]ducation programmes and services for the peoples concerned shall be developed and implemented *in co-operation* with them to address their special

198 American Convention on Human Rights, 22 November 1969, OASTS no. 36 (entered into force 18 July 1978) [ACHR].

199 "Thus, the 'indigenisation' of the general right to property was based on more specific instruments on the rights of indigenous peoples. From this perspective, the Inter-American Court's progressive approach seems to indicate that the most positive development regarding the content of human rights discourse in relation to indigenous peoples comes from the ILO Convention 169 and the UN and OAS Declarations." Gilbert, *supra* note 169 at 211. See also Malgosia Fitzmaurice, "The New Developments Regarding the Saami People of the North" (2009) 16 Int'l J Minority & Group Rights 67 at 69-70. See further discussion of these developments below, text accompanying notes 253-71.

200 See Barsh, *supra* note 20 at 213, 234.

201 See Gudmundur Alfredsson and Erika Ferrer, *Minority Rights: A Guide to United Nations Procedures and Institutions* (London: Minority Rights Group International, Raoul Wallenberg Institute of Human Rights and Humanitarian Law, 1998) at 15.

202 Convention no. 169, *supra* note 44, Article 26 [emphasis added]. See Klaus Dieter Beiter, *The Protection of the Right to Education by International Law* (Leiden: Martinus Nijhoff, 2006) at 310; Thornberry, *supra* note 11 at 361-62.

needs, and shall incorporate their histories, their knowledge and technologies, their value systems and their further social, economic and cultural aspirations."[203] Indeed, in the framework of the devolution it promotes, the convention requires competent authorities to "ensure the training of members of these peoples and their involvement in the formulation and implementation of education programmes, *with a view to the progressive transfer of responsibility* for the conduct of these programmes to these peoples as appropriate."[204] It continues: "In addition, governments shall recognise the right of these peoples to establish their own educational institutions and facilities, provided that such institutions meet minimum standards established by the competent authority in consultation with these peoples. *Appropriate resources shall be provided for this purpose.*"[205] This last clause is of particular significance since the onus for providing resources for education seems to lie with the government.[206]

In regard to the major issue of mother tongue, the convention provides that children belonging to the peoples concerned "shall,

203 Convention no. 169, *supra* note 44, Article 27(1) [emphasis added]. See Jose Paulo Kastrup, "The Internationalization of Indigenous Rights from the Environmental and Human Rights Perspective" (1997) 32 Tex Int'l LJ 97 at 115; Thornberry, *supra* note 11 at 362, observing that "[t]he provision represents the most demanding requirement for an indigenous or minority-sensitive educational programme generated by an international treaty."

204 Convention no. 169, *supra* note 44, Article 27(2) [emphasis added]. See ILO, *ILO Convention on Indigenous and Tribal Peoples, 1989 (no.169): A Manual*, revised edition (Geneva: ILO, 2003) at 12, where it is noted that "the transfer of responsibility should take place only when indigenous and tribal peoples decide it is the right time for them to assume management and control of these issues. However once this is done, governments cannot simply walk away and avoid any further responsibility. They have to maintain an overview of the activities to make sure that they are running smoothly, and that they are properly financed." Thornberry notes that "there is no properly comparable provision in other international instruments." Thornberry, *supra* note 11 at 363.

205 Convention no. 169, *supra* note 44, Article 27(3) [emphasis added]. See Marian Van Den Vosch and Willem Van Genugten, "International Legal Protection of Migrant Workers, National Minorities and Indigenous Peoples — Comparing Underlying Concepts" (2002) 9 Int'l J on Minority & Group Rights 195 at 216.

206 Strelein, *supra* note 107 at 72. Thornberry argues that this provision "contrasts vividly with the bleak negation of any State financial responsibility for such institutions in the FCNM [Framework Convention for the Protection of National Minorities, 10 November 1994, ETS no. 157] and the more guarded freedom to seek public contributions in the OSCE Copenhagen Document." Thornberry, *supra* note 11 at 363. See also Barsh, *supra* note 20 at 230, observing that "in any event, states would bear fiscal responsibility for language education."

wherever practicable, be taught to read and write in their own indigenous language or in the language most commonly used by the group to which they belong."[207] Although the convention does not clarify the precise content of the word "practicable," it has been interpreted as meaning that even if the number of indigenous children asking for public education in their own language is relatively small, this factor should not constitute a complete barrier to the implementation of the provision.[208] On the other hand, it has also been argued that there are cases where application of the clause is objectively difficult to implement — for example, where a language exists only in oral form or where the number of users is so small that it would be inconvenient to spend large sums of money on the creation of teaching materials in that language, especially if the state has only limited funds available for education.[209] In cases where education in an indigenous language is not practicable, the convention requires, in the spirit of Article 6, that the authorities should undertake consultations with the people concerned with a view to adopting measures to achieve the objective stated.[210]

However, while the convention emphasizes the right of indigenous peoples to maintain their cultural distinctiveness, preserve their language, and not be assimilated against their will, it also recognizes the benefits of integration when this takes place in an atmosphere of respect for indigenous culture.[211] It thus provides that "[t]he imparting of general knowledge and skills that will help children belonging to the peoples concerned to participate fully and on an equal footing in their own community and in the national community shall be an aim of education for these peoples."[212] In this spirit, the convention is "highly supportive of a bilingual education

207 Convention no. 169, *supra* note 44, Article 28(1) [emphasis added]. See UNESCO, *Education in a Multilingual World: UNESCO Education Position Paper* (Paris: UNESCO, 2003) at 23; Thornberry, *supra* note 11 at 363.

208 See Fernand de Varennes, *Languages, Minorities and Human Rights* (The Hague: Martinus Nijhoff, 1996) at 266.

209 *Ibid.*

210 Convention no. 169, *supra* note 44, Article 28(1). See Lauri Hannikainen, "The Status of Minorities, Indigenous Peoples and Immigrant and Refugee Groups in Four Nordic Countries" (1996) 65 Nordic J Int'l L 1 at 20-21.

211 See Noam Schimmel, "Indigenous Education and Human Rights" (2007) 14 Int'l J on Minority and Group Rights 425 at 430.

212 Convention no. 169, *supra* note 44, Article 29. See Cynthia Price Cohen, "International Protection of the Rights of the Indigenous Child" (1995) 7 St Thomas L Rev 557 at 559.

that values both indigenous languages and the national language,"[213] and provides that "[a]dequate measures shall be taken to ensure that these peoples have the opportunity to attain fluency in the national language or in one of the official languages of the country."[214] Finally, Article 31 provides that

> educational measures shall be taken among all sections of the national community, and particularly among those that are in most direct contact with the peoples concerned, with the object of eliminating prejudices that they may harbour in respect of these peoples. To this end, efforts shall be made to ensure that history textbooks and other educational materials provide a fair, accurate and informative portrayal of the societies and cultures of these peoples.[215]

THE CRITICS OF THE CONVENTION

In addition to the criticisms canvassed earlier — regarding non-recognition of indigenous peoples as "peoples" proper,[216] refusal to recognize a right of prior consent in decisions concerning indigenous peoples, non-recognition of a right of ownership of the natural resources pertaining to indigenous lands, and, finally, conditional recognition of indigenous customs[217] — the convention has also been attacked on the basis of further shortcomings in its substantive provisions. Specifically, it has been seen as failing to provide protection for indigenous intellectual property rights,[218] and, indeed, it

213 Lynda Frost, "The Bilingual Education of Indigenous Children in Nicaragua under the 1987 Autonomy Statute: The Effective Limits of Legal Change" (1995) 3 Int'l J Child Rts 51 at 58.

214 Convention no. 169, *supra* note 44, Article 28(2). See WK Hastings, "International Law and Education in a Minority Language," in Ruth Wodak and David Corson, eds, *Language Policy and Political Issues in Education*, volume 1 (Dordrecht: Kluwer Academic, 1997) 67 at 72; Thornberry, *supra* note 11 at 364.

215 Convention no. 169, *supra* note 44, Article 31. See Patrick Thornberry and Dianne Gibbons, "Education and Minority Rights: A Short Survey of International Standards" (1997) 4 Int'l J on Minority & Group Rights 115 at 139.

216 See Mauro Barelli, "The Role of Soft Law in the International Legal System: The Case of the United Nations Declaration on the Rights of Indigenous Peoples" (2009) 58 ICLQ 957 at 958.

217 See Katie O' Bryan, "The Appropriation of Indigenous Ecological Knowledge: Recent Australian Developments" (2004) 1 Macq J Int'l and Comp Envtl L 29 at 35.

218 Lars-Anders Baer, "The Rights of Indigenous Peoples: A Brief Introduction in the Context of the Sámi" (2005) 12 Int'l J on Minority & Group Rights 245 at 252.

makes no clear reference to the protection of cultural property.[219] It has also been noted that many of its provisions are not framed in terms of rights of indigenous peoples as such but, rather, as obligations for state authorities.[220] Further cause for concern is the fact that the wording of several of its provisions is extremely broad and vague,[221] rendering the thrust of their application uncertain[222] and leading to the criticism that the convention leaves states with a very wide margin of discretion.[223] This state of affairs is perhaps extended by the provision — corresponding, it must be said, to real needs — that "[t]he nature and scope of the measures to be taken to give effect to this Convention shall be determined in a flexible manner, having regard to the conditions characteristic of each country."[224]

Such observations have led several indigenous organizations to see the convention as "inadequate to meet indigenous aspirations."[225] Indeed, some of these organizations adopted a negative position in the deliberations taking place in the UN Working Group

219 See Lakshman Guruswamy, Jason C Roberts, and Catina Drywater, "Protecting the Cultural and Natural Heritage: Finding Common Ground" (1999) 34 Tulsa LJ 713 at 730, noting however that "although the Convention does not expressly address cultural property protection, it has been interpreted as a safeguard for the heritage of indigenous peoples."

220 Traci L McClellan, "The Role of International Law in Protecting the Traditional Knowledge and Plant Life of Indigenous Peoples" (2001) 19 Wis Int'l LJ 249 at 261.

221 In the words of one critic, "Convention no. 169 contains few clear norms and virtually no sanctions." Martin A Geer, "Foreigners in Their Own Land: Cultural Land and Transnational Corporations: Emergent International Rights and Wrongs" (1998) 38 Va J Int'l L 331 at 367.

222 "Many of the provisions in the Convention are qualified by terms such as 'as appropriate,' 'as necessary,' 'whenever practicable' or 'to the extent possible.' These terms provide flexibility to the Convention, although critics say that they may have the effect of limiting or obscuring the obligations of ratifying Governments." Tanja Joona, "The Political Recognition and Ratification of ILO Convention no. 169 in Finland, with Some Comparison to Sweden and Norway" (2005) 23 Nordic J Human Rights 305 at 311.

223 See Dean B Suagee, "Human Rights of Indigenous Peoples: Will the United States Rise to the Occasion?" (1997) 21 Am Indian L Rev 365 at 368.

224 Convention no. 169, *supra* note 44, Article 34. See Hans Petter Graver and Geir Ulfstein, "The Sami People's Right to Land in Norway" (2004) 11 Int'l J on Minority & Group Rights 337 at 347; Thornberry, *supra* note 11 at 365-66. Regarding the issue of the Convention's "flexibility," see Peris Jones and Malcolm Langford, "Between Demos and Ethos: The Nepal Constitution and Indigenous Rights" (2011) 18 Int'l J on Minority & Group Rights 369 at 375.

225 Garth Nettheim, "'The Consent of the Natives': Mabo and Indigenous Political Rights" (1993) 15 Sydney L Rev 223 at 233.

on the Rights of Indigenous Populations when they were asked about the possibility of incorporating a reference to the convention in the draft UNDRIP then being considered, fearing that doing so could lead to constraints on the recognition of their rights.[226] For their part, some scholars have argued that, while the convention is an improvement, it still does not pay sufficient attention to the rights and aspirations of indigenous peoples[227] and is, in fact, little more than a baseline for discussions concerning those rights.[228] Finally, skepticism over the effectiveness of the convention has been exacerbated by its small number of ratifications (only twenty-two at the time of writing).[229] The most critical issue, however, seems to be the objective fact that "indigenous peoples do not have direct access to submitting reports to the ILO supervisory bodies."[230]

226 See Russel Lawrence Barsh, "Indigenous Peoples and the UN Commission on Human Rights: A Case of the Immovable Object and the Irresistible Force" (1996) 18 Hum Rts Q 782 at 789-90. See also Rodríguez-Piñero, *supra* note 117 at 319, commenting that Convention no. 169 was virtually ignored by indigenous representatives involved in the drafting of UNDRIP.

227 See Michael Kirby, "Protecting Cultural Rights: Some Developments," in Margaret Wilson and Paul Hunt, eds, *Culture, Rights and Cultural Rights: Perspectives from the South Pacific* (Wellington: Huia, 2000) 145 at 149.

228 Darrell Addisson Posey, "Can Cultural Rights Protect Traditional Cultural Knowledge and Biodiversity?" in Halina Nieć, ed, *Cultural Rights and Wrongs* (Paris: UNESCO, Institute of Article and Law, 1998) 42 at 47.

229 See Mauro Barelli, "The Interplay between Global and Regional Human Rights Systems in the Construction of the Indigenous Rights Regime" (2010) 32 Hum Rts Q 951 at 955, n 16, observing that "the poor ratification record had inevitably undermined the global impact of ILO no. 169," since the majority of indigenous peoples find themselves unable to rely on its legal framework. Compare UN Commission on Human Rights, "Human Rights and Indigenous Issues: Report of the Special Rapporteur on the situation of human rights and fundamental freedoms of indigenous people, Mr. Rodolfo Stavenhagen, submitted pursuant to Commission Resolution 2001/57," 4 February 2002, UN Doc E/CN.4/2002/97 at para 16, where the special rapporteur argues that "while Convention 169 has received only a limited number of ratifications up to now, it is rapidly becoming a vibrant instrument for use by both States and indigenous organizations." Convention no. 169 has been ratified (as of 15 February 2012) by Argentina, Bolivia, Brazil, the Central African Republic, Chile, Colombia, Costa Rica, Denmark, Dominica, Ecuador, Fiji, Guatemala, Honduras, Mexico, Nepal, the Netherlands, Nicaragua, Norway, Paraguay, Peru, Spain, and Venezuela. See "Ratifications of C169 — Indigenous and Tribal Peoples Convention, 1989 (no. 169)," online: <http://www.ilo.org/dyn/no.rmlex/en/f?p=NO.RMLEXPUB:11300:0::NO.:11300:P11300_INSTRUMENT_ID:312314:NO.>.

230 See International Labour Office, *Indigenous and Tribal Peoples' Rights in Practice: A Guide to ILO Convention no. 169* (Geneva: ILO, 2009) at 179.

The ILO's Supervisory System and Indigenous Peoples: Weaknesses and Dynamics

The ILO has been praised for having a very well-developed system for supervising the implementation of its conventions and recommendations.[231] However, it has been observed that the ILO "has yet to establish a forum within the Organization for indigenous representatives to be involved in the development of international policies regarding indigenous rights."[232] Bartolomé Clavero's comment pinpoints the fundamental weakness of the convention, which goes beyond the somewhat inevitable compromises found in every international text on human/minority/indigenous rights, for it fails to provide for any direct, official, indigenous monitoring of its implementation, a flaw attributable to the general structure of the ILO.[233]

Concretely, the ILO's supervisory system for monitoring the application of its conventions is based on Articles 22-24 of its Constitution.[234] Under the terms of Article 22, members are required to submit regular reports (every five years unless requested sooner) on the measures they have taken to give effect to the provisions of conventions to which they are a party,[235] while Article 23(2) requires them to communicate copies of these reports to the most representative employers' and workers' organizations in their countries for their comments.[236] These reports are scrutinized by the independent twenty-member Committee of Experts on the Application of Conventions and Recommendations, which after review makes two types of comments: (1) "observations," which are comments on fundamental questions in cases of a serious and persistent

231 Hurst Hannum, "Human Rights" in Joyner, *supra* note 54, 131 at 149.

232 Bartolomé Clavero, "The Indigenous Rights of Participation and International Development Policies" (2005) 22 Ariz J Int'l and Comp L 41 at 46.

233 See Athanasios Yupsanis, "ILO Convention no. 169 Concerning Indigenous and Tribal Peoples in Independent Countries 1989-2009: An Overview" (2010) 79 Nordic J Int'l L 433 at 448.

234 ILO Constitution, *supra* note 3.

235 *Ibid*, Article 22. See Lee Swepston, "The International Labour Organization and Human Rights: Access to the ILO," in Gudmundur Alfredsson et al, eds, *International Human Rights Monitoring Mechanisms: Essays in Honour of Jacob Th. Möller*, 2nd edition (Leiden: Martinus Nijhoff, 2009) 291 at 294.

236 ILO Constitution, *supra* note 3, Article 23(2). See Erika de Wet, "Governance through Promotion and Persuasion: The 1998 ILO Declaration on Fundamental Principles and Rights at Work," in Armin von Bogdandy et al, eds, *The Exercise of Public Authority by International Institutions — Advancing International Institutional Law* (Heidelberg: Springer, 2010) 377 at 396.

failure of a state to comply with the obligations of a convention, and (2) "direct requests," which are requests to the governments concerned for further information or concerning technical matters.[237] The former are published in the committee of experts' report to the International Labour Conference, whereas the latter are not. Next, the Conference Committee on the Application of Standards, a body comprising government, labour, and employers' representatives, examines the committee of experts' report, discusses thoroughly any problems or issues of special interest, and makes its own annotated report to the conference.[238]

In addition to this process, which forms the core of the ILO supervisory system, the ILO Constitution also provides for other mechanisms for giving effect to its conventions. First of all, any state member has the right to file a complaint with the International Labour Office if in its view some other member is not effectively meeting its obligations.[239] Article 26(4) extends this same right to the Governing Body and to all workers' and employers' delegations to the conference.[240] In all cases, the Governing Body may appoint a three-member Commission of Inquiry, whose recommendations can be referred to the International Court of Justice by the government concerned. Otherwise, they become legally binding.[241] Second, any industrial association of employers or workers can make "representations" to the ILO that a state has failed to implement its commitments.[242] The Governing Body can then appoint an ad hoc

237 See Eric Gravel and Chloé Charbonneau-Jobin, *The Committee of Experts on the Application of Conventions and Recommendations: Its Dynamic and Impact* (Geneva: ILO, 2003) at 13.

238 Francis Wolf, "Human Rights and the International Labour Organization," in Theodor Meron, ed, *Human Rights in International Law: Legal and Policy Issues*, volume 2 (Oxford: Clarendon Press, 1984) 273 at 284.

239 ILO Constitution, *supra* note 3, Article 26(1). See Robert Howse and Brian A Langille with Julien Burda, "The World Trade Organization and Labour Rights: Man Bites Dog," in Virginia O'Leary and Daniel Warner, eds, *Social Issues, Globalisation and International Institutions: Labour Rights and the EU, ILO, OECD and WTO* (Leiden: Martinus Nijhoff, 2006) 157 at 194.

240 ILO Constitution, *supra* note 3, Article 26(4). See Virginia O'Leary, *International Labour Conventions and National Law* (Dordrecht: Martinus Nijhoff, 1982) at 18.

241 ILO Constitution, *supra* note 3, Article 28. See Henrik Karl Nielsen, "The Supervisory Machinery of the International Labour Organization" (1995) 64 Nordic J Int'l L 129 at 138-39.

242 ILO Constitution, *supra* note 3, Article 24. See Lorenzo Nesti, "The Mapuche-Pehuenche and the Ralco Dam on the Biobio River: The Challenge of Protecting Indigenous Land Rights" (2002) 9 Int'l J on Minority & Group Rights 1 at 26.

tripartite committee charged with reporting its findings and recommendations to the Governing Body. If the Governing Body finds the clarifications made by the state in question to be unsatisfactory, it may publish that statement together with the comments of the tripartite committee.[243]

It is clear from this brief outline of the different mechanisms for monitoring implementation of ILO conventions within the ILO framework that there are no means by which indigenous peoples can make complaints or representations directly.[244] It has, however, been pointed out that there are some ways in which indigenous peoples can ensure that their concerns are to an extent taken into account. These include: (1) participating in ILO meetings and other activities as representatives of governments or workers'/employers' organizations, or as representatives of a non-governmental organization (NGO) on the ILO Special List of Non-Governmental International Organizations (as the Four Directions Council, Indigenous World Association, and Saami Council have done);[245] (2) sending information directly to the ILO with respect to a new national policy, law, or court decision, since the texts of laws and court decisions are considered to be verifiable, objective information;[246] or (3) sending information to the ILO via friendly workers' or employers' organizations.[247] While these avenues should by no means be disparaged, it is open to question just how far they can go towards meeting the demands and aspirations of indigenous peoples.

243 ILO Constitution, *supra* note 3, Article 25. See Harriet Ketley, "Exclusion by Definition: Access to International Tribunals for the Enforcement of the Collective Rights of Indigenous Peoples" (2001) 8 Int'l J on Minority & Group Rights 331 at 343.

244 R Pitty, "Indigenous Peoples, Self-Determination and International Law" (2001) 5 Intl J Human Rights 44 at 58.

245 See *ILO Convention on Indigenous and Tribal Peoples, 1989 (no. 169): A Manual*, *supra* note 204 at 78; Joona, *supra* note 99 at 225.

246 See International Labour Office, *Eliminating Discrimination against Indigenous and Tribal Peoples in Employment and Occupation: A Guide to ILO Convention no. 111* (Geneva: ILO, 2007) at 26.

247 See Chandra Roy and Mike Kaye, *The International Labour Organization: A Handbook for Minorities and Indigenous Peoples* (London: Minority Rights Group International, Anti-Slavery International, 2002) at 8, 25, noting that it is vital for indigenous peoples to develop and foster good relations with workers' and employers' organizations, since they play a key role in monitoring the implementation of ILO Conventions.

The Influence of Convention no. 169

As James Anaya explains, "[t]o be sure, the text of Convention No. 169 includes several qualifiers that can be seen as leaving substantial state discretion intact, and it undoubtedly falls short of indigenous peoples' full aspirations."[248] He continues: "But whatever its shortcomings, the Convention succeeds in affirming the value of indigenous communities and cultures and in setting forth a series of basic precepts in that regard."[249] Anaya's assessment is one of the most concise and most accurate appreciations of the convention. Specifically, Convention no. 169, despite its small number of ratifications and the initial ambivalence of several indigenous peoples towards it, has played a major role in the development of international recognition of indigenous rights,[250] serving as an important point of reference in the formulation of rights contained in the UNDRIP and in the proposed Organization of American States' American Declaration on the Rights of Indigenous Peoples.[251] It has also significantly influenced the practice of UN human rights treaty monitoring bodies, which, on the one hand, constantly urge states to use the convention as a guideline even if they are not parties to it and, on the other, encourage them to ratify it.[252]

Moreover, Convention no. 169 has had a decisive impact in Latin America with respect to the practice of both the bodies of the inter-American human rights system and the region's national judiciaries. More specifically, since the *Case of the Mayagna (Sumo) Awas Tingni*

248 S James Anaya, "Divergent Discourses about International Law, Indigenous Peoples, and Rights over Lands and Natural Resources: Toward a Realist Trend" (2005) 16 Colo J Int'l Envtl L & Pol'y 237 at 246.

249 S James Anaya, "Indigenous Rights Norms in Contemporary International Law" (1991) 8 Ariz J Int'l & Comp L 1 at 8.

250 Jennifer E Brady, "The Huaorani Tribe of Ecuador: A Study in Self-Determination for Indigenous Peoples" (1997) 10 Harv Hum Rts J 291 at 309.

251 See UNDRIP, *supra* note 128; OAS Working Group to Prepare the Draft American Declaration on the Rights of Indigenous Peoples, *Record of the Current Status of the Draft American Declaration on the Rights of Indigenous Peoples*, 2 May 2012, Doc OEA/Ser.K/XVI/GT/DADIN/doc.334/08 rev.7 (2012). See also Andrew Erueti, "The Demarcation of Indigenous Peoples' Traditional Lands: Comparing Domestic Principles of Demarcation with Emerging Principles of International Law" (2006) 23 Ariz J Int'l & Comp L 543 at 588.

252 See S James Anaya, Moira Gracey, and Leonardo Alvarado, *The Rights of the Pygmy People in the Republic of Congo: International Legal Context* (London: Rainforest Foundation, 2005) at 19, n 84.

Community (Nicaragua),[253] both the Inter-American Commission on Human Rights and the Inter-American Court of Human Rights have used the convention as an interpretive tool in specifying the obligations of states under the ACHR and the American Declaration of the Rights and Obligations of Man, specifically regarding indigenous peoples' right to (communal) property.[254]

For example, in the *Case of the Yakye Axa Indigenous Community (Paraguay)*,

> [t]he Commission alleged that the State has not ensured the ancestral property rights of the Yakye Axa Indigenous Community and its members, because said Community's land claim has been processed since 1993 but no satisfactory solution has been attained. According to the Commission in its application, this has made it impossible for the Community and its members to own and possess their territory, and has kept it in a vulnerable situation in terms of food, medical and public health care, constantly threatening the survival of the members of the Community and of the latter as such.[255]

In this context, Paraguay was said to have violated Article 4 (right to life), Article 8 (right to a fair trial), Article 21 (right to property), and Article 25 (right to judicial protection), in connection with Article 1(1) (obligation to respect rights), of the ACHR.[256] The Inter-American Court of Human Rights, in its analysis, referred, *inter alia*, to Article 14(3) of Convention no. 169 regarding the requirement that "adequate measures shall be established within the national

253 *Case of the Mayagna (Sumo) Awas Tingni Community (Nicaragua)* (2001), Inter-Am Ct HR (Ser C) no. 79; also reported as Inter-American Court of Human Rights, "The Case of the Mayagna (Sumo) Awas Tingni Community v. Nicaragua, Judgement of August 31, 2001" (2002) 19 Ariz J Int'l & Comp L 395.

254 ACHR, *supra* note 198, Article 21; American Declaration of the Rights and Duties of Man, OAS Res XXX, adopted by the Ninth International Conference of American States (1948), reprinted in *Basic Documents Pertaining to Human Rights in the Inter-American System*, Doc OEA/Ser.L/V/II.82/doc.6 rev.1 at 17 (1992), Article 23 [American Declaration]. See Mario Mello, "Recent Advances in the Justiciability of Indigenous Rights in the Inter-American System of Human Rights" (2006) 4 Sur-Int'l J Human Rights 31 at 35.

255 *Case of the Yakye Axa Indigenous Community (Paraguay)* (2005), Inter-Am Ct HR (Ser C) no. 125 at para 2 [*Yakye Axa* case].

256 ACHR, *supra* note 198, Articles 1(1), 4, 8, 21, 25. See Mónica Feria Tinta, *The Landmark Rulings of the Inter-American Court of Human Rights on the Rights of the Child: Protecting the Most Vulnerable at the Edge* (Leiden: Martinus Nijhoff, 2008) at 284-85.

legal system to resolve land claims by the peoples concerned."[257] The court stressed that "[t]his international provision, in combination with Articles 8 and 25 of the American Convention, places the State under the obligation to provide an effective means with due process guarantees to the members of the indigenous communities for them to claim traditional lands, as a guarantee of their right to communal property."[258] Further, in its consideration of the scope of Article 21 of the ACHR, the court deemed it "useful and appropriate to resort to other international treaties, aside from the American Convention, such as ILO Convention no. 169, to interpret its provisions in accordance with the evolution of the inter-American system, taking into account related developments in International Human Rights Law."[259] Moreover, the court pointed out that "ILO Convention No. 169 contains numerous provisions pertaining to the right of indigenous communities to communal property, which is addressed in this case, and said provisions can shed light on the content and scope of Article 21 of the American Convention."[260] The court emphasized the fact that

> [t]he culture of the members of the indigenous communities directly relates to a specific way of being, seeing, and acting in the world, developed on the basis of their close relationship with their traditional territories and the resources therein, not only because they are their main means of subsistence, but also because they are part of their worldview, their religiosity, and therefore, of their cultural identity.[261]

This circumstance, said the court, "relates to the provision set forth in Article 13 of ILO Convention No. 169, that the States must respect 'the special importance for the cultures and spiritual values of the peoples concerned of their relationship with the lands or territories,

257 Convention no. 169, *supra* note 44, Article 14(3).

258 *Yakye Axa* case, *supra* note 255 at paras 95-96.

259 *Ibid* at para 127.

260 *Ibid* at para 130. See also Manuel Eduardo Góngora-Mera, *Inter-American Judicial Constitutionalism: On the Constitutional Rank of Human Rights Treaties in Latin America Through National and Inter-American Adjudication* (San José, Costa Rica: Inter-American Institute of Human Rights, 2011) at 224.

261 *Yakye Axa* case, *supra* note 255 at para 135. See also Jo M Pasqualucci, "International Indigenous Land Rights: A Critique of the Jurisprudence of the Inter-American Court of Human Rights in the Light of the United Nations Declaration on the Rights of Indigenous Peoples" (2009) 27 Wis Int'l LJ 51 at 80.

or both as applicable, which they occupy or otherwise use, and in particular the collective aspects of this relationship.'"[262]

Next, regarding the issue of return of indigenous peoples to the territories from which they had been displaced, the court took note of Article 16(4) of Convention no. 169, observing that the

> [s]election and delivery of alternative lands, payment of fair compensation, or both, are not subject to purely discretionary criteria of the State, but rather, pursuant to a comprehensive interpretation of ILO Convention No. 169 and of the American Convention, there must be a consensus with the peoples involved, in accordance with their own mechanism of consultation, values, customs and customary law.[263]

In the end, the court found that Paraguay had violated Article 21 of the ACHR and unanimously ordered the state to identify the traditional territory of the members of the Yakye Axa Indigenous Community, to grant it to them free of cost, and to take such domestic legislative, administrative, and other steps as may be necessary, within a reasonable term, to guarantee the effective exercise of their right to property.[264]

Similarly, in the *Case of the Sawhoyamaxa Indigenous Community (Paraguay)*, the Inter-American Court of Human Rights had to decide whether Paraguay had violated Articles 4 (right to life), 5 (right to humane treatment), 8 (right to a fair trial), 21 (right to property), and 25 (right to judicial protection), in relation to Articles 1(1) and (2) of the ACHR,[265] to the detriment of the Sawhoyamaxa Indigenous Community of the Enxet-Lengua people and its members.[266] The community alleged that Paraguay had not ensured its ancestral

262 *Yakye Axa* case, *supra* note 255 at para 136.

263 *Ibid* at paras 150-51. See also Inter-American Commission of Human Rights, *Indigenous and Tribal Peoples' Rights over Their Ancestral Lands and Natural Resources: Norms and Jurisprudence of the Inter-American Human Rights System*, 30 December 2009, Doc OEA/Ser.L/V/II/doc.56 (2009) at para 147.

264 See Lilly G Ching-Soto, "Reparations in the Inter-American System of Human Rights: An Analysis of the Jurisprudence on Collective Cases of Indigenous Peoples and the Economic, Social and Cultural Aspects of Their Reparations" (2010) 10 Revista do Instituto Brasileiro des Direitos Humanos 219 at 223-24.

265 ACHR, *supra* note 198, Articles 1(1), 2, 4, 5, 8, 21, 25.

266 *Case of the Sawhoyamaxa Indigenous Community (Paraguay)* (2006), Inter-Am Ct HR (Series C) no. 146 [*Sawhoyamaxa* case]. See Anikó Raisz, "Indigenous Communities before the Inter-American Court of Human Rights: New Century, New Era?" (2008) 5 Miskolc J Int'l L 35 at 46.

property right and that of its members, inasmuch as their claim to territorial rights had been pending since 1991 and had not been satisfactorily resolved. As stated in the commission's application, this lack of action had barred the community and its members from title to, and possession of, their lands, resulting in a state of nutritional, medical, and health vulnerability for the community that constantly threatened its survival and integrity.[267]

In this case, the court also referred to ILO Convention no. 169 in order to reaffirm the special relationship between indigenous peoples and their lands.[268] Specifically,

> [i]n analyzing the content and scope of Article 21 of the Convention in relation to the communal property of the members of indigenous communities, the Court has taken into account Convention No. 169 of the ILO in the light of the general interpretation rules established under Article 29 of the Convention, in order to construe the provisions of the aforementioned Article 21 in accordance with the evolution of the Inter-American system considering the development that has taken place regarding these matters in international human rights law.[269]

Thus, in referring, as in the *Yakye Axa* case, to Article 13 of Convention no. 169, the court stressed that

> indigenous communities might have a collective understanding of the concepts of property and possession, in the sense that ownership of the land "is not centered on an individual but rather on the group and its community" [footnote omitted]. This notion of ownership and possession of land does not necessarily conform to the classic concept of property, but deserves equal protection under Article 21 of the American Convention.[270]

The court ultimately concluded that Paraguay had violated Article 21 of the ACHR, in conjunction with Article 1(1), and ordered it to adopt all legislative, administrative, and other measures necessary

267 *Sawhoyamaxa* case, *supra* note 266 at para 2.

268 See Ana María Suárez Franco, "Effectively Realizing ESCR: The Sawhoyamaxa Decision of the Inter-American Court of Human Rights" (2007) 2 Right to Food Quarterly 2 at 2.

269 *Sawhoyamaxa* case, *supra* note 266 at para 117.

270 *Ibid* at paras 119-120. See also Olivier De Schutter, "The Green Rush: The Global Race for Farmland and the Rights of Land Users" (2011) 52 Harv Int'l LJ (2011) 503 at 536, n 129.

to formally and physically convey to the members of the Sawhoyamaxa Community their traditional lands.

It is thus clear from these leading cases that the Inter-American Court of Human Rights has embraced a broad conception of the right to property enshrined in Article 21 of the ACHR, reading it in the light of ILO Convention no. 169 in order to highlight the special link that indigenous peoples have with their traditional lands.[271] On the domestic level, too, the convention's provisions — particularly those concerning indigenous land rights, rights over natural resources, and participatory rights — have, to a greater or lesser degree, inspired progressive judgments and corresponding constitutional reviews and amendments, particularly in Latin American states.[272] A recent, characteristic example is the *Alejandro Papic Dominguez Con Comunidad Indigena Aymara Chusmiza v Usmagama* case (known as the *Aymara water rights* case).[273] The case involved a long-standing conflict in the Taparaca region in northern Chile between two Aymara communities and Agua Mineral Chusmiza, a private water bottling company seeking the right to bottle and sell freshwater from a source historically used by the Aymara for traditional irrigation practices.[274]

In its consideration of the merits of the case, the Supreme Court of Chile relied in part on the provisions of Convention no. 169, which Chile had ratified in September 2008, giving it constitutional status — that is, the highest hierarchical value in the Chilean legal system.[275]

271 See Christian Courtis, "The Right to Food as a Justiciable Right: Challenges and Strategies" (2007) 11 Max Planck YB UN L 317 at 333.

272 Rainer Grote, "The Status and Rights of Indigenous Peoples in Latin America" (1999) 59 Heidelberg J Int'l L 497 at 526-27; Rodríguez-Piñero, *supra* note 117, noting that "indigenous policies in Latin America gave way to a new paradigm of 'multicultural constitutionalism'" (at 326) and that "Convention 169 is, in many respects, a Latin America indigenous code" (at 338). For a detailed analysis, see ILO International Standards Department, *Application of Convention no. 169 by Domestic and International Courts in Latin America: A Casebook* (Geneva: ILO, 2009). See also Courtis, *supra* note 108 at 64-67, 70-75.

273 *Alejandro Papic Dominguez Con Comunidad Indigena Aymara Chusmiza v Usmagama*, no. 2840-2008, 25 November 2008 (Supreme Court of Chile).

274 See Michelle Platt Bassi, *Ethical Issues of Water Resource Management in a Changing Climate: Equity and Legal Pluralism in Chile* (MA Thesis, Department of International Studies and the Graduate School of the University of Oregon, 2010) at 77-80 [unpublished].

275 George S McGraw, "Defining and Defending the Right to Water and Its Minimum Core: Legal Construction and the Role of National Jurisprudence" (2011) 8 Loyola University Chicago Int'l L Rev 127 at 182, n 347.

The court found that the Aymara communities had customary rights to the Chusmiza spring, despite the fact that it was located on land that belonged to Agua Mineral, reasoning that "the recognition of these rights ... in favour of the Aymara and Atacamena communities, does not only involve the waters found in the land that is registered as property of these communities but also the waters that feed the indigenous communities despite being found in lands that belong to third parties."[276] Thus, the court, in a landmark ruling, granted a water flow of nine litres per second to the Aymara communities based on the "duty of society in general and of the State in particular, to protect, respect, and promote the development of the indigenous peoples, their cultures, families and communities."[277]

The convention has also been invoked to challenge the constitutionality of laws that, contrary to constitutional guarantees, have been adopted without prior consultation with the indigenous peoples they may affect. Such was the case, for example, in an application that asked the Constitutional Court of Colombia to determine the constitutionality of the Colombian General Forestry Act.[278] The act contained provisions regulating forestry matters that had been adopted without prior consultations with indigenous representatives but which, even if not directly applicable to indigenous territories, could affect the areas where these communities were generally located and therefore have an impact on their lifestyle and close relationship with the forest.

In its decision, the Constitutional Court of Colombia stressed that, with regard to indigenous and tribal communities, the right to consultation is one of the forms of democratic participation provided for in the Colombian Constitution.[279] This right was supported by ILO Convention no. 169, which had been legislatively integrated into the national legal order in 1991. The court, citing its own case law, noted that Convention no. 169 is part of the "Constitutionality Block."[280] It thus focused emphatically on Article 6 of the convention regarding the need to consult indigenous peoples though

276 See Sarah A Altschuller, Amy Lehr, and Suzanne A Spears, "Corporate Social Responsibility" (2010) 44 Int'l Lawyer 213 at 228.

277 *Ibid.*

278 General Forestry Act, Act 1021 of 2006 (Colombia).

279 *Decision C-030/08*, 23 January 2008, Case File D-6837 (Constitutional Court of Colombia).

280 The "Constitutional Block" doctrine holds that human rights conventions ratified by the Colombian State are part of the Constitution and should be used to

appropriate procedures whenever consideration is given to legislative measures that may directly affect them:[281]

> In order to have complied with the consultation requirement, it would have been necessary to inform the indigenous communities about the bill, illustrate its scope and how it could affect them, and give them opportunities to effectively state their opinions about the bill. [The State] did not comply with this process. For this reason the Court concluded, that given that the bill is about a matter that profoundly affects the worldview of these communities and their relationship with the earth, there is no alternative than to declare this law unconstitutional.[282]

Thus, it was made clear in the court's reasoning that the role of the convention in sustaining indigenous participatory rights was crucial since "the Court endorsed the suggestion that the consult was compelled, at least in part, by the obligations of ILO Convention 169."[283]

The same path has also been followed by the Constitutional Court of Guatemala, which, in a December 2009 decision regarding similar issues, strongly reaffirmed that the consultation and all other rights under Convention no. 169 have domestic constitutional status — in other words, they are considered part of the set of human rights protected by Articles 1-149 (also known as the dogmatic part) of the Political Constitution of Guatemala.[284] As such, all of the mining and hydroelectric licences granted by the Guatemalan Ministry of Energy and Mining without consulting the relevant indigenous peoples were illegal and in violation of the Constitution.[285]

---

determine the constitutionality of lower-ranking acts or laws. According to this doctrine, Convention no. 169 has, in Colombia, a constitutional status and is obligatory for legislators, administrative officers, and judges. See Ana María Suárez Franco, "Unconstitutionality Declaration of the Forestry Law in Colombia" (2008) 3 Right to Food Quarterly 10 at 10.

281 See Eugenia Ponce de León, "Colombia's New Forest Law Rejected" (2008) 36 Arborvitae 5 at 5.

282 See Republic of Colombia, Constitutional Court, Presidency, "Press Release no. 1 (Press Release translated by ELAW and AIDA from the original Spanish version issued by the Colombian Constitutional Court)" (23 January 2008), online: <http://www.elaw.org/system/files/Constitutional+Court+consultation+Forestry+Act.pdf>.

283 Colin Crawford, "Environmental Benefits and the Notion of Positive Environmental Justice" (2011) 32 U Pennsylvania J Intl L 911 at 927.

284 *Case 3878-207*, 21 December 2009 (Constitutional Court of Guatemala).

285 See Indigenous Peoples Issues and Resources, "Guatemalan Constitutional Court States that ILO Convention 169 has Constitutional Status," online:

Furthermore, the convention has even served as a useful, legally binding guide in criminal cases where the social, cultural, religious, or spiritual values and practices of indigenous peoples have been at stake. In one such case, for example, a Mayan priest was accused by agents of the national police of trading objects of archaeological value, transporting them from one community to another. The judge dismissed the case on the basis that the accused was a Mayan priest and, in this context, transported the objects for use in Mayan rituals and ceremonies. The court relied heavily on relevant provisions of Convention no. 169 (Articles 5, 8, and 9) in giving reasons in support of its decision.[286]

In the more general public policy context, the convention has acted as a benchmark for indigenous peoples of states that have ratified it, giving them grounds to demand reforms (for example, Bolivia, and Colombia),[287] to establish claims to ancestral lands (for example, Honduras),[288] to conclude agreements for the protection of their identity and cultural rights (for example, Mexico),[289] to entrench the obligation on the state to consult with them before taking decisions concerning them (for example, Norway),[290] and so on. The position that the convention "constitutes a valuable contribution to the legal protection of indigenous peoples living in the countries that have duly ratified it" is thus solidly documented.[291]

<http://indigenouspeoplesissues.com/index.php?option=com_content andview=Articleandid=3990:guatemalan-constitutional-court-states-that-ilo-convention-169-has-constitutional-statusandcatid=30andItemid=63>.

286 See Christian Courtis, "Notes on the Implementation by Latin American Courts of the ILO Convention no. 169 on Indigenous Peoples" (2011) 18 Int'l J on Minority & Group Rights 433 at 457-58.

287 See Michael J Miller, "Biodiversity Policy Making in Costa Rica: Pursuing Indigenous and Peasant Rights" (2006) 15 J Environment & Development 359 at 375-76.

288 See Keri Vacanti Brondo and Laura Woods, "Garifuna Land Rights and Ecotourism as Economic Development in Honduras' Cayos Cochinos Marine Protected Area" (2007) 3 Ecological & Environmental Anthropology 2 at 8.

289 See Ana Filipa Vrdoljak, "Self-Determination and Cultural Rights," in Francioni and Scheinin, *supra* note 74, 41 at 73, n 195.

290 See Láilá Susanne Vars, "Political Aspects of the Sami's Right to Self-Determination" (2008) 2 Gáldu Čála / J Indigenous Peoples' Rights 62 at 69.

291 Erica-Irene A Daes, "An Overview of the History of Indigenous Peoples: Self-Determination and the United Nations" (2008) 21 Cambridge Rev Int'l Affairs 7 at 11.

The convention also serves as a benchmark for the basic land, participatory, and other rights of indigenous peoples, both in terms of litigation and policy setting, even for states that are not parties to it.[292] An illustrative example is that of the decision of Belize's Supreme Court in *Cal v Attorney General*. In this case, the Maya claimants of two villages sought redress for alleged violations of sections 3, 3(a), 3(d), 4, 16, and 17 of the Belize Constitution. These violations, they claimed, arose "from the failure of the Government of Belize to recognize, protect and respect their customary land rights, which … are based on the traditional land use and occupation of the Maya people."[293] As Willem van Genugten notes, among the interesting aspects of the decision in the case was the court's reference to Convention no. 169 notwithstanding the fact that Belize is not party to the convention.[294] The court emphasized that "although Belize has yet to ratify Convention No 169 … it is not in doubt that Article 14 of this instrument contains provisions concerning indigenous peoples' right to land that resonate with the general principles of international law regarding indigenous peoples."[295] It was in part on this basis that the Supreme Court rendered its landmark decision recognizing the collective and individual rights of the Maya claimants to their land and resources, which they had used and occupied in conformity with their customary practices, as "property" within the meaning of the Belize Constitution and requiring the government to determine, demarcate, and provide official documentation to those lands as well as to abstain from issuing any concessions, permits, or contracts authorizing logging, prospecting, or exploration, mining, or similar activities unless such acts were pursuant to the Maya's informed consent and in conformity with Belize's constitutional guarantees.[296]

[292] S James Anaya, "Keynote Address: Indigenous Peoples and Their Mark on the International Legal System" (2007) 31 Am Indian L Rev 257 at 261.

[293] *Cal v Attorney General*, Claim no. 171 of 2007, Supreme Court of Belize (18 October 2007) (2007) 46 ILM 1022 at para 2.

[294] See Willem van Genugten, "Protection of Indigenous Peoples on the African Continent: Concepts, Position Seeking, and the Interaction of Legal Systems" (2010) 104 AJIL 29 at 52.

[295] *Cal v Attorney General*, *supra* note 293 at para 130. See also Maia S Campbell and S James Anaya, "The Case of the Maya Villages of Belize: Reversing the Trend of Government Neglect to Secure Indigenous Land Rights" (2008) 8 Hum Rts L Rev 377 at 398.

[296] *Cal v Attorney General*, *supra* note 293 at para 136. See also Cathal Doyle, "Indigenous Peoples and the Millennium Development Goals — 'Sacrificial Lambs' or Equal Beneficiaries?" (2009) 13 Int'l JHR 44 at 52-53.

Another recent, indicative example is the judgment of the High Court of Kenya — a country that is also not party to Convention no. 169 — in *Lemeiguran v Attorney General*.[297] In this case, the applicants, members of a community of 30,000 persons known as Il Chamus (that is, people who see far), claimed that since the creation of the Baringo Central Constituency in 1963 no person from their community had been elected as a member of the Parliament. Further, bearing in mind the nature of the constituency boundaries and the voting patterns in the constituency, it was not statistically likely that a candidate from their community would be elected in the following decades.[298] In these circumstances, they claimed, the members of their community had been denied their fundamental right of representation in the National Assembly under sections 1 and 1A of the Kenyan Constitution, and they further argued that their community constituted a "special interest" under section 33 of the Constitution or an indigenous minority qualifying for representation through a nominated member of parliament. They also argued that such representation was more than necessary to prevent their exclusion from receiving proper benefits and to protect them from needless and exploitative development and/or irreversible destruction of their values, traditions, and social patterns in the event that oil or other mineral wealth were to be found within their areas.[299] For these reasons, the applicants sought a declaration from the court entitling them to a specially nominated seat in the National Assembly.[300]

In its decision of 18 December 2006, the court referred explicitly to Articles 3 and 7 of Convention no. 169 regarding the right of indigenous peoples to enjoy the full measure of human rights without discrimination and their right to participate in the formulation, implementation, and evaluation of plans and programs for development that may affect them.[301] In part on this basis, the court held that

297 *Lemeiguran v Attorney General*, [2008] 3 Kenya LR 325 [*Lemeiguran*].

298 See Kenya National Commission on Human Rights, *Submission to the Committee on the Elimination of Racial Discrimination in Response to the Periodic Report of Kenya* (June 2011) at 13, online: <http://www2.ohchr.org/english/bodies/cerd/docs/ngos/KNCHR_Kenya_CERD79.pdf>.

299 See *Lemeiguran*, *supra* note 297 at 325-26, 344.

300 UN Human Rights Committee, *Consideration of Reports Submitted by States Parties under Article 40 of the Covenant: Third Periodic Report of States Parties: Kenya*, UN Doc CCPR/C/KEN/3 (13 January 2011) at para 203.

301 *Lemeiguran*, *supra* note 297 at 365-66.

minorities such as the Il Chamus have the right to influence the formulation and implementation of public policy, and to be represented by people belonging to the same social, cultural and economic context as themselves ... For a political system to be truly democratic, it has to allow minorities a voice of their own, to articulate their distinct concerns and seek redress and thereby lay a sure base for deliberative democracy.[302]

The court further ruled that the Il Chamus community constituted a special interest for the purposes of nomination as contemplated by section 33 of the Kenyan Constitution and that the Electoral Commission must take into account the need to ensure adequate representation of minorities, especially the Il Chamus of the Baringo Central Constituency.[303] Thus, the High Court of Kenya was inspired in part by Convention no. 169 and endorsed its participatory standards even though Kenya is not a party to the convention.[304]

The convention has also influenced policy making in states that are not parties to it. Germany, for example, which has not ratified the convention, has declared itself bound by its principles in its development policy regarding co-operation with the indigenous and tribal peoples of Latin America and the Caribbean.[305] Finally, it may more generally be argued that the convention has officially sealed the rejection of assimilation policies, establishing a basic agenda of legally binding minimum standards for the further elaboration of indigenous issues and rights.[306]

302 *Ibid* at 367. See also International Labour Organization and African Commission on Human and Peoples' Rights, *Kenya: Constitutional, Legislative and Administrative Provisions Concerning Indigenous Peoples* (Geneva: International Labour Office, 2009) at 26.

303 *Lemeiguran, supra* note 297 at 386-87.

304 Gaetano Pentassuglia, "Towards a Jurisprudential Articulation of Indigenous Land Rights" (2011) 22 EJIL 165 at 190.

305 "The cross-sectoral Strategy on Cooperation with Indigenous Peoples in Latin America and the Caribbean is a binding guideline adopted by the Federal Ministry for Economic Cooperation and Development (BMZ) for the formulation of development co-operation (DC) in Latin America and the Caribbean by official bilateral implementing agencies ... Its principles are derived directly from the provisions of ILO Convention (no. 169) Concerning Indigenous and Tribal Peoples in Independent Countries." Federal Ministry for Economic Cooperation and Development (Germany), Development Education and Information Division, "Development Cooperation with Indigenous Peoples in Latin America and the Caribbean (Strategies 141)" (2006) at 4, online: <http://www.bmz.de/en/publications/type_of_publication/strategies/konzept141.pdf>.

306 See Lisa Valenta, "Disconnect: The 1998 Brazilian Constitution, Customary International Law, and Indigenous Land Rights in Northern Brazil" (2003) 38

Conclusion: The ILO, Pioneer in the Protection of Indigenous Peoples

"It has never been realized by the public, as has been the case with the UN or UNESCO, that the International Labour Organization (ILO) has, since 1919, assigned an important place to human rights in its fields of competence ... This is especially true in connection with the protection of indigenous peoples."[307] Hans-Joachim Heintze was perfectly correct in this observation, for, indeed, the ILO's invaluable contribution to establishing norms for the protection and promotion of indigenous rights is not particularly well known to either the general public or to sections of the international legal academy. This article has attempted to demonstrate some elements of the ILO's extremely important contributions in this respect. Beyond elaborating norms, however, the ILO has also succeeded in gaining the confidence of many indigenous peoples through its development of, and support for, national and regional projects promoting indigenous interests and raising indigenous peoples' awareness of their rights.[308] In light of what is currently feasible and despite past and — to a lesser degree — present reservations on the part of some indigenous groups and academics, the ILO has become a central pillar of the international community's as yet partial response to indigenous demands by establishing a solid floor of basic, minimum prerequisites for the protection of the dignity of these most disadvantaged peoples.

Sommaire

Depuis sa création, l'Organisation internationale du travail (OIT) a été un pionnier sur les questions touchant les peuples autochtones,

---

Tex Int'l LJ 643 at 659. See also Chidi Oguamanam, "Indigenous Peoples and International Law: The Making of a Regime" (2004) 30 Queen's LJ 348 at 364; Rodríguez-Piñero, *supra* note 117 at 328, noting that "Convention 169 is now widely regarded as an important foundation of indigenous peoples' rights in international law, and most indigenous organizations now actively promote the ratification of the convention."

307 Heintze, *supra* note 9 at 310. As Thornberry also notes, "[t]he ILO can claim much of the credit for bringing rights of indigenous peoples - as such, and not as derivatives of other rights or applications of them — into the forefront of contemporary discussion." Thornberry, *supra* note 11 at 320.

308 See Alexandra Xanthaki, "Indigenous Rights in International Law over the Last Ten Years and Future Developments" (2009) 10 Melbourne J Int'l L 27 at 29.

quoiqu'originalement à partir d'une perspective culturellement biaisée et intégrationniste. Ses contributions ont progressé de la préparation d'études sur les conditions de travail des peuples autochtones dans les années 1920, à l'élaboration de recommandations et de conventions sur les droits des travailleurs autochtones dans les années 1940 et 1950, et plus récemment à l'adoption d'instruments juridiquement contraignants qui reconnaissent un plus large éventail de droits des peuples autochtones, telles que celles relatives au territoire et aux ressources, questions au sommet de l'ordre du jour des peuples autochtones. Cet article passe en revue et évalue ces développements avec un accent particulier sur les Conventions no. 107 (1957) et 169 (1989) de l'OIT. L'auteur conclut que, mettant de côté son orientation originalement assimilationniste, l'OIT a apporté une contribution inestimable à la satisfaction partielle des revendications autochtones, et a réussi à établir un minimum de standards essentiels à la sauvegarde de la dignité et des droits de ces peuples des plus défavorisés.

Summary

From its very inception, the International Labour Organization (ILO) has been a pioneer in addressing indigenous peoples' issues, albeit initially from a culturally biased, integrationist perspective. Its contributions have progressed from the preparation of studies on the working conditions of indigenous peoples in the 1920s, to the elaboration of recommendations and conventions on indigenous labour rights in the early 1940s and 1950s, and most recently to the adoption of legally binding instruments recognizing a broader range of indigenous rights, such as those pertaining to land and resources, which are at the top of indigenous peoples' agendas. This article reviews and assesses these developments with a particular focus on ILO Convention nos. 107 (1957) and 169 (1989). The author concludes that, setting aside its initially assimilationist orientation, the ILO has made invaluable contributions in partial satisfaction of indigenous demands and has succeeded in establishing a solid floor of basic, minimum prerequisites for the safeguarding of the dignity and rights of these most disadvantaged, both historically and presently, peoples.

Private Rights, the Use of Maps, State Responsibility, and Other Issues in the International Court of Justice's Boundary Jurisprudence: 2000-10

ALBERTO ALVAREZ-JIMENEZ

Introduction

One of Margaret Atwood's characters points out that "[a] boundary was a boundary only if you could defend it."[1] The idea of the fragility of frontiers implied in this statement is located at the opposite pole of how international law deals with international boundaries. Power is, and always will be, a component in the creation and development of international law. For example, traces of power are still present, to a certain extent, in the principle of *uti possidetis juris*, according to which newly created states preserve the boundaries set under colonial law and in the relevance of the notion of *effectivités* in the absence of legal title over territory. However, the role of power in frontier issues is no longer determinant — once there is a boundary under international law, its existence does not depend on the power to defend it, as one of the most prominent decisions of the International Court of Justice (ICJ) in the first decade of the twenty-first century reveals.

Boundary disputes constitute one of the most delicate issues for states, given their security, economic, human, and social dimensions. It is, then, not surprising to see that frontier issues are among the

Alberto Alvarez-Jimenez, LL.D., School of International Development and Global Studies, University of Ottawa. This article forms part of a series of articles dealing with the International Court of Justice's boundary jurisprudence from 2000 to 2010, including Alberto Alvarez-Jimenez, "Boundary Treaties in the International Court of Justice's Jurisprudence: 2000-2010" (2012) 23 EJIL 495; and Alberto Alvarez-Jimenez, "The International Court of Justice's Use of the Vienna Convention in the Interpretation of Boundary Agreements: 2000-2010" (2012) 3 J Int'l Dispute Settlement 409.

1 Margaret Atwood, *Moral Disorder and Other Stories* (Toronto: McClelland and Stewart, 2006) at 131.

most recurrent before the ICJ and have given rise to a very rich jurisprudence. This jurisprudence comprises traditional areas: consent in boundary treaties, the already mentioned principle of *uti possidetis juris*, the notion of *effectivités*, acquiescence in boundary controversies, and maritime delimitation. However, this jurisprudence also includes other topics that usually receive less attention from international law scholars, but which are nonetheless important to states and sometimes underlie their significant interest in boundary disputes. This article deals with such topics in order to show how the ICJ has handled them in its boundary jurisprudence of the first decade of the new millennium.[2]

The article is divided into seven parts. The first part discusses the ICJ's decisions that identify the kind of territory that cannot be appropriated and those related to *terra nullius*. The second part reviews the cases in which the Court has recognized and protected private rights, which is a very unusual situation. The third part assesses the Court's pronouncements related to state succession and unilateral donations as sources of title to territory. The fourth part considers criteria that the ICJ has rejected as irrelevant in establishing title to territory — paramount among them being the notion of historical consolidation. The fifth part examines the different ways in which the Court has made use of maps. The sixth part evaluates the Court's pronouncements regarding state responsibility in connection with boundary disputes, and, finally, the seventh part presents some conclusions.[3]

[2] Although some scholars seem to make a distinction between boundary and territorial disputes (eg, Malcolm N Shaw, "The Heritage of States: The Principle of *Uti Possidetis Juris* Today" (1996) 67:1 Brit YB Int'l L 77 at 79), this article uses the term "boundary disputes" as comprising territorial disputes. As the chamber of the International Court of Justice (ICJ) stated in *Frontier Dispute (Burkina Faso v Republic of Mali)*, [1986] ICJ Rep 554 at 563 [*Burkina Faso/Mali*], "the effect of any judicial decision rendered either in a dispute as to attribution of territory or in a delimitation dispute is necessarily to establish a frontier."

[3] This article includes a judgment of a chamber of the Court as part of the case law. Although it seems that this ruling cannot be formally equated with those rendered by the full Court, the judgment is relevant for this article's purposes. The reasons are twofold. First, as Judge Oda once stated, "the chamber is a component of the Court, bound by its Statute and Rules" (see *Land, Island and Maritime Frontier Dispute (El Salvador v Honduras), Constitution of Chamber*, Order of 8 May 1987, [1987] ICJ Rep 10 at 13). And, second, the Court draws no distinction between its judgments and those of chambers when providing justifications for its legal reasoning.

Territory That Cannot Be Appropriated and Territory That Has Not Been Appropriated (*Terra Nullius*)

What Cannot Be Regarded as Territory Susceptible to Appropriation

Virtually all kinds of territory can be appropriated by any of the modes of acquisition: by way of treaty, state succession, occupation, the principle of *uti possidetis juris* (according to which the boundaries that colonial powers imprinted on their colonies are preserved after independence),[4] and *effectivités* (understood as public actions carried out with sovereign intent by a state on a certain territory, sometimes in the absence of any formal title).[5] However, the ICJ has recognized two exceptions to this rule over the first decade of the twenty-first century: low-tide elevations in the sea and islands located in areas of highly changeable geographical conditions.

In *Maritime Delimitation and Territorial Questions between Qatar and Bahrain*,[6] the ICJ dealt with the issue of whether low-tide elevations

4 The Chamber of the Court in *Frontier Dispute (Benin v Niger)* noted the principle of *uti possidetis juris* as defined in *Burkina Faso/Mali, supra* note 2 at 566: "[I]ts essence lies 'in its primary aim of securing respect for the territorial boundaries at the moment when independence is achieved,' including former administrative delimitations established during the colonial period that became international frontiers." See *Frontier Dispute (Benin v Niger)*, [2005] ICJ Rep 90 at 108 [*Benin/Niger*].

5 In *Territorial and Maritime Dispute between Nicaragua and Honduras in the Caribbean Sea (Nicaragua v Honduras)*, the ICJ affirmed the long-standing definition of the elements of *effectivités* articulated by the Permanent Court of International Justice: "A sovereign title may be inferred from the effective exercise of powers appertaining to the authority of the State over a given territory. To sustain a claim of sovereignty on that basis, a number of conditions must be proven conclusively. As described by the Permanent Court of International Justice, 'a claim to sovereignty based not upon some particular act or title such as a treaty of accession but merely upon continued display of authority, involves two elements each of which must be shown to exist: the intention and will to act as sovereign, and some actual exercise or display of such authority.'" *Legal Status of Eastern Greenland*, Judgment, 1933, PCIJ, Series A/B, No. 53, pp. 45-46). See *Territorial and Maritime Dispute between Nicaragua and Honduras in the Caribbean Sea (Nicaragua v Honduras)*, [2007] ICJ Rep 659 at 712 [*Nicaragua/Honduras*].

6 See *Maritime Delimitation and Territorial Questions between Qatar and Bahrain* (*Qatar v Bahrain*), [2001] ICJ Rep 40 [*Qatar/Bahrain*]. For assessments of this judgment, see Glen Plant, "International Decisions" (2002) 96:1 AJIL 198; Malcolm D Evans, "Decisions of International Tribunals: The International Court of Justice" (2002) 51:03 ICLQ 709; Yoshifumi Tanaka, "Reflections on Maritime Delimitation in the *Qatar/Bahrain* Case" (2003) 52:1 ICLQ 53; Emmanuel Decaux, "Affaire de

could be appropriated,[7] a topic neither regulated by treaty nor customary international law.[8] These elevations are defined by Article 13(1) of the United Nations Convention on the Law of the Sea (UNCLOS) as "a naturally formed area of land which is surrounded by and above water at low tide but submerged at high tide."[9] One of the issues in dispute in this case was whether an elevation of this kind, Fasht ad Dibal, could be regarded as territory and susceptible to appropriation. Bahrain argued that this was possible and claimed sovereignty over it by virtue of some acts of authority that Bahrain had carried out there,[10] whereas Qatar held the opposite view.[11] The Court sided with the latter and expressed the view that low-tide elevations could not be assimilated to islands for the purpose of acquisition of sovereignty absent specific international law norms.[12] Among other reasons, this holding was so because, while islands have a territorial sea under the conventions on the law of the sea, low-tide elevations generally do not.[13] Consequently, low-tide elevations cannot be appropriated as territory and are considered part of the seabed.[14] However, the Court also clarified that the fact that low-tide elevations could not be appropriated under the principles

la *Délimitation maritime et des questions territoriales entre Qatar at Bahreïn*, Fond (arrêt du 16 mars 2001 Qatar c Bahreïn)" (2001) 47 AFDI 177.

7 For an analysis of the ICJ's pronouncements regarding this topic, see Tanaka, *supra* note 6 at 71.

8 See *Qatar/Bahrain*, *supra* note 6 at 101-2.

9 United Nations Convention on the Law of the Sea, 10 December 1982, 1833 UNTS 3, Article 13(1).

10 See *Qatar/Bahrain*, *supra* note 6 at 100.

11 See *ibid*.

12 See *ibid* at 102. This holding was ratified by the ICJ in *Nicaragua/Honduras*, *supra* note 5 at 92.

13 See *Qatar/Bahrain*, *supra* note 6 at 102. The impact of this conclusion on this dispute was that Fasht ad Dibal, which was located within the territorial seas of either Qatar or Bahrain, was not taken into account by the ICJ when it drew the equidistance line to construct the single maritime boundary between the two states. See *ibid* at 102-3. See further in this regard Plant, *supra* note 6 at 202. The Court ultimately concluded that Qatar had sovereignty over Fasht ad Dibal as it fell on its side of the single maritime boundary thus drawn. See *Qatar/Bahrain*, *supra* note 6 at 117. For an analysis of the Court's decision on this point, see Decaux, *supra* note 6 at 230-33.

14 For instance, the 1978 Torres Strait Treaty between Australia and Papua New Guinea in Regard to Low-Tide Elevations as Part of the Seabed, 18 December 1978, 18 ILM 291 (1979). See Tanaka, *supra* note 6 at 73.

governing the acquisition of territory did not mean that states could not have sovereignty over low-tide elevations. In fact, a state could do so when such elevations were within its territorial sea.[15]

The ICJ in *Territorial and Maritime Dispute between Nicaragua and Honduras in the Caribbean Sea* tacitly recognized other kinds of territory that cannot be appropriated, in particular, islands located in areas of highly changeable geographical conditions.[16] In this dispute, both parties claimed sovereignty over an island in the mouth of the River Coco. However, the Court refused to pronounce on the issue for the following reason: "For the last century the unstable nature of the river mouth has meant that larger islands are liable to join their nearer bank and the future of smaller islands is uncertain. Because of the changing conditions of the area, the ICJ makes no finding as to sovereign title over islands in the mouth of the River Coco."[17]

TERRA NULLIUS

The ICJ's discussions or assessments of *terra nullius* — that is, the land of no one — were concentrated on tiny, uninhabited islands during the first decade of the new millennium. The notion is important because the categorization of a territory as *terra nullius* may well determine the mode of acquisition of sovereignty over the given territory. If it is *terra nullius*, it can be acquired by the state that shows most *effectivités*. If it is not, sovereignty may be determined

15 See *Qatar/Bahrain, supra* note 6 at 101. The ICJ thus followed its previous case law, specifically *The Minquiers and Ecrehos Case (France v United Kingdom)*, [1953] ICJ Rep 47, and the *Land, Island and Maritime Frontier Dispute (El Salvador v Honduras: Nicaragua intervening)*, [1992] ICJ Rep 351, in which it had recognized that certain kinds of territory could not be appropriated. See Tanaka, *supra* note 6 at 73. Finally, it is worth mentioning that the ICJ affirmed these findings in its judgment in *Sovereignty over Pedra Branca/Pulau Batu Puteh, Middle Rocks and South Ledge (Malaysia v Singapore)*, [2008] ICJ Rep 12 at 100-1 [*Malaysia/Singapore*], regarding another low-tide elevation named South Ledge.

16 The core of the controversy was the determination of a single maritime boundary between the parties in the Caribbean Sea as well as sovereignty over some islands in the disputed area, namely Bobel Cay, South Cay, Savanna Cay, Port Royal Cay, and other rocks, banks, and reefs. See *Nicaragua/Honduras, supra* note 5 at 685. The ICJ could not determine sovereignty over the islands on the basis of *uti possidetis juris*, but it ruled in favour of Honduras on the sovereignty issue on the basis of its *effectivités* (at 721). For an assessment of this judgment, see Coalter G Lathrop, "International Decisions" (2008) 102:1 AJIL 113; Elizabeth A Kirk, "Decisions of International Courts and Tribunals" (2008) 57:3 ICLQ 701.

17 *Nicaragua/Honduras, supra* note 5 at 704.

on the bases of either state succession from a prior titleholder, *uti possidetis juris*, or even *effectivités.*

The ICJ has not, however, easily declared the existence of *terra nullius* and has used conceptual tools to avoid such a conclusion, even if title has not explicitly been found to exist at a certain point in time. For instance, the Court in *Nicaragua/Honduras* dealt with sovereignty over the islands of Bobel Cay, South Cay, Savanna Cay, and Port Royal Cay, as well as other rocks, banks, and reefs, which one of the parties claimed had been attached to it during colonial times. The Court faced the fact that Spain, the relevant colonial power, had never made any mention of the islands in any document, nor had it exercised any authority there. The Court nevertheless affirmed previous arbitral jurisprudence, according to which a territory can be regarded as having belonged to a colonial power even if it neither specifically identified the territory as its own nor exercised any authority there.[18] Acting on this premise, the Court confirmed that the islands were not *terra nullius* and proceeded to determine which of the parties had sovereignty over them after independence on the basis, first, of *uti possidetis juris* and, second, of *effectivités.*[19]

On another occasion, the ICJ simply inferred the non-existence of *terra nullius* based on the facts of the case. In *Sovereignty over Pedra Branca/Pulau Batu Puteh, Middle Rocks and South Ledge (Malaysia/Singapore)*,[20] the Court stated that the Island of Pedra Branca could

18 See *Affaire des frontières colombo-vénézuéliennes (Colombie c Vénézuéla)*, (1922) I RIAA 223 at 228, as quoted by the Court in *Nicaragua/Honduras, supra* note 5 at 701. It is important to mention that the significance of this finding is not diminished by the fact that both parties to this dispute had agreed that the islands were not *terra nullius* at the time of independence (at 687). It is not for parties, but for the Court, to make the final determination in this regard.

19 See *Nicaragua/Honduras, supra* note 5 at 708.

20 See *Malaysia/Singapore, supra* note 15 at 100-1. The parties agreed to submit to the ICJ their dispute related to sovereignty over Pedra Branca/Pulau Batu Puteh, Middle Rocks, and South Ledge. The Court found that title to Pedra Branca belonged to Malaysia but that it had been transferred to Singapore due to the latter's *effectivités* and the former's acquiescence, as evidenced by Malaysia's actions, unilateral statements recognizing Singapore as the titleholder, and, of paramount importance, Malaysia's omissions and lack of any act of sovereignty over the island for decades (at 95-96). The Court also ruled that Middle Rocks belonged to Malaysia (at 99) and that South Ledge belonged to the state in whose territorial waters it was located (at 101). For evaluations of this decision, see Coalter G Lathrop, "International Decisions" (2008) 102:4 AJIL 828; Cleméntine Bories, "L'arret de la Cour internationale de Justice du 23 mai 2008 dans l'affaire *Souveraineté sur Pedra Branca/Pulau Batu Puteh, Middle Rocks et South Ledge (*Malaisie/Singapour)" (2008) 54 AFDI 227.

not be regarded as *terra incognita*, given its important location, and, therefore, it had to be assumed that the island belonged to the Sultanate that had control over the area in which the island was located, even if no explicit title had been proven to exist.[21] Title was thereafter determined on the basis of succession from this original titleholder.

The only recognition of *terra nullius* by the ICJ during the period 2000-10 took place in *Sovereignty over Pulau Ligitan and Pulau Sipadan (Indonesia/Malaysia)*, regarding the islands at issue in that case.[22] There was no document proving that the islands belonged to the pre-colonial ruler in the area, the Sultan of Sulu.[23] The islands were not mentioned in the 1878 Protocol between Spain and Sulu Confirming the Bases of Peace and Capitulation by virtue of which the Sultan ceded all of his possessions to Spain.[24] Nor was there any mention of Pulau Ligitan/Sipadan in the 1885 Protocol between Spain, Germany, and Great Britain that dealt with their possessions in the area.[25] The ICJ also held that there was no evidence of Spain's interest in these territories nor was there proof of any occupation by this state.[26] Consequently, Pulau Ligitan/Sipadan were not disposed of by Spain in its 1900 Treaty with the United States, in which the former relinquished to the latter all title and claim of title to

21 See *Malaysia/Singapore*, *supra* note 15 at 35.

22 *Sovereignty over Pulau Ligitan and Pulau Sipadan (Indonesia v Malaysia)*, [2002] ICJ Rep 625 at 634 [*Indonesia/Malaysia*]. Ligitan is a very small island, with just a few trees and not permanently inhabited. Sipadan is also small but is densely wooded, and it has been a tourist resort since the 1980s (at 4). Indonesia claimed that it had sovereignty over the two islands by virtue of a 1981 convention between the Netherlands and Great Britain, on the basis of *effectivités* carried out by both the Netherlands and Indonesia and as successor of the Sultan of Bulungan, who previously had authority over the islands. Malaysia, for its part, argued that its sovereignty existed by virtue of its being the last link in a chain of transfers of title (which included Spain, the United States, and the United Kingdom) from the original sovereign, the Sultan of Sulu. The ICJ, however, held that the treaty the parties were relying on did not establish sovereignty over the islands and that title did not pass to any of the parties as successors (at 678). The Court then relied on *effectivités* and concluded that the islands belonged to Malaysia (at 686). For an analysis of this judgment, see Delphine Perri, "Titre conventionnel et effectivités: L'affaire de la *Souveraineté sur Pulau Ligitan at Pulau Sipadan (Indonésie c Malaisie)*" (2002) 48 AFDI 322.

23 See *Indonesia/Malaysia*, *supra* note 22 at 674-75.

24 *Ibid* at 675.

25 *Ibid.*

26 *Ibid.*

any island in the Philippine archipelago.[27] A 1930 convention between the United States and the United Kingdom did not mention the islands either.[28] The Court also found that an 1891 convention between the Netherlands and the Sultan of Bulungan did not constitute title over Pulau Ligitan/Sipadan.[29] On these bases, the ICJ concluded that any decision pertaining to sovereignty over the islands had to be made on the basis of *effectivités* as "an independent and separate issue,"[30] and it determined that the islands belonged to Malaysia.[31] Implicit in the use of *effectivités* was the *terra nullius* character of the islands.

There is no contradiction between the method used for the assessment of *terra nullius* by the ICJ in *Nicaragua/Honduras*, in which the islands were not regarded as such — even if the colonial power, Spain, had never explicitly identified them as part of its kingdom — and that deployed by the Court in *Indonesia/Malaysia*, in which the islands in question were regarded as *terra nullius* precisely because successive treaties between local rulers and colonial powers failed to identify them as falling under the authority of any of them. The facts of each case justify the different approaches. In *Nicaragua/Honduras*, there was only a single, undisputed colonial power in the area for centuries, until Nicaragua and Honduras achieved independence. It was therefore legally plausible for the Court to assume that, in the absence of any other in a position to raise a similar claim, the islands belonged to this power. On the contrary, in *Indonesia/Malaysia*, the Court faced the situation of islands located in an area under the influence of many colonial powers — old and new — over time, each power defining the confines of its dominion there on several occasions. The fact that not one of these powers ever claimed that the islands belonged to it illustrated that the islands were *terra nullius*.

The Recognition and Protection of Private Rights

International boundary agreements only create rights and obligations for states. This is certainly the general rule, but, in exceptional situations, these agreements may also create rights for individuals,

[27] *Ibid* at 676.

[28] *Ibid* at 677.

[29] *Ibid* at 669, 678.

[30] *Ibid* at 678.

[31] *Ibid* at 686.

as the judgment of the ICJ in *Dispute Regarding Navigational and Related Rights (Costa Rica v Nicaragua)* evidences.[32] In this dispute, the Court determined that Costa Rica had navigational rights for commercial purposes on the San Juan River, on the basis of Article VI of the 1858 Treaty of Limits.[33] Such a provision excluded, by implication, navigational rights for non-commercial purposes. However, the further question the Court had to address was whether the inhabitants of the Costa Rican bank of the San Juan River had navigational rights for the purpose of their everyday life.[34] The question was relevant because the boundary between the countries was the said bank — that is, Nicaragua had sovereignty over the entirety of the river.[35] The Court concluded that the treaty did contemplate non-commercial navigational rights for this Costa Rican community:

> The Court is of the opinion that it cannot have been the intention of the authors of the 1858 Treaty to deprive the inhabitants of the Costa Rican bank of the river, where the bank constitutes the boundary between the two States, of the right to use the river to the extent necessary to meet their essential requirements, even for activities of a non-commercial nature, given the geography of the area. While choosing, in Article II of the Treaty, to fix the boundary on the river bank, the parties must be presumed, in view of the historical background to the conclusion of this Treaty and of the Treaty's object and purpose as defined by the Preamble and Article I, to have intended to preserve for the Costa Ricans living on that bank a minimal right of navigation for the purpose of continuing to live a normal life in the villages along the river. The Court considers that while such a right cannot be derived from the express language of Article VI, it can be inferred from the provisions of the Treaty as a whole and, in particular, the manner in which the boundary is fixed.[36]

[32] See *Dispute Regarding Navigational and Related Rights (Costa Rica v Nicaragua)*, [2009] ICJ Rep 213 at 265 [*Costa Rica/Nicaragua*]. For commentary on this judgment, see Eirik Bjorge, "Current Developments: International Courts and Tribunals" (2011) 60:1 ICLQ 271.

[33] See *Costa Rica/Nicaragua, supra* note 32 at 244. 1858 Treaty of Limits, 15 April 1858, reproduced in *Dispute Regarding Navigational and Related Rights (Costa Rica v Nicaragua)*, written submissions of Costa Rica, 29 September 2005, at 221.

[34] *Costa Rica/Nicaragua, supra* note 32 at 245.

[35] *Ibid* at 226.

[36] *Ibid* at 246. Judge ad hoc Guillaume considered that there was no basis in the treaty for the non-commercial navigational right the ICJ declared to exist for the benefit of the inhabitants of the Costa Rican bank of the San Juan River. See

A different situation involving private individuals obtaining rights as a result of the settlement of a boundary dispute arose in *Land and Maritime Boundary between Cameroon and Nigeria (Cameroon v Nigeria: Equatorial Guinea intervening).*[37] Given the existence of more than three million Nigerians living in the contested Bakassi peninsula, who were wholly integrated within the Cameroonian society, Cameroon made the following unilateral statement before the Court: "Faithful to its traditional policy of hospitality and tolerance, Cameroon will continue to afford protection to Nigerians living in the [Bakassi] Peninsula and in the Lake Chad area."[38] As a result of having found that the disputed peninsula and lake areas

---

Dispute Regarding Navigational and Related Rights (Costa Rica v Nicaragua), Declaration of Judge ad hoc Guillaume, [2009] ICJ Rep 290 at 300. This view is supported by Sarah Cassella, who also considers that this right was created by the Court for equity reasons (*ex aequo et bono*). See Sarah Cassella, "Rééquilibrer les effets inéquitables d'une délimitation territoriale: l'arrêt de la Cour internationale de Justice du 13 juillet 2009 dans l'affaire du *Différend relatif à des droits de navigation et des droits connexes (Costa Rica c Nicaragua)*" (2009) 55 AFDI 253 at 266. Finally, Coalter Lathrop deems that this holding of the Court may well mean that riparian rights may well become part of customary international law related to the navigational uses of international boundary waters. See Coalter G Lathrop, "International Decisions" (2010) 104 AJIL 454 at 459.

37 See *Land and Maritime Boundary between Cameroon and Nigeria (Cameroon v Nigeria: Equatorial Guinea intervening)*, [2002] ICJ Rep 303 [*Cameroon/Nigeria*]. The main point of contention in this case, for the purpose of this article, was sovereignty over the Bakassi peninsula and a parcel in the area of Lake Chad that included thirty-three villages. The ICJ was also called on to determine the course of the maritime boundary between the two countries. The case had a significant natural resource dimension, given the oil concessions granted by both parties. The judgment left the concessions mostly untouched. The Court's judgment was severely criticized by Nigeria, which was disappointed with the outcome, in particular, the Court's conclusion that the Bakassi peninsula belonged to Cameroon, since this was the most important issue between the parties. The intervention of the UN Secretary General was requested by the parties to implement the decision. For assessments of this judgment, see John H Crook, "The 2002 Judicial Activity of the International Court of Justice" (2003) 97:2 AJIL 352 at 354; Pieter HF Bekker, "International Decisions" (2003) 97:2 AJIL 387; JG Merrills, "Decisions of International Tribunals: International Court of Justice" (2003) 52:3 ICLQ 775 at 788; Pierre D'Argent, "Des frontières et des peuples: l'affaire de la *Frontière terrestre et maritime entre le Cameroun et le Nigéria, arrêt sur le fond*" (2002) 48 AFDI 281. For an additional evaluation of the judgment from the perspective of counsel for Cameroon, see Maurice Mendelson, "The *Cameroon – Nigeria Case* in the International Court of Justice: Some Territorial Sovereignty and Boundary Delimitation Issues" (2004) 75:1 Brit YB Int'l L 223.

38 *Cameroon/Nigeria*, *supra* note 37 at 452.

belonged to Cameroon, the ICJ held that this declaration was an international undertaking and included it in the operative part of the judgment.[39]

Not only did the ICJ recognize new international rights for the benefit of individuals, but it also protected pre-existing private rights when settling boundary disputes. In effect, as a result of the delimitation of Lake Chad and the Bakassi peninsula, the Court found in *Cameroon/Nigeria* that each party to the dispute was occupying territory that belonged to the other. The Court thus imposed on the parties the obligation to withdraw their administration and military and police forces from such territory.[40] However, the Court's order did not require relocation of the citizens of the occupying parties living in the said areas, thereby protecting their right to remain and to continue to enjoy their existing rights.

A slightly similar situation took place in *Frontier Dispute (Benin v Niger)*, where a Chamber of the ICJ had to decide to whom certain islands on the Niger River belonged.[41] The Chamber determined the issue with respect to each relevant island but, in doing so, specifically stated that its declaration left pre-existing property rights intact.[42] In sum, the Court's boundary jurisprudence of the first decade of the new millennium illustrates that international

39 *Ibid* at 455.

40 *Ibid* at 451-52.

41 Both parties, which had formerly been part of French West Africa, requested that the ICJ form a Chamber to adjudicate their dispute related to the course of their boundary in the Niger River sector and in the Mekrou River sector, as well as with respect to sovereignty over the islands in the river, particularly Lété Island. The island was one of the most complex issues of the controversy and had been in dispute for decades. See *Benin/Niger, supra* note 4 at 107. The Chamber stated that no party had legal title on the basis of the principle of *uti possidetis juris* and decided the case on the basis of *effectivités* (at 127). The Chamber declared that the boundary between the parties followed the main navigable channel of the Niger River at the time of independence and that those islands that were to the right of the channel belonged to Benin and those on the left to Niger (at 133). While this conclusion granted the island of Lété to Niger, the Chamber ruled in favour of Benin regarding the course of the boundary in the region related to the River Mekrou (at 144, Sketch Map no 5, 148-49). For commentary on this judgment, see Stephen Mathias, "The 2005 Judicial Activity of the International Court of Justice" (2006) 100:3 AJIL 629 at 634; Stephen Allen, "Decisions of International Tribunals: International Court of Justice" (2006) 55 ICLQ 729; Anne-Thida Norodom, "L'arrêt de la Chambre de la Cour internationale de Justice dans l'affaire *du Différend frontalier (Bénin/Niger)*" (2005) 51 AFDI 185.

42 See *Benin/Niger, supra* note 4 at 140.

boundary agreements and settlements of boundary disputes may exceptionally create specific international rights for private individuals or protect their pre-existing private rights in situations in which the judgment implies a change in the state administering the territory inhabited by the given private individuals.[43]

State Succession and Unilateral Donations as Title to Territory

acquisition of title over territory by succession

Acquisition of territory by succession means that a state has sovereignty over a territory by virtue of being the successor to its past titleholder. After decolonization and the disintegration of the Soviet Union, it is not surprising that state succession is a frequent mode of acquisition and one that has repeatedly been at issue in the ICJ's case law over the first decade of the new millennium. Three issues were particularly important for the application of state succession as a mode of acquisition of territory in this jurisprudence. They are, first, whether a local ruler had authority over territory centuries ago; second, whether a local ruler had legal authority over a territory but transferred it to a first colonial power; and, third, what are the requirements for demonstrating a chain of title leading to the last successor in cases of state succession? The Court applied practical legal approaches to the first two and a strict legal test to the third.

Regarding the first issue, the question of whether a territory was under the authority of a local ruler many centuries ago may be a complex matter to prove in a territorial dispute. The ICJ recognized, in *Malaysia/Singapore*, that a ruler could be found to have had title over territory even in the absence of a specific document that indicated so. In this case, Malaysia claimed that the Island of Pedra Branca had always belonged to the Sultanate of Johor, to which Malaysia was a successor. Although Malaysia was able to demonstrate that the United Kingdom had tacitly recognized such a fact in the

43 However, some authors have criticized the ICJ for not always fully taking into consideration the important human dimension of boundary disputes. According to Emmanuel Decaux, this was the case with the Court's decision in *Qatar/Bahrain*, *supra* note 6. He says: "[L]a Cour semble s'être raccrochée à ce qui était pour elle le terrain le plus familier, plaquant une grille de lecture étatique sur les émirats du Golfe, en négligeant les réalités humaines qui ont longtemps marquée la région, comme la mobilité des groupes nomades et la non-appropriation des bien rares du désert ou des richesses de la mer." See Decaux, *supra* note 6 at 211.

nineteenth century, Malaysia was unable to prove specific title over the island by the Sultanate.[44]

The ICJ nevertheless found an alternate means of reaching such a conclusion as a matter of law. First, the Court used an inference. Although Pedra Branca was not explicitly designated in any title, it could not have been regarded as unknown territory (*terra incognita*), owing to its important location in the Straits of Singapore. Thus, given that the Sultanate of Johor had control over the area, it had to be inferred that the island was also under its control.[45] Second, the Court found that there was no competing claim to the island during the centuries of presumed control by the Sultanate. The absence of such claim, in the Court's view, showed that the island did, in fact, belong to the Sultanate.[46] Third, the ICJ reinforced its conclusion by accepting that the ties of loyalty between the Sultanate and a nomadic fishing community operating in the area that included Pedra Branca was also an expression of the exercise of authority by the former over the island.[47] In the result, as can be seen, the Court recognized a distant title over the island through indirect means, although it was supported by colonial evidence. This was one of the bases of the Court's conclusion that Malaysia, as the successor of the Sultanate, had title over Pedra Branca.

The second issue was whether a treaty between a local ruler and a colonial power involved a transfer of authority or sovereignty over territory from the former to the latter, such that this treaty could found the claim of the party claiming title on the basis of its being the successor to the given colonial power. This question was addressed by the ICJ in *Cameroon/Nigeria*. The core of the dispute was, as seen earlier, sovereignty over the Bakassi peninsula.

The peninsula had belonged to the kings and chiefs of Old Calabar, and the question was whether they had transferred sovereignty over it when they signed the Treaty of Protection with Great Britain in 1884. Nigeria argued that this treaty did not include a transfer of sovereignty over territory, since the kings and chiefs retained the power to enter into international agreements with other powers (albeit subject to the approval of Great Britain). The effect of this omission, according to Nigeria, was that the peninsula

44 See *Malaysia/Singapore*, *supra* note 15 at 33.

45 *Ibid* at 35.

46 *Ibid* at 35-37.

47 *Ibid* at 37-38.

could not have been transferred to Germany by virtue of the 1913 Anglo-German Agreement.[48]

The ICJ stated that the nature of the treaty could not be derived from its title alone.[49] It said that this kind of treaty sometimes preserved the international legal personality of the party being granted protection but was sometimes also made with indigenous rulers who were not states.[50] The Court held that the 1884 Treaty of Protection was of the latter kind — that is, it did not establish an international protectorate — and that Great Britain administered the territories and was not just protecting them.[51] Moreover, Nigeria was not able to produce evidence supporting the existence of the kings and chiefs of Old Calabar as international legal subjects after the 1884 treaty.[52] In addition, it was not demonstrated to the Court's satisfaction that the rulers had protested against the 1913 Anglo-German Agreement or that they had transferred their territory to Nigeria.[53] On these bases, the Court concluded that, although it had to be considered a derivative root of title,[54] the Court had to give effect to the 1884 treaty, which meant that the territory formerly under the control of the rulers was then under that of Great Britain.[55] Consequently, Great Britain had transferred the territory to Germany by virtue of the 1913 Anglo-German Agreement, and Cameroon had title as a result of the succession of titles. In sum, the ICJ was somewhat flexible in its approach to acquisition of title over the peninsula by Great Britain from the chiefs and kings of Old Calabar. While formal transfer of sovereignty could not be established, the former was nevertheless found to have become the titleholder of the said territory.

Finally, some of the requirements for the demonstration of title over territory as a result of state succession can be inferred from

48 See *Cameroon/Nigeria, supra* note 37 at 402. 1913 Anglo-German Agreement, Treaty Series No. 13 (1913). United Kingdom Cd. 7056 (with maps).

49 See *Cameroon/Nigeria, supra* note 37 at 404.

50 *Ibid* at 405.

51 *Ibid.*

52 *Ibid.*

53 *Ibid* at 406.

54 *Ibid* at 404.

55 *Ibid* at 404, 407. Judge Koroma, for instance, dissented as to this conclusion. In his view, a correct interpretation of the text of the treaty led to the conclusion that it had only a protective nature and involved neither cession nor transfer of territory. See the dissenting opinion of Judge Koroma (at 479-81).

the Court's judgment in *Indonesia/Malaysia.* Malaysia claimed that it had title over the disputed islands by virtue of its being successor to their original titleholder. However, as Malaysia was not able to identify and prove a title specifically referring to the islands in question, it invited the ICJ to declare the existence of title on the basis of inferences from related transfers.[56] Nonetheless, the Court was not prepared to draw any such inferences and explicitly stated that "the islands in dispute are not mentioned by name in any of the international legal instruments presented by Malaysia to prove the alleged consecutive transfers of title."[57] On this basis, the Court concluded that Malaysia could not have inherited a treaty-based title from the United Kingdom.[58] As can be seen from this ruling, state succession over territory can be found only where there is a title that specifically alludes to it. The Court is not willing to make inferences regarding the transfer of sovereignty in a state succession context in the absence of titles of this character.

There is a difference between the approaches of the ICJ in *Malaysia/Singapore* and *Indonesia/Malaysia* in finding the existence of title over territory. The Court is somewhat flexible regarding the recognition of the title of local rulers in distant times, and such title can be found on the basis of inferences. However, the Court is not flexible regarding claims by subsequent colonial and post-colonial titleholders based on state succession — title must be specifically proved in the chain of transfers.

Regarding the approach taken by the Court in *Cameroon/Nigeria,* it is one that responds to the realities of colonialism, despite how much one may dislike it. In this regard, it accords with Maurice Mendelson's standpoint. He points out that, although the argument is ethnocentric and racist in light of contemporary views, the fact is that in the nineteenth century international law was what colonial powers meant it to be. Consequently, even if the treaty with the chiefs and kings of Old Calabar did not transfer sovereignty at the time of its conclusion, nothing prevented the United Kingdom from subsequently converting it into a British colony.[59] Further, Pierre D'Argent rightly points out that, even if Judge Koroma were right in his interpretation of the treaty,[60] the fact that the kings and

56 See *Indonesia/Malaysia, supra* note 22 at 669-74.

57 *Ibid* at 674; see also 678.

58 *Ibid.*

59 See Mendelson, *supra* note 37 at 232-33.

60 See the dissenting opinion of Judge Koroma in *Cameroon/Nigeria, supra* note 37.

chiefs of Old Calabar disappeared as separate entities after the treaty was concluded would have opened the door to acquisition of the territory by the United Kingdom in any event.[61]

Finally, the categorization of treaties between local rulers that lacked international legal personality and colonial powers as derivative roots of title does not appear to have a meaningful consequence. The effects of these treaties are the same as those of normal treaties for the purpose of the succession of titles and the transfer of sovereignty over territory. In sum, with respect to state succession, it can be said that the ICJ was flexible when dealing with the first two links in the process: recognition of title in the original sovereign (*Malaysia/Singapore*) and transfer of title by this original sovereign to a colonial power (*Cameroon/Nigeria*). However, a strict approach to title was applied from this point forward in the chain of events until the point of transfer to the last title holder (*Indonesia/Malaysia*).

UNILATERAL DONATIONS

Unilateral donations of territory are undoubtedly rare events. They may have taken place in the past, and donor states or their successors may well have subsequently wanted to narrow the scope of the donation, thereby triggering disputes. The ICJ assessed the issue of a unilateral donation of territory in *Malaysia/Singapore.* Regarding the dispute over who had sovereignty over the island of Pedra Branca, one of the issues was the extent of a renunciation of claims over certain territory made by Sultan Abdul Rahman to Sultan Hussein.[62] The Court tacitly determined that the requirements for territorial donations are the following: first, proof of title over the concerned territory by the donor; and, second, explicit identification or identification by implication of the territory subject to the donation.[63]

Impermissible Modes of Acquisition of Title to Territory

Cases defining the bases of title to territory are as important to states as those in which the ICJ denies title on the basis of a particular factual situation. It could be said that the contours of the boundary jurisprudence are determined by two dimensions: those notions that qualify as modes of acquisition of title to territory and those

61 See D'Argent, *supra* note 37 at 308.

62 See *Malaysia/Singapore, supra* note 15 at 47.

63 *Ibid* at 49.

that do not. The Court's case law of the first decade of the new millennium dealt particularly with the latter, with positive long-lasting consequences, as will be seen in the next section.

THE REJECTION OF HISTORICAL CONSOLIDATION AS A BASIS OF TITLE

In *Cameroon/Nigeria*, the ICJ rejected the notion of historical consolidation — that is, the prolonged occupation of territory belonging to another state — as a basis of title to territory. Nigeria claimed that it had acquired sovereignty over a series of villages and islands located in a specific area of Lake Chad by virtue of historical consolidation of its actions there, without Cameroon's opposition.[64] Although the Court had recognized the relevance of such consolidation to maritime delimitations in its judgment in *Fisheries (United Kingdom v Norway)*, it had refused to extend it beyond that context.[65] It stated:

> The Court notes that the theory of historical consolidation is highly controversial and cannot replace the established modes of acquisition of title under international law, which take into account many other important variables of fact and law. It further observes that nothing in the *Fisheries* Judgment suggests that the "historical consolidation" referred to, in connection with the external boundaries of the territorial sea, allows land occupation to prevail over an established treaty title.[66]

The Court also stated that, in any case, the duration of the purportedly sovereign acts by Nigeria, which encompassed close to twenty years, was not enough under the said notion even if its applicability were to be considered in the case.[67] In the absence of the notion of historical consolidation, the Court said, the legal test had to be whether the titleholder had acquiesced to passing title to the other state.[68]

Judge Koroma was of the view that historical consolidation should have been recognized in *Cameroon/Nigeria*.[69] However, it seems that

64 See *Cameroon/Nigeria, supra* note 37 at 346.

65 *Fisheries (United Kingdom v Norway)*, [1951] ICJ Rep 130 at 137.

66 *Cameroon/Nigeria, supra* note 37 at 352.

67 *Ibid.*

68 *Ibid* at 352-54.

69 See the dissenting opinion of Judge Koroma in *Cameroon/Nigeria, supra* note 37 at 485. As to the length of time required for historical consolidation, Judge

his notion of historical consolidation included the transfer of title due to acquiescence on the part of the titleholder,[70] a situation to which the ICJ did give effect in *Malaysia/Singapore*.[71]

In *Cameroon/Nigeria*, then, the court closed the door to a weakening of the legal value of title over territory. *Effectivités* never prevail over valid title, which is a significant holding of this decision.[72]

GEOGRAPHIC PROXIMITY IS NOT ALWAYS ENOUGH TO CONFER TITLE

In *Malaysia/Singapore*, the ICJ decided not to apply the doctrine according to which, regarding a group of islands, the fate of the principal island determines that of the rest.[73] Singapore, in this case, claimed that it had sovereignty over Pedra Branca, the main island and, thus, over the maritime features named Middle Rocks (respectively 0.6 and 1.2 metres high and located 0.6 and 2.2 nautical miles from Pedra Branca).[74] As noted earlier, the Court declared that the Sultanate of Johor had had authority over Pedra Branca, but it also found that sovereignty had passed from its successor, Malaysia, to Singapore by virtue of the latter's acts as sovereign and the former's acquiescence.[75] However, the Court regarded Middle Rocks as distinctive territory from Pedra Branca and, therefore, found that the facts supporting the transfer of sovereignty over Pedra Branca to Singapore did not apply to Middle Rocks. Consequently, sovereignty over them fell to Malaysia.[76] Thus, the Court did not apply the doctrine described in the preceding paragraph, but this fact does not necessarily mean that it completely rejected it.[77]

Koroma held that this would depend on the particular facts of the case and on the area, and he suggested that shorter periods of time should be recognized in certain circumstances (*ibid*).

70 *Ibid* at 484-85.

71 See note 20 and accompanying text in this article.

72 Merrills, *supra* note 37 at 796.

73 *Island of Palmas Case (Netherlands v United States of America)*, (1928) II RIAA 829 at 855 [*Island of Palmas*].

74 *Malaysia/Singapore, supra* note 15 at 95-97.

75 *Ibid* at 95-96.

76 *Malaysia/Singapore, supra* note 15 at 99.

77 Bories, *supra* note 20 at 231.

The Use of Maps

GENERAL CONSIDERATIONS

Maps play an important role in boundary delimitations.[78] They can be defined as "portrayal[s] of geographical facts, and usually also of political facts associated with them; for a cartographer commonly endeavors to reveal not only what nature has wrought, but also what states have decreed with respect to her works."[79] Maps may be public, private, or semi-public, and states may use them in different ways in connection with boundaries. States can incorporate maps within their boundary treaties, include them as annexes, or simply make reference to them.[80] Domestic and international courts and tribunals were, until recently, reluctant to accept them as evidence, for lack of accuracy among many other reasons.[81] This reluctance was even more significant in the case of maps published by private persons.[82]

The legal value of a given map will vary depending on the relationship between that map and the boundary agreement in question. The highest value is when maps are incorporated or annexed to the agreement. It is equally important to note that maps may also have value as evidence, depending on their geographical accuracy. In addition, although such value can be diminished if maps have inconsistencies, they may still be useful to courts and tribunals as evidence for different purposes.[83] On the other hand, conflicts or

78 For a previous assessment of the role of maps in boundary delimitations, see Sakeus Akweenda, "The Legal Significance of Maps in Boundary Questions: A Reappraisal with Particular Emphasis on Namibia" (1989) 60 Brit YB Int'l L 205.

79 Charles Cheney Hyde, "Maps as Evidence in International Boundary Disputes" (1933) 27 AJIL 311 at 311.

80 Akweenda, *supra* note 78 at 206-11.

81 *Ibid* at 212-18.

82 *Ibid* at 219. For instance, the sole arbitrator in the *Island of Timor* case declared that a private map "could not be weighed in value with the two official maps signed by the commissioners or delegates of the two states." See Judicial Decisions Involving Questions of International Law, *Arbitral Award Rendered in Execution of the Compromis Signed at the Hague, April 3, 1913 between the Netherlands and Portugal Concerning the Subject of the Boundary of a Part of Their Possessions in the Island of Timor*" (1915) 9 AJIL 240 at 259.

83 For instance, in the *Minquiers and Ecrehos Case (France v UK)*, Judge Carneiro stated in his individual opinion that the maps at issue in that dispute were not decisive in settling the legal question regarding territorial sovereignty. However, he pointed out that maps could be used as evidence showing that exercises of

discrepancies between maps and the text of the treaty to which they are related are possible. In the absence of specific treaty provisions addressing this situation, the outcome that best reflects the parties' intentions has been adopted.[84] Conflicts between boundary agreements and maps can also arise when the latter are produced after the former have entered into force, and the map may even prevail, as the Court's judgment in the *Case Concerning the Temple of Preah Vihear (Cambodia v Thailand)* showed a few decades ago.[85] In this case, a map that contained an error in relation to a treaty's terms, according to Thailand, was upheld by the ICJ against this party because, in the Court's view, Thailand had accepted the error by not raising it and by circulating the map widely.[86] By virtue of such acceptance, the Court said, the map contained an interpretation of the treaty, not an error.[87]

Maps can also be regarded as part of the negotiating process of boundary treaties[88] or as subsequent practice under Article 31(3)(b) of the Vienna Convention on the Law of Treaties (VCLT).[89] Maps playing any of these roles may also constitute a valuable aid in determining boundaries when the basis of title does not sufficiently define them. In particular, the Chamber of the ICJ in *Frontier Dispute (Burkina Faso v Republic of Mali)* stated in this regard: "[H]aving regard to the ... neutrality of the source, the Chamber considers that where all other evidence is lacking, or is not sufficient to show an exact line, the probative value of the ... map becomes decisive."[90]

---

sovereignty were known. See *The Minquiers and Ecrehos Case (France v United Kingdon)*, Individual Opinion of Judge Levi Carneiro, [1953] ICJ Rep 85 at 105. See also Akweenda, *supra* note 78 at 220.

84 *Ibid* at 211.

85 *Case Concerning the Temple of Preah Vihear (Cambodia v Thailand)*, [1962] ICJ Rep 6 [*Preah Vihear*].

86 Akweenda, *supra* note 78 at 223.

87 *Preah Vihear, supra* note 85 at 34. As to the claim of error, the ICJ held that "the plea of error cannot be allowed as an element vitiating consent if the party advancing it contributed by its own conduct to the error, or could have avoided it, or if the circumstances were such as to put that party on notice of a possible error" (at 26).

88 Akweenda, *supra* note 78 at 210.

89 Vienna Convention on the Law of Treaties, 23 May 1969, 1155 UNTS 331, Article 31(3)(b) [VCLT].

90 *Burkina Faso/Mali, supra* note 2 at 586. It is important to mention that this finding of the Chamber took place in the context of the application of the *uti possidetis*

THE USE OF MAPS BY THE COURT, 2000-10

During the period under consideration, the ICJ pronounced on the circumstances in which maps have legal significance and on their value and limitations as evidence. In *Indonesia/Malaysia*, quoting previous decisions, the Court stated:

> [M]aps merely constitute information which varies in accuracy from case to case; of themselves, and by virtue solely of their existence, they cannot constitute a territorial title, that is, a document endowed by international law with intrinsic legal force for the purpose of establishing territorial rights. Of course, in some cases maps may acquire such legal force, but where this is so the legal force does not arise solely from their intrinsic merits: it is because such maps fall into the category of physical expressions of the will of the State or States concerned. This is the case, for example, when maps are annexed to an official text of which they form an integral part. Except in this clearly defined case, maps are only extrinsic evidence of varying reliability or unreliability which may be used, along with other evidence of a circumstantial kind, to establish or reconstitute the real facts.[91]

The Chamber of the ICJ in *Benin/Niger* reiterated that, when maps do not constitute an expression of the parties' intention, they must be considered only as evidence, and, given that they do not confer title, they cannot be allowed to create legal presumptions shifting the burden of proof.[92] The Court also affirmed in *Nicaragua/Honduras* that the assessment of maps produced by any of the parties depends on "the neutrality of the sources towards the dispute in question and the parties to that dispute."[93] Finally, the Court dealt with a specific kind of map in *Nicaragua/Honduras* — old maps related to little-known areas without administrative control. The Court embraced prior arbitral jurisprudence attaching little probative value to such maps.[94]

---

juris principle, which had initially not yielded a boundary. See also Akweenda, *supra* note 78 at 225.

91 *Indonesia/Malaysia, supra* note 22 at 667. See also *Benin/Niger, supra* note 4 at 119-20; *Nicaragua/Honduras, supra* note 5 at 723.

92 See *Benin/Niger, supra* note 4 at 119.

93 See *Nicaragua/Honduras, supra* note 5 at 723 (reaffirming the ICJ's previous holding in *Burkina Faso/Mali, supra* note 2 at 583.

94 See *Nicaragua/Honduras, supra* note 5 at 722-33 (citing *Honduras Borders* (*Guatemala v Honduras*), (1933) II RIAA 1307 at 1325).

The Court's Use of Maps as Expressions of the Will of the Parties

Maps that constitute expressions of the parties' will were used by the ICJ during the period 2000–10 for three purposes: (1) to eliminate indeterminacies in the relevant agreement; (2) to correct a mistake in the agreement; and (3) to confirm an interpretation thereof. The Court also defined the conditions that maps, which have been agreed on by the parties, have to meet to be regarded as context for the interpretation of the relevant treaty under Article 31(2) of the VCLT.

To begin with, maps that serve as expressions of the will of the parties played an important role in the ICJ's decision in *Cameroon/Nigeria*. Nigeria claimed that the boundary in the Lake Chad area was indeterminate because of a lack of precision in the definition of the boundary in one of the relevant agreements and because of subsequent geographical changes.[95] Faced with a change in a geographic feature existing at the time of the delimitation,[96] the Court made use of the maps attached to the relevant agreements between France and the United Kingdom (namely the 1919 Milner-Simon Declaration and the 1931 Henderson-Fleuriau Exchange of Notes) to suppress a minor indeterminacy contained in the League of Nations' mandate and to determine the intention of the parties in this exchange of notes.[97]

Maps appended to boundary agreements were also used to determine the parties' intentions when the text of the agreement contained mistakes. This situation arose in *Cameroon/Nigeria*, in which the ICJ used an appended map to determine the parties' intention regarding the Sapeo area, whose boundary description in the 1929-30 Thomson-Marchand Declaration included errors.[98] Maps fully agreed to by the parties in *Indonesia/Malaysia* were used to confirm an interpretation that the Court had reached regarding

95 See *Cameroon/Nigeria, supra* note 37 at 337-38.

96 *Ibid* at 345-46.

97 *Ibid* at 345. 1919 Milner-Simon Declaration, 10 July 1919, reproduced in *Land and Maritime Boundary between Cameroon and Nigeria (Cameroon v Nigeria: Equatorial Guinea intervening)*, written submissions of Cameroon, 29 March 1994, at 318; 1931 Henderson-Fleuriau Exchange of Notes, 9 January 1931, reproduced in *Land and Maritime Boundary between Cameroon and Nigeria (Cameroon v Nigeria: Equatorial Guinea intervening)*, written submissions of Cameroon, 29 March 1994, at 318.

98 *Cameroon/Nigeria, supra* note 37 at 383. Thomson-Marchand Declaration, 29 December 1929 and 31 January 1930, written submissions of Cameroon, 29 March 1994, at 318.

the applicable treaty. In this case, a series of agreements had been concluded within the framework of the 1891 United Kingdom–Netherlands convention defining the boundaries between the Netherlands' possessions in the Island of Borneo and the states on that island under British protection. Each of the agreements had maps annexed to them,[99] and the ICJ relied on them to reinforce its conclusion concerning the inability of the convention, and of any subsequent agreement, to determine sovereignty over the disputed islands.[100]

However, maps included as part of treaties have not been the only ones used by the ICJ to ascertain the parties' will. The Court has also made use of maps prepared by them only for the purpose of negotiating international agreements. This is what occurred in *Cameroon/Nigeria*, where the Court was faced with a mistake in the identification of a river in the Thompson-Marchand Declaration and consequent difficulty in identifying the boundary. The declaration did not provide a definitive answer, nor did the maps submitted by the parties.[101] The Court recognized that, in such circumstances, it "had to have recourse to other means of interpretation" and relied on a sketch map prepared by French and British officials during the negotiation of the declaration — but not finally annexed to it — to determine the boundary line in the specific section at issue.[102]

Finally, the case law of the first decade of the new millennium gave the ICJ the opportunity to clarify when maps could be used as context for the interpretation of treaties according to Article 31 of the VCLT. Article 31(2) provides:

> 2. The context for the purpose of the interpretation of a treaty shall comprise, in addition to the text, including its preamble and annexes:
>
> (*a*) any agreement relating to the treaty which was made between all the parties in connection with the conclusion of the treaty;
>
> (*b*) any instrument which was made by one or more parties in connection with the conclusion of the treaty and accepted by the other parties as an instrument related to the treaty.[103]

99 *Indonesia/Malaysia, supra* note 22 at 661-62.

100 *Ibid* at 662.

101 *Cameroon/Nigeria, supra* note 37 at 366-67.

102 *Ibid* at 367.

103 VCLT, *supra* note 89, Article 31(2).

In *Indonesia/Malaysia*, Indonesia relied on a map to support its interpretation of a convention between the United Kingdom and the Netherlands according to which Indonesia had title over the islands disputed in the case. The map was prepared by the Dutch government, attached to an explanatory memorandum, and forwarded by the British agent to the UK Foreign Office, which did not express any view. On this basis, Indonesia claimed that the map constituted context for the interpretation of the convention in light of either Article 31(2)(a) or (b) of the VCLT.[104] Malaysia argued that the map was never promulgated by the Netherlands, that the ratification of the convention made no reference to it, and that the map was never the subject of negotiations.[105]

The ICJ sided with Malaysia. It started by noting that the map did not make any specific allusion to the tiny islands in issue. The Court went on to say that there was no evidence of a dispute between the Netherlands and the United Kingdom related to the islands at the time of negotiation of the convention, so the map could not be taken as attributing the islands to the Netherlands.[106] The Court then assessed the circumstances under which the map had reached the United Kingdom and said:

> The Court observes that the Explanatory Memorandum and map was never transmitted by the Dutch Government to the British Government, but were simply forwarded to the latter by its diplomatic agent in The Hague ... This agent specified that the map had been published in the Official Journal of the Netherlands and formed part of a Report presented to the Second Chamber of the States-General. He added that "the map seems to be the only interesting feature of a document which does not otherwise call for special comment." However, [the agent] did not draw the attention of his authority to the red line drawn on the map among other lines. The British Government did not react to this internal transmission. In these circumstances, such a lack of reaction to this line on the map appended to the Memorandum cannot be deemed to constitute acquiescence in this line.[107]

The Court thus concluded that, for these reasons, the map did not come within Articles 31(2)(a) or (b).[108]

104 *Indonesia/Malaysia, supra* note 22 at 648-49.

105 *Ibid* at 649.

106 *Ibid* at 650.

107 *Ibid* at 650-51; see also 663-64.

108 *Ibid* at 664.

It can be inferred from these findings that, for a map to assume the status of context within the meaning of Article 31(2) of the VCLT, it is necessary to demonstrate that the map relates to an agreement between the parties dealing with the specific object of the dispute. Alternatively, it must relate to a clear position by one of the parties on the specific issue and acceptance of it by the other. Failure to respond in the absence of such a clearly expressed position is not acquiescence under Article 31(2)(b). As can be seen, the ICJ in *Indonesia/Malaysia* established a strict threshold for maps to serve as context under the interpretation provisions of the VCLT.

The Court's Use of Maps That Are Not the Expression of the Parties' Will

As mentioned earlier, maps that have not been agreed to by the parties may play a role as evidence. Sometimes, during the period under review, the Court attached no value to them; in others, it did. In effect, maps of this nature were disregarded by the Chamber of the ICJ in *Benin/Niger*. In this case, the parties relied on a set of unattached maps as evidence to support their *effectivités* over the disputed islands on the River Niger. The Chamber refused to give any probative weight to these maps.[109] A similar situation took place in *Nicaragua/Honduras*. There, Nicaragua claimed that its negotiations with the United Kingdom regarding turtle fishing rights in the area were *effectivités* over the islands in dispute. To support its contentions, Nicaragua provided a map produced by a British hydrographer. The Court found that the United Kingdom had not commissioned the map and attached little value to it.[110]

In *Territorial and Maritime Dispute (Nicaragua v Colombia)*, Colombia relied on maps that it had produced to show that the parties had adopted the eighty-second meridian as the maritime delimitation line between the parties in the 1928 Treaty Concerning Territorial Questions at Issue between Colombia and Nicaragua and the 1930 Protocol of Exchange of Ratifications. Nicaragua contested this position.[111] The ICJ stated that the maps were ambiguous in identifying the meridian as the delimitation line and did not contain

109 *Cameroon/Nigeria, supra* note 37 at 358.

110 *Nicaragua/Honduras, supra* note 5 at 718-19.

111 See *Territorial and Maritime Dispute (Nicaragua v Colombia)*, Preliminary Objections, [2007] ICJ Rep 832 at 865-67 [*Nicaragua/Colombia* (Preliminary Objections)]. For an evaluation of this judgment, see Stephen Mathias, "Current Developments: The 2007 Judicial Activity of the International Court of Justice" (2008) 102:3 AJIL 588 at 602. Treaty Concerning Territorial Questions at Issue

any explanatory legend. For these reasons, the Court concluded that the maps could not prove the allegation by Colombia.[112]

In *Nicaragua/Honduras*, the ICJ also assessed maps produced by the parties in support of their respective claims. Both Nicaragua and Honduras produced official maps that included some maritime features but not the islands in dispute in the case. For this reason, the Court did not attach any value to the maps in attributing sovereignty over the islands.[113] The Court in *Nicaragua/Honduras* also refused to attach probative value to maps that did show the disputed islands but that failed to indicate their political affiliation.[114] Other similar maps submitted by the parties in *Nicaragua/Honduras* received little consideration since, as the Court stated, "none ... was part of a legal instrument in force nor more specifically part of a boundary treaty concluded between Nicaragua and Honduras."[115] However, the Chamber in *Benin/Niger* slightly mitigated the extent of a similar holding by giving some weight to maps that were not annexed to any administrative instrument, but only because they confirmed the Chamber's conclusions based on relevant colonial regulations.[116]

There is nevertheless a kind of map that has not been agreed to by the parties but that may play an important role as evidence in boundary disputes — a map produced by one party or its predecessors that contradicts its claims before the Court. The evidentiary value of maps of this nature was explicitly endorsed by the ICJ in *Malaysia/Singapore*. In this case, the Court adopted the words of the Eritrea-Ethiopia Boundary Commission in *Decision Regarding Delimitation of the Border between the State of Eritrea and the Federal Democratic Republic of Ethiopia*: "The map still stands as a statement of a geographical fact, especially when the State adversely affected had

---

between Colombia and Nicaragua, 24 March 1928, reproduced in *Territorial and Maritime Dispute (Nicaragua v Colombia)* (Preliminary Objections), written submissions of Colombia, 21 July 2003, at 842; Protocol of Exchange of Ratifications, signed on 5 May 1930, reproduced in *Territorial and Maritime Dispute (Nicaragua v Colombia)* (Preliminary Objections), written submissions of Colombia, 21 July 2003, at 843.

112 *Nicaragua/Colombia* (Preliminary Objections), *supra* note 111 at 868.

113 *Nicaragua/Honduras, supra* note 5 at 722, 723.

114 *Ibid* at 723 (citing *Island of Palmas, supra* note 73 at 852-53).

115 *Nicaragua/Honduras, supra* note 5 at 724.

116 *Benin/Niger, supra* note 4 at 147-48.

itself produced and disseminated it, even against its own interest."[117] As this kind of map was at issue in *Malaysia/Singapore*, it gave the Court the opportunity to expand on this issue. Singapore had submitted six official maps, produced by the Malaysian surveyor general and the director of national mapping in the 1960s and 1970s, in which it was unquestionably stated that the Island of Pedra Branca fell under Singapore's sovereignty.[118] Malaysia responded that maps not incorporated into treaties or not part of inter-state negotiations could not contain admissions and that the maps in question contained a disclaimer.[119] The ICJ made a distinction between a map recognizing title and a map stating an official position. The Malaysian maps did not create a title for Singapore on Pedra Branca, but they indicated Malaysia's position as to Singapore's sovereignty there.[120] The maps were part of the evidence on which the Court based its conclusion that Malaysia had acquiesced to the transfer of title to the island to Singapore.

Maps of this character were also submitted by Indonesia in *Indonesia/Malaysia* and allowed the ICJ to shed still further light on the characteristics required to increase their probative weight. The Court gave the Malaysian and British maps little credit since they contained important inconsistencies and were therefore inconclusive in supporting Indonesia's position.[121] The lessons that can be drawn from these findings regarding maps produced by a party but that oppose its position before the ICJ are the following. First, to be of value, the maps must be uniform in respect of the particular issue in dispute. Second, they must be directly related to the territory in dispute. When this set of characteristics is present, one party may benefit from the maps produced by the other. Those maps do not prove title but constitute important evidence in determining it.

117 *Malaysia/Singapore, supra* note 15 at 95 (citing *Decision Regarding Delimitation of the Border between the State of Eritrea and the Federal Democratic Republic of Ethiopia*, Eritrea-Ethiopia Boundary Commission, 13 April 2002, at 28, online: UN High Commissioner for Refugees <http://www.unhcr.org/refworld/docid/4a54bbeco.htm>).

118 *Malaysia/Singapore, supra* note 15 at 94.

119 *Ibid.*

120 *Ibid* at 95.

121 *Indonesia/Malaysia, supra* note 22 at 667-68. It is important to mention that Indonesia was also relying on maps produced by the United Kingdom, Malaysia's predecessor, which, in Indonesia's view, contradicted Malaysia's claims (at 28, 40).

The Court's Use of Maps with Disclaimers

Maps with disclaimers may have little value if they are produced by a party in support of its position before the ICJ. A map of this nature was relevant in *Nicaragua/Honduras*, where Honduras produced a map prepared by the Pan-American Institute of Geography and History that included some of the islands in dispute and supported its claim before the Court. However, the Court noted that the map had a disclaimer and did not assess it for this reason.[122]

The situation seems different with respect to maps with disclaimers produced by one party but used against it by the other — these maps may still have evidentiary value. This situation arose in *Malaysia/Singapore* where, as mentioned earlier, Singapore submitted maps produced by Malaysia declaring that Pedra Branca was under Singapore's sovereignty. The maps clearly supported Singapore's claim, but they had a disclaimer according to which they were not to be considered authoritative on the delimitation of international or other boundaries.[123] The Court narrowly interpreted the disclaimer, holding that it "is not here concerned with a boundary but with a distinct island" and concluding that the maps *tended* to confirm that Malaysia had deemed the island to be Singapore's.[124] In sum, on the basis of this holding, parties may not expect the ICJ to disregard maps only because of the existence of a disclaimer, at least when the map is used against the party that prepared it. Rather, the Court may interpret the disclaimer narrowly and find the map useful in resolving issues falling outside the scope of that disclaimer.

State Responsibility

The ICJ was prudent during the first decade of the twentieth-first century in terms of state responsibility arising out of boundary disputes. The Court consistently regarded its judgments concerning boundaries as sufficient to address any reparation claims, and, on this basis, it refused to award damages or to require assurances of non-repetition.

NO AWARDS OF DAMAGES

The ICJ refused to award damages twice during the time period covered by this article. The Court in *Cameroon/Nigeria* addressed

122 *Nicaragua/Honduras, supra* note 5 at 722.

123 *Malaysia/Singapore, supra* note 15 at 94-95.

124 *Ibid* at 95.

Cameroon's claim of material and non-material damages suffered as a result of Nigeria's occupation.[125] It ruled that both the judgment and the order of evacuation issued therein against Nigeria sufficiently addressed the injury and concluded that "the Court will not therefore seek to ascertain whether and to what extent Nigeria's responsibility to Cameroon has been engaged as a result of the occupation."[126]

Commenting on this finding, D'Argent says that the ICJ may have left some injury uncompensated without explaining the legal reasons for such a result. However, he argues that the Court's solution had the advantage of not jeopardizing the settlement of the boundary dispute with a further, and perhaps dilated, controversy over damages. D'Argent concludes that the solution was politically wise and legally sound since it allowed the Court to ensure peace, justice, and international security.[127]

In *Costa Rica/Nicaragua*, Costa Rica also made a claim for damages.[128] The ICJ reiterated that an order of cessation of a continuing transgression constituted a form of reparation for the aggrieved state, and it rejected the damage claims since Costa Rica had not offered any proof supporting them.[129] Sarah Cassella summarizes well the outcome in *Costa Rica/Nicaragua*: "Un certain équilibre entre les droits et les obligations des États en cause a été rétabli, en partie par un jugement en équité."[130]

ASSURANCES OF NON-REPETITION

In *Cameroon/Nigeria*, Cameroon asked the ICJ for assurances of non-repetition by Nigeria, but the Court refused this remedy as it considered it unnecessary. The Court pointed out:

> [T]he Judgment ... today specifies in definitive and mandatory terms the land and maritime boundary between the two States. With all uncertainty

125 *Cameroon/Nigeria*, *supra* note 37 at 316-17.

126 *Ibid* at 452. Bekker has criticized this conclusion. See Bekker, *supra* note 37 at 397.

127 D'Argent, *supra* note 37 at 318.

128 *Costa Rica/Nicaragua*, *supra* note 32 at 222-24.

129 *Nicaragua/Honduras*, *supra* note 5 at 705. In this case, Nicaragua reserved its right to make a damage claim but did not develop it during the proceedings, such that the ICJ did not rule on it (at 666-67, 760-64).

130 Cassella, *supra* note 36 at 277.

dispelled in this regard, the Court cannot envisage a situation where either Party, after withdrawing its military and police forces and administration from the other's territory, would fail to respect the territorial sovereignty of that Party. Hence Cameroon's submission on this point cannot be upheld.[131]

Costa Rica also asked the Court to order assurances of non-repetition in *Costa Rica/Nicaragua*.[132] The Court, affirming its previous holdings on this issue, declared that this remedy was exceptional as "there is no reason to suppose that a State whose act or conduct has been declared wrongful by the Court will repeat that act or conduct in the future, since its good faith must be presumed."[133] The Court concluded that there was no evidence in *Costa Rica/Nicaragua* of exceptional circumstances justifying the ordering of assurances of non-repetition.[134]

The ICJ's conclusions in the earlier-mentioned cases seem well thought out. The remedy of assurances of non-repetition is justifiable only under very exceptional circumstances — for example, those of *LaGrand (Germany v United States of America)*, where a convicted alien, whose rights under the Vienna Convention on Consular Relations had not been respected, was sentenced to death in the United States.[135] A similar degree of gravity has certainly not been present in the boundary cases before the court over the last decade.

Conclusions

The ICJ's boundary jurisprudence of the first decade of the twenty-first century discloses multiple important facets that go well beyond those more conventionally associated with boundary cases — such as the interpretation of boundary treaties, the principle of *uti*

131 *Cameroon/Nigeria, supra* note 37 at 452.

132 *Costa Rica/Nicaragua, supra* note 32 at 222-24.

133 *Ibid* at 267.

134 *Ibid.*

135 Vienna Convention on Consular Relations, 24 April 1963, entered into force on 19 March 1967, 596 UNTS 261. Germany sought assurances that the United States would not repeat these unlawful acts regarding the detention of, or criminal proceedings against, German citizens. The ICJ declared that a program designed and put in place by the United States to strengthen the consular notification at the state and local level addressed this concern. See *LaGrand (Germany v United States of America)*, [2001] ICJ Rep 466 at 511-13, 516.

possidetis juris, effectivités, or maritime delimitation. This article has focused on the former, less conventional, aspects of this jurisprudence and distilled a number of lessons that flow therefrom.

First, although, in principle, all kinds of territory can be appropriated, the ICJ has declared two exceptions to this rule over the first decade of the twenty-first century: low-tide elevations beyond the territorial sea (*Qatar/Bahrain* and *Nicaragua/Honduras*) and, at least by implication, islands located in areas of highly changeable geographical conditions within rivers (*Nicaragua/Honduras*). In addition, the Court did not easily declare the existence of *terra nullius* and used conceptual tools to avoid such findings, even if formal title was not clearly found to have been established at a specific point in time. To this end, the Court affirmed previous arbitral jurisprudence according to which territory can be regarded as having belonged to a colonial power even if the former neither specifically identified the territory as its own nor exercised any authority there (*Nicaragua/Honduras*). On another occasion, the ICJ simply inferred the inexistence of *terra nullius* based on the facts of the case — for example, the location of the territory, the existence of rulers controlling the general area where the territory was situated, or the absence of claims to the territory by other rulers for significant periods of time (*Malaysia/Singapore*). Nonetheless, the Court recognized the existence of *terra nullius* when no colonial or post-colonial power exerting influence in the area where the disputed territory was located could prove title over it (*Indonesia/Malaysia*).

Second, the ICJ's jurisprudence over the period under analysis reveals that, although international boundary agreements and settlements of boundary controversies primarily create rights for states, they may also give rise to specific international rights for the benefit of private individuals (*Costa Rica/Nicaragua*) or protect pre-existing private rights in situations in which the Court's judgment compels a change in the state administering territory inhabited by private individuals (*Cameroon/Nigeria* and *Benin/Niger*). This is certainly a positive development in the case law and one that parallels the increasing concern in multiple branches of international law for the individual, as a subject of, and therefore a holder of rights at, international law. Such outcomes also constitute an appropriate response to the pressing reality of boundary disputes on the ground, which sometimes affect the fate of millions of people.

Third, regarding state succession as a basis of title to territory, the ICJ has adopted a flexible approach when dealing with the first two links in the chain of succession. In particular, title of an original sovereign over territory was recognized on the basis of factual inferences (*Malaysia/Singapore*) and transfer of title by this original sovereign to a colonial power was recognized even where the relevant agreement was not explicit in this regard (*Cameroon/Nigeria*). A strict approach regarding title was, however, adopted by the Court in evaluating subsequent links in the chain of transfers down to the last titleholder — title had to be proven in relation to the specific territory in dispute (*Indonesia/Malaysia*). Whether or not one agrees with the results of these approaches in particular cases, the ICJ's positions s themselves generally seem to be right. Proof of title held by original sovereigns in forms most known today (treaties and other international agreements) may sometimes be difficult to find, and the well-reasoned use of inferences by the Court based on fully proven facts may be a good substitute in order to arrive at conclusions about the identity of the original sovereign over the disputed territory. The same can be said of the ICJ's practical approach to transfer of title by this titleholder to colonial powers at a time when power often played a more significant role in the lawful transfer of sovereignty. Although post-colonial observers may object to such an approach — for many good reasons — the fact remains that it is difficult for the Court, with its important institutional constraints (such as a lack of general compulsory jurisdiction or enforcement mechanisms, to mention but two), to attempt to reverse the effects of colonization by refusing to recognize in law the reality that sometimes underlies past agreements between small, local rulers and colonial powers. To do so would require the Court to uphold pre-colonial rulers' title when such rulers had virtually disappeared from the international scene and their territory had been fully controlled by one or more colonial powers throughout decades or centuries. It may well be useful to recall what Sir Robert Jennings, then president of the ICJ, once expressed in conveying the Court's report to the UN General Assembly: "[A] court must indeed apply legal rules and be seen clearly to be doing so ... Nevertheless, a good and useful court will not be ignorant of the political issues involved or of the political consequences of the decision it takes."[136] Finally, the strict approach taken by the Court following this first transfer of title, when addressing claims based on state succession, is both sound and the only admissible one in light of developments in international law in the last century.

[136] Sir Robert Yewdall Jennings, "Speech by Sir Robert Yewdall Jennings on the Report of the International Court of Justice," UN Doc A/46/PV.44 (1991), reprinted in "Official Documents" (1992) 86 AJIL 249 at 252.

Clearly reflecting this evolution is the ICJ's rejection in *Cameroon/Nigeria* of the notion of historical consolidation as a basis of title. Thus, the Court closed the door to any impairment of the legal value of title over territory. *Effectivités* never take precedence over valid title absent acquiescence, and this finding undoubtedly constitutes one of the most important by the Court during the period under analysis — power no longer trumps international boundary agreements.

Regarding the ICJ's use of maps in boundary disputes during the first decade of the new millennium, it is not surprising to find that the case law is so rich. Its most salient features are the following. First, maps constituting an expression of the parties' will may be relevant in eliminating indeterminacies in, confirming interpretations of, and correcting errors in related agreements. Second, the conditions that maps have to meet to be deemed context for the purposes of interpreting related treaties under Article 31(2) of the VCLT have been clarified. These conditions are that the map must relate to a specific issue in dispute under an agreement between the parties or pursuant to a clear position taken by one of the parties and accepted by the other. Third, the parties' intentions can be ascertained from maps attached to international agreements and from non-attached maps produced as part of the preparatory work for the treaty. Fourth is the important evidentiary value of maps that do not support a party's position before the ICJ. When produced by said party, they act not as evidence of title but, rather, as important evidence of official positions contradicting the party's own claims before the Court. Fifth, the requirements that a map must meet to possess such value have been identified by the ICJ. The map must be specifically related to the issue in dispute, and, in the event of several maps, they must be consistent in respect of that issue. Sixth, disclaimers in such maps do not prevent the Court from using them as evidence. The Court may interpret the scope of the disclaimer and use the map as evidence regarding issues not covered by the disclaimer. This rich array of pronouncements on the value of maps in resolving boundary disputes, doubtless the result of skillful litigation by the parties to the relevant cases, provides states with important guidance when negotiating boundary agreements or settlements.

Finally, the ICJ exercised some restraint during the first decade of the twentieth-first century regarding declarations of state responsibility stemming from boundary controversies. The Court repeatedly stated that its judgments concerning boundaries were sufficient to address the aggrieved party's reparation claim (see mainly *Cameroon/Nigeria*) and, on this basis, refused to award damages or order assurances of non-repetition (*Cameroon/Nigeria* and *Costa Rica/Nicaragua*). In this author's view, the Court's approach in this regard is right — these remedies should be exceptional in boundary disputes. It must be kept in mind that, although deciding cases according to law, the ICJ must nonetheless do all within its power and the limits of the judicial function to assist the parties in finally resolving their dispute as a result of the judgment. Awarding remedies in state responsibility as a consequence of adjudication of the underlying boundary dispute may make this final resolution more difficult to achieve and preserve. As Judges Bedjaoui, Ranjeva, and Koroma said in relation to the judgment in *Qatar/Bahrain* — words also applicable to other cases:

> [I]n deciding solely in accordance with international law, the Court was nevertheless duty-bound to seek out, from among the possible solutions, that which appeared to be the most pacifying and likely to cause the least dissatisfaction on either side.[137]

In sum, boundary disputes are among the most complex and delicate in international adjudication, and the Court's decisions and reasoning on the topics selected for this article reveal that the Court continues to make valuable contributions to the development of the law in this area for the benefit of the community of states. What is the ICJ's formula for achieving this outcome? Law is the guiding criterion and paramount objective, but reality — past and present — is not ignored by the Court when adjudicating these controversies.

Sommaire

Les différends frontaliers posent des problématiques des plus délicats pour les États. Il n'est donc pas surprenant que les questions frontalières sont parmi les plus récurrentes devant la Cour internationale de Justice (CIJ) et ont donné lieu à une abondante jurisprudence qui traite de domaines traditionnels: le consentement dans les traités de délimitation, le principe de l'*uti possidetis juris,*

137 *Maritime Delimitation and Territorial Questions between Qatar and Bahrain* (*Qatar v Bahrain*), Joint Dissenting Opinion of Judges Bedjaoui, Ranjeva and Koroma, [2001] ICJ Rep 145 at 150.

la notion d'effectivités, et la délimitation maritime. Mais cette jurisprudence aborde également d'autres sujets connexes, moins saillants mais néanmoins d'intérêt pour les États. Cet article discute du traitement de ces derniers sujets par la CIJ dans sa jurisprudence sur les frontières de la première décennie du nouveau millénaire. L'auteur passe en revue les décisions de la CIJ qui traitent des types de territoire que les États ne peuvent s'approprier, de la *terra nullius,* des droits privés, de la succession d'États, des dons unilatéraux, des critères non-pertinents dans l'établissement d'un titre territorial (notamment la notion de consolidation historique), de l'usage des cartes géographiques, et de la responsabilité des États dans le cadre de différends frontaliers.

Summary

Boundary disputes constitute one of the most delicate issues for states, such that it is not surprising that frontier issues are among the most recurrent before the International Court of Justice (ICJ) and have given rise to a rich jurisprudence. This jurisprudence comprises traditional areas: consent in boundary treaties, the principle of *uti possidetis juris,* the notion of *effectivités,* and maritime delimitation. However, it also includes other topics that usually receive less attention, but which are nonetheless important to states and sometimes underlie their significant interest in boundary disputes. This article deals with such topics in order to show how the ICJ has handled them in its boundary jurisprudence of the first decade of the new millennium. The author discusses ICJ decisions addressing types of territory that cannot be appropriated, *terra nullius,* private rights, state succession, unilateral donations as sources of title to territory, irrelevant criteria in establishing title to territory (particularly historical consolidation), the use of maps, and state responsibility in connection with boundary disputes.

The Arctic Environment and International Humanitarian Law

ASHLEY BARNES AND CHRISTOPHER WATERS

Introduction

Given the increasing legal scrutiny of the deployments and actions of armed forces in the West generally, the scant attention given to the potential role of international humanitarian law (IHL), or the law of armed conflict, in the Arctic is curious.[1] The UN Convention on the Law of the Sea (UNCLOS) is rightly viewed by policymakers and defence practitioners as the primary legal regime for the management of Arctic waters.[2] Regional powers (Canada, Russia, Denmark, Norway, and the United States) have agreed to abide by this law in the resolution of territorial disputes in the Arctic.[3] Their recent rhetoric has stressed the need for co-operative approaches in dealing with distinct regional challenges related to security, development, and environmental protection. These themes are reflected in a *Statement on Canada's Arctic Foreign Policy*, which

---

Ashley Barnes, Barrister and Solicitor, formerly a law clerk at the Federal Court. Christopher Waters, Faculty of Law, University of Windsor. The views expressed are solely those of the authors and in no way reflect the opinion of the court. The authors thank Michael Byers and Rob Huebert for their helpful comments on earlier drafts. This article builds on a brief paper by the authors entitled "The Arctic Environment and the Law of Armed Conflict" (2011) 6:4 Canadian Naval Review 16.

1 On the legalization of war — including in terms of international humanitarian law (IHL) — see David Kennedy, *Of War and Law* (Princeton, NJ: Princeton University Press, 2006). Though for a view suggesting that the legalisation paradigm can be misleading, see Christopher Waters, "Beyond Lawfare: Juridical Oversight of Western Militaries" (2009) 46 Alberta Law Review 885.

2 United Nations Convention on the Law of the Sea, 10 December 1982, 1833 UNTS 3, Article 13(1).

3 A formal commitment was made by Arctic nations in the Ilulissat Declaration, 29 May 2008, online: <http://www.oceanlaw.org/downloads/arctic/Ilulissat_Declaration.pdf>.

was released in 2010.[4] While there is a continued focus on asserting national sovereignty, according to this statement, Canada aims to promote "a stable, rules-based region" and work program with its partners in the Arctic Council, a multinational group dedicated to regional concerns.[5] It would, however, be short-sighted not to give adequate consideration to IHL as a relevant legal regime if co-operation is replaced by international armed conflict. As Christopher Penny puts it, referring to antecedents from the Second World War, "[c]onflict in the Arctic isn't a doomsayer's dark fantasy. It is something that has already happened. And it could easily happen again."[6]

Talk of co-operation is in stark contrast to the ongoing expansion of military activities in the Arctic.[7] As the warmer climate makes valuable resources increasingly accessible, nations are eager to protect their economic and security interests. Not surprisingly, they have all taken steps to develop their capabilities for operating in the region. In recent years, Russia has angered its neighbours by reinstating reconnaissance flights over the area and deploying vessels adjacent to a Norwegian offshore oil rig. While top officials have ruled out war, Russia's 2008 policy statement on the Arctic makes clear that it will position itself militarily to defend its interests in the region.[8] Similarly, while Denmark is a proponent of peaceful regional negotiations, it is simultaneously developing naval equipment designed specifically for the Arctic seas.[9] The United States already possesses submarines capable of operating in the region, and its policy statements increasingly emphasize the importance of

4 Canada, *Statement on Canada's Arctic Foreign Policy 2010: Exercising Sovereignty and Promoting Canada's Northern Strategy Abroad*, online: Department of Foreign Affairs and International Trade <http://www.international.gc.ca/polar-polaire/assets/pdfs/CAFP_booklet-PECA_livret-eng.pdf> [*Canada's Arctic Foreign Policy*].

5 *Ibid* at 3, 10.

6 Christopher Penny, "International Humanitarian Law and the Arctic," online: <http://ccil-ccdi.squarespace.com/ccil-conference-papers/2010/> at 2.

7 Rob Huebert called attention to the continuing military expansion in the region. Rob Huebert, *The Newly Emerging Arctic Security Environment* (Calgary: Canadian Defence and Foreign Affairs Institute, 2010).

8 See James Kraska, "From Pariah to Partner: Russian-American Security Cooperation in the Arctic Ocean" (2009) 16 ILSA J Int'l & Comp L 517 at 525-26; Dmitri Trenin and Pavel Baev, *The Arctic: A View from Moscow* (Moscow, Russian Federation: Carnegie Endowment for International Peace, 2010) at 9.

9 Huebert, *supra* note 7 at 9-12.

the Arctic to national security.[10] China's new Arctic vision also presents the prospect of future competition.[11]

With its Northern-oriented defence strategy, Canada forms part of this "co-operation with militarization" trend. Indeed, reinforcing sovereignty remains one of the core pillars of Canadian policy and includes plans to invest in equipment and training that would improve Northern surveillance and response capabilities.[12] The Canadian Forces, in conjunction with other government departments, regularly participate in regional military exercises as part of Operation Nanook. The latest instalment took place in August 2011 and involved responding to an actual, instead of a fictional, air disaster.[13] In addition, a recent poll revealed that Canadians consider the Arctic to be the nation's highest foreign policy priority. Many would like to see existing military resources shifted to defending northern interests, even if it comes at the expense of responding to conflicts abroad.[14] In all likelihood, the Canadian Forces — and their regional counterparts — will focus on supporting law enforcement, search and rescue, and promoting sovereignty in accordance with UNCLOS.[15]

10 *Ibid* at 20-22.

11 Bill Schiller, "China Warming Up to Be an Arctic Player," *Toronto Star* (1 March 2010), online: <http://www.thestar.com/news/world/china/article/773148–china-warming-up-to-be-an-arctic-player>.

12 *Canada's Arctic Foreign Policy, supra* note 4 at 5-7. This policy trend is also evident in the *Canada First Defence Strategy* (May 2008) at 6, online: Department of National Defence <http://www.forces.gc.ca/site/pri/first-premier/June18_0910_CFDS_english_low-res.pdf>: "[C]hanges in the Arctic could also spark an increase in illegal activity, with important implications for Canadian sovereignty and security and a potential requirement for additional military support."

13 See Department of National Defence, Operation Nanook 2011, online: Department of National Defence <http://www.forces.gc.ca/site/feature-vedette/2011/08/nanook11/index-eng.asp>.

14 Jill Maloney, "In the Arctic, Canada Willing to Fight to Keep the True North Free," *Globe and Mail* (25 January 2011), online: <http://www.theglobeandmail.com/news/politics/in-the-arctic-canada-willing-to-fight-to-keep-the-true-north-free/article1881683/>. Interestingly, the poll also revealed that more Canadians were willing to take a strong stance on defending the North than their American counterparts.

15 This role was analyzed specifically for the Canadian Navy in Office of the Judge Advocate General, "The Operational Legal Challenges of Naval Operations in Canada's Arctic Waters," Strategic Legal Papers Series Issue 3, online: Department of National Defence <http://www.forces.gc.ca/jag/publications/oplaw-loiop/slap-plsa-3/index-eng.asp>. Although this article conducted an extensive analysis of security concerns and corresponding operations in Arctic waters, it did not mention any IHL-related issues in the event tensions were to escalate.

Given the mix of resource exploitation and militarization, however, some level of uncertainty is unavoidable. Although the likelihood of outright armed conflict over resources or sovereignty in the Arctic appears remote, Arctic-centred conflict is a possibility, as is the prospect that conflict could spill into the Arctic from a conflict started elsewhere. In this light, the distinct restraints that IHL imposes on military activities in the Arctic context require consideration. Should fighting break out, IHL would become a relevant legal regime. This article therefore explores two aspects of the law of armed conflict that would pose challenges for militaries fighting in the Arctic. First, it discusses the specific prohibition of serious damage to the natural environment. Second, it considers broader IHL principles, notably proportionality and distinction, in relation to regional environmental factors. As we will show, the application of IHL to the unique and precarious Arctic environment would prohibit some military action that might be legal in armed conflict in other geographic regions.

The Prohibition of Serious Damage to the Environment

IHL provides specific protection for the environment from "widespread, long-term, and severe" damage. It also imposes an obligation to have "due regard" for the surrounding environment in the conduct of hostilities. A review of these principles demonstrates their particular relevance to any Arctic military operation.

The Widespread, Long-Term, and Severe Threshold

While all armed conflicts invariably have some impact on the natural environment, IHL specifically prohibits such damage over a certain threshold. This concept was first expressed in the 1976 Convention on the Prohibition of Military or Any Hostile Use of Environmental Modification Techniques (ENMOD), which requires states "not to engage in military or any other hostile use of environmental modification techniques having widespread, long-lasting or severe effects as the means of destruction."[16] Though significant for its influence on the development and interpretation of subsequent legal restrictions, this convention has limited application — it is only relevant

16 Convention on the Prohibition of Military or Any Hostile Use of Environmental Modification Techniques, 10 December 1976, 1108 UNTS 151, Article 1 [ENMOD].

in cases of deliberate, and rarely used, environmental manipulation techniques.[17]

By far the most prominent protection for the environment under IHL is contained in Additional Protocol I to the Geneva Conventions.[18] Article 35(3) prohibits the use of "methods or means of warfare which are intended, or may be expected, to cause widespread, long-term and severe damage to the natural environment."[19] Similarly, Article 55 requires that "[c]are shall be taken in warfare to protect the natural environment against widespread, long-term and severe damage."[20] The main element of these provisions is the repeated reference to damage that is widespread, long term, and severe. Beyond the implication that the harm contemplated must be of a particularly serious nature, Additional Protocol I unfortunately provides limited guidance on the precise meaning of this threshold. For example, it is unclear exactly how much territory has to be impacted to constitute "widespread" damage or how long this damage would have to last before it would be considered "long term." Until an authoritative practical analysis of the provisions is conducted or states provide clarification through further agreement, their meaning must be discerned from discussions during negotiation as well as subsequent practice and commentary.[21] Most legal analysts agree that states intended the threshold to be extremely high since it requires the presence of all three conjunctive elements — widespread, long term, and severe — before coming into play.[22] Generally speaking, the damage caused would have to resemble a shock on "the balance of the ecosystem."[23]

17 Yoram Dinstein, *The Conduct of Hostilities under the Law of International Armed Conflict*, 2nd edition (Cambridge: Cambridge University Press, 2010) at 199.

18 Protocol I Additional to the Geneva Conventions of 12 August 1949, and Relating to the Protection of Victims of International Armed Conflict, 12 December 1977, 1125 UNTS 3, 16 ILM 139 [Additional Protocol I].

19 *Ibid*, Article 35(3).

20 *Ibid*, Article 55.

21 Vienna Convention on the Law of Treaties, 23 May 1969, 1155 UNTS 331, Articles 31-32.

22 See, for example, Michael Bothe, Karl Josef Partsch, and Waldemar A Solf, *New Rules for Victims of Armed Conflict: Commentary on the Two Protocols Additional to the Geneva Conventions of 1949* (Leiden: Martinus Nijhoff Publishers, 1982) at 346.

23 This terminology, found in the preparatory work to Additional Protocol I, *supra* note 18, was highlighted in Karen Hulme, *War Torn Environment: Interpreting the Legal Threshold* (Leiden: Martinus Nijhoff Publishers, 2004) at 20.

Apart from these initial observations, however, there is continuing debate as to the appropriate approach to interpretation. In drafting the provisions, states indicated that "long term" would refer to decades, but they did not specify anything relating to other aspects of the threshold.[24] While similar terminology was the subject of formal "understandings" during the negotiation of ENMOD, states appear to have rejected their direct application to the interpretation of Additional Protocol I.[25] This is in part because ENMOD is more lenient in not requiring all three elements to be present at the same time, as evidenced in the use of the disjunctive widespread, long-lasting, *or* severe.[26] Nevertheless, ENMOD remains an important starting point in analyzing the Additional Protocol I provisions. Karen Hulme suggests that the deliberate failure of states to adopt the ENMOD standard necessarily implies that they were seeking a higher threshold for Additional Protocol I.[27] The "decades-long" interpretation that was proposed for "long term" in Additional Protocol I is straightforward. To constitute "widespread," Hulme argues the damage would have to exceed the several hundred square kilometres standard under ENMOD.[28] Moreover, only a significant disruption to environment and human life would qualify as "severe."[29] Although Hulme's approach is persuasive, some analysts are not convinced that Additional Protocol I should be interpreted so restrictively. For instance, Julian Wyatt argues that since no further interpretation has been provided by states, the existing ENMOD standard has been incorporated into the Additional Protocol I threshold by default.[30] As these differing approaches suggest, there has yet to be a definitive interpretation of the Additional Protocol I

[24] International Committee of the Red Cross (ICRC), *Commentary on the Additional Protocols of 8 June 1977 to the Geneva Conventions of 12 August 1949* (Dordrecht: Martinus Nijhoff, 1987) at para 1452, online: <http://www.icrc.org/ihl.nsf/COM/470-750044?OpenDocument>.

[25] See "Understandings Regarding the Convention [ENMOD]," in *Report of the Conference of the Committee on Disarmament*, UNGAOR, 31st Sess, Supp No 27, vol 1, UN Doc A/31/27 (1976) at 91-92 [ENMOD Understandings]; Bothe, Partsch, and Solf, *supra* note 22 at 348.

[26] ENMOD, *supra* note 16 [emphasis added].

[27] Hulme, *supra* note 23.

[28] ENMOD Understandings, *supra* note 25 at 91.

[29] Hulme, *supra* note 23 at 89-90.

[30] Julian Wyatt, "Law-Making at the Intersection of International, Environmental, Humanitarian and Criminal Law" (2010) 59 IRRC 593 at 624.

threshold. Accordingly, it is possible to justify employing either the ENMOD standard or a more restrictive threshold.

It could also be argued that quantifying the threshold, in terms of the number of square kilometres affected by the damage, the number of years it persists, or the number of individuals affected is not as important as recognizing the purpose of the provision as a whole. The threshold is clearly directed at the most serious instances of environmental damage in wartime that would be recognizable when the integrity of some aspect of the environment is threatened or there is general condemnation from the international community. To the extent that it impacts on the application of the "widespread, long-term, and severe" threshold, slightly different wording in Article 55 of Additional Protocol I must also be taken into consideration. Unlike the Article 35(3) provision, Article 55 focuses attention on damage that would "prejudice the health or survival of the population."[31] Not only is environmental harm caused by conflict an issue, but so too is its potential impact on the ability of human beings to inhabit that environment or make use of it in a particular way. This human-centred approach implies that, for the prohibition to become operative, there must be at least a link to, or identifiable impact on, a nearby human population. Although the most serious damage to the environment might be measured in relation to its direct impact on human life, this addition to Article 55 need not be interpreted too strictly. The wording can be viewed as merely recognizing the interrelationship between human beings and their environment. Any damage to the world's ecosystems could be seen as affecting the quality of human life as a whole.

Furthermore, Article 55 provides that "care" be taken to "protect" the natural environment from serious damage.[32] An often neglected distinction between the Additional Protocol I provisions, this terminology has recently received greater consideration. It may ultimately place an additional onus on militaries during wartime to take reasonable steps to keep the environment safe from damage.[33] This requirement, in turn, may imply that proactive measures are required to prevent environmental damage where it is more likely to occur. As a consequence, slight differences in Article 55 may impose further requirements on militaries to choose methods of

31 Additional Protocol I, *supra* note 16, Article 55(1).

32 *Ibid.*

33 Karen Hulme, "Taking Care to Protect the Environment against Damage: A Meaningless Obligation?" (2010) 92 IRRC 879 at 680-81.

warfare that respect environmental conditions and avoid serious consequences.

The customary law status of the "widespread, long-term, and severe" threshold should also be recognized. Initially, there was some debate among states over the basis for the Additional Protocol I provisions, as they represented novel formulations for the explicit protection of the environment under IHL. The United States and the United Kingdom, for example, were concerned about the possibility of a broad application that might result in outright prohibition of many military activities, such as the use of nuclear weapons.[34] It is, however, now appropriate to regard the Additional Protocol I provisions as having attained status as customary international law. This is partly evidenced by the inclusion of a prohibition on "widespread, long-term, and severe" damage to the environment in Rule 45 of the International Committee of the Red Cross' (ICRC) authoritative study on the customary principles of IHL.[35] It is also apparent in the threshold's wide dissemination. It should come as no surprise then that this standard is reflected in the Canadian Forces' manual on the law of armed conflict.[36] Perhaps most important was the inclusion of intentionally causing "widespread, long-term, and severe damage" to the natural environment in the definition of war crimes under the Rome Statute of the International Criminal Court in 1998.[37] Not only is serious damage to the environment prohibited by treaty and customary rules governing the conduct of warfare, but it can also attract international criminal sanction.

In most circumstances, however, the "widespread, long-term, and severe" threshold continues to provide sufficient leeway for military operations. While these restrictions come into play in extreme circumstances, incidental environmental effects are able to escape the application of the Additional Protocol I threshold and related

[34] See Michael N. Schmitt, "Green War: An Assessment of the Environmental Law of International Armed Conflict" (1997) 22 Yale J Int'l L 1 at 74-75.

[35] Jean-Marie Henckaerts and Louise Doswald-Beck, *Customary International Humanitarian Law*, volume 1 (Cambridge: Cambridge University Press, 2005), Rule 45. However, the study notes that the United States and United Kingdom continue to object to its application to the use of nuclear weapons specifically.

[36] Office of the Judge Advocate General, *Law of Armed Conflict at the Operational and Tactical Levels* (Ottawa: Department of National Defence, 2001) at 53.

[37] See Rome Statute of the International Criminal Court, 17 July 1998, 2187 UNTS 3, Article 8(2)(b)(iv).

customary principles. These exceptions make a distinction between military activities that simply lead to unintended environmental consequences and those that would, by their very nature or as a function of the location of the attack, be expected to have a devastating impact. From an environmental perspective, it is not surprising that this approach is heavily criticized. Many commentators claim that the environment remains vulnerable in wartime as the threshold is difficult to surpass and, in more serious cases, is challenging to apply without further precision.[38] Admittedly, to provide strong protection for the environment in most situations, the law would have to be more restrictive. As will be seen, however, these concerns are less significant in an Arctic environment that is highly susceptible to "widespread, long-term, and severe" environmental damage. In that context, IHL serves to constrain military activities significantly, particularly when reinforced by the principle of "due regard" for the natural environment.

THE NEED FOR "DUE REGARD"

Explicit protection for the environment under IHL is not exclusive to the "widespread, long-term, and severe" threshold. The 1994 *San Remo Manual on International Law Applicable to Armed Conflict at Sea,* which is broadly regarded as authoritative, provides that "[m]ethods and means of warfare should be employed with due regard for the natural environment taking into account the relevant rules of international law."[39] This standard includes a prohibition on "[d]amage to or destruction of the natural environment not justified by military necessity and carried out wantonly."[40] Formulated differently than

38 For arguments that this area of law is insufficiently restrictive, see Adam Roberts, "The Law of War and Environmental Damage," in Jay Austin and Carl E Bruch, *The Environmental Consequences of War: Legal, Economic, and Scientific Perspectives* (Cambridge: Cambridge University Press, 2000) 47.

39 Louise Doswald-Beck, ed, *San Remo Manual on International Law Applicable to Armed Conflicts at Sea,* International Institute of Humanitarian Law (Cambridge: Cambridge University Press, 1995), Article 44 [*San Remo Manual*]. The text of the manual is also available online: International Committee of the Red Cross <http://www.icrc.org/eng/resources/documents/misc/57jmst.htm>. The British defence manual describes the *San Remo Manual* as "a valuable reference work." UK Ministry of Defence, *Manual of the Law of Armed Conflict* (Oxford: Oxford University Press, 2004) at para 13.2. More generally, the British defence manual's chapter on maritime warfare (chapter 13) broadly relies on the *San Remo Manual* as authoritative on customary international law principles.

40 *San Remo Manual, supra* note 39, Article 44.

Additional Protocol I, it focuses on recklessly causing any environmental damage in naval warfare. The need for "due regard" is understood as requiring a balancing of different interests.[41] The assessment of the potential for environmental damage is therefore crucial in conducting military operations.

In some respects, the obligation to have "due regard" appears less restrictive than the Additional Protocol I threshold. This is because it includes a justification for causing environmental destruction. It only requires that the environment be taken into consideration. As long as the damage caused has a legitimate and overriding military purpose, it may still be legally acceptable. Viewed from a different perspective, however, it is possible to conceive of situations where the balancing required under the "due regard" concept could weigh in favour of environmental preservation such that military action would not be justified. This is particularly the case where there is an awareness of heightened environmental risks or sensitivities. More importantly, the San Remo manual does not contain an express threshold requirement as does Additional Protocol I. Not doing so opens up the possibility that lesser damage — damage that falls short of the "widespread, long-term, and severe" threshold — caused by recklessness or without "due regard" for the environment could still be restricted.[42]

Interestingly, the notion of "due regard" is also reflected in the ICRC's study but without any specific reference to military justification. Rule 44 seems to propose a more robust obligation than its San Remo counterpart when it states:

> Methods and means of warfare must be employed with due regard to the protection and preservation of the natural environment. In the conduct of military operations, all feasible precautions must be taken to avoid, and in any event to minimise, incidental damage to the environment. Lack of scientific certainty as to the effects on the environment of certain military operations does not absolve a party to the conflict from taking such precautions.[43]

According to this particular formulation, the need for "due regard" relates to taking measures to limit the extent of any damage to the environment. It goes as far as to explicitly recognize the possibility

[41] *Ibid* at 84.

[42] This is alluded to in Hulme, *supra* note 33 at 686.

[43] *San Remo Manual, supra* note 39, Rule 44.

of incidental damage. Perhaps more surprising is that it seeks to eliminate any potential rationalization for environmental damage rooted in scientific uncertainty. Where military commanders are uncertain of the exact environmental consequences, they are still expected to take a precautionary approach. Some commentators remain skeptical of the inclusion in the ICRC's study of this particular "due regard" formulation as it may not be reflective of customary international law.[44] However, since it draws on a range of basic IHL principles and provides additional detail on the "due regard" concept, it cannot be ignored.

Irrespective of the exact wording of this "due regard" concept, it addresses wanton environmental destruction. In this respect, the concept reflects a goal similar to that of Additional Protocol I. This obligation poses significant challenges for militaries operating in the Arctic, as the next subsection shows.

Potential Damage to the Arctic Environment

However the foregoing legal principles are formally worded, one cannot ignore the potential for environmental damage in the Arctic in general, let alone during armed conflict. This environment is characterized by extreme conditions. In the coldest regions, air temperatures only reach as high as 4 degrees Celcius in July and fall below minus 60 degrees Celcius in winter. These temperatures slow chemical reactions and biological processes.[45] They lead to low soil temperatures and permafrost. The growing season for plants is extremely short — as little as three to four months in the Low Arctic and around two and a half months in the High Arctic.[46] These low temperatures also result in extensive ice cover on freshwater and marine habitats. This amount of ice promotes a large variety of physiological and behavioural adaptations in Arctic biota. Low light levels are common as the region receives only one-third to one-half of the annual solar radiation received in temperate climates.[47] Low absolute productivity and recent glaciations result in low species

44 George H Aldrich, "Customary International Humanitarian Law: An Interpretation on Behalf of the International Committee of the Red Cross" (2005) 76 BYIL 515.

45 Arctic Monitoring and Assessment Programme (AMAP), *AMAP Assessment Report: Pollution Issues* (Oslo: Arctic Monitoring and Assessment Programme, 1998) at 117, online: <http://amap.no/>.

46 *Ibid.*

47 *Ibid* at 118.

diversity and often simple food chains. The Arctic Ocean is one of the most complex regions in the world's oceans and is unique among marine ecosystems for the presence of ice cover, a high proportion of continental shelves, and the influence of fresh water.[48] This situation is further complicated by the wide range of variations in climate and physical geography throughout the region's terrestrial, freshwater, and marine environments.[49]

Numerous studies have shown that this exceptional environment is highly sensitive to contamination and other disruptions.[50] Persistent organic pollutants (POPs), for example, that find their way to the Arctic from other parts of the world disappear considerably more slowly than in southern areas because of colder temperatures.[51] Since these pollutants bio-accumulate and bio-magnify in Arctic conditions, they pose a serious threat to polar organisms.[52] The Arctic terrestrial environment is also susceptible to physical destruction, and the impact of human activity can be seen hundreds of years after the fact.[53] As one group of scientists has asserted,

> [t]he Arctic basin plays a unique role in global environmental processes, giving a number of useful feedbacks for the Earth's climatic system. Low temperatures, intensity of atmospheric circulation and the availability of large ice-covered water systems are notable for high latitudes, quite unlike other areas of the globe (apart from Antarctica). The intensive industrial development of the northern hemisphere has led to significant environmental change in these regions ... Further adverse impacts on Arctic ecosystems may well lead to an increase in regional or even global scale negative consequences ... It is known that the ecosystems of the Arctic seas are

48 *Ibid* at 128.

49 For discussion of the variability of the environment across the region, see *ibid* at 9-23.

50 A detailed analysis of the unique pollution dynamics in the Arctic is provided by Eiliv Steinnes, "Pathways and Effects of Contaminants in the Arctic," in Sarah J Woodin and Mick Marquiss, eds, *Ecology of Arctic Environments*, British Ecological Society (Oxford: Blackwell Science, 1997) 209.

51 *Canadian Arctic Contaminants Assessment Report II*, volume I (Ottawa: Indian and Northern Affairs Canada, 2003) at 16; Arctic Monitoring and Assessment Programme, *AMAP Assessment 2009: Persistent Organic Pollutants* (Oslo: Arctic Monitoring and Assessment Programme, 2009), online: <http://amap.no/>.

52 See, eg, BM Jenssen, "Effects of Environment Changes and Pollution on Arctic and Antarctic Organisms,"Part A: Molecular and Integrative Physiology (2010) 157 Comparative Biochemistry and Physiology S40-S41.

53 AMAP, *supra* note 45 at 118.

considerably more vulnerable than the ecosystems of other seas. The processes that clean the Arctic Ocean are slower. Marine organisms of the Arctic ecosystem live in the polar climate, where the vegetation period is seriously restricted. Some feedback mechanisms operate with significant time delays and the capacity to neutralize the effects of human activity appears to be weak. In addition to these reasons the Arctic ecosystem has specific boundary conditions connected with the sea ice boundary that reduces its ability to recover.[54]

These assertions are supported by assessments of the impact of industrial development associated with the oil and gas sector in the Arctic. In a report from the US National Research Council, it was noted that there could be effects on hydrologic processes, vegetation, and animal populations up to several kilometres from the physical footprint of a structure. The Arctic tundra has proven to be easily impacted by vehicle travel.[55] The report concludes by proposing measures needed to mitigate the impact of this development on the surrounding environment. The potential for negative effects is compounded by the strain placed on the Arctic environment by global climate change.[56]

These assessments of the environmental impact of contaminants and increased development in the region provide insight into the "widespread, long-term, and severe" damage that would be likely to occur as a result of any military action. Militaries fighting on land or at sea would have to take into account unique regional considerations. Any increased military activity, even in peacetime, could have a direct impact on the environment. For example, the use of military vehicles could add to the erosion of the Arctic tundra. It is not surprising that in the United States there have already been concerns expressed about the environmental consequences of the peacetime military development of radar stations, air traffic control, and warning systems, and support for ground forces and naval patrols using

54 K Ya Kondratyev, VF Krapivin, and GW Phillips, "Arctic Basin Pollution Dynamics," in Leonid P Bobylev, Kirill Ya Kondratyev, and Ola M Johannessen, eds, *Arctic Environment Variability in the Context of Global Change* (Chichester, UK: Praxis Publishing, 2003) 309 at 309-10.

55 National Research Council, *Cumulative Environmental Effects of Oil and Gas Activities on Alaska's North Slope* (Washington, DC: National Academies Press, 2001) at 5.

56 See, eg, John E Walsh, "Climate of the Arctic Marine Environment" (2008) 18:2 Ecological Applications S3; F Stuart Chapin III et al, "Responses of Arctic Tundra to Experimental and Observed Changes in Climate" (1995) 76:3 Ecology 694.

nuclear submarines.[57] Increased naval traffic in the area could adversely affect marine ecosystems. Although on a lower scale, similar risks have been identified in connection with an increase in commercial shipping in newly accessible ice-free Arctic straits.[58]

The risks posed by the use of any munitions would be even more troubling. Explosions could leave chemicals and oil seeping into the ocean floor or allow them to be carried away by currents. Since these chemicals would persist for longer periods than in many other environments, they would pose an ongoing danger to Arctic aquatic life, including marine mammals. As we have also seen, it would be more difficult for the region's environment to regenerate.

Another likely cause of damage that might meet the "widespread, long-term, and severe" threshold would be oil spills. Sunken ships could result in oil seepage as could attacks on oil infrastructure aimed at accessing untapped reserves in the region. Research on the impact of previous oil spills in the region sheds light on these possible consequences. Slower growth rates and shorter growing seasons make the rate of biological recovery from oil damage much slower than in other regions. As a consequence, the effects of oil pollution may be more severe and persistent in the Arctic environment than elsewhere.[59] In particular, oil damage tends to be more pronounced in near-shore ecosystems, including soft-sediment environments in sheltered bays where higher concentrations of oil can be found more than eight years following a spill.[60] Oil released under ice cover can cause melting. Droplets that collect under ice can form a slick and spread outwards, significantly increasing the area affected by the spill.[61] It should also be noted that as much as 60 percent of the ecological impact of oil spills in the Arctic is

57 Norman A Chance and Elena N Andreeva, "Sustainability, Equity and Natural Resources in Northwest Siberia and Arctic Alaska" (1995) 23:2 Ecology 217 at 229.

58 Discussions have centred around improving overall capabilities of ships to operate in Arctic waters. See United States Arctic Research Commission (USARC), *The Arctic Ocean and Climate Change: A Scenario for the US Navy* (Arlington, VA: USARC, 2002) at 15, online: <http://www.arctic.gov/publications/arctic_and_climate_change.pdf>.

59 AMAP, *supra* note 45 at 661.

60 Thomas A Dean and Stephen C Jewett, "Habitat-Specific Recovery of Shallow Subtidal Communities Following the Exxon Valdez Oil Spill" (2001) 11:5 Ecological Applications 1456.

61 AMAP, *supra* note 45 at 671-72.

transmitted indirectly.[62] This impact relates to the long-term effects on the habitat and the survival of different species.

By far the most significant issue with respect to oil contamination would be the complications associated with clean-up efforts in remote locations. The territory is so vast that it would lengthen the time needed to respond to a spill, allowing the oil to spread further before it could be cleaned up. There would also be fewer locations available from which to launch recovery missions.[63] Up to 30 percent of oil can be recovered in ideal conditions, but many scientists suspect that the figure would be much lower in the Arctic.[64] Buried oil could persist for decades as ice could envelop and transport it considerable distances. Some oil would also sink and contaminate the seafloor, making it impossible to remedy.[65] In addition, there is a great deal of concern that current clean-up techniques have not been designed or tested to operate effectively in the Arctic environment. This situation has prompted increased research into regional responses to oilspills.[66] During Operation Nanook in 2010, the Canadian Forces participated in a simulated emergency response to a petrochemical leak.[67] This operation demonstrated that states are already aware of the environmental risks posed by the presence of oil infrastructure in the Arctic. These risks would only be heightened in the context of an armed conflict.

There are also states capable of deploying nuclear submarines to the region. Engaging in warfare with submarines of this nature could lead to radioactive fallout in the Arctic seas. Due to extreme temperatures and seasonal fluctuations, the effects of radionuclides on the environment and their transfer to Arctic organisms are highly complex processes that have only recently received substantial

62 RT Paine et al, "Trouble on Oiled Waters: Lessons from the Exxon Valdez Oil Spill" (1996) 27 Ann Rev Ecology & Systematics 197 at 227.

63 Michael Torrice, "Science Lags on Saving the Arctic from Oil Spills" (2009) 325 Science 1335.

64 *Ibid.*

65 Jeffrey Short and Susan Murray, "A Frozen Hell" (2011) 472 Nature 162 at 162-63.

66 USARC, *Advancing Oil Spill Response in Ice-Covered Waters* (Arlington, VA: USARC, 2004), online: <http://www.arctic.gov/publications/oil_in_ice.html>.

67 Department of National Defence, "Operation Nanook Reaches Successful Conclusion," News Release (30 August 2010), online: Government of Canada <http://www.forces.gc.ca/site/news-nouvelles/news-nouvelles-eng.asp?cat=00&id=3521>.

scientific consideration.[68] The environmental effects of such fallout would be significant in any part of the world, but their consequences in the Arctic would be even more difficult to predict.

States must refrain from using methods of warfare that are intended, or may be expected, to cause damage beyond a certain threshold in order to comply with the standards of Additional Protocol I. While a commander's intentions would have to be addressed in each specific instance, an individual cannot be wilfully blind to well-recognized environmental risks. States are aware of the potential risks — this is evident in their efforts to address Arctic-specific environmental issues outside of armed conflict. The Arctic Council engages in significant environmental assessment and research programs, which takes place under the auspices of the Arctic Monitoring and Assessment Programme (AMAP).[69] A prime example of the Arctic Council's work is the preparation of a comprehensive study on the nature of the environment and the impact of climate change in the Arctic.[70] Also relevant is the Working Group on Protection for the Arctic Marine Environment (PAME), which conducts research and develops strategies for the protection of Arctic species.[71] In addition to these scientific research programs is recognition of environmental dangers at the policy level. Among Canadian priorities in the Arctic are the promotion of ecosystem-based management and enhancing efforts on these pressing environmental issues.[72]

In analyzing the protection of the environment under IHL, some military commentators have raised concerns that an obligation to minimize damage could lead to uncertainty and thereby unnecessarily constrain military activity.[73] In the Arctic context, however,

68 AMAP, *AMAP Assessment 2009: Radioactivity in the Arctic* (Oslo: AMAP, 2009), online: <http://amap.no/>.

69 See Arctic Council, "Arctic Monitoring and Assessment Programme (AMAP)," online: Arctic Council <http://www.arctic-council.org/index.php/en/amap>.

70 Arctic Climate Impact Assessment (ACIA), *Arctic Climate Impact Assessment* (Cambridge: Cambridge University Press, 2005), online: <http://www.acia.uaf.edu/>.

71 See Arctic Council, "PAME: Protection of the Arctic Marine Environment," online: Arctic Council <http://www.arctic-council.org/index.php/en/pame>.

72 *Canada's Arctic Foreign Policy*, *supra* note 4 at 5.

73 For example, it has been suggested that "[a]n absolute ban on environmental damage caused by military operations is inconceivable. War by definition is a 'no holds barred affair.' Thus, the real issue is how best to minimize the environmental impact of military operations without constraining the military commander with

there should be less uncertainty or difficulty applying the law in the course of hostilities than in a less sensitive environment. As demonstrated, many states have recognized the high degree of vulnerability in the physical environment and in the organisms in this region. Although the exact consequences of a particular attack might not be known with scientific certainty, there is sufficient global knowledge of environmental susceptibilities in the region to require the exercise of caution. Disruptions to the Arctic environment spread across more territory, tend to persist longer, and have more devastating impacts on the region, which all take longer to recover from than in other places in the world. Applying the "widespread, long-term, and severe" threshold, it is conceivable that damage would last for decades, spread over more than several hundred square kilometres, and cause significant disruption to the environment and human life.

Similarly, failing to avoid environmental damage where it can easily occur in the Arctic would be problematic, since Additional Protocol I and the San Remo manual stipulate obligations to exercise "care" or have "due regard." The fragile nature of the Arctic environment itself and the greater potential for damage in this area should encourage states to refrain from certain wartime activities on the basis of these obligations. How could a state ignore that, given the fragility of Arctic waters and highly complex ecosystems, almost any military action could be considered wanton and in conflict with the need to exercise "due regard"?

Furthermore, there are potential restrictions relating to the location of military activities. Specific to naval operations under the San Remo manual is a provision encouraging parties to agree not to engage in hostile actions in marine areas containing rare or fragile ecosystems or the habitat of endangered species or other forms of marine life.[74] This encouragement would undoubtedly apply to the unique maritime environment of the Arctic where efforts are already underway to ensure its protection and sustainability in the face of

---

policies that have little chance of serious consideration in wartime. But most importantly, we must not create uncertainty or risk aversion in the minds of our commanders regarding environmental considerations that could be exploited by their adversaries." See William H Wright, "Naval Warfare and the Environment," in Richard Grunawalt, John E King, and Ronald S McClain, eds, *Protection of the Environment during Armed Conflict and Other Military Operations* (Newport, RI: US Naval War College, 1996) 35 at 35.

74 *San Remo Manual, supra* note 39, Article 11.

increased development.[75] The provision demonstrates the desire of states to preserve the most sensitive areas of the natural environment, even in carrying out military actions. It also reinforces the proposition that precarious regions, such as the Arctic, enjoy a form of specially protected status. The provision is nonetheless fairly deferential to states and merely encourages them to agree to protect these areas rather than establishing an outright prohibition.

The connection made under Article 55 between the protection of the natural environment during warfare and the human population also remains relevant. One might be tempted to consider remote areas, such as the Arctic, as being more preferable locations for armed conflict precisely because they are more sparsely populated. However, this thinking does not reflect the increased awareness of, and concern associated with, the destruction and wide-ranging, long-term effects caused by modern armed conflicts. Indeed, the IHL environmental provisions are emblematic of developing legal constraints on warfare directed at adverse consequences beyond immediate threats to the civilian population. No matter where it occurs, the dangers of armed conflict cannot be treated lightly, but this concern is particularly warranted in vulnerable regions. Accordingly, the restrictions placed by IHL on methods of warfare in the Arctic are in no way undermined where military actions occur in areas completely isolated from human settlement. For example, Inuit peoples who inhabit the Arctic may be affected, even though they may not be directly adjacent to a particular attack or adverse

[75] For a discussion of the need to preserve the distinct Arctic marine ecosystem in the face of ongoing challenges, see, eg, Arctic Council, *Arctic Marine Strategic Plan* (24 November 2004) at 5-7, online: <http://www.pame.is/images/stories/AMSP_files/AMSP-Nov-2004.pdf>. At the same time, it should be recognized that the Arctic is not the pristine environment portrayed in the popular imagination. The Arctic is not immune from much of the pollution and resource degradation experienced in other parts of the world. As David Carron has noted, there are various images regarding the current and future state of the Arctic. It is at once an impassable and remote area, a ring of water where nations focus on bilateral relations, or a semi-enclosed area with increasing activity and governance challenges (as well as what might be considered symbolic militarization). See David D Caron, "Politics, Law and Three Images of the Arctic," in *Proceedings of the 102nd Annual Meeting of the American Society of International Law*, Washington, 2008 (Washington: ASIL, 2008) 157 at 158. Considering any of these images independently does not truly address the extent to which the political and legal landscape is changing. The first image of the Arctic as an impassable area will never be eliminated, but critically evaluating all other images will be necessary to understanding the role of law in the region.

environmental consequence. There is scientific evidence that Northern settlements are particularly susceptible to environmental intrusions. In a comprehensive report, the Canadian Department of Indian and Northern Affairs notes that contaminants enter the food web and bio-accumulate in the Arctic. Since a larger proportion of Northerners rely on traditional food sources than their southern counterparts, they are exposed to a higher degree of contaminants.[76] Similarly, any pollution caused by military activity could have an adverse impact on human health in the region. As a prime example, contamination of fishing grounds would have a significant impact.

It is also worth considering the broader integration of Inuit livelihoods, traditions, and culture within their surrounding environment. As the chair of the Inuit Circumpolar Conference noted in 2004, the "Inuit generally look holistically on issues" and "[c]ulture, economy and environment are all woven into our tapestry."[77] She went on to suggest that although the Inuit are small in number, they "use and occupy huge areas of land."[78] Recognizing the interconnectedness of the Inuit and their environment, she remarked that "people have lost the understanding that their own human activity can have severe negative impacts on their neighbours," and it is these "negative impacts that challenge our efforts to preserve in our homeland, our cultural heritage."[79] Potential military operations in the Arctic could affect the balance between Inuit culture and the environment. Given the high level of interaction between the two, environmental damage is likely to have a direct impact on the lives of the Inuit population.

It should finally be noted that in the separate but related legal regime of international human rights law, states have also agreed to restrictions on military activities in the UN Declaration on the Rights of Indigenous Peoples.[80] Although originally opposed to

76 *Canadian Arctic Contaminants Assessment Report II, supra* note 51 at 16.

77 Sheila Watt-Cloutier, "Bringing Inuit and Arctic Perspectives to the Global Stage: Lessons and Opportunities," in Robert O van Everdingen, ed, *Proceedings of the Fourteenth Inuit Studies Conference, Calgary, 2004* (Calgary: Arctic Institute of North America, 2004) 301 at 302, online: <http://pubs.aina.ucalgary.ca/aina/14thiscproceedings.pdf>.

78 *Ibid.*

79 *Ibid.*

80 United Nations Declaration on the Rights of Indigenous Peoples, GA Res 61/295, UNGAOR, 61st Sess, Supp No 53, UN Doc A/RES/61/295 (2007) [UNDRIP].

aspects of the declaration, Canada eventually endorsed this "soft law" instrument in November 2010.[81] The declaration does not permit military activities on lands of indigenous peoples without a public interest justification or prior agreement. Before using their lands for military activities, there is a requirement that states consult with indigenous peoples.[82] This obligation reinforces IHL limitations on environmental destruction as it relates to indigenous Arctic inhabitants. Although it is unclear to what extent these provisions would apply in times of armed conflict (as Canada has implied in public statements), they suggest still further restrictions on a state's potential military activities in the Arctic.[83]

Broader IHL Principles and Regional Environmental Factors

In addition to the specific tests for environmental harm that are contained in Additional Protocol I and the San Remo manual, broader principles of IHL also have a bearing on warfare in the Arctic context.

PROPORTIONALITY

IHL establishes requirements for the selection of military targets. Principal among them is the requirement that the incidental effects of attacks be proportionate to their overall military objectives. In assessing proportionality, various factors must be taken into consideration with a focus on harm caused to the civilian population. While it does not receive the attention it should in practice, the environment remains a relevant aspect of target selection. In the *Legality of the Threat or Use of Nuclear Weapons*, the International Court of Justice affirmed that "[s]tates must take environmental considerations into account when assessing what is necessary and proportionate in the pursuit of legitimate military objectives."[84] This advisory opinion demonstrates that protection of the environment is part

[81] "Canada Endorses Indigenous Rights Declaration," *CBC News* (12 November 2010), online: CBC News <http://www.cbc.ca/news/canada/story/2010/11/12/indigenous-declaration.html>.

[82] UNDRIP, *supra* note 80, Article 30.

[83] Aboriginal Affairs and Northern Development Canada, *Canada's Statement of Support on the United Nations Declaration on the Rights of Indigenous Peoples* (12 November 2010), online: <http://www.ainc-inac.gc.ca/ap/ia/dcl/stmt-eng.asp>.

[84] *Legality of the Threat or Use of Nuclear Weapons*, Advisory Opinion, [1996] ICJ Rep 226 at 242.

of the broader IHL framework and not confined solely to express provisions with extremely high thresholds. Thus, environmental factors assume a great deal of significance in the assessment of military targets in the Arctic. The exceptional characteristics of this region necessarily alter the proportionality calculation that takes place in conflicts in most other regions.

Proportionality is intimately connected to the concept of military necessity. As it is often articulated, militaries must refrain from an attack where harm to the civilian population, and indirectly the environment, would be excessive in relation to the anticipated military advantage.[85] It is much easier to articulate this concept than it is to apply. What constitutes a "military advantage" inevitably requires some form of value judgment, and harm may be difficult to gauge.[86] Some commentators argue that military advantage can be interpreted too broadly so as to provide justification for almost any harm.[87] However, this does not necessarily mean that military objectives cannot be selected in a way that minimizes collateral damage and loss of life while still targeting the most highly valued elements of an adversary's military potential.[88] An assessment of proportionality must distinguish disproportionate harm from the collateral damage that is permissible in all armed conflicts.[89]

Making these determinations already poses challenges with respect to civilians and civilian objects, but it becomes more complex with the addition of environmental factors. This is particularly so given that assessing the likely impact of an attack on the environment requires at least rudimentary scientific awareness. Significantly,

85 Additional Protocol I, *supra* note 18, Article 57.

86 Schmitt, *supra* note 34 at 56.

87 See Schmitt, *supra* note 34 at 54. For a critical discussion of the predominance of military necessity in IHL, see generally Chris Jochnick and Roger Normand, "The Legitimation of Violence: A Critical History of the Laws of War" (1994) 35 Harv Int'l LJ 49.

88 Understanding concepts such as "military objectives" or necessity is discussed in detail by Jefferson D Reynolds, "Collateral Damage on the Twenty-First Century Battlefield: Enemy Exploitation of the Law of Armed Conflict, and the Struggle for a Moral High Ground" (2005) 56 AFL Rev 1 at 82-87. It is also worth noting that military necessity does not trump specific IHL prohibitions, including Article 35(3) of Additional Protocol I. As the British Defence Manual states: "Necessity cannot be used to justify action prohibited by law." See British Ministry of Defence, *supra* note 39 at para 2.3.

89 Michael Bothe et al, "International Law Protecting the Environment during Armed Conflict: Gaps and Opportunities" (2010) 92 IRRC 569 at 577-78.

decision making may take place in the heat of battle without sufficient time to assess accurately what will occur. In many cases, the consequences of an attack on the environment will only become apparent in hindsight.[90]

While there are challenges associated with accounting for environmental factors in the proportionality calculation, they are not insurmountable. Despite the potential for different interpretations, proportionality serves as a practical guideline in all military targeting. There is no reason to believe that adequate consideration cannot also be given to the environment. While there are situations where environmental damage might be appropriately termed collateral damage, it should not automatically be dismissed in this manner. IHL makes clear that consideration of the potential for environmental damage is essential in the initial assessment of the proportionality of a proposed attack. And it is also worthy to note that there is increased awareness, on the part of soldiers and commanders, of the long-term effects of military operations and the need for environmental stewardship and pollution prevention, or what has been termed an "ethos of responsibility."[91] This recognition suggests that environmental considerations are already integrated into military planning and target assessment.

Applying the proportionality principle in the Arctic leads to various complications in assessing targets. Since the likelihood of adverse environmental effects of most attacks is considerably higher than in other environments, the possibility of such attacks would weigh heavily against military advantage on the proportionality fulcrum. Practically speaking, scientific knowledge regarding the exact consequences of these attacks is less important than a broad-based awareness of the precarious nature of the Arctic environment. This awareness should be sufficient to restrict military operations. For example, attacking an oil installation would pose serious risks to an already fragile environment. While disrupting oil supplies may be of military significance, it is not likely to outweigh the harm that could be caused indirectly to the civilian population by way of environmental impact. By contrast, let us take the example of the potential environment effects of the destruction of an average size,

90 Mark JT Caggiano, "The Legitimacy of Environmental Destruction in Modern Warfare: Customary Substance over Conventional Form" (1993) 20 BC Envt'l Aff L Rev 479 at 497.

91 See, eg, William M Arkin, "The Environmental Threat of Military Operations," in Grunawalt, King, and McClain, *supra* note 73, 116 at 131.

non-nuclear vessel. Some adverse environmental consequences of pollutants entering the sea may not represent "widespread" damage within the meaning of Additional Protocol I. Nevertheless, there is no reason why the adverse effects of the attack could not still be considered disproportionate in relation to the military advantage gained where, for example, the significance of the vessel is not great. In these and similar cases, environmental impacts in the Arctic could weigh heavily against engaging such targets. On the other hand, it is conceivable that a high degree of military utility could tilt the scales in the opposite direction.

The important point is that environmental factors must have a prominent presence in the minds of military commanders and their legal advisors in assessing Arctic targets. Complicating the proportionality calculation is the fact that scientific knowledge or certainty regarding environmental effects may not be available at the time. Such absence of information, however, does not relieve those responsible from meeting their basic legal obligations. In light of these environmental considerations, the best approach is probably a restrictive one, suggesting that most military action would ultimately be circumscribed in the Arctic once the environment is factored into the target assessment.

THE ENVIRONMENT AS "CIVILIAN OBJECT"

A related principle of IHL that has bearing on the conduct of Arctic hostilities is the avoidance of civilian objects during an attack. Deeply entrenched in customary international law, this principle is articulated in Article 48 of Additional Protocol I. It stipulates that there must be a distinction made between military and civilian objects in the course of an attack.[92] This principle is also supported by Article 57, which requires that precautionary measures be taken to spare civilian objects.[93] There is wide recognition that this protection of civilian objects also applies to the environment.[94] Consequently, militaries are prohibited from attacking environmental assets that are not related to an opposing side's war effort. A naval vessel could

92 Additional Protocol I, *supra* note 18, Article 48.

93 *Ibid*, Article 57.

94 See, eg, International Committee of the Red Cross, *Guidelines for Military Manuals and Instructions on the Protection of the Environment in Times of Armed Conflict* (30 April 1996), online: International Committee of the Red Cross <http://www.icrc.org/eng/resources/documents/misc/57jn38.htm> [*Guidelines for Military Manuals*].

not, for example, directly target glaciers, fragile coastlines, or nearby native communities in the Arctic.

Of course, protection for the environment as a civilian object is far from absolute. Civilian objects can be transformed by use into military ones, and this possibility is particularly relevant in the environmental context. For example, establishing a military outpost on that same fragile coastline would terminate its civilian protection from deliberate targeting. Similarly, using the Arctic landscape or seas to provide cover for military assets would also change their status. Recent commentary on the protection of the environment as a civilian object therefore suggests that this protection must go further. For example, any military presence might have to be excluded from environmentally sensitive areas in order to extend their civilian protection and prevent loss of their immunity from attack in the future.[95]

In addition, implying that environmental protection is synonymous with civilian safeguards is a purely anthropocentric approach. It is possible to debate whether principles designed for civilian preservation can truly translate into real protection for the environment itself.[96] For present purposes, however, the protection of the environment as a civilian object provides an additional legal constraint and seems to preclude any military actions directed against, or that would negatively affect, the Arctic environment. This notion is also apparent from Article 54(2) of Additional Protocol I, which provides that

> [i]t is prohibited to attack, destroy, remove or render useless objects indispensable to the survival of the civilian population, such as foodstuffs ... crops, livestock, drinking water installations and supplies and irrigation works, for the specific purpose of denying them for their sustenance value to the civilian population or to the adverse Party, whatever the motive, whether in order to starve out civilians, to cause them to move away, or for any other motive.[97]

95 Bothe et al, *supra* note 89 at 577. For some of the other challenges facing recognition of the environment as a civilian object, see Betsy Baker, "Legal Protections for the Environment in Times of Armed Conflict" (1992) 33 Va J Int'l L 351 at 364.

96 The dominance of the anthropocentric approach in matters of IHL and the environment is considered in Schmitt, *supra* note 34 at 13.

97 Additional Protocol I, *supra* note 18, Article 54(2).

This prohibition takes on particular significance in the Arctic where the Inuit population is highly dependent on the surrounding natural environment for its survival. Military activities that would adversely affect the availability of food sources would therefore seem to be restricted.

IHL's protection of cultural property is also potentially relevant to the environment, especially in the case where natural factors constitute "the cultural or spiritual heritage of peoples."[98] It is not difficult to make a link between the heritage of Inuit peoples and certain aspects of the Arctic environment. Indeed, despite the emphasis on expanding military defence, most Canadians place a great deal of emphasis on their connection to the Northern landscape. This connection is reflected in Canada's Arctic Foreign Policy Statement, which highlights the need for "healthy and productive ecosystems" and prioritizes "protecting our environmental heritage."[99] It would therefore be difficult to justify an attack on widely recognized natural wonders in the Arctic since any offensive would amount to the destruction of significant aspects of Canada's cultural heritage (although this is admittedly more of a stretch for Southerners than it is for Northerners).

Taken together, all of these broader principles relating to the environment as a civilian object would impose considerable further restrictions on the range of permissible military activities in the Arctic. They reflect the overwhelming regional environmental considerations that would come into play in the Arctic. As environmental factors are assessed pursuant to these broader principles of IHL, it becomes evident that a good number of traditional war-fighting activities would not meet minimum standards in the Arctic.[100]

This conclusion is problematic. It is often suggested that IHL will be ignored by war-fighters if it becomes unrealistic. Furthermore,

98 See *Guidelines for Military Manuals*, *supra* note 94; Michael D Diedrich, Jr, "Law of War and Ecology: A Proposal for a Workable Approach to Protecting the Environment through the Law of War" (1992) 136 Mil L Rev 137 at 146-48.

99 *Canada's Arctic Foreign Policy*, *supra* note 4 at 3-4.

100 While not the primary focus of this article, the nature of the Arctic environment may be relevant to IHL beyond restrictions on the means and methods of warfare. An area of concern for compliance with IHL is in the treatment of detainees where inhospitable Arctic conditions and a lack of infrastructure would pose particular challenges. States are expected to ensure humane treatment for detainees, including medical assistance and a favourable climate for internment. Convention (III) Relative to the Treatment of Prisoners of War, Geneva, 12 August 1949, 75 UNTS 135, Articles13, 15, 22, 30-31, and 46. Clearly, it would be more difficult to provide these basic necessities while adrift in Arctic waters or

if the law is obeyed, it might cause the feuding parties to carry out military actions outside of the Arctic, spreading what might otherwise have been a geographically limited war. Clearly, the lesson is that peaceful means should be used to resolve Arctic conflicts. If warfare does break out in the Arctic, the environmental and legal results could well be catastrophic. Nonetheless, burying one's head in the sand (or ice) is not an option.

Conclusion

The Arctic is a unique and exceptionally fragile region. States should continue their co-operative approach to address the challenges it poses, and UNCLOS provides a suitable legal framework for doing so. As recent commentary suggests, perhaps it is time to start exploring the means of developing an Arctic presence that is less focused on the military.[101] Although the stated purpose of the current military build-up in the region is generally constabulary, it would be foolish to dismiss its potential significance too quickly. Arctic states are becoming more assertive in an area with potential that is only just beginning to be understood. The implications of IHL for potential conflict in the Arctic necessitate a more proactive analytical approach, particularly in light of the underlying insecurities in the region. Moreover, discussing the issue should not be considered tantamount to preparing for military action in the region. Being aware of the implications now enables states to be responsible in the future. Realizing the extent of the restrictions that IHL would impose in the event of Arctic conflict, in order to protect the environment, ultimately reinforces the importance of co-operative approaches.

As demonstrated, the particular vulnerability of the Arctic environment to human activity is relevant to the application of IHL in the region. It would most likely preclude many war-fighting actions that might reasonably be contemplated elsewhere. IHL expressly prohibits the use of various means and methods of warfare that may

---

at an isolated outpost. While the notion of Arctic detainees may seem somewhat fanciful, it underscores the range of obligations IHL imposes and their potential consequences in this regional context.

101 Canadian International Council, "Should Canada Strengthen Its Military Presence in the Arctic?" Canadian International Council, online: <http://www.opencanada.org/rapid-response/should-canada-strengthen-its-military-presence-in-the-arctic/>.

be expected to cause serious damage to the natural environment, which comprises the prohibition of "widespread, long-term, and severe" damage to the environment and the obligation to have "due regard." In the Arctic context, where the impact of human activity is more significant and lasts longer, there is real potential for contravening both this prohibition and obligation. Also relevant are broader principles of IHL that require that the environment be taken into consideration when targeting. Regional factors would weigh heavily in the assessment of proportionality or the protection of civilian objects, and these factors should provide an additional layer of protection for the Arctic environment in wartime. Any environmental damage would have a significant effect on Arctic inhabitants.

States need to pay greater attention to the manner in which IHL would impose overarching legal constraints on any Arctic conflict. The same Canadian public that is eager to defend Northern interests must also consider the Arctic a pristine and protected environment central to the country's identity. When considering the significance of IHL to the Arctic, these perspectives seem almost incompatible. Where does this apparent paradox leave us?

At the very least, the Canadian Forces — commendably, a military that takes IHL seriously — should show leadership in planning and training for legal means and methods of warfare in the Arctic. To begin with, military doctrine and training could address the legal constraints and potential means of mitigating environmental harm through appropriate targeting and choice of weaponry. However, beyond highlighting the need for military doctrine and training on fighting in the Arctic, this article invites further reflection along three lines. Canadians and their Arctic neighbours need to consider (1) the extent to which the militarization of the Arctic increases the possibility of armed conflict there; (2) the difficulty and impracticality of engaging in armed conflict in a legal manner in that region; and (3) the catastrophic consequences that could result from not fighting in a legal manner in the Arctic, if fighting there must be.

Sommaire

Alors qu'il appert à juste titre que le droit de la mer est le régime juridique international le plus approprié pour le règlement des différends dans l'Arctique, il n'en demeure pas moins que cette région subit une ère non seulement de changement climatique mais aussi de militarisation. Or il est curieux que peu d'attention ait été accordée aux contraintes qu'imposerait le droit international humanitaire (DIH) en cas de conflit armé dans l'Arctique — aussi peu probable soit-il. Ces contraintes comprennent notamment l'interdiction de causer des dommages étendus, durables et graves à l'environnement naturel en vertu du Protocole additionnel I aux Conventions de Genève, ainsi que l'obligation connexe de "ten[ir] dûment compte" de l'environnement naturel, obligation reconnue, par exemple, par le *Manuel de San Remo sur les conflits armés en mer.* De même, des facteurs environnementaux doivent jouer dans l'évaluation militaire des cibles en vertu des principes généraux du DIH liés au ciblage. Les auteurs commentent l'application de ces diverses obligations juridiques dans le contexte de l'Arctique. Se référant à la littérature scientifique et à la nature particulièrement fragile de l'environnement de cette région, ils en arrivent à la conclusion que plusieurs techniques de combat classiques conduiraient à des dommages qui seraient juridiquement inadmissibles. Cette conclusion devrait constituer une incitation supplémentaire, pour ceux qui élaborent des politiques en lien avec l'Arctique, de démilitariser cette région et d'y favoriser la résolution pacifique des différends liés à la souveraineté, la navigation ou les ressources.

Summary

While the law of the sea is rightly viewed as the most suitable international legal regime for the settlement of disputes in the Arctic, the militarization of this region in an era of climate change is also observable. Yet curiously, scant attention has been paid to the constraints the international humanitarian law (IHL) would impose on armed conflict in the Arctic, as unlikely as such conflict may be. These constraints include the specific prohibition on causing widespread, long-term, and severe environmental damage under Additional Protocol I to the Geneva Conventions as well as the related obligation to have "due regard" for the natural environment, as referred to in, for example, the *San Remo Manual on International Law Applicable to Armed Conflict at Sea.* Similarly, environmental factors must play into military assessments of targets based on the general principles of IHL related to targeting. The authors explore how these various legal obligations could be applied in the Arctic context. Referring to the scientific literature, they suggest that, due to the particularly vulnerable nature of this regional environment, many traditional war-fighting techniques would lead to damage that is not legally permissible. This conclusion should provide an additional incentive to policy makers to demilitarize the Arctic and to solve peacefully any disputes that may arise over sovereignty, navigation, or resources.

Notes and Comments / Notes et commentaires

Responsabilité pénale des agents ou fonctionnaires internationaux et immunité de juridiction

Introduction

"*Véritable maladie du corps social, le phénomène criminel frappe l'observateur à la fois par sa permanence et par son importance.*"[1] C'est énoncer un lieu commun que de souligner que le criminel ou le délinquant ne se caractérise ni par son âge, ni par son sexe, encore moins par sa profession: on le retrouve un peu partout. Cette situation exige l'organisation d'une réaction sociale en vue de préserver l'ordre public. Compte tenu de l'importance qu'il y a à le préserver, la réaction de la société face au crime, quoique souvent assortie de nombreuses exceptions, s'adresse à tous les criminels, y compris aux agents ou fonctionnaires internationaux. Le présent article se propose de traiter l'organisation de la réaction sociale dans cette dernière hypothèse. Un bref arrêt sur les spécificités du statut des agents internationaux permettra d'aborder judicieusement la question de la répression des infractions dont ils se seraient rendus coupables.

Spécificités du statut des agents ou fonctionnaires internationaux

Avant de préciser l'étendue des immunités de l'agent international, une identification de la notion s'impose. Il n'entre pas dans nos intentions d'esquisser ici une théorie de l'agent international.

---

1 Jean Pradel, *Manuel de droit pénal général*, 17e éd, Paris, Editions Cujas, 2008 à la p 17.

LA NOTION D'AGENT INTERNATIONAL

Selon la Cour internationale de Justice (CIJ) est agent international quiconque, fonctionnaire rémunéré ou non, employé à titre permanent ou non, a été chargé par un organe de l'organisation d'exercer ou d'aider à exercer l'une des fonctions de celle-ci. Bref, toute personne par qui l'organisation agit.[2]

Bien que reprise par la Commission du droit international (CDI),[3] force est cependant d'admettre que cette définition est trop extensive. Tout soutien ou toute collaboration dans l'accomplissement des missions d'une organisation internationale ne fait pas nécessairement de son auteur un agent de celle-ci.[4] Tout est ici, semble-t-il, une question d'espèce. De nos jours, la doctrine semble considérer que les fonctionnaires internationaux sont des agents exerçant, de façon exclusive et continue, une fonction publique au service d'une organisation internationale et soumis à un régime juridique d'origine internationale.[5]

En tout état de cause, le vocable agent est par conséquent un terme générique qui inclut toutes les personnes et entités qui travaillent pour une organisation internationale. Parmi celles-ci, outre les fonctionnaires internationaux *stricto sensu*, figurent d'autres catégories de personnels, notamment les experts et les membres des opérations de maintien de la paix.

L'ÉTENDUE DE LEUR IMMUNITÉ DE JURIDICTION PÉNALE

L'immunité peut trouver sa source formelle dans une loi étatique, comme elle peut avoir été garantie par une norme internationale.[6] S'il n'existe aucun État capable d'accorder des immunités à une

[2] *Réparation des dommages subis au service des Nations Unies*, Avis consultatif, [1949] CIJ rec 174 à la p 177.

[3] *Rapport sur la soixante et unième session*, Doc off CDI NU, 2009, supp n° 10, Doc NU A/64/10, aux pp 44, 52.

[4] La situation des membres des conseils des personnes accusées devant les tribunaux pénaux internationaux *ad hoc* illustre parfaitement cette remarque. Ils sont choisis et rémunérés par les Nations Unies. Cependant, ils ne sont pas des agents internationaux. Voir *Turner c Secretary General of the United Nations* (2010), Tribunal du contentieux administratif des Nations Unies, Doc. n° UNDT/2010/170.

[5] Pierre-Marie Dupuy et Yann Kerbrat, *Droit international public*, 10e éd, Paris, Dalloz, 2010 à la p 223.

[6] Antonio Cassese et al, *International Criminal Law: Cases and Commentary*, Oxford, Oxford University Press, 2011 à la p 76.

organisation internationale — en matière d'administration internationale de territoire notamment — celle-ci peut s'auto-octroyer les immunités qu'elle estime indispensables pour l'accomplissement de sa mission. L'exemple du Kosovo illustre bien cette hypothèse.[7] En effet, en vertu d'un règlement[8] s'inspirant largement de la Convention de 1946 sur les privilèges et immunités des Nations Unies, la Mission d'administration intérimaire des Nations Unies au Kosovo (MINUK) s'est auto-octroyé un régime relativement étendu en matière d'immunités juridictionnelles.

Le droit des organisations internationales, rigoureusement parlant, distingue deux catégories d'immunités: d'une part les immunités reconnues aux organisations internationales elles-mêmes en tant que personnes juridiques — leurs agents, au sens large, les individus invités par elles à titre privé, entre autres, sont également bénéficiaires de ces immunités — et, d'autre part, celles accordées aux représentants des États membres et aux observateurs publics.[9] Seules les premières immunités sont abordées dans le présent article et uniquement en ce qui concerne les agents internationaux. Elles peuvent se subdiviser, à leur tour, en matière pénale[10] comme civile, en deux catégories:[11] les immunités diplomatiques ou personnelles (*ratione personae*) et les immunités fonctionnelles (*ratione materiae*).[12]

7 Frederick Rawski "To Waive or Not to Waive: Immunity and Accountability in UN Peacekeeping Operations," dans Boris Kondoch, dir, *International Peacekeeping*, Burlington, Ashgate, 2007 à la p 553.

8 *On the Status, Privileges and Immunities of KFOR and UNMIK and Their Personnel in Kosovo*, UNMIK Reg n° 2000/47 (18 août 2000). Ce texte résulte d'une déclaration conjointe de la MINUK et de la KFOR quant à leur statut juridique. La déclaration et le règlement sont reproduits dans la *Revue générale de droit international public* 2000 aux pp 1132-37.

9 La question du titulaire, par opposition au simple bénéficiaire, de toutes ces immunités n'est pas abordée dans cet article. C'est un examen auquel nous ne procéderons pas ici, voulant nous borner à préciser l'étendue des immunités.

10 Robert Cryer et al, *An Introduction to International Criminal Law and Procedure*, 2e éd, Cambridge, Cambridge University Press, 2010 aux pp 531-60; Robert Kolb, *Droit international pénal: précis*, Bâle, Helbing Lichtenhahn, 2008 aux pp 202-3.

11 Paola Gaeta, "Official Capacity and Immunities," dans Antonio Cassese, Paola Gaeta, et John RWD Jones, dir, *The Rome Statute of the International Criminal Court: A Commentary*, vol 1, Oxford, Oxford University Press, 2002 aux pp 975-79.

12 L'expression "immunités fonctionnelles" est entendue ici au sens strict. Sinon, toutes les immunités reconnues aux organisations internationales et à leurs agents sont fonctionnelles en ce sens qu'elles visent à assurer un accomplissement adéquat des fonctions confiées aux premières.

Les agents internationaux membres de la haute direction bénéficient d'immunités juridictionnelles très étendues. Ils jouissent des immunités et facilités reconnues aux agents diplomatiques conformément au droit des gens et aux usages internationaux. Comme ces derniers, leur immunité de juridiction pénale est "absolue,"[13] contrairement à leur immunité de juridiction civile qui connaît au moins trois exceptions.[14] Par ce statut qui leur est offert par renvoi,[15] les accords de siège (ou autres instruments) assimilent les agents internationaux concernés à des agents diplomatiques. Ils bénéficient ainsi des garanties coutumières et conventionnelles internationales qui sont celles des agents diplomatiques,[16] notamment l'applicabilité de l'article 31 de la Convention de Vienne du 18 avril 1961 sur les relations diplomatiques. Le caractère absolu de l'immunité de juridiction pénale des agents membres de la haute direction est néanmoins assorti de plusieurs exceptions.[17] D'abord, en cas de flagrant délit, ils peuvent être brièvement détenus à des fins préventives.[18] Ensuite, si un agent international bénéficiaire d'immunités pénales diplomatiques conduit en état d'ivresse, il est admis que les autorités compétentes peuvent arrêter le véhicule et conduire l'agent dans un poste de police jusqu'à ce qu'il ne soit plus un danger ni pour lui-même ni pour les tiers. Enfin, il est également admis qu'il peut

13 Cassese et al, *supra* note 6 à la p 88; Jean Salmon, "Les immunités diplomatiques dans la tourmente" dans *Le procès international: Liber amicorum Jean-Pierre Cot*, Bruxelles, Bruylant, 2009, 215 à la p 216; Jean Salmon, *Manuel de droit diplomatique*, Bruxelles, Bruylant, 1994 à la p 303; Joe Verhoeven, "Les immunités propres aux organes ou autres agents des sujets du droit international" dans Joe Verhoeven, dir, *Le droit international des immunités: contestation ou consolidation?*, Bruxelles, Larcier, 2004, 61 aux pp 72-75; Philippe Cahier, *Le droit diplomatique contemporain*, Genève, Librairie Droz, 1964 aux pp 244-46.

14 Convention de Vienne sur les relations diplomatiques, 18 avril 1961, 500 RTNU 95, §1, art 31 [Conventionne de Vienne].

15 Le renvoi est souvent implicite par le simple usage des termes "immunités diplomatiques" dans les textes. Toutefois, il est de plus en plus explicite. Exemple de Protocole sur les privileges et immunités de l'organisation européenne pour la recherche nucléaire, 2004, CERN, art 12 qui mentionne que "le Directeur général jouit pendant la durée de ses fonctions des privilèges et immunités reconnus par la Convention de Vienne du 18 avril 1961 sur les relations diplomatiques aux agents diplomatiques de rang comparable."

16 Salmon, *supra* note 13 aux pp 588-89.

17 *Ibid* aux pp 294-96.

18 *Affaire relative au personnel diplomatique et consulaire des États-Unis* à *Téhéran (États-Unis d'Amérique c Iran)*, [1980] CIJ Rec 3 au para 86.

être arrêté et désarmé s'il venait à porter une arme de manière illicite.

Peut-être y aurait-il lieu de soulever à cette place la question des limites de cette assimilation de certains fonctionnaires internationaux à des diplomates. On sait par exemple que les diplomates ne jouissent pas des mêmes privilèges et immunités dans leur État de nationalité. A cet égard, des auteurs se demandent s'il en est de même des agents internationaux bénéficiaires des immunités diplomatiques.[19] Une réponse affirmative se retrouve dans certains manuels.[20] Dans la pratique actuelle, trois types de traitements sont réservés aux agents internationaux lorsqu'ils travaillent dans le pays dont ils portent la nationalité: un refus, complet ou partiel, des privilèges et immunités, ou un traitement identique à celui des autres agents internationaux.

Les autres agents internationaux bénéficient uniquement des immunités nécessaires afin d'assurer, en toute circonstance, le libre fonctionnement de l'organisation et la complète indépendance des personnes concernées dans l'exercice de leurs fonctions en rapport avec elle. Les immunités sont ici dites fonctionnelles, car elles ne sont reconnues aux agents internationaux que pour les actes accomplis par eux en leur qualité officielle.[21] Les actes privés sont ainsi exclus du domaine couvert par les immunités.

Il découle de ce qui précède que les immunités d'un agent international, quand elles existent, sont toujours soit diplomatiques ou personnelles, soit fonctionnelles. Elles ne devraient pas, cela se conçoit sans trop de peine, empêcher la répression des infractions imputables aux agents internationaux, soit par les tribunaux étatiques, soit par les tribunaux internationaux.[22]

19 Simon Chesterman et al, *Law and Practice of the United Nations: Documents and Commentary*, New York, Oxford University Press, 2008 à la p 530.

20 Philippe Sands QC et Pierre Klein, *Bowett's Law of International Institutions*, 6e ed, London, Sweet & Maxwell, 2009 à la p 490.

21 La notion d'immunités fonctionnelles fait l'objet de diverses interprétations, notamment devant les tribunaux nationaux. Voir August Reinisch, *International Organizations before National Courts*, Cambridge, Cambridge University Press, 2000 aux pp 205-14; Jan Klabbers, *An Introduction to International Institutional Law*, 2e éd., Cambridge, Cambridge University Press, 2009 à la p 151.

22 La répression des infractions commises par les agents internationaux par les tribunaux étatiques comporte à la fois des avantages et des inconvénients. Voir Wolfgang Münch, "Wrongdoing of International Civil Servants — Referral of Cases to National Authorities for Criminal Prosecution" (2006) 10 *Max Planck Yearbook of United Nations Law*, 71 aux pp 82-86.

La répression des infractions imputables aux agents internationaux

Est considéré comme infraction, aux fins du présent article, "*l'acte (ou l'omission) interdit(e) sous la menace d'une peine prononcée par le juge pénal.*"[23] C'est la loi pénale de chaque État qui érige des comportements humains en infractions punissables.[24] Cette tâche n'est plus une exclusivité des ordres juridiques étatiques. Désormais, la définition des incriminations pénales est aussi une réalité en droit international. Mieux, il existe même des juridictions internationales pénales chargées de juger les individus coupables de commission d'un crime international. Un agent international, à l'instar de tout individu, peut donc se voir reprocher le non-respect d'une incrimination prévue soit par une loi étatique soit par une norme internationale. Compte tenu du fait qu'il est très difficile de parler de "droit pénal des organisations internationales," à tout le moins à cette étape de l'évolution du droit international, on ne s'attardera pas, dans le présent article, sur les mécanismes internes des organisations internationales relatives aux infractions pénales, notamment les enquêtes ou investigations internes. Du reste, les réflexions de Wolfgang Münch consacrées à la question, malgré quelques légères évolutions çà et là, restent largement pertinentes.[25]

La répression des infractions de droit interne

Si les principes posent l'aptitude de chaque État à réprimer les infractions prévues par son droit pénal, cette compétence varie, en se rétrécissant, jusqu'à disparaître lorsque l'auteur de l'infraction bénéficie d'une immunité de juridiction pénale, même si les infractions commises restent punissables et le seront (dans certains cas) devant un autre juge pénal.

Le principe: la compétence territoriale des États

La doctrine admet que "le droit international public laisse à chaque État une grande latitude dans la définition du droit applicable sur son territoire."[26] Chaque État exerce sur son territoire la plénitude

23 Jean Pradel, *Droit pénal comparé*, 3e éd, Paris, Dalloz, 2008 à la p 55.

24 Eric David, *Eléments de droit pénal international et européen*, Bruxelles, Bruylant, 2009 à la p 9.

25 Münch, *supra* note 22 aux pp 73-77.

26 Evelyne Lagrange "Les titres de compétence," dans Société française pour le droit international, *Les compétences de l'Etat en droit international*, Paris, Pedone, 2006 à la p 99.

des pouvoirs législatifs, exécutifs et juridictionnels.[27] Cette compétence territoriale implique généralement que le droit pénal d'un État donné s'applique à l'ensemble des infractions commises sur son territoire,[28] qu'elles l'aient été par un étranger ou par un national, qu'elles l'aient été au préjudice d'un étranger ou d'un national.[29] Les États peuvent ensuite prévoir l'applicabilité de leur droit pénal et la compétence de leurs tribunaux pour la répression d'infractions commises par leurs nationaux ou au détriment de ceux-ci à l'étranger,[30] sous réserve du respect du principe *ne bis in idem.* Enfin, "le droit international leur attribue aussi, dans des cas déterminés, le pouvoir de protéger, par la voie de la répression pénale, les intérêts de la communauté internationale et de l'humanité. C'est ce qu'on appelle la compétence universelle."[31] C'est surtout le souci d'éviter l'impunité qui incite les États à prévoir la compétence universelle.[32]

Le droit international impose des limites à ces différentes facettes de la compétence des Etats.

L'exception: l'obstacle tenant aux immunités

Compte tenu du fait que la quasi-totalité des infractions commises par les agents internationaux comporte un élément d'extranéité — soit à cause de la nationalité de l'agent international délinquant, soit en raison de la nationalité de la victime — se pose la question de la compétence internationale des tribunaux répressifs étatiques. Autrement dit, les juridictions répressives de l'État sur le territoire duquel une infraction a été commise peuvent-elles se voir empêchées d'exercer leurs pouvoirs lorsque l'auteur est un agent international?

27 David, *supra* note 24 à la p 11.

28 Henri Donnedieu de Vabres, *Les principes modernes du droit pénal international,* Paris, Editions Panthéon-Assas, 2004 à la p 11.

29 Bernard Bouloc, *Procédure pénale,* 22e éd, Paris, Dalloz, 2010 aux pp 498-99.

30 Renée Koering-Joulin, "La conception française de la compétence personnelle passive," dans *Les compétences, supra* note 26, 151 aux pp 151-57.

31 Dupuy et Kerbrat, *supra* note 5 à la p 600.

32 Le terme "impunité" est entendu dans cet article dans son sens large, c'est-à-dire qu'il renvoie à une absence de punition, de châtiment. Dans un sens étroit, il peut signifier "le défaut d'exécution d'une peine prononcée par l'autorité compétente sur la base d'une incrimination préétablie," voir Carlo Santulli, "Pourquoi combattre l'impunité dans un cadre international? La Cour pénale internationale: de l'impunité à la répression?" dans Simone Gaboriau et Hélène Pauliat, dir, *La justice pénale internationale,* Limoges, Pulim, 2002, 179 à la p 182.

Une réponse affirmative s'impose dans la plupart des cas au regard du droit positif. En effet, de manière générale, le pouvoir répressif des Etats est limité de nos jours par les normes internationales relatives aux droits de l'homme.[33] Les lois répressives étatiques doivent être conformes au droit international des droits de l'homme.[34] A côté de cette limitation générale relative au pouvoir normatif des Etats, il existe des limitations plus spécifiques qui, elles, portent sur les pouvoirs de leurs tribunaux.[35] Un exemple de ces dernières limitations est fourni par la situation des agents internationaux bénéficiaires des immunités juridictionnelles. Cet obstacle lié aux immunités comporte deux aspects: il empêche non seulement l'exercice du pouvoir juridictionnel, mais en plus il paralyse le pouvoir d'exécution qui est la suite logique des pouvoirs législatifs et juridictionnels de l'État.[36]

Quoique très répandue, l'immunité de juridiction pénale n'est cependant pas reconnue à tous les agents internationaux de toutes les organisations internationales, et pas de manière identique quand elle l'est. Savoir si un agent international donné bénéficie de l'immunité de juridiction pénale dans une affaire précise est une question qui s'apprécie au cas par cas. Il faut vérifier si une norme de droit international[37] ou de droit national[38] reconnaît à l'agent soupçonné d'avoir commis l'infraction pénale une telle immunité.

La réponse peut être affirmative: en pareil cas, l'étendue de l'immunité peut ne concerner que les actes officiels de l'agent, ou couvrir également ses actes privés s'il s'agit d'une immunité absolue octroyée par renvoi au droit diplomatique.[39]

La réponse peut également être négative: dans une telle hypothèse, rare il faut le reconnaître, l'agent international est un justiciable ordinaire sous la juridiction de l'État concerné.

33 David, *supra* note 24 aux pp 56-57.

34 *Ibid.*

35 D'autres limites spécifiques résultent du lieu de commission de l'infraction. Elles ne retiendront pas plus avant ici notre attention.

36 David, *supra* note 24 aux pp 154-55.

37 Droit coutumier, acte constitutif de l'organisation internationale, accord multilatéral relatif au statut d'une ou de plusieurs organisations internationales, accord de siège ou tout autre accord pertinent.

38 Lois, jurisprudence et pratique de l'État concerné.

39 Le renvoi au droit diplomatique, opéré par un accord de siège ou par un autre texte, rend l'article 31 de la Convention de Vienne sur les relations diplomatiques applicable. Il rend le droit coutumier aussi applicable.

LA RÉPRESSION DES INFRACTIONS DE DROIT INTERNATIONAL

On retrouve l'obstacle immunitaire lorsque des tribunaux étatiques souhaitent réprimer une infraction internationale imputable à un agent international. En revanche, en principe, il disparaît dans l'hypothèse où la charge de la répression est confiée à une juridiction internationale.

Par les tribunaux nationaux

Qu'il s'agisse des incriminations coutumières ou conventionnelles, les Etats sont plus ou moins tenus d'établir leur juridiction afin de permettre leur répression par leurs tribunaux. Ils le sont en ce qui concerne les premières en raison de leur qualité de sujet du droit international: ils doivent respecter le droit international général. La pratique semble néanmoins indiquer que les modalités de l'obligation coutumière ne sont pas toujours familières aux juges étatiques. D'un naturel prudent, ils préfèrent s'en tenir au prescrit de leur droit national, y compris les traités en vigueur dans leur ordre juridique.[40] Les États sont tenus d'établir leur juridiction, s'agissant des secondes, parce qu'ils sont parties aux traités qui prévoient les incriminations en cause.[41] Cependant, l'établissement de leur juridiction ne permet pas toujours aux États de réprimer les infractions internationales. Encore faut-il que leur auteur ne bénéficie pas d'immunités juridictionnelles en matière pénale, comme c'est généralement le cas des agents internationaux.

Si la tendance est à un assouplissement de cet obstacle en ce qui concerne les représentants des États, force est néanmoins de noter que l'équilibre dans les jurisprudences étatiques semble privilégier la qualité officielle des criminels par rapport à la lutte contre l'impunité, par l'admission de l'immunité de juridiction pénale.[42] Quoique critiquée par une partie de la doctrine,[43] la jurisprudence de la Cour

40 David, *supra* note 24 à la p 699.

41 Patrick Daillier, Mathias Forteau, et Alain Pellet, *Droit international public*, 8e éd, Paris, LGDJ, 2009 à la p 792; Serge Sur, "Le droit international pénal entre l'État et la société internationale" dans Marc Henzelin et Robert Roth, dir, *Le droit pénal à l'épreuve de l'internationalisation*, Genève, Georg, 2002, 49 aux pp 50 et 51; David, *supra* note 24 aux pp 696-97.

42 Isabelle Fouchard, *Crime international: entre internationalisation du droit pénal et pénalisation du droit international*, thèse de doctorat en droit, Université de Genève, Institut de Hautes Etudes Internationales et du Développement, 2008, aux pp 228-41 [non publiée].

43 Dupuy et Kerbrat, *supra* note 5 aux pp 597-99; Daillier, Forteau, et Pellet, *supra* note 41 à la p 795; Dominique Carreau, "La compétence universelle au regard

internationale de Justice confirme cet équilibre favorable à la reconnaissance de la qualité officielle devant les tribunaux étatiques.[44] La réponse de la jurisprudence de la Cour européenne des droits de l'homme n'est pas encore d'une grande fermeté en la matière. Dans l'affaire *Al-Adsani*, elle a admis le bénéfice de l'immunité de juridiction devant un tribunal étatique parce qu'elle "ne concerne pas, comme c'était le cas des décisions Furundzija et Pinochet, la responsabilité pénale d'un individu."[45] A *contrario*, selon une partie de la doctrine, la Cour admettrait que l'obstacle immunitaire n'aurait pas pu s'élever s'il s'était agi d'une procédure pénale contre une personne physique.[46] Cette interprétation n'a pas encore été confirmée par la Cour et n'est pas non plus admise de manière unanime en doctrine. Ainsi, selon l'Institut de droit international, "le chef d'État bénéficie de l'immunité de juridiction devant le tribunal d'un État étranger pour toute infraction qu'il aurait pu commettre, quelle qu'en soit la gravité."[47] En somme, la pratique enseigne que les deux conceptions coexistent, faisant de la situation actuelle une situation confuse.[48] Quoi qu'il en soit, si les tribunaux étatiques font encore prévaloir l'immunité de juridiction pénale des représentants des États sur la lutte contre l'impunité, leur attitude, vraisemblablement, sera similaire lorsque l'accusé est un agent international.

Le juge répressif international peut, quant à lui, se passer du statut officiel de l'auteur d'une infraction internationale.

---

du droit international," dans *Les droits et le Droit — Mélanges dédiés à Bernard Bouloc*, Paris, Dalloz, 2007, 89 aux pp 90-92; Maurice Kamto, "Une troublante 'Immunité totale' du ministre des Affaires étrangères" (Sur un aspect de l'arrêt du 14 février 2002 dans l'affaire relative au *Mandat d'arrêt du 11 avril 2000*)" (2002) 1-2 Rev BDI 518 aux pp 523-30.

44 *Mandat d'arrêt du 11 avril 2000 (République démocratique du Congo c Belgique)*, [2002] CIJ Rec 3 au para 58.

45 *Al Adsani c Royaume-Uni* (2001), 35763/97 CEDH à la p 25 para 61.

46 Eric David, *Principes de droit des conflits armés*, 4e éd, Bruxelles, Bruylant, 2008 à la p 938.

47 *Les immunités de juridiction et d'exécution du chef d'État et de gouvernement en droit international*, Vancouver, Résolution de Session de Vancouver, 2001, art 2, à comparer avec sa Résolution de Naples de 2009.

48 Mireille Delmas-Marty, "La responsabilité pénale en échec (prescription, amnistie, immunités)" dans Antonio Cassese et Mireille Delmas-Marty, dir, *Juridictions nationales et crimes internationaux*, Paris, Presses Universitaires de France, 2002, 613 aux pp. 637-639.

Par la justice pénale internationale

La seule juridiction répressive internationale dont la compétence *ratione personae* inclut les agents internationaux au sens large, reste la Cour pénale internationale. Son Statut ne comporte pas de restriction à cet égard.[49] Envisagée dans un premier temps, l'idée d'exclure certaines catégories d'agents internationaux de sa juridiction a finalement été abandonnée.[50] Par ailleurs, il se conçoit facilement que les crimes qui relèvent de sa compétence puissent être commis par les agents internationaux.[51] Elle a par conséquent été habilitée pour juger toute personne physique, quelle que soit sa qualité officielle,[52] y compris les membres du personnel militaire des opérations de maintien de la paix.[53] La question de la répression internationale des infractions commises par les agents internationaux demeure encore ouverte relativement au choix du régime de répression.[54] Toutefois, si les États venaient à confier cette tâche, partiellement ou entièrement, à la Cour pénale internationale, l'obstacle lié aux immunités perdrait toute pertinence.[55] Cette mise à l'écart des immunités devant le juge répressif international par le Statut de la Cour cristallise une longue pratique internationale dont l'origine remonte au lendemain de la Deuxième Guerre mondiale.[56] Il s'agirait là d'une règle déclaratoire du droit

[49] Statut de Rome de la cour pénale internationale, 17 juiliet 1998, Doc NU A/CONF.183/9 à l'art 25 [Statut de Rome].

[50] Geert-Jan Alexander Knoops, *The Prosecution and Defense of Peacekeepers Under International Criminal Law,* Ardsley, Transnational Publishers, 2004, aux pp 318-21.

[51] Paul C Szasz et Thordis Ingadottir, "The UN and the ICC: The Immunity of the UN and Its Officials" in Thordis Ingadottir, dir, *The International Criminal Court: Recommendations on Policy and Practice: Financing, Victims, Judges, and Immunities,* Ardsley, Transnational Publishers, 2003, 183 à la p 198.

[52] Gaeta, *supra* note 11 à la p 991.

[53] Marten Zwanenburg, *Accountability of Peace Support Operations,* Leyde, Nijhoff, 2005 à la p 175; Carsten Stahn, "The Ambiguities of Security Council Resolution 1422 (2002)" (2003) 14: 1 EJIL 85 aux pp 94-97.

[54] Les Etats membres des Nations Unies ont encore de la peine à s'accorder sur la question.

[55] Statut de Rome, *supra* note 49, art 27. Voir également Paola Gaeta, "Does President Al Bashir Enjoy Immunity from Arrest?" (2009) 7: 2 J Int'l Crim J 315 aux pp 320-22.

[56] Fouchard, *supra* note 42 aux pp 224-27.

international coutumier.[57] Il en découle qu'en cas de silence du statut d'une juridiction répressive internationale, la règle reste le défaut de pertinence des immunités pénales.[58]

Cette norme coutumière relative à l'inexistence de l'immunité pénale devant les juridictions internationales rend la relation qui lie les Nations Unies à la Cour pénale techniquement très discutable, voire problématique. En effet, l'article 19 de l'Accord négocié entre les deux organisations internationales se lit comme suit:

> Lorsque la Cour souhaite exercer sa compétence à l'égard d'une personne ... qui, en la circonstance, jouit, en vertu de la Convention sur les privilèges et immunités des Nations Unies et des règles pertinentes du droit international, de privilèges et d'immunités ... l'Organisation s'engage à coopérer pleinement avec la Cour ... en particulier en levant ces privilèges et immunités.[59]

Or, l'idée selon laquelle la Cour pénale internationale serait liée par les normes qui garantissent les immunités aux Nations Unies et à ses agents semble difficilement défendable. Premièrement, elle l'est parce que la Cour n'est pas partie aux traités qui octroient lesdites immunités, qu'il s'agisse de la Charte ou de la Convention générale sur les privilèges et immunités des Nations Unies. Le droit conventionnel pertinent ne met donc pas à la charge de la Cour une obligation d'abstention, comme il le fait à l'égard des tribunaux des Etats parties. Deuxièmement, l'idée paraît difficile à soutenir parce que, à l'instar du droit conventionnel, le droit coutumier non plus, en ne reconnaissant pas d'immunités pénales aux agents des Nations Unies, n'enjoint pas la Cour pénale internationale de s'abstenir d'exercer son pouvoir juridictionnel à leur égard. Troisièmement, elle l'est parce que "l'immunité accordée par le droit international ... n'a de sens que devant le juge national," "elle ne se conçoit guère devant un juge international."[60] Aussi peut-on

57 *Prosecutor v Anto Furundzija*, IT-95-17/1-T, Jugement de première instance (10 décembre 1998) (Tribunal pénal international pour l'ex-Yugoslavie), disponible à: ICTY <http://www.icty.org> [*Furundzija*].

58 Antonio Cassese, *International Criminal Law*, 2e éd, Oxford, Oxford University Press, 2008 aux pp 311-13.

59 Accord négocié régissant les relations entre la Cour pénale internationale et l'Organisation des Nations Unies, ICC-ASP/3/Res.1, 2004, disponible à <http://www.icc-cpi.int.>.

60 Joe Verhoeven, "Mandat d'arrêt international et statut de ministre" (2002), en ligne: Actualité et Droit International < http://www.ridi.org/adi/articles/2002/200205ver.htm>.

éprouver quelque doute sur la portée exacte de l'article 19 ci-dessus mentionné.

En matière civile, malgré les réserves d'une partie minoritaire de la doctrine,[61] un nombre grandissant d'auteurs soutient, explicitement ou implicitement, l'existence d'immunités d'organisations internationales à statut coutumier notamment en ce qui concerne les Etats membres, parfois uniquement en faveur des organisations universelles du système onusien et de leurs agents.[62] Des juridictions nationales partagent ce point de vue: tel est le cas des tribunaux néerlandais,[63] italiens,[64] et israéliens.[65] Telle serait aussi la position

61 Pour une réserve générale, voir Hazel Fox, *The Law of State Immunity*, 2e ed, Oxford, Oxford University Press, 2008 à la p 726. Pour une réserve particulière relative aux membres militaires des opérations de maintien de la paix, voir Róisín Burke, "Status of Forces Deployed on UN Peacekeeping Operations: Jurisdictional Immunity" (2011) 16: 1 J Confl & Sec L 63 aux pp 94-102.

62 Dupuy et Kerbrat, *supra* note 5 aux pp 221-22; Sands et Klein, *supra* note 20 à la page 493; David Ruzié, "La protection des agents internationaux" dans SFDI, *Les agents internationaux*, Paris, Pedone, 1985, 281 à la p 311; Antonio Cassese, *International Law*, Oxford, Oxford University Press, 2005 à la p 138; Gérard Cahin, *La coutume internationale et les organisations internationales: l'incidence de la dimension institutionnelle sur le processus coutumier*, Paris, Pedone, 2001 à la p 436; Christian Dominice, "L'immunité de juridiction et d'exécution des organisations internationales," (1984) 187 Rec des Cours 145 à la p 220; Eric David, *Droit des organisations internationales*, 16e éd, Bruxelles, Presses Universitaires de Bruxelles, 2005 à la p 360; Pierre Klein, *La responsabilité des organisations internationales dans les ordres juridiques interne et international*, Bruxelles, Bruylant, 1998 à la p 228; Reinisch, *supra* note 21 à la p 2; Florence Poirat, "Les immunités des sujets du droit international (État et organisations internationales)," dans Verhoeven, *supra* note 13, 11 à la p 13; Jean-François Flauss, "Droit des immunités et protection internationale des droits de l'homme" (2000) SZIER 298 à la p 320; Ignaz Seidl-Hohenveldern, "Functional immunity of international organizations and human rights" dans Wolfgang Benedek et al, dir, *Development and Developing International and European Law: Essays in Honour of Konrad Ginther on the Occasion of his Sixty-Fifth Birthday*, Francfort-sur-le-Main, Lang, 1999, 137 à la p 138.

63 *Stichting Greenpeace Nederland v Euratom* (2007), 136 ILR 429 (CS Pays-Bas); *Iran-United States Claims Tribunal v AS* (1985), 94 ILR 321 (CS Pays-Bas); *Eckhardt v European Organization for the Safety of Air Navigation (Eurocontrol)* (1984), 94 ILR 331 (Dist Ct Maastricht).

64 *FAO v INPDAI* (1982), 87 ILR 1 (Cass it); *Cristiani c Italian Latin-American Institute* (1985), 87 ILR 20 (Cass it).

65 En mars 2009, les tribunaux israéliens ont rejeté la plainte de deux particuliers qui avaient assigné la Commission européenne. Ils l'ont fait, semble-t-il, en vertu du caractère coutumier des immunités dont jouit la Commission en tant qu'organe d'une organisation internationale. En ligne: <http://www.diplomaticlaw.com>.

des tribunaux allemands.[66] En matière pénale, une telle unanimité ne semble pas encore constatable. Mais même si l'on supposait, en matière pénale également, l'existence d'une coutume internationale celle-ci lierait exclusivement les États qui se verraient obligés de reconnaître l'immunité pénale aux agents internationaux. Certes, en tant que sujet du droit international, les organisations internationales doivent observer le droit international coutumier compatible avec leurs moyens ainsi qu'avec le principe de spécialité.[67] Cependant, même si les immunités ne sont pas par nature étrangères aux juridictions internationales,[68] une norme coutumière ici ne lierait pas la Cour pénale internationale: d'une part, parce que la pratique dont elle est issue ne concernerait que les tribunaux étatiques[69] et, d'autre part, parce qu'elle se heurterait à une autre norme coutumière, à savoir le défaut de pertinence de l'immunité devant le juge pénal international.[70]

En définitive, force est, semble-t-il, de noter l'inexistence de normes en droit international interdisant à la Cour pénale internationale d'exercer son pouvoir de juger lorsque des agents internationaux sont poursuivis devant elle. Parler dès lors de la nécessité pour les Nations Unies de lever l'immunité de ses agents afin que la Cour puisse les juger, paraît ne relever au mieux que d'une commodité de langage.[71] Si les deux organisations concernées regardaient

66 Voir Ignaz Seidl-Hohenveldern "Failure of Controls in the Sixth International Tin Agreement" dans Niels Blokker et Sam Muller, dir, *Towards More Effective Supervision by International Organizations — Essay in Honour of Henry G. Schermers*, vol 1, Boston and London, Dordrecht, 1994, 255 à la p 271.

67 Matthieu Aldjima Namountougou, *Droits de l'homme et immunités des organisations internationales: essai de conciliation en droit international*, thèse de doctorat en droit, Université de Genève, Institut de Hautes Etudes Internationales et du Développement, 2011 aux pp 232-234 [non publié].

68 Jean Salmon "Libres propos sur l'arrêt de la C.I.J. du 14 février 2002 dans l'affaire relative au *Mandat d'arrêt du 11 avril 2000* (*R.D.C. c. Belgique*)" (2002) 35: 1-2 Rev BDI 512 aux pp 514-15.

69 L'immunité est accordée aux agents internationaux contre l'intervention des organes étatiques, notamment les tribunaux, et non contre celle des juridictions internationales.

70 *Furundzija*, *supra* note 57.

71 L'ONU et la Cour auraient dû faire précéder l'article 19 d'un autre article par lequel elles conviendraient que les agents de la première jouissent de l'immunité de juridiction pénale devant la seconde. Il deviendrait alors pertinent de parler de la levée de cette immunité. En l'absence d'immunité, on peut reconnaître officiellement cette inexistence et le signifier aux autorités, en l'occurrence à la Cour. Mais on ne lève pas l'immunité.

malgré tout l'article 19 de l'Accord négocié comme ayant une quelconque pertinence juridique, il conviendrait alors de conclure qu'il s'agit là d'un moyen purement politique, traduit ou exprimé de manière discutable au plan juridique, mis à la disposition des Nations Unies afin qu'elles puissent empêcher le jugement de ses agents devant la Cour si tel venait à être leur souhait pour des raisons qui peuvent par ailleurs être légitimes.

LE CAS PARTICULIER DES OMP

Un regard rétrospectif permet de se rendre compte que les prospectives actuelles en matière de responsabilité pénale des agents internationaux ont surtout eu pour élément déclencheur les scandales (sexuels) à répétition dont plusieurs opérations de maintien de la paix ont été le théâtre.

Aspects rétrospectifs

C'est au cours des années 2000 que des révélations faites notamment par des médias et des associations de défense des droits de l'homme ont montré que des membres des opérations de maintien de la paix s'étaient rendus coupables d'infractions graves, commises le plus souvent de manière répétitive. L'exploitation et les abus sexuels avaient été signalés comme étant les infractions les plus courantes.[72] Le Secrétariat des Nations Unies a établi un rapport qui a révélé le caractère systématique de ces infractions dans les opérations de maintien de la paix.[73] La majorité de ces infractions n'ont pas donné lieu à des poursuites.[74] Ce double constat — la commission des infractions graves par les personnels des opérations de maintien

72 Toutefois, de manière générale, il semble que la fraude, le détournement, le vol et la corruption sont les infractions les plus répandues dans les organisations internationales. Voir Münch, *supra* note 22 aux pp 77-81.

73 UN General Assembly, "Report of the Secretary-General's Special Advisor, Prince Zeid Ra'ad Zeid al-Hussein on 'A comprehensive strategy to eliminate future sexual exploitation and abuse in United Nations peacekeeping operations,'" *Fifty-ninth Session*, Doc NU A/59/710 (24 mars 2005).

74 Ne pouvant pas être jugés par les tribunaux de l'État hôte, d'une part en raison des immunités et, d'autre part parce qu'ils relèvent de la juridiction exclusive de leur État de nationalité en vertu d'accords conclus avec l'ONU, les agents indélicats étaient renvoyés dans leur pays, où ils sont rarement poursuivis. Voir Vanessa Kent, "Protecting civilians from UN peacekeepers and humanitarian workers: Sexual exploitation and abuse" dans Chiyuki Aoi, Cedric de Coning, et Ramesh Thakur, dir, *Unintended Consequences of Peacekeeping Operations*, Tokyo/ New York/ Paris, United Nations University Press, 2007, 44 à la p 49.

de la paix et l'impunité presque générale qui avait toujours prévalu — a remis au grand jour la question de la répression des infractions commises par les agents internationaux. Le rapport à l'origine de ce double constat n'a d'ailleurs pas manqué de souligner qu'il "importe de chercher sérieusement à éliminer les lacunes qui permettent aux auteurs d'infractions de se soustraire parfois à leurs responsabilités."[75] C'est ainsi que les Nations Unies mirent en place un groupe d'experts juridiques pour approfondir la réflexion sur la question.

Dans son rapport, ce groupe d'experts juridiques recommanda aux Nations Unies de favoriser la répression desdites infractions par l'État hôte, c'est-à-dire l'État du lieu de leur commission.[76] "Le Groupe estime que l'État hôte doit, dans la mesure du possible, exercer sa compétence en ce qui concerne les infractions commises par du personnel participant aux opérations de maintien de la paix sur son territoire."[77] En cas de défaillance de cet ordre juridique, le groupe préconisa la répression par d'autres États.[78] Toutefois, cette seconde solution ne va pas sans difficultés. En effet, les États qui entendent réprimer les infractions imputables aux agents internationaux alors même que celles-ci n'ont pas été commises sur leur territoire peuvent se retrouver face à des obstacles d'ordre juridique tels que la variété des définitions des crimes dans les différents ordres juridiques étatiques, la question de l'admission des preuves, le problème de l'extradition des présumés coupables ou encore celui de l'obtention d'une entraide judiciaire. Pour le dépassement de ces difficultés le groupe d'experts juridiques se montra favorable à l'adoption d'une convention internationale qui les aplanira.[79]

Aspects prospectifs

Le traitement de la question de la répression des infractions imputables aux personnels des opérations de maintien de la paix est encore en cours au niveau de plusieurs enceintes des Nations Unies. Une solution envisageable serait de confier à la Cour pénale

75 UN General Assembly, *supra* note 73 au para 90.

76 UN General Assembly "Ensuring the Accountability of United Nations Staff and Experts on Mission with Respect to Criminal Acts Committed in Peacekeeping Operations," *Sixtieth Session,* Doc NU A/60/980 (16 août 2006) § 27.

77 *Ibid.*

78 *Ibid* aux para 45 et s.

79 *Ibid* aux para 62-63.

internationale la charge de réprimer ces infractions. Cela serait indiqué pour les infractions particulièrement graves qui relèvent de sa compétence et qui n'ont pas été adéquatement jugées par un tribunal étatique. Néanmoins la solution comporte deux inconvénients majeurs. D'une part, "s'agissant de l'exercice de la compétence par la Cour pénale internationale, il est à noter que de nombreux États ne sont pas parties au Statut de Rome de la Cour et qu'en l'absence d'une décision du Conseil de sécurité prise en vertu du Chapitre VII de la Charte des Nations Unies, la Cour ne peut pas se déclarer compétente si ni l'État hôte ni l'État de nationalité ne sont parties au Statut ou n'ont accepté la juridiction de la Cour."[80] D'autre part, "il est peu probable que la juridiction actuelle de la Cour lui donne compétence à l'égard de tous les crimes qui doivent être jugés,"[81] la majorité de ceux-ci restant des crimes ordinaires.[82] S'il convient que la solution définitive fasse de la place à la Cour pénale internationale, cette dernière solution devrait non seulement rester complémentaire, mais en plus elle ne devrait pas permettre aux auteurs des crimes ordinaires d'échapper aux conséquences de leurs actes.

Une seconde solution techniquement concevable serait l'institution d'une nouvelle juridiction internationale — soit par voie conventionnelle, soit par la voie éprouvée du Conseil de sécurité agissant en vertu du Chapitre VII de la Charte des Nations Unies — ayant vocation à connaître des crimes commis par les personnels des opérations de maintien de la paix. "Les difficultés que soulève l'institution d'un organe judiciaire par traité sont globalement les mêmes que celles que poserait l'attribution de ladite compétence à la Cour pénale internationale."[83] En revanche, l'établissement d'un nouvel organe judiciaire international par le Conseil de sécurité "permettrait d'aplanir un certain nombre de ces difficultés étant donné que tous les États Membres des Nations Unies seraient

80 *Ibid* au para 71 (d).

81 *Ibid* au para 71 (e). "Le viol, par exemple, ne relève pas de la compétence de la Cour à moins qu'il constitue un crime contre l'humanité du fait qu'il a été commis dans le cadre d'une 'attaque généralisée ou systématique lancée contre toute population civile,' comme le prévoit le Statut de la Cour."

82 Marco Odello, "Tackling Criminal Acts in Peacekeeping Operations: The Accountability of Peacekeepers" (2010) 15: 2 J Confl & Sec L 347 à la p 358.

83 UN General Assembly, *supra* note 76 au para 73: "La difficulté majeure réside dans l'incertitude quant à la participation des États au traité et donc à la situation qui prévaudrait du point de vue juridictionnel dans les cas où ni l'État hôte ni l'État de nationalité de l'auteur présumé ne seraient parties au traité."

alors automatiquement tenus de s'y conformer et auraient notamment l'obligation de coopérer avec l'entité créée par cette décision."[84] La question de la compétence du Conseil de sécurité pour créer une telle juridiction internationale paraît susciter encore des interrogations.[85] Une variante de cette seconde solution consisterait à faire juger le personnel militaire des opérations de maintien de la paix par un tribunal mixte.[86] Cette éventualité a fait l'objet de nombreux débats lors de l'établissement du Tribunal spécial pour la Sierra Leone.[87] Mais elle ne bénéficie pas encore des faveurs des Nations Unies, en particulier de celles du Conseil de sécurité qui semble privilégier la répression par les Etats dont les soldats sont les nationaux.[88]

Une troisième solution internationale serait la solution purement normative, à savoir l'adoption d'une convention internationale relative à la répression des infractions imputables aux agents internationaux. Les deux principaux inconvénients de cette solution — la relativité du droit conventionnel et l'éventualité qu'un long temps s'écoule avant l'entrée en vigueur du traité — peuvent être tempérés par divers mécanismes.[89] L'importance des avantages liés à l'adoption d'un traité pour l'efficacité de la répression des infractions qui nous intéressent ici par les ordres juridiques étatiques implique que les Etats devraient redoubler d'efforts pour que cette entreprise aboutisse.[90]

Conclusion

Le système répressif international, qui est en plein développement, n'a pas encore déployé toutes ses potentialités en ce qui concerne la responsabilité pénale des agents internationaux. Il reste encore une voie complémentaire, d'autant plus que les Etats "voient dans

84 *Ibid* au para 74.

85 *Ibid* aux para 75-76.

86 Knoops, *supra* note 50 aux pp 311-12.

87 *Ibid*, aux pp 314-18.

88 Dans le cas sierra-léonais, une complémentarité a été instituée: le Tribunal spécial pour la Sierra Leone ne peut juger les forces des opérations de maintien de la paix que dans l'hypothèse où l'Etat national de la personne soupçonnée d'être coupable ne veut pas ou ne peut pas la juger. Voir Statut du tribunal spécial pour la Sierra Leone, Rés CS 1315, 2000, aux arts 1 (2) et (3).

89 UN General Assembly, *supra* note 76 au para 65.

90 *Ibid* au para 63.

la faculté de punir un attribut de la souveraineté."[91] De même, l'expérience des Nations Unies enseigne qu'il est irréaliste d'attendre des Etats de nationalité des agents internationaux délinquants un quelconque "zèle" dans la répression des infractions dont ceux-ci se seraient rendus coupables.[92] En outre, en pareil cas, les organisations internationales ne disposent pas d'instruments de contrôle.[93] Il ne reste donc que la voie du lieu de commission des faits répréhensibles qui devrait, semble-t-il, être privilégiée.[94] Cette solution qui fait de la justice pénale internationale une sorte de justice complémentaire paraît la plus appropriée dans la mesure où "l'idée qui fonde la justice pénale internationale [permanente] n'est pas de bâtir une justice supranationale excluant la justice nationale, mais de montrer l'exemple."[95] Elle est au contraire "appelée à épauler les juridictions nationales lorsque celles-ci ne sont pas en mesure d'exercer leurs fonctions répressives."[96]

S'il convient de privilégier la répression par les tribunaux de l'État hôte, les autres possibilités ne doivent cependant pas être complètement écartées. Elles devraient au contraire — un peu comme une "épée de Damoclès" — pouvoir être activées dans l'hypothèse où la première voie s'avèrerait inopérante ou inefficace. Les diverses carences de nombre d'ordres juridiques étatiques, en particulier ceux qui traversent une crise et qui accueillent pour cette raison une opération de maintien de la paix, invitent à la mise au point d'un système de complémentarité entre les ordres juridiques étatique et international. L'exclusion catégorique et systématique des crimes commis par les membres du personnel militaire des opérations de maintien de la paix de la connaissance des juridictions

91 Daillier, Forteau, et Pellet, *supra* note 41 à la p 794.

92 UN General Assembly, *supra* note 73 au para 67.

93 Robert Kolb, Gabriele Porretto, et Sylvain Vite, *L'application du droit international humanitaire et des droits de l'homme aux organisations internationales: Forces de paix et administrations civiles transitoires*, Bruxelles, Bruylant, 2005 à la p 407.

94 Une autre voie efficace serait celle des autres États disposés à réprimer les infractions qui nous intéressent. Mais, jusque-là, elle n'est pas moins incertaine que celle des Etats de nationalité.

95 Mireille Delmas-Marty, "La CPI et les interactions entre droit international pénal et droit pénal interne à la phase d'ouverture du procès pénal" (2005) Revue de science criminelle, 473 à la p 477. Voir également Cassese, *supra* note 58 aux pp 342-44.

96 Joe Verhoeven, "Considérations sur ce qui est commun: Cours général de droit international public (2002)" (2008) 334 Rec des Cours 9 à la p 421.

internationales ou mixtes est discutable car elle paraît donner à croire, sans doute à tort, que la justice internationale pénale est une justice qui pratique du "deux poids, deux mesures."[97] Cette complémentarité des juges nationaux et internationaux autorise à penser qu'avec un peu de volonté politique les États disposeraient des voies et moyens pour fermer complètement la porte à l'impunité qui, faut-il le rappeler, ici comme ailleurs, nourrit sérieusement le crime. En tout état de cause, la co-opération entre les organisations internationales et leurs Etats hôtes est un aspect crucial dans le combat contre l'impunité.

MATTHIEU ALDJIMA NAMOUNTOUGOU
Docteur en droit, Institut de hautes études internationales et du développement, Genève

Summary

According to the International Court of Justice, any person through whom an international organization acts is an agent of that organization. However, this definition is too broad. Any participation in the fulfilment of the mission of an international organization does not necessarily make the person an agent of the international organization. After detailing the particularities of the status of international agents, this article considers the issue of accountability for wrongs attributable to them. It recommends in this respect the development of a system of accountability that combines national and international justice responses with priority to the former based on the location of the offence.

97 Selon le modèle onusien d'accord sur le statut des forces des opérations de maintien de la paix, les soldats d'un contingent relèvent de la justice pénale du pays qui a fourni ce contingent. Voir UN General Assembly, "Comprehensive Review of the Whole Question of Peace-Keeping Operations in All Their Aspects," *Fifty-fifth Session*, Doc NU A/45/594 (9 octobre 1990) au para 47(b). Le risque que les membres du personnel militaire ne soit pas jugés dans leur pays d'origine en raison d'obstacles juridiques a été considérablement réduit par les évolutions récentes. Tous les Etats membres des Nations Unies ont été formellement priés d'adapter leur droit pénal.

Sommaire

Selon la Cour internationale de justice, est agent d'une organisation internationale toute personne par qui l'organisation agit. Force est cependant d'admettre que cette définition est trop extensive. Toute collaboration dans l'accomplissement des missions d'une organisation internationale ne fait pas nécessairement de son auteur un agent de celle-ci. Après avoir précisé les particularités du statut d'agent international, le présent article aborde la question de la répression des infractions imputables aux agents internationaux. Il préconise à cet égard la mise au point d'un système de répression qui combine justice nationale et justice internationale, tout en reconnaissant une primauté à la première, notamment celle du lieu de commission des faits incriminés.

The Entry into Force of the Lisbon Treaty: The European Union in Retrospect and Prospect

Introduction

On 1 December 2009, after several ups and downs in the negotiations and a struggle lasting almost a decade, the Treaty of Lisbon Amending the Treaty on European Union and the Treaty Establishing the European Community (Lisbon Treaty), which was aimed at improving the functioning of the European Union (EU), finally entered into force.[1] The Lisbon Treaty significantly amends the treaty basis of the EU as a supranational organization; makes the EU a legal entity under public international law; strengthens the role of the European Parliament; and significantly reforms the role of the High Representative of the Union for Foreign Affairs and Security Policy (HR), which is now supported by the recently established European External Action Service (EEAS). The treaty has also made the EU Charter on Fundamental Rights legally binding and enforceable.[2] It further expands the competences of the EU

The author wishes to thank Trevor C Hartley (London School of Economics and Political Science), Joseph HH Weiler (New York University), Damian Chalmers (London School of Economics and Political Science), Neil Walker (European University Institute), Jose M de Areliza (Instituto de Empresa, Madrid), Kieran St C Bradley (European Parliament), Imola Streho (Sciences Po, Paris), and Marie-Pierre Granger (Central European University) from whose lectures the author has derived a great deal. The views expressed herein are personal.

1 Treaty of Lisbon Amending the Treaty on European Union and the Treaty Establishing the European Community, 13 December 2007, [2007] OJ C 306/1, online: <http://eur-lex.europa.eu/JOHtml.do?uri=OJ:C:2007:306:SOM:en:HTML> [Lisbon Treaty].

2 Charter of Fundamental Rights of the European Union, [2010] OJ C 83/389, online: <http://eur-lex.europa.eu/LexUriServ/LexUriServ.do?uri=OJ:C:2010:083:0389:0403:EN:PDF> [EU Charter].

in the field of trade and other external commercial relations by providing it exclusive competence to conduct the EU's Common Commercial Policy (CCP), including not only all aspects of trade in goods and services as well as commercial aspects of intellectual property rights (IPRs) but also foreign direct investment (FDI) — a completely new element.[3]

This article focuses on the Lisbon Treaty and its implications for the EU and international law. It will first provide a brief overview of the background to adoption of the Lisbon Treaty, and then it will describe the critical hurdles that were overcome during the treaty's ratification process. The important changes brought about by the treaty, and some of its underlying implications for the EU, will then be discussed. Finally, some concluding observations will be made.

Background

In concluding the Treaty of Nice Amending the Treaty on European Union, the Treaties Establishing the European Communities and Certain Related Acts (Treaty of Nice) on 11 December 2000, the EU member states declared that there would be another intergovernmental conference (IGC) in 2004 to consider the significant issues that the Treaty of Amsterdam Amending the Treaty on European Union, the Treaties Establishing the European Communities and Certain Related Acts and the Treaty of Nice had left unresolved.[4] In particular, member states called "for a deeper and wider debate about the future of the European Union," which would involve "wide-ranging discussions with all interested parties: representatives of national parliaments and all those reflecting public opinion,

[3] For excellent discussions of the Lisbon Treaty, see Y Devuyst, "The European Union's Institutional Balance after the Treaty of Lisbon: 'Community Method' and 'Democratic Deficit' Reassessed" (2008) 39 Geo J Int'l L 247; P Craig, "The Treaty of Lisbon: Process, Architecture and Substance" (2008) 33 Eur L Rev 137; M Dougan, "The Treaty of Lisbon 2007: Winning Minds Not Hearts" (2008) 45 CML Rev 617. For a more succinct overview of the Lisbon Treaty, see Nikolaos Lavranos, "The Entering into Force of the Lisbon Treaty: A European Odyssey" (14 December 2009) 13:26 ASIL Insights, online: <http://www.asil.org/insights091214.cfm>; Christoph Hermann, "The Treaty of Lisbon Expands the EU's External Trade and Investment Powers" (21 September 2010) 14:28 ASIL Insights, online: <http://www.asil.org/insights 100921pdf.cfm>.

[4] Treaty of Amsterdam Amending the Treaty on European Union, the Treaties Establishing the European Communities and Certain Related Acts, 2 October 1997, [1997] OJ C 340/1 (entered into force 1 May 1999), online: <http://eur-lex.

namely political, economic and university circles, representatives of civil society, etc."[5] As a result, member states began considering wide-ranging institutional reforms. In December 2001 in Laeken, Belgium, where the member states had convened to discuss preparations for the 2004 IGC, it became apparent that the scope of reforms by then under consideration would require considerable preparatory work prior to this conference. Thus, in the 2001 Laeken Declaration on the Future of the European Union, the European Council, composed of EU heads of state and government, announced the convening of a convention on the future of Europe.[6]

---

europa.eu/en/treaties/dat/11997D/tif/JOC_1997_340__1_EN_0005.pdf> [Treaty of Amsterdam]; Treaty of Nice Amending the Treaty on European Union, the Treaties Establishing the European Communities and Certain Related Acts, 11 December 2000, [2001] OJ C 80/1 (entered into force 2 February 2003), online: <http://eur-lex.europa.eu/en/treaties/dat/12001C/pdf/12001C_EN.pdf> [Treaty of Nice]; Declaration on the Future of the Union, Declaration no. 23 to the Treaty of Nice, Final Act of the Conference of the Representatives of the Governments of the Member States, Annex, [2001] OJ C 80/77 at 85-86.

5 *Ibid* at 85, para 3. The Treaty of Nice failed to address several contentious issues, in particular, the delimitation of powers between the European Union (EU) and member states; the status of the EU Charter, *supra* note 2; simplification of the various treaties constituting the EU; and expanding the role of national parliaments in the European architecture. See generally M Gray and A Stubb, "The Treaty of Nice: Negotiating a Poisoned Chalice?" (2001) 39 J Common Market Studies 5; W Wessels, "The Millennium IGC in the EU's Evolution" (2001) 39 J Common Market Studies 197; Joschka Fischer, "From Confederacy to Federation: Thoughts on the Finality of European Integration" (Speech delivered at Humboldt University, Berlin, 12 May 2000), reprinted in Christian Joerges, Yves Mény, and HH Weiler, eds, *What Kind of Constitution for What Kind of Polity? Responses to Joschka Fischer* (Florence: European University Institute, 2000) 19, online: <http://www.cvce.eu/viewer/-/content/4cd02fa7-d9d0-4cd2-91c9-2746a3297773/en>. Fischer argued: "These three reforms — the solution of the democracy problem and the need for fundamental reordering of competences both horizontally, i.e. among the European institutions, and vertically, i.e. between Europe, the nation state and the regions — will only be able to succeed if Europe is established anew with a constitution. In other words, through the realization of the project of a European constitution centred around basic, human, and civil rights, an equal division of powers between the European institutions and a precise delineation between European and nation state level. The main axis for such a European constitution will be the relationship between the Federation and the nation state." For a series of detailed responses, see Joerges, Mény, and Weiler (*ibid*). See also N Walker, "Europe's Constitutional Passion Play" (2003) 28 Eur L Rev 905; N Walker, "Big 'C' or Small 'c'?" (2006) 12 Eur LJ 12; Pavlos Eleftheriadis, "The Idea of a European Constitution" (2007) 27 Oxford J Legal Studies 1.

6 Laeken Declaration on the Future of the European Union, European Council, 15 December 2001, reprinted in Laeken European Council, *Presidency Conclusions,*

Although the convention's initial mandate was merely to identify options for consideration by the subsequent IGC, by the time the convention opened in February 2002, the great majority of participants were willing to pursue an ambitious agreement.[7] During the first session of the convention, its chair, Valéry Giscard d'Estaing, stated that the goal of the convention should be to produce a single proposal opening the way for a "Constitution for Europe" that would replace the various treaties constituting the European Communities (EC) and EU.[8] Sixteen months later, on 18 July 2003, the convention had submitted a draft Treaty Establishing a Constitution

---

Annex I, EU Doc SN 300/1/01 REV 1 (14-15 December 2001) 19 at 24, online: <http://ec.europa.eu/governance/impact/background/docs/laeken_concl_en.pdf> [Laeken Declaration]. For an excellent overview, see P Magnette, "In the Name of Simplification: Coping with Constitutional Conflicts in the Convention on the Future of Europe" (2005) 11 Eur LJ 432; C Skach, "We the Peoples? Constitutionalising the European Union" (2005) 43 J Common Market Studies 149. Ever since the Laeken Declaration used the word "constitution" in a subsection entitled "Towards a Constitution for European Citizens," the adoption of a "constitutional text in the Union" was regarded as imminent by the EU (Laeken Declaration, at 23-24).

7 The main task of the Convention on the Future of Europe was to consider the key issues arising for the EU's future development and to try to identify the possible responses to them by conducting a wide public consultation. In addition to its chair (Valéry Giscard D'Estaing) and two vice-chairs (Giuliano Amato and Jean Luc Dehaene), the Convention on the Future of Europe comprised 102 delegates from national governments and parliaments (including from the then accession candidate states), the European Parliament, and the European Commission. Civil society representatives were invited to attend as observers. The convention met in plenary session, with all members present, once a month. It was the final decision-making body, responsible for adopting any agreed text. Its decisions were taken in public by consensus rather than by vote. See generally the archived website of the convention, online: <http://european-convention.eu.int/EN/bienvenue/bienvenue2352.html?lang=EN>.

8 "Introductory Speech by President V. Giscard D'Estaing to the Convention on the Future of Europe," reprinted in European Convention Secretariat, *Speeches Delivered at the Inaugural Meeting of the Convention on 28 February 2002*, EU Doc CONV 4/02 (2002), Annex 4, 12 at 20. (It is to be noted that at that time there were still three communities (the European Community, the European Atomic Energy Community, and the European Coal and Steel Community). The Coal and Steel Community Treaty expired in 2002, after fifty years. The Treaty on European Union was concluded in Maastricht in 1992. Treaty on European Union, 7 February 1992, [1992] OJ C 191/1 (in force 1993), online: <http://eur-lex.europa.eu/en/treaties/dat/11992M/tif/JOC_1992_191__1_EN_0001.pdf> (TEU). See also N Walker, "Europe's Constitutional Momentum and the Search for Polity Legitimacy" (2005) 4 Int'l J Constitutional L 211; and M Maduro, "The Importance of Being Called a Constitution" (2005) 4 Int'l J Constitutional L 332.

for Europe to the European Council.[9] Following a series of amendments to this original draft, the Treaty Establishing a Constitution for Europe (Constitutional Treaty) was finally signed by member states in Rome in October 2004.[10]

Indeed, the aptly named Constitutional Treaty did provide for almost all major elements of a national constitution, including a charter of fundamental rights, a list of exclusive and shared competences, institutional provisions (establishing, for example, the offices of the president of the European Council as well as the European minister of foreign affairs), and a number of EU symbols, such as an official anthem and a flag.

Although the Constitutional Treaty was signed by all member states in 2004, it still needed to be ratified by each of them.[11] It was hoped that ratification would proceed as usual and that there would be no turbulence in the EU constitutionalization process.[12] However, the unexpected rejection of the European Constitution by Dutch and French voters in 2005 brought this process to a complete halt. Following these defeats, many viewed the process as being dead.[13]

However, the "reflection pause" of almost two years that followed this unexpected rejection gave European leaders an opportunity

[9] Draft Treaty Establishing a Constitution for Europe, 18 July 2003, EU Doc CONV 850/03 (2003), online: <http://european-convention.eu.int/docs/Treaty/cv00850.en03.pdf>.

[10] Treaty Establishing a Constitution for Europe, 29 October 2004, [2004] OJ C 310/1, online: <http://eur-lex.europa.eu/JOHtml.do?uri=OJ:C:2004:310:SOM:EN:HTML> [Constitutional Treaty].

[11] *Ibid*, Article IV-447.

[12] It is noteworthy, however, that soon after the signing of the Constitutional Treaty in Rome in October 2004 ten member states decided to hold referenda to determine whether or not they should ratify it. The first such referendum was held in Spain, where the treaty was approved with an overwhelming majority of 76.72 percent in a 42.32 percent voter turnout. See EOS Gallup Europe, *The European Constitution: Post Referendum Survey in Spain* (Brussels: European Commission, 2005) at 2, online: <http://ec.europa.eu/public_opinion/flash/fl_168_en.pdf>.

[13] In the referenda held in France (on 29 May 2005) and in the Netherlands (on 1 June 2005), the Constitutional Treaty was rejected by 55 percent and 62 percent of voters respectively. See Jens-Peter Bonde, *From EU Constitution to the Irish Referendums on the Lisbon Treaty*, 2nd edition (Brussels: Foundation for EU Democracy, 2009) at 58, online: <http://en.euabc.com/upload/from_eu_constitution.pdf>. Arguably, the reasons for such rejections were protests against globalization, the consequences of the 2004 EU enlargement, fear of eventual Turkish membership in the EU, and (in the Netherlands) anger over the perceived power of the larger EU member states.

to analyze the various reasons for this rejection.[14] As a result of that analysis, it was realized that the word "Constitution," with its connotation of creating a "federal United States of Europe" (much like the United States of America), did not resonate well in domestic political constituencies and was viewed as going a step too far. Thus, in March 2007 — the fiftieth anniversary of the Treaty Establishing the European Community (Treaty of Rome) — the presidents of the Council of the European Union, European Parliament, and European Commission agreed to place "the European Union on a renewed common basis before the European Parliament elections in 2009.[15] However, realizing the gravity, sensitivity, and importance of the matter, member states agreed that all references to the word "constitution" should be redacted and that provisions relating to all other state-like symbols, such as the European flag and anthem, be removed. At the same time, the parties decided to leave the substance of the European Constitution in place.[16] After all of these deliberations and changes, a text had been agreed informally between the member states by 19 October 2007, and on 13 December 2007 the Lisbon Treaty was finally signed by all member states.[17]

Critical Hurdles in the Ratification Process

The Lisbon Treaty, like the Constitutional Treaty, had to be ratified by all member states before it could come into force. However, by

14 See Luxembourg Presidency of the Council of the European Union, "Jean-Claude Juncker states that there will be a period for reflection and discussion but the process to ratify the Constitutional Treaty will continue with no renegotiation," Press Release (17 June 2005), online: <http://www.eu2005.lu/en/actualites/communiques/2005/06/16jclj-ratif/index.html>.

15 Declaration on the Occasion of the Fiftieth Anniversary of the Signature of the Treaties of Rome," 25 March 2007, Part III, online: <http://europa.eu/50/docs/berlin_declaration_en.pdf>. Treaty Establishing the European Community, 25 March 1957, [2002] OJ C 325/33, online: <http://eur-lex.europa.eu/en/treaties/dat/12002E/pdf/12002E_EN.pdf> [Treaty of Rome].

16 In terms of substance, the strategy involved using the Constitutional Treaty as a starting point while addressing the question of what had to be altered to make the treaty acceptable to all. The heads of government met on 21-23 June 2007 to consider the process and produced a sixteen-page mandate that was to provide the basis for an inter-governmental conference (IGC) to be completed by December 2007. The mandate indicated that the new treaty was to follow the text of the Constitutional Treaty except as specified in the mandate. Accordingly, the scope of the subsequent IGC was highly limited. See Council of the European Union, "IGC 2007 Mandate," EU Doc 11218/07 (26 June 2007), Annex, online: <http://register.consilium.europa.eu/pdf/en/07/st11/st11218.en07.pdf>.

17 Lisbon Treaty, *supra* note 1.

no stretch of the imagination was the process of ratification a constitutional moment in which, through referenda, the "people" of Europe participated in the creation of a new pan-European democracy. Many contentious issues, such as the enlargement of the EU, steadily decreasing enthusiasm and support for European integration, the emergence over the prior decade of more "Euroskeptic," nationalistic governments, and growing public ambivalence about European constitutionalization (caused by increasing anxieties about security, immigration, religion, and, most recently, the economy) took centre stage, eclipsing the progress made on several such fronts in the Lisbon Treaty. As a result, the ratification process was not straightforward.

Hungary set a record by ratifying the Lisbon Treaty within four days after its signature. Learning from the past French and Dutch "no" votes, France, the Netherlands, and most other member states decided against holding referenda. Yet the hurdles for the coming into force of the Lisbon Treaty remained manifold. While parliamentary approval was sufficient in some member states, others required referenda and/or approval by their constitutional courts. Ireland, in particular, held a referendum, as it was required to do under its constitution. And challenges in the constitutional courts of Germany and the Czech Republic were in addition to the parliamentary approval in those countries.

THE IRISH REFERENDUM

Ireland required a second referendum to ratify the Lisbon Treaty, after the treaty was rejected by the Irish people the first time around.[18] The rejection in the first referendum could be attributed to a lack of information about the Lisbon Treaty, coupled with concerns about perceived threats to Irish abortion laws and neutrality as well as possible conscription to a pan-European army.[19] Ironically, none of these concerns appeared to be rooted in the terms of the Lisbon Treaty amendments themselves. The only actual amendment

[18] In the first referendum held on 12 June 2008, 53.4 percent of Irish voters rejected the Lisbon Treaty. See Bonde, *supra* note 13 at 11, 17.

[19] For a detailed analysis of the Irish "no" vote commissioned by the Irish Department of Foreign Affairs, see Millward Brown IMS, "Post Lisbon Treaty Referendum Research Findings," September 2008, online: <http://www.dfa.ie/uploads/documents/Publications/Post%20Lisbon%20Treaty%20Referendum%20Research%20Findings/final%20-%20post%20lisbon%20treaty%20referendum%20research%20findings.pdf>.

that seemed to weigh heavily in the outcome was the possible loss of an Irish commissioner generated by the Lisbon Treaty's proposed reduction in the size of the Commission.[20] Responding to this concern, in December 2008, the EU governments agreed that, upon the entry into force of the Lisbon Treaty, they would take a decision providing that the Commission would retain one commissioner from each member state.[21] Some other guarantees were also subsequently offered in June 2009.[22]

During the second referendum, due to the ongoing economic crisis, Irish voters seemed to realize that, without the safety net offered by Brussels, Ireland could find itself in a position similar to that of the virtually bankrupt Iceland, which for the very same reason had applied for EU membership.[23] Consequently, the Irish approved the Lisbon Treaty in the second referendum, which was held on 2 October 2009, by a clear majority of 67 percent.[24]

CONDITIONAL APPROVAL BY THE FEDERAL GERMAN CONSTITUTIONAL COURT

As with the Treaty on European Union (Maastricht Treaty) in 1993, the Federal German Constitutional Court was called upon to address the earlier-mentioned concerns with regard to the Lisbon Treaty.[25]

20 *Ibid* at 14.

21 Presidency Conclusions, Brussels European Council, EU Doc 17271/1/08 REV 1 (11-12 December 2008) at 2, online: <http://consilium.europa.eu/uedocs/cms_data/docs/pressdata/en/ec/104692.pdf>.

22 Presidency Conclusions, Brussels European Council, EU Doc 11225/2/09 REV 2 (18-19 June 2009), online: <http://www.consilium.europa.eu/uedocs/cms_data/docs/pressdata/en/ec/108622.pdf>. The member states set out three sets of guarantees — that is, that nothing in the Lisbon Treaty would (1) affect the scope or applicability of the rights to life, protection of the family, or in respect of education as set out in the Irish Constitution; (2) change in any way, for any member state, the extent or operation of EU competence in respect of taxation; and (3) prejudice the security and defence policy of any member state, provide for the creation of a European army or conscription or affect a state's right to decide whether or not to participate in a military operation: Annex I (at 17-19).

23 Iceland submitted its EU membership application on 23 July 2009. See Swedish Presidency of the European Union, *Iceland and EU Set Out Together*, Press Release (23 July 2009), online: <http://www.se2009.eu/en/meetings_news/2009/7/23/iceland_and_the_eu_set_out_together_23_july.html>.

24 See Bonde, *supra* note 13 at 17.

25 Treaty on European Union, 7 February 1992, [1992] OJ C 191/1 [Maastricht Treaty].

And just as it did with the Maastricht Treaty in 1993, the court took quite a balanced view and did not disappoint either the "eurosceptics" or the pro-European integration movement.[26] In its judgment dated 30 June 2009 on the Lisbon Treaty, the court unambiguously formulated limits and "no go" areas for any future European integration process.[27] The court made it quite clear that it would not accept any transfer of competences in areas such as education, taxation, and culture.[28] It took the view that the Lisbon Treaty is essentially a treaty that improved, where necessary, the functioning of the EU without changing its fundamental nature — that is, nothing less, but certainly nothing more, than a co-operation forum between sovereign states in a limited number of clearly identified areas.

THE CZECH PRESIDENT'S OPT OUT

Czech President Václav Klaus threatened to refuse to ratify the Lisbon Treaty unless the Czech Republic obtained an opt-out regarding application of the EU Charter of Fundamental Rights. Klaus claimed that the charter, which would become legally binding upon entry into force of the Lisbon Treaty, would expose his country to property claims by the 2.5 million ethnic Germans and their descendants who had been expelled after the Second World War from the then Czechoslovakia under the "Benes Decrees."[29]

After intense and elaborate discussions, the Czech Republic received a political promise in the European Council that it would get the same opt-out provided to the United Kingdom and Poland in Protocol no. 30 on the Application of the Charter of Fundamental Rights of the European Union to Poland and to the United Kingdom.[30] This opt-out may not have achieved the legal effect that

26 The court gave only conditional approval to the Maastricht Treaty in 1993. See *Maastricht Decision,* (1993) BverfGE 89, 155 (Federal Constitutional Court of Germany).

27 *Lisbon Decision,* 2 BvE 2/08 (30 June 2009) (Federal Constitutional Court of Germany), online: <http://www.bverfg.de/entscheidungen/es20090630_2bve000208en.html>.

28 The court was particularly critical of the fiction fostered in past decades that the European decision-making process was essentially comparable to that of member states in terms of democratic representation. See *ibid* at paras. 271-72.

29 For a detail account on the Benes Decrees, see <http://www.americanhungarianfederation.org/news_benesdecrees.htm>.

30 Brussels European Council, *Presidency Conclusions,* EU Doc 15265/1/09 REV 1 (29-30 October 2009) at 2 and Annex I, online: <http://www.consilium.

the United Kingdom and Poland had expected.[31] However, it was understood, at the time of the promised opt-out, that no mention was to be made of the Benes Decrees or anything related to the past. After the Czech opt-out was approved, the Czech Constitutional Court approved the Lisbon Treaty.[32]

Changes Introduced by the Lisbon Treaty and Their Implications

The Lisbon Treaty establishes two revised treaty regimes governing the EU — that is, the Treaty on European Union (TEU) and the Treaty on the Functioning of the European Union (TFEU).[33] The post-Lisbon TEU is an amended version of the 1992 Maastricht Treaty.[34] Similarly, the TFEU is an amended and renamed version of the Treaty of Rome.[35] This pedigree is important because the Lisbon Treaty was presented as a series of technical amendments to the Treaties of Maastricht and Rome rather than as a completely new treaty such as the ill-fated Constitutional Treaty.[36]

---

europa.eu/uedocs/cms_data/docs/pressdata/en/ec/110889.pdf>; Protocol no. 30 on the Application of the Charter of Fundamental Rights of the European Union to Poland and to the United Kingdom, [2010] OJ C 83/313, online: <http://eur-lex.europa.eu/LexUriServ/LexUriServ.do?uri=OJ:C:2010:083:0201:0328:EN:PDF> [Protocol no. 30].

31 See *NS v Secretary of State for the Home Department, C-411/10; ME v Refugee Applications Commissioner,* Case C-93/10 (21 December 2011), online: <http://curia.europa.eu/juris/document/document.jsf?text=&docid=117187&pageIndex=0&doclang=EN&mode=doc&dir=&occ=first&part=1&cid=1900719>. The European Court of Justice (ECJ) observed that an asylum seeker may not be transferred to a member state where he risks being subjected to inhuman treatment and ruled that EU law does not permit a conclusive presumption that member states observe the fundamental rights conferred on asylum seekers. The court stated that its answers did not have to be qualified in any respect so as to take account of Protocol no. 30, *supra* note 30 at para 122.

32 Treaty of Lisbon II, Doc Pl Ús 29/09 (3 November 2009), online: <http://www.usoud.cz/view/pl-29-09> (Czech Republic Constitutional Court).

33 See Treaty on European Union, [2010] OJ C 83/13, online: <http://eur-lex.europa.eu/LexUriServ/LexUriServ.do?uri=OJ:C:2010:083:0013:0046:EN:PDF> [TEU]; Treaty on the Functioning of the European Union, [2010] OJ C 83/47, online: <http://eur-lex.europa.eu/LexUriServ/LexUriServ.do?uri=OJ:C:2010:083:0047:0200:EN:PDF> [TFEU].

34 Maastricht Treaty, *supra* note 25.

35 Treaty of Rome, *supra* note 15.

36 The Lisbon Treaty involved amendments to all of the articles of the Maastricht Treaty and to 216 provisions of the Treaty of Rome.

While the TEU mainly deals with the mission, values, democratic principles, neighbourhood policy, composition, central functions, external action, legal personality, and so on of the EU, the TFEU sets out its explicit competences.[37] The following paragraphs will outline the main changes to each, and the implications arising therefrom, brought about by the Lisbon Treaty.

THE EU AS A LEGAL ENTITY UNDER PUBLIC INTERNATIONAL LAW

From a purely public international law point of view, the Lisbon Treaty has ended the peculiar, highly contentious "double identity" of the European Community (EC) and EU. This step was accomplished by explicitly granting the EU legal personality[38] and providing that the EU succeeds to all EC rights and obligations under public international law.[39] Previously, although the EC and two other communities had been granted legal personality, the legal personality of the EU remained unregulated such that, by and large, its legal personality remained disputed. This problem, which had cast doubt on the EU's capacity to conclude treaties, had divided legal scholars between two lines of thinking. One supported the view that the EU possessed implicit treaty-making authority, derived from the EC, since the EU was created in 1993. This view relied for support on the advisory opinion of the International Court of Justice (ICJ) in *Reparation for Injuries Suffered in the Service of the*

[37] The TEU, *supra* note 33, deals with the following matters, *inter alia*:

- the mission and values of the EU: respect for the rule of law, the principle of limited powers, respect for national identities, and upholding democracy and fundamental rights;
- the democratic principles of the EU and providing for the active contribution of national parliaments to the functioning of the EU;
- a neighbourhood policy, whereby the EU is to develop a special relationship with neighbouring countries;
- the composition and central functions of EU institutions;
- detailed provisions on the EU's external action, in particular, its common foreign and security policy and its common security and defence policy;
- procedures for its own amendment as well as amendment of the TFEU;
- the legal personality of the EU;
- provisions governing asymmetric integration, including circumstances in which a member state may leave or be expelled from the EU and, when states engage in enhanced co-operation, the procedure whereby some member states may develop EU legislation among themselves where there is no sufficient will for such legislation by all member states.

[38] TEU, *supra* note 33, Article 47.

[39] *Ibid*, Article 1.

United Nations,[40] in which the ICJ held that an international organization, such as the United Nations, may have legal personality (albeit limited), in order to fulfil its functions even if legal personality is not explicitly mentioned in the founding instrument of the international organization. The other line of thinking supported the view that it is only with the coming into force of the Lisbon Treaty that the EU actually obtained legal personality and, hence, treaty-making powers.

However, one cannot lose sight of the fact that, in practice, many states had concluded treaties with the EU prior to the Lisbon Treaty. Thus, there is no denying the fact that the EU exercised treaty-making power in the past without being explicitly granted legal personality.[41] In this sense, then, the Lisbon Treaty merely reaffirms the existing position.[42] At most, therefore, by explicitly granting legal personality to the EU, the Lisbon Treaty simply clarifies that the EU has the capacity to conclude treaties. The EU's organs have advised states and international organizations, such as the World Trade Organization (WTO), of this clarified status and its underling implications.[43]

40 *Reparation for Injuries Suffered in the Service of the United Nations,* Advisory Opinion, [1949] ICJ 174, online: <http://www.ICJ-cij.org/docket/files/4/1835.pdf>.

41 See, eg, Agreement between the European Union and the Federal Republic of Yugoslavia on the Activities of the European Union Monitoring Mission (EUMM) in the Federal Republic of Yugoslavia, 25 April 2001, [2001] OJ L 125/2, online: <http://eur-lex.europa.eu/LexUriServ/LexUriServ.do?uri=CELEX:22001A0505(01):EN:HTML>; Agreement between the European Union and the Republic of Croatia on the Participation of the Republic of Croatia in the European Union Military Operation to Contribute to the Deterrence, Prevention and Repression of Acts of Piracy and Armed Robbery off the Somali Coast (Operation Atlanta), 27 July 2009, [2009] OJ L 202/84, online: <http://eur-lex.europa.eu/LexUriServ/LexUriServ.do?uri=OJ:L:2009:202:0084:0089:EN:PDF>.

42 On the other hand, just hours before the Lisbon Treaty entered into force, the EU signed a treaty with the United States on access by US law enforcement agencies to the SWIFT database. Agreement between the European Union and the United States of America on the Processing and Transfer of Financial Messaging Data from the European Union to the United States for Purposes of the Terrorist Finance Tracking Program, 30 November 2009, [2009] OJ L 008/11. The timing was criticized in that it avoided greater participation by the European Parliament in the treaty-making process that would have been required had the Lisbon Treaty already been in force. See Valentina Pop, "Bank Data Transfer Deal with US Reached," *EU Observer* (30 November 2009), online: <http://euobserver.com/22/29072>.

43 See, eg, *Verbal Note from the Council of the European Union and the Commission of the European Communities,* WTO Doc WT/L/779 (30 November 2009), online: <http://trade.ec.europa.eu/doclib/docs/2009/december/tradoc_145573.pdf>.

DISTRIBUTION OF EXCLUSIVE, SHARED, AND SUPPORTIVE COMPETENCES BETWEEN THE EU AND ITS MEMBER STATES

In order to provide greater clarity and avoid possible confusion, the Lisbon Treaty sets out a catalogue of competences. While such catalogues are quite prevalent in typical federal state constitutions such as those of the United States, Australia, and India, this is the first such comprehensive catalogue for the EU. The Lisbon Treaty catalogue governs the distribution of exclusive, shared, and supportive competences between Brussels and the member states and also enumerates the policies that come within the purview of each of these categories.[44] In areas where EU competence is exclusive, policy and legislation are made only by the EU institutions collectively; where it is shared, member state governments may also make rules; and where it is supportive, member states take the lead and the EU may only play a supporting role. In addition to setting out

44 See TFEU, *supra* note 33, Articles 2-6. Article 3 enumerates the exclusive competences as follows:

1. The Union shall have exclusive competence in the following areas:
   (a) customs union;
   (b) the establishing of the competition rules necessary for the functioning of the internal market;
   (c) monetary policy for the member states whose currency is the euro;
   (d) the conservation of marine biological resources under the common fisheries policy;
   (3) common commercial policy.
2. The Union shall also have exclusive competence for the conclusion of an international agreement when its conclusion is provided for in a legislative act of the Union or is necessary to enable the Union to exercise its internal competence, or in so far as its conclusion may affect common rules or alter their scope.

Article 4 enumerates the shared competences:

1. The Union shall share competence with the member states where the Treaties confer on it a competence which does not relate to the areas referred to in Articles 3 and 6.
2. Shared competence between the Union and the member states applies in the following principal areas:
   a) internal market;
   b) social policy, for the aspects defined in this Treaty;
   c) economic, social and territorial cohesion;
   d) agriculture and fisheries, excluding the conservation of marine biological resources;
   e) environment;
   f) consumer protection;
   g) transport;
   h) trans-European networks;
   i) energy;
   j) area of freedom, security and justice;

the competences of the EU, the TFEU also sets out detailed procedures to be followed in exercising these competences in each policy field.[45]

It is significant to note that the Lisbon Treaty extends the areas of exclusive competence of the EU, which clearly means that it will now be able to conclude more treaties acting alone rather than as a co-party with other member states.[46] In particular, the EU is explicitly given the exclusive competence to conclude an international agreement if doing so is necessary to enable the EU to exercise an internal competence, or if it may affect EU rules, or if EU legislation so provides.[47] This change is quite significant with wide-ranging ramifications for the powers of the member states. It is also somewhat ironic, since the main purpose of the catalogue of competences is to reduce the tendency of centralization, which, in the past, has led to a consistent, gradual transfer of competences from member states to Brussels without any clear legal basis. In this context, it remains to be seen whether this catalogue will contribute to more clarity or, rather, lead to more disputes between European institutions and the member states regarding their respective competences.

NEW POSTS: PRESIDENT OF THE EUROPEAN COUNCIL AND HIGH REPRESENTATIVE FOR FOREIGN AFFAIRS

The Lisbon Treaty has introduced two new positions: the president of the European Council, who represents the EU *vis-à-vis* third states at the level of heads of state and government as far as the Common

---

k) common safety concerns in public health matters, for the aspects defined in this Treaty.

3. In the areas of research, technological development and space, the Union shall have competence to carry out activities, in particular to define and implement programmes; however, the exercise of that competence shall not result in member states being prevented from exercising theirs.
4. In the areas of development co-operation and humanitarian aid, the Union shall have competence to carry out activities and conduct a common policy; however, the exercise of that competence shall not result in member states being prevented from exercising theirs.

[45] *Ibid*, Articles 5-6.

[46] In this context, see the ECJ's opinion on the distribution of powers between the EC and the member states regarding the modification of General Agreement on Trade in Services (GATS) commitments. *Opinion 1/08 – Opinion Pursuant to Article 300(6) EC – General Agreement on Trade in Services (GATS)*, [2009] ECR I-11129, online: <http://curia.europa.eu/juris/document/document.jsf?text=&docid=72655&pageIndex=0&doclang=EN&mode=doc&dir=&occ=first&part=1&cid=1907583> [*Opinion 1/08*].

[47] TFEU, *supra* note 33, Article 216.

Foreign and Security Policy (CFSP) is concerned,[48] and the high representative for foreign affairs and security policy (HR), which is a merger of the two prior external relations positions of high representative for common foreign and security policy and the commissioner for external relations.[49]

The main task of the president of the European Council will be to chair, co-ordinate, and implement the work of the European Council as well as to facilitate co-operation between the various European institutions. Further, the president must ensure the external representation of the EU concerning issues of common foreign and security policy, without prejudice to the powers of the HR. The president shall have a tenure of two-and-a-half years, renewable only once.[50] In addition to chairing the Foreign Affairs Council, the HR's main task will be to conduct the EU's CFSP. At the moment, the HR straddles the Council and the Commission in the sense that she is a vice-president of the Commission and also chairs the Council of Ministers when it meets in its composition of ministers of foreign affairs.[51] As there appears *prima facie* to be a degree of overlap between the tasks assigned to the president and the HR, it will be interesting to see how these two functionaries co-ordinate their respective roles and how effective these two offices will prove to be at the international level.

THE EU'S EXPLICITLY EXCLUSIVE COMPETENCE OVER THE CCP

The Lisbon Treaty lists the CCP as an exclusive competence of the EU,[52] thereby prohibiting member states from legislating or adopting legally binding instruments (including international agreements) within this domain without EU approval.[53] Unmistakably, this development means that, unlike the previous legal position (where the EC's exclusive competence only included trade in goods, cross-border trade in services (Mode 1), and border measures against counterfeit or pirated goods),[54] the EU's exclusivity now includes all

48 *Ibid*, Article 15(6).

49 *Ibid*, Article 18.

50 *Ibid*, Article 15(5)-(6).

51 *Ibid*, Article 18.

52 TFEU, *supra* note 33, Article 3(1)(e).

53 *Ibid*, Article 2(1).

54 *Opinion 1/94, Competence of the Community to Conclude International Agreements Concerning Services and the Protection of Intellectual Property – Article 228 (6) of the EC Treaty*, [1994] ECR I-5267 (ECJ).

aspects of trade in goods and services as well as commercial aspects of intellectual property rights. In addition, foreign direct investment (FDI) has now been made part of the CCP.[55]

Thus, an agreement amending the EU's schedule of specific commitments under the General Agreement on Trade in Services (GATS) of the WTO can now be concluded by the EU alone, an action that previously would have required agreement by the EC as well as its member states.[56] This position raises a very contentious legal issue as to whether the EU alone could adopt a Final Act of the Doha Round of Multilateral Trade Negotiations (although there is no immediate prospect of finishing this round soon). Member states are still calling for mixed agreements (that is, agreements adopted by both the EU as well as member states) for WTO-related agreements, based on the remaining shared competences in transport services and criminal sanctions in the field of intellectual property protection.[57] Legal scholars, such as Christoph Hermann, have vehemently argued that if the Doha Round ever produces a final act, this issue may eventually have to be resolved by the European Court of Justice (ECJ).[58]

Further, the Lisbon Treaty strengthens the EU's CCP with robust economic policy goals such as "market opening"[59] and calls for the CCP to be conducted in the context of broader EU external policy "objectives" ranging from democracy to good global governance.[60] Many scholars have suggested that, given the generality and potential for contradiction between these goals, the organs responsible for the conduct of the CCP must enjoy wide discretion in pursuing such objectives. The ECJ is therefore unlikely to strike down particular measures for being inconsistent with them. Their normative power must nevertheless not be underestimated, and the European

55 TFEU, *supra* note 33, Article 207(4). For a detailed assessment of this, see Julien Chaisse, "Promises and Pitfalls of the European Union Policy on Foreign Investment: How Will the New EU Competence on FDI Affect the Emerging Global Regime?" (2012) 15 J Int'l Econ L 51.

56 *Opinion 1/08*, *supra* note 46. General Agreement on Trade in Services, See Annexe 1B of the Agreement Establishing the World Trade Organization, online: <http://www.wto.org/english/docs_e/legal_e/26-gats.pdf>.

57 TFEU, *supra* note 33, Article 207(5).

58 See Hermann, *supra* note 3.

59 TFEU, *supra* note 33, Articles 205, 207(1).

60 TEU, *supra* note 33, Article 21(2).

Parliament will most likely closely supervise the Commission and the Council in this regard.[61]

This view derives further support from the fact that the Lisbon Treaty, in the context of the CCP, has given much greater say to the European Parliament in the negotiation and conclusion of international treaties.[62] The European Parliament, which previously had only an opportunity to be heard, which was voluntarily granted by the Commission, is now entitled to full participation in the negotiation of all matters falling within the CCP (trade in goods, services, commercial aspects of IPRs, and FDI). Further, under the EU regulations defining the framework for the conduct of the CCP (adopted according to the ordinary legislative procedure), the consent of the European Parliament (without the right to ask for amendments, *ergo* "fast track") has now become necessary for concluding any international agreement based on the trade competence of the EU, irrespective of whether the agreement affects the "framework" of the CCP.[63]

At the functional level, the Lisbon Treaty mandates that it is the responsibility of the HR (rather than the president of the European Council) to ensure that the EU's external actions are coherent and to co-ordinate the CFSP and other external dimensions of the EU's policy, including the CCP.[64] In this regard, the HR is to be supported by the EEAS. However, it is important to note that the HR does not preside over meetings of the EU's Foreign Affairs Council when the council deals with CCP matters.[65] Thus, the CCP remains the domain of the Council, dominated by member states and the Commission's directorate general for trade. Practically speaking, while

61 See Hermann, *supra* note 3.

62 See Andrew Willis, "EU Treaty Implications for Trade Unclear," *EU Observer* (8 December 2009), online: <http://euobserver.com/9/29119>. The author argues that the role of the European Parliament has been stepped up considerably in many areas, including trade policy, since the Lisbon rules came into force on 1 December 2009.

63 TFEU, *supra* note 33, Articles 207(2), 218(6)(a)(v), 288. For a different view, see Markus Krajewski, "External Trade Law and the Constitution Treaty: Towards a Federal and More Democratic Common Commercial Policy?" (2005) 42 CML Rev 91 at 122.

64 TEU, *supra* note 33, Article 18(4).

65 See *Council Decision of 1 December 2009 Adopting the Council's Rules of Procedure*, [2009] OJ L 325/35, Article 2(5) at 38, n 1, Annex, online: <http://eur-lex.europa.eu/LexUriServ/LexUriServ.do?uri=OJ:L:2009:325:0035:0061:EN:PDF>.

EU delegations report to the HR as head of the EEAS, they report to the trade commissioner on trade matters.

EXPANSION OF THE EU'S COMPETENCE IN TRADE AND INVESTMENT LAWS

As noted earlier, the Lisbon Treaty gives the EU exclusive competence for trade in services and commercial aspects of IPRs, whereas this competence had previously been shared, in part, by the EC and its member states. The treaty also confers on the EU a completely new competence for FDI, even though the EC already had some legislative powers in the field of establishment and free movement of capital.[66]

Not surprisingly, most academic and political commentary on the Lisbon Treaty has been directed at the scope and consequences of the EU's new powers in the area of investment.[67] Some issues that have been raised deserve particular attention and possibly even legislative action. Does the EU's new competence in this area cover all investment? No. There is far-reaching consensus among scholars that the treaty's text does not give the EU competence over portfolio investments.[68] Since many international investment agreements do not distinguish between direct and portfolio investment, it will therefore be necessary to draw a line between the two for EU purposes.

Legal scholars also disagree on which types of investment measures fall within the EU's competence over FDI, given that it forms part of the CCP.[69] Three types of measures may be distinguished: (1) market access; (2) post-establishment standards of treatment; and (3) protection against expropriation. Many support an extensive interpretation covering all three types of measures. The EU's new competence for FDI has the unambiguous effect that member states can no longer conclude bilateral investment treaties (BITs) without

[66] TFEU, *supra* note 33, Articles 206, 207(1).

[67] For excellent insights, see Joachim Karl, "The Competence for Foreign Direct Investment: New Powers for the European Union?" (2004) 5 J World Investment & Trade 413; Jan Ceyssens, "Towards a Common Foreign Investment Policy? Foreign Investment in the European Constitution" (2005) LIEI 259; Marc Bungenberg, "Going Global? The EU Common Commercial Policy after Lisbon" (2010) Eur YB Int'l Econ L 123.

[68] Karl, *supra* note 67 at 433; Bungenberg, *supra* note 67 at 144.

[69] *Ibid* at 142.

the EU's prior consent.[70] The Commission has recently published a proposed regulation that would provide a permission procedure and specify the consequences of such a permission.[71] The proposed regulation would require member states to provide notification of all of their existing investment agreements, which would then benefit from a general (but revocable) permission. In light of the estimated 1,300 BITs involving member states, this development is extremely significant. Building upon its "minimum platform on investment," the EU will now try to negotiate its own investment agreements (EU BITs) with major third countries, such as China and India.[72] Since the EU lacks competence over portfolio investment, these EU BITs will need to be concluded as "mixed agreements," with member states concluding the agreements alongside the EU.

Despite the transfer of competences to the EU, the BITs previously concluded remain uncontested. Under public international law, they benefit from the *pacta sunt servanda* principle.[73] Similarly, EU law allows member states to fulfil their obligations towards third states despite possible conflicts with EU law.[74] This principle will remain the same under the proposed regulation mentioned earlier.[75] However, insofar as the member states' BITs are in substantive

70 TFEU, *supra* note 33, Article 2(1).

71 European Commission, *Proposal for a Regulation of the European Parliament and of the Council Establishing Transitional Arrangements for Bilateral Investment Agreements Between Member States and Third Countries*, EU Doc COM(2010)344 (7 July 2010), online: <http://trade.ec.europa.eu/doclib/docs/2010/july/tradoc_146308.pdf> [*Commission Proposal*]. See also European Commission, *Communication from the Commission to the Council, the European Parliament, the European Economic and Social Committee and the Committee of the Regions: Towards a Comprehensive European International Investment Policy*, EU Doc COM(2010)343 (7 July 2010), online: <http://trade.ec.europa.eu/doclib/docs/2010/july/tradoc_146307.pdf> [*Commission Communication*].

72 Niklas Maydell, "The European Community's Minimum Platform on Investment or the Trojan Horse of Investment Competence," in August Reinisch and Christina Knahr, eds, *International Investment Law in Context* (The Hague: Eleven International Publishing, 2007) 73.

73 Vienna Convention on the Law of Treaties, 23 May 1969, 1155 UNTS 331, Article 26.

74 TFEU, *supra* note 33, Article 351.

75 *Ibid.* See also *Commission Proposal, supra* note 71; and *Commission Communication, supra* note 71.

conflict with EU law — for example, because they lack a regional economic integration clause or a clause ensuring the effectiveness of EU restrictions on capital movements — member states will have to either renegotiate or terminate these BITs.[76]

Generally speaking, as a result of the amendments to the CCP brought about by the Lisbon Treaty in the field of FDI, the era of member states' BITs is coming to an end. Under future mixed EU–member state BITs, new questions will have to be answered, including those regarding accession of the EU to the International Centre for Settlement of Investment Disputes (ICSID), the allocation of liability under mixed BITs, and — perhaps most fundamentally — why such future treaties need to be "mixed" at all.

COMPETITION LAW: BUSINESS AS USUAL

While mainly perceived as "business as usual" by most competition lawyers, the Lisbon Treaty provides for three set of amendments in the area of competition law.[77] First, it modifies the numbering and wording of EU competition rules. Second, *prima facie*, it downgrades the status of competition policy in the EU's legal architecture, as former Article 3(1)(g) of the Treaty of Rome has been repealed.[78] The TEU's new Article 3 does not make any reference

[76] *Commission v Austria*, Case C-205/06, [2009] ECR I-1301; *Commission v Sweden*, Case C-249/06, [2009] ECR I-1335; *Commission v Finland*, Case C-118/07, [2009] ECR I-0000.

[77] See, eg, N Parr and N Cuninghame, "Treaty of Lisbon Enters into Force," *Ashurst Competition Newsletter* (December 2009), online: <http://www.ashurst.com/publication-item.aspx?id_Content=4901>; G Sproul, "The Coming into Force of the Lisbon Treaty and Its Impact on Competition Law," *Mayer Brown Newsletter* (2 December 2009), online: <http://www.mayerbrown.com/publications/The-coming-into-force-of-the-Lisbon-Treaty-and-its-impact-on-competition-law-12-02-2009/>; Linklaters LLP, "The Lisbon Treaty Comes into Force," *Stop Press* (14 December 2009); Nicolas Petit and Norman Neyrinck, "A Review of the Competition Law Implications of the Treaty on the Functioning of the European Union," *CPI Antitrust Chronicle* (17 February 2010), online: <https://www.competitionpolicyinternational.com/a-review-of-the-competition-law-implications-of-the-treaty-on-the-functioning-of-the-european-union/>.

[78] Concerns were raised during the negotiations with respect to repeal of Article 3 of the Treaty of Rome, *supra* note 15,which listed the EU's objectives. Article 3(1)(g) mandated the EU to implement "a system ensuring that competition in the internal market is not distorted." Thus, its repeal may affect the future application of the main provisions of competition law.

to "competition" as such.[79] Third, the Lisbon Treaty provides for a number of changes in the field of state aid.

In the context of former Article 3(1)(g) of the Treaty of Rome, it is pertinent to note that the ECJ had used this provision to give a teleological interpretation to Articles 81-86 of the Treaty of Rome. For example, in *Europemballage Corporation and Continental Can Company v Commission*, the ECJ, keeping an eye to "the spirit, general scheme and wording of Article [82], as well as to the system and objectives of the Treaty," divided the definition of the expression "abuse of a dominant position," which is contained in Article 82 of the Treaty of Rome, from EC policy as stated in Article 2 (which declared that the objective of the EC was to establish a common market) and Article 3(1)(g) of the Treaty of Rome.[80] Nevertheless, new Article 3(b) of the TFEU makes "the establishment of competition rules necessary for the functioning of the internal market" one of the EU's exclusive competences. Thus, removal of the reference to "competition" from the list of EU objectives does not appear to be particularly problematic.[81]

THE EU CHARTER OF FUNDAMENTAL RIGHTS: LEGALLY BINDING AND ENFORCEABLE

With the coming into force of the Lisbon Treaty, the EU Charter of Fundamental Rights became legally binding and enforceable.[82]

79 TEU, *supra* note 33, Article 3 states that one of the EU's objectives will be to "establish an internal market. It shall work for sustainable development of Europe based on balanced growth and price stability, a highly competitive social market economy, aiming at full employment and social progress, and a high level of protection and improvement of the quality of the environment. It shall promote scientific and technological advance."

80 *Europemballage Corporation and Continental Can Company v Commission*, Case 6/72, [1973] ECR 215.

81 Such removal of the reference "competition" could be considered a political attempt by some member states (such as France) to undermine the European Commission's battle against protectionist policies and anti-competitive state aid. For example, it might be argued that the absence of free competition as a central EU objective could be used as an argument before the ECJ by a member state in defence of actions to bolster national firms.

82 TEU, *supra* note 33, Article 6. The EU Charter, *supra* note 2, is not an integral part of the treaty. It was originally adopted as a non-binding declaration in 2000 during negotiation of the Treaty of Nice, *supra* note 4. However, the EU Charter is incorporated by reference, and made binding, by the TEU, Article 6.

This charter, which is widely regarded as a mirror image of the European Convention on Human Rights (ECHR), is the first legally binding fundamental rights instrument that binds all EU institutions. It necessarily follows that all EU measures must now be in accordance with the charter.[83]

Moreover, the Lisbon Treaty introduces an explicit requirement that the EU accede to the ECHR.[84] Accordingly, Europe will have two distinct but highly similar fundamental rights treaties supervised and enforced by two independent European courts — the European Court of Human Rights (ECtHR), which is based in Strasbourg, and the ECJ, which is based in Luxembourg. The accession of the EU to the ECHR will necessarily result in the ECtHR being able to review the judgments of the ECJ in light of the EU's obligations under the ECHR. However, Article 52(3) of the EU Charter of Fundamental Rights prescribes concordance of interpretation in the case of corresponding provisions as between the two instruments. Looking at their past experiences, it will be interesting to see how these two fundamental rights systems will interact and how they will accommodate any divergence in their jurisprudence in the future.

DEMOCRATIC REFORM OF INSTITUTIONS AND QUALIFIED MAJORITY VOTING (QMV)

Undoubtedly, the institutional set-up of the EU is one of the main focuses of the Lisbon Treaty, which extends the participatory rights of the European Parliament in the so-called "ordinary legislative procedure."[85] Further, apart from strengthening the European Parliament's position by making it a co-legislator with the Council in additional policy areas, national parliaments of member states will be more closely involved in the European decision-making process.[86] Notably, national parliaments will be informed about all

83 European Convention for the Protection of Human Rights and Fundamental Freedoms, as amended by Protocols nos. 11 and 14, 4 November 1950, ETS 5, online: <http://www.unhcr.org/refworld/docid/3ae6b3b04.html>.

84 TEU, *supra* note 33, Article 6(2).

85 TFEU, *supra* note 33, Articles 289(1), 291.

86 Protocol no. 1 on the Role of National Parliaments in the European Union, [2010] OJ C 83/203, online: <http://eur-lex.europa.eu/LexUriServ/LexUriServ.do?uri=OJ:C:2010:083:0201:0328:EN:PDF>; Protocol no. 2 on the Application of the Principles of Subsidiarity and Proportionality, [2010] OJ C 83/206, online:

legislative proposals at the same time they are sent to the European Parliament. In addition, national parliaments will be allowed to complain to the European Commission if they consider that the subsidiarity principle is infringed. If national parliaments muster sufficient support among themselves, they may, albeit indirectly, bring a case before the ECJ to review a potentially infringing act.[87]

The Lisbon Treaty also fundamentally changes the requirements for a "qualified majority" in the European Council, starting on 1 November 2014.[88] When the Council authorizes the negotiation and conclusion of agreements with third states, authorizes trade sanctions, and makes most of its decisions on legislation, it acts by a qualified majority. Importantly, however, the European Council has now been converted into a European institution with explicitly defined powers. Indeed, these powers have been significantly extended, returning to member states, as represented in the European Council, powers they had lost over time to the Commission and European Parliament.

Further, the merger of the so-called third pillar — which governs police and judicial co-operation — with the first pillar will allow the European Commission and the European Parliament to participate in the decision-making process regarding all future policing and criminal legislation. In addition, decisions of the Council of Ministers in this area will now be taken by a qualified majority vote rather than by consensus. This change should facilitate the legislative process.

Concluding Observations

The strengthening of European institutions brought about by the Lisbon Treaty is clearly a shift towards a more supranational decision-making process under increased parliamentary and judicial scrutiny. The greater participatory role of the European Parliament will likely have a major impact on EU policy making, given the fact that the European Parliament has in the past remained much more responsive to environmental or other social policy demands voiced by divergent stakeholders. At the same time, it is also beyond doubt that member states have retained and even increased their influence

---

<http://eur-lex.europa.eu/LexUriServ/LexUriServ.do?uri=OJ:C:2010:083:0201:0328:EN:PDF> [Protocol no. 2].

87 Protocol no. 2, *supra* note 86, Article 8.

88 TEU, *supra* note 33, Article 16(4).

in the European decision-making process through reforms to the European Council.

Selling institutional reform to the public is indeed a hard job. As the German Constitutional Court rightly pointed out, EU procedures are hybrid ones, oscillating in appearance between those found in national democracies and those characteristic of intergovernmental organizations. If the Lisbon Treaty differs significantly from the Constitutional Treaty in the nature of its reform of the EU, the process by which such reform was negotiated was more closed and more accelerated than in the case of any other such initiative to date. There was a lack of transparency and an exclusion of national parliaments from the process that still remains to be justified. The "u-turn" in the Irish referenda vividly illustrates the lack of knowledge about, and popular interest in, the European integration project, thus throwing into question the very democratic legitimacy of the entire process.

Similarly, both the German and Czech constitutional courts focused on whether excessive powers had been granted to the EU, although the bases for their concern were distinct. For the Czech Constitutional Court, this concern derived from the Czech Republic being a democratic state based upon the rule of law, which entails that unlimited powers could not be transferred to another body such as the EU. For the German Constitutional Court, the issue lay in the principle of self-determination, inherent in the right of each German citizen to be represented in the Bundestag (the German Parliament). Thus, the competences central to Germany's constitutional identity could not be transferred to the EU, as the latter lacked sufficient democratic structures to safeguard this principle. While allowing for the ratification of the Lisbon Treaty, both courts expressed concerns about individual provisions, thereby holding out the possibility of future review. Both courts also expressed serious concerns about the vagueness, and the possibility for abuse of, the simplified revision procedure. Notably, the German Constitutional Court considered that any revision using this procedure would constitute a formal amendment that would be open to constitutional review and require ratification by both German parliamentary chambers, the Bundestag, and the Bundesrat. The Czech Constitutional Court, for its part, was unhappy about the lack of clarity surrounding the EU's treaty-making powers. The concerns voiced by these two constitutional courts unmistakably suggest that use of these procedures is likely to be the subject of particular scrutiny by these (and perhaps other) constitutional courts in the future.

Europhiles have often swung between optimism and disillusion, and, in the capitals of Europe, Euro-skepticism seems to follow on the heels of EU-phoria just as often as the reverse occurs.[89] The history of European integration shows that it has progressed step by step and is indeed an ongoing and irreversible process. Notwithstanding all of its great achievements so far, there are ever-growing demands that issues of the "legitimacy gap" be addressed and that some credibility be given to the idea of building an EU "close to the people." The citizens of the EU all have legitimate expectations that EU institutions will address the mounting pressures of globalization, international security, immigration, transnational crime and terrorism, social security, and climate change. If EU institutions are able to do so, it may be that the Lisbon Treaty will have achieved its goal of enabling Europe to better shoulder the ever-growing challenges of governance.

AVINASH SHARMA
Visiting Research Fellow, Max Planck Institute for Comparative Public Law and International Law, Heidelberg, Germany

Sommaire

L'histoire de l'intégration européenne révèle un processus qui est irréversible et qui se poursuit toujours, étape par étape. Une telle étape récente est la conclusion du Traité de Lisbonne, qui est entré en vigueur le 1er décembre 2009, suite à des négociations couvrant près d'une décennie. Le traité vise notamment à améliorer le fonctionnement de l'Union européenne (UE) et modifie de façon significative les fondements conventionnels de l'UE qui en font une organisation supranationale. Le Traité de Lisbonne dote expressément l'UE de la personnalité juridique internationale, renforce le rôle du Parlement européen, et apporte des réformes significatives au rôle du haut représentant de l'Union pour les affaires étrangères et la politique de sécurité. En outre, le Traité de Lisbonne fait de la Charte européenne des droits fondamentaux un instrument juridiquement contraignant et exécutoire; et élargit les compétences de l'UE dans les domaines du commerce et d'autres relations

89 Francesca Astengo and Nanette Neuwahl, "Adoption of the Treaty on the Constitution for Europe," *ASIL Insights* (June 2004), online: <http://www.asil.org/insigh137.cfm>.

commerciales extérieures en lui fournissant une compétence exclusive dans le domaine de la politique commerciale commune. L'auteur passe en revue ces innovations, et d'autres, du Traité de Lisbonne et évalue brièvement le Traité et ses implications pour l'UE.

Summary

The history of European integration unmistakably shows that it has progressed step by step and is indeed an ongoing and irreversible process. One such step is the conclusion of the Lisbon Treaty, which came into force on 1 December 2009, following negotiations spanning nearly a decade. The treaty aims, *inter alia,* at improving the functioning of the European Union (EU) and significantly amends the treaty basis of the EU as a supranational organization. It formally establishes the EU as a legal entity under public international law, strengthens the role of the European Parliament, and significantly reforms the role of the high representative of the union for foreign affairs and security policy. Moreover, the treaty has made the EU Charter on Fundamental Rights a legally binding and enforceable instrument and has expanded the competences of the EU in the fields of trade and other external commercial relations by providing it with exclusive competence to conduct the EU's Common Commercial Policy. The author reviews these and other innovations of the Lisbon Treaty and briefly evaluates the treaty and its implications for the EU.

Leslie C. Green
(1920-2011)

The Board of Editors records with sadness the passing of Leslie Green, a long-standing member of the board (volume 12, 1974 to volume 36, 1998) and an honorary editor since volume 37 (1999).

Leslie Green was a renowned expert on military law and the law of armed conflict. He studied under Georg Swarzenberger at the University of London, was dean of law at the University of Singapore, and then for almost thirty years taught at the University of Alberta. He also held the Stockton Chair of International Law at the United States Naval War College and advised both the Canadian and American governments on issues relating to armed conflict, terrorism, and international crimes.

The recipient of an honorary LL.D. from the University of Alberta in 1994, Leslie Green received the John E. Read Medal from the Canadian Council on International Law in 1997 and was a fellow of the Royal Society of Canada. Green contributed regularly to the *Canadian Yearbook of International Law,* his last contribution being a note on "The Role of Discipline in the Military" in volume 42 (2004).[1] He was a founding member of the Canadian Council on International Law and, for many years, an active participant in its meetings, someone who could always be expected to challenge speakers from the floor and not let what he regarded as error or heresy pass.

A dedicated teacher and scholar, one who held strong opinions and was ready to voice them forcefully, Leslie Green enriched the Canadian international legal community and made a lasting contribution to his fields of expertise. His works are read worldwide,

1 Leslie C Green, "The Role of Discipline in the Military" (2004) 42 Can YB Int'l Law 385.

and he influenced the development of government policy in respect of legal issues relating to war, armed conflict, terrorism, and crimes against humanity.

The Editors

Charles B. Bourne
(1921-2012)

It was with great regret that the Board of Editors learned of the death of the *Canadian Yearbook of International Law*'s founding editor-in-chief, Charles Bourne.

Charles Bourne had a long and distinguished career as an international lawyer. A graduate of the University of Toronto, Cambridge University, and the Harvard Law School, he taught initially at the University of Saskatchewan and then for many years at the University of British Columbia, where he was at the forefront of the international law program for over thirty years. Many of his former students went on to have distinguished careers in the field of international law, including several legal advisers to the Canadian Department of External (later Foreign) Affairs. His intellectual rigour, his clarity of thought, his attention to detail, and his high professional standards were all passed on, and they stayed with those taught by him or indeed anyone who came into contact with him.

As a scholar, Charles was renowned for his work in the field of international water resources law. A long-time chair of the International Law Association Committee on Water Resources Law, Charles was one of the authors of the Helsinki Rules, which set the standard for the field and remain a hallmark today. As Academic-in-Residence in the Department of External Affairs in the early 1970s, Charles worked on the Great Lakes Water Quality Agreement, and he was an authority on the Columbia River Treaty as well.

In addition to his numerous articles on international law, Charles' great scholarly contribution was as the founding editor-in-chief of this Yearbook. Starting with little and working with a group of other Canadian scholars who were committed to the project, Charles built the Yearbook over the thirty years he served as editor-in-chief to the place in international legal scholarship it holds today. Charles had high standards — articles had to meet those standards in order to be accepted and then they were subjected to a rigorous, if at times idiosyncratic, editorial process. The objective was to publish work of high quality and to provide a forum for the work of Canadian scholars and Canadian practice in international law. The result, as the volumes of the past and this volume show, speaks for itself. The Yearbook bears the indelible imprint of Charles Bourne, the scholar, and of Charles Bourne, the man.

A full account of the career and contribution of Charles Bourne is found in the article in volume 34 of the *Canadian Yearbook of International Law* by Ronald St. J. Macdonald, "Charles B. Bourne: Scholar, Teacher, and Editor, Innovator in the Development of the International Law of Water Resources."[1] The opening line of this article provides a fitting tribute: "Charles B. Bourne is a role model for anyone pursuing a career in public international law in Canada."[2]

On a personal note, Charles Bourne was a man I admired, a mentor, a scholar to emulate, and one whose standards were ideals to live up to — he was a true role model. He fostered my career as an international lawyer and then paid me the honour of inviting me to succeed him as editor-in-chief of this yearbook. Charles Bourne's passing saddens, but his contribution was immense and his legacy endures.

Donald M. McRae
Editor-in-Chief (1993-2010)

[1] Ronald St J Macdonald, "Charles B. Bourne: Scholar, Teacher, and Editor, Innovator in the Development of the International Law of Water Resources" (1996) 34 Can YB Int'l Law 3.

[2] *Ibid* at 3.

Chronique de droit international économique en 2010-11 / Digest of International Economic Law in 2010-11

I Commerce

RICHARD OUELLET ET HERVÉ A. PRINCE

I. Introduction

Un regard de droit international économique sur l'activité commerciale des années 2010-2011 touchant le Canada permet de constater que l'on n'arrêtera pas de sitôt l'ouverture des marchés. L'impossibilité de conclure le cycle de Doha ne ralentit pas le phénomène de l'intégration économique. Elle l'amène à prendre d'autres formes. Autant au plan régional ou continental qu'au sein même du système commercial multilatéral, on verra que les années 2010 et 2011 ont amené leurs lots de progrès dans la négociation et la mise en œuvre des accords économiques internationaux.

L'année 2010 a commencé avec la célébration du 25ème anniversaire de l'adhésion du Canada à l'Organisation des États Américains (OEA).[1] Si le membership du Canada à l'OEA ne relève pas directement de sa politique commerciale, il n'est pas sans lien avec la stratégie appliquée ces années-ci par le gouvernement canadien

Richard Ouellet est professeur titulaire de droit international économique à la Faculté de droit de l'Université Laval. Hervé A. Prince est professeur adjoint à la Faculté de droit de l'Université de Montréal. Les auteurs sont respectivement membres du Centre de recherche en droit public (CRDP) et du Centre de droit des affaires et du commerce international. Ils sont tous les deux membres du Centre d'études en droit économique (CÉDÉ). Les auteurs tiennent à remercier Mme Lilian Balderas Morales pour sa collaboration à la préparation de cette chronique.

1 Pour mémoire, il faut rappeler que les origines de l'OEA remontent à la Première Conférence internationale tenue à Washington d'octobre 1889 à avril 1890 et qui avait permis la création de l'Union Internationale des Républiques américaines, devenue par la suite Union panaméricaine, puis OEA en 1948 grâce à la Charte de l'OEA, entrée en vigueur en 1951. Les objectifs de l'Organisation sont plutôt de nature politique, en ligne: <http://www.oas.org/fr/a_propos/qui_nous_sommes.asp>.

quant à l'ouverture des marchés. Considérée comme l'ancêtre des institutions régionales, l'OEA n'a pas véritablement de compétence en matière commerciale comme l'indique bien l'article 1er de sa charte constitutive.[2] Il est toutefois prévu que le Secrétariat de l'Organisation fournisse aux Membres de l'aide en matière de renforcement des capacités humaines et l'amélioration des opportunités commerciales et de la compétitivité des entreprises. En effet, la politique économique et commerciale canadienne menée dans les années qui ont suivi ce 25ème anniversaire semble faire écho à cette recherche de nouveaux marchés. Depuis 2010, le gouvernement Harper affiche une détermination dans la recherche de nouveaux débouchés pour les entreprises canadiennes, le resserrement des partenariats économiques et s'implique davantage sur la scène mondiale dans les domaines économiques et commerciaux.

L'illustration de cette détermination peut se retrouver tant dans la politique menée au niveau national qu'international. Au plan national, on note que la politique canadienne menée au cours des années 2010 et 2011 aura insisté sur deux leviers essentiels en termes d'opportunités pour nos entreprises: la multiplication des programmes d'appuis aux entreprises et aux collectivités locales dans le but d'y créer des conditions favorables à l'investissement étranger[3] d'un côté et une accentuation des programmes d'aides aux entreprises canadiennes désireuses d'étendre leurs activités dans les pays en développement de l'autre. Sur le premier aspect de cette politique, on se contentera de souligner les actions menées dans le cadre d'Investissement Canada — Initiative des communautés" (ICIC).[4] Ce dispositif découlant du Programme de soutien au commerce mondial[5] a eu pour objectif d'aider les communautés locales à attirer des investisseurs étrangers sur leurs territoires et y créer des conditions de croissance et d'emploi. Entre 2010 et 2011,

2 *Charter of the Organization of American States (A-41)*, en ligne: <http://www.oas.org/dil/treaties_A-41_Charter_of_the_Organization_of_American_States.htm>.

3 Nous n'insisterons pas davantage sur cet aspect de la politique commerciale canadienne qui sera abordée dans une autre partie de cette chronique, celle portant sur les investissements étrangers.

4 Affaires étrangères et Commerce international, "Investissement Canada — Initiative des Communautés," en ligne: <http://www.international.gc.ca/funding-financement/investment-investissement/index.aspx?lang=fra&menu_id=12&view=d>.

5 Affaires étrangères et Commerce international, "Programme de soutien au commerce mondial," en ligne: <http://www.deleguescommerciaux.gc.ca/fra/financement/accueil.jsp>.

plusieurs communautés[6] à travers le pays, dont la Nouvelle-Écosse,[7] la Colombie-Britannique,[8] et des associations relevant de divers secteurs,[9] du Québec,[10] de l'Ontario,[11] de l'Île-du-Prince Édouard,[12] ou de l'Alberta[13] ont ainsi pu bénéficier de ce programme.

Sur le deuxième aspect de cette politique au plan national, on peut relever les actions menées à partir de 2010 au sein du Programme de coopération pour l'investissement développé dans le cadre de la stratégie globale de réduction de la pauvreté. Le nouveau programme remplaçait en 2010 le Programme de coopération

6 Affaires étrangères et Commerce international, "Le gouvernement Harper aide les collectivités locales à attirer des investissements étrangers pour stimuler la création d'emplois et de croissance et assurer la prospérité des Canadiens," en ligne: <http://www.international.gc.ca/media_commerce/comm/news-communiques/2011/318.aspx?lang=fra&view=d>.

7 Affaires étrangères et Commerce international, "Les collectivités attirent l'investissement étranger et créent des emplois avec le soutien du gouvernement du Canada," en ligne: <http://www.international.gc.ca/media_commerce/comm/news-communiques/2010/241.aspx?lang=fra&view=d>.

8 Affaires étrangères et Commerce international, "Le gouvernement du Canada appuie divers groups de la Colombie-Britannique pour les aider à attirer des investissements étrangers et créer des emplois," en ligne: <http://www.international.gc.ca/media_commerce/comm/news-communiques/2010/258.aspx?lang=fra&view=d>.

9 Affaires étrangères et Commerce international, "Le gouvernement du Canada aide les entreprises canadiennes à se mesurer à la concurrence mondiale afin de créer des emplois et de favoriser la prospérité," en ligne: <http://www.international.gc.ca/media_commerce/comm/news-communiques/2010/260.aspx?lang=fra&view=d>.

10 Affaires étrangères et Commerce international, "Le gouvernement du Canada accorde son appui à divers organismes communautaires du Québec pour les aider à attirer des investissements étrangers et créer des emplois," en ligne: <http://www.international.gc.ca/media_commerce/comm/news-communiques/2010/263.aspx?lang=fra&view=d>.

11 Affaires étrangères et Commerce international, "Le gouvernement Harper aide les collectivités de l'Ontario à attirer des investissements étrangers et à créer des emplois," en ligne: <http://www.international.gc.ca/media_commerce/comm/news-communiques/2010/288.aspx?lang=fra&view=d>.

12 Affaires étrangères et Commerce international, "Le gouvernement Harper ouvre de nouveaux marchés pour l'Île-du-Prince Édouard," en ligne: <http://www.international.gc.ca/media_commerce/comm/news-communiques/2010/315.aspx?lang=fra&view=d>.

13 Affaires étrangères et Commerce international, "Le gouvernement Harper aide les collectivité de l'Alberta en matière d'investissements étrangers," en ligne: <http://www.international.gc.ca/media_commerce/comm/news-communiques/2010/377-1.aspx?lang=fra&view=d>.

industrielle de l'Agence canadienne de développement économique (PCI-ACDI)[14] qui avait notamment pour objectif d'"inciter les entreprises du secteur privé canadien à établir des relations d'affaires à long terme avec les partenaires des pays en développement."[15] Une nouvelle façon pour le gouvernement Harper de permettre aux entreprises d'ici de nouer des partenariats nouveaux avec des marchés autrefois moins attractifs.[16]

Sur le plan international, le maître-mot des années 2010 et 2011 de la politique du gouvernement Harper aura été l'accentuation des politiques d'intégration économique. Il s'agit surtout pour ce gouvernement de miser sur des mesures de renforcement de ses relations économiques et commerciales. Au-delà des États-Unis, partenaire historique du Canada, la politique commerciale canadienne au cours de ces deux dernières années aura surtout été marquée par des actions tous azimuts pour un bilatéralisme commercial renforcé à côté d'un multilatéralisme qui progresse à petits pas à l'Organisation mondiale du commerce (OMC).

II. Le commerce canadien aux plans bilatéral et régional

Au cours des deux années écoulées, le commerce canadien aux plans bilatéral et régional aura été marqué par un effort soutenu du gouvernement fédéral à ouvrir de nouveaux marchés grâce à l'établissement de partenariats nouveaux et au renforcement des liens économiques et commerciaux classiques.

A. l'intégration économique à l'échelle planétaire

1. L'intégration nord-américaine

Au cours des années 2010 et 2011, un constat domine les relations commerciales du Canada avec ses partenaires nord-américains: le renforcement des liens de co-opération économique.

14 Il faut rappeler qu'en 1978, avait été institué le Programme de coopération industrielle de l'Agence canadienne de développement économique (PCI-ACDI) qui prenait en charge le volet de la coopération industrielle de l'ACDI.

15 Agence canadienne de développement international — Direction de l'évaluation — Direction générale de la gestion du rendement et des connaissances, Rapport administratif de l'évaluation du Programme de coopération industrielle (ACDI-PCI) de l'ACDI, décembre 2007, à la p 2.

16 Affaires étrangères et Commerce international, "Nouvelle initiative visant à aider les entreprises canadiennes à étendre leurs activités dans les pays en développement," en ligne: <http://www.international.gc.ca/media_commerce/comm/news-communiques/2010/010.aspx?lang=fra&view=d>.

Dès l'hiver 2010, la volonté canadienne de maintenir des liens privilégiés de co-opération et d'entente cordiale avec les États-Unis s'est exprimée dans l'accord sur les marchés publics passé, on s'en souviendra, en réaction à l'insertion d'une clause "*Buy American*" dans le Plan de relance Obama de 2009.[17] Cet accord éliminant les mesures du Plan de relance Obama affectant le commerce canadien est entré en vigueur en février 2010.[18] Grâce à cet accord, les entreprises canadiennes pourront participer aux projets d'infrastructures états-uniens financés par l'American Recovery and Reinvestment Act. Les fournisseurs états-uniens et canadiens pourront ainsi bénéficier d'un accès permanent et garanti aux approvisionnements de leurs marchés publics respectifs. Cette entente cordiale va également se traduire par la publication en décembre 2011 d'un Plan d'action conjoint sur la sécurité du périmètre et la compétitivité économique[19] dont le chapitre sur le commerce insiste sur la facilitation des mouvements et le commerce transfrontalier.

Dans la même veine, on peut noter l'aboutissement des discussions canado-américaines sur la gestion transfrontière de l'eau ou sur les dispositions "*Buy American*" du "*American Jobs Act*" (projet de loi sur les emplois américains).[20] En fait, les relations avec le voisin du Sud sont demeurées bonnes nonobstant les craintes qu'a pu susciter au Canada l'entrée en vigueur aux États-Unis des dispositions relatives au "*Buy American.*" Aujourd'hui, le débat sur les marchés publics peut être considéré comme un sujet clos si l'on s'en tient aux discussions ayant mené à la conclusion d'un nouvel accord plurilatéral sur les marchés publics dans le cadre

17 Voir Richard Ouellet, "Chronique de droit international économique en 2009," (2010) 48 ACDI 255 à la p 258.

18 Accord entre le Gouvernement du Canada et le Gouvernement des États-Unis d'Amérique en matière de marchés publics, en ligne: <http://www.international.gc.ca/trade-agreements-accords-commerciaux/assets/pdfs/FRE-Canada-USA_Government_Procurement.pdf>. On sait que cet accord comportait des obligations temporaires dont l'application a cessé en septembre 2011.

19 Gouvernement du Canada, "Plan d'action — Par-delà la frontière: une mission commune de la sécurité du périmètre et de la compétitivité économique," en ligne: <http://www.borderactionplan-plandactionfrontalier.gc.ca/psec-scep/assets/pdfs/bap_report-paf_rapport-fra-dec2011.pdf>.

20 Affaires étrangères et Commerce international, "Déclaration du ministre du commerce international, Ed Fast, sur les dispositions "*Buy American*" de l'*American Jobs Act*," en ligne: <http://www.international.gc.ca/media_commerce/comm/news-communiques/2011/307.aspx?lang=fra&view=d>.

de l'Organisation mondiale du commerce.[21] Le nouvel accord innove sur un point de discorde essentiel, à savoir l'élargissement de son champ d'application à de nouvelles entités gouvernementales y compris les entités des gouvernements locaux, les entités souscentrales, les services ainsi que d'autres activités faisant l'objet de marchés publics.[22]

Avec le Mexique, la bonne entente s'est traduite par la signature de l'Accord de reconnaissance mutuelle pour l'évaluation de la conformité du matériel de télécommunication. Il s'agit là d'un réel succès pour le gouvernement Harper mais surtout pour les entreprises canadiennes de télécommunication, qui pourront désormais s'implanter au Mexique sans devoir se soumettre aux procédures supplémentaires d'évaluation de la conformité mexicaine. Cet accord traduit surtout la volonté de co-opération des Membres de l'ALÉNA puisque les discussions en vue de la signature de l'accord ont été menées dans le cadre du Sous-comité des normes de télécommunication de l'ALÉNA.

2. *Le commerce canadien dans les Amériques*

En 2008, le Canada lançait sa nouvelle "stratégie commerciale mondiale"[23] dans laquelle il avait identifié 13 marchés prioritaires qui offriraient de meilleurs débouchés et un grand potentiel de croissance pour le Canada. Au nombre de ces marchés, apparaissaient les Amériques (Brésil, Amérique latine et Caraïbes, Mexique et États-Unis) au premier rang. Le document indiquait notamment que l'intérêt canadien dans cette région serait d'approfondir l'accès aux marchés grâce à des pourparlers commerciaux et la négociation d'une approche continentale à l'intégration, au développement et à la compétitivité économique.[24]

[21] OMC, Les Conférences ministérielles, Note d'information: L'Accord sur les marchés publics (AMP), en ligne: <http://www.wto.org/french/thewto_f/minist_f/min11_f/brief_gpa_f.htm>. Nous traiterons plus longuement de cet accord plurilatéral plus bas.

[22] OMC, Comité des marchés publics, Révision de l'Accord sur les marchés public — situation au 13 décembre 2010, OMC Doc GPA/W/313 du 16 décembre 2010.

[23] Richard Ouellet, "Chronique de Droit international économique en 2007" (2008) 46 ACDI 433, à la p 343.

[24] Affaires étrangères et Commerce international, "La stratégie commerciale mondiale pour assurer la croissance et la prospérité," en ligne: <http://www.international.gc.ca/commerce/assets/pdfs/GCS-fr.pdf> à la p 14.

Au cours des années 2010 et 2011, cette volonté du gouvernement fédéral s'est concrétisée à travers les négociations ou la conclusion de plusieurs accords d'intégration économique avec les pays des Amériques. On peut ainsi signaler la signature avec la Colombie d'un Accord de libre-échange dont la loi de mise en œuvre a reçu la sanction royale en juin 2010.[25] Cet accord de libre-échange auquel s'ajoutent les accords de co-opération dans le domaine de l'environnement et du travail établit des conditions préférentielles d'échanges commerciaux entre les deux pays dans les domaines du commerce des marchandises et des services, les marchés publics, les investissements et la politique de concurrence, en plus de prévoir un mécanisme de règlement des différends.[26] La signature de cet accord avec la Colombie relance la co-opération économique canadienne avec ce pays. En effet, l'accord fait suite à la reprise des exportations de bovins canadiens en direction de la Colombie. Depuis 2003, le bœuf canadien était sous embargo suite à la découverte d'un cas de vache folle en Alberta. Et la réouverture du marché colombien au bovin canadien constituait une première en Amérique du Sud depuis l'embargo. C'est donc le signe d'une confiance retrouvée entre les deux pays. Cette réouverture était d'autant plus attendue que pour la seule Colombie, les importations de bovins canadiens sont évaluées à 6 millions de dollars par le *Canada Beef Export Federation*.[27] Il s'agit là donc d'un marché important pour l'industrie canadienne de l'élevage bovin et pour le secteur agricole en entier, qui pourra désormais, grâce à l'accord de libre-échange, exporter en franchise de droits vers la Colombie les bovins vivants, des lentilles, l'orge, le pois et certaines coupes de viande de bœuf.

Parallèlement, le bilatéralisme commercial canadien va poursuivre son enracinement dans les Amériques. Cet encrage prend au cours des années 2010 et 2011 la forme d'un accord de libre-échange avec le Panama qui est entré en vigueur le 14 mai 2010.[28] L'accord avec

25 Loi de mise en œuvre de l'Accord de libre-échange Canada-Colombie, LC 2010, c 4.

26 Voir, Accord de libre-échange Canada-Colombie, en ligne: <http://www.international.gc.ca/trade-agreements-accords-commerciaux/agr-acc/colombia-colombie/can-colombia-toc-tdm-can-colombie.aspx?lang=fra&view=d>.

27 Affaires étrangères et Commerce international, Communiqué du 9 avril 2010, en ligne: <http://www.international.gc.ca/media_commerce/comm/news-communiques/2010/131.aspx?lang=fra&view=d>.

28 Accord de libre-échange Canada-Panama, en ligne: <http://www.international.gc.ca/trade-agreements-accords-commerciaux/agr-acc/panama/panama-toc-panama-tdm.aspx?lang=fra&view=d>.

le Panama offre des conditions préférentielles de commerce des marchandises, de commerce des services, des conditions favorables à l'investissement étranger et un meilleur accès aux marchés publics. Dans le même temps, le Canada engage des pourparlers avec le Costa Rica en vue d'élargir la portée de l'accord de libre-échange qui le lie à ce pays. L'accord actuellement en vigueur entre le Canada et le Costa Rica ne portait que sur le commerce des marchandises.[29] Le lancement des négociations avec le gouvernement Costaricain devrait permettre d'élargir l'accord entré en vigueur en 2002 au commerce des services, ainsi qu'aux marchés publics. Le nouvel accord devrait également couvrir le commerce électronique, les télécommunications, les investissements et les obstacles techniques au commerce.

Mais au-delà du continent, le Canada aura déployé au cours de la période 2010-2011 les mêmes efforts pour conclure ou pour accélérer les négociations en vue de la conclusion d'accords de libre-échange avec des pays situés en dehors de la région des Amériques.

3. *Le bilatéralisme commercial canadien avec l'Europe*

Le commerce bilatéral du Canada avec l'Europe a été principalement marqué au cours des années 2010 et 2011 par les négociations en vue de la conclusion d'un Accord économique et commercial global entre le Canada et l'Union Européenne (AECG). Ces négociations se dérouleront dans la plus grande discrétion, comme on pouvait déjà le pressentir dans les déclarations conjointes issues des Sommets de Québec[30] et de Prague[31] respectivement en 2008 et 2009.

Ce qui est certain, c'est que les négociations lancées à Prague en 2009 entre le Canada et l'Union Européenne devraient aboutir à la conclusion d'un accord économique de large portée, incluant notamment la libéralisation du commerce des marchandises et des services, l'investissement, les marchés publics des gouvernements

29 Accord de libre-échange Canada-Costa Rica, en ligne: <http://www.international.gc.ca/trade-agreements-accords-commerciaux/agr-acc/costarica/Costa_Rica_toc.aspx?lang=fr&menu_id=7&view=d>.

30 Gouvernement du Canada, Déclaration du Sommet Canada-UE de 2008, en ligne: <http://www.canadainternational.gc.ca/eu-ue/bilateral_relations_bilaterales/2008_10_17_statement-declaration.aspx?lang=fra&view=d>.

31 Gouvernement du Canada, Déclaration du Sommet Canada-UE de 2008, en ligne: <http://www.canadainternational.gc.ca/eu-ue/bilateral_relations_bilaterales/2009_05_06_statement-declaration.aspx?lang=fra&view=d>.

centraux et sous-centraux, la propriété intellectuelle, le renforcement de la co-opération en matières de règlementation, de politique de concurrence, de développement durable et de règlement des différends.[32] Depuis la première réunion de 2009, neuf séries de négociations auront été tenues soit dans un pays Membre de l'Union Européenne, soit au Canada où la neuvième série de négociations s'est déroulée du 17 au 21 octobre 2011 à Ottawa.[33] Le communiqué laconique qui suit cette négociation ne laisse rien entrevoir de ce qui a pu y être débattu.[34]

Il apparaît toutefois que le Gouvernement fédéral, les gouvernements d'États européens engagés dans la négociation ainsi que les milieux d'affaires des deux côtés de l'Atlantique semblent assez convaincus des retombées économiques positives de l'AECG dont la conclusion est désormais envisagée pour 2012.[35] Cet optimisme vient à être renforcé par les données publiées par Statistiques Canada. En effet, d'après les chiffres rapportés par le Ministère des Affaires étrangères et du Commerce international du Canada, avec une population de plus 500 millions d'habitants, l'Union Européenne constitue le plus grand marché commun du monde et arrive en deuxième position des partenaires commerciaux du Canada pour le commerce des marchandises et des services. Pour la seule année 2010, par exemple, les exportations canadiennes de marchandises et de services vers l'Europe ont représenté 49,2 milliards de dollars, alors que les exportations européennes vers le Canada ont représenté 55,3 milliards de dollars.[36] Il est donc clair que le marché européen constitue l'une des priorités du

[32] Premier ministre du Canada, "Le Canada et l'Union Européenne: Vers un accord sur un partenariat économique approfondi," en ligne: <http://www.pm.gc.ca/fra/media.asp?id=2560>.

[33] Affaires étrangères et Commerce international, "Le Canada et l'Union Européenne concluent la neuvième série de négociations en vue d'un accord historique de libre-échange," en ligne: <http://www.international.gc.ca/media_commerce/comm/news-communiques/2011/312.aspx?lang=fra&view=d>.

[34] *Ibid.*

[35] Affaires étrangères et Commerce international, "Le ministre Van Loan conclut une visite de promotion du libre-échange en Europe," en ligne: <http://www.international.gc.ca/media_commerce/comm/news-communiques/2010/157.aspx?lang=fra&view=d>.

[36] Affaires étrangères et Commerce international, "Négociations en vue d'un accord économique et commercial global entre le Canada et l'union européenne," en ligne: <http://www.international.gc.ca/trade-agreements-accords-commerciaux/agr-acc/eu-ue/can-eu.aspx?lang=fra&view=d>.

bilatéralisme commercial canadien. Ceci est d'autant plus vrai que l'offensive canadienne ne s'arrête pas seulement aux portes des Membres de l'Union Européenne.

Pour preuve, le Canada a entamé en 2010 parallèlement aux négociations avec l'Europe, des discussions avec l'Ukraine dans le but de parvenir avec ce pays à la conclusion d'un accord de libre-échange. Fort des relations culturelles qu'entretiennent les deux pays, le Canada entend s'appuyer sur ces liens pour développer des relations commerciales plus étroites avec l'Ukraine. Cet accord pour lequel la deuxième série de négociations a eu lieu en mai 2011 devrait favoriser les exportations canadiennes des produits de la mer, la machinerie y compris le commerce de véhicules, les matières plastiques et les produits du fer et d'acier.[37]

4. *L'offensive commerciale canadienne dans le reste du monde*

Avec les difficultés du cycle de Doha dans le cadre des négociations commerciales multilatérales de l'OMC, le Canada semble avoir misé sur le bilatéralisme commercial. Le bilatéralisme commercial canadien s'est ainsi ouvert au cours de ces dernières années à des marchés autrefois délaissés ou avec lesquels ses échanges commerciaux sont quasiment nuls. Il en est ainsi notamment des pays africains avec lesquels le Canada entreprend de plus en plus des négociations en vue d'y établir des partenariats économiques. La concrétisation de ce type de partenariat reste encore à ses débuts et les actions concrètes posées par le gouvernement au cours de ces deux dernières années ne sont pas spectaculaires même si elles marquent le début d'une offensive. Il en est ainsi de la visite du ministre Van Loan en mars 2010 au Kenya au cours de laquelle il réaffirmait l'appui du Canada en faveur de l'intégration économique dans la région de l'Afrique de l'Est. Le ministre avait alors souligné les intentions canadiennes par sa participation à la signature d'un protocole d'entente entre la Corporation commerciale canadienne, l'Agence canadienne de passation des contrats et d'approvisionnement internationaux et Muringa Holdings Ltd., un consortium dans le secteur de l'énergie dont le siège se trouve à Nairobi au Kenya.[38]

[37] Affaires étrangères et Commerce international, "Le Canada mène des négociations de libre-échange avec l'Ukraine," en ligne: <http://www.international.gc.ca/media_commerce/comm/news-communiques/2010/190.aspx?lang=fra&view=d>.

[38] Affaires étrangères et Commerce international, "Visite ministérielle en Afrique," en ligne: <http://www.international.gc.ca/commerce/visit-visite/africa-2010-afrique.aspx?lang=fra&view=d>.

Cette offensive s'est poursuivie d'abord à Toronto en mars 2011 avec la Conférence intitulée *L'Afrique en essor: aux frontières de l'entreprenariat et de l'innovation* qui réunissait des dirigeants du monde des affaires, des scientifiques et des représentants du gouvernement dans le but de réfléchir sur les aspects déterminants de la croissance économique en Afrique.[39] Depuis, des négociations ont été engagées entre le Gouvernement canadien et le Maroc en vue de la conclusion d'un accord de libre-échange. Le premier cycle des négociations s'est déroulé du 11 au 14 octobre 2011 à Ottawa.[40] La conclusion d'un accord de libre-échange avec le Maroc constituera le premier du genre du gouvernement canadien avec un pays africain. Il ouvrira une porte vers les pays de la Méditerranée mais également vers l'Afrique subsaharienne.

Au-delà de l'Afrique, le gouvernement canadien renforce sa coopération économique avec les pays du Moyen-Orient comme en témoignent les discussions exploratoires engagées avec Israël en vue d'élargir l'accord de libre-échange existant avec ce pays (ALECI).[41] L'ALECI, entré en vigueur en 1997, aura permis de doubler le commerce bilatéral avec Israël. Entre 1996 et 2010, la valeur des échanges commerciaux entre les deux pays est passée de 507 millions de dollars à 1,4 milliard de dollars.[42] Le Canada a l'intention d'élargir davantage cet accord afin d'y intégrer le commerce des services, les marchés publics, l'investissement, les questions environnementales et le travail.

C'est surtout vers l'Asie que l'offensive canadienne aura été plus significative notamment grâce au resserrement des liens économiques, commerciaux et d'investissement avec les pays d'Asie. Plus globalement, le renforcement de ces liens se fera dans le cadre des

[39] Affaires étrangères et Commerce international, "Le gouvernement Harper s'engage à ouvrir de nouveaux marchés en Afrique," en ligne: <http://www.international.gc.ca/media_commerce/comm/news-communiques/2011/103.aspx?lang=fra&view=d>.

[40] Affaires étrangères et Commerce international, "Début des négociations en vue d'un accord de libre-échange avec le Maroc," en ligne: <http://www.international.gc.ca/trade-agreements-accords-commerciaux/agr-acc/morocco-maroc.aspx?lang=fra&view=d>.

[41] Accord de libre-échange entre le Gouvernement du Canada et le Gouvernement de l'État d'Israël, en ligne:< http://www.international.gc.ca/trade-agreements-accords-commerciaux/agr-acc/israel/toc-tdm.aspx?lang=fra&view=d>.

[42] Affaires étrangères et Commerce international, "Accord de libre-échange entre le Gouvernement du Canada et le Gouvernement de l'État d'Israël," en ligne: <http://www.international.gc.ca/trade-agreements-accords-commerciaux/agr-acc/israel/index.aspx?lang=fra&view=d>.

relations du Canada avec les pays Membres de la Coopération économique pour l'Asie-Pacifique (APEC)[43] et des pays Membres de l'Association des Nations d'Asie du Sud-Est (ANASE).[44] Dans un cadre plus restreint, ces deux dernières années auront été marquées par le lancement des négociations en vue de la conclusion d'un accord de libre-échange avec l'Inde[45] ainsi que la promotion du commerce international avec la Chine.

B. LES DIFFÉRENDS LIÉS À L'ALÉNA IMPLIQUANT LE CANADA

L'Accord sur le bois d'œuvre résineux signé en 2006 entre le Canada et les États-Unis[46] devait, comme le rappelait un groupe spécial, mettre un terme à tout recours juridictionnel entre les parties et ôter à tout tribunal canadien et états-unien tout pouvoir consultatif en cette matière.[47]

Alors que l'accord arrive bientôt à échéance, on peut considérer qu'il a plutôt bien fonctionné. Toutefois, depuis son entrée en vigueur, le tribunal arbitral de Londres a dû se prononcer sur plusieurs de ses dispositions.[48] Au cours de l'année 2011, le tribunal aura eu à donner suite à un recours états-unien déposé en janvier 2008 et portant sur la conformité des programmes de l'Ontario et

43 Affaires étrangères et Commerce international, "18ème réunion des dirigeants de l'APEC- 13 et 14 novembre 2010," en ligne: <http://www.international.gc.ca/apec/apec_2010_declaration.aspx?lang=fra&view=d>. Voir aussi Affaires étrangères et Commerce international, "19ème Réunion des dirigeants de l'APEC-12 et 13 novembre 2011," en ligne: <http://www.international.gc.ca/apec/apec_2011_declaration.aspx?lang=fra&view=d>.

44 Affaires étrangères et Commerce international, "Déclaration conjointe sur le partenariat renforcé ANASE-Canada," en ligne: <http://www.international.gc.ca/asia_pacific-asie_pacifique/highlights-faits/JointDeclaration-AseanCanadaAnase-DeclarationConjointe.aspx?lang=fra&view=d>.

45 Affaires étrangères et Commerce international, "Le lancement des négociations de libre-échange est le point dominant de la visite du ministre Van Loan en Inde," en ligne: <http://www.international.gc.ca/media_commerce/comm/news-communiques/2010/367.aspx?lang=fra&view=d>.

46 Accord sur le bois d'œuvre résineux entre le Gouvernement du Canada et le Gouvernement des États-Unis, en ligne: <http://www.international.gc.ca/controls-controles/assets/pdfs/softwood/SLA-fr.pdf>.

47 *Groupe spécial, Certains produits de bois d'œuvre résineux en provenance du Canada: décision définitive sur le champ d'application concernant les importations classes dans la sous-position 4409.10.05 du HTSUS,* Dossier du Secrétariat n° USA-CDA-2006-1904-05 [Rapport du Groupe spécial].

48 London Court of International Arbitration (LCIA), 3 March 2008, *The United States of America v Canada,* Case n° 7941, en ligne: <http://www.international.gc.ca/controls-controles/assets/pdfs/softwood/Award03-03-2008.pdf>; London

du Québec relativement à l'accord sur le bois d'œuvre résineux.[49] Dans sa décision, le tribunal a considéré que les programmes des gouvernements provinciaux désignés n'étaient pas conformes à l'Accord de 2006. Il conclut à la violation par le Canada de l'article XVII(1) de l'accord relatif aux mesures anti-contournement.[50] Cette décision d'arbitrage est à peine rendue qu'une nouvelle procédure est introduite par les États-Unis au cours de la même année, 2011. Cette fois, il s'agit d'une requête visant à vérifier la conformité du système d'établissement des prix du bois imposés en Colombie-Britannique. En l'occurrence, les États-Unis considéraient que la Colombie-Britannique a vendu pour moins cher que requis par le système de tarification de l'accord de 2006, son bois d'œuvre à ses producteurs nationaux. Ce qui confère à ceux-ci d'importants avantages additionnels et par le fait même, violerait l'accord de 2006 puisque la sous-évaluation opérée contourne les mesures à l'exportation prévues par l'accord sur le bois d'œuvre conclu entre le Canada et les États-Unis en 2006. Par ce fait, le Canada violerait le mécanisme de tarification mis en place par l'accord de 2006.[51] L'affaire devra dans les prochains mois faire l'objet d'une décision par le tribunal de Londres.

III. Le commerce canadien et l'Organisation mondiale du commerce (OMC)

A. Les développements dans le système commercial multilatéral en 2010-2011

Bien que l'impasse dans les négociations devant mener à la conclusion de l'engagement unique dans le cadre du Programme de Doha pour le développement, les années 2010-11 ont été fertiles pour les

Court of International Arbitration (CIA), 23 February 2009, *The United States of America v Canada*, Case n° 7941, en ligne: <http://www.international.gc.ca/controls-controles/assets/pdfs/softwood/USAvCanada09219AwardonRemedies.pdf>; London Court of International Arbitration (LCIA), 28 September 2009, *The United States of America v Canada*, Case n° 91312, en ligne: <http://www.international.gc.ca/controls-controles/assets/pdfs/softwood/CanadavUSA_Award21092009.pdf>.

[49] London Court of International Arbitration, 28 January 2012, *United States of America v Canada*, Case n° 81010, en ligne: <http://www.international.gc.ca/controls-controles/assets/pdfs/softwood/ruling-London_Court_pub_ver-decision.pdf>.

[50] *Ibid.*

[51] Request for Arbitration, *The United States of America v Canada*, in the LCIA, n° 111790, 18 January 2011, en ligne: <http://www.scribd.com/doc/47111464/

Membres de l'OMC. Quelques évolutions tangibles du système commercial multilatéral ont vu le jour. On peut d'ailleurs soupçonner que c'est dans un nouvel esprit ou avec une nouvelle stratégie que travaille désormais l'OMC, ses Membres, son secrétariat et son directeur général. Faute d'arriver au grand soir et de conclure le cycle de Doha, on met l'accent sur les petits gains concrets et utiles. C'est visiblement dans cet esprit que s'est préparée et tenue la huitième Conférence ministérielle qui a lieu en décembre 2011 à Genève. La présente section de cette chronique sera aussi écrite dans cet esprit et nous insisterons sur les résultats les plus intéressants plutôt que sur les travaux et les négociations qui ne livrent pas leurs fruits.

Avant d'observer ces progrès amenés à l'occasion de la dernière Conférence ministérielle de l'OMC, il faut mentionner des nouvelles liées à la vie et à l'évolution de l'organisation proprement dite. Relevons d'abord que le 12 septembre 2011, la première pierre du nouveau bâtiment de l'OMC a été posée. Fruit d'un accord entre l'OMC et la Confédération suisse, ce bâtiment sera normalement prêt fin 2012. La construction de ce bâtiment était nécessaire, l'OMC manquant d'espace pour son personnel et pour l'accueil des délégués qui s'y réunissent tous les jours. Mentionnons aussi l'arrivée de deux nouveaux membres à l'Organe d'appel, en décembre 2011. Pour remplacer Mmes Lilia R. Bautista et Jennifer A. Hillman, toutes deux parties à la retraite à l'issue de leurs mandats, l'Organe d'appel a accueilli en ses rangs MM. Ujal Singh Bhatia de l'Inde et Thomas Graham des États-Unis. Parmi les autres nouvelles survenues en 2010-11 liées au fonctionnement de l'OMC, l'une était d'intérêt pour les Canadiens alors que John Gero fut président du Conseil Général de l'OMC pour l'année 2010.

1. Les accessions

L'une des fonctions les plus importantes de la Conférence ministérielle est sans doute d'adopter les modalités d'accession de nouveaux Membres de l'organisation. La Conférence ministérielle a été très fructueuse à cet égard. La Russie,[52] le Samoa,[53] et le

LCIA-111790-Request-Arbitrationhttp://www.international.gc.ca/controls-controles/assets/pdfs/softwood/Req_%20Arbitration_US_2011_01_18.pdf>.

52 *Accession de la Fédération de Russie, Décision du 16 décembre 2011*, OMC Doc WT/MIN(11)/24, en ligne: <http://docsonline.wto.org/DDFDocuments/u/wt/l/839.doc>

53 *Accession du Samoa, Décision du 15 décembre 2011*, OMC Doc WT/MIN(11)/27, en ligne: <http://docsonline.wto.org/DDFDocuments/u/wt/l/840.doc>.

Monténégro[54] ont vu leurs conditions d'accession adoptées par la Conférence ministérielle. Ils devraient normalement devenir formellement Membres de l'OMC au cours de l'année 2012.

Il devrait en aller de même du Vanuatu qui a vu ses conditions d'accession approuvées par le Conseil général le 26 octobre, quelques semaines avant la Conférence ministérielle. En vue de servir la vocation universelle de l'OMC, la Conférence ministérielle a aussi adopté une décision visant à renforcer les Lignes directrices sur l'accession des Pays moins avancés (PMA) adoptées en 2002. Par cette décision, le Sous-comité des PMA s'est vu demander "de formuler des recommandations pour davantage renforcer, rationnaliser et rendre opérationnelles les Lignes directrices de 2002, notamment en incluant des points de repère, en particulier dans le domaine des marchandises, qui tiennent compte du niveau des engagements contractés par les PMA Membres existants. Des points de repère dans le domaine des services devraient aussi être examinés."[55] Ces travaux et l'assistance technique mieux ciblée qui devrait en découler devraient faciliter l'accession des PMA à l'OMC.

2. *Traitement différencié pour les PMA en matière de services*

En vue de favoriser le commerce des services des PMA, la Conférence ministérielle a adopté une dérogation à l'AGCS.[56] Pour l'essentiel, cette dérogation prévoit que:

> Nonobstant les dispositions de l'article II:1 de l'AGCS, les Membres pourront accorder un traitement préférentiel aux services et fournisseurs de services des pays les moins avancés pour ce qui est de l'application des mesures visées à l'article XVI et de toutes autres mesures pouvant être annexées à la présente dérogation, par rapport aux services similaires et fournisseurs de services similaires des autres Membres. Un tel traitement sera accordé immédiatement et sans condition aux services similaires et fournisseurs de services similaires de tous les pays les moins avancés Membres. Un traitement préférentiel pour ce qui est de l'application de mesures

[54] *Accession du Monténégro, Décision du 15 décembre 2011*, OMC Doc WT/MIN(11)/28, en ligne: <http://docsonline.wto.org/DDFDocuments/u/wt/l/841.doc>.

[55] *Accession des pays les moins avancés, Décision du 17 décembre 2011*, OMC Doc WT/L/846, en ligne: <http://docsonline.wto.org/DDFDocuments/u/wt/l/846.doc>.

[56] *Traitement préférentiel pour les services et fournisseurs de services des pays les moins avancés, Décision du 17 décembre 2011*, OMC Doc WT/L/847, en ligne: <http://docsonline.wto.org/DDFDocuments/u/wt/l/847.doc>.

autres que celles qui sont visées à l'article XVI sera approuvé par le Conseil du commerce des services conformément à ses procédures et sera annexé à la présente dérogation."[57]

Cette dérogation devrait avoir pour effet de permettre aux PMA de prendre une part plus intéressante de la croissance mondiale du marché des services.

3. La révision de l'Accord plurilatéral sur les marchés publics

Les Parties à l'Accord sur les marchés publics (AMP) ont profité de la Conférence ministérielle de décembre 2011 pour achever la révision de cet accord plurilatéral. C'est en fait quelques heures avant l'ouverture officielle de la huitième conférence ministérielle que les 42 Parties à l'Accord ont adopté l'Accord révisé et ses annexes.

L'AMP a comme objectif d'ouvrir autant que possible les marchés publics des Parties à la concurrence internationale.[58] Il participe du même esprit que le reste des accords de l'OMC et, donc, s'appuie sur les mêmes valeurs: non-discrimination, transparence, flexibilité et libre concurrence. Toutefois, étant donné la complexité du sujet, la participation à cet accord est facultative et l'Accord est plurilatéral. Dans cette veine, les Parties ont aussi le droit d'exclure des secteurs sensibles de l'application de cet accord.

Les négociations pour l'amélioration de l'AMP ont été entreprises en 1997, en vertu de son article XXIV:7 b) qui comporte un mandat en ce sens.[59] Les premières modifications, achevées en décembre 2010, font de l'accord un outil de gouvernance des marchés publics et ménagent aux Parties de nouvelles flexibilités en termes d'engagements procéduraux.[60] Ainsi, l'accord concerne l'atteinte de

57 *Ibid* au para 1.

58 OMC, Les Conférences ministérielles, Note d'information: L'Accord sur les marchés publics, en ligne: <http://wto.org/french/thewto_f/minist_f/min11_f/brief_gpa_f.htm>.

59 "Au plus tard à l'expiration de la troisième année à compter de la date d'entrée en vigueur du présent accord, et par la suite de façon périodique, les Parties engageront de nouvelles négociations en vue d'améliorer l'Accord et d'en étendre le plus possible la portée entre toutes les Parties sur une base de réciprocité mutuelle, compte tenu des dispositions de l'article V relatif aux pays en développement." OMC, Accord sur les marchés publics. Article XXIV:7 b), en ligne: <http://wto.org/french/docs_f/legal_f/gpr-94_02_f.htm#articleXXIV>.

60 *Ibid.*

l'équilibre entre l'obtention du meilleur rapport qualité-prix et le marge de manœuvre politique.[61]

Juste avant l'ouverture officielle de la huitième conférence ministérielle en décembre 2011, les Parties à l'Accord sur les marchés publics ont clos les négociations servant à élargir les termes de cet accord.[62] Cette deuxième partie des négociations touche les aspects relatifs à la couverture et à l'accès aux marchés. Les dispositions de l'accord ont été réélaborées pour faciliter son application et pour mieux s'adapter à l'évolution des besoins des marchés publics.[63]

En même temps, de nouvelles entités gouvernementales de différents niveaux administratifs, et des nouveaux services et secteurs faisant l'objet des marchés publics ont été ajoutés aux annexes de l'appendice I.[64] Pour plusieurs pays, des marchés publics d'entités fédérées sont désormais couverts par l'Accord. Pour le Canada, par exemple, des marchés publics des provinces et des entités provinciales sont couverts.

De nouvelles dispositions en matière de transparence ont aussi été incluses avec l'intention de mieux agir contre la corruption dans ce domaine.[65] Le traitement spécial et différencié des PVD a également été précisé, ce qui facilitera leur accès à l'Accord.[66] Un des résultats prévisibles de cette révision sera celui d'accélérer la signature et la ratification des huit candidats qui discutent leur accession à l'AMP, c'est-à-dire: l'Albanie, la Chine, la Géorgie, la Jordanie, Moldova, l'Oman, le Panama, la République Kirghize et l'Ukraine.[67]

Toujours dans la prospective, une des modifications les plus importantes apportée à l'AMP est l'élaboration de programmes de travail

61 *Ibid.*

62 OMC, Nouvelles 2011, 15 décembre 2011, Marchés Publics — Une étape historique, en ligne: <http://wto.org/french/news_f/news11_f/gpro_15dec11_f.htm>.

63 OMC, La renégociation de l'Accord sur les marchés publics, *infra* note 69.

64 "Par exemple, une Partie a convenu d'étendre la portée de l'Accord à l'ensemble de ses provinces et territoires. Considérées conjointement, les autres Parties à l'Accord ont ajouté au moins 200 entités additionnelles dans leurs listes. Trois Parties de premier plan vont revoir la portée des accords de "construction-exploitation-transfert de propriété" (CET). De plus, presque toutes les Parties ont étendu la portée de l'Accord à des services supplémentaires, et trois Parties ont convenu d'abaisser certains de leurs valeurs de seuil." OMC, La renégociation de l'Accord sur les marchés publics, *infra* note 69.

65 *Ibid.*

66 OMC, La renégociation de l'Accord sur les marchés publics, *infra* note 69.

67 OMC, Les Conférences ministérielles, *supra* note 58.

futurs afin "de faciliter la compréhension mutuelle des approches adoptées par les Parties pour mettre en œuvre l'Accord révisé et d'améliorer au fil du temps l'administration de l'Accord."[68] Les programmes de travail futurs sont les suivants: programme de travail pour les PME; programme de travail sur la collecte et la communication de données statistiques; programme de travail sur les marchés durables; programme de travail sur les exclusions et restrictions énoncées dans les Annexes concernant les Parties; et programme de travail sur les normes de sécurité dans les marchés publics internationaux.[69]

B. LES DIFFÉRENDS DEVANT L'OMC IMPLIQUANT LE CANADA

Plusieurs différends importants impliquant le Canada ont connu des développements intéressants en 2010 ou 2011.

1. *Communautés européennes – Mesures concernant les viandes et produits carnés (hormones) (DS48)*

Cette affaire longue et complexe qui a connu quelques rebondissements inédits depuis une quinzaine d'années a semblé connaître une issue tout aussi particulière en 2011. Le 17 mars 2011, les délégations de l'Union européenne et du Canada ont adressé à la Présidente de l'Organe de règlement des différends (ORD) une communication à laquelle est joint ce que les parties ont appelé un Mémorandum d'accord.[70] Ce Mémorandum d'accord comporte un Protocole d'entente et une annexe. Le Protocole d'entente, au sujet duquel les parties ont pris soin de dire qu'il "ne constitue pas un accord international entre le Canada et la Commission, et [qu'] il ne crée par ailleurs aucune obligation juridique entre le Canada et l'UE, ni entre ses signataires," prévoit que "le Canada

68 OMC, Comité des marchés publics. Réunion au niveau ministériel du comité des marchés publics (15 décembre 2011). Décision sur les résultats des négociations au titre de l'article XXIV:7 de l'Accord sur les marchés publics, OMC Doc GPA/112, 16 décembre 2011, en ligne: <http://wto.org/french/tratop_f/gproc_f/overview_f.htm>.

69 OMC, Marchés Publics: L'Accord plurilatéral sur les marchés publics. La renégociation de l'Accord sur les marchés publics, en ligne: <http://wto.org/french/tratop_f/gproc_f/negotiations_f.htm>.

70 *Communautés européennes – Mesures concernant les viandes et les produits carnés (hormones)*, Communication conjointe de l'Union européenne et du Canada (22 mars 2011), OMC Doc WT/DS 48/26, en ligne: <http://docsonline.wto.org/DDFDocuments/u/WT/DS/48-26.doc>.

et la Commission envisagent d'entamer les procédures internes nécessaires à la prise des mesures envisagées dans le présent protocole. Après que ces mesures auront été prises, le Canada et l'UE envisagent de notifier le présent protocole, à titre de solution convenue d'un commun accord, à l'Organe de règlement des différends ("ORD")."[71]

Ce protocole ne trouve son sens que quand on prend connaissance de son annexe. On apprend à la lecture de cette annexe que l'Union européenne et le Canada "envisagent" la prise, en trois phases, d'une série de mesures internes par lesquelles l'UE accroitra l'accès à son marché pour la viande bovine canadienne, et le Canada suspendra les droits qu'il avait majorés sur certains produits de l'UE, conformément à l'autorisation qui lui avait été donnée de faire en 1999.

Au cours de la première phase, qui doit durer jusqu'au 1er août 2012, il est envisagé que l'UE permette "un accroissement de l'accès au marché de l'UE pour la viande bovine de haute qualité" i.e. "une augmentation d'un volume annuel de 1 500 tonnes métriques du contingent tarifaire autonome pour la viande bovine de haute qualité, soumis à un taux de droit contingentaire nul (0 pour cent), établi par l'UE dans le règlement (CE) no 617/2009 du Conseil du 13 juillet 2009."[72] L'expression "viande bovine" fait l'objet d'une définition au paragraphe 1d) du Protocole.

En contrepartie, est envisagée:

> [d]ès que possible dans les semaines qui suivront la signature du présent protocole, la suspension de tous les droits majorés imposés sur certains produits de l'UE en application du *Décret imposant une surtaxe à l'Union européenne* du Canada ... Le Canada entamera le processus interne aux fins de cette suspension dès la signature du présent protocole.[73]

Pour la phase 2, "une augmentation à un volume de 3 200 tonnes métriques (poids du produit) du contingent tarifaire autonome visé à l'alinéa 2a), soumis à un taux de droit contingentaire nul, est envisagée."[74]

La phase 3, quant à elle, consiste en une consolidation des mesures prises lors des deux premières phases. On est frappé, à l'analyse,

71 *Ibid* à la p 2.

72 *Ibid* à la p 4.

73 *Ibid.*

74 *Ibid.*

non seulement par le caractère graduel de la mise en œuvre des mesures convenues entre les parties mais aussi par les mécanismes de surveillance, d'examen et de consultations prévus dans ce protocole aux articles 4, 5 et 6. La fragilité de cet accord entre l'UE et le Canada est palpable à la seule lecture du texte. Il est à souhaiter que la mise en œuvre de cet accord, dont des étapes cruciales auront lieu en 2012, se passera comme souhaité. On peut espérer que la perspective d'un accord économique et commercial global (AECG) entre les deux parties contribuera à apaiser les tensions et à favoriser la mise en place des mesures internes envisagées.

2. *Communautés européennes – Certaines mesures prohibant l'importation et la commercialisation de produits dérivés du phoque (DS369)*

Le 14 février 2011, le Canada a demandé la constitution d'un groupe spécial dans cette affaire.[75] Cette demande est intervenue près de trois ans et demi après la demande par le Canada de consultations avec les Communautés européennes au sujet de certaines mesures prises par la Belgique et les PaysBas concernant l'importation, le transport, la fabrication, la commercialisation et la vente de produits dérivés du phoque.

Cette plainte canadienne ne doit pas être confondue avec celle présentée par le Canada dans l'affaire DS/400 dont nous traiterons plus bas. Les mesures visées dans la demande d'établissement d'un groupe spécial dont il est question ici sont les suivantes: (i) la Loi relative à l'interdiction de fabriquer et de commercialiser des produits dérivés de phoques, F. 2007 – 1590 [C – 2007/11138], 16 mars 2007, ("[l']interdiction commerciale belge"); (ii) l'Arrêté ministériel modifiant l'arrêté ministériel du 15 septembre 1995 soumettant à licence l'importation de certaines marchandises, F. 2004 – 1983 [C – 2004/11258], 28 mai 2004 (la "prescription belge en matière de licences d'importation"); et (iii) les articles 5 et 13 de la Loi sur la flore et la faune néerlandaise, lus conjointement avec le Décret du 4 juillet 2007 modifiant le Décret sur la désignation des espèces animales et végétales (Loi sur la flore et la faune) et le Décret sur les espèces animales et végétales protégées (exemptions) en relation avec l'interdiction du commerce de produits dérivés de

75 *Communautés européennes – Certaines mesures prohibant l'importation et la commercialisation de produits dérivés du phoque* (Demande d'établissement d'un groupe spécial présentée par le Canada) (14 février 2011), OMC Doc WT/DS/369/2, en ligne: <http://docsonline.wto.org/DDFDocuments/u/WT/DS/369-2.doc>.

phoques du Groenland et de phoques à capuchon (l'"interdiction commerciale néerlandaise").

Le Canada considère que ces mesures, ou parties de ces mesures, sont incompatibles avec les articles I:1, III:4 et XI:1 du GATT de 1994 et avec les articles 2.1 et 2.2 de l'Accord sur les obstacles techniques au commerce.[76]

3. États-Unis d'Amérique – Certaines prescriptions en matière d'étiquetage indiquant le pays d'origine (EPO) (DS/384)

Le rapport du Groupe spécial chargé de cette affaire est tombé le 18 novembre 2011.[77]

On se rappellera que le Canada contestait un système d'étiquetage états-unien mis en place à compter de 2008 et qui visait des produits alimentaires, notamment des produits carnés. Cette mesure, mieux connue sous les acronymes EPO en français (étiquetage du pays d'origine) et COOL en anglais (*Country of Origin Labelling*), était, selon le Canada, composée des dispositions suivantes: "la *Loi sur la commercialisation des produits agricoles de 1946*, modifiée par la *Loi sur la sécurité des exploitations agricoles et l'investissement rural de 2002* ("*Loi sur l'agriculture de 2002*") et la *Loi sur les produits alimentaires, la conservation et l'énergie de 2008* ("*Loi sur l'agriculture de 2008*"); la règle finale provisoire relative à l'étiquetage obligatoire indiquant le pays d'origine des viandes de bœuf, de porc, d'agneau, de poulet et de chèvre, des denrées agricoles périssables, des arachides, des noix de pécan, du ginseng et des noix de macadamia, publiée le 1er août 2008 dans 7 CFR, partie 65 ("règle finale provisoire (AMS)"); et à l'étiquetage obligatoire indiquant le pays d'origine des morceaux de chair musculaire de bœuf (y compris de veau), d'agneau, de poulet, de chèvre et de porc, et de la viande hachée de bœuf, d'agneau, de poulet, de chèvre et de porc publiée le 28 août 2008 dans 9 CFR, parties 317 et 381 ("règle finale provisoire (FSIS)"); la règle finale relative à l'étiquetage obligatoire indiquant le pays d'origine des viandes de bœuf, de porc, d'agneau, de poulet et de chèvre, des denrées agricoles périssables, des arachides, des noix de pécan, du ginseng et des noix de macadamia, publiée le 15 janvier 2009 dans 7 CFR, partie 65 (la "règle finale de 2009 (AMS)");

[76] *Ibid.*

[77] *États-Unis – Certaines prescriptions en matière d'étiquetage indiquant le pays d'origine* (EPO) (Rapport du Groupe spécial pour les affaires DS 384 et DS386) (18 novembre 2011), OMC Doc WT/DS384/R, en ligne: <http://docsonline.wto.org/DDFDocuments/u/WT/DS/386R-01.doc>.

la lettre adressée par le Secrétaire à l'agriculture des États-Unis, Thomas J. Vilsack, au "représentant de la branche de production," datée du 20 février 2009 (la "lettre Vilsack"); et toutes modifications, indications administratives, directives ou annonces de politique publiées en relation avec les points a) à d) cidessus."[78]

L'EPO créait cinq catégories d'étiquettes qui pouvaient être apposées sur les produits visés: Étiquette A — "Produit des États-Unis" — utilisée uniquement pour les morceaux de chair musculaire provenant d'animaux nés, élevés et abattus aux États-Unis; Étiquette B — "Produit des États-Unis et du pays X" — utilisée pour les morceaux de chair musculaire provenant d'animaux nés dans le pays X, mais élevés et abattus aux États-Unis; Étiquette C — "Produit du pays X et des États-Unis" — utilisée pour les morceaux de chair musculaire provenant d'animaux nés et élevés dans le pays X et importés pour abattage immédiat aux États-Unis; Étiquette D — "Produit du pays X" — utilisée pour les morceaux de chair musculaire importés; Étiquette E — "Produit du pays X, du pays Y, du pays Z" — utilisée pour la viande hachée; l'étiquette doit indiquer tous les pays d'origine de la viande contenue dans la viande hachée ou qui peut raisonnablement y être contenue.[79]

La mesure prévoyait aussi que chaque détaillant devait tenir registre de l'origine exacte de ses marchandises visées. Les fournisseurs devaient fournir l'information nécessaire aux détaillants et aussi tenir registre de l'origine du bétail transformé.

Les États-Unis prétendaient que la mesure EPO était nécessaire à une bonne information du consommateur. Ils insistaient notamment sur le haut niveau d'acceptation de ce type de mesure parmi les Membres de l'OMC. Selon les États-Unis, la mesure conciliait bien les intérêts des consommateurs et des producteurs puisqu'elle était sans effet sur les coûts de production des producteurs étrangers et ne leur imposait aucune action spécifique.[80] Ils faisaient aussi valoir que la lettre Vilsack n'était ni un règlement technique, ni une loi, un règlement ou une prescription et n'est donc visé ni par l'Accord OTC ni par l'article III:4 du GATT.[81]

78 *Ibid* au para 2.2.

79 *Ibid,* Annexe A-1, para 6. Résumé analytique de la première communication écrite du Canada.

80 *Ibid,* Annexe A-3, aux para 1-39. Résumé analytique de la première communication écrite des États-Unis.

81 *Ibid* aux para 10-12, 55, 58.

Le Canada prétendait quant à lui que la mesure EPO a eu comme résultat une forte diminution des exportations de bovins et de porcs canadiens vers les États-Unis, et une réduction des prix des animaux canadiens aux États-Unis.[82] Le Canada expose que les États-Unis sont les principaux importateurs de bovins et de porcs canadiens et que, depuis l'adoption de l'EPO, les exportations de bovins sont tombées de 1,4 millions de têtes à 1,1 millions de têtes (23%); pour les porcs, les exportations sont tombées de 10 millions de têtes à 6,4 millions de têtes (36%).[83]

La mesure en cause, selon le Canada, établit une différence de traitement basée sur le pays d'origine du produit. Les coûts de séparation et d'identification du bétail canadien font en sorte que la charge économique a augmenté pour les abattoirs états-uniens en ce qui concerne l'utilisation d'animaux canadiens. Ceci a eu comme conséquence que plusieurs abattoirs ne prennent plus du tout les animaux canadiens et que d'autres abattoirs les prennent seulement dans des journées ou des horaires spéciaux, provoquant aux exportateurs canadiens des charges économiques supplémentaires liées, d'abord, à la limitation des exportations et, après, aux problèmes de logistique qu'entraîne la restriction horaire. Le Canada ajoute que les abattoirs ont, aussi, modifié leurs pratiques en matière de contrats au détriment des animaux canadiens.

Selon le Canada, l'EPO constitue un règlement technique[84] et viole l'article 2.1 de l'Accord OTC en prévoyant un traitement moins favorable aux produits importés que celui qui est prévu pour les produits similaires nationaux.[85]

Le Canada ajoute que l'EPO va à l'encontre des dispositions de l'article 2.2 du même accord car son véritable objectif (la protection de la branche de production nationale) n'est pas légitime.[86] Dans le cas où son objectif soit bien celui que les États-Unis déclarent (l'information du consommateur), l'EPO n'en permet pas la réalisation, car les étiquettes ne sont pas suffisamment informatives.[87] Pour conclure au sujet de l'article 2.2, le Canada est d'avis que les

82 *Ibid,* Annexe A-1 au para 2. Résumé analytique de la première communication écrite du Canada.

83 *Ibid* au para 13.

84 *Ibid* au para 19.

85 *Ibid* aux para 20-21.

86 *Ibid* aux para 25-26.

87 *Ibid* au para 27.

mesures en cause sont plus restrictives que nécessaire pour arriver à l'objectif officiel de la mesure, car des mesures de rechange moins restrictives pour le commerce international sont disponibles.[88]

En ce qui concerne l'article III:4 du GATT, le Canada affirme que le bétail canadien et le bétail états-unien sont des produits similaires et que le traitement offert par les États-Unis au bétail canadien est moins favorable que celui offert au bétail national.[89] Le Canada affirme ensuite que la lettre Vilsack constitue une application déraisonnable de la règle finale de 2009 et est contraire aux dispositions de l'article X:3 du GATT.[90] Le Canada allègue, au titre de l'article XXIII:1 (b), que les actions états-uniennes compromettent ou annulent les avantages du Canada liés aux accords de l'OMC.[91] Dans son rapport qui fait au total plus de 450 pages en langue française, le Groupe spécial donne raison au Canada sur la plupart des questions soulevées.

Le groupe spécial a d'abord creusé la question de savoir si la mesure EPO, et la lettre Vilsack, étaient un règlement. Le Groupe spécial commence son analyse en déterminant les mesures qui relèvent de son mandat, c'est-à-dire: la loi EPO, la règle finale de 2009, la règle finale provisoire (AMS) et la lettre Vilsack.[92]

Les plaignants sont d'avis que les mesures en cause se traitent comme étant une seule mesure. Pour décider à ce sujet, le Groupe spécial considère les facteurs pris en compte auparavant,[93] soit:

> (i) la manière dont le plaignant a présenté son (ses) allégation(s) en ce qui concerne les instruments en cause [note de bas de page omise]; (ii) la position du défendeur; et (iii) le statut juridique des prescriptions ou instrument(s), y compris le fonctionnement des prescriptions ou instruments et le lien entre eux, c'est-à-dire la question de savoir si une prescription ou un instrument donné a un statut autonome [note de bas de page

[88] *Ibid* aux para 28.

[89] *Ibid* aux para 31-35.

[90] *Ibid* aux para 35-37.

[91] *Ibid* aux para 38-39.

[92] OMC, *États-Unis – Certaines prescriptions en matière d'étiquetage indiquant le pays d'origine* (EPO), *supra* note 77 au para 7.17.

[93] Dans l'affaire *États-Unis – Restrictions à l'exportation* au para 8.82-8.131). Dans l'affaire *Japon – Pellicule* aux para 10.90-10.94 et 10.350-10.367. Rapport de l'Organe d'appel *CE – Amiante* au para 64; rapport du Groupe spécial *États-Unis – Restrictions à l'exportation* au para 8.85.

omise] Nous examinerons les mesures en cause dans les présents différends à la lumière de ces facteurs."[94]

Donc, un lien doit être établi entre les mesures en cause pour être en mesure de les traiter comme étant une seule. Ce lien est évident pour la loi EPO et la règle finale; elles sont étroitement liées car l'une constitue le cadre et le fondement de l'autre. La règle finale n'a pas de statut juridique autonome, elle doit donc être examinée toujours à la lumière de l'EPO.[95] D'un autre côté, la lettre Vilsack n'a pas de lien juridique formel avec ces instruments et n'a pas le même statut juridique.[96] Même si la lettre a été envoyée par le Secrétaire à l'agriculture (ce que lui confère une certaine importance) et même si celle-ci parle de la mise en œuvre de la règle finale, il n'y a pas d'éléments qui puissent indiquer qu'elle jouit du même statut juridique que les deux autres instruments.[97] Ainsi, il n'est pas possible de la traiter sur un pied d'égalité par rapport à la loi EPO et à la règle finale.[98]

Les produits en cause sont les viandes de bœuf et de porc produites aux États-Unis à partir de bovins et de porcs importés du Canada pour élevage et abattage ou exclusivement pour abattage immédiat.[99] Le Groupe spécial analyse les plaintes concernant l'Accord OTC. La première question est celle de savoir si l'EPO et la lettre Vilsack sont des règlements techniques. L'EPO impose un système d'étiquetage, où le détaillant est obligé d'informer le consommateur de l'origine de la viande.[100] Elle propose différentes catégories d'étiquettes pour le classement des produits.[101] Elle compte un système d'audit qui l'aide à garantir le respect des normes établies[102] et elle a établi une démarche en cas d'infraction.[103] Le Groupe spécial en déduit que, au vu de ce que l'article 2.1 prescrit,

94 OMC, *États-Unis – Certaines prescriptions en matière d'étiquetage indiquant le pays d'origine* (EPO), *supra* note 77 au para 7.50.

95 *Ibid* au para 7.54.

96 *Ibid* au para 7.55.

97 *Ibid* au para 7.62.

98 *Ibid.*

99 *Ibid* au para 7.65.

100 *Ibid* au para 7.88.

101 *Ibid* aux para 7.89-7.100.

102 *Ibid* aux para 7.116-7.120.

103 *Ibid* au para 7.122.

l'EPO constitue un règlement technique[104] étant donné qu'elle s'applique à un groupe de produits identifiables (les produits carnés),[105] qu'elle énonce une caractéristique des produits visés[106] (les étiquettes[107]) et qu'elle est obligatoire.[108]

La situation est différente pour la lettre Vilsack. Celle-ci propose trois pratiques[109] plus strictes que la règle finale, certes, mais d'adoption volontaire. Le Groupe spécial rappelle le commentaire de l'Organe d'appel lors de l'affaire *Amiante* où il est mentionné que les règlements pourraient être obligatoires *de facto* même s'ils ne le sont pas *de jure*.[110] Cependant, le Groupe spécial considère que rien dans la lettre en question n'établit que son contenu soit obligatoire *de facto*. Le Groupe spécial conclut que la lettre Vilsack demeure distincte de la loi EPO[111] et ne constitue pas un règlement technique.[112] Évidemment, cette conclusion exclut ensuite la lettre Vilsack de toute autre analyse à la lumière de l'Accord OTC.

Le Groupe spécial s'attaque ensuite à l'analyse de la mesure EPO en cause à la lumière de l'article 2.1 de l'Accord OTC. Cet article impose les obligations de traitement national et de traitement NPF en ce qui concerne les règlements techniques. Il y a donc trois conditions cumulatives à remplir pour démontrer un cas de violation de l'article 2.1: que la mesure en question soit un règlement technique ; que les produits en cause soient similaires; et qu'il soit accordé aux produits importés un traitement moins favorable qu'aux produits similaires nationaux ou d'autres pays.[113] Il est important de signaler que les deux dernières conditions énumérées

[104] *Ibid* au para 7.216.

[105] *Ibid* au para 7.207.

[106] *Ibid* au para 7.214.

[107] *Ibid* au para 7.213. Le Groupe spécial cite un commentaire de l'Organe d'appel dans l'affaire *Amiante*, qui dit que l'étiquetage est une caractéristique du produit. Le Groupe spécial de l'affaire *CE – Marques de commerce et indications géographiques (Australie)* "a ajouté qu'une prescription explicite imposant d'indiquer le pays d'origine sur l'étiquette du produit était effectivement une prescription en matière d'étiquetage aux fins de la définition d'un règlement technique."

[108] *Ibid* au para 7.162.

[109] *Ibid* aux para 7.124-7.127.

[110] *Ibid* au para 7.176.

[111] *Ibid* au para 7.180.

[112] *Ibid* au para 7.195.

[113] *Ibid* au para 7.219. Citation du Groupe spécial de l'affaire *CE – Marques de commerce et indications géographiques (Australie)*.

par l'article n'avaient jamais fait l'objet d'une interprétation jurisprudentielle.[114] Le Groupe spécial a ainsi jugé qu'il serait approprié[115] d'interpréter ces dispositions dans le contexte jurisprudentiel de l'article III:4 du GATT, étant donné que les termes de cet article sont semblables à ceux de l'article 2.1 de l'Accord OTC,[116] et que le préambule de ce dernier indique qu'il a pour but de "favoriser la réalisation des objectifs du GATT de 1994."[117]

En ce qui concerne les conditions cumulatives pour démontrer l'incompatibilité d'une mesure avec l'article 2.1 de l'Accord OTC, premièrement, le Groupe spécial rappelle qu'il avait déjà déclaré l'EPO comme étant un règlement technique,[118] alors que la lettre Vilsack ne l'était pas. Il a annoncé que son analyse toucherait l'EPO mais ne toucherait pas la lettre Vilsack.

Les États-Unis alléguaient que, malgré le fait que l'EPO soit un règlement technique, celle-ci ne touchait pas les produits en cause, car il s'agit bien d'un règlement qui vise la viande et non pas le bétail. Le Groupe spécial estime, toutefois, que l'EPO concerne aussi le bétail, puisque toute la chaîne de production est touchée par l'obligation de fournir des informations justes pour l'étiquetage postérieur.[119]

Deuxièmement, le Groupe spécial a déterminé que le bétail canadien est bel et bien similaire au bétail états-unien car, dans le contexte de la mesure, la seule distinction qui existe entre ces produits est l'origine.[120] Ainsi, deux produits dont la seule différence est l'origine sont considérés comme similaires dans le sens de l'article III:4 du GATT.

Pour la troisième question, le Groupe spécial a cité le rapport de l'Organe d'appel dans le différend *Corée – Viande de bœuf* qui dit que "un traitement [non] moins favorable' signifi[ait] ... ne pas soumettre le produit importé à des conditions de concurrence moins favorables que celles dont bénéficie le produit national similaire."[121] Le Groupe spécial estime que, pour savoir si les États-Unis

114 *Ibid* au para 7.228.

115 *Ibid* au para 7.234.

116 *Ibid* au para 7.230.

117 *Ibid* au para 7.233.

118 *Ibid* au para 7.236.

119 *Ibid* au para 7.246.

120 *Ibid* aux para 7.253-7.254.

121 *Ibid* au para 7.276.

accordent un traitement moins favorable au bétail canadien, il est nécessaire de savoir: (a) si l'EPO accorde un traitement différencié au bétail importé par le biais des différentes étiquettes; (b) si la mesure EPO implique une séparation des bétails et, en conséquence, des coûts plus hauts pour le bétail importé; et (c) si, en raison des coûts reliés à la mise en œuvre de la mesure en cause, il existe une incitation à transformer le bétail national réduisant, de cette manière, les possibilités de concurrence du bétail importé.[122]

D'abord, du fait que la viande provenant du bétail canadien ne peut pas porter la même étiquette que la viande provenant du bétail états-unien, le Groupe spécial estime que l'EPO impose un traitement différencié au bétail canadien par rapport au bétail états-unien.[123] Ceci n'est toutefois pas forcément incompatible avec l'article 2.1 si cette différence de traitement n'entraîne pas un désavantage concurrentiel.[124]

En ce qui touche le deuxième point, le Groupe spécial observe que l'EPO assume elle-même l'existence de coûts reliés à la mise en conformité de la mesure. Ces coûts doivent être supportés par toute la chaîne de production.[125] Les coûts de mise en conformité ne peuvent être déclarés illégaux que si ceux-ci sont supportés uniquement par les produits importés et non par les produits nationaux similaires.[126] Le Groupe spécial a trouvé que la séparation du bétail était le choix de tous les abattoirs où l'on acceptait encore le bétail canadien. Effectivement, cette méthode a été fortement encouragée par la mesure même et par les autorités.[127] Il s'agit, cependant, d'une méthode qui impose des coûts élevés aux abattoirs et aux importateurs et il semble qu'elle soit un défi important pour les fournisseurs.[128] Les abattoirs cherchent à abaisser ces coûts en achetant le bétail moins cher[129] et en limitant les horaires et les jours de semaine où ils reçoivent du bétail étranger. Du côté des importateurs, ils doivent supporter en plus des charges économiques supplémentaires liées à la logistique et à la mortalité du bétail qui

122 *Ibid* au para 7.279.

123 *Ibid* au para 7.295.

124 *Ibid* au para 7.296.

125 *Ibid* aux para 303-309.

126 *Ibid* au para 7.313.

127 *Ibid* au para 7.323.

128 *Ibid* aux para 7.335-7.336.

129 *Ibid* au para 7.352.

doit attendre les horaires indiqués pour être pris. Le Groupe spécial observe que, pour fonctionner, l'EPO a besoin de la méthode de séparation[130] et que celle-ci impose une lourde charge au bétail importé.[131] Ainsi, il est remarquable qu'il revient toujours moins cher pour le fournisseur de ne transformer que le bétail national.[132] De cette façon se résout aussi le troisième point: la mesure EPO encourage la transformation du bétail national plutôt que du bétail étranger;[133] le résultat le plus frappant à cet égard est la décision de plusieurs grands transformateurs de bétail états-uniens d'apposer uniquement l'étiquette A sur leurs produits carnés après l'adoption des prescriptions EPO.[134]

"Le Groupe spécial conclut que la mesure EPO modifie les conditions de concurrence sur le marché des États-Unis au détriment du bétail importé."[135] Après l'entrée en vigueur de l'ALÉNA, le bétail circule librement dans toute la zone, la mesure en cause a modifié ces circonstances à l'aide d'une incitation économique à utiliser le bétail national.[136] Le Groupe spécial considère aussi que, en ce qui concerne la chair musculaire, l'EPO crée une discrimination *de facto* à l'encontre du bétail importé.[137]

Le cas de l'étiquette pour la viande hachée est particulier. Il y a une seule étiquette pour la viande hachée de bœuf et/ou de porc, importée ou nationale. Cette étiquette, d'après la mesure EPO, doit énumérer tous les pays d'origine de la viande hachée et tous les pays d'origine raisonnablement possibles de la viande, ce qui résulte dans une séparation de la viande hachée en fonction de l'origine et, tout comme pour la chair musculaire, cette séparation entraîne des coûts.[138] Toutefois, la règle finale de 2009 dit que: "lorsqu'une matière première d'une origine spécifique ne reste pas dans les stocks d'un transformateur pendant plus de 60 jours, ce pays ne sera plus inclus en tant que pays d'origine possible."[139]

130 *Ibid* au para 7.327.

131 *Ibid* au para 7.347.

132 *Ibid* au para 7.350.

133 *Ibid* au para 7.357.

134 *Ibid* aux para 7.360-7.361.

135 *Ibid* au para 7.372.

136 *Ibid* au para 7.390.

137 *Ibid* au para 7.420.

138 *Ibid* aux para 7.421-7.427.

139 *Ibid* au para 7.425.

Cette règle de tolérance des stocks rend plus flexible (et même superflu) le processus de séparation de la viande hachée et limite les coûts additionnels de la mise en œuvre de la mesure EPO. Donc, en ce qui concerne la viande hachée, le Groupe spécial considère que les États-Unis n'accordent pas un traitement moins favorable au bétail importé.[140]

Le Groupe spécial, se laissant guider par le commentaire de l'Organe d'appel dans l'affaire *Corée – Viande de bœuf*,[141] a estimé nécessaire d'évaluer les effets réels sur le commerce de la mesure en cause. Ceci même s'il est considéré que le manque d'effets réels sur le commerce n'empêche pas un Membre de présenter avec succès une allégation de violation au titre des accords visés.[142] Le Groupe spécial a affirmé qu'il était de son devoir d'analyser tous les éléments de preuve amenés par les parties et que les effets négatifs de la mesure dans le commerce constituaient une question qui était étroitement liée à la conclusion de l'affaire.[143] Donc, deux études économétriques ont été analysées par le Groupe spécial, l'une offerte par le Canada (Étude économétrique de Sunmer) et l'autre par les États-Unis (Rapport Informa). Le Groupe spécial a déclaré vouloir évaluer surtout la robustesse des études sans, pour autant, faire une étude économétrique lui-même. Le Groupe spécial a trouvé que les deux études se sont avérées très utiles pour observer les différentes variantes du même sujet, mais il a considéré que l'étude fournie par le Canada (Sunmer) était plus robuste et avait bien identifié et illustré un effet économique négatif bien réel de la mesure EPO.[144] Or, cette incidence économique s'est masquée dans l'étude Informa (États-Unis) et l'analyse reste peu rigoureuse et les conclusions obscures.[145]

Finalement, le Groupe spécial a conclu que la mesure EPO était contraire à l'article 2.1, particulièrement en ce qui concerne les morceaux de chair musculaire.[146]

Le Groupe spécial a ensuite examiné les arguments liés à l'article 2.2 de l'Accord OTC. Pour montrer l'incompatibilité de la mesure

140 *Ibid* au para 7.437.

141 *Ibid* au para 7.438.

142 *Ibid* au para 7.440.

143 *Ibid* aux para 7.745-7.746.

144 *Ibid* aux para 7.514-7.517, 7.539-7.542.

145 *Ibid* au para 7.543-7.545.

146 *Ibid* au para 7.548.

avec cet article, il incombe au plaignant de prouver que: (a) le règlement technique est restrictif pour le commerce;[147] (b) identifier l'objectif de la restriction et indiquer s'il est légitime ou pas;[148] (c) si l'objectif est légitime, établir si le règlement en question permet de réaliser cet objectif[149] et d) déterminer si le règlement est plus restrictif au commerce que nécessaire (test des mesures de rechange).[150]

Le Groupe spécial a voulu éclaircir la question à savoir si la non-conformité d'un règlement avec l'article 2.1 supposait automatiquement la non-conformité avec l'article 2.2.[151] Ensuite, le Groupe spécial rappelle que d'autres Groupes spéciaux ont établi que l'on peut déterminer le caractère restrictif d'une norme en observant si celle-ci réduit les possibilités de concurrence des produits étrangers.[152] Or, le caractère restrictif de la norme EPO a déjà été établi.[153]

Par rapport à l'objectif de la mesure, le Groupe spécial considère que, malgré les accusations des plaignants, il est nécessaire d'user du principe de bonne foi en croyant la parole de la partie défenderesse.[154] D'ailleurs, il ajoute qu'il serait logique qu'un Membre qui impose une mesure soit capable d'identifier l'objectif qu'il recherche.[155] Ainsi, les États-Unis déclarent que l'objectif de leur mesure est celui de fournir aux consommateurs des renseignements sur l'origine de la viande qu'ils achètent.[156] Le Groupe spécial présume, donc, que celui-ci est l'objectif de la mesure EPO.[157]

Le Canada allègue que, même si celui-là était le véritable objectif de la mesure, il n'est pas évident qu'il soit un but légitime, car l'information sur l'origine de la viande peut provoquer une prise de décision discriminatoire, à cause du contexte particulier de l'EPO. C'est-à-dire que, si les consommateurs états-uniens ont besoin de

147 *Ibid* au para 7.554.

148 *Ibid* au para 7.555.

149 *Ibid* au para 7.556.

150 *Ibid* au para 7.557.

151 *Ibid* au para 7.573.

152 *Ibid* au para 7.571.

153 *Ibid* au para 7.575.

154 *Ibid* au para 7.605.

155 *Ibid* au para 7.592.

156 *Ibid* au para 7.591.

157 *Ibid* au para 7.620.

cette information pour faire un choix fondé seulement sur l'origine de la viande et non pas selon une différence qualitative, alors l'objectif ne peut pas être légitime, d'après le Canada.[158]

Le Groupe spécial a déterminé que l'objectif déclaré par les États-Unis était un objectif légitime.[159] Cette conclusion partielle fut inspirée des décisions prises par les Groupes spéciaux dans les affaires *CE – Sardines* et *Canada – Brevets pour les produits pharmaceutiques*.[160]

Sur la question de savoir si la mesure EPO était plus restrictive que nécessaire pour le commerce le Groupe spécial a décidé de faire

> référence au critère juridique établi au titre des dispositions pertinentes d'autres accords visés, y compris l'article XX du GATT de 1994 [note de bas de page omise] et l'article 5:6 de l'Accord SPS, dans la mesure appropriée [note de bas de page omise]. À cet égard, nous trouvons des éléments à l'appui de notre approche dans la déclaration faite par l'Organe d'appel dans le différend *Australie – Pommes.* Dans le contexte de l'analyse d'une disposition de l'Accord SPS, l'Organe d'appel a constaté que le sens attribué à une disposition du GATT de 1994 lui apportait une aide en matière d'interprétation puisque les deux dispositions faisaient partie intégrante du même traité en vertu de l'article II:2 de l'Accord sur l'OMC."[161]

Le Groupe spécial considère que, à cette fin, la mesure doit être évaluée d'après sa conception, sa structure et son objectif d'information.[162] Le Groupe spécial cite l'Organe d'appel dans l'affaire *Brésil – Pneus rechapés* pour dire que la mesure contribue à la réalisation de son but lorsqu'il existe une véritable relation entre l'objectif et la mesure en cause.[163] Le Groupe spécial estime ainsi que pour savoir si la mesure EPO est efficace, il faudrait établir si les étiquettes en question apportent des renseignements clairs et exacts sur l'origine de la viande.[164] Par le biais de l'étude de la signification des étiquettes,[165] le Groupe spécial conclut que les informations

158 *Ibid* au para 7.623.

159 *Ibid* au para 7.651.

160 *Ibid* au para 7.650.

161 *Ibid* au para 7.667, pour voir plus d'explications concernant cette décision du Groupe spécial voir aussi le para 7.670.

162 *Ibid* au para 7.685.

163 *Ibid* au para 7.693.

164 *Ibid* au para 7.695.

165 *Ibid* aux para 7.696-7.707.

contenues sur les étiquettes B, C et D sont très obscures et ne donnent qu'une idée très approximative de l'origine de la viande.[166]

De cette manière, le Groupe spécial constate que la mesure EPO n'est pas efficace. Il déclare aussi qu'il n'est pas nécessaire de continuer avec l'analyse de l'article 2.2 de l'Accord OTC, car les éléments dont il dispose sont suffisants pour établir l'incompatibilité de la mesure EPO avec ledit article.[167]

Le Groupe spécial met en évidence le fait que les articles III:4 et X:3 du GATT s'occupent de différents types de mesures. L'article III: 4 s'applique plutôt aux mesures elles-mêmes i.e. lois, règlements, etc, alors que l'article X:3 ne vise que l'application de ces lois, règlements et mesures.[168]

Les allégations liées à l'article III:4 du GATT touchent la mesure EPO et la lettre Vilsack. Le Groupe spécial a jugé inutile d'examiner la mesure EPO à la lumière de cet article, car elle a déjà été jugée comme étant incompatible avec des dispositions très similaires dans l'Accord OTC.[169] Les allégations liées à l'article X:3 du GATT se rapportent à la mesure EPO ainsi qu'à la lettre Vilsack. Partant, le Groupe spécial a décidé de commencer son analyse par l'article X:3, d'abord avec la mesure EPO et ensuite avec la lettre Vilsack. Dans le cas où la lettre Vilsack ne relève pas de l'article X:3 le Groupe spécial l'aurait examiné à la lumière de l'article III:4, puisqu'elle ne peut pas relever des deux en même temps pour les raisons qui ont été exposées au paragraphe précédent.

Les plaignants allèguent que la mesure EPO a été appliquée de manière déraisonnable et va à l'encontre de l'article X:3 du GATT. Pour établir une violation de X:3, il faut prouver qu'existe l'application d'un des instruments visés dans l'article X:1 du GATT et que cette application est déraisonnable.[170] Toutes les parties étaient d'accord pour dire que l'EPO est une mesure visée par ledit article et qu'elle était en train d'être appliquée. Il est alors nécessaire que les parties plaignantes signalent l'acte d'application de cette mesure qu'elles estiment constituer une application déraisonnable.[171]

166 *Ibid* au para 7.715.

167 *Ibid* aux para 7.719-7.720.

168 *Ibid* au para 7.806.

169 *Ibid* au para 7.807.

170 *Ibid* aux para 7.812-7.813.

171 *Ibid* aux para 7.814-7.816

Le Canada dit que la lettre Vilsack constitue une application déraisonnable de l'EPO.[172] Le Groupe spécial observe que "la question de savoir si un acte d'application peut être considéré comme raisonnable au sens de l'article X:3 a) suppose l'examen des circonstances factuelles propres à chaque affaire."[173] Le Groupe spécial observe que la lettre a été écrite avec le but de confirmer la mise en œuvre de la règle finale de 2009 et de faire certaines suggestions à la branche de production.[174] Ces suggestions, de caractère volontaire, visent à réduire la flexibilité ménagée par la règle finale, en plus d'aller au-delà des bornes et des exceptions que la même règle finale a imposées. Ces recommandations sont: (a) "d'inclure des renseignements sur l'étape de production réalisée dans chaque pays lorsque plusieurs pays sont mentionnés sur l'étiquette. La lettre Vilsack donne les exemples suivants au sujet de la manière dont ces renseignements pourraient être mentionnés sur les étiquettes: "Né et élevé dans le pays X et abattu dans le pays Y" ou "né dans le pays X et élevé et abattu dans le pays Y";[175] (b) "même lorsque des produits sont traités par salaison, fumage, ébouillantage, cuisson au gril ou cuisson à la vapeur, un étiquetage volontaire devrait être effectué";[176] et (c) par rapport à la viande hachée, "ramener à dix jours cette tolérance concernant les stocks."[177]

Le Groupe spécial ne voit pas de raisons valables de suggérer des pratiques plus strictes que la norme. D'ailleurs, cet acte est d'autant plus particulier qu'il se fait dans le même document où s'annonce l'entrée en vigueur de ladite norme.[178] Ceci est susceptible d'engendrer de la confusion et peut avoir des incidences néfastes sur l'application de la règle.[179] En vertu de quoi, le Groupe spécial considère que la lettre Vilsack constitue une application déraisonnable de la règle finale de 2009 et, en conséquence, la juge incompatible avec l'article X:3 du GATT.[180]

172 *Ibid* au para 7.822.

173 *Ibid* au para 7.851.

174 *Ibid* au para 7.852.

175 *Ibid* au para 7.854.

176 *Ibid* au para 7.855.

177 *Ibid* au para 7.856.

178 *Ibid* au para 7.859.

179 *Ibid* aux para 7.860-7.861.

180 *Ibid* aux para 7.863-7.864.

Au vu des résultats de son analyse, le Groupe spécial a décidé de ne pas analyser les mesures à la lumière de l'article XXIII:1 du GATT.[181] Le Groupe spécial conclut donc, quant à l'affaire WT/DS 384 et quant aux allégations canadiennes au titre du GATT de 1994, que:

> (a) la mesure EPO est un 'règlement technique' au sens de l'Annexe 1.1 de l'Accord OTC, alors que la lettre Vilsack n'en est pas un; (b) la mesure EPO, en particulier s'agissant des étiquettes pour les morceaux de chair musculaire, viole l'article 2.1 parce qu'elle soumet le bétail importé à un traitement moins favorable que celui qui est accordé au bétail national similaire; et (c) la mesure EPO viole l'article 2.2 parce qu'elle ne réalise pas l'objectif consistant à fournir aux consommateurs des renseignements sur l'origine en ce qui concerne les produits carnés.[182]

Quant aux allégations canadiennes au titre de l'Accord OTC, il conclut que:

> (a) nous n'avons pas besoin de formuler de constatation sur la mesure EPO au titre de l'article III:4 compte tenu de notre constatation selon laquelle cette même mesure était contraire à l'obligation de traitement national énoncée à l'article 2.1 de l'Accord OTC; (b) la lettre Vilsack viole l'article X:3 (a) parce qu'elle ne constitue pas une application raisonnable de la mesure EPO; et (c) ayant constaté que la lettre Vilsack était visée par l'article X:3 (a), nous nous abstenons d'examiner si elle est incompatible avec l'article III:4.[183]

On peut, sans crainte de se tromper, avancer que ce rapport fera l'objet d'un appel en 2012.

4. *République de Corée – Mesures visant l'importation de viande bovine et de produits à base de viande bovine en provenance du Canada (DS391)*

Dans cette affaire amorcée en avril 2009, le Canada a adressé, le 7 juillet 2011, une communication à la Présidente de l'ORD. Cette communication à laquelle la République de Corée a souscrit "a pour objet de confirmer le mémorandum [qui suit] sur la question

181 *Ibid* au para 7.907.

182 *Ibid* au para 8.3.

183 *Ibid* au para 8.4.

de l'accès au marché coréen pour la viande bovine en provenance du Canada."[184]

En plus de quelques dispositions formelles d'ordre procédural en vue de la bonne application de l'accord intervenu, ce mémorandum contient les prescriptions sanitaires que le Canada s'engage à respecter pour pouvoir exporter de la viande de bœuf et des produits de viande de bœuf vers la Corée.

L'une des idées maîtresses de ce mémorandum est que le Canada peut exporter de la viande de bœuf et des produits à base de viande bovine s'il est indemne depuis 12 mois de la fièvre aphteuse et indemne depuis 24 mois de la peste des petits ruminants, de la pleuropneumonie contagieuse des bovins, de la dermatose nodulaire et de la fièvre de la Vallée du Rift. Il ne doit pas non plus y avoir eu de vaccination contre ces maladies. Si le Canada arrive à faire reconnaître par le gouvernement coréen qu'il met en œuvre une politique d'éradication efficace, la période requise pour reconnaître que le Canada est indemne peut être raccourcie.[185] Le Canada devra aussi maintenir en permanence des mesures pour déceler et prévenir l'introduction et la propagation de l'encéphalite spongiforme bovine (ESB).[186] Des mesures d'information, d'inspection et de quarantaine sont aussi prévues en cas d'apparition de cas d'ESB au Canada.[187]

Le mémorandum contient aussi quelques autres prescriptions générales, des prescriptions relatives aux établissements de traitement de la viande et des prescriptions relatives à la viande de bœuf.[188]

On peut espérer que le marché coréen restera ouvert longtemps et durablement à la viande de bœuf canadienne.

5. *Communautés européennes – Mesures prohibant l'importation et la commercialisation de produits dérivés du phoque (Plaignant: Canada) (DS/400)*

Le 17 août 2010, la Commission européenne a publié le Règlement (UE) n° 737/2010 de la Commission portant modalités d'application

184 *République de Corée – Mesures visant l'importation de viande bovine et de produits à base de viande bovine en provenance du Canada (DS391(Communication du Canada))* (7 juillet 2011), OMC Doc WT/DS391/8, en ligne: <http://docsonline.wto.org/DDFDocuments/u/WT/DS/391-8.doc>.

185 *Ibid* à la p 4, art 2.

186 *Ibid* à la p 4, art 4.

187 *Ibid* à la p 4, art 5.

188 *Ibid*, art 3-21.

du Règlement (CE) nº 1007/2009 du Parlement européen et du Conseil sur le commerce des produits dérivés du phoque. Le Canada a, dans la foulée, demandé la tenue de nouvelles consultations au sujet du Règlement (CE) n. 1007-2009 que nous avons longuement décrit dans cette chronique l'an dernier et du Règlement d'application nouvellement adopté.[189] Dans cette nouvelle demande de consultations, le Canada complète ses prétentions en indiquant être d'avis que: "la mesure d'application, prise isolément ou conjointement avec le Règlement (CE) nº 1007/2009, est incompatible avec les obligations de l'Union européenne au titre de l'Accord de Marrakech instituant l'Organisation mondiale du commerce, y compris: i) les articles I:1, III:4 et XI:1 du GATT de 1994; ii) les articles 2.1, 2.2, 5.1, 5.2, 5.4, 5.6, 6.1, 6.2, 7.1, 7.2, 7.4, 7.5, 8.1 et 8.2 de l'Accord OTC; iii) l'article 4:2 de l'Accord sur l'agriculture."[190]

Tout comme dans l'affaire DS369 décrite plus haut, le Canada a demandé l'établissement d'un groupe spécial le 14 février 2011.[191]

6. *Canada – Certaines mesures affectant le secteur de la production d'énergie renouvelable (DS/412)*

Le 16 septembre 2010, le Japon a demandé l'ouverture de consultations avec le Canada au sujet de mesures prises "en relation avec le Programme FIT établi en 2009 par la province canadienne de l'Ontario, qui prévoit la fixation de prix à long terme garantis pour la production des installations de production d'énergie renouvelable qui contiennent un pourcentage défini d'éléments d'origine nationale."[192] Ces mesures comprennent, mais non exclusivement, ce qui suit:

189 *Communautés européennes – Mesures prohibant l'importation et la commercialisation de produits dérivés du phoque (Demande de consultations présentée par le Canada, Addendum)* (21 octobre 2010), OMC Doc WT/DS400/1 /Add.1, en ligne: <http://docsonline.wto.org/DDFDocuments/u/G/AG/GEN87A1.doc>.

190 *Ibid.*

191 *Communautés européennes – Certaines mesures prohibant l'importation et la commercialisation de produits dérivés du phoque (Demande d'établissement d'un groupe spécial présentée par le Canada)* (14 février 2011), OMC Doc WT/DS400/4, en ligne: <http://docsonline.wto.org/DDFDocuments/u/WT/DS/400-4.doc>.

192 *Canada – Certaines mesures affectant le secteur de la production d'énergie renouvelable (Demande de consultations présentée par le Japon)* (16 septembre 2010), OMC Doc WT/DS412/1, en ligne: <http://docsonline.wto.org/DDFDocuments/u/G/SCM/D84-1.doc>.

(1) la Loi de 1998 sur l'électricité, telle qu'elle a été modifiée, y compris en particulier la partie II.1 (Office de l'électricité de l'Ontario) et la partie II.2 (Gestion de l'approvisionnement en électricité, de la capacité de production et de la demande d'électricité) de la Loi, y compris en particulier l'article 25.35 (programme de tarifs de rachat garantis);

(2) la Loi édictant la Loi de 2009 sur l'énergie verte et visant à développer une économie verte, abrogeant la Loi de 2006 sur le leadership en matière de conservation de l'énergie et la Loi sur le rendement énergétique et modifiant d'autres lois (la "Loi de 2009 sur l'énergie verte et l'économie verte"), y compris en particulier l'annexe B modifiant la Loi de 1998 sur l'électricité;

(3) la Loi modifiant la Loi de 1998 sur l'électricité, la Loi de 1998 sur la Commission de l'énergie de l'Ontario et apportant des modifications corrélatives à d'autres lois (la "Loi de 2004 sur la restructuration du secteur de l'électricité"), y compris en particulier l'annexe A, article 28, promulguant la partie II.1 de la Loi de 1998 sur l'électricité;

(4) la directive FIT, datée du 24 septembre 2009 et adressée par M. George Smitherman, VicePremier Ministre et Ministre de l'énergie et de l'infrastructure à M. Colin Anderson, Directeur général de l'Office de l'électricité de l'Ontario, enjoignant l'OEO d'élaborer un programme FIT et d'inclure une prescription exigeant que les requérants présentent un plan pour réaliser les objectifs concernant la teneur en éléments d'origine nationale (c'estàdire ontarienne) énoncés dans les règles FIT;

(5) les règles FIT, version 1.3.1 publiée le 2 juillet 2010 et modifiée le 13 août 2010 par l'OEO, et les règles microFIT, version 1.5, publiée le 25 août 2010;

(6) le contrat FIT, version 1.3.1 (2 juillet 2010), y compris les modalités et conditions générales, pièces, et définitions types, publiée par l'OEO, et le contrat microFIT, version 1.5 (25 août 2010), y compris les Appendices, publiée par l'OEO, ainsi que les contrats FIT et microFIT individuels exécutés par l'OEO avec des fournisseurs d'énergie renouvelable en Ontario;

(7) le formulaire de demande FIT (1er décembre 2009) et le formulaire de demande microFIT en ligne, publiés par l'OEO;

(8) le barème FIT (13 août 2010) et le barème microFIT (13 août 2020), publiés par l'OEO;

(9) les interprétations aux fins du programme FIT des prescriptions concernant la teneur en éléments d'origine nationale (14 décembre 2009), publiées par l'OEO; et

(10) toutes modifications ou prorogations de ce qui précède, toutes mesures de remplacement, toutes mesures de reconduction, toutes mesures de mise en œuvre, et toutes mesures connexes."[193]

Après analyse des documents rendus publics par le gouvernement de l'Ontario et l'Office de l'électricité de l'Ontario, notamment sur le site web du programme FIT, le Japon est d'avis que les mesures canadiennes sont incompatibles avec les articles III:4 et III:5 du GATT de 1994, l'article 2:1 de l'Accord sur les mesures concernant les investissements et liées au commerce (Accord sur les MIC) et de l'article 3:2 de l'Accord sur les subventions et mesures compensatoires (Accord SMC). Le gouvernement japonais croit que les mesures en cause créent une discrimination à l'encontre du matériel pour installations de production d'énergie renouvelable produit à l'extérieur de l'Ontario et constituent une subvention prohibée au sens de l'Accord SMC.[194]

Le 6 octobre 2011, le Groupe spécial a été constitué et son mandat lui a été attribué. Le 4 novembre 2011, le Canada a présenté au Groupe spécial une demande de décision préliminaire au sujet des demandes d'établissement de groupe spécial faites dans ce dossier ainsi que dans l'affaire DS/426 dont il sera question plus bas. Le Canada prétend que ces demandes n'indiquent pas suffisamment les fondements juridiques à la base de la plainte et n'indiquent pas suffisamment les éléments factuels constitutifs qui feraient de la "contribution financière" une subvention prohibée. Une décision sur cette demande préliminaire du Canada devrait être rendue par le groupe spécial en 2012.

7. *Canada – Mesures relatives au programme de tarifs de rachat garantis (DS/426)*

Cette affaire est très voisine de l'affaire 412 que nous avons décrite plus haut. On peut d'ailleurs anticiper que, pendant l'année 2012, le Groupe spécial chargé de l'affaire 412 se verra aussi confier la présente affaire. Le 16 août 2011, l'Union européenne a demandé l'ouverture de consultations avec le Canada au sujet, à peu de choses près, des mêmes mesures que celles visées par la demande de

193 *Ibid* aux 1-2.

194 *Ibid* aux 2-3.

consultations du Japon dans l'affaire 412.[195] L'UE considère que ces mesures sont incompatibles avec les articles 3:1)b) et 3:2 b) de l'Accord SMC, l'article III:4 du GATT de 1994 et l'article 2:1 de l'Accord sur les MIC.

IV. Conclusion

Faute d'avoir vu le fameux cycle de Doha se conclure, le Canada n'est pas resté les bras croisés en 2010 et en 2011. Comme plusieurs grandes nations commerçantes, il a trouvé de nouveaux vecteurs de développement de sa politique commerciale. Au plan multilatéral, une certaine résignation qu'on avait pu sentir dans un passé récent semble avoir fait place à une politique de petits pas. Si les progrès du système commercial multilatéral sont modestes, ils n'en sont pas moins présents.

[195] *Canada – Mesures relatives au programme de tarifs de rachat garantis (Demande de consultations présentée par l'Union européenne)* (16 août 2011), OMC Doc WT/DS426/1, en ligne: <http://docsonline.wto.org/DDFDocuments/u/G/SCM/D87-1.doc>.

II. Le Canada et le système financier international en 2010-11

BERNARD COLAS

Sur fond de reprise modeste à l'échelle mondiale en 2010, puis de l'écueil vécu par la zone Euro, plus particulièrement en 2010 puis en 2011, l'ensemble des intervenants et décideurs du système financier international ont tenté d'en renforcir l'architecture à tous les niveaux. Le Canada s'illustre clairement auprès (I) du Groupe des 20 (G20), des institutions financières internationales (II), des organismes de contrôle des établissements financiers (III), du groupe d'action financière (IV) et du Joint Forum (V). Les règles internationales en matière de saine gouvernance financière se déploient et s'articulent avec plus d'autorité. Le Canada, fort de la qualité et de la performance de son système financier dont son système bancaire quasi-exemplaire, contribue par sa participation à en asseoir la légitimité.

I. Le Groupe des 20

Les visées du G20 sont (1) la promotion d'une croissance allant de pair avec la stabilité macro financière et la création d'emplois, (2) la réforme du système monétaire international ainsi que le rééquilibrage de la demande extérieure et (3) l'adaptation continue de l'appui aux pays membres à faible revenu. Ces domaines d'actions prioritaires traduisent une prise de conscience plus générale de la nécessité de renforcer, voire de transformer, la surveillance de l'économie mondiale pour aider les gouvernements à anticiper les événements.[1]

Bernard Colas est avocat associé de l'étude Colas Moreira Kazandjian Zikovsky (CMKZ) à Montréal et Docteur en droit. L'auteur remercie Isabelle Gauvreau, Flore Kouadio, LL.M. et Xavier Mageau, LL.M. de la même étude pour leur importante contribution à la préparation de cet article.

1 Fonds Monétaire International (FMI), *Rapport annuel 2011, Vers une croissance équitable et équilibrée*, à la p 17.

A. LES RENCONTRES DE 2010-11

Au cours des années 2010-2011, les chefs d'états du G20 se sont rencontrés à trois reprises. Au sein du G20, les chefs d'états et de gouvernements exercent leur influence et créent des échéances pour faire avancer les travaux des institutions financières internationales, et des organismes regroupant les régulateurs nationaux (OICV, CBCB, Joint Forum) en vue de renforcer la gouvernance économique et financière mondiale.

À Toronto, fin juin 2010, les pays du G20 se sont engagés à réduire de moitié leurs déficits budgétaires en trois ans, tout en essayant de soutenir la reprise; et à lutter contre les pratiques risquées de leurs banques.[2] Les chefs d'États et de gouvernements ont aussi mis de l'avant le principe de l'inclusion financière de deux milliards de personnes défavorisées sans accès aux services financiers. Cette mesure est vue comme favorisant la protection simultanée de la stabilité financière et des consommateurs.[3] À Séoul, en novembre 2010, les chefs d'États et de gouvernements ont souhaité mettre de l'avant des plans d'assainissement des finances publiques afin d'assurer une reprise soutenue, une croissance durable et améliorer la stabilité des marchés financiers.[4] À Cannes, début novembre 2011, le G20 a lancé un appel aux Institutions financières internationales (IFIs), aux banques régionales de développement, à la Conférence des Nations Unies sur le commerce et le développement (CNUCED), à l'Organisation de Coopération et de Développement Économiques (OCDE), à la Banque des règlements internationaux (BRI) et au Conseil de la stabilité financière (CSF) de lui proposer

2 "Nous avons convenu que de renforcer les fonds propres et les liquidités et de prévenir l'effet de levier excessif sont au cœur de la réforme du secteur financier. Nous sommes convenus d'accroître la qualité la quantité et la cohérence internationale du capital, de renforcer les normes de liquidités, de prévenir les recours excessifs aux leviers financiers et la prise de risques inconsidérés et de réduire la procyclicalité." G20 Sommet de Toronto 2010, *Déclaration des chefs d'État et de gouvernement,* 26 et 27 juin 2010, Annexe II au para 5, en ligne: <http://canadainternational.gc.ca/g20/summit-sommet/2010/toronto-declaration-toronto.aspx?lang=fra&view=d>.

3 *Ibid. Principes de l'inclusion financière novatrice* Toronto, le 27 juin, 2010, en ligne: <http://www.g20.utoronto.ca/2010/to-principles-fr.html>.

4 G20 Sommet de Séoul, *Déclaration des chefs d'État et de gouvernement,* 11 et 12 novembre 2010, au para 9, en ligne: <http://www.canadainternational.gc.ca/g20/summit-sommet/2010/g20_seoul_declaration.aspx?lang=fra&menu_id=41&menu=L&view=d > [G20 Sommet de Séoul, *Déclaration des chefs*].

un plan d'actions pour soutenir le développement et l'approfondissement des marchés obligataires en monnaie locale.[5]

Le G20 a aussi prévu l'élaboration de règles visant la stabilité financière des pays émergents en collaboration avec le CSF et Banque Mondiale.[6]

B. UNE NOUVELLE INSTANCE À PRENDRE EN COMPTE: LE CONSEIL DE STABILITÉ FINANCIÈRE

Créé par le G20 en 2009, le CSF joue un rôle de premier plan pour évaluer les vulnérabilités du système financier international, ainsi que pour identifier et contrôler les actions nécessaires pour y remédier. De ce fait, le CSF complète le travail du Comité de Bâle sur le contrôle bancaire et des autres instances internationales pour la mise en œuvre de la surveillance micro prudentielle du secteur financier par pays et contribue plus avant l'adhésion des juridictions nationales aux normes élaborées par les instances internationales. Le CSF réunit des autorités nationales responsables de la stabilité financière dans d'importants centres financiers internationaux, des institutions financières internationales, de secteurs spécifiques, des regroupements internationaux de régulateurs et de superviseurs et des comités d'experts des banques centrales. Le FMI, ayant un rôle complémentaire à celui du Conseil de Stabilité financière, collabore à celui-ci et a joint ses rangs en 2010.

Le CSF, parrainé par la BRI et logé à la même adresse que le Comité de Bâle sur le contrôle bancaire deviendrait, suivant les vœux du G20, une entité juridique distincte. Les ressources du CSF doivent être accrues pour l'assister dans sa mission de principal interlocuteur des instances régulatrices nationales en ce qui concerne l'intégration du dispositif normatif international dans les juridictions nationales.[7] Le Conseil de stabilité financière a notamment émis des recommandations afin de réduire la dépendance des organismes de normalisation, des participants au marché, des

5 G20 Sommet de Cannes, *Déclaration des chefs d'État et de gouvernement,* 3 et 4 novembre 2011, au para 11, en ligne: <http://www.canadainternational.gc.ca/g20/summit-sommet/2011/cannes_declaration_20111104.aspx?lang=fra&view=d> [G20 Sommet de Cannes, *Déclaration des chefs*].

6 *Ibid* au para 9.

7 G20 Sommet de Cannes, *Déclaration finale du Sommet de Cannes,* aux para 37-39, en ligne: <http://www.canadainternational.gc.ca/g20/summit-sommet/2011/cannes_declaration_20111104.aspx?lang=fra&view=d>.

organismes de surveillance et des banques centrales envers les agences de notations externes.[8]

II. Les Institutions financières internationales

A. Le Fonds monétaire international

De son côté, le FMI s'est vu imparti, au cours des sommets du G20 tenus en 2010 et 2011, des mandats qui ont trait à l'organisation de la gouvernance financière, la mise en place de moyens pour évaluer les risques de dérèglements du système financier international, de ses outils de financement et la révision de son propre financement, de sa propre gouvernance et de sa représentativité. Ces propositions doivent aussi prévoir une surveillance et une supervision plus efficaces. Le FMI travaille de concert avec la BRI et le CSF pour poursuivre les travaux sur les cadres stratégiques macro prudentiels.

1. *Réformes, représentativité, financement, et instruments de prêts*

Le FMI représente 187 pays membres depuis juin 2010. L'accord des quotes-parts de 2008 est entré en vigueur en mars 2011; ainsi le total des quotes-parts s'élève maintenant à 238.4 milliards de DTS. La quote-part du Canada s'élève à 6,37 milliards de DTS pour 2,88 % des droits de vote ce qui lui assure le neuvième rang des actionnaires du FMI.[9] L'administrateur élu au FMI pour le groupe de pays comprenant le Canada, l'Irlande et les pays des Caraïbes est le Canadien Thomas A. Hockin, qui a mené une carrière dans les services financiers.

Les administrateurs du FMI prévoient une autre réforme des quotes-parts, recommandée en décembre 2010. Ses aménagements auront pour effet de doubler les quotes-parts pour les porter à environ 476,8 milliards de DTS (environ 773 milliards de dollars), et d'en transférer plus de 6 % vers les pays émergents et en développement dynamique. Cette réforme préserve les quotes-parts relatives des pays membres les plus pauvres et le nombre de voix qui leur est attribué. Suite à ce réalignement, le Brésil, la Fédération de Russie, l'Inde et la Chine figureront parmi les dix plus gros actionnaires

[8] G20 Sommet de Séoul 2010, *Déclaration des dirigeants*, au para 38, en ligne: <http://www.canadainternational.gc.ca/g20/summit-sommet/2010/g20_seoul_declaration.aspx?lang=fra&menu_id=41&menu=L&view=d>.

[9] Ministère des Finances Canada, *Le Canada au FMI et à la Banque mondiale: Rapport sur les opérations effectuées en vertu de la Loi sur les accords de Bretton Woods et des accords connexes* (Ottawa: Ministère des Finances Canada, 2010), à la p 6.

du FMI.[10] Cette réforme admise par le FMI prendra effet suite à la ratification des pays membres et l'approbation des modifications des Statuts du FMI, nécessitant le trois cinquième des pays membres représentant 85 % du total des voix attribués.[11]

À ces réformes de la représentativité des actionnaires et du financement du FMI, le Canada préconise celle du conseil d'administration: une instance élue dont deux sièges seraient retirés à la représentation globale des pays européens avancés au bénéfice des pays émergents.

Le FMI a également négocié un accroissement substantiel des accords permanents d'emprunts conclus avec les pays membres, sous la forme de Nouveaux accords d'emprunt (NAE), entrés en vigueur en mars 2011, afin de palier à l'intense crise financière frappant la zone euro. Cet élargissement des accords s'est traduit, dans un premier temps, par un décuplement de la capacité d'emprunt ainsi portée à 367,5 milliards de DTS (environ 596 milliards de dollars). Les administrateurs du FMI, pour préserver le caractère de l'institution financée par quotes-parts, insistent afin que les NAE soient revus en baisse dès la mise à disposition des ressources correspondant à la mise en place des nouvelles quotes-parts prévue en 2010 pour sa mise en place en 2012.[12]

Le FMI, troisième plus important détenteur des réserves d'or au monde (96 millions d'onces en janvier 2010), a aussi accru ses moyens financiers en procédant à des ventes successives pour soutenir ses activités de financement dans le cadre de la crise financière mondiale.[13]

La nouvelle réforme des quotes-parts s'accompagnera d'une réforme du panier des devises des DTS qui doit elle-même entrer en vigueur en 2015 ou plus tôt, au fur et à mesure que les devises respecteront les critères définis pour intégrer le panier des devises clés formant les DTS.[14]

10 FMI, *Rapport Annuel 2011*, à la p 10, en ligne: <http://www.imf.org/external/french/pubs/ft/ar/2011/pdf/ar11_fra.pdf>.

11 FMI, *Fiche technique — Quotes-parts au FMI*, le 30 mars 2011, en ligne: <http://www.imf.org/external/np/exr/facts/fre/pdf/quotasf.pdf>.

12 FMI, *Rapport Annuel 2010*, à la p 12, en ligne: <http://www.imf.org/external/french/pubs/ft/ar/2010/ar10_fra.pdf>.

13 FMI, *Fiche technique — Les ressources du FMI*, en ligne: <http://www.ieo-imf.org/external/np/exr/facts/fre/pdf/finfacf.pdf>.

14 G20 Sommet de Cannes, *Déclaration des chefs, supra* note 5 au para 5.

Au cours des deux dernières années, le FMI a révisé, à nouveau, ses instruments d'aide financière. Pour les pays bénéficiant de fondamentaux économiques solides et d'un cadre institutionnel robuste le FMI a mis en place une ligne de crédit de précaution et de liquidité (LPL), à six mois, pouvant représenter cinq fois la quote-part du pays concerné afin de palier à la crise des paiements. L'instrument de financement rapide (IFR) pour les pays soumis à des chocs exogènes (soulèvements politiques, catastrophes naturelles, etc.) est une aide financière temporaire représentant cent pourcent de la quote-part et pour les pays pauvres, les facilités élargies de crédit (FECs).[15]

2. *Interventions*

Face à la crise des paiements de la Grèce, en 2010, le FMI a contribué à la restructuration de la dette à la hauteur de 26,43 milliards de DTS sur les 85 milliards DTS qui ont été rassemblés à titre de mesures temporaires de financement. Pour l'Irlande, aux prises avec un déficit de 32 % de son PIB généré par son soutien à ses banques nationales, le FMI a allongé 19,47 milliards de DTS. Au final l'ensemble des avances du FMI pour soutenir la zone euro en 2010 et en 2011 ont été de 75,6 milliards de DTS.[16] En 2009, le Canada avait consenti au FMI un prêt bilatéral temporaire de 10 milliards de dollars américains. Ce prêt s'est avéré crucial pour soutenir les interventions mentionnées ci-haut.[17]

En 2011, face à sa propre crise des paiements, l'Italie a invité le FMI à procéder à une vérification publique de la mise en œuvre de ses politiques sur une base trimestrielle.[18]

Outre un financement, sans précédent des pays avancés, le FMI a accru son aide aux pays les plus pauvres. Le FMI a procédé à une réforme de la structure de la conditionnalité et des conditions financières des facilités de financement concessionnel en créant un

15 FMI, *Fiche technique – Les ressources du FMI, supra* note 13. Voir également l'article paru sur le site du quotidien Le Point.fr en date du 23/11/2011, "Crise de la dette: le FMI étoffe ses instruments de crédit," en ligne: <http://www.lepoint.fr/economie/crise-de-la-dette-le-fmi-etoffe-ses-instruments-de-credit-23-11-2011-1399294_28.php>.

16 FMI, *Rapport Annuel 2011, supra* note 10 à la p 5.

17 Ministère des finances Canada, au *Le Canada au FMI et au Groupe de la Banque mondiale,* à la p 25, en ligne: <http://www.fin.gc.ca/bretwood/pdf/bretwd10-fra.pdf>.

18 G20 Sommet de Cannes, *Déclaration des chefs, supra* note 5 au para 5.

nouveau fonds fiduciaire pour la réduction de la pauvreté et pour la croissance.[19] L'encours des prêts concessionnels s'est élevé à environ 5 milliards de DTS au cours de l'année 2010 et puis à 6 milliards pour l'année 2011.[20]

3. *Surveillance, diffusion des données, et assistance technique*

Les crises successives depuis 2008 ont montré que le risque total du système financier dans son ensemble est supérieur à l'agrégation des risques individuels, et a mis en lumière l'insuffisance des moyens dont disposent les autorités pour mesurer le risque systémique.[21] Ces constats incitent les régulateurs dans leur ensemble à vouloir améliorer la surveillance macro prudentielle et la collecte des données.[22]

Afin que le FMI puisse assurer le fonctionnement effectif du système monétaire international (surveillances bilatérales et multilatérales), sa nouvelle directrice générale prône l'établissement de politiques claires de partage de données des États membres.[23] À ce jour, 68 pays ont adhéré à la norme spéciale de diffusion des données (NSDD), créée en mars 1996, avec pour objectif d'aider les pays membres à communiquer leurs données économiques et financières au public. D'un autre côté, 98 pays-membres ont joint le système général de diffusion des données (SGDD), offrant le "tableau de bord" créé en 1997.[24]

Le FMI s'allie avec la Banque mondiale pour les données sur les dettes publiques et collabore avec la BRI pour les statistiques relatives aux titres. Par ailleurs, le FMI a approfondi son analyse en

19 FMI, *Fiche technique, Le soutien du FMI aux pays à faible revenu,* le 31 mars 2011, en ligne: <http://www.imf.org/external/np/exr/facts/fre/poorf.htm>.

20 FMI, *Rapport Annuel 2011, supra* note 10 à la p 26.

21 Le risque systémique peut être défini comme le risque d'une déficience du système financier d'une telle ampleur qu'elle puisse affecter l'économie réelle. Les lacunes se sont manifestées en ce qui concerne à la fois le cadre analytique et les données qu'utilisent, sur chaque établissement et au niveau agrégé, les autorités et les marchés dans leur processus de décision.

22 Banque des Règlements Internationaux, *81ème rapport annuel,* 1er avril 2010 au 31 mars 2011, à la p 95, en ligne: <http://www.bis.org/publ/arpdf/ar2011_fr.pdf>.

23 En mars 2011, le FMI et le CSF ont organisé à Washington une conférence relative aux déficits de données. Le recensement exhaustif des données et partant, la collaboration des états et des juridictions à les partager, est un enjeu primordial pour permettre aux institutions financières internationales de jouer leur rôle prédictif et de précaution.

24 FMI, *Rapport Annuel 2011, supra* note 10 à la p 48.

examinant les bilans des secteurs non financiers dont ceux des entreprises et des ménages, le prix des logements et d'autres données relatives à l'immobilier et les instruments de transfert de risques de crédit et sur le risque ultime favorisé par les produits dérivés et les processus dits de "titrisation."[25]

Le FMI se penche sur les équilibres budgétaires des États ou les moyens de les améliorer, la qualité des dettes souveraines, les impacts des agences de notation et les données macroéconomiques afin de repérer les indicateurs propres à exercer une surveillance plus proactive des risques systémiques. Le FMI collabore avec le CSF à l'exercice semestriel d'alerte avancée (EAA). L'EAA vise à déceler les facteurs de vulnérabilité et les déclencheurs qui pourraient précipiter des crises systémiques, et à déterminer comment ces risques pourraient être atténués, notamment par une action internationale concertée.

4. Contribution canadienne

Le Canada fait partie des 25 pays membres du FMI dont les secteurs financiers représentent 90 % de l'activité financière mondiale. Le Canada se prête depuis septembre 2010, en application de l'article IV des Statuts du FMI, au PESF (Programme d'évaluation du secteur financier). Ces évaluations analysent la structure, la solidité du système financier et ses liens avec le reste de l'économie en rapport avec les normes internationales ainsi que la capacité des autorités de gérer et de résoudre une crise financière.[26]

En matière d'assistance technique, le Canada assume le leadership du Centre régional d'assistance technique des Caraïbes en y consacrant 25 millions de dollars au cours de la période 2010-2013. De plus, l'Agence canadienne de développement international (ACDI) offre son aide en matière de gestion fiscale, douanière et financière à long terme destinée aux administrations publiques des pays des Caraïbes. L'ACDI contribue à hauteur de 19,2 millions de dollars au cours de la durée de trois ans de ce programme.

B. LE GROUPE DE LA BANQUE MONDIALE

La Banque Mondiale intervient aussi suite à des catastrophes comme le séisme d'Haïti début 2010 ou celui de Japon en 2011 tout en poursuivant les Objectifs du Millénaire pour le développement

25 *Ibid* à la p 42.

26 *Ibid* à la p 48.

(OMD) convenus lors du Sommet du Millénaire en 2000. La Banque Mondiale cible les populations pauvres et vulnérables et se concentre sur les pays qui sont mal partis pour atteindre les OMD en 2015.[27] Elle crée des opportunités de croissance, promeut l'action collective au niveau mondial de même que renforce la gouvernance et met une emphase particulière sur la lutte à la corruption.

Deux des cinq instances de la Banque Mondiale, la Banque internationale pour la reconstruction et le développement (BIRD) et l'Association internationale de développement (IDA) ont consenti des prêts et crédits totaux de 58.7 milliards de dollars américains pour l'exercice 2010 et de 42 milliards pour l'exercice 2011. Malgré la décroissance apparente, les sommes allouées en 2011 étaient supérieures à celles attribuées en 2007, année dite pré-crise.

1. Représentativité et réforme de la gouvernance

Lors du Sommet de Toronto des dirigeants du G20, le Canada a instamment demandé que l'augmentation du capital de la Banque Mondiale concorde avec la révision de la gouvernance de l'organisation et de nouvelles façons de gérer les résultats, les contributions financières et leur suivi ainsi que de tenir compte des impacts environnementaux.

Ainsi, l'Administratrice représentant le Canada à la Banque Mondiale a présidé le Comité de la gouvernance et des affaires administratives (CGAA) lequel dirige le processus de réforme de la représentation au sein de la Banque. Les travaux ont reçus l'approbation du Conseil des Gouverneurs en mars 2011 et a permis de porter les voix des pays en développement et des pays en transition à 47.19 % à la BIRD et à la SFI à 39,48 %. Les pays d'Afrique sont maintenant représentés par trois Administrateurs. En fonction des ces réformes la Banque est tenue de réexaminer son capital tous les cinq ans à compter de 2015.[28]

Dans la foulée des efforts consentis pour une plus grande transparence des activités de la Banque aussi bien que pour contribuer à la mise en commun des informations financières qui serviront à mieux cerner les impacts systémiques touchant le système financier international, la Banque mondiale a mis en ligne l'accès à 7000 séries de données.[29]

27 *Ibid* à la p 27.

28 *Ibid* à la p 61.

29 Voir en ligne: <http://data.worldbank.org/data-catalog>.

2. *Collaboration soutenue de la part du Canada*

Le Canada a versé en 2010 une cotisation 384 millions de dollars à l'Association internationale de développement (IDA), une autre instance de la Banque Mondiale, dans le cadre de la reconstitution triennale de ses fonds. Le Canada a aussi consenti des crédits dans le cadre des programmes et des fonds fiduciaires par l'entremise de l'ACDI à la hauteur de 91 millions au cours de l'année 2010.[30]

À titre ponctuel, le Canada a soutenu Haïti en préconisant l'élimination de sa dette de 825 millions auprès des institutions financières internationales dont la Banque Mondiale. Le Canada a été le premier pays à verser la somme de 32,6 millions de dollars américains aux fins d'effacer cette dette.

La SFI, chargée des opérations avec le secteur privé, a bénéficié de la part du Canada de 50 millions pour le Programme mondial pour l'agriculture et la sécurité alimentaire. Le Canada a aussi apporté 20 millions au soutien de 14 propositions d'affaires de petites et moyennes entreprises provenant des quatre coins du monde dans le cadre d'un concours institué lors du G20 de Toronto.[31]

Cependant le Canada n'a pas encore adhéré au Centre international pour le règlement des différents (CIRDI) malgré la nomination d'une ressortissante canadienne au poste de Secrétaire générale de l'organisation.[32]

III. Les Organismes de contrôle des établissements financiers

A. Le comité de Bâle sur le contrôle bancaire (CBCB)

1. *Contexte*

Les règles prudentielles des institutions financières, basées sur les prémisses de la discipline de marché et la dispersion des risques, qui devaient pourvoir suite à la déréglementation des vingt dernières années, ont failli à la tâche. Le G20 et le Conseil de Stabilité

30 Ministère des finances Canada, *Le Canada au FMI et à la Banque mondiale: Rapport sur les opérations effectuées en vertu de la Loi sur les accords de Bretton Woods et des accords connexes* (Ottawa: Ministère des Finances Canada, 2010), à la p 57.

31 *Ibid* à la p 70.

32 L'élection de Meg Kinnear au Secrétariat general du CIRDI, en ligne: <http://icsid.worldbank.org/ICSID/FrontServlet?requestType=CasesRH&actionVal=OpenPage&PageType=AnnouncementsFrame&FromPage=Announcements&pageName=Announcement15>.

Financière ont appelé à une réforme en profondeur des pratiques dans le secteur bancaire international.[33]

Les risques de crédits, qui devaient être jugulés par la panoplie de produits dérivés entre autres et le resserrement des critères de Bâle II, se sont matérialisés et ont déséquilibré le système financier international. La déclaration finale du G20 de Séoul a été sévère pour le milieu bancaire dans son ensemble.[34]

Le FMI incite vivement les États à intégrer Bâle II. Rappelons que Bâle II ajoutait à la norme de fonds propres des institutions bancaires, des obligations de surveillance supplémentaire de la stabilité des ratios dans le temps, dit Pilier II. Les banques devront être en mesure de démontrer la qualité de leurs ratios de fonds propres non seulement en tenant compte de la qualité de leurs actifs mais également de leurs segments de clientèle.

2. *L'état de la réglementation canadienne en matière de fonds propres*

Au Canada, le Bureau du surintendant des institutions financières (BSIF) a émis ses directives faisant respecter les ratios actif/fonds propres et de fonds propres basés sur le risque de Bâle II. Elles sont entrées en vigueur en janvier 2012.[35]

Le BSIF met de l'avant un ratio actif/fonds propres obtenu en divisant l'actif total de l'institution (l'ensemble des prêts consentis comprenant certains éléments hors bilan), par le total de ses fonds propres nets rajustés. La cible de ce ratio est de 20.

Les fonds propres, suivant les lignes directrices de Bâle II, sont classés en trois catégories (en anglais "*tier*"): essentiellement, la catégorie 1 des fonds propres est constituée du capital-actions et des bénéfices non-réparties des banques; la catégorie 2 de fonds propres est constituée de l'ensemble des réserves latentes, de réserves de réévaluation, des provisions générales, d'instruments hybrides de capital et de dette, de dettes subordonnées (amortissement

33 Comité de Bâle sur le contrôle bancaire, *Réponse du Comité de Bâle à la crise financière: Rapport au Groupe des Vingt* (Bâle, Suisse: Banque des Règlements Internationaux, Octobre 2010), en ligne: <http://www.bis.org/publ/bcbs179_fr.pdf>.

34 G20 Sommet de Séoul, *Déclaration des chefs*, *supra* note 4, au para 27.

35 Bureau du surintendant des institutions financières, *Ligne directrice Objet: Normes de fonds propres No: A-1 Date d'entrée en vigueur:* Janvier 2012, en ligne: <http://www.osfi-bsif.gc.ca/app/DocRepository/1/fra/directrices/fonds/directrices/CAR_A1_f.pdf>. Les prérogatives du BSIF lui sont imparties par l'article 485 (1) de la Loi sur les banques et l'article 473 (1) de la Loi sur les sociétés de fiducie et de prêts.

minimum de dix ans). Les fonds propres de catégorie 3 désignent les titres de créance subordonnée qui remplissent les conditions suivantes: leur échéance initiale est d'au moins deux ans; le paiement de l'intérêt ou du principal est retardé (même à l'échéance) s'il risque d'entraîner la chute des fonds propres de l'institution au-dessous de son exigence minimale, ils ne peuvent être rachetés avant l'échéance sans l'accord préalable du BSIF. Cette dernière catégorie ne sert que dans le ratio de fonds propres basé sur le risque.[36]

Le ratio actif/fonds propres commande donc que l'actif total ne puisse excéder 20 fois les fonds propres des catégories 1 et 2. Toutefois, avec l'approbation préalable du surintendant, il y a certaines mesures de flexibilité. En fixant le ratio actif/fonds propres d'une institution, le BSIF tient compte de facteurs comme l'expérience de gestion et d'exploitation, la solidité de la société mère, la diversification de l'actif, le genre d'actif et la propension à prendre des risques.

Pour le deuxième ratio de fonds propres, le ratio de fonds propres basé sur les risques, les institutions financières canadiennes doivent respecter des normes de fonds propres minimales axées sur le risque en fonction de leur exposition au risque de crédit, de leurs risques opérationnels et, si elles exercent d'importantes activités de négociation, de leurs risques de marché. Le ratio de fonds propres basé sur les risques, intègre au numérateur une notion élargie de fonds propres en additionnant les fonds propres de catégorie 3. Le diviseur de ce ratio inclut les actifs pondérés en fonction des risques (APR) suivant des méthodes d'évaluation dites standard, des méthodes d'évaluation de notation interne, auxquels on additionne le risque opérationnel et le risque de marché de l'institution financière visée. Les exigences minimales en matière de fonds propres, qui doivent être respectées en tout temps, s'établissent à un ratio de propres de catégorie 1 de 4 %, et à un ratio total des fonds propres de 8 %. Le BSIF peut fixer des ratios cibles de fonds propres plus élevés pour l'ensemble du secteur.[37]

3. Bâle III

Les règles de Bâle III, émises par le CBCB en septembre 2010, visent leur intégration par les juridictions entre 2013 et 2019.

[36] Bureau du surintendant des institutions financières, *Ligne directrice Objet: Normes de fonds propres No: A-1 Date d'entrée en vigueur:* janvier 2012, *supra* note 35, à la p 26.

[37] *Ibid* à la p 9.

Dans l'esprit d'un processus continu de surveillance du secteur bancaire, Bâle III instaure des normes rehaussées de liquidité, de vigie constante des risques de crédit et de qualité et de quantité des fonds propres.

Les normes de liquidités LCR (Liquidity Coverage Ratio) et NSFR (Net Stable Funding Ratio) visent deux temporalités différentes. La première, dite LCR, pallie au besoin de liquidité de l'institution bancaire sur une période de trente jours et tient compte des scénarios connus de chocs et d'impacts les plus sévères. Le second, NSFR, s'adresse au besoin de liquidité des banques sur un an. Bâle III prévoit dans son échéancier que les banques rencontrent ces normes de liquidité, qui tiennent compte autant des éléments du bilan que des engagements hors bilan, en 2015.[38]

Les exigences minimales du ratio de fonds propres passent à 4,5 % lorsque le numérateur soit les actions ordinaires et assimilées, soit bien plus que le ratio minimal de 2 % prévu par Bâle II. De même, le ratio minimal de fonds propres T1 (T pour "*tier*" comme ci-haut) qui comprend d'autres éléments, soit les bénéfices non répartis et certaines réserves qualifiées, sera porté à 6 %, alors qu'il n'est que de 4 % en application de Bâle II. Le total des fonds propres (T1 plus T2) doit, à tout moment, être au moins égal à 8,0 % des actifs pondérés.[39]

De plus, pour faire face à de futures périodes de tensions, les banques seront tenues de disposer d'un volant supplémentaire de 2,5 %, dit "de conservation," en actions ordinaires. Le volant permettra aux banques de continuer de disposer des fonds propres nécessaires pour soutenir leurs opérations en période de tensions. C'est ainsi que, en temps normal, les exigences totales pour la composante d'actions ordinaires seront effectivement portées à au moins 7 %. Ne pas remplir cette exigence aura des conséquences directes: plus les fonds propres d'une banque seront proches des exigences minimales, plus cette banque sera limitée en matière de distribution de bénéfices (dividendes, rachat d'actions et primes, par exemple), jusqu'à ce qu'elle les reconstitue.

La vigilance sera accrue sur les actifs au regard desquels les fonds propres sont mesurés. Bâle III instaure un ratio de levier minimal

38 Comité de Bâle sur le contrôle bancaire, Bâle III: *Dispositif réglementaire mondial visant à renforcer la résilience des établissements et systèmes bancaires,* Décembre 2010 (document révisé juin 2011) Annexe 4, en ligne: <http://www.bis.org/publ/bcbs189_fr.pdf>.

39 *Ibid* à la p 13.

de 3 % pour ces mêmes fonds propres dits T1 — soit le ratio des fonds propres de base, calculé selon la nouvelle définition, plus stricte, de Bâle III, en rapport à la somme des actifs totaux non pondérés d'une banque et de ses expositions de hors-bilan — durant une période préliminaire qui débutera en janvier 2013. Le Comité de Bâle suivra l'évolution du ratio de levier tout au long du cycle économique et étudiera ainsi son impact sur les modèles opérationnels des banques et son interaction avec les exigences fondées sur le risque.[40]

Lorsque les autorités jugeront que l'expansion du crédit crée la menace d'un risque systémique, elles pourront imposer un volant supplémentaire de 0 à 2,5 % des fonds propres supplémentaires du total des actifs pondérés des risques.[41]

En bref, le niveau de fonds propres exigé des banques à l'échelle mondiale va considérablement augmenter dans les années à venir. Les exigences de Bâle III feront l'objet d'observations et de révisions continues. La surveillance portera sur les profits, le risque, les modèles opérationnels des banques et la conjoncture économique.

B. L'ORGANISATION INTERNATIONALE DES COMMISSIONS DES VALEURS

Sous les hospices du Président Directeur général de l'Autorité des marchés financiers du Québec, Montréal a accueilli l'OICV du 6 au 10 juin 2010. L'OICV préconise la coopération internationale afin de maintenir des marchés équitables, efficaces et transparents, et chercher à résoudre les risques systémiques par des normes cohérentes et internationalement reconnues afin de protéger les investisseurs. L'OICV a mis de l'avant en juin 2010 huit nouveaux principes qui s'ajoutent aux trente principes de normes internationales déjà publiées. Ces huit nouveaux principes portent notamment sur les moyens d'atténuer les risques systémiques et prévoient l'assujettissement des vérificateurs et des agences de notation à la surveillance des autorités.

[40] Allocution de Jaime Caruana, Directeur Général de la Banque des Règlements Internationaux, *Bâle III: vers un système financier plus sûr,* à l'occasion de la 3e Conférence bancaire internationale Santander, Madrid, le 15 septembre 2010, en ligne: <http://www.bis.org/speeches/sp100921_fr.pdf>.

[41] Comité de Bâle sur le contrôle bancaire, *Bâle III: Dispositif réglementaire mondial visant à renforcer la résilience des établissements et systèmes bancaires,* Décembre 2010 (document révisé juin 2011) à la p 64, en ligne: <http://www.bis.org/publ/bcbs189_fr.pdf>.

FINet, CME Clearing, Eurex Clearing, et LCH.Clearnet sont des contreparties centrales de la négociation des produits dérivés dans divers marchés financiers, dont ceux des pensions, des options et des swaps. Leur conception ne fait pas l'objet de normes internationales. Des arbitrages inhérents à un certain nombre de questions ainsi que les critères de comparaison internationaux seront analysés et auront des répercussions sur les travaux du CBCB.[42]

La méthodologie d'évaluation de la mise en œuvre des Principes de l'OICV est utilisée lors des Programmes d'évaluation du secteur financier (PESF) menés par le FMI dans le cadre de sa mission de surveillance.[43]

IV. Le groupe d'action financiere

Le GAFI exerce une surveillance sur les juridictions qui présentent des défaillances stratégiques du point de vue de la lutte contre le blanchiment de capitaux et le financement du terrorisme (LBC/FT), phénomène qui participe au risque de déséquilibre pour le système financier international.

L'Inde a joint les rangs des 34 pays membres du GAFI en 2010. De ce nombre, 31 se sont soumis au troisième cycle d'évaluation mutuelle des mesures de LBFC/FT.[44]

Les Quarante (+ Neuf) Recommandations du GAFI ont eu vingt ans en 2010. Ces Recommandations accompagnées de leurs Notes interprétatives constituent un ensemble exhaustif de stratégies et de mesures destinées à combattre le blanchiment de capitaux et le financement du terrorisme. Ces normes sont approuvées au total par 130 juridictions à travers des associations régionales parentes du GAFI.

Le GAFI a étudié en 2011 une typologie sur le blanchiment des produits de la corruption et de son effet sur les économies en se

42 Comité de Bâle sur le contrôle bancaire, Bâle III: *Dispositif réglementaire mondial visant à renforcer la résilience des établissements et systèmes bancaires,* Décembre 2010 (document révisé juin 2011) à la p 50, en ligne: <http://www.bis.org/publ/bcbs189_fr.pdf>. Voir aussi Banque du Canada, *Lessons from International Central Counterparties: Benchmarking and Analysis,* juin 2011, Alexandre Lazarow, en ligne: <http://www.bankofcanada.ca/wp-content/uploads/2011/06/dp2011-04.pdf>.

43 Conférence de l'OICV à Cape Town en Afrique Final Update, *36th Annual Conference of the International Organization of Securities Commissions Cape Town,* 20 April 2011 à la p 2, en ligne: <http://www.cmvm.pt/CMVM/Cooperacao%20Internacional/Docs%20Iosco/Documents/ComFinal36ConfAnualIOSCO.pdf>.

44 2010 GAFI/OCDE, *Groupe d'Action Financière, Rapport Annuel 2009-2010,* en ligne: <http://www.oecd.org/dataoecd/12/5/46084991.pdf>.

référant à diverses études qui en analysent les impacts négatifs et démontrent les mécanismes de freinage de la croissance. Le rapport constate également que les économies les plus avancées sont celles qui sont le moins sous l'emprise de la corruption.[45]

Outre les mesures d'évaluation mutuelle, d'application des Recommandations, le principe de l'inclusion financière, favorisant l'accès du plus grand nombre aux services financiers, semble être un autre moyen de juguler à moyen et à long terme les pratiques de blanchiment d'argent et de financement du terrorisme.[46]

Le CANAFE (Centre d'analyse des opérations et déclarations financières du Canada) a été établi dans le cadre de la Loi sur le recyclage des produits de la criminalité et le financement des activités terroristes du Canada. Les entités visées par la Loi sont obligées de faire les déclarations au CANAFE pour les opérations présentant des caractéristiques suspectes.[47]

Au cours de l'exercice 2010-2011 le CANAFE a communiqué 777 cas aux autorités canadiennes et aux unités du renseignement financier étrangères (URF).[48] Le CANAFE peut maintenant échanger des renseignements tactiques concernant le blanchiment d'argent et le financement d'activités terroristes avec les pays suivants: le Belize, les îles Vierges britanniques, la Dominique, la Grenade, la Macédoine, la République de Malte, les Antilles néerlandaises, Sainte-Lucie, Saint-Martin, le Sénégal et la Serbie ce qui porte à 73 URFs avec lesquelles le CANAFE peut collaborer.

V. Le joint forum

En tant qu'acteur veillant à l'intégration des réglementations touchant le domaine bancaire, les valeurs mobilières, le secteur des assurances sur le plan transjuridictionnel, le Joint Forum s'est penché, à travers trois rapports émis dans la période 2010-11, sur les sujets suivants: une revue comparative des réglementations afférentes, les modèles de risques et les impacts de la titrisation.

45 2011 FATF/OECD, *Laundering the Proceeds of Corruption*, July 2011, en ligne: <http://www.fatf-gafi.org/media/fatf/documents/reports/Laundering%20the%20Proceeds%20of%20Corruption.pdf>.

46 2010 GAFI/OCDE, *supra* note 44.

47 Loi sur le recyclage des produits de la criminalité et le financement des activités terroristes, LC 2000, c17, notamment aux articles 5-6, 7-7.1.

48 Centre d'analyse des opérations et déclarations financières du Canada, *Rapport Annuel 2011*, à la p 6, en ligne: <http://www.canafe.gc.ca/publications/ar/2011/ar2011-fra.pdf>.

Le premier rapport émis en janvier 2010 s'attarde aux questions des différences de réglementations entre les trois secteurs: bancaire, valeur mobilière, et assurance quant aux produits financiers similaires. Le rapport traite également du lien entre les fonds de couverture et les normes de souscription minimales des prêts hypothécaires résidentiels, et du transfert de risque de crédit, en se concentrant sur les swaps sur défaillance de crédit et d'assurance de garantie financière (CDS).[49]

Le second rapport s'adresse à la qualité des modèles de risques qui sont employés par les institutions financières. Il recommande l'amélioration des techniques de mesures d'évaluation d'agrégation des risques, en fonction de la nature de l'entreprise financière, en mettant de l'avant la suffisance du capital et la solvabilité afin de contrer les événements extrêmes. Les instances régulatrices sont interpellées afin de conscientiser les preneurs de risque aux avantages d'une meilleure calibration du risque et d'un processus décisionnel.[50]

Selon le Joint Forum, les autorités doivent encourager un alignement cohérent de la rémunération et des incitatifs des gestionnaires des institutions financières avec la qualité des actifs à long terme et une prise de risque prudente.[51]

VI. Conclusion

Les sommets du G20 créent un ordonnancement des actions des intervenants de la scène financière internationale. Le Conseil de la stabilité financière, dont les capacités politiques sont plus importantes, compte-tenu de sa proximité avec les chefs d'états et du gouvernement du G20, joue un rôle accru pour la coordination des mandats impartis par le G20 aux organismes de contrôle des établissements financiers. Le CSF est appelé à jouer un rôle prépondérant pour faire avancer les principes de gouvernance aux pratiques des institutions financières réglementées ou non.

Trois idées semblent progresser dans les discussions récentes en vue de l'assainissement du système financier international: l'acces-

[49] Joint Forum, *Review of the Differentiated Nature and Scope of Financial Regulation Key Issues and Recommendations,* January 2010, en ligne: <http://www.bis.org/publ/joint24.pdf>.

[50] Joint Forum, *Developments in Modelling Risk Aggregation,* October 2010, en ligne: <http://www.bis.org/publ/joint25.pdf>.

[51] Joint Forum, *Report on Asset Securitisation Incentives,* July 2011, en ligne: <http://www.bis.org/publ/joint26.pdf>.

sibilité aux services financiers aux populations les plus défavorisés, une certaine normalisation des rémunérations et des incitatifs des preneurs de risques et l'indépendance des vérificateurs et des agences de notation sur l'objet de leurs prestations.

Les pratiques fiscales et les meilleures pratiques comptables sont autant d'éléments qui créent des impacts sur la bonne marche du système financier international; à ceux-là s'ajoute la nécessité des juridictions de partager des données financières. Les organismes de contrôle des établissements financiers doivent instaurer des modèles prédictifs plus performants. Par ailleurs, un consensus se fait autour du principe que les pertes doivent être assumées par les institutions soit les dirigeants, les actionnaires et les créanciers, et non par les contribuables.[52]

Le Canada, fort de la bonne tenue de son système financier pris globalement, assume un leadership créé par la force de son exemple. Le Canada, dont plusieurs ressortissants assument des responsabilités importantes au sein des institutions internationales, est un interlocuteur crédible, susceptible de faire avancer auprès de ses partenaires du G20, l'alignement des pratiques réglementaires menant à la confiance, condition essentielle du rétablissement du système financier international.

52 OICV, Montréal, 10 juin 2010, Discours avec Mark Carney, gouverneur de la Banque du Canada, en ligne: <http://www.bankofcanada.ca/wp-content/uploads/2010/09/disc100610.pdf>.

III. Investissement

préparé par

CÉLINE LÉVESQUE

I. Introduction

Cette chronique portant sur l'investissement met les bouchées doubles: elle couvre les années 2010 et 2011. Cette façon de se rapprocher de l'actualité exige toutefois un traitement moins détaillé et plus synthétique. Aussi la chronique est-elle consacrée à l'analyse de l'approche de tribunaux — à la fois des tribunaux arbitraux et des tribunaux judiciaires qui ont à rendre des décisions au sujet de demandes d'annulation de sentences arbitrales.

Dans la première partie, l'approche des tribunaux dans trois affaires rendues sous le régime du chapitre 11 (Investissement) de l'Accord de libre-échange nord-américain (ALENA)[1] est étudiée. L'accent mis sur la prise de décision et sur les modes de raisonnement juridique, plutôt que sur le fond, permet de mettre en relief la grande marge de manœuvre dont disposent les tribunaux dans un système *ad hoc* d'arbitrage international. Bien que, dans les cas étudiés, les investisseurs aient tous été déboutés, la variété des

---

Céline Lévesque est professeure agrégée à la Faculté de droit, Section de droit civil, de l'Université d'Ottawa. L'auteur tient à remercier Samantha McKenzie pour son assistance de recherche et le conseil de recherche en sciences humaines du Canada pour son soutien financier. En 2008-09, la professeure Lévesque occupait le poste d'universitaire en résidence à la Direction générale du droit commercial international, Ministère des Affaires étrangères et du Commerce international. Elle a alors été impliquée dans deux des affaires qui font l'objet d'un commentaire dans cette chronique (*Chemtura* et *Merrill & Ring*). Les opinions exprimées dans cette chronique sont celles de l'auteur et ne reflètent pas nécessairement celles du gouvernement du Canada.

[1] Accord de libre-échange nord-américain entre le gouvernement du Canada, le gouvernement du Mexique et le gouvernement des États-Unis d'Amérique, 17 décembre 1992, RTCan 1994 n° 2, 32 (3) ILM 605 (entrée en vigueur: 1er janvier 1994) [ALENA].

approches est remarquable. Il s'agit des affaires *Grand River Enterprises et al. c United States,*[2] *Chemtura Corporation c Canada,*[3] *Merrill & Ring Forestry L.P. c Canada.*[4]

Dans la deuxième partie, il est question de l'approche des tribunaux judiciaires canadiens concernant les demandes d'annulation de sentences arbitrales rendues en vertu du chapitre 11 de l'ALENA. Dans les chroniques précédentes, la trilogie des affaires mexicaines concernant les édulcorants a fait l'objet d'une étude détaillée.[5] On se rappellera que le Mexique a uniquement fait une demande d'annulation de la sentence dans l'une de ces affaires, soit *Cargill c Mexico.*[6] En août 2010, la Cour supérieure de l'Ontario a rejeté la demande mexicaine.[7] La Cour d'appel de l'Ontario, dans un arrêt rendu en octobre 2011, a également refusé d'annuler la sentence.[8] Cette dernière décision est notable, car elle a le mérite de clarifier la norme de contrôle applicable, bien qu'elle sème le doute sur une question importante d'interprétation des traités. Comparée aux autres décisions canadiennes, elle offre une approche améliorée.

Il ne faudrait toutefois pas passer sous silence deux développements, liés au contentieux d'investissement, qui méritent d'être soulignés. En premier lieu, étant donné qu'il existe relativement peu de sentences arbitrales rendues en vertu d'accords canadiens de promotion et de protection des investissements (ou APIE), il vaut la peine de s'arrêter sur la sentence dans l'affaire *Alasdair Ross Anderson et al c Costa Rica,* rendue en 2010.[9] Dans cette affaire, 137

2 *Grand River Enterprises et al. c United States* (Award, 12 janvier 2011) [*Grand River*]. Il est à noter que les sentences arbitrales mentionnées dans cette chronique sont disponibles en ligne: <http://italaw.com/>. Les sites internet des Parties à l'ALENA contiennent également les sentences rendues en vertu du chapitre 11. Voir MAECI, disponible en ligne à: <http://www.international.gc.ca/trade-agreements-accords-commerciaux/disp-diff/nafta.aspx?lang=fra>.

3 *Chemtura Corporation c Canada* (Award, 2 août 2010) [*Chemtura*].

4 *Merrill & Ring Forestry L.P. c Canada* (Award, 31 mars 2010) [*Merrill & Ring*].

5 Voir C Lévesque, "Chronique de Droit international économique en 2008: Investissement" (2009) XLVII ACDI aux pp 385-410 et C Lévesque, "Chronique de Droit international économique en 2009: Investissement" (2010) XLVIII ACDI aux pp 292, 314-34.

6 *Cargill, Incorporated c Mexico* (Award, 18 septembre 2009) ICSID Case N° ARB(AF)/05/2 [*Cargill*].

7 *United Mexican States c Cargill, Incorporated,* 2010 ONSC 4656.

8 *Mexico c Cargill, Incorporated,* 2011 ONCA 622.

9 *Alasdair Ross Anderson et al c Costa Rica* (Award, 19 mai 2010) [*Alasdair*]. Une autre décision sur la compétence a été rendue en vertu d'un APIE en 2010 dans

Canadiens avaient investi dans ce qui s'est avéré un "*Ponzi scheme*" illégal au Costa Rica. Alléguant que le gouvernement avait manqué de vigilance et fait défaut dans la supervision de son système financier, ces individus ont porté plainte contre le Costa Rica pour manquement à ses obligations conventionnelles de protection et de sécurité, de traitement juste et équitable, et en matière d'expropriation.[10] Le Costa Rica a soulevé un déclinatoire de compétence fondé sur cinq motifs, dont un à été retenu par le Tribunal. Après avoir analysé les définitions d'investisseur et d'investissement dans l'APIE Canada-Costa Rica, le Tribunal a conclu qu'il n'avait pas la compétence *ratione materiae* pour trancher ce différend au fond. En effet, pour répondre à la définition d'investissement, les avoirs des canadiens devaient être détenus ou contrôlés "en conformité avec les lois" du Costa Rica, ce qui n'était pas le cas en l'espèce, car les transactions étaient illégales. Pour le Tribunal, il s'agissait d'une exigence objective. Qui plus est, les demandeurs n'avaient pas fait preuve de diligence raisonnable afin de s'assurer que leurs dépôts d'argent se conformaient aux lois du Costa Rica.[11]

Cette sentence est à noter, car elle s'inscrit dans la tendance de certains tribunaux à appliquer de façon stricte l'exigence "de conformité aux lois" afin de se prononcer sur les cas d'illégalité ou de mauvaise conduite de la part des investisseurs étrangers.[12] D'ailleurs, le Tribunal est clair dans ses motifs: "*[t]he Tribunal's interpretation of the words 'owned in accordance with the laws' of Costa Rica reflects both sound public policy and sound investment practice. Costa Rica, indeed any country, has a fundamental interest in securing respect for its law.*"[13]

En second lieu, il faut prendre note du règlement par le Canada d'au moins deux affaires dans le cadre du chapitre 11 de l'ALENA

---

l'affaire *Nova Scotia Power Incorporated (NSPI) c Venezuela* (Decision on Jurisdiction, 22 avril 2010) (en espagnol). Au moins une sentence au fond a aussi été rendue en 2010, mais son texte n'a pas encore été rendu public: *Frontier Petroleum Services (FPS) c Czech Republic* (Final Award, 12 Novembre 2010).

[10] *Ibid* aux para 15-16. Voir, l'Accord entre le gouvernement du Canada et le gouvernement de la République du Costa Rica pour l'encouragement et la protection des investissements, 18 mars 1988 (entrée en vigueur: 29 septembre 1999) [APIE Canada-Costa Rica (1988)].

[11] *Ibid* aux para 44-47, 51-61.

[12] Voir Andrew Newcombe, "Investor Misconduct" dans Armand de Mestral et Céline Lévesque, dir, *Improving International Investment Agreements*, Routledge [à paraître en 2012].

[13] *Alasdair*, *supra* note 9 au para 58.

en 2010 et 2011. Dans l'affaire *Abitibi Bowater c Canada,* le Tribunal a rendu un "*Consent Award*" en décembre 2010, en vertu duquel le Canada s'engage à verser 130 millions de dollars canadiens à l'investisseur américain.[14] Ce règlement fait suite à l'expropriation de l'investissement d'Abitibi Bowater par la province de Terre Neuve et Labrador en 2008. Suite à ce règlement, le Premier Ministre Harper a indiqué que son gouvernement ne tenterait pas de recouvrer l'argent de la province, mais qu'il envisageait de mettre en place un mécanisme qui pourrait le permettre à l'avenir.[15] Ce dossier, qui implique les relations fédéro-provinciales et l'impact des accords commerciaux au Canada, est à suivre avec attention.

Dans un tout autre répertoire, le Canada a conclu un "accord de règlement" dans l'affaire qui l'opposait à la compagnie américaine Dow Agrosciences, le 25 mai 2011.[16] Dans ce cas, aucune compensation n'est accordée à la demanderesse, qui apparaît battre en retraite. En effet, la contestation par Dow de mesures du gouvernement du Québec interdisant certaines utilisations de pesticides pour pelouse (contenant du 2,4 D) avait soulevé les passions. L'accord, conclu avec l'assentiment du Québec, contient une reconnaissance, favorable à la compagnie, concernant la dangerosité de ses produits, mais confirme à la fois le droit de la province et des municipalités de réglementer les pesticides de façon plus restrictive que ne le fait le fédéral.[17]

Ces deux règlements sont à remarquer, car le dernier règlement public, par le gouvernement fédéral, d'une affaire dans le cadre du chapitre 11 de l'ALENA remonte à 1998. Les critiques avaient alors été nombreuses du règlement dans l'affaire *Ethyl Corporation c Canada,* qui concernait l'additif MMT pour l'essence.[18] Les années

14 *Abitibi Bowater Inc c Canada* (Consent Award, 15 décembre 2010).

15 Voir par ex Bertrand Marotte et John Ibbitson, "Provinces on hook in future trade disputes: Harper," *Globe and Mail* (26 août 2010).

16 *Dow Agrosciences LLC c Canada* (Accord de règlement, 25 mai 2011).

17 *Ibid* à la p 2.

18 Voir MAECI, disponible en ligne à: <http://www.international.gc.ca/trade-agreements-accords-commerciaux/disp-diff/ethyl.aspx?lang=en&view=d>. Voir aussi *Ethyl Corporation c Canada* (Decision on jurisdiction, 24 juin 1998). Au sujet des critiques, voir ex Shawn McCarthy, "Failed ban becomes selling point for MMT Not enough scientific evidence to prove additive a risk, minister says, promising to give manufacturers $19-million," *Globe and Mail* (21 July 1998) A3; "Ethyl vs Canada or Investor vs State," en ligne: Suns <http://www.sunsonline.org/trade/areas/environm/06030297.htm>; Stephen J Kobrin, "The MAI and the Clash of Globalizations," *Foreign Policy* (September 1998) 97 at 102-4, en

passées sans autre règlement pouvaient laisser craindre que le gouvernement fédéral ne soit plus disposé à régler même les affaires qui méritaient de l'être. Cette crainte ne semble plus fondée.[19]

II. La diversité des approches dans l'arbitrage investisseur-État: Les affaires *Grand River, Chemtura et Merrill & Ring*

Dans le cadre de l'arbitrage investisseur-État, le choix des arbitres est une décision d'une importance qui ne peut être sous-estimée. En vertu du chapitre 11 de l'ALENA, l'investisseur et l'État font leur choix et, ensuite, ils tentent de s'entendre sur le président du tribunal. À défaut d'entente, le secrétaire général du Centre international pour le règlement des différends relatifs aux investissements (CIRDI) procédera à la nomination.[20] Une fois le tribunal constitué, une dynamique à trois s'établira entre les arbitres. Les trois sentences rendues sur le fond en 2010-2011 démontrent à quel point cette dynamique peut influencer l'approche du tribunal (sans parler du résultat).

Dans l'affaire *Grand River,* le Tribunal adopte une approche "modèle," faisant preuve d'une certaine retenue, dans le cadre d'une approche généralement empreinte de justesse.[21] Dans l'affaire *Chemtura,* le Tribunal fait preuve d'une très (pourra-t-on dire, trop) grande retenue.[22] Hormis au sujet d'une question (discutée plus bas), cette sentence contribue peu à la résolution de plusieurs questions juridiques pourtant controversées. Dans l'affaire *Merrill & Ring,* l'approche du Tribunal est troublante à plusieurs égards.[23] Notamment, la sentence, quoiqu'unanime, révèle des désaccords parmi les membres du Tribunal qui sont de nature à saper la conviction qu'elle aurait pu emporter.

---

ligne: <http://chenry.webhost.utexas.edu/civil/resources/maiclashof globalizations.pdf>; voir aussi Julie A Soloway, "Environmental Trade Barriers under NAFTA: The MMT Fuel Additives Controversy" (1999) 8:1 Minn J Global Trade à la p 88.

19 Sur la question du règlement alternatif des différends investisseur-État et sur l'expérience canadienne, voir C. Lévesque, "Increasing the Use of Alternative Dispute Resolution in IIAs," dans de Mestral et Lévesque, *supra* note 12.

20 ALENA, *supra* note 1, art 1124.

21 *Grand River, supra* note 2.

22 *Chemtura, supra* note 3.

23 *Merrill & Ring, supra* note 4.

A. *GRAND RIVER ENTERPRISES ET AL. C UNITED STATES*

Cette affaire a commencé en mars 2004 et il aura fallu presque sept ans avant d'avoir une sentence finale. Cette durée s'explique notamment par la bifurcation des procédures[24] et une demande de récusation d'un des arbitres.[25] Le Tribunal était constitué de Fali S. Nariman (président — nommé par le Secrétaire Général du CIRDI),[26] James Anaya (nommé par les demandeurs) et John R. Crook (nommé par les États-Unis).

La sentence sur le fond compte 63 pages et pourrait être qualifiée de sentence "modèle." Le Tribunal conçoit bien son mandat et offre un raisonnement clair et convaincant.[27] Il fait preuve d'économie judiciaire, en évitant de se prononcer sur des questions qu'il n'a pas à trancher pour régler ce différend en particulier, mais s'assure toutefois de répondre à tous les arguments des demandeurs (même lorsque ceux-ci ne sont pas limpides). Le Tribunal se montre aussi très habile dans son interprétation et son application de certains concepts controversés, dont celui des "attentes légitimes des investisseurs."

Avant de fournir quelques illustrations, il est utile de rappeler le contexte et les faits de cette affaire. Les demandeurs, Grand River Enterprises Six Nations Ltd (Grand River), Jerry Montour, Kenneth Hill et Arthur Montour, sont tous impliqués dans l'industrie du tabac. En 1998, afin de régler des poursuites judiciaires opposant certains États américains aux grands producteurs de tabac, une

24 La décision sur la compétence a été rendue en juillet 2006. Le Tribunal avait alors rejeté plusieurs allégations des demandeurs, parce que la compétence *ratione temporis* lui manquait pour en décider au fond. Voir *Grand River Enterprises Six Nations, Ltd., et al. c United States* (Decision on Objections to Jurisdiction, 20 juillet 2006) aux para 53-83, 103.

25 En mars 2007, les États-Unis ont fait une demande de récusation de l'arbitre Anaya. Cette demande a finalement été rejetée par le Secrétaire-Général du CIRDI, après que le professeur Anaya eut cessé toute implication dans une affaire (hors-ALENA) impliquant les États-Unis. *Ibid* aux para 28-31.

26 *Ibid* au para 25.

27 Le Tribunal explique clairement (mais brièvement) la façon dont il conçoit son mandat et les limites de sa compétence. Voir, par exemple, sur la question du précédent (para 61), ou encore sur l'interprétation de l'article 31(3)(c) de la Convention de Vienne sur le droit des traités et l'obligation de tenir compte d'autres règles pertinentes de droit international (para 71). Son traitement fait preuve d'équilibre. Selon le Tribunal, par exemple, certains termes, tel que "investissement," ne doivent pas être interprétés largement ou restrictivement, car l'ALENA implique un équilibre entre les droits et obligations (para 69).

entente a été conclue, soit le "Master Settlement Agreement" (MSA).[28] Grand River n'a pas adhéré au MSA et a donc conservé le statut de manufacturier non participant.[29] Différentes mesures ont été prises dans la mise en œuvre de cet accord, afin que les producteurs de tabac non participants se soumettent à des obligations similaires. Éventuellement, une lacune, dans les législations, qui avait profité à Grand River, a été comblée.[30] Ces événements ont mené à la plainte des demandeurs.

Grand River est une entreprise qui produit des cigarettes au Canada. Jerry Montour et Kenneth Hill possèdent le contrôle de la compagnie Grand River. Ils résident tous les deux dans une réserve autochtone en Ontario. Arthur Montour, également canadien, réside pour sa part dans l'État de New York, où il gère une compagnie de distribution de cigarettes.[31] Les demandeurs se plaignent que les États-Unis ont manqué à leurs obligations en vertu du chapitre 11 de l'ALENA. Ils allèguent que certaines mesures adoptées dans la mise en œuvre du MSA constituent une expropriation de leurs investissements au sens de l'article 1110, une violation du principe de traitement national et de la nation la plus favorisée (articles 1102 et 1103), ainsi qu'une violation de la norme minimale de traitement (article 1105).

Le Tribunal a d'abord jugé qu'il n'avait pas compétence pour décider des plaintes de Grand River, Jerry Montour et Kenneth Hill, car ceux-ci n'avaient pas effectué d'investissement aux États-Unis.[32] Par contre, la plainte d'Arthur Montour était recevable, car sa compagnie importait des cigarettes manufacturées par Grand River et les distribuait à des grossistes et des points de vente au détail dans des réserves indiennes aux États-Unis.[33]

28 *Grand River, supra* note 2 aux para 8-10.

29 *Ibid* au para 11.

30 *Ibid* au para 12-21.

31 *Ibid* au para 2.

32 Le Tribunal a jugé que l'investissement le plus important des demandeurs (leur "*manufacturing plant*") était situé au Canada et que ces derniers ne géraient pas d'entreprise aux États-Unis. Il n'a pas non plus admis que certaines dépenses, telles que la location d'un camion et d'une remorque pour quelques mois aux États-Unis, soient suffisantes pour constituer un investissement au sens de l'ALENA. À ce sujet, le Tribunal fait une remarque qui pourra s'avérer pertinente dans d'autres cas, en comparant le montant modeste des dépenses alléguées aux centaines de millions de dollars réclamées au titre des dommages. Voir *ibid* aux para 85-122, sur le dernier point aux para 121-22.

33 *Ibid* au para 6.

Le Tribunal a ensuite rejeté une à une les allégations de manquement — vis-à-vis d'Arthur Montour — aux articles 1110, 1102, 1103 et 1105 de l'ALENA. Le Tribunal est judicieux dans son choix des questions auxquelles il estime ne pas avoir besoin de répondre, par exemple celles qui ne concernent pas la situation spécifique d'Arthur Montour, et de celles auxquelles il va répondre, malgré le fait que les allégations manquaient de précision quant à Arthur Montour.[34]

La meilleure illustration de l'approche exemplaire du Tribunal est sans doute sa manière d'appréhender les arguments concernant les "attentes légitimes" d'Arthur Montour. Étant donné que les deux parties s'entendaient pour dire que ce concept pouvait jouer un rôle dans l'interprétation de l'article 1110 (expropriation) de l'ALENA, le Tribunal en a traité à ce titre, plutôt que dans le cadre de l'article 1105 (norme minimale de traitement).[35] Confronté à des arguments contradictoires sur l'interprétation du droit interne américain concernant les autochtones et la vente de cigarettes dans les réserves et à l'extérieur de celles-ci, le Tribunal a refusé de trancher. Son approche vaut d'être notée:

> *The Tribunal believes that both Parties advanced positions regarding the state of U.S. federal Indian law that were unjustifiably categorical. Both posited legal "bright lines" in situations where they do not exist. ... What is clear from the Parties' submissions and their experts' reports is that U.S. domestic law is currently far from conclusive about the question raised here of the extent of permissible state regulation. ... Both parties apparently would have the Tribunal resolve this highly contested question of U.S. domestic law, which the Tribunal declines to do.*[36]

Après avoir décrit brièvement le concept d' "attente légitimes" dans le contexte de l'ALENA, le Tribunal s'est servi de l'incertitude, en droit interne, pour justifier sa conclusion que les attentes d'Arthur Montour n'étaient pas légitimes ou raisonnables dans les circonstances. En d'autres mots, un investisseur prudent ne pouvait s'attendre à ce que le régime entourant le MSA ne lui soit pas appliqué

[34] Voir par ex *ibid* aux para 170-71 (sur articles 1102 et 1103), et au para 204 (sur la norme minimale de traitement) où le Tribunal a fait preuve d'économie judiciaire. Voir aussi les para 160 et 178, où le tribunal s'est assuré de répondre à toutes les allégations (mêmes incomplètes, sur les articles 1102 et 1105 respectivement).

[35] Les États-Unis contestent que la violation des attentes légitimes des investisseurs fasse partie de la norme minimale de traitement. Voir *ibid* au para 127.

[36] *Ibid* aux para 137-39.

sur le fondement d'un droit interne incertain.[37] Ce raisonnement est très habile, car il a permis au Tribunal de rendre une décision convaincante, tout en évitant de trancher des questions délicates relevant du droit interne américain.[38]

La sentence est un peu moins exemplaire quant au traitement de l'obligation de consulter les peuples autochtones en droit international coutumier. À cet égard, le Tribunal s'avance d'une façon qui ne semblait pas nécessaire, compte tenu de sa conclusion dans les faits.[39]

Somme toute, cette sentence fait preuve d'une rigueur digne de remarque. Elle témoigne d'une approche réfléchie et équilibrée.

B. *CHEMTURA CORPORATION C CANADA*

La sentence, en date d'août 2010, a été rendue presque huit ans après le dépôt de la première demande en arbitrage de l'investisseur.[40] En pratique, les procédures arbitrales ont vraiment pris leur envol durant l'année 2007. Le Tribunal était constitué de Gabrielle Kaufmann-Kohler (présidente),[41] Charles Brower (nommé par la compagnie Chemtura) et James Crawford (nommé par le Canada). Ces trois arbitres sont des figures dominantes de l'arbitrage investisseur-État et comptent parmi les arbitres les plus prisés au monde. Malgré leur calibre, la sentence apporte une contribution somme toute mineure à l'éclaircissement des obligations juridiques du chapitre 11 de l'ALENA.

Peut-être que les espoirs d'une sentence "phare" étaient déplacés. En effet, l'une des façons pour le Tribunal d'éviter des désaccords semble avoir été de se concentrer sur les faits et de limiter au maximum les énoncés de droit. Il s'agissait peut-être là de la seule façon de rendre une décision unanime. Cela étant, "l'économie judiciaire" dont fait preuve le Tribunal (si l'on peut qualifier ainsi son approche) laisse planer le doute sur d'importantes questions. Par exemple, l'analyse du contenu juridique de la norme minimale de traitement est succincte, diffuse et peu approfondie.

37 *Ibid* au para 142.

38 Voir aussi *ibid* para 234.

39 *Ibid* au para 210. Voir aussi les para 183-85 où des désaccords entre les membres du Tribunal sont exprimés. Voir aussi l'impact sur la répartition des frais (para 247).

40 Cette demande, déposée en octobre 2002, a été suivie d'une autre demande en février 2005. Voir *Chemtura, supra* note 3 aux para 50-61.

41 Nommée par accord entre les parties.

Il convient d'abord de procéder à un rappel des faits. Chemtura est une compagnie chimique constituée dans l'état du Delaware aux États-Unis. Chemtura Canada, sa filiale, produit notamment le lindane, un insecticide utilisé surtout en agriculture pour traiter les semences. Le lindane a été homologué au Canada depuis la fin des années 30, mais son utilisation est devenue de plus en plus controversée avec le temps de part le monde,[42] à cause des dangers posés à la santé et à l'environnement.[43]

Après des évaluations, l'Agence de réglementation de la lutte antiparasitaire (ARLA) de Santé Canada a procédé au retrait graduel de l'utilisation du lindane en vertu de la Loi sur les produits antiparasitaires. Suite à des rebondissements divers, les homologations de Chemtura ont finalement été suspendues.[44]

La plainte de Chemtura allègue le manquement du Canada à ses obligations en vertu des articles 1103, 1105 et 1110 de l'ALENA. De manière générale, les allégations concernent l'évaluation des risques présentés par le lindane et le déroulement du retrait d'homologation de ce produit.[45] Le Tribunal a rejeté toutes ces allégations et ordonné le paiement de l'entièreté des frais de l'arbitrage et de la moitié des frais de représentation du Canada à la compagnie Chemtura. Compte tenu de ses propres frais, la procédure arbitrale aura coûté à la compagnie environ 5 millions de dollars.[46]

La meilleur illustration de l'approche "*in concreto*" du Tribunal se trouve dans son traitement du manquement à l'article 1105. Le Tribunal note d'abord, plutôt sommairement, que la détermination de la portée de l'article 1105 devait tenir compte de l'évolution du droit international coutumier et de l'impact des traités bilatéraux d'investissement sur cette évolution.[47] Il dit ensuite qu'il en tiendra compte, lorsque nécessaire, dans son évaluation spécifique de chaque mesures.[48] Le Tribunal s'est ensuite tourné vers la question de la "marge d'appréciation" potentielle, dont bénéficieraient les

[42] Voir la liste, reproduite dans la sentence, des pays qui ont adopté des restrictions concernant le lindane. *Chemtura, supra* note 3 au para 135.

[43] *Ibid* aux para 133-163. Voir aussi *Chemtura Corporation c Canada* (Counter memorial, 20 octobre 2008) au para 1.

[44] *Ibid* aux para 32, 34.

[45] Voir la liste des mesures détaillées, *ibid* au para 110.

[46] *Ibid* aux para 268-73.

[47] *Ibid* au para 121.

[48] *Ibid* au para 122.

agences réglementaires nationales. C'est dans ce contexte qu'il a énoncé son approche analytique:

> *Having reviewed the arguments of the Parties, the Tribunal is of the opinion that the assessment of the facts is an integral part of the review under Article 1105 of NAFTA. In assessing whether the treatment afforded to the Claimant's investment was in accordance with the international minimum standard, the Tribunal must take into account all the circumstances, including the fact that certain agencies manage highly specialized domains involving scientific and public policy determinations. This is not an abstract assessment circumscribed by a legal doctrine about the margin of appreciation of specialized regulatory agencies. It is an assessment that must be conducted* in concreto*. The Tribunal will proceed to such assessment* in concreto *when reviewing the specific measures challenged by the Claimant.*[49]

L'analyse est par la suite dominée par les faits et la sentence contient de nombreuses références à la preuve écrite et aux témoignages durant les audiences. Le Tribunal parsème son analyse de conclusions juridiques autours des concepts suivants: "*bad faith*,"[50] "*unfairness*,"[51] "*breach of due process*,"[52] "*discriminatory manner*."[53] L'une de ses conclusions concerne aussi les attentes raisonnables ou légitimes de Chemtura, en lien avec l'objectif de "*regulatory fairness*" de l'article 1105.[54]

L'une des difficultés de cette approche est son manque de profondeur. Par exemple, le Tribunal n'explore pas la question de savoir si l'obligation de non-discrimination ou celle du respect des attentes légitimes des investisseurs fait partie de la norme minimale de traitement en droit international coutumier. Sauf à un endroit, il n'explore pas non plus la question du seuil requis pour conclure

49 *Ibid* au para 123. Le Tribunal s'est tout de même dit d'accord avec le Canada que son rôle n'était pas de trancher la question de la dangerosité du lindane, en d'autres mots, de remettre en question les conclusions scientifiques d'une agence réglementaire spécialisée (aux para 134 et 153-54). Sur le traitement de la preuve scientifique en droit international des investissements, voir C Lévesque, "Science in the Hands of International Investment Tribunals: A Case for Scientific Due Process" (2009) 20 Finnish YB Int'l L aux pp 259-90; Marcos Orellana, "The Role of Science in Investment Arbitrations Concerning Public Health and the Environment" (2006) 17 YB Int'l Env L aux pp 48-72.

50 *Ibid* aux para 148, 152-53, 162, 184, 224.

51 *Ibid* aux para 152-53, 179, 184, 224.

52 *Ibid* au para 148, en termes de sérieuse "procedurally improper behavior," et 162.

53 *Ibid* au para 221.

54 *Ibid* au para 179.

à une violation de la norme minimale de traitement. Ce n'est que dans l'une des dernières pages de l'analyse portant sur l'article 1105 que l'on peut trouver la mention qu'un manquement n'a pas à être "*outrageous*" pour constituer une violation. Ce rejet de la norme dans l'affaire *Neer,* malgré son caractère controversé, s'opère sans plus d'explications.

Le Tribunal fait également preuve d'"économie judiciaire" dans son analyse des articles 1103 et 1110. Après avoir relaté les arguments des parties quant au traitement de la nation la plus favorisée et soulevé quelques lacunes au niveau de la preuve, le Tribunal a dit ne pas avoir à décider de la question de principe, à savoir si une norme plus favorable pouvait être "importée" d'un autre traité en vertu de l'article 1103. De l'opinion du Tribunal, indépendamment de la norme, la conclusion en fait demeurerait la même.[55]

En ce qui concerne l'article 1110, le Tribunal a également choisi de ne pas se prononcer sur le degré d'ingérence nécessaire pour constituer une expropriation. Pour lui, il était suffisant d'appliquer le critère du degré élevé de privation ("*substantial deprivation*") aux faits, sans plus d'élaboration en droit.[56] Le Tribunal a toutefois mis de côté sa retenue, lorsqu'il a accepté l'argument du Canada sur la doctrine du pouvoir de police. Même s'il avait déjà conclu que l'ingérence alléguée ne constituait pas une expropriation (et qu'il n'avait donc pas à se prononcer sur la question), il a tout de même indiqué que: "*the Tribunal considers in any event that the measures challenged by the Claimant constituted a valid exercise of the Respondent's police powers.*"[57] Cet énoncé est bienvenu.

A certains égards, cette sentence est irréprochable. Son style est clair, son traitement des faits précis et complet. On ne peut remettre en question les aptitudes de ses auteurs. Il demeure que sur le plan du droit, la sentence révèle une retenue qu'on peut juger excessive. En évitant de discuter de questions pourtant controversées, le Tribunal a manqué l'occasion de contribuer à l'avancement du droit. Cela dit, pour être réaliste, il faut admettre que ce silence aura probablement été le prix de l'unanimité.

C. *MERRILL & RING FORESTRY L.P. C CANADA*

Cette affaire a commencé avec la demande en arbitrage de l'investisseur américain, le 17 décembre 2006, et est arrivée à terme le

55 *Ibid* aux para 233-36.

56 *Ibid* au para 249.

57 *Ibid* au para 266.

31 mars 2010. Le Tribunal était constitué de Francisco Orrego Vicuña (président — nommé par le Secrétaire Général du CIRDI), Kenneth W. Dam (nommé par Merrill & Ring) et J. William Rowley (nommé par le Canada).[58]

Cette sentence n'est pas un exemple à suivre. La première moitié de la sentence, qui compte 108 pages, n'est pas irréprochable sur le fond, mais son approche est peu critiquable. Il en va tout autrement de la deuxième moitié, où le Tribunal adopte une approche qui appelle de nombreuses critiques. En particulier, en ce qui a trait à la question du manquement à l'article 1105, que le Tribunal qualifie de "*most complex and difficult question*,"[59] le Tribunal a été incapable de trancher.

Un rappel des faits s'impose. Merrill & Ring Forestry L.P. est une société en commandite constituée dans l'État de Washington, aux États-Unis.[60] Active dans la foresterie, elle opère notamment en Colombie Britannique, où elle possède des terres. Ses activités comprennent, entre autres, la vente de billes de bois sur le marché canadien et sur les marchés internationaux.[61] La compagnie se plaint de l'effet sur ses opérations de mesures provinciales et fédérales mettant en œuvre le régime canadien d'exportation des billes de bois (*Canada's Log Export Regime*).[62] En particulier, Merrill & Ring se plaint de certaines mesures qui l'obligent à se soumettre à une procédure de calcul de l'excédent avant de pouvoir exporter ses billes; procédure qui, selon elle, permet à des acheteurs locaux de lui soutirer des prix réduits.[63] Selon l'investisseur, l'effet cumulatif des mesures oblige ce dernier à vendre ses billes de bois en dessous de leur juste valeur marchande.[64] En conséquence, Merrill & Ring réclame des dommages d'au moins 25 millions de dollars, pour le manquement du Canada aux articles 1102, 1105, 1106, et 1110 de l'ALENA.[65]

58 Président nommé à défaut d'accord entre les parties, voir *Merrill & Ring*, *supra* note 4 au para 2.

59 *Ibid* au para 182.

60 *Merrill & Ring Forestry L.P c Canada* (Notice of Arbitration, 27 décembre 2006) au para 2 [*M&R NOA*].

61 *Ibid* aux para 13-16.

62 *Merrill & Ring*, *supra* note 4 au para 26.

63 *Ibid* aux para 26-29, 34-36.

64 *Ibid* au para 49.

65 *M&R NOA*, *supra* note 60 au para 66. L'article 1103 y est mentionné, mais il n'en est pas question dans la sentence.

Le Tribunal a rejeté, sans trop de difficultés, les allégations de manquement aux articles 1102, 1106 et 1110. Toutefois, sur la question de la violation de l'article 1105, aucune décision n'est rendue de prime abord, car les membres du Tribunal ne s'entendent pas sur la norme, ni sur son application aux faits. Le Tribunal évite tout de même l'impasse en passant directement à la question des dommages. Sa conclusion que Merrill & Ring n'a pas fait la preuve d'un dommage lui permet de conclure que la preuve du manquement à l'article 1105 n'a pas été faite non plus. Selon lui: "*an international wrongful act will only be committed in international investment law if there is an act in breach of an international legal obligation, attributable to the Respondent that also results in damages.*"[66] À la toute fin de la sentence, le Tribunal décide également qu'il n'est pas nécessaire pour lui de décider de la question de la prescription, car sans manquement et sans dommage, sa résolution est inutile.[67]

Deux problèmes principaux peuvent être identifiés quant à l'approche du Tribunal.[68] Premièrement, la progression normale des décisions (c'est-à-dire, compétence — fond — dommage) est inversée. Deuxièmement, la façon dont le Tribunal expose les désaccords entre ses membres est susceptible de retirer toute force de conviction à la sentence. D'abord, l'ordre suivi par le Tribunal pour rendre sa décision est déroutant. On peut déduire du texte que c'était la seule façon pour le Tribunal de se sortir d'une impasse sur le fond — mais à quel prix! Le Tribunal note, en début de sentence, qu'il doit analyser l'objection juridictionnelle du Canada au sujet de la prescription. En effet, le Canada a plaidé que le Tribunal n'avait pas compétence pour entendre cette affaire, car les plaintes de M&R étaient prescrites par l'article 1116(2) de l'ALENA.[69] Comme on l'a vu plus haut, le Tribunal n'a pas rendu de décision sur cette

66 *Merrill & Ring, supra* note 4 au para 266.

67 *Ibid* aux para 268-69.

68 On aurait pu aussi décrire cette tendance malheureuse du Tribunal à s'exprimer sur des questions qui ne se posent pas en l'espèce ou qui ne relèvent pas de sa compétence. Le meilleur (ou pire!) exemple concerne la question des subventions (au para 222). Après avoir admis que cette affaire n'impliquait pas de subventions ou de transferts de fonds directs, le Tribunal suggère, dans une note, que *si* c'était le cas, cela pourrait constituer un manquement à l'Accord sur les subventions et les mesures compensatoires de l'OMC.

69 *Ibid* au para 58. Voir ALENA, *supra* note 1, art 1116(2): "Un investisseur ne pourra soumettre une plainte à l'arbitrage si plus de trois ans se sont écoulés depuis la date à laquelle l'investisseur a eu ou aurait dû avoir connaissance du manquement allégué et de la perte ou du dommage subi."

question. Dans les trois paragraphes consacrés à la prescription, il ne décidera pas non plus de la question de savoir si l'objection du Canada était véritablement juridictionnelle.[70] Pourtant, la question était controversée et avait fait l'objet d'arguments contradictoires de la part des parties.[71] Qui plus est, s'il s'agissait bien d'une objection de compétence, il était impératif pour le Tribunal d'en décider.[72]

Le Tribunal ne tranchera pas non plus (en droit ou en fait) la question du manquement à l'article 1105. En apparence, le raisonnement du Tribunal procède en deux parties: l'analyse du droit applicable et son application aux faits. Toutefois, la lecture de la sentence révèle une tout autre démarche, qui fait l'objet de commentaires plus bas.

Étant donné le désaccord des membres du Tribunal sur l'article 1105, ils ont cru bon de décider d'abord de la question des dommages.[73] La justification de cette démarche surprenante se limite à deux paragraphes.[74] Après avoir reconnu qu'aucune règle générale de droit international n'existe à savoir si un acte illicite peut exister en l'absence d'un dommage, le Tribunal conclut qu'en droit international des investissements, les obligations (primaires) sont indissociables de l'existence d'un dommage. Le Tribunal affirme, sans plus, que: "*a finding of liability without a finding of damage would be difficult to explain in the context of investment law arbitration and would indeed be contrary to some of its fundamental tenets.*"[75] Aucune explication n'est donnée au sujet de ces tenants pourtant fondamentaux. Aucune discussion n'est offerte d'affaires où un Tribunal serait arrivé à une décision contraire.[76] Ainsi, non seulement la façon de procéder est critiquable, mais le manque de justification l'est tout autant.

70 *Ibid* aux para 267-69.

71 Voir par ex *Merrill & Ring Forestry L.P. c Canada* (Counter memorial, 13 mai 2008) aux para 144-262.

72 Voir l'approche différente des Tribunaux dans les affaires *Methanex Corporation c United States* (Final Award of the Tribunal on Jurisdiction and Merits, 3 août 2005) et *Loewen Group, Inc. and Raymond L Loewen c United States* (Award, 26 juin 2003) ICSID Case N° ARB(AF)/98/3.

73 *Merrill & Ring, supra* note 4 aux para 243 et 246.

74 *Ibid* aux para 244-45.

75 *Ibid* au para 245.

76 Voir l'affaire *Biwater Gauff (Tanzania) Ltd. c United Republic of Tanzania* (Award, 24 juillet 2008) ICSID Case N° ARB/05/22. Dans cette affaire, le Tribunal a

Au minimum, on aurait pu s'attendre à une discussion des termes de certains articles du chapitre 11 de l'ALENA. Par exemple, l'article 1131(1) prévoit qu': "[u]n tribunal établi en vertu de la présente section tranchera les points en litige conformément au présent accord et aux règles applicables du droit international" (en anglais: "...*shall decide the issues in dispute*").[77] Un autre exemple est l'article 1135(1) qui prévoit que: "[t]out tribunal qui rend une sentence finale à l'encontre d'une Partie pourra accorder uniquement, de façon séparée ou combinée: a) des dommages pécuniaires."[78] À la lecture de ces articles, on pourrait prétendre que le tribunal se doit de trancher les points en litige ou de rendre sa sentence *avant* de se prononcer sur la question des dommages.

Le deuxième problème majeur de l'approche du Tribunal est sa façon de traiter des désaccords importants entre ses membres. La sentence révèle beaucoup trop tard ces désaccords, et ces derniers ont pour effet de remettre en question l'entièreté de l'exposé du droit auquel s'est livré le Tribunal (ou à tout le moins l'un de ses membres avec l'assentiment des autres).

Dans son analyse de l'article 1105, le Tribunal présente d'abord un exposé du droit de 13 pages qui surprend, tant par son style que par son contenu.[79] L'exposé, plutôt cavalier, a la prétention de résoudre des questions hautement complexes et controversées de droit international coutumier portant sur la norme minimale de traitement des investisseurs étrangers. Le Tribunal élabore une théorie de développement du droit international en cette matière selon deux axes principaux. Le premier concerne les cas mettant en jeu les notions de "*personal safety, denial of justice and due process.*"[80] Dans ces cas, le seuil de violation est élevé; selon l'affaire *Neer*, le

---

conclu au manquement de la Tanzanie à plusieurs de ses obligations en vertu de l'accord portant sur l'investissement entre le Royaume-Uni et la Tanzanie. Toutefois, le Tribunal a rejeté la demande en dommages pour défaut de causalité. Voir les para 464-66 (discussion sur l'expropriation), para 778-87 (sur la causalité) et para 812-14 (conclusion). Voir aussi l'opinion concurrente et dissidente en certains points de Gary Born, qui opine que "*there is no right without a remedy*" (para 32) et que le Tribunal aurait dû octroyer une forme de réparation autre que des dommages.

[77] ALENA, *supra* note 1, art 1131(1).

[78] *Ibid*, art 1135(1).

[79] *Merrill & Ring, supra* note 4 aux para 182-213.

[80] *Ibid* au para 204; également décrit comme suit "*due process, denial of justice and physical mistreatment*" au para 197.

comportement doit être "*outrageous*" pour constituer un manquement à la norme minimale de traitement.[81] Le deuxième axe concerne le traitement des étrangers dans le contexte des affaires ("*business, trade and investments*").[82] Dans ces cas, la norme serait beaucoup plus libérale, plus "*open-minded.*"[83] Le Tribunal conclut, sans retenue, que "*this standard provides for the fair and equitable treatment of aliens within the confines of reasonableness.*"[84]

Lorsque vient le temps d'appliquer le droit aux faits, on est surpris de constater que le Tribunal examine deux "scénarios" selon le droit applicable — plutôt que d'appliquer la norme qu'il vient d'exposer. La démarche est décrite de la façon suivante:

> *The Tribunal has considered a possible breach of the protections provided by Article 1105(1) under two different scenarios. The first is based on the Investor's view that the protection provided by Article 1105(1) is significant and that the threshold to be applied to establish breach is a comparatively low one, and thus the log export regime's interference with its business could readily result in a breach of Article 1105(1). The second scenario, while not relying on the Neer standard or some other similarly high threshold, is based on the view that for there to be an 1105(1) breach, a state's wrongful conduct or behavior must be sufficiently serious as to be readily distinguishable from an ordinary effect of otherwise acceptable regulatory measures.*[85]

Le Tribunal procède ensuite à l'analyse de la preuve dans le cadre du premier scénario. Dans cette analyse, la critique des politiques publiques du Canada est évidente.[86] Pourtant, dans l'analyse du second scénario, on note que le Tribunal n'a pas pour tâche de juger de la légitimité du régime canadien sur l'exportation des billes de bois.[87] Même l'évaluation de la preuve, des faits de l'espèce, est différente dans ce scénario.[88]

81 *Ibid* aux para 204-5.

82 Voir par ex *ibid* au para 205.

83 *Ibid* aux para 205, 207.

84 *Ibid* au para 213.

85 *Ibid* au para 219. Il faut noter que ces deux scénarios sont décrits de façon contradictoire plus loin. Au para 236, le Tribunal note: "*Such a policy could not be fairly described in this context as meeting any of the adjectives that have been used over the years, such as egregious, outrageous, arbitrary, grossly unfair or manifestly unreasonable.*" Voir au para 266.

86 Voir par ex *ibid* aux para 224, 226, 229-30, 233.

87 Voir *ibid* au para 236.

88 Voir par ex *ibid* au para 238, où le contraste est évident avec les para 227-29.

L'explication de l'approche boiteuse du Tribunal arrive à la page 95 de la sentence (à environs dix pages de la fin), où on apprend que les membres du Tribunal ne s'entendent pas sur la norme à appliquer ou sur son application en fait! C'est pourquoi le Tribunal a choisi de se prononcer sur la question des dommages, une matière qui, elle, faisait l'unanimité.[89]

Compte tenu de l'incongruité de cette approche, il est difficile d'imaginer que cette sentence arrive à convaincre quiconque du bien fondé de l'analyse du Tribunal concernant l'évolution et le contenu de la norme minimale de traitement en droit international coutumier. Somme toute, il s'agit d'un exemple à éviter.

III. L'approche des tribunaux canadiens concernant l'annulation de sentences arbitrales: L'apport de l'affaire *Cargill c Mexico*

Les tribunaux canadiens ont rendu des décisions au sujet de demandes d'annulation de sentences arbitrales rendues en vertu du chapitre 11 de l'ALENA à cinq reprises: une fois en Colombie-Britannique,[90] trois fois en Ontario[91] et une fois en Cour fédérale.[92] La décision la plus récente, celle qui émane de la Cour d'appel de l'Ontario dans l'affaire *Cargill*, a le mérite de clarifier la norme de contrôle applicable à de tels cas d'annulation. Comparée à certains tribunaux l'ayant précédée, la Cour d'appel évite l'importation en bloc (et inappropriée) de concepts tirés du droit administratif interne concernant le contrôle judiciaire. Elle a aussi le mérite d'élucider la norme applicable lorsque la compétence du tribunal pour décider de certaines questions est contestée, en adoptant la norme de la décision "correcte." Le soin que prend la Cour d'appel de "naviguer" entre la retenue et l'exercice du mandat de contrôle pour excès de compétence est également notable.[93] Tout de même imparfaite

[89] Voir *ibid* aux para 243 et 246.

[90] *The United Mexican States c Metalclad Corporation*, 2001 BCSC 664.

[91] *The United Mexican States c Feldman Karpa*, 2005 ONCA 249, *Bayview Irrigation District #11 et al c United Mexican States*, 2008 ONSC 22120 et *Mexico c Cargill Incorporated*, *supra* note 7 and 8.

[92] *Canada (Attorney General) c S.D. Myers Inc.*, 2004 FC 38.

[93] *Mexico c Cargill, Incorporated*, *supra* note 8; "*One challenge for the reviewing court is to navigate the tension between the discouragement to courts to intervene on the one hand, and on the other, the court's statutory mandate to review for jurisdictional excess, ensuring that the tribunal correctly identified the limits of its decision-making authority. Ultimately, when deciding its own jurisdiction, the tribunal has to be correct*" (para 48).

(notamment en ce qui a trait à l'application de la norme en l'espèce et au rôle attribué aux "interprétations" des Parties à l'ALENA), cette décision fait preuve d'une approche améliorée.

Une mise en contexte s'impose. Durant les années 2007 à 2009, le Mexique a été condamné à payer un montant cumulatif de plus de 168 millions de dollars à des investisseurs américains pour avoir manqué à ses obligations en vertu du chapitre 11 de l'ALENA, notamment à l'obligation de traitement national.[94] Seule une des trois sentences arbitrales (celle rendue dans l'affaire *Cargill*) a fait l'objet d'une demande d'annulation de la part du Mexique. Le motif principal de cette demande est que le Tribunal a outrepassé ses compétences en octroyant 41 millions de dollars (sur 77 millions) pour des dommages subis par Cargill aux États-Unis, et non pas directement par sa filiale au Mexique.[95] En d'autres mots, selon le Mexique, le Tribunal a erré en décidant que les pertes de Cargill en rapport avec les ventes à l'exportation à partir des États-Unis vers Cargill de Mexico (sa filiale) pouvaient être indemnisées en vertu du chapitre 11 de l'ALENA.

Étant donné que le lieu de l'arbitrage était Toronto, la demande d'annulation a été faite en Cour supérieure de l'Ontario. Cette demande a été rejetée en août 2010.[96] Le Mexique a fait appel de la décision auprès de la Cour d'appel de l'Ontario, qui a également rejeté la demande en octobre 2011.[97] Dans un recours ultime, le 2 décembre 2011, le Mexique a demandé la permission d'en appeler à la Cour suprême du Canada, en raison de l'importance nationale

94 *Archer Daniels Midland Company and Tate & Lyle Ingredients Americas, Inc. c Mexico* (Award, 21 novembre 2007) ICSID Case N° ARB(AF)/04/05; *Corn Products International, Inc c Mexico* (Decision on Responsibility, 15 janvier 2008) ICSID Case N° ARB(AF)/04/01; *Cargill, supra* note 6. La trilogie des affaires mexicaines concernant les édulcorants a fait l'objet d'une étude détaillée dans nos chroniques précédentes, voir *supra* note 5.

95 Voir *Mexico c Cargill Incorporated, supra* note 8 au para 10 (quant au montant de dommages). Dans la sentence, le Tribunal a jugé utile de considérer les profits perdus à la frontière en deux groupes, soit les *upstream losses* (celles attribuables à l'impossibilité pour Cargill de vendre le sirop de maïs à haute teneur en fructose à Cargill de Mexico) et les *downstream losses* (celles attribuables aux pertes directes de Cargill de Mexico). Après réflexion, le Tribunal a décidé que tant les pertes en amont que les pertes en aval pouvaient être incluses dans le calcul des dommages pouvant être octroyés en vertu du chapitre 11. *Cargill, supra* note 6 aux para 519-26.

96 *United Mexican States c Cargill, supra* note 7.

97 *Mexico c Cargill, Incorporated, supra* note 8.

et même "supra-nationale" des questions posées.[98] Tout comme dans la première partie de cette chronique, l'accent sera mis sur l'approche des tribunaux, surtout celle adoptée par la Cour d'appel.

L'un des mérites de l'approche retenue par la Cour d'appel est de ne pas prôner l'application directe des normes de droit administratif interne concernant le contrôle judiciaire. Dans l'affaire *S.D. Myers*, la Cour fédérale a été influencée par l'approche "pragmatique et fonctionnelle,"[99] et dans l'affaire *Feldman*, la Cour d'appel de l'Ontario avait même appliqué les facteurs de l'approche "pragmatique et fonctionnelle," développés par la Cour suprême dans l'affaire *Pushpanathan c Canada*, afin de déterminer le degré de déférence dû aux tribunaux assujettis au contrôle judiciaire.[100]

Selon la Cour d'appel dans l'affaire *Cargill*, "*importing and directly applying domestic concepts of standard of review, both from administrative law and from domestic review by appeal courts of trial decisions, may not be helpful to courts when conducting their review process of international arbitration awards under Article 34 of the* Model Law."[101] Cela dit, la Cour d'appel s'est tout de même inspirée de la décision de la Cour suprême du Canada dans l'affaire *Dunsmuir* (la décision récente la plus importante sur la norme de contrôle judiciaire), mais sans toutefois retenir les critères d'application de l'analyse relative à la norme de contrôle.[102]

Il revenait ensuite à la Cour d'appel d'identifier la norme de contrôle applicable. La référence ci-dessus à l'article 34 de la "Loi type" (*Model Law*) vise la Loi type de la CNUDCI sur l'arbitrage commercial international,[103] qui prévoit les motifs limitatifs permettant l'annulation d'une sentence arbitrale. Le motif d'annulation allégué dans l'affaire *Cargill* est celui prévu au paragraphe (2) (a) (iii): "Que la sentence porte sur un différend non visé dans le compromis ou n'entrant pas dans les prévisions de la clause compromissoire, ou

[98] *United Mexican States c. Cargill, Incorporated*, leave to appeal to SCC requested, filed 2 December 2011.

[99] *Canada (Attorney General) c S.D. Myers Inc*, *supra* note 92 au para 59. Le Canada avait notamment encouragé la Cour à adopter cette norme.

[100] *United Mexican States c Feldman Karpa*, *supra* note 91 au para 38.

[101] *Mexico c Cargill, Incorporated*, *supra* note 8 au para 30.

[102] *Ibid* aux para 35, 40-42, 44-46.

[103] Loi type de la CNUDCI sur l'arbitrage commercial international (1985). Toutes les provinces canadiennes et le fédéral ont adopté des lois mettant en œuvre la Loi type.

qu'elle contient des décisions qui dépassent les termes du compromis ou de la clause compromissoire."[104]

L'approche de la Cour d'appel se distingue de celle de la Cour supérieure dans la même affaire, mais aussi de celle des autres tribunaux canadiens. Dans l'affaire *Metalclad*, la Cour suprême de la Colombie-Britannique a refusé l'importation (en bloc) de l'approche "pragmatique et fonctionnelle" dans un contrôle en vertu de l'article 34 de la Loi type.[105] Toutefois, la décision de la Cour laisse à croire que la norme appliquée est celle de la décision correcte. En effet, la Cour a conclu que le Tribunal arbitral avait rendu une décision qui dépassait les termes de la soumission à l'arbitrage, en indiquant incorrectement que le droit applicable incluait une obligation de transparence ("*misstated the applicable law to include*").[106]

A l'opposé, la Cour supérieure de l'Ontario dans l'affaire *Bayview Irrigation* semble rejeter la norme de la décision correcte:

> *My role on judicial review is not to conduct a hearing* de novo *of the merits of the Tribunal's decision on jurisdiction. The standard of review is narrower in scope than that governing the review by a domestic court of the decision of a domestic administrative tribunal. The Supreme Court of Canada in a recent judgment held there are only two standards — correctness and reasonableness simpliciter. [Dunsmuir].*[107]

La Cour ajoute qu'elle doit faire preuve de retenue et qu'il existe une présomption forte que le Tribunal a agi à l'intérieur de son mandat.[108] Aussi considère-t-elle que les motifs d'annulation doivent être interprétés restrictivement et que les demandeurs doivent satisfaire à un "*high threshold*" pour obtenir l'annulation de la sentence.[109]

104 *Ibid*, art 34(2)(iii).

105 *United Mexican States c Metalclad Corporation*, 2001 BCSC 664 au para 54.

106 *Ibid* au para 70. Cette décision a été l'objet de plusieurs critiques. Voir par ex E. Gaillard, "Centre international de règlement des différends relatifs aux investissements (CIRDI) — Chronique des sentences arbitrales" (2002) 1 JDI 189, aux pp. 191-193 et G. Sacerdoti, "Investment Arbitration under ICSID and UNCITRAL Rules: Prerequisites, Applicable Law, Review of Awards" (2004) 19 ICSID Review 1 aux pp. 40-41.

107 *Bayview Irrigation District #11 et al c United Mexican States*, *supra* note 91 au para 60.

108 *Ibid* aux para 62-63.

109 *Ibid* au para 63.

Dans l'affaire *S.D. Myers,* la Cour fédérale (inspirée de l'approche "pragmatique et fonctionnelle") adopte une approche mixte. Elle a estimé que, sur une question de compétence, "la norme de contrôle applicable à la pure question de droit est la décision correcte et, à la question mixte de droit et de fait, la décision raisonnable."[110]

Établissant une norme différente à nouveau, la Cour supérieure de l'Ontario dans l'affaire *Cargill* a retenu la norme de la décision raisonnable (même en droit, semble-t-il). L'approche de la Cour est décrite sommairement et laisse à désirer. Dans un jugement comptant vingt pages, la Cour consacre deux pages à la norme de contrôle. Il s'agit essentiellement de citations tirées de trois décisions judicaires portant sur la "présomption forte" qu'un tribunal arbitral agit à l'intérieur de son mandat et sur le "degré de déférence" élevé dû aux décisions des tribunaux arbitraux.[111] Sans plus d'analyse, la Cour arrive à la conclusion que: "*The weight of authority supports the respondent's submission that the court's approach should be one of restraint and deference and that [sic] standard of review in considering whether the tribunal has exceeded its jurisdiction is one of reasonableness.*"[112]

L'approche de la Cour d'appel diffère et l'amène à conclure que, pour une question de compétence, la norme de contrôle est celle de la décision "correcte" (et non pas "raisonnable"). Pour en venir à cette conclusion, la Cour a analysé les termes de l'article 34 (2) de la Loi type, les termes de la soumission à l'arbitrage, ainsi que les décisions pertinentes des tribunaux judiciaires, surtout canadiens, mais aussi une décision anglaise.[113] Malgré son affirmation au sujet de l'utilité limitée des décisions de droit administratif interne, la Cour ne semble avoir pu s'empêcher d'établir un parallèle avec la démarche analytique de la Cour Suprême dans l'affaire *Dunsmuir,* qui établit également une distinction entre la norme de la décision "raisonnable" et celle de la décision "correcte."[114] La Cour d'appel note ainsi qu'une décision de "pure" compétence serait assujettie à la norme de la décision "correcte."[115] Elle ajoute

110 *Canada (Attorney General) c S.D. Myers Inc, supra* note 92 au para 59.

111 *United Mexican States c Cargill, supra* note 7 aux para 49-55.

112 *Ibid* au para 55.

113 *Mexico c Cargill, Incorporated, supra* note 8 aux para 31 et ss. En référence à l'affaire *Dallah Real Estate and Tourism Holding Co. c Ministry of Religious Affairs of the Government of Pakistan,* 2011 1 AC 763, que la Cour distingue de la présente affaire (au para 39).

114 *Ibid* aux para 35, 40, 45.

115 *Ibid* au para 35.

que les tribunaux judiciaires dans les affaires *Metalclad* et *S.D. Myers* avaient aussi adopté cette norme.[116]

En définitive, la Cour d'appel estime qu'étant donné que la question relevant de l'article 34 (2)(a)(iii) est de savoir si le Tribunal "*acted within its jurisdiction*" (et qu'aucun terme de l'article n'impose de limites à la démarche de la Cour), il n'existe aucune raison d'ignorer la règle "normale" selon laquelle, sur une question de compétence, un tribunal ne peut outrepasser son mandat.[117] En d'autres mots: "*The tribunal therefore had to be correct in the sense that the decision it made had to be within the scope of the submission and the NAFTA provisions ... It has no authority to expand its jurisdiction by incorrectly interpreting the submission or the NAFTA, even if its interpretation could be viewed as a reasonable one.*"[118]

De façon notable, la Cour d'appel rejette la norme de la décision raisonnable car, selon elle, un contrôle du caractère raisonnable d'une décision mène nécessairement à une analyse du fond. En d'autres mots, la question n'est pas de savoir si une décision est acceptable parce que raisonnable, mais plutôt si elle l'est parce qu'elle a été rendue à l'intérieur du mandat du tribunal.[119]

La Cour d'appel a également clarifié le sens à donner à l'expression "*powerful presumption,*" maintes fois citée par les tribunaux judiciaires mais rarement analysée:

> *In my view, the principle underlying the concept of a 'powerful presumption' is that courts will intervene rarely because their intervention is limited to true jurisdictional errors. To the extent that the phrase 'powerful presumption' may suggest that a reviewing court should presume that the tribunal was correct in determining the scope of its jurisdiction, the phrase is misleading. If courts were to defer to the decision of the tribunal on issues of true jurisdiction, that would effectively nullify the purpose and intent of the review authority of the court under Article 34(2)(a)(iii).*[120]

Dans cette citation, tout comme dans son raisonnement, la Cour d'appel met l'accent sur le concept de "*true question of jurisdiction.*"[121] Cet accent témoigne de la préoccupation de limiter le contrôle aux

[116] *Ibid.*

[117] *Ibid* au para 40.

[118] *Ibid* au para 41.

[119] *Ibid* au para 51.

[120] *Ibid* au para 46.

[121] *Ibid* aux para 40, 44, 46-47, 52-53.

questions touchant véritablement à la compétence du tribunal arbitral et d'éviter de trancher sur le fond.[122] Selon la Cour, cette démarche devrait mener les tribunaux judiciaires à intervenir uniquement dans de rares circonstances.[123]

Dans ce contexte, la Cour d'appel note, avec justesse, que le défi pour les tribunaux est de "naviguer" entre la retenue et l'exercice du mandat de contrôle pour excès de compétence.[124] Finalement, la Cour fournit un mode d'emploi permettant de bien "naviguer":

> *Another way to define the proper approach is to ask the following three questions:*
> - *What was the issue that the tribunal decided?*
> - *Was the issue within the submission to arbitration made under Chapter 11 of the NAFTA?*
> - *Is there anything in the NAFTA, properly interpreted, that precluded the tribunal from making the award it made?*

La démarche proposée par la Cour d'appel constitue une amélioration par rapport à celles adoptées antérieurement par les tribunaux canadiens. Elle est plus analytique, réfléchie et moins ancrée dans les concepts de droit administratif interne. Elle n'en demeure pas moins imparfaite. D'abord, il est beaucoup plus aisé de parler de "véritable question de compétence" que de trancher dans un cas d'espèce. Dans le contexte particulier du chapitre 11 de l'ALENA, la qualification de plusieurs questions comme relevant de la compétence du tribunal demeure incertaine. L'examen *de novo* par un tribunal judiciaire, non spécialisé, de questions complexes de droit international public et économique n'est pas non plus sans poser des difficultés. L'application de la norme de la décision correcte en l'espèce et le refus par la Cour d'appel d'accorder de l'importance aux "interprétations" des Parties à l'ALENA illustrent bien ces difficultés.

En l'espèce, la Cour d'appel a estimé que les allégations du Mexique relevaient du fond et non pas de la compétence du Tribunal.[125] Dans son raisonnement, la Cour a cité ou paraphrasé le texte de plusieurs dispositions de l'ALENA, pour ensuite conclure qu'il revient au tribunal arbitral de juger des faits et d'appliquer les faits aux articles pertinents afin de juger si les dommages, en l'espèce,

122 *Ibid* aux para 45-47.

123 *Ibid* aux para 44, 46.

124 *Ibid* au para 48.

125 *Ibid* au para 66.

"*fall within the defined criteria.*"[126] La Cour, en faisant référence à la conclusion de la Cour supérieure, énonce le critère applicable et conclut que le Tribunal arbitral a correctement décidé des limites à sa capacité d'octroyer des dommages.[127] Sa conclusion en droit repose fondamentalement sur l'absence, au chapitre 11 de l'ALENA, de mots limitant l'octroi des dommages sur une base territoriale.[128]

Finalement, la Cour s'est penchée sur l'argument du Mexique selon lequel les Parties à l'ALENA s'étaient entendues sur une interprétation du chapitre 11 qui excluait l'octroi de dommages en amont ("*upstream damages*"). Cet argument est fondé sur l'article 31(3) a) et b) de la Convention de Vienne sur le droit des traités qui prévoit que:

3. Il sera tenu compte, en même temps que du contexte:
   a) De tout accord ultérieur intervenu entre les parties au sujet de l'interprétation du traité ou de l'application de ses dispositions;
   b) De toute pratique ultérieurement suivie dans l'application du traité par laquelle est établi l'accord des parties à l'égard de l'interprétation du traité.[129]

Ce qui est notable, en l'espèce, c'est que les trois Parties à l'ALENA sont intervenues devant la Cour d'appel pour confirmer l'interprétation à donner au chapitre 11. Toutes les trois ont plaidé que la Cour devait en tenir compte en application de la norme de contrôle. Toutefois, la Cour a refusé de le faire. Elle a jugé que les écritures *passées* des Parties ne constituaient pas un accord spécifique selon lequel, dans tous les cas, les dommages étaient limités à ceux subis par l'investisseur dans le territoire où il a investi.[130] Après avoir cité l'opinion des Parties, la Cour conclut, dans un passage qui laisse perplexe, ce qui suit:

I agree that if that position of the three Parties was a clear, well-understood, agreed common position, in accordance with Article 31(3)(b) of the Vienna Convention,

[126] *Ibid* aux para 67-69.

[127] *Ibid* aux para 69-70.

[128] *Ibid* au para 72.

[129] Cité *ibid* au para 75. Voir Convention de Vienne sur le droit des traités, 1155 RTNU 331 (23 mai 1969).

[130] *Ibid* aux para 79-82.

> *that prohibited the award of any losses suffered by the investor in its home business operation, even caused by the breach, it would be an error of jurisdiction for the tribunal to fail to give effect to that interpretation of the relevant provisions of Chapter 11. However, that does not appear to be the case.*[131]

En particulier, l'expression "*clear, well-understood, agreed common position*" n'est pas explicitée ou analysée. Pourtant, cette question d'interprétation des traités revêt une importance considérable en l'espèce. A preuve, dans sa demande pour permission d'en appeler à la Cour suprême du Canada, le Mexique conteste l'application erronée, par la Cour d'appel, de la Convention de Vienne.[132] Sans entrer dans une discussion du bien fondé de cette position, les allégations mexicaines illustrent bien l'insuffisance de l'analyse de la Cour d'appel.

Il en va de même au sujet de l'autre motif principal allégué par le Mexique, concernant l'étendue de la protection offerte aux investisseurs étrangers dans le cadre de l'ALENA. En particulier, le Mexique allègue que la Cour d'appel a appliqué la bonne norme de contrôle, mais aux mauvaises questions:[133]

> *A NAFTA Chapter Eleven tribunal's jurisdiction is not defined by simply asking, as the Court of Appeal did, whether the claimed investment fits within the definition provided in Article 1139, and whether the damages claimed were incurred 'by reason of, or arising out of' the breach ... Nor, contrary to what the Court of Appeal thought, was the issue before the reviewing courts whether there are any 'territorial limitations' on the location in which damages must be incurred in order to be compensable under NAFTA Chapter Eleven (para 69).*[134]

Après avoir posé ce qu'il estime être la "bonne question," à savoir si les Parties à l'ALENA ont des obligations quelconques vis-à-vis d'investisseurs en lien avec des investissements dans leur pays d'origine, le Mexique souligne l'importance de comprendre la structure et les objectifs de l'ALENA, qui sont ensuite expliqués.[135]

En définitive, bien que son approche soit plus recommandable que celles des autres tribunaux judiciaires canadiens, la décision

131 *Ibid* au para 84.

132 *United Mexican States c. Cargill, Incorporated,* leave to appeal, *supra* note 98.

133 *Ibid* au para 36.

134 *Ibid.*

135 *Ibid* au para 37.

de la Cour d'appel de l'Ontario dans l'affaire *Cargill,* ainsi que les arguments du Mexique la concernant, illustrent bien les défis que l'arbitrage investisseur-État pose aux tribunaux judiciaires internes.

Canadian Practice in International Law / Pratique canadienne en matière de droit international

At the Department of Foreign Affairs and International Trade in 2010–11 / Au ministère des Affaires étrangères et du Commerce international en 2010–11

compiled by / préparé par

ALAN H. KESSEL

AIR AND SPACE LAW

Requirement to Deposit a Bond or Guarantee upon Entry of an Aircraft into a Foreign State

In September 2010, in response to the question of whether the requirement to deposit a bond or guarantee upon entry of an aircraft into a foreign state is inconsistent with Article 24 of the Convention on International Civil Aviation (Chicago Convention), done at Chicago on 7 December 1944, the Legal Branch wrote:

There is at least a reasonable argument that the foreign State has not violated the Chicago Convention, which deals with international civil aviation, primarily the transportation of passengers, cargo and mail across international borders, as well as air navigation generally. Article 24(a) states:

Allan H. Kessel, The Legal Adviser, Department of Foreign Affairs and International Trade, Ottawa, Canada. The extracts from official correspondence contained in this survey have been made available by courtesy of the Department of Foreign Affairs and International Trade. Some of the correspondence from which extracts are given was provided for the general guidance of the enquirer in relation to specific facts that are often not described in full in the extracts within this compilation. The statements of law and practice should not necessarily be regarded as definitive.

> Aircraft on a flight to, from, or across the territory of another contracting State shall be admitted temporarily free of duty, subject to the customs regulations of the State.

It is debatable whether Article 24 was meant to apply to aerial services other than the transportation of passengers, mail or cargo. Even if it was intended to apply to such situations, it is unclear how long an aircraft can remain in a foreign State under the status of "admitted temporarily." An aircraft transporting passengers or cargo would only remain in a foreign State for the purpose of unloading and loading for the return or onward voyage. This may take more than a day but it is a temporary stay for logistical reasons only. In this case, the purpose of the aircraft's stay is not to facilitate international transportation, but appears to be to perform a domestic service within the country. This service may require the aircraft to be in the State for an extended period of time, which would bring into question its status as "admitted temporarily." In such cases, it is at least arguable that the aircraft is not simply being admitted temporarily and that Article 24 no longer shields it from the imposition of customs duties.

In the event that Article 24 of the Chicago Convention does apply to such aerial services and the aircraft can be said to be admitted temporarily, there does not appear to be any rule forbidding the receiving country from requiring a refundable bond or guarantee from the operator to cover its potential customs liabilities. In fact, Annex 9 (Facilitation) to the Chicago Convention states as follows:

> A. Bonds and exemption from requisition or seizure
>
> 8.1 Recommended Practice – If a Contracting State requires bonds of an aircraft operator to cover his liabilities under the customs, immigration, public health, animal and plant quarantine, or similar laws of the State, it should permit the use of a single comprehensive bond whenever possible.

DIPLOMATIC LAW

Establishment of Voting Stations on Foreign Diplomatic and Consular Premises in Canada

In November 2011, in response to the question of whether the establishment of voting stations on foreign diplomatic and consular premises in Canada without the express consent of the government of Canada violates international law, the Legal Branch wrote:

Article 3 of the Vienna Convention on Diplomatic Relations (VCDR) enumerates the functions of a diplomatic mission, while Article 5 of the

Vienna Convention on Consular Relations (VCCR) enumerates those of a consular post. Neither article specifically grants to the sending State the right to hold voting stations in the territory of the host country.

In the case of the VCCR, non-enumerated consular functions are possible under Article 5(m) of that convention, provided they are not prohibited by host state's laws or regulations, or provided that the host state does not object to the functions being carried out. Foreign missions carrying out voting activities for foreign elections, within their premises or elsewhere in Canada, must obtain Canada's consent prior to proceeding.

Further, Article 55 of the VCCR provides that premises of a consular post must not be used in any manner incompatible with the exercise of consular functions. If a foreign voting activity is arranged by a foreign mission but is not authorized by Canada, this would be incompatible with the exercise of consular functions (for more information, consult the following link: <http://www.international.gc.ca/protocol-protocole/circular_1264_circulaire.aspx?lang=eng&view=d>).

Screening of Diplomatic Bags

Through Circular Note no. XDC-0144 dated 28 January 2011, the Legal Branch reiterated Canada's policy and practice on the screening of diplomatic bags:

The Department of Foreign Affairs and International Trade (Office of Protocol) presents its compliments to Their Excellencies the Heads of Diplomatic Missions and notified Chargés d'affaires, a.i. accredited to Canada, and the Heads of International Organizations and other Offices established in Canada, and has the honour to reiterate the Government of Canada's policy and related expectations on the treatment and status of diplomatic bags.

Article 27 of the Vienna Convention on Diplomatic Relations (VCDR) exempts the diplomatic bag from opening and detention. This exemption derives from the fundamental principle of protection of free communication that is owed to diplomatic missions for official purposes. Canada considers that x-ray or any other form of electronic scanning of diplomatic bags constitutes a constructive opening of the bag. Such opening can adversely affect the integrity and the confidentiality of the documents and articles contained in the bag and therefore impair the inviolability of the bag, and is thus regarded by Canada as creating an unacceptable breach of the VCDR.

Within the framework of its diplomatic relations, Canada continues to ensure, through domestic legislation and enabling regulation, that foreign diplomatic pouches, when these visibly bear external marks of their status and are appropriately sealed, are exempt from manual search, or any form of electronic scanning (by x-ray device or other method) and cannot be opened or detained. However, recognizing the importance of public safety and civil aviation security considerations and the need to safeguard against abuses, relevant Canadian authorities which may have serious reasons to suspect that a diplomatic pouch could constitute a threat are instructed to notify the authorities of the sending State and request that the bag be opened in their presence. If the sending State refuses the examination, the bag will be returned to its place of origin.

Therefore, the Department urges the Heads of Mission to bring to the attention of their Capitals the Government of Canada's above policy with the goal of exempting Canadian diplomatic bags abroad from any policy, current or future, of x-ray or any other form of electronic scanning.

Since Canada does not, in the pursuance of its interests and activities as sending State, allow its diplomatic bags to be opened or screened by x-ray or any other method, the inability to send diplomatic bags via certain airports causes serious operational challenges. In fact, the Department stresses that its decision to send a Circular Note at this time was made necessary by the concern that rules and practices of certain States effectively permit the regular use of electronic devices, such as x-rays, for the examination and screening of diplomatic bags. In this regard, Canada continues to work bilaterally and in common approach with other concerned States to object to these actions taken by certain States.

The Department of Foreign Affairs and International Trade (Office of Protocol) avails itself of this opportunity to renew to Their Excellencies the Heads of Diplomatic Missions and notified Chargés d'affaires, a.i. accredited to Canada, and to the Heads of International Organizations and other Offices established in Canada, the assurances of its highest consideration.

Requirement to Contribute to the Social Security Programs of Foreign States for Locally Engaged Staff Working at Canadian Missions

In a legal opinion dated 20 September 2011, the Legal Branch wrote:

The principles of state immunity law offer a number of reasons why Canada would not be required to contribute into the social security system of a foreign state for Locally Engaged Staff (LES) hired by [a] Canadian diplomatic or consular mission ...[1]

1 Canadian diplomatic and consular missions do not have a distinct legal personality from that of their sending State, Canada. This explains why state immunity law is the source to the answers sought.

Canada would not find relief from the requirements of [local] labour laws in the Vienna Convention on Diplomatic Relations (VCDR). The portion of the Vienna Convention relating to social security contributions, specifically article 33, exempts diplomats from making social security contributions in the receiving state. The article has an exception … requiring diplomats to pay into the social security program of the receiving state for personal servants. This hiring of a personal servant … is not the same as the Government of Canada employing an LES to work at a Canadian diplomatic mission. The VCDR concerns itself with the case of an employee hired by a diplomat, not an employee hired by a foreign state ...

Absolute immunity means that a state can claim immunity from the jurisdiction of the state of the forum for all its acts.[2] In contrast, restrictive immunity means that a state is generally not entitled to immunity in cases where it behaves in a manner similar to that of a private enterprise, such as in the case of a commercial transaction ... the trend in the jurisprudence has been in support of an increasing acceptance of the notion that a contract of employment was similar to a commercial contract, and therefore not subject to state immunity[3] ... While restrictive immunity may apply to Canada in matters of employment contracts, social security matters remain ... subject to state immunity ...

The relevant body of law in the case of the social security contributions of a foreign state for its LES is not the VCDR but rather the law of State Immunity ... [C]ontributions to social security for LES in the receiving state are a matter of state immunity, and the sending state, which employs the LES, is not subject to local laws requiring social security contributions ...

Support for the position that states have immunity from making social security contributions for their LES can be found in the International Law Commission's *Final Draft Articles and Commentary on Jurisdictional Immunities of States and Their Property (1991)* ... Paragraph 11(1) of these draft articles ... reads:

> Unless otherwise agreed between the States concerned, a State cannot invoke immunity from jurisdiction before a court of another State which is otherwise competent in a proceeding which relates to a contract of employment between the State and an individual for work performed or to be performed, in whole or in part, in the territory of that other State.[4]

2 Richard Garnett, "State Immunity in Employment Matters" (1997) 46 Int'l & Comp LQ 81 at 82.

3 *Ibid* at 82-83.

4 A Dickinson et al, *State Immunity* (Toronto: Oxford University Press, 2004) at 120, 122.

The drafters' commentary ... explains that the original version of this text in the ILC articles contained a reference to "social security" ... [M]ention of "social security" was ... deliberately removed from the final draft ... the term "contract of employment" ... is not meant to include matters related to social security ...

Paragraph 11(1) creates a category of instances from which a state cannot claim immunity. That social security was deliberately removed from this category ... implies that state immunity does continue to cover social security. Its intentional deletion appears to indicate that in the view of the ILC social security is not a matter that would be considered an element of a labour contract and therefore subject to restricted state immunity ...

Canada is immune, at international law, from the obligation to contribute to the [receiving state's] social security programme for its LES ... [C]ustomary international law does not accept that social security is an exception to the rule of state immunity ... Canada ... in its own state practice ... does not require any foreign state to make contributions to Canadian social security programmes ... this decision is entirely one to be made by the foreign state.

INTERNATIONAL CRIMINAL LAW

Requirement to Establish Nationality Jurisdiction under the OECD Anti-Bribery Convention

In a legal opinion dated 23 September 2010, the Legal Branch wrote:

Canada generally does not exercise enforcement jurisdiction on the basis of nationality — that is, simply on the basis that a crime was committed by a Canadian, regardless of where that crime was committed in the world. In the Phase 2 Report on Canada, the OECD Anti-Bribery Working Group recommended that Canada "reconsider the decision not to establish nationality jurisdiction over the offence of bribing a foreign public official." Similarly, a recommendation to establish nationality jurisdiction over the foreign bribery offence resulted from the National Roundtables on Corporate Social Responsibility and the Canadian Extractive Sector in Developing Countries, a series of stakeholder consultations hosted by DFAIT [Department of Foreign Affairs and International Trade] in 2006.

On May 15, 2009, the Minister of Justice introduced Bill C-31 (*An Act to amend the Criminal Code, the Corruption of Foreign Public Officials Act and the Identification of Criminals Act and to make a consequential amendment to another Act*). If passed, this Bill would have amended the CFPOA [the *Corruption of Foreign Public Officials Act*] to allow Canada to prosecute

Canadian companies or Canadian individuals for offences under the CFPOA without having to provide evidence of a link between Canada and the offence ... The Bill died on the order papers ...

Canada continues to take the position ... that enforcement jurisdiction based on territorial jurisdiction, which includes the possibility of prosecuting bribery by Canadians or Canadian companies of foreign public officials that occurs abroad but that [has] a "real and substantial connection" to Canada (known as the "Libman test"), is adequate for ... meeting Canada's obligations under Article 4.1 of the Convention.

Canada's position is that Article 4.2 of the Convention does not create any obligations for Canada. Because Canada is not a party "which has jurisdiction to prosecute its nationals for offences committed abroad," it is unnecessary for Canada to "take such measures as may be necessary to establish its jurisdiction to do so in respect of the bribery of a foreign public official, according to the same principles," as required by Article 4.2 ... [B]ased on the negotiating history of the Convention, Article 4.2 is intended to create obligations for states parties which cannot, either by law or by operation of policy, extradite their own nationals to face trial for offences committed abroad, and thus would require the additional "hook" of nationality jurisdiction to ensure that foreign bribery committed by their own nationals abroad would not go unpunished.

Though we cannot point to an international legal obligation on Canada to create an ability in law to exercise enforcement jurisdiction over the crime of foreign bribery on the basis of nationality, the RCMP [Royal Canadian Mounted Police] and federal prosecutors have indicated that the nationality jurisdiction amendment to the Corruption of Foreign Public Officials Act could eliminate a potential barrier to enforcement of the foreign bribery offence in Canada, though the question of jurisdiction has not hampered their ability to date to prosecute and enforce the CFPOA.

INTERNATIONAL ECONOMIC LAW

Règlement sur l'application de la résolution des Nations Unies sur la Libye et les mesures économiques spéciales

Le 14 mars 2011, le Secteur juridique a émis, par l'entremise du Bureau du surintendant des institutions financières (BSIF) et du ministère des Finances du Canada, les conseils suivants quant à l'interprétation du Règlement sur l'application de la résolution des Nations Unies sur la Libye et les mesures économiques spéciales (maintenant le Règlement sur l'application de la résolution des Nations Unies sur la Libye), ci-après appelé le "règlement sur la Libye":

Le ministère des Affaires étrangères et du Commerce international (MAECI) a transmis au BSIF les renseignements suivants pour guider les IFF [institutions financières fédérales] dans l'application du règlement sur la Libye.

Le MAECI a avisé le BSIF que la *Loi sur les mesures économiques spéciales* autorise le gouverneur en conseil à restreindre ou à interdire certaines activités à l'égard d'un État étranger. Elle n'autorise pas la restriction ou l'interdiction d'opérations effectuées avec des nationaux d'un État autre que l'État à l'égard duquel le règlement est pris, à moins que la personne se trouve dans cet État ou qu'elle agisse au nom ou pour le bénéfice de cet État ou d'une personne qui s'y trouve. Les faits à cet égard doivent être établis.

Par nationaux d'un pays, on entend, dans le cas d'une personne morale, une personne morale constituée ou prorogée sous le régime du droit de l'État en question.

Opérations effectuées avec des banques constituées en dehors de la Libye, dont la Banque centrale de la Libye est propriétaire, en totalité ou en partie, directement ou indirectement

En raison de la limite susmentionnée, l'alinéa *b*) de la définition de "personne désignée" à l'article 1 du règlement sur la Libye n'inclut pas une banque ou autre institution financière constituée ou prorogée sous le régime du droit d'un pays autre que la Libye, à moins qu'on puisse établir qu'il s'agit dans les faits d'un ministère, d'une institution ou d'une agence du gouvernement de la Libye. Le fait que le gouvernement de la Libye est propriétaire de la banque ou de l'institution financière ne suffit pas aux fins de cette démonstration.

Faute d'une telle démonstration, les opérations effectuées avec des banques et des institutions financières constituées dans un pays autre que la Libye ne sont pas interdites, à moins qu'elles ne portent sur l'une des activités interdites aux articles 7 ou 8.

S'agissant d'une opération donnée, la question de savoir si cette opération tomberait sous le coup des interdictions décrétées dans ces articles, y compris une opération portant sur un bien détenu par une personne désignée ou en son nom, consistant à mettre des biens à la disposition d'une personne désignée, ou à fournir des services financiers à une personne désignée ou à son profit, est une question de fait.

Établir si une opération implique une personne désignée

Les IFF doivent procéder à cette vérification en se fondant sur les deux définitions prévues dans le règlement sur la Libye. Veuillez noter que pour les besoins de l'alinéa b) de la définition de "personne désignée," la question de savoir si une personne donnée est un ministère, une institution ou une agence du gouvernement de la Libye est une question de fait, et ne relève pas du MAECI. Malheureusement, ni le BSIF ni le MAECI sont en mesure de donner un avis juridique ou autre directive sur le gel de fonds. Nous renvoyons les IFF au Guide d'instructions du BSIF intitulé Lois visant les personnes et entités inscrites et frappées de sanctions, publié en juin 2010 et qu'on peut consulter sur le site Web du BSIF (<http://www.osfi-bsif.gc.ca/app/DocRepository/1/fra/enjeux/sanctions/bsif590/dsninstr_f.pdf>)

Opération portant sur un bien détenu par une personne désignée ou en son nom, ou consistant à faciliter la conclusion d'une telle opération ou à fournir des services financiers s'y rapportant

Il importe pour les IFF de ne pas perdre de vue que les interdictions prévues dans le règlement sur la Libye diffèrent selon les types de personne désignée. Par exemple, l'alinéa 7(2)(*a*) interdit d'effectuer, "directement ou indirectement, une opération portant sur un bien se trouvant au Canada le 26 février 2011 ou après cette date dont est propriétaire ou que contrôle toute personne désignée, toute personne agissant pour le compte ou sur les instructions d'une telle personne ou toute personne dont est propriétaire ou que contrôle une personne désignée". Par comparaison, l'alinéa 8(2)(*a*) interdit "d'effectuer une opération portant sur un bien, indépendamment de la situation de celui-ci, détenu par une personne désignée ou en son nom". On retrouve une énumération exhaustive des interdictions frappant les opérations sur des biens à l'article 7 (pour les personnes désignées visées à l'alinéa (*a*) de la définition), et à l'article 8 (pour les personnes désignées visées à l'alinéa (*b*) de la définition).

Entrée en vigueur du règlement sur la Libye

Le règlement sur la Libye ne s'applique pas aux activités ou aux opérations ayant eu lieu avant son entrée en vigueur. Toutefois, dans le cas de contrats non encore pleinement exécutés concernant des biens interdits ou des personnes désignées, les mesures prévues s'appliqueront. De plus, l'alinéa 7(2)(*a*) du règlement interdit expressément les opérations portant sur des biens se trouvant au Canada le 26 février 2011 ou après cette date dont est propriétaire ou que contrôle une personne désignée.

Exceptions et permis

Les articles 14 à 16 du règlement sur la Libye prévoient la délivrance d'attestations d'erreur sur l'identité, d'attestations de dépenses ordinaires et extraordinaires et d'attestations autorisant de procéder à certaines opérations découlant de contrats existant avant la prise du règlement. Il est à noter que ces exceptions s'appliquent uniquement aux activités visées à l'article 7 du règlement, et qu'elles requièrent pour la plupart l'approbation préalable du Conseil de sécurité des Nations Unies.

La procédure à suivre pour demander la délivrance de ces attestations est établie aux articles 14 à 16 du règlement que vous pouvez consulter à l'adresse suivante: <http://www.international.gc.ca/sanctions/libya-libye.aspx?lang=fra>.

L'IFF qui détermine qu'elle s'apprête à procéder à une opération interdite à l'article 8 du règlement peut demander au ministre des Affaires étrangères de lui délivrer un permis l'autorisant à entreprendre ou à poursuivre l'opération. Vous pouvez consulter le Décret concernant l'autorisation par permis à l'adresse suivante: <http://www.international.gc.ca/sanctions/libya-libye.aspx?lang=fra>.

Traitement des opérations financières vers ou en provenance de [la] Libye

Les sanctions mises en place contre la Libye n'imposent pas de restrictions sur toutes les opérations financières vers ou en provenance de la Libye; ces opérations demeurent permises, pourvu qu'elles ne tombent pas sous le coup de l'une des interdictions prévues aux articles 7 et 8. Habituellement, les opérations interdites impliquent des personnes désignées ou leurs biens, ou sont effectuées au nom et au profit d'une personne désignée. Il faut examiner chaque opération individuellement, en tenant compte des différences, expliquées précédemment, entre les articles 7 et 8. Toutes opérations portant sur des fonds ou autres biens d'une personne désignée, tel le gouvernement de la Libye (y compris la Banque centrale de la Libye), est interdite.

Les interdictions prévues dans le règlement s'appliquent aux personnes au Canada ainsi qu'aux Canadiens à l'étranger. Les termes "personne" et "Canadien" sont définis dans la *Loi sur les mesures économiques spéciales.*

Les succursales étrangères d'IFF qui ne sont pas dotées d'une personnalité juridique distincte d'une IFF constituée ou prorogée sous le régime de la *Loi sur les banques* ou de la *Loi sur les sociétés d'assurances* sont assujetties aux obligations prévues par le règlement.

Les filiales étrangères d'IFF peuvent également être assujetties aux obligations prévues dans le règlement suivant leur structure juridique, la nature des opérations qu'elles facilitent (soit la mesure dans laquelle l'opération est effectuée exclusivement par l'institution mère) et la mesure dans laquelle des Canadiens participent à l'exploitation de la filiale étrangère.

Déclaration à la Gendarmerie royale du Canada

Une institution financière canadienne qui constate l'existence de biens se trouvant en sa possession ou à sa disposition dont elle a des motifs de croire qu'ils appartiennent à une personne désignée ou sont à la disposition de celle-ci, ou qui détient des renseignements au sujet d'une opération, prévue ou ayant déjà eu lieu, portant sur des biens visés par le règlement sur la Libye, est tenue d'en faire la déclaration sur-le-champ à la Gendarmerie royale du Canada (GRC) et au Service canadien du renseignement de sécurité (SCRS).

INTERNATIONAL ENVIRONMENTAL LAW

Relationship between the International Joint Commission and the Department of the Environment Act

On 30 August 2011, the Legal Branch commented in the following terms on the relationship between the International Joint Commission (IJC) and the Department of the Environment Act in the context of two legal opinions written in the past and also an unattributed assertion that Canada and the United States have, to some extent, surrendered their authority to the IJC:

We had the opportunity of considering a 1999 opinion as further considered in 2007 and especially took interest in the various legislative changes that this section has undergone through the decades. As you know, the current version of Section 4 (1) (e) of the *Department of the Environment Act* (DEA) gives the Minister of the Environment a power to enforce rules or regulations by the IJC [International Joint Commission] "in so far as they related to the preservation and enhancement of the quality of the natural environment" (that particular language was adopted by Parliament in 1978). To our knowledge this power has never been practically exercised in any instance; nor are we aware of any earlier versions of this section being put to a practical use by any Minister.

We would have the following preliminary comments. First, the power to enforce under the DEA is subject to the qualification that it cannot be a power assigned by law to any other department, a significant fact acknowledged in the 2007 piece. Now the *International Boundary Waters Treaty Act* (IBWTA) has a licensing provision (albeit also not yet exercised) and also somewhat obscure language in Section 3 that purports to "amend and alter the laws of Canada and the provinces to permit, authorize and sanction the performance of the obligations undertaken by [Canada], and so as to sanction, confer and impose the various rights, duties, obligations intended by the treaty to be conferred or imposed or to exist within Canada." The 1999 opinion did not consider the possible interplay between Section 4 (1) (e) of the DEA and Section 3 of the IBWTA and of course could not compare Section 4 to the IBWTA licensing regime since [the] opinion was written prior to the adoption of that regime, though such an enactment was contemplated when the 1999 opinion was being written. The 2007 opinion agrees that the Minister of the Environment's authority is limited by whatever authority is given to the Minister for Foreign Affairs under the IBWTA and we would naturally agree.

The authority given to enforce originally related to pollution, *which is strictly limited to the second arm of Article IV* of the Boundary Waters Treaty, and the Orders of Approval issued over the years by the IJC only dealt with levels and flows as contemplated in Articles III and the first arm of Article IV, not the second arm of Article IV. The language is certainly broader today ("preservation and enhancement of the quality of the natural environment"), but we would be cautious to conclude that this concept is a central one to the Orders of Approval issued under Articles III and IV. The IJC is grappling today in its review of the Saint Lawrence/Lake Ontario Order to consider if it has any jurisdiction to consider environmental effects and that might reflect upon the extent of the authority of the Minister of the Environment under the DEA as well.

Given the licensing power and also the language of Section 3, there is an interesting question of what residual authority remains to the Minister of the Environment under Section 4 of his statute. We would not be surprised if the IBWTA has substantially occupied the field but would hesitate to conclude that today.

Given our views, and those expressed in 1999 and 2007, we can see no merit in the following statement which asserts that both Canada and the USA somehow gave up their sovereign power to the IJC in the sense of providing resources to enforce the IJC's Orders:

> Canada and the United States gave up part of their sovereign power to the IJC when they signed the Boundary Waters Treaty, and anything that flows from IJC Orders is for the two governments to provide resources to enforce the Orders. Thus the 1914 Orders and subsequent supplementary orders led to not just one of quasi-judicial enforcer who but [*sic*]also participates in actual day-to-day operations in Lake Superior and (Lake Ontario as per 1952 and 1956 Orders) outflow regulation. These responsibilities cannot be delegated to provincial or municipal agencies, and definitely not to utilities (self-regulating).

Certainly both countries desired the IJC to issue orders of approval to manage jointly held bodies of water rather than each country unilaterally doing so as they did prior to the conclusion of the Treaty. The IJC is an institution that is neither a creature of Canada nor the USA and as such has played a highly useful role in managing the two nations' shared water resources. But in the matter of providing resources in the form of personnel or financial support, the IJC has no compulsive authority to demand either from the two governments. The negotiating history of the Boundary Waters treaty illustrates again and again that the USA Administration was quite cautious in the authority given to the IJC and as illustrated by Article X, would only provide an arbitral authority to the IJC if the USA Senate provided its advice and consent, thereby ensuring it would never take place. There is no language in the treaty that would enable us to conclude that the USA legislative branch surrendered any of its appropriation power to the IJC, let alone to the USA Administration on the IJC's behalf.

We also contest the suggestion that the IJC is a *quasi-judicial* enforcer. In fact, as recognized both in 1999 and 2007, the IJC's Orders of Approval are not enforceable at all in either Canadian or US Courts, which is an essential characteristic of a quasi-judicial act. They can become enforceable in Canadian courts if a parallel license is issued by the Minister under the regime of the IBWTA but then it is the license being enforced, not the Order of Approval. In the USA, enforcement is tied to a license issued by the USA Federal Energy Regulatory Commission (FERC) without which IJC Orders in the USA have no practical legal effect. Therefore, to describe them as quasi-judicial, is simply in error.

INTERNATIONAL HUMAN RIGHTS LAW

Pakistan's Reservations with Regard to the International Covenant on Civil and Political Rights

On 27 June 2011, the Legal Branch submitted the following objection to Pakistan's reservations with regard to the International Covenant on Civil and Political Rights:

The Government of Canada has carefully examined the reservations made by the Government of the Islamic Republic of Pakistan upon ratification of the *International Covenant on Civil and Political Rights*, which declare that:

- the provisions of Articles 3, 6, 7, 18 and 19 shall be so applied to the extent that they are not repugnant to the Provisions of the Constitution of Pakistan and the Sharia laws;
- the provisions of Articles 12 shall be so applied as to be in conformity with the Provisions of the Constitution of Pakistan;
- With respect to Article 13, the Government of the Islamic Republic of Pakistan reserves its right to apply its law relating to foreigners;
- the provisions of Articles 25 shall be so applied to the extent that they are not repugnant to the Provisions of the Constitution of Pakistan; and

- the Government of the Islamic Republic of Pakistan does not recognize the competence of the Committee provided for in Article 40 of the Covenant.

The Government of Canada considers that reservations that consist of a general reference to national law or to the prescriptions of the Islamic Sharia constitute, in reality, reservations with a general, indeterminate scope. This makes it impossible to identify the modifications to obligations under the Covenant that each reservation purports to introduce and impossible for the other States Parties to the Covenant to know the extent to which Pakistan has accepted the obligations of the Covenant, an uncertainty that is unacceptable, especially in the context of treaties related to human rights.

The Government of Canada further considers that the competence of the Committee to receive, study and comment on the reports submitted by States Parties as provided for in Article 40 of the Covenant is essential to the implementation of the Covenant. Through its function and its activity, the Human Rights Committee plays an essential role in monitoring the fulfilment of the obligations of the States Parties to the Convention. Participation in the reporting mechanism outlined in Article 40, which is aimed at encouraging more effective implementation by States Parties of their treaty obligations, is standard practice of States Parties to the Covenant.

The Government of Canada notes that the reservations made by the Government of the Islamic Republic of Pakistan, addressing many of the most essential provisions of the Covenant, and aiming to exclude the obligations under those provisions, are incompatible with the object and purpose of the Covenant, and thus inadmissible under article 19(c) of the *Vienna Convention on the Law of Treaties.* In addition, Articles 6, 7 and 18 of the Covenant are among the provisions from which no derogation is allowed, according to Article 4 of the Covenant. The Government of Canada therefore objects to the aforesaid reservations made by the Government of the Islamic Republic of Pakistan.

This objection does not preclude the entry into force in its entirety of the Covenant between Canada and the Islamic Republic of Pakistan.

Pakistan's Reservations with Regard to the Convention against Torture

On 27 June 2011, the Legal Branch submitted the following objection to Pakistan's reservations with regard to the Convention against Torture:

The Government of Canada has carefully examined the reservations made by the Government of the Islamic Republic of Pakistan upon ratification of the Convention against Torture and Other Cruel, Inhuman or Degrading Treatment or Punishment, in accordance with which the government of the Islamic Republic of Pakistan declares that:

> [T]he provisions of Articles 4, 6, 12, 13 and 16 shall be so applied to the extent that they are not repugnant to the Provisions of the Constitution of Pakistan and the Sharia laws.

The Government of Canada considers that a reservation that consists of a general reference to national law or to the prescriptions of the Islamic Sharia constitutes, in reality, a reservation with a general, indeterminate scope. Such a reservation makes it impossible to identify the modifications to obligations under the Convention that it purports to introduce and impossible for the other States Parties to the Convention to know the extent to which Pakistan has accepted the obligations of the Convention, an uncertainty that is unacceptable, especially in the context of treaties related to human rights.

The Government of Canada notes that the above-mentioned reservations made by the Government of the Islamic Republic of Pakistan, addressing many of the most essential provisions of the Convention, and aiming to exclude the obligations under those provisions, are incompatible with the object and purpose of the Convention, and thus inadmissible under article 19(c) of the *Vienna Convention on the Law of Treaties*. The Government of Canada therefore objects to the aforesaid reservations made by the Government of the Islamic Republic of Pakistan.

This objection does not preclude the entry into force in its entirety of the Convention between Canada and the Islamic Republic of Pakistan.

INTERNATIONAL LAW OF TREATIES

Russia's Unilateral "Suspension" of Implementation of Its Obligations under the Conventional Forces in Europe Treaty – The Case for Counter-Measures

In a legal opinion dated 24 November 2011, the Legal Branch wrote:

Under customary international law, counter-measures are permitted against a party to a treaty, by another party or parties, as a response to a breach of treaty obligations. They must be distinguished from the alternative actions provided for in the Vienna Convention on the Law of Treaties.

The test for the appropriate application of counter-measures was set out by the International Court of Justice in the 1997 *Gabčíkovo* case, where the conditions that must be satisfied were outlined as follows:

1. Counter-measures must be taken in response to a previous international wrong of another state and directed against that state;
2. The injured state must have called on the other state to discontinue its wrongful conduct or make reparation for it;
3. The purpose must be to induce the other state to comply with its obligations; and
4. The effects of the counter-measure must be proportionate to the injury suffered, taking account of the rights in question, and therefore the counter-measure must be reversible.[5]

An analysis of the current situation indicates that counter-measures are an appropriate response to Russia's purported unilateral "suspension" of its obligations under the *Treaty on Conventional Armed Forces in Europe* (CFE Treaty)[6] in December 2007, as well as its non-compliance since with its CFE Treaty obligations regarding data exchange, notifications and inspections. Detailed analysis follows below.

I. Previous wrongful act

To be considered legal under international law, counter-measures must be imposed in response to a "wrongful act" by one state, in this case, Russia's December 2007 unilateral "suspension" of its obligations under the CFE Treaty and, since then, continuing non-compliance with the Treaty's requirements involving information exchange, notifications and inspections. In order to determine whether counter-measures can be justified, it must first be determined that Russia's actions were wrongful at international law.

A. Illegal "suspension"

On July 14, 2007, Russian President Putin officially decreed that "[e]xceptional circumstances surrounding the CFE Treaty have led the Russian Federation to consider suspending its participation in the Treaty until NATO members ratify the Adapted Treaty and begin to implement the document in good faith." The announcement did not invoke Article XIX (the "Extraordinary Events" clause) of the CFE Treaty, but offered the following six "exceptional circumstances that affect the security of the Russian Federation" in support of Russia's decision to "suspend":

1. The failure of Bulgaria, Hungary, Poland, Romania, Slovakia and the Czech Republic to make the necessary changes in the composition

[5] *Case Concerning the Gabčíkovo-Nagymaros Project (Hungary v Slovakia)*, [1997] ICJ Rep 7 [*Gabčíkovo-Nagymaros* case].

[6] Treaty on Conventional Armed Forces in Europe, 19 November 1990, 30 ILM 6 (1991),online: <http://www.osce.org/documents/doclib/1990/11/13752_en.pdf>.

of group of states party to the Treaty on the accession of these countries to NATO;

2. The excessive parties to the CFE Treaty that belong to NATO, and the exclusive group that formed among CFE Treaty members as a result of the widening of the alliance;
3. The negative impact of the planned deployment of U.S. conventional forces in Bulgaria and Romania because of this exclusive group mentality;
4. The failure of a number of parties of the CFE Treaty to comply with the political obligations contained in the Istanbul Agreements relating to the early ratification of the Adapted Treaty;
5. The failure of Hungary, Poland, Slovakia and the Czech Republic to comply with commitments accepted in Istanbul to adjust their territorial ceilings;
6. Estonia, Latvia and Lithuania's failure to participate in the CFE Treaty has adverse effects on Russia's ability to implement its political commitments to military containment in the northwestern part of the Russian Federation. Estonia, Latvia and Lithuania's actions result in a territory in which there are no restrictions on the deployment of conventional forces, including other countries' forces.

The statement also indicated that the "suspension" is "in conformity with international law."[7]

B. "Suspension" in accordance with VCLT

The termination of treaty obligations is governed by the *Vienna Convention on the Law of Treaties* (VCLT).[8] The VCLT provides for a series of circumstances under which a state may terminate or suspend its treaty obligations. The first is in accordance with the treaty itself.

a. Treaty provisions

The CFE Treaty does not provide for its unilateral suspension. Article XIX(2) of the Treaty does provide for withdrawal from the Treaty if a party "decides that extraordinary events related to the subject matter of the Treaty have jeopardised its national interests."

Russia has argued that the withdrawal provision allows for the lesser action of Treaty suspension. This argument has been widely repudiated by

7 President of Russia, "Information on the Decree On Suspending the Russian Federation's Participation in the Treaty on Conventional Armed Forces in Europe and Related International Agreements," 14 July 2007, online: <http://kremlin.ru/eng/text/docs/2007/07/137839.shtml>.

8 Vienna Convention on the Law of Treaties, 23 May 1969, 1155 UNTS 331 [VCLT].

treaty law scholars and experts. The general customary international law norm that applies is "to express one thing implies the exclusion of the other." In other words, if the drafters had wanted to allow for suspension of the Treaty through Article XIX(2), they would have made it explicit.

b. Consent of the parties

The VCLT also provides that the operation of a Treaty may be suspended with the consent of the parties. This is not the case here. Clearly, the parties to the CFE Treaty did not consent to the "suspension"; a NATO statement dated December 12, 2007, declared that "NATO Allies deeply regret" Russia's decision.[9] This sentiment has been consistently echoed by Allies in their official statements. At the 2009, Strasbourg-Kehl Summit, Allies expressed deep concern:

> that since 12 December 2007, Russia has continued its unilateral "suspension" of its legal obligations under the CFE Treaty ... These actions run counter to our common objective of preserving the long-term viability of the CFE regime and we call upon Russia to resume its implementation without further delay. Because of our commitment to cooperative security and fulfilment of international agreements as well as the importance we attach to the confidence that results from military transparency and predictability, we have continued fully to implement the Treaty despite Russia's "suspension." However, the current situation, where NATO CFE Allies implement the Treaty while Russia does not, cannot last indefinitely.[10]

Most recently, at the 2010 NATO Summit in Lisbon, Allies reiterated that "the current situation, where NATO CFE Allies implement the Treaty while Russia does not, cannot continue indefinitely."[11]

The suspension with consent provision also requires consultation between the state seeking to suspend the treaty and the other parties to the

9 Alliance statement on the Russian Federation's "suspension" of its CFE obligations, NATO Press Release no 139 (12 December 2007), online: <http://www.nato.int/cps/en/natolive/news_15500.htm?mode=pressrelease>.

10 Strasbourg/Kehl Summit Declaration issued by the Heads of State and Government participating in the meeting of the North Atlantic Council in Strasbourg/Kehl, NATO Press Release no 044 (2009), 4 April 2009, online: <http://www.nato.int/cps/en/natolive/news_52837.htm?mode=pressrelease>.

11 Lisbon Summit Declaration issued by the Heads of State and Government participating in the meeting of the North Atlantic Council in Lisbon, NATO Press Release no 155 (2010), 20 November 2010, online: <http://www.nato.int/cps/en/natolive/official_texts_68828htm?mode=pressrelease>.

treaty. Despite being announced beforehand, Russia's intended "suspension" was not a topic at a June 2007 Extraordinary CFE Conference, so there appears to effectively have been no "consultation with the other contracting states" as required by the VCLT.

c. Supervening treaty

The VCLT also provides that a treaty may be suspended if a supervening treaty on the same subject matter is concluded between the parties. Again, this is not the case here. The 1999 CFE Adaptation Agreement[12] might have qualified as a supervening treaty as it was conceived as an update to the CFE Treaty and Russia and the other CFE Parties were the intended parties. The Agreement, however, has not entered into force due to a lack of ratifications. To date, only four states have ratified the Adaptation Agreement, which would require ratification by all 30 CFE state parties to enter into force.

d. Impossibility

The VCLT also provides that a party may invoke impossibility of performance as a means of terminating, withdrawing from or suspending a treaty due to at least temporary "disappearance or destruction of an object indispensible for the execution of the treaty."[13] In terms of what circumstances might render a treaty's operation impossible, the International Law Commission has mentioned as possibilities the submergence of an island or the destruction of a dam.[14] No such indispensible object has been lost here, even temporarily. The six circumstances offered by President Putin in July 2007 are in the nature of political objections. As important as these concerns are from the Russian perspective, they do not reflect a missing "indispensible object" that would render Russia incapable of performing its obligations under the treaty.

e. Fundamental change in circumstances

The VCLT also provides that a fundamental change in circumstances can be invoked for terminating, withdrawing or suspending a treaty under strictly defined conditions. This ground may not be invoked unless the change is of circumstances existing at the time of the conclusion of the

12 Agreement on the Adaptation of the Treaty on Conventional Armed Forces in Europe, 19 November 1999, online: <http://www.osce.org/documents/doclib/1999/11/13760_en.pdf>.

13 VCLT, *supra* note 8, Article 61(1).

14 Cited in Anthony Aust, *Modern Treaty Law and Practice,* 2nd edition (Cambridge: Cambridge University Press, 2007) at 297.

treaty; the change is "fundamental;" the change was not foreseen by the parties when they concluded the treaty; the existence of the circumstances constituted an essential basis of the consent of the parties to be bound by the treaty and the effect of the change was "radically to transform the extent of the obligations still to be performed under the treaty."[15]

The fundamental change in circumstances language has been invoked many times, but so far it has not been applied by an international tribunal. In *Gabčíkovo,* the ICJ rejected Hungary's argument that profound political changes which diminish the economic viability of a project, progress in environmental knowledge or the development of new norms of international law constituted a fundamental change in circumstances. The Court emphasised that the stability of treaty relations dictates that this VCLT provision only be applied in exceptional cases.[16] Given the strictness of the VCLT requirements as interpreted by the ICJ, it is extremely unlikely that any of the six factors cited by Russia would qualify.

f. Material breach

The VCLT also provides for a party to a multilateral treaty that is "specially affected" by a material breach of the treaty by another party to suspend operation of the treaty vis-à-vis the defaulting party. In this case, Russia has suspended operation of the treaty vis-à-vis all other parties.[17] To justify its "suspension" under the VCLT, Russia would need to argue that all other CFE parties were in material breach. A material breach is defined by the VCLT as "a repudiation of the Treaty not sanctioned by the VCLT," or "the violation of a provision essential to the accomplishment of the object and purpose of the treaty."[18] It is worth noting that the test for establishing a material breach is a high one. In the *Gabčíkovo* case, the ICJ interpreted the relevant VCLT article 60 in a rigorous manner:

> [T]he Court is of the view that it is only a material breach of the treaty itself, by a State party to that treaty, which entitles the other party to rely on it as a ground for terminating the treaty. The violation of other treaty rules or of rules of general international law may justify the taking of certain measures, including countermeasures, by the injured State, but it does not constitute a ground for termination under the law of treaties.[19]

15 VCLT, *supra* note 8, Article 62.

16 *Gabčíkovo-Nagymaros* case, *supra* note 5 at para 104.

17 VCLT, *supra* note 8, Article 60.

18 *Ibid.* Article 60(3).

19 *Gabčíkovo-Nagymaros* case, *supra* note 5 at para 106.

While Russia has not argued material breach, do any of the six exceptional circumstances proffered by Putin qualify as a material breach of the CFE Treaty by the other parties? Clearly the other CFE States Parties have not repudiated the CFE Treaty. Given the definition of material breach, and the ICJ's strict interpretation of the material breach concept, it is difficult to see how any of the six political circumstances outlined by Russia could amount to a violation of an essential provision of the Treaty, given that they related to ongoing states of affairs or issues outside the ambit of the Treaty. Since the circumstances enumerated by Russia existed for several years before Russia implemented its unilateral "suspension" an argument could also be made that Russia in essence acquiesced to their existence. This would weaken any case made by Russia to the effect that these circumstances constituted either a "fundamental change in circumstances" or a material breach of the CFE's provisions by the other States Parties.

In short, Russia's "suspension" does not conform to the CFE Treaty's provisions, nor is Russia's "suspension" salvaged under the provisions of the VCLT.

In addition to Russia's unlawful "suspension" of its obligations under the CFE treaty — as outlined above, a wrongful act in itself that would allow for the lawful imposition of counter-measures — Russia has, since December 2007, ceased complying with specific provisions of the CFE Treaty related to annual data exchange, notifications and inspections. As there is no basis in international law for these actions, they would also constitute wrongful acts justifying the imposition of counter-measures in accordance with the first part of the *Gabčíkovo* test.

II. Call to discontinue

The second element of the *Gabčíkovo* test for the lawful application of counter-measures involves a requirement for the state seeking to impose counter-measures to first have called upon the other state to discontinue its wrongful conduct. This element is satisfied in the present case by the public statements, since December 2007, by NATO Allies that express deep regret at Russia's unilateral "suspension" of its obligations under the CFE Treaty and call on Russia to resume implementing its obligations under the Treaty.

III. Induce compliance

The third element of the *Gabčíkovo* test requires that the purpose of counter-measures must be to induce the other state to comply with its obligations. This would be satisfied by those Parties imposing counter-measures to confirm and emphasise, in any public statements or notifications to the Treaty depositary, that the counter-measures are intended to induce Russia to comply with its obligations under the Treaty. Those countries imposing counter-measures should also review the situation on a regular basis to ensure that counter-measures continue to serve the purpose of inducing Russia to return to compliance with the Treaty.

IV. Proportionality/reversibility

The final element of the *Gabčíkovo* test requires any counter-measures to be proportional to the original wrongful act, and therefore reversible. In this case, should each Party seeking to impose counter-measures cease implementing vis-à-vis Russia the obligations that Russia unilaterally ceased implementing in December 2007, namely the annual data exchange on conventional arms holdings in Europe provided for under the CFE Treaty, notifications under the Treaty and the acceptance of inspections by Russia, they would appear proportional to the wrongful act they are intended to address. They would also be reversible, in that they would create no impediment to resuming these activities vis-à-vis Russia upon Russia's return to compliance with its CFE Treaty obligations. In this regard, the Russian MFA released a statement elaborating on President Putin's decree announcing its unilateral "suspension" in December 2007. The statement intimated the practical effects of the "suspension" on the Russian Federation's obligations under the CFE Treaty: "[I]n particular, providing information and receiving and conducting inspections will be temporarily suspended."[20] (Note that notifications are an integral part of the inspections regime and would also be captured by the Russian MFA's statement.)

V. ILC elements

The International Law Commission's (ILC) Articles on state responsibility, adopted by the UN General Assembly in 2002, also address counter-measures.[21] These essentially aim to codify the *Gabčíkovo* test with additional procedural conditions. These additional elements may not constitute customary international law and it is difficult to determine the exact weight to be attributed to the work of the ILC.

The ILC Articles require an injured state, before taking counter-measures, to (1) call upon the responsible State to fulfil its relevant obligations, (2) to notify the wrongdoing State of any decision to take counter-measures and (3) to offer to negotiate with that State. The first of these requirements has been discussed above. Absent a compelling rationale to the contrary,

20 Ministry of Foreign Affairs of the Russian Federation, *Statement by Russia's Ministry of Foreign Affairs Regarding Suspension by Russian Federation of Treaty on Conventional Armed Forces in Europe*, 12 December 2007, online: <http://www.mid.ru/brp_4.nsf/e78a48070f128a7b43256999005bcbb3/10da6dd509e4d164c32573af004cc4be?>.

21 UNGA Resolution A/RES/56/83, adopted on 28 January 2002.

the second and third parts would likely be satisfied with language in the statements notifying Russia of a country's decision to impose counter-measures to the effect that that country remains committed to conventional arms control and ready to continue to engage with Russia on the issue, including on addressing the issue of Russia's ongoing non-compliance with its Treaty obligations.

The ILC Articles also require that counter-measures may not be taken, and if already taken must be suspended without undue delay if (1) the internationally wrongful act has ceased; and (2) the dispute is pending before a court or tribunal which has the authority to make decisions binding on the parties. Neither of these appears to be the current case, but it is important to note that any counter-measures applied should be suspended in good time should Russia return to implementing its CFE obligations.

Finally, the ILC Articles require that counter-measures shall be terminated as soon as the responsible State has complied with its obligations under international law.

INTERNATIONAL TRADE LAW

World Trade Organization — Agreement on Technical Barriers to Trade — Definition of "Technical Regulation"

In Canada's Executive Summary of its Third Party Oral Submission to the WTO panel dated 29 October 2010 in the case of *United States – Measures Concerning the Importation, Marketing and Sale of Tuna and Tuna Products*, the Legal Branch wrote:

The second sentence of the definition of "technical regulation" sets out categories of subject matter that are not examples of "product characteristics." Rather, these categories are independent of those found in the first sentence. Thus, the Appellate Body's requirement that a "technical regulation" must lay down one or more product characteristics should be expanded. The construction of the definition of "technical regulation" supports this interpretation.

First, the two sentences of the definition each contain a number of categories of subject matter that address different aspects or characteristics of the product at issue. The categories in the first sentence address characteristics intrinsic to the product itself and process or production methods (PPMs) that are related to those intrinsic product characteristics. The categories in the second sentence address characteristics extrinsic to the product; they encompass presentational or informational aspects of the product.

Second, the use of "also" and "deal exclusively with" at the beginning of the second sentence indicate that the categories covered by the second sentence are additional to, and distinct from those covered by the first sentence.

Third, the use of the word "it" as the subject of the second sentence instead of the word "they" indicates that the subject of the second sentence is the "document" rather than the "product characteristics." Thus, there is no connotation that the subject matter categories covered by the second sentence are in some way related to or constitute "product characteristics."

Finally, the use of the disjunctive word "or" in the first sentence indicates that the first sentence also refers to categories of subject matter that could be separate and distinct from one another. Thus, there are categories within the first sentence, such as some PPMs, that may be the subject of a technical regulation without constituting product characteristics.

World Trade Organization – Agreement on Technical Barriers to Trade – Interpretation of Article 2.1

In a written response to questions from the Panel dated 4 October 2010 in the case of *United States – Certain Country of Origin Labelling (COOL) Requirements*, the Legal Branch wrote:

Article 2.1 of the *TBT Agreement* mirrors the non-discrimination requirement under Article III:4 of the *GATT 1994*, which prohibits less favourable treatment of imported products. In fact, the wording of the actual obligation is identical, *i.e.*, that a WTO Member is prohibited from according treatment less favourable than that accorded to like products of national origin. Both provisions apply to internal regulatory measures and therefore the interpretation of the terms found in those provisions, as developed by the jurisprudence under Article III:4, should be the same. Much like the WTO Agreement (including all the covered agreements), those provisions should be interpreted harmoniously, in keeping with the second recital in the preamble to the *TBT Agreement* that states that the Agreement is to further the objectives of the *GATT 1994*.

Article 2.1 of the *TBT Agreement* includes the no-less-favourable-treatment requirement of domestic and imported "like" products, and extends the scope of the obligation to "like" products originating from any country. Thus, Article 2.1 combines the National Treatment and Most-Favoured-Nation (MFN) obligations. Article III:4 of the *GATT 1994* does not do this. However, Article I:1 of the *GATT 1994*, which contains the MFN obligation, applies to the subject matter of Article III:4.

The *TBT Agreement* does not have a stand-alone MFN obligation like the *GATT 1994* and therefore both the MFN and National Treatment obligation are combined in the provision that addresses discriminatory technical regulations. If the drafters of the *TBT Agreement* had a different understanding of the terms "like product" or "less favourable treatment" as they apply to national treatment or MFN, they could have drafted two separate provisions on national treatment and MFN.

Nevertheless, in terms of "like products," the Appellate Body has said that the "accordion of 'likeness' stretches and squeezes in different places as different provisions of the WTO Agreement." It is therefore possible that the test for "likeness" within the meaning of *TBT* Article 2.1 may be slightly different as compared to the test for "likeness" under *GATT 1994* Articles I:1 or III:4. However, in this case, it is well established that products and service suppliers are "like" when they are the same except for origin. That principle is well accepted in *GATT* Article III:2 and III:4, and *GATS* Article XVII. There is no reason to find otherwise for *TBT* Article 2.1. Since the COOL measure makes labelling distinctions on livestock based only on where that livestock is born, raised, and slaughtered, imported livestock must be "like" domestic born and raised livestock.

The term "treatment no less favourable" has the same meaning in relation to national treatment and MFN under both the *TBT Agreement* and the *GATT 1994*. The fact that Article 2.1 combines national treatment and MFN does not warrant a different interpretation depending on whether the violation is on a national treatment or MFN basis. The MFN clause under Article I:1 as well as the national treatment obligation in Article III:4, cover instances of both *de jure* and *de facto* discrimination. There is no reason to adopt a different approach under *TBT* Article 2.1 to the scope of the "less favourable treatment" obligation when the MFN and national treatment bases are combined.

World Trade Organization — Agreement on Technical Barriers to Trade — Interpretation of Article 2.2

In a written submission to the World Trade Organization dated 29 October 2010 in the case of *United States – Certain Country of Origin Labelling (COOL) Requirements*, the Legal Branch wrote:

[T]he proper interpretation of a technical regulation's compliance with this Article requires a five-step test:

1. Determine if the technical regulation restricts international trade. If it does not, the measure cannot violate Article 2.2.

2. Identify the objective of the technical regulation.
3. Determine if the objective of the technical regulation is legitimate. If it is not, the technical regulation violates Article 2.2.
4. Determine if the technical regulation, alone or in connection with other measures, fulfils the legitimate objective. If it does not do that, the technical regulation violates Article 2.2.
5. Assess other alternative measures that would fulfil the legitimate objective in a less trade restrictive way, "taking into account the risks non-fulfillment would create." If there are such alternative measures, the technical regulation violates Article 2.2.

...

If a technical regulation does not restrict international trade it cannot violate *TBT* Article 2.2 since such a measure would never create "unnecessary obstacles to international trade" or be "more trade restrictive than necessary." Technical regulations are not by definition "trade restrictive." However, if a technical regulation imposes any restriction on international trade it meets this element of the test.

[T]he Panel should determine the objective of a measure ... This determination should focus on the "design, the architecture and the structure" of that measure ... [T]hat focus should be supplemented as necessary with additional information to determine the objective of the measure, including its legislative history ... [I]n the context of *GATT* Article III:2 what is key is whether the measure affords protection[;] intent is irrelevant. But in the context of *TBT* Article 2.2, intent is important, since the Article requires an assessment not only of the effect of a measure, but also its "objective" — something not required in *GATT* Article III:2 ...

Use of legislative history in statutory interpretation is not the same as using legislative history to determine the objective of a measure for purposes of *TBT* Article 2.2. Nevertheless, to the extent that there is an analogy, use of legislative history, including statements by those who design laws and regulations, is in keeping with the modern practice of statutory interpretation of many domestic tribunals, including civil law countries, common law countries generally, and the United States in particular. It is also consistent with the interpretation of treaty obligations in international law ...

If the objective of a measure is ... not specifically listed in *TBT* Article 2.2, then in order to determine its legitimacy in the next step of analysis, it is necessary to define the objective with an appropriate level of specificity, which in this instance needs to be high. It needs to be high in this case because "consumer information" as an objective can be for both legitimate and illegitimate purposes. For example, it would not be a legitimate objective to provide information to consumers in order to discriminate on the basis of race, to further protectionist purposes, or to require the provision of "information" that is false. Whether a given objective is defined with a sufficiently high level of specificity can only be determined on a case-by-case basis ...

A general term such as "*inter alia*" followed by specific terms means that the general term is limited to the type of items listed in the specific terms (a principle often referred to by the Latin term *ejusdem generis*). Thus, in order to determine whether an objective that is not specifically listed in Article 2.2 is a legitimate objective it is necessary to look to the specifically listed legitimate objectives. They are all important objectives recognized elsewhere in the covered agreements:

- national security requirements;
- protection of human health or safety, animal or plant life or health;
- protection of the environment; and
- the prevention of deceptive practices.

These listed objectives are reflected in the general exceptions in other covered agreements. It would therefore be reasonable to conclude that the type of items listed in the specific terms (and therefore the type to which the general term *inter alia* is restricted) covers objectives set out as general exceptions or other similar situations in the covered agreements. For example the important objective of protecting national treasures of artistic value (included in *GATT* Article XX(f)) might be legitimate within the meaning of *TBT* Article 2.2 ...

[E]ven if the Panel finds that [an] objective of the COOL measure is "providing information to consumers," this is not an objective of the type listed in *TBT* Article 2.2. "Consumer information" is a broad term, covering potentially hundreds of pieces of information about a product. At that level of generality it is not at the same level of importance as the legitimate objectives covered under *TBT* Article 2.2. It is therefore particularly important to define the objective with more precision for the analysis under *TBT* Article 2.2 ...

One potential purpose for providing information to consumers is to encourage them to favour U.S. domestic producers of livestock over foreign competitors. The use of such information for protectionist purposes is not legitimate, just as a direct protectionist objective is not ...

If the Panel finds that the COOL measure has a legitimate objective that it does fulfill, then it is still necessary to consider whether other alternative measures would fulfill that objective in a less trade-restrictive way. The assessment of alternative measures against the challenged technical regulation requires a focus on the risks non-fulfillment would create. Applying that test, both voluntary labelling and labelling based on substantial transformation would fulfill the legitimate objective, if one exists, of the COOL measure, while creating an equal or lesser risk of non-fulfillment of that objective.

World Trade Organization — GATT Article XI:2(a)'s Exception for Export Restrictions

In a written submission to the World Trade Organization dated 29 September 2011 in the case of *China-Measures Related to the Exportation of Various Raw Materials,* the Legal Branch wrote:

Article XI:2(a) permits WTO Members to temporarily apply restrictions to essential products such as food to prevent or relieve critical shortages.

The Panel concluded that the term "critical" in Article XI:2(a) indicates that a shortage must be of decisive importance or grave, or even rising to the level of a crisis or catastrophe. The Panel also found that Article XI:2(a) requires that measures in the form of restrictions or bans may be used on a temporary basis either to "prevent" or otherwise "relieve" such a shortage. The Panel found further that the requirement that measures be applied "temporarily" contextually informs the notion of "critical shortage." As a result, the Panel found that Article XI:2(a) does not permit a WTO Member to impose long-term measures to address an inevitable depletion of a finite resource.

China suggests that the Panel's interpretation excludes from the scope of the provision of Article XI:2(a) export restrictions on non-renewable, exhaustible natural resources. China errs in this criticism.

The Panel's finding on "critical shortage" permits a WTO Member to relieve a critical shortage of an exhaustible natural resource through temporary application of an export restriction. Consider the following: oil is a non-renewable resource. Suppose there is a conflict that has a negative impact on the capacity of several major oil producing countries. As a result, there is a shortage of oil over a period of years, causing significant effects on pricing and the global economy. A WTO Member with limited oil reserves, the producing capacity of which was not affected by the conflict, decides to take measures in the form of export restrictions to address the oil crisis. In that situation, the measures could be justified as applied to relieve a critical shortage of an essential product because the shortage is not caused only by the very fact that the resource is by its nature non-renewable. To assume otherwise would mean that any exhaustible resource could be subject to continued restrictions that would ignore the object and purpose of the express exception to trade rules concerning exhaustible natural resources set out in Article XX(g).

In its submission to the Panel, Canada emphasized that while the general focus of XI:2(a) is similar to GATT Article XX(g), the test is quite different. Notably, as there are no *chapeau* requirements that the measure not be "arbitrary or unjustifiable discrimination" or a "disguised restriction on international trade," there is a "heightened need to be attentive in considering whether a member meets the requirements of a paragraph in Article XI:2."

It its submissions, China mischaracterized Canada's position, parsing Canada's language to argue for a more liberal interpretation of Article XI:2 exceptions — the exact opposite of Canada's point.

Canada considers that the Panel correctly found that an interpretation of Article XI:2(a) that permits the application of a measure for a limited time under limited circumstances "would be in harmony with the protection that may be available to a Member under Article XX(g), which addresses the conservation of exhaustible natural resources." The Panel's finding that the absence in Article XI:2(a) of the safeguards found in the *chapeau* of GATT Article XX(g) "lends support to our view that a restriction or ban applied under Article XI:2(a) must be of a limited duration and not indefinite."

There is also no merit to China's suggestion that the Panel found Article XI:2(a) and Article XX(g) of the GATT to be mutually exclusive. The Panel did not come to that conclusion. Rather, the Panel concluded that a Member cannot use the exception.set out in Article XI:2(b) where the facts dictate that the Article XX(g) exception — conservation of exhaustible natural resources – is applicable.

Let us return to the WTO Member with limited oil reserves. Suppose that Member applies export restrictions as well as domestic restrictions to ensure the oil reserves will last 50 years. The export restrictions are challenged at the WTO as violating GATT Article XI:1. The Member could at that point invoke the GATT Article XX(g) exception on the basis that the restrictions "relate to the conservation of exhaustible natural resources" and "are made in conjunction with restrictions on domestic production or consumption." Suppose, further, that some years after the imposition of the initial export and domestic restrictions the conflict posited above erupts to affect the global production capacity. The Member decides to further limit exports of oil to relieve the critical shortage until the conflict is over. That additional export limit could potentially be justified under GATT Article XI:2(a) which permits "[e]xport prohibitions or restrictions temporarily applied to prevent or relieve critical shortages of foodstuffs or other products essential to the exporting [Member]." Both Article XX(g) and Article XI:2(a) could apply cumulatively in harmony with WTO practice. In other words, a critical shortage caused by a factor other than the resource's inherent exhaustibility can potentially support an export ban under Article XI:2(a).

World Trade Organization — China's Obligations in Its Accession Protocol Relating to Export Charges and the Application of GATT Article VIII to Export Charges

In a written submission to the World Trade Organization dated 29 September 2011 in the case of *China-Measures Related to the Exportation of Various Raw Materials,* the Legal Branch wrote:

The Panel found that payments made to the Chinese Government for the right to export are not subject to Article VIII:1(a), neither are they "charges applied to exports" subject to paragraph 11.3 of China's Accession Protocol. The United States appeals this finding, arguing that the payments violate GATT Article VIII:1(a) and paragraph 11.3 of the Accession Protocol.

Canada agrees with the United States that the Panel erred in finding that the export quota allocation charge complies with China's WTO obligations. Canada considers further that the charge constitutes a violation of paragraph 11.3 of China's Accession Protocol, or, in the alternative, a violation of GATT Article VIII:1(a).

Drawing from jurisprudence in relation to charges "on or in connection with" importation, Canada starts from the proposition that any state-imposed charge on exports falls within the scope of Article VIII. To interpret the provision otherwise would be to create a hole in the coverage of WTO law regulating exports.

Article VIII:1(a) provides in relevant part:

> All fees and charges of whatever character (other than import and export duties ...) imposed by contracting parties on or in connection with importation or exportation shall be limited in amount to the approximate cost of services rendered.

The Panel collapsed its analysis of whether the export quota allocation charge is a "fee" or "charge" within the meaning of GATT Article VIII with the question of whether the charge is imposed in connection with exportation. Canada considers that these matters should have been addressed separately: determine whether the export quota allocation charge is a "fee" or "charge," and then determine whether that fee or charge is imposed "on or in connection with" importation.

The Panel rightly found that the terms "fee" or "charge" cover "pecuniary burden, cost[s]" or "expense[s]" to an exporting enterprise. This is in keeping with findings that the term "charge" or "charges" in the GATT means "a pecuniary burden" and a "liability to pay money." Canada considers that on the facts of this case there is no dispute that the export quota allocation charge is both a "pecuniary burden" and a "liability" to pay money, and therefore is a "fee" or "charge" within the meaning of GATT Article VIII:1(a). The only issue, therefore, should be whether that fee or charge is imposed "on or in connection with" exportation.

The Panel agreed with the Parties that the term "on or in connection with" exportation has a broad temporal scope, including charges that are associated with, linked or logically related to exportation. Yet the Panel then erred in adding a restriction that "in connection with" exportation should be limited to "customs-related activities." This conclusion is not supported by the text of the provision, or the context provided by the rest of the GATT. Notably, the panel in *China – Auto Parts* found that the phrase "on or in connection with importation" covers a broader scope than the words "on importation." The latter requires a stricter temporal connection to the time when a product passes a Member's border, though the relevant charge may be collected or assessed at a later time. Yet the Panel further noted that the fact that a charge is administered by a customs authority is not determinative of its nature. Following this logic, a charge imposed as a requirement for importation would be considered "in connection" with importation, regardless of who administers it or when it is charged. There is no reason for a different analysis to apply in relation to exportation.

The Panel effectively read in a requirement that only charges collected in exchange for a "service rendered" may be considered as falling within the scope of Article VIII:1(a). The Panel further erred in placing undue emphasis on its finding that the export quota allocation charge is paid "in expectation of a future return" and that consequently it is not imposed "in connection with" exportation. These findings contradict the Panel's earlier conclusion that a broad temporal view is supported by the language "on or in connection with," and its factual finding that the remittance of the export quota allocation charges are a non-negotiable element of the exportation process. Further, acceptance of the Panel's reasoning would mean a WTO Member could circumvent its obligations under GATT Article II by imposing a charge for a "right to import" with related import licence requirements.

As noted above, unless the export quota allocation charge is an export duty it must violate GATT Article VIII:1(a) since it is not a charge that is limited to the approximate cost of a service rendered. However, if it is an export duty, then it would by definition fall within the scope of paragraph 11.3 of China's Accession Protocol as a tax or charge applied to exports. Canada considers that the charge is an export duty.

The term "export duty" is not defined in the GATT, nor has the term been considered in detail. However, the limited interpretation the term has received points to it having a broad scope. In the context of imports, it is well established that "other duties or charges" covers charges imposed for a variety of reasons, including payments that discriminate against imports, but excluding charges equivalent to internal taxes, anti-dumping or countervailing duties, or fees or charges commensurate with the costs of services rendered. A broad scope for the term "duty" is also consistent with usage in the Anti-Dumping Agreement, where a panel has found that a duty exists where there is a transfer of money from the importer (or, here, exporter) to the government.

Canada submits that the term "duty" in GATT Article XI similarly refers to all transfers of money from an exporter to the government that are not purportedly imposed for services rendered or applied in relation to the sale of goods and services inside a customs territory. This interpretation is analogous to the one adopted by the panel and Appellate Body in *India – Additional Import Duties*, where the term "other duties and charges" referred to in GATT Article II:1 was "defined in relation to" "ordinary customs duties" such that "other duties and charges" would only encompass charges that were not "ordinary customs duties."

Paragraph 11.3 of China's Accession Protocol obliges China to "eliminate all taxes and charges applied to exports unless specifically provided for in Annex 6 of [the] Protocol or applied in conformity with the provisions of Article VIII of the GATT 1994." None of the materials subject to the export quota allocation charge is listed in Annex 6 and, as set out above, the charge is not applied in conformity with Article VIII.

The Panel erred in finding that the export quota allocation charges are not "charges applied to exports" for the purposes of paragraph 11.3 of the Accession Protocol. The Panel based this conclusion on two key elements of reasoning.

First, the Panel found that the collection of the export quota allocation charge does not amount to the imposition of a fee or charge "in connection with" exportation within the meaning of Article VIII.

Second, the Panel found that paragraph 11.3 shares the same "thrust" of Article VIII such that no distinction should be made between "charges applied to exports" and "fees or charges imposed ... on or in connection with ... exportation." Canada agrees with this conclusion generally; however, since the Panel erred in finding that the export quota allocation charge is not imposed "on or in connection with" exportation, it came to the wrong conclusion regarding the applicability of paragraph 11.3 as a result. More specifically, it found that the export quota allocation charge is not a charge applied to exports.

As the Panel correctly noted, "... paragraph 11.3 deals with an obligation that does not otherwise exist in the GATT 1994: namely the prohibition on the use of export duties." In this regard, paragraph 11.3 specifically addresses what Article VIII does not — China's commitment to eliminate all taxes and charges applied to exports that are not provided for in Annex 6, and that are not approximate costs for services rendered as provided for in Article VIII.

GATT Article VIII and paragraph 11.3 of China's Accession Protocol together create a tightly woven mesh that catches all charges imposed by the Chinese government in connection with exportation. It is not possible for China to impose an export charge that is subject to neither Article VIII nor paragraph 11.3. The export allocation charge is paid to the Chinese government to obtain an export quota allocation. That allocation is required to obtain an export licence. That export licence is required to export products. Consequently, the export allocation charge must fall within the scope of one of these provisions. The fact that China has structured its exportation process such that a charge on exports has been administratively distanced from the actual act of exportation should not result in China being allowed to evade its obligations under WTO law.

World Trade Organization — Procurement for "Governmental Purposes"

In a written submission to the World Trade Organization dated 22 December 2011 in the case of *Canada – Certain Measures Affecting the Renewable Energy Sector*, the Legal Branch wrote:

The procurement of renewable electricity ... falls within the scope of GATT Article III:8(a). That Article removes laws, regulations and requirements that govern certain procurements from the obligations of Article III of the GATT and the TRIMs Agreement ...

Japan's claim that the FIT Program, including its contracts, is inconsistent with the national treatment obligation contained in GATT Article III:4 is unfounded. The FIT Program, including its contracts, is a program for the procurement of renewable electricity by the Government of Ontario in pursuit of its policy mandate to provide adequate and reliable electricity to the Ontario public from clean sources. Consequently, under GATT Article III:8(a), the FIT Program is not subject to the obligations of GATT Article III, including III:4 ...

When GATT Article III was being developed, some parties sought to have its obligations apply broadly to purchases by government. However, this proposal to expressly extend the national treatment obligation to government purchases was rejected. Instead, certain government procurements were removed from the scope of the national treatment obligation through what eventually became Article III:8(a) ...

Article III:8(a) preserves governments' flexibility to pursue public policy objectives through their procurements ...

Article III:8(a) does not exclude all laws, regulations and requirements that govern procurement from the national treatment obligations of Article III. The conditions in the provision, such as the requirement that the procurement is for "governmental purposes," impose limits on its scope. However, where a law, regulation or requirement falls within those limits, it is not subject to the national treatment obligations of Article III. Thus ... a Member is free to use the purchases within that law, regulation or requirement "as a policy tool to promote smaller business, local industry or advanced technologies." The Member is free to condition those purchases on the use of domestic goods or services without thereby breaching its Article III national treatment obligations. ...

On its face, Article III:8(a) provides that the obligations of Article III do not apply to:

- a law, regulation or requirement;
- which governs procurement by a governmental agency of a product which that agency purchases,

where that purchase is:

- for governmental purposes; and
- not with a view to commercial resale or with a view to use the product in the production of goods for commercial sale.

The Oxford Online Dictionary defines "product" as "[a]n object produced by a particular action or process; the result of mental or physical work or effort." Renewable electricity is such an "object," produced by the actions and processes at renewable electricity production facilities ...

The ordinary meaning of "procurement" is "[t]he action of obtaining something; acquisition ..." In Article III:8(a), this meaning is confirmed by the context, which refers to the "procurement by governmental agencies of products *purchased* ..." The ordinary meaning of "purchase" is "[t]o acquire in exchange for payment in money or an equivalent; to buy."

Thus, Article III:8(a) applies to the governmental acquisition of products by payment. The Ministerial Direction, and the terms of the FIT and microFIT Rules and contracts, confirm that the [Ontario Power Authority] (OPA) is acquiring renewable electricity by purchase: it is paying money in return for the delivery of that electricity into the transmission grid.

To fall in the scope of Article III:8(a), the FIT Program laws and requirements must *govern* the procurement of electricity ...

The ordinary meaning of "govern," endorsed by the panel in *EC – Customs Matters* in the context of Article X:3(b) of the GATT, is to "control, regulate, or determine (a person, another's actions, the course or issue of events)." There is nothing in the context of the word "govern" in Article III:8(a) that is inconsistent with this ordinary meaning. Nor is this ordinary meaning inconsistent with the object of Article III:8(a) to allow Members to use government procurement to pursue public policy. Thus, for the purposes of Article III:8(a), a measure "governing the procurement" is one that controls, regulates or determines that procurement ...

Section 25.35 of the *Electricity Act, 1998*, the Ministerial Direction and the FIT and microFIT Rules and contracts satisfy this definition. Together they provide the rules that are binding on, and control, regulate or determine, the OPA's purchases of renewable electricity under the FIT Program ...

To fall within the scope of Article III:8(a), the purchase governed by the law, regulation or requirement must be for "governmental purposes" ...

The ordinary meaning of "purpose" is "[t]he reason for which something is done or made, or for which it exists; the result or effect intended or sought; the end to which an object or action is directed; aim." The ordinary meaning of "governmental" is "[o]f or pertaining to government ..." Thus, a "purchase for governmental purposes" is a purchase for an aim of the government. Governments express their aims through legislation, regulations, policies and executive directions. Consequently, a purchase by a governmental agency, which is directed in legislation, regulations, policy or an executive direction is a purchase for governmental purposes. There is nothing in the context to the phrase "governmental purposes" that is inconsistent with this ordinary meaning. This ordinary meaning in context is also consistent with the object of Article III:8(a) to allow governments to use government procurement to pursue public policy ...

The OPA's purchase of renewable electricity under section 25.35 of the *Electricity Act, 1998*, the Ministerial Direction and the FIT and microFIT rules and contracts is a purchase in furtherance of an aim of the Government of Ontario. Specifically, the OPA purchases renewable electricity to help secure the supply of adequate and reliable electricity in Ontario from clean sources, as directed by the then Minister of Energy and Infrastructure, George Smitherman, in the Ministerial Direction. In that Direction, Minister Smitherman identified "[t]he objectives of the FIT Program" as including the objective to "[i]ncrease capacity of renewable energy supply to ensure adequate generation and reduce emissions." By purchasing renewable electricity, the OPA is furthering this aim of the Government of Ontario and, thereby, is purchasing for "governmental purposes" ...

To fall within the scope of Article III:8(a), a purchase must be for "governmental purposes" as well as not "with a view to commercial resale" ...

The ordinary meaning of "commercial," endorsed by the Appellate Body in *United States – Anti-Dumping and Countervailing Duties (China)* in the context of the SCM Agreement, is "interested in financial return rather than artistry; likely to make a profit; regarded as a mere matter of business." The ordinary meaning of "with a view to" is "with the aim of attaining; with the hope or intention of." Thus, the ordinary meaning of a purchase "with a view to commercial resale" is a purchase with an aim to resell for profit. There is nothing in the context to the phrase that is inconsistent with this ordinary meaning. It is also consistent with the object of Article III:8(a) to allow Members to use government procurement to pursue public policy ...

The OPA purchases renewable electricity with the aim to help secure a sufficient and reliable supply of electricity for Ontario consumers and to protect the environment – it does not purchase with an aim to resell for profit. Indeed, the *Electricity Act, 1998* prevents the Authority from doing anything with the aim to profit. Subsection 25.2(2) is entitled "Not for profit" and states that "[t]he business and affairs of the OPA shall be carried on without the purpose of gain ..." Consistent with subsection 25.2(2), the OPA does not aim to profit, nor does it profit in fact, from the sale of renewable electricity — the OPA simply recovers the cost of purchasing that renewable electricity. Thus, the OPA does not purchase renewable electricity with a view to its commercial resale ...

To fall within the scope of Article III:8(a), a purchase cannot be "with a view to commercial resale" but also cannot be "with a view to use in the production of goods for commercial sale" ...

As explained above, the ordinary meaning of "commercial" is with the aim of profit and the ordinary meaning of "with a view to" is "with the aim of attaining; with the hope or intention of." The ordinary meaning of "production" is "[t]he action or an act of producing, making, or causing anything; generation or creation *of* something; the fact or condition of being produced." Thus, the ordinary meaning of a purchase by a governmental agency of a product "with a view to use in the production of goods for commercial sale" is a purchase by the governmental agency of a product with the aim of making a good to sell for profit. There is nothing in the context to the phrase, or the object and purpose of Article III:8(a) or the GATT, which is inconsistent with this interpretation ...

The OPA is not purchasing renewable electricity with the aim of making a good to sell for profit. First, neither the OPA, nor any other part of the Government of Ontario, is using the renewable electricity which is purchased by the OPA to make any goods. The Government of Ontario, through the OPA, purchases the electricity for transmission into the grid. Thus, there is no production of goods for commercial sale.

Section 25.35 of the *Electricity Act, 1998* [S.O. 1998, c 15], the Ministerial Direction and the FIT and microFIT Rules and contracts are laws or requirements that satisfy the elements of Article III:8(a) of the GATT. Together, they provide the rules for the OPA's purchase of renewable electricity to secure the adequate and reliable supply of electricity for Ontario from clean sources. The OPA's purchase is a government procurement that fits squarely within the scope of Article III:8(a).

As such, section 25.35, the Ministerial Direction and the FIT and microFIT Rules and contracts are not subject to the national treatment obligations of GATT Article III. Consistent with the purpose behind the procurement exception, the Government of Ontario is free to use that procurement to pursue its policy objectives. Thus, the Government is free to condition the procurement of renewable electricity on production of that electricity through the use of local content. Those local content requirements, which are challenged by Japan in this dispute, are not subject to the obligations in GATT Article III and, therefore, cannot breach Article III:4.

LAW OF THE SEA

Northern Canada Vessel Traffic Services Zone Regulations (NORDREG)

On 22 September 2010, the United States and the International Association of Independent Tanker Owners (INTERTANKO) made a submission to the Maritime Safety Committee of the International Maritime Organization (IMO) requesting that the committee determine that Canada's Northern Canada Vessel Traffic Services Zone Regulations (NORDREG) were not established in accordance with applicable IMO requirements for the establishment of mandatory ship reporting and vessel traffic services systems. Through a written submission presented by Transport Canada to the Maritime Safety Committee dated 5 October 2010, the Legal Branch outlined Canada's authority under international law to implement NORDREG in the following terms:

Article 234 of UNCLOS provides for the right of coastal States to adopt and enforce non-discriminatory laws and regulations for the prevention, reduction and control of marine pollution from vessels in ice-covered areas within the limits of the Exclusive Economic Zone (EEZ). Article 234 permits States to enact these laws and regulations without seeking prior IMO approval. Accompanying the right to enact such laws is a general obligation under Article 192 to protect and preserve the marine environment.

Article 234 can be compared and contrasted with other provisions in the Convention dealing with the protection of the marine environment such as Article 211, paragraphs 5 and 6 which require the coastal State to conform to "generally accepted international rules and standards established through the competent international organization." In contrast, no such requirement is included in Article 234, which establishes its own *sui generis* code for appropriate unilateral coastal State measures. Article 234 overrides Article 211 in ice-covered areas. The uniqueness of Article 234 is apparent by the fact that it was not included within other sections dealing with the protection of the marine environment; rather, it stands distinct, as the only Article in Section 8 of Part XII.

Article 234 provides a complete legal justification in international law for NORDREG. Further, NORDREG is consistent with SOLAS Chapter V, Regulation 11.4, which provides that "Ship reporting systems not submitted to the Organization for adoption do not necessarily need to comply with this regulation" and Regulation 12, which provides that "use of VTS may only be made mandatory in sea areas within the territorial sea," qualified by "nothing in this regulation shall prejudice the rights and duties of governments under international law ..." Canada's rights and duties under Article 234 of UNCLOS take precedence over the 12NM limitation.

Parliamentary Declarations in 2011 / Déclarations parlementaires en 2011

compiled by / préparé par
ALEXANDRA LOGVIN

Statements made on the introduction of legislation / Déclarations sur l'introduction de la législation

C-3 (Supporting Vulnerable Seniors and Strengthening Canada's Economy Act / Loi visant le soutien aux aînés vulnérables et le renforcement de l'économie canadienne)
C-4 (Preventing Human Smugglers from Abusing Canada's Immigration System Act / Loi visant à empêcher les passeurs d'utiliser abusivement le système d'immigration canadien)
C-10 (Safe Streets and Communities Act / Loi sur la sécurité des rues et des communautés)
C-13 (Keeping Canada's Economy and Jobs Growing Act / Loi sur le soutien de la croissance de l'économie et de l'emploi au Canada)
C-18 (Marketing Freedom for Grain Farmers Act / Loi sur le libre choix des producteurs de grains en matière de commercialisation)
C-23 (Canada-Jordan Economic Growth and Prosperity Act / Loi sur la croissance économique et la prospérité — Canada-Jordanie)
C-24 (Canada-Panama Economic Growth and Prosperity Act / La croissance économique et la prosperité — Canada-Panama)

Alexandra Logvin is a layer at Fasken Martineau DuMoulin LLP in Ottawa. This compilation covers parliamentary declarations made during the first session of the 41st Parliament (2 June - 15 December 2011). Earlier declarations made in 2011, during the third session of the 40th Parliament, are compiled in the previous volume (volume 48) of this Yearbook.

Statements in Response to Questions / Déclarations en réponse aux questions

environment / environnement

Climate change / Changements climatiques
Energy / Énergie
Hazardous Chemicals / Substances chimiques dangereuses
Keystone XL pipeline / Pipeline Keystone XL
Ozone Layer / Couche d'ozone

foreign affairs / affaires étrangères

Arctic Sovereignty / Souveraineté dans l'Arctique
G-8 and G-20 Summits / Sommets du G-8 et du G-20
Iran
Japan / Japon
Libya / Libye
Palestine
Poland / Pologne
Tunisia / Tunisie
Ukraine
United States / États-Unis

health / santé

Food Inspection / Système d'inspection des aliments
HIV-AIDS / VIH-SIDA
World Health Organization / Organisation mondiale de la Santé

human rights / droits de la personne

Aboriginal Women / Femmes autochtones
Anti-semitism / Antisémitisme
Congo
Egypt / Égypte
Employment / Emploi
Health / Santé
Immigration
  Deportation / Déportation
  Newcommers / Nouveaux arrivants
  Permanent Residency / Résidence permanente
  Visitors' Visas / Visas de visiteurs
Iran
Iraq / Irak

Persons with Disabilities / Personnes handicapées
Protecting Canadians Abroad / Protection des Canadiens à l'étranger
Religion
Rights of Women / Droits des femmes
Sexual Minorities / Minorités sexuelles
Sri Lanka
Syria / Syrie
Ukraine

INTERNATIONAL CRIMINAL LAW / DROIT PÉNAL INTERNATIONAL

International Child Abduction / Enlèvements internationaux d'enfants
International Transfer of Offenders / Transfèrement international des délinquants
Transportation of Dangerous Goods / Transport des marchandises dangereuses

INTERNATIONAL HUMANITARIAN LAW / DROIT INTERNATIONAL HUMANITAIRE

Humanitarian Intervention and Aid / Aide et intervention humanitaire
- Afghanistan
- Africa / Afrique
- Libya / Libye
- Pakistan
- Turkey / Turquie

International Transfer of Detainees / Transfert international des détenus
Refugees / Réfugiés

TRADE AND ECONOMY / COMMERCE ET ÉCONOMIE

Aerospace / Industrie aérospatiale
Agriculture
GMO / OGM
Asia-Pacific Gateway / Porte d'entrée de l'Asie-Pacifique
Buy Local Policy / Politique d'achat local
Canada-U.S. Border / Frontière canado-américaine
Canada's Economy / Économie du Canada
Copyright / Droit d'auteur
Foreign Investment / Investissement étranger

Science and Technology / Sciences et la technologie
Steel Industry / Industrie de l'acier
Stock Markets / Bourses et les marchés de capitaux
Tariffs / Tarifs
Taxation / Fiscalité
Telecommunications / Télécommunications
Trade Agreements / Accords commerciaux
  Asia / Asie
  European Union / Union européenne
  Kuwait / Koweït
  Panama and Jordan / Panama et la Jordanie
  Trans-Pacific Partnership / Partenariat transpacifique
WTO / OMC

LAW OF THE SEA / DROIT DE LA MER

Fisheries/ Pêches
Sustainability / Durabilité

SPORTS

Statements Made on the Introduction of Legislation / Déclarations sur l'introduction de la législation

BILL C-3: SUPPORTING VULNERABLE SENIORS AND STRENGTHENING CANADA'S ECONOMY ACT / LOI C-3: LOI VISANT LE SOUTIEN AUX AÎNÉS VULNÉRABLES ET LE RENFORCEMENT DE L'ÉCONOMIE CANADIENNE[1]

Mrs. Shelly Glover (Parliamentary Secretary to the Minister of Finance):

This [Bill] would implement key measures from budget 2011, the next phase of Canada's economic action plan, a low tax plan for jobs and growth.

Without a doubt, our government is on the right track for job creation, economic growth and keeping Canada among the best economic positions in the industrialized world ... Overall, since July 2009, Canada has created over 560,000 net new jobs, the strongest record of job growth among all the G7 countries. Even better, over 80% of those 560,000-plus net new jobs have been full-time positions ...

1 Editor's note*:* An Act to Implement Certain Provisions of the 2011 Budget as updated on 6 June 2011 / Loi portant exécution de certaines dispositions du budget de 2011 mis à jour le 6 juin 2011; introduced in the House of Commons on 14 June 2011. The bill received Royal Assent on 26 June 2011; SC 2011, c 15.

[T]here is more. For the third straight year, the World Economic Forum rated our banking system the best and the safest in the world. Also, both the OECD and the IMF have recently forecast Canada's economic growth will be among the strongest in the G7 for both 2011 and 2012. In the words of the independent Conference Board of Canada:

> Canada's economic fundamentals — fiscal policies, tax policy, monetary policy and management of the exchange rate — are arguably in the best shape in the developed world.

While all of this is positive news, we must remain cautious and focused on the economy, for we all recognize that too many Canadians are still looking for work and the global economic recovery still remains fragile. Now is the time to stay focused on the economy and on supporting job growth. That is why we need to stay the course with the Supporting Vulnerable Seniors and Strengthening Canada's Economy Act ...

The Supporting Vulnerable Seniors and Strengthening Canada's Economy Act contributes to the successful and swift implementation of the next phase of Canada's economic action plan by proposing to legislate into law several of its key measures. Prominent among such measures include the following: help for vulnerable seniors by enhancing the guaranteed income supplement, also known as the GIS, for seniors who may be at risk of experiencing financial difficulties; support for provincial front line delivery of health care and social programs by extending the temporary total transfer protection to 2011-12, representing nearly $1 billion in support to affected provinces; encouragement for Canada's young entrepreneurs by providing $20 million to help the Canadian Youth Business Foundation; enhanced federal assistance for part-time students by reducing the in-study interest rate to zero, bringing them in line with full-time students; improvements to the registered disability savings plan, also known as the RDSP, by increasing flexibility to access RDSP assets for beneficiaries with shortened life expectancies, and ensuring that individuals can appeal in every single case a determination concerning their eligibility for the disability tax credit; support for Canada's veterans by providing tax relief for Legion purchases of Remembrance Day poppies and wreaths; support for Canada's leadership in genomics research by providing $65 million to Genome Canada to launch a new competition in the area of human health, and sustain the operating costs of Genome Canada and genome centres; strengthened oversight of Canada's mortgage insurance industry to ensure the continued stability of Canada's housing finance system; and much more.

(House of Commons Debates, 15 June 2011, pp. 404-7)
(Débats de la Chambre des Communes, le 15 juin 2011, pp. 404-7)

BILL C-4: PREVENTING HUMAN SMUGGLERS FROM ABUSING CANADA'S IMMIGRATION SYSTEM ACT / LOI C-4: LOI VISANT À EMPÊCHER LES PASSEURS D'UTILISER ABUSIVEMENT LE SYSTÈME D'IMMIGRATION CANADIEN[2]

Hon. Vic Toews (Minister of Public Safety):

[T]he legislation before us today [was] first introduced [on] October 2, 2010, as part of an overall strategy to help put an end to human smuggling ...

Canadians ... want our borders to stay open to newcomers who play by the rules when they come to our country, but firmly shut against those who would abuse our generosity, threaten the integrity of our immigration system and pose a risk to our safety and security.

[T]hey want Canada to remain the welcoming country it has always been for newcomers. ... The arrival of two migrant vessels from Southeast Asia over the past two years, the MV *Ocean Lady* and the MV *Sun Sea*, have proved the reach and determination of organized human smuggling networks in their efforts to target Canada.

We have heard from experts in the field that Canada is the destination of choice for human smugglers and that criminal networks are evolving and adapting to utilize more sophisticated ways of moving their cargo.

Canada, therefore, needs to be ever more vigilant and more aggressive in cracking down on the ringleaders of this worldwide criminal operation, not less, as some have suggested ...

One way our government intends to do that is by passing legislation this fall to, among other things, tackle organized drug crimes and establish tougher sentences and mandatory jail terms for child molesters and those who use the Internet for this purpose.

We will end house arrest for serious and violent offenders. We will bring measures to ensure pardons can be refused in cases involving serious crimes against children. We will equip our police with new investigative powers designed for the computer age.

Our government was quite clear in our 2011 platform that such legislation would be passed within 100 sitting days of the return of the House, and ours is a government that delivers on its commitments.

We were equally clear in our platform that another way our government would continue to stand on guard for Canada and protect the safety and

2 Editor's note: An Act to Amend the Immigration and Refugee Protection Act, the Balanced Refugee Reform Act and the Marine Transportation Security Act / Loi modifiant la Loi sur l'immigration et la protection des réfugiés, la Loi sur des mesures de réforme équitables concernant les réfugiés et la Loi sur la sûreté du transport maritime; introduced in the House of Commons on 16 June 2011.

security of Canadians would be by cracking down on human smuggling. That is why we are here today. Bill C-4 is all about that ...

Bill C-4 would, first and foremost, crack down on those criminals who would abuse our generous immigration system and endanger the safety and security of our Canadian communities.

We are providing a strong deterrent to those who are organizing human smuggling operations to jump the queue into Canada and we are ensuring the integrity and fairness of Canada's immigration system for years to come.

Under this act, our government would enable the Minister of Public Safety to designate the arrival of a group of persons as an irregular arrival and make those involved subject to the act's measures. It would make it easier to prosecute human smugglers. It would impose mandatory minimum prison sentences on convicted human smugglers. It would hold shipowners and operators to account for the use of their ships in human smuggling operations.

As part of the legislation, designated arrivals would face mandatory detention for up to one year to allow Canadian authorities to determine admissibility and illegal activity. In short, the detention period would provide more time to identify those who had arrived in our country and whether they posed a threat to our national security ...

Under the act, our government is also reducing the attraction of coming to Canada by way of illegal human smuggling operations. This includes measures like preventing those who come to Canada as part of an irregular arrival, including those who subsequently obtain refugee status, from applying for permanent resident status for a period of five years.

The act would ensure that the health benefits participants receive would not be more generous than those received by other members of the Canadian public. It would enhance the ability to terminate refugee applications of those who would return to their country of origin for a vacation or would demonstrate in other ways that they were not legitimately in need of Canada's protection. It would also prevent individuals who participate in human smuggling events from sponsoring family members for a period of five years.

Bill C-4 is virtually identical to the legislation our government introduced in the House of Commons last year. There are minor revisions, most notably one which puts the responsibility for designating an irregular arrival event in the exclusive purview of the minister rather than delegating it.

(House of Commons Debates, 21 June 2011, pp. 595-97)
(Débats de la Chambre des Communes, le 21 juin 2011, pp. 595-97)

BILL C-10: SAFE STREETS AND COMMUNITIES ACT / LOI C-10: LOI SUR LA SÉCURITÉ DES RUES ET DES COMMUNAUTÉS[3]

Hon. Rob Nicholson (Minister of Justice and Attorney General of Canada):

The bill ... fulfills the commitment in the June 2011 Speech from the Throne to ... reintroduce law and order legislation to combat crime and terrorism. This commitment, in turn, reflects the strong mandate that Canadians have given us to protect society and to hold criminals accountable ... We have a duty to stand up for ... victims, which we are doing by bringing in this legislation.

The objective of our criminal law reform agenda over the past few years has been to build a stronger, safer and better Canada. This comprehensive legislation is another important step in the process to achieve this end ... There are five parts to Bill C-10. Part 1 includes reforms to deter terrorism by supporting victims of terrorism and amending the *State Immunity Act*. Part 2 includes sentencing reforms that will target sexual offences against children and serious drug offences, as well as prevent the use of conditional sentences for serious violent and property crimes. Part 3 includes post-sentencing reforms to increase offender accountability, eliminate pardons for serious crimes and strengthen the international transfer of offenders regime. Part 4 includes reforms to better protect Canadians from violent young offenders. Lastly, part 5 includes immigration reforms to better protect vulnerable foreign workers against abuse and exploitation, including through human trafficking ...

Part 1 is comprised of clauses 2 through 9. These amendments seek to deter terrorism by enacting the *Justice for Victims of Terrorism Act*. As reflected in the proposed preamble to the new act, these reforms recognize that, "terrorism is a matter of national concern that affects the security of the nation," and that it is a "priority to deter and prevent acts of terrorism against Canada and Canadians." As Canadians recently marked the 10th anniversary of the 9/11 attacks on New York, Virginia and Pennsylvania, it

3 Editor's note: An Act to Enact the Justice for Victims of Terrorism Act and to amend the State Immunity Act, the Criminal Code, the Controlled Drugs and Substances Act, the Corrections and Conditional Release Act, the Youth Criminal Justice Act, the Immigration and Refugee Protection Act and other Acts / Loi édictant la Loi sur la justice pour les victimes d'actes de terrorisme et modifiant la Loi sur l'immunité des États, le Code criminel, la Loi réglementant certaines drogues et autres substances, la Loi sur le système correctionnel et la mise en liberté sous condition, la Loi sur le système de justice pénale pour les adolescents, la Loi sur l'immigration et la protection des réfugiés et d'autres lois; introduced in the House of Commons on 20 September 2011. The bill received Royal Assent on 13 March 2012; SC 2012, c 1.

was a stark reminder that the threat of terrorism remains and that we must continue to be vigilant.

Accordingly and with a view to deterring terrorism, part 1 proposes to create a cause of action for victims of terrorism to enable them to sue perpetrators and supporters of terrorism, including listed foreign states, for loss or damage that occurred as a result of an act of terrorism or omission committed anywhere in the world on or after January 1, 1985. It also would amend the *State Immunity Act* to lift immunity of those states that the government has listed for support of terrorism.

Part 2 is comprised of clauses 10 through 51. It proposes sentencing amendments to the Criminal Code and the *Controlled Drugs and Substances Act* to ensure that the sentences imposed for child sexual exploitation, serious drug offences, as well as for other serious violent and property crimes, adequately reflect the severity of these crimes. The exploitation of children is a most serious crime, one that is incomprehensible and must be met with appropriate punishment ... These reforms seek to consistently and adequately condemn all forms of child sexual abuse through the imposition of new and higher mandatory sentences of imprisonment, as well as some higher maximum penalties. They also seek to prevent the commission of sexual offences against children through the creation of two new offences and by requiring courts to consider imposing conditions to prevent suspected or convicted child sex offenders from engaging in conduct that could facilitate or further their commission of sexual offences against children ...

We are also addressing the serious issue of drug crimes in this country, particularly those involving organized crime and those that target youth because we all know the impact that such crimes have on our communities.

Part 2's proposals to address drug crime include amendments to the *Controlled Drugs and Substances Act* to impose mandatory minimum sentences of imprisonment for the offences of production, trafficking or possession for the purposes of trafficking or importing, and exporting or possession for the purpose of exporting of schedule I drugs, such as heroin, cocaine and methamphetamine, and schedule II drugs, such as marijuana. These mandatory minimum sentences would apply where there was an aggravating factor, including where the production of the drug constituted a potential security, health or safety hazard, or the offence was committed in or near a school ...

Part 3, which is comprised of clauses 52 through 166, proposes post-sentencing reforms to better support victims and to increase offender accountability ...

Part 4, which is found at clauses 167 through 204, proposes reforms to the *Youth Criminal Justice Act* to strengthen its handling of violent and repeat young offenders. These reforms include: highlighting the protection of the public as a principle, making it easier to detain youth charged with serious offences pending trial; ensuring that prosecutors consider seeking adult sentences for the most serious offences; prohibiting youth under the age of 18 from serving a sentence in an adult facility; and requiring police to keep records of extrajudicial measures ...

Last, part 5, which is found at clauses 205 through 207, proposes amendments to the *Immigration and Refugee Protection Act* to authorize immigration officers to refuse work permits to foreign nationals and workers where it would protect them against humiliating and degrading treatment, including sexual exploitation and human trafficking.

(House of Commons Debates, 21 September 2011, pp. 1297-1300)
(Débats de la Chambre des Communes, le 21 septembre 2011, pp. 1297-1300)

BILL C-13: KEEPING CANADA'S ECONOMY AND JOBS GROWING ACT / LOI C-13: LOI SUR LE SOUTIEN DE LA CROISSANCE DE L'ÉCONOMIE ET DE L'EMPLOI AU CANADA[4]

Hon. Ted Menzies (for the Minister of Finance):

This act represents a key component of the next phase of Canada's economic action plan. Today's legislation represents an ambitious, substantive, and positive response to the economic challenges of today and the opportunities of tomorrow. Indeed, the global economic recovery is challenged, as demonstrated by ongoing events in Europe and in the United States. While the roots of these global challenges are not from within our borders, they could nevertheless impact Canada ...

In our initial response, Canada's economic action plan, we delivered $60 billion in extraordinary investments to support jobs and growth during the worst of the global recession. It was a plan that helped families and businesses deal with the short-term challenges, while also supporting Canada's long-term prosperity through, for instance, landmark infrastructure investments in roads, bridges, universities, colleges, and many more. It was a plan that, according to countless independent observers, worked. As BMO economist Doug Porter publicly declared, it was, "arguably one of the most successful stimulus programs in the industrialized world." Earlier

[4] Editor's note: An Act to Implement Certain Provisions of the 2011 Budget as updated on 6 June 2011 and Other Measures/ Loi portant exécution de certaines dispositions du budget de 2011 mis à jour le 6 juin 2011 et mettant en oeuvre d'autres mesures; introduced in the House of Commons on 4 October 2011. The Bill received Royal Assent on 15 December 2011; SC 2011, c 24.

this year, our ... government built on that record of accomplishments with the next phase of Canada's economic action plan: a low tax plan for jobs and growth. The next phase seeks to foster positive conditions for long-term economic prosperity, while staying on track to return to balanced budgets, while helping Canadian families.

The *Keeping Canada's Economy and Jobs Growing Act* represents a vital component of the next phase as it implements many of its key elements. For instance, the act would promote job creation and economic growth by: providing a temporary hiring credit for small business, to encourage additional hiring; expanding tax support for clean energy generation, to encourage green investments; extending the mineral exploration tax credit for flow-through share investors by one year to support Canada's mining sector; simplifying customs tariffs in order to facilitate trade and lower the administrative burden for businesses; extending the accelerated capital cost allowance treatment for investments in productivity-improving machinery and equipment for Canada's manufacturing sector; and eliminating the mandatory retirement age for federally regulated employees in order to give older workers wishing to work the option to remain in the workforce.

The [A]ct would support communities from coast to coast to coast by: legislating a permanent annual investment of $2 billion in the gas tax fund to provide predictable long-term infrastructure funding for municipalities; enhancing the wage earner protection program to cover more workers affected by employer bankruptcy or receivership; introducing a volunteer firefighters tax credit for volunteer firefighters; and increasing the ability of Canadians to give more confidently to legitimate charities, by helping combat fraud and other forms of abuse by illegitimate charities.

The *Keeping Canada's Economy and Jobs Growing Act* would help families by: introducing a new family caregiver tax credit to assist caregivers of all types of infirm, dependent relatives; removing the limit on the amount of eligible expenses caregivers can claim for their financially dependent relatives under the medical expense tax credit; and introducing a new children's arts tax credit for programs associated with children's arts, cultural, recreational and developmental activities.

The [A]ct would invest in education and training by: forgiving loans for new doctors and nurses in underserved rural and remote areas; helping apprentices in the skilled trades, as well as workers in regulated professions, by making occupational trade and professional examination fees eligible for tuition tax credit; improving federal financial assistance for students; and making it easier to allocate registered education savings plan assets among siblings, without incurring tax penalties or forfeiting Canada education savings grants.

Finally, it would respect taxpayers by: phasing out the direct subsidy for political parties and closing numerous tax loopholes that allow a few businesses and individuals to avoid paying their fair share of tax ... Before spotlighting a couple of the numerous and very positive measures in today's legislation, let me underline that, while indeed the global economy is in a period of turbulence and there are challenges that lie ahead, Canada has performed relatively well ...

The facts are indisputable. Canada is standing tall. On economic growth, both the IMF and the OECD forecast that we will have among the strongest economic growth in the G7 in the years ahead. On jobs, Canada has the strongest job creation record in the G7 with nearly 600,000 net new jobs created since July 2009, with over 80% of those being full-time jobs.

On our financial sector, the World Economic Forum has, for the fourth straight year, rated our banking system the best in the world. On our fiscal situation, Canada has, and will continue to have, by far the lowest total government net debt to GDP ratio in the entire G7 based on IMF projections.

On fiscal and economic fundamentals, Canada's credit rating, unlike numerous other countries, has been affirmed as being the highest possible by major rating agencies. Indeed, Moody's recently renewed Canada's triple A credit rating, praising our "economic resiliency, very high government financial strength, and a low susceptibility to event risk." On our competitiveness, *Forbes*, the influential business magazine, ranked Canada as the best country in the world for business to grow and create jobs, largely due to our low tax plan for Canadian businesses. The list goes on. There is little wonder that *The Economist* and global leaders have singled out Canada's economy and our Conservative government's economic leadership for repeated praise. BMO economist, Doug Porter, testifying before the finance committee this last week, declared, "compared to policy making in the rest of the world, Canada's economic policy-making has been exemplary. I don't think there has been a significant misstep in recent years." We recall the words of U.K. Prime Minister David Cameron before this chamber:

> In the last few years, Canada has got every major decision right. Look at the facts ... Your economic leadership has helped the Canadian economy to weather the global storms far better than many of your international competitors.

As encouraging and positive as those facts and quotes may be, they should not serve as an invitation to rest on our laurels, especially in the light of the ongoing global economic turmoil in the EU and United States ...

The *Keeping Canada's Economy and Jobs Growing Act* is a very substantive piece of legislation at over 640 pages. While there is no way I can spotlight each and every great measure in the bill, I would like to spotlight a couple of them, one of which garnered strong attention to date, and another that some have overlooked.

First, I would like to talk about a measure that has garnered pretty strong attention, that being the new volunteer firefighters tax credit ... While there is no way we can every truly repay them, we can show them we value all of the nearly 85,000 volunteer firefighters who keep our communities safe. That is why I am proud that we have proposed the volunteer firefighters tax credit in this legislation. It will help volunteer firefighters by providing them with a 15% nonrefundable tax credit of $3,000 ...

Second, and lastly, I would like to briefly talk about a measure that has not received a lot of attention: tax relief to help apprentices in the skilled trades and workers in regulated professions with the cost of occupational trade and professional examination fees. As we all know, apprentices in the skilled trades must complete certification exams at the end of their apprenticeship to practice their trade. Likewise, students in fields like nursing, medicine, law and accounting are also required to complete examinations to practice their occupations. Until now, the cost of these certification examinations were generally not eligible for tax relief. The [Act] will now make all occupational trade and professional examination fees eligible for the tuition tax credit where the examination is required to obtain a professional status, certification or licence in a trade recognized by federal or provincial law that allows the individual to practice that profession or trade within Canada.

Examples of eligible occupations, trades and professions include: architects, machinists, bakers, bricklayers, carpenters, chartered accountants, dental technicians, hair stylists, motor vehicle body repairers, welders and much more. In fact, it is estimated that more than 30,000 individuals would benefit just this year.

(House of Commons Debates, 5 October 2011, pp. 1888-91)
(Débats de la Chambre des Communes, le 5 octobre 2010, pp. 1888-91)

BILL C-18: MARKETING FREEDOM FOR GRAIN FARMERS ACT / LOI C-18: LOI SUR LE LIBRE CHOIX DES PRODUCTEURS DE GRAINS EN MATIÈRE DE COMMERCIALISATION[5]

Hon. Gerry Ritz (Minister of Agriculture and Agri-Food and Minister for the Canadian Wheat Board):

[5] Editor's note: An Act to Reorganize the Canadian Wheat Board and to Make Consequential and Related Amendments to Certain Acts / Loi réorganisant la Commission canadienne du blé et apportant des modifications corrélatives et connexes à certaines lois; introduced in the House of Commons on 18 October 2011. The bill received Royal Assent on 15 December 2011; SC 2011, c 25.

We believe that all Canadian farmers should be able to position their businesses to capture the marketing opportunities that will be open to them. We live in a free country and giving farmers the freedom to choose is the right thing to do. Currently, by law, western Canadian wheat, durum and barley growers do not have the same rights as other producers in Canada about where and how they sell their products. For export or domestic human consumption, they have no other option but to market through the Canadian Wheat Board, the monopoly that was established in 1943 by an order in council, not by producers or for producers at that time.

By allowing marketing freedom, western wheat and barley growers will be able to market based on what is best for their own bottom line of their own business ... With this proposed legislation, we would provide marketing choice to western grain farmers once and for all. To avoid market disruption, the goal is for farmers and grain marketers, including the new entity, to be able to start forward contracting in January 2012. Farmers, grain companies and customers need this assurance. As we well know, market certainty and clarity underpins stability in the marketplace domestically and internationally.

The bill would remove the monopoly of the Canadian Wheat Board and allow for the new Canadian wheat board to continue as a voluntary marketing organization for up to five years as it makes the transition to full private entity. During the transition period, this new voluntary organization would still be called the Canadian wheat board. It would continue to offer farmers the option of pooling their crops. It would continue to benefit from a borrowing guarantee backed by the federal government and it would develop a business plan for privatization, which will be reviewed no later than 2016.

This new freedom is not only good for farmers, it also has many economic benefits for communities across western Canada. New processing plants would be able to open their doors for business and look to hire new employees unfettered by the current ridiculous requirement to buy wheat and barley only from the Canadian Wheat Board.

Canada's grain industry is a powerhouse that brings $16 billion to the farm gate and makes up almost half of our agricultural exports. What was once Canada's signature crop, hard red spring wheat, has fallen behind. Wheat and barley innovation has become stagnate. Competition for acres has weakened and newer crops, such as canola, have surpassed wheat in value.

A C.D. Howe report released this past spring confirmed that Canada's share of annual worldwide wheat production has fallen by 50% in the last 50 years. It is a staggering number. Equally, Canadian market share and world barley exports have declined by 40% since the 1980s. With the reduced market share, the Canadian Wheat Board has less influence on the world stage and, as a result, has become a price taker.

We have seen tremendous growth in value added opportunities across the Prairies over the past 20 years for crops that do not have a monopoly marketer, including oats, pulses, flax and, of course, canola. We would see these same opportunities open up for wheat and barley as we implement market freedom ...

Canada will continue to sell wheat and barley and maintain its reputation as a quality, reliable supplier. The international grain trade works largely on forward contracting for future purchases and sales. If there is uncertainty in the market about the rules of who can sell Canadian wheat and barley, there is a high risk that buyers will turn to other countries to buy that wheat and barley. The Canadian wheat and barley sector can continue to supply domestic and world markets with high quality wheat and barley, but they look to us to provide the certainty they need to plan and carry out their business decisions.

(House of Commons Debates, 19 October 2011, pp. 2223-26)
(Débats de la Chambre des Communes, le 19 octobre 2011, pp. 2223-26)

BILL C-23: CANADA-JORDAN ECONOMIC GROWTH AND PROSPERITY ACT / LOI C-23: LOI SUR LA CROISSANCE ÉCONOMIQUE ET LA PROSPÉRITÉ — CANADA-JORDANIE[6]

Mr. Gerald Keddy (Parliamentary Secretary to the Minister of International Trade, for the Atlantic Canada Opportunities Agency and for the Atlantic Gateway):

Our government is committed to securing and deepening access to traditional markets, like the United States, and broadening and expanding access to more markets, like Jordan.

Trade accounts for over 60% of our annual GDP and, with one in five Canadian jobs generated by trade, it is a matter of fundamental importance to the financial security of hard-working Canadians and their families ...

We continue to see fierce competition in the global marketplace, with emerging economies and global players continuing to climb the value

[6] Editor's note: An Act to Implement the Free Trade Agreement between Canada and the Hashemite Kingdom of Jordan, the Agreement on the Environment between Canada and the Hashemite Kingdom of Jordan and the Agreement on Labour Cooperation between Canada and the Hashemite Kingdom of Jordan/ Loi portant mise en oeuvre de l'Accord de libre-échange entre le Canada et le Royaume hachémite de Jordanie, de l'Accord sur l'environnement entre le Canada et le Royaume hachémite de Jordanie et de l'Accord de coopération dans le domaine du travail entre le Canada et le Royaume hachémite de Jordanie; introduced in the House of Commons on 15 November 2011. The bill received Royal Assent on 29 June 2012; SC 2012, c 18.

chain and establishing themselves in a wide range of sectors. This government will do everything it can to ensure that Canadian workers and Canadian businesses have the tools and opportunities to build the links needed to succeed in today's global economy. Our government is committed to bringing continued economic prosperity to Canadians by pursuing bilateral and regional free trade relationships.

Negotiating and implementing trade agreements with our international partners will also help to level the playing field for our companies in an increasingly complex and competitive environment. Pursuing free trade agreements sends a clear signal that protectionism is not the right way to achieve increased global stability and prosperity. In these challenging times, deeper trade ties are the best way to create jobs and economic growth. Our government will get that done. That is why we have an ambitious, job creating, pro-trade plan. The Canada-Jordan Economic Growth and Prosperity Act is a key part of this plan.

The Canada-Jordan free trade agreement also demonstrates Canada's support for an Arab state that, like Canada, supports peace and security in the Middle East. We will recall that in 2007, the Rt. Hon. Prime Minister joined His Majesty King Abdullah II in a commitment to take our commercial relationship to the next level. The Canada-Jordan free trade agreement, along with related agreements on labour co-operation and the environment, signed in 2009, are a direct result of this commitment.

Canada's economy is export driven ... We know it is in our best economic interest to seek out new opportunities for our producers, workers and exporters in as many foreign markets as possible. Moreover, negotiating free trade agreements allows for Canadian firms to specialize and increase their comparative advantage in the global marketplace. By improving access to foreign markets for Canadian workers and businesses, this government is keeping its commitment to support economic growth and create new jobs for Canadian workers.

In a number of countries, Canadian firms are at a competitive disadvantage because their foreign competitors have preferential market access under some form of a free trade agreement. The Canada-Jordan free trade agreement addresses this serious issue by leveling the playing field with key competitors who are already benefiting from free trade agreements with Jordan, namely competition from the United States and the European Union. Through the Canada-Jordan Economic Growth and Prosperity Act, our government is ensuring that Canadian workers and firms are on equal footing to compete with firms from across the world in the Jordanian market. Opening doors to trade and investment is the right approach for creating opportunities for Canadian workers and businesses in global markets ...

The free trade agreement with Jordan would benefit both Canadians and Jordanians by giving Canadian and Jordanian exporters unprecedented access to our respective markets and eliminating tariffs on a number of key products. World leading Canadian sectors, like forestry, manufacturing and agriculture and agri-food would benefit.

Over the years, Canada and Jordan have built a strong, mutually beneficial relationship. This free trade agreement continues to build on that important start. It is a relationship grounded in common aspirations, like peace, stability and prosperity for our citizens. This new free trade agreement would help to move these aspirations forward.

Despite the recent economic downturn experienced by the global economy, our bilateral trade with Jordan increased to $85.9 million in 2010 from $82.5 million in 2009, indicating that the longer-term trend of our trade relationship is one of growth. For example, Canada's 2010 merchandise exports to Jordan of $66 million were more than double the $31 million total in 2003. This free trade agreement would provide the opportunity to further enhance this trend of upward growth.

Jordan's current average applied tariff is 11%, with peaks of up to 30% applied on some Canadian exports of interest. In fact, 67% of Jordan's tariff lines, covering over 99% of Canadian exports, will be eliminated when the agreement is first implemented. This is a huge step forward in the growing economic partnership between Canada and Jordan and will help to ensure that Canadian firms remain competitive globally. Jordan's remaining tariff reductions will then take place over three or five years.

Let me give a better idea of the specific sectors that will benefit if the Canada-Jordan Economic Growth and Prosperity Act is quickly moved through the House. Top exports in 2010 included paper and paperboard, vegetables, wood, vehicles and machinery. In 2010 Canada imported some $20 million in goods from Jordan, including both knit and woven apparel, inorganic chemicals, precious stones, mainly jewellery, and vegetables, cucumbers. Our trade relationship has clearly been growing, despite Jordan's most favoured nation applied average tariff of 11% and peaks of up to 30% on many key Canadian exports. The Canada-Jordan free trade agreement aims to remedy this situation and promote continued prosperity for Canadian workers, producers and exporters. Once this agreement is brought into force, Canada will immediately benefit from duty-free access for over 99% of current Canadian exports by value.

What does this new agreement mean for individual exporters? Permit me to run through some specific examples, starting with the agricultural sector. Canadian exporters of pulses, lentils, chickpeas, beans and peas will benefit from the immediate elimination of Jordan's tariffs of 5% to 10% on these products. Of Canada's $7 million of vegetable exports to Jordan in 2010, the majority were lentils and chickpeas, which currently face a 5% tariff, and peas that are subject to a 10% tariff, both of which go to duty-free access immediately upon implementation of the agreement.

In 2010 exports of frozen potato products to Jordan totalled some $88,000. These exporters will benefit from the immediate elimination of a 20% Jordanian tariff and place them on a level playing field with competitors in the U.S. and the E.U., which currently benefit from duty-free access to the Jordanian market.

Canadian beef exporters will benefit from the immediate elimination of Jordanian tariffs, which range from 5% to 23% on all beef products, including fresh chilled frozen and preserved meat and offal and processed products such as sausages and jerky. Jordan lifted its restrictions on Canadian beef products in February 2009, which will allow this sector to benefit from these lower tariffs.

Animal feed will also benefit from the elimination of Jordanian tariffs of up to 23% and some of these are currently subject to an additional 10% tariff that will be eliminated immediately upon implementation of the free trade agreement.

The Canada-Jordan free trade agreement is certainly more than just agricultural products. The elimination of Jordanian tariffs, ranging from 15% to 30% on certain wood products, could benefit Canadian exporters of doors, frames, joinery, shakes and shingles and other building materials.

...

With $9.7 million in exports in 2010, mainly light passenger vehicles, Jordan is a growing market for Canadian auto and auto parts exports. The elimination of Jordan's tariffs ranging from 10% to 30% will help Canadian exporters to further expand into this market.

Canada exports a variety of mechanical and electrical machinery to Jordan, $9.2 million in 2010, including heavy construction and mining equipment, communications equipment, filtration or purification devices, pumps, machinery and components. The elimination of Jordanian tariffs, ranging from 10% to 30% on a variety of current and potential Canadian machinery exports, will certainly help our machinery manufacturing sector.

Canada's exports of pharmaceuticals to Jordan totalled just shy of a million dollars in 2010, of which 80% were subject to a 5% Jordanian tariff. That will be eliminated upon implementation of this free trade agreement.

Although Jordan is currently a small market for Canadian fish and seafood exports, the elimination of Jordan's 10% to 30% tariffs on fish and seafood could help Canadian exporters expand their presence in the Jordanian market.

(House of Commons Debates, 14 December 2011, pp. 4445-48)
(Débats de la Chambre des Communes, le 14 décembre 2011, pp. 4445-48)

BILL C-24: CANADA-PANAMA ECONOMIC GROWTH AND PROSPERITY ACT / LOI C-24: LOI SUR LA CROISSANCE ÉCONOMIQUE ET LA PROSPERITÉ — CANADA-PANAMA[7]

Mr. Gerald Keddy (Parliamentary Secretary to the Minister of International Trade, for the Atlantic Canada Opportunities Agency and for the Atlantic Gateway):

Trade is the key to ... financial success. One in five Canadian jobs and over 60% of our annual GDP is generated by trade. Trade is a matter of fundamental importance to workers, as it helps put food on the table and helps families make ends meet.

In the past few months we have seen a vivid reminder to all of us that the world economy remains in the grip of a global economic crisis. The fragility of global markets has emphasized the importance and urgency of continuing to diversify our trade relationships and expanding our exports with emerging market economies like Panama.

These are challenging economic times. Problems in the global economic situation continue to persist. That is why our government is taking action today to create jobs and help our businesses and their workers succeed in the years ahead. That includes our ambitious protrude plan to help businesses expand their presence around the world.

In these tough economic times, Canadians expect their government to do everything it can to enhance the ability of Canadian firms to participate in global markets and to create an advantage for Canadian businesses. That is why our government took action on our budget 2010 commitment to make Canada a tariff-free zone for industrial manufacturers.

Eliminating tariffs on goods used in manufacturing helps Canadian companies lower their production costs and increase their competitiveness. This contributes to a stronger economy, creates jobs and growth here at home, and reinforces our G20 leadership in the fight against protectionism ...

With this legislation we are one step closer to giving Canadian businesses the access they need in Panama. By improving access to foreign markets for Canadian businesses, we are supporting the Canadian recovery and creating new jobs for Canadian workers ...

7 Editor's note: An Act to Implement the Free Trade Agreement between Canada and the Republic of Panama, the Agreement on the Environment between Canada and the Republic of Panama and the Agreement on Labour Cooperation between Canada and the Republic of Panama / Loi portant mise en oeuvre de l'Accord de libre-échange entre le Canada et la République du Panama, de l'Accord sur l'environnement entre le Canada et la République du Panama et de l'Accord de coopération dans le domaine du travail entre le Canada et la République du Panama; introduced in the House of Commons on 15 November 2011.

Canada is an export-driven economy, and pursuing bilateral and regional trade agreements is essential to bringing continued job prosperity and economic growth to Canadians ...

A free trade agreement with Panama is also a part of our government's efforts to strengthen Canada's engagement in the Americas. Panama occupies a unique and influential position in the global trading system, thanks to the Panama Canal. This vital gateway is currently being twinned. Our government recognizes that Canadian firms are well placed to help. It should be noted that when the twinning of the Panama Canal is finished, it will carry approximately 5% of the entire trade on the planet. That is an opportunity Canada cannot turn its back on.

The Canada-Panama Economic Growth and Prosperity Act would generate increased export and investment opportunities for Canadians by creating a preferential and more predictable trade and investment environment. For example, for exporters of Canadian goods, Panamanian tariffs on over 90% of Canadian goods exported to that country would be eliminated upon entry into force of the free trade agreement. Most remaining tariffs would be eliminated over a period of between five to fifteen years.

For Canadian service providers, the free trade agreement would help expand market access opportunities in areas such as information and communications technology, energy and financial services. This agreement would benefit workers in every region of this country. For example, Quebec would benefit from the elimination of Panamanian tariffs on key exports, such as machinery, vehicles, pork products, pharmaceuticals and aerospace products.

Investment and services provisions would benefit the engineering, construction and transportation sectors. Ontario would benefit from the elimination of Panamanian tariffs on key exports, such as pharmaceuticals, machinery, information and communications technology products, and electrical and electronic equipment.

Financial services provisions would benefit Canadian banks and financial service providers operating in Panama.

Western provinces would benefit from the elimination of Panamanian tariffs on key export interests, such as fats and oils, processed food, pork, information and communications technology products, pulses and cereals.

The Atlantic provinces would benefit from the elimination of Panamanian tariffs on key export interests such as frozen potato products, trees and plants, fish and seafood, and forestry products.

For Canadians looking to invest in Panama, the free trade agreement includes a chapter of comprehensive rules governing investment. The rules provide greater protections and predictability for Canadian investors and their investments in Panama.

The free trade agreement also provides Canadian exporters of goods and services greater market access to Panama's government procurement opportunities, including those related to the Panama Canal expansion and other infrastructure projects ...

[I]n July 2011 the OECD formally placed Panama on its list of jurisdictions that have substantially implemented the international standard for exchange of tax information, commonly known as the white list. This is an extremely important achievement. It demonstrates Panama's commitment to combat international tax evasion. Panama is committed to the implementation of this free trade agreement and has already completed its domestic ratification process.

Canada is not the only country with whom Panama has negotiated a free trade agreement. Panama is deepening its regional economic partnerships and is expanding its global reach through the negotiation of trade agreements with countries such as the United States and the European Union ...

Just last year, the Government of Panama laid out a five-year strategic plan in which it plans to spend $13.6 billion on the country's infrastructure. Under this plan, $9.6 billion would be allocated to infrastructure investments and other economic programs designed to stimulate further growth. Some examples of projects the government is looking to undertake include airport construction, expansions and upgrades, a new convention centre, a new water treatment plant, power generation projects, agriculture irrigation systems, and a $1.5 billion metro system.

I am pleased to say that the Canada-Panama free trade agreement includes strong government procurement provisions that guarantee Canadian suppliers will have non-discriminatory access to a broad range of procurement opportunities, including those under the Panama Canal authority.

(House of Commons Debates, 12 December 2011, pp. 4286-89)
(Débats de la Chambre des Communes, le 12 décembre 2011, pp. 4286-89)

Statements in Response to Questions / Déclarations en réponse aux questions

environment / environnement

Climate Change / Changements climatiques

Ms. Megan Leslie (Halifax):

The fight for a climate change plan in Canada has an unlikely ally, the loyal executives at Suncor. They agree that the government's piecemeal approach to regulating emissions is expensive and ineffective. The government has always had an open door policy for oil executives. Will the minister now commit to dropping his expensive and ineffective approach and introduce a legally binding plan to combat emissions?

Hon. Peter Kent (Minister of the Environment):

[The] Alberta industry ... creates so many jobs and generates ... great wealth for the Canadian economy. [W]e have a plan and the plan is working. We addressed transportation emissions first. We moved on to the coal-fired electricity generating sector, and we are about to begin consultations with other heavy emitters, including the oil and gas sector.

(House of Commons Debates, 8 June 2011, p. 128)
(Débats de la Chambre des Communes, le 8 juin 2011, p.128)

Ms. Kirsty Duncan (Etobicoke North):

The government was required to submit two greenhouse gas emissions reports in the last month, one to the UN and one to Parliament. The government told the UN that its climate change policies are up to 10 times more effective than what it told Parliament. The government is telling the UN one thing, while telling Parliament another. Will the minister tell us which report is accurate and who ordered the changes?

Hon. Peter Kent (Minister of the Environment):

The two reports are based on two different compilations of data. With regard to the inventory report to the United Nations framework convention on climate change, we reported that in 2009 the oil sands contributed 6.5% of Canada's total emissions. As reported, this fact is accurate.

(House of Commons Debates, 9 June 2011, pp. 206-7)
(Débats de la Chambre des Communes, le 9 juin 2011, pp. 206-7)

Ms. Kirsty Duncan (Etobicoke North):

The National Round Table on the Environment and the Economy predicts that climate change will cost Canadians up to $43 billion by 2050. The government's own advisory panel found that catastrophic climate change could wipe out up to 25% of Canada's GDP. Right now, the government has no plan to meet 75% of its greenhouse gas reduction targets. As we lead up to the world conference in Durban, when will Canadians get a real plan?

Hon. Peter Kent (Minister of the Environment):

Our government is indeed balancing the need for a cleaner and healthier environment with protecting jobs and economic growth. The Kyoto protocol does not include major emitters such as China, India or even the United States and therefore does not work. Canada will not sign on to any new agreement that does not include all major emitters. We remain committed to reducing Canada's greenhouse gas emissions by 17% below 2005 levels and we are achieving that goal.

(House of Commons Debates, 15 November 2011, pp. 3103-4)
(Débats de la Chambre des Communes, le 15 novembre 2011, pp. 3103-4)

Energy / Énergie

Mme Megan Leslie (Halifax):

La semaine du ministre de l'Environnement a été difficile. Le commissaire à l'environnement a démoli son travail et l'Europe propose une directive sur la qualité des carburants. Le message est clair: les sables bitumineux sont trop polluants pour faire concurrence aux énergies propres ... Quand le gouvernement va-t-il s'en rendre compte?

Mr. David Anderson (Parliamentary Secretary to the Minister of Natural Resources and for the Canadian Wheat Board):

We do not agree with the energy directive that has come out from the EU. We are going to continue to work to represent and to protect Canadian oil sands interests and Canadian economic interests. We will stand with the workers [and ...] the industry. We are going to protect the environment at the same time.

(House of Commons Debates, 7 October 2011, p. 2007)
(Débats de la Chambre des Communes, le 7 octobre 2011, p. 2007)

Hazardous Chemicals / Substances chimiques dangereuses

M. Romeo Saganash (Abitibi — Baie-James — Nunavik — Eeyou):

Le Canada a passé plus d'une décennie à tenter d'empêcher que l'amiante soit inscrite sur la liste des produits dangereux de la *Convention de Rotterdam [sur la procédure de consentement préalable en connaissance de cause applicable à certains produits chimiques et pesticides dangereux qui font l'objet d'un commerce international]*. Nous apprenons maintenant que Santé Canada avait averti le gouvernement des dangers liés à l'amiante et avait recommandé que ce produit soit ajouté à la liste ... Ce gouvernement va-t-il se raviser et accepter que l'amiante soit ajoutée à la liste de la Convention de Rotterdam?

L'hon. Christian Paradis (ministre de l'Industrie et ministre d'État (Agriculture)):

Depuis plus de 30 ans, le Canada fait la promotion de l'utilisation sécuritaire et contrôlée du chrysotile sur la scène nationale et internationale. En outre, les revues scientifiques démontrent que le chrysotile peut effectivement être utilisé de façon sécuritaire dans des conditions contrôlées.

(House of Commons Debates, 14 June 2011, pp. 349-50)
(Débats de la Chambre des Communes, le 14 juin 2011, pp. 349-50)

Keystone XL Pipeline / Pipeline Keystone XL

M. Romeo Saganash (Abitibi — Baie-James — Nunavik — Eeyou):

L'Agence de protection de l'environnement des États-Unis a rejeté l'étude sur le pipeline Keystone XL et la considère, et je cite, "insuffisante." Près d'un million de barils de pétrole de plus voyageront par ce pipeline. Selon l'agence, cela entraînera une augmentation des émissions de gaz à effet de serre provenant des sables bitumineux. Est-ce que le ministre peut confirmer ces faits et dévoiler toute étude relative aux émissions de GES et le pipeline Keystone?

Mr. David Anderson (Parliamentary Secretary to the Minister of Natural Resources and for the Canadian Wheat Board):

The National Energy Board is a strong independent regulator that ensures pipeline safety. It is mandated to ensure the safety and the security of pipelines from when they are first proposed until they are abandoned. Canada and the U.S. trade oil, natural gas and electricity across our boarders every day. The Keystone XL pipeline will provide a substantial economic benefit to Canada.

(House of Commons Debates, 8 June 2011, p. 129)
(Débats de la Chambre des Communes, le 8 juin 2011, p. 129)

Ozone Layer / Couche d'ozone

Ms. Elizabeth May (Saanich — Gulf Islands):

[T]he minister says we will streamline and optimize our ozone measurements [...] I would like to ask the honourable minister [...] to withdraw the letters threatening the jobs of the World Ozone and Ultraviolet Radiation Centre program manager [... and] the ozone sonde program.

Hon. Peter Kent (Minister of the Environment):

[W]e are not cutting any ozone monitoring services or closing the centre. Yes, we are optimizing and streamlining the way we collect data to ensure that taxpayers' dollars are spent in the most prudent but still environmentally correct way. That is what we were elected to do.

(House of Commons Debates, 21 September 2011, pp. 1294-95)
(Débats de la Chambre des Communes, le 21 septembre 2011, pp. 1294-95)

FOREIGN AFFAIRS / AFFAIRES ÉTRANGÈRES

Arctic Sovereignty / Souveraineté dans l'Arctique

Mr. Dennis Bevington (Western Arctic):

Two weeks ago the U.S. government issued permits for Shell Oil to release 250 metric tonnes of pollution in the Beaufort Sea, along the disputed territorial waters between Canada and the U.S. The so-called environmental standards developed by the Americans were clearly intended to apply to these Canadian waters ... Has the government been involved in setting these environmental standards?

Hon. John Baird (Minister of Foreign Affairs):

We have ongoing discussions with our neighbours to the south on this and other issues that are important to the Arctic. Obviously, this government will always stand up for Canadian sovereignty and fight for what is right. We have an incredibly important responsibility to ensure that our environment is protected and nowhere is that responsibility more important than in the Arctic, which has a very fragile ecosystem.

(House of Commons Debates, 6 October 2011, p. 1951)
(Débats de la Chambre des Communes, le 6 octobre 2011, p. 1951)

G-8 and G-20 Summits / Sommets du G-8 et du G-20

Hon. Gerry Byrne (Humber — St. Barbe — Baie Verte):

G8 and G20 summits are held, supposedly, to demonstrate to the world collective leadership ... and global stability created by fiscal prudence and respect for democratic institutions ... If the government could do it all over again, could it ... tell Canadians now [what] it would do ... differently?

Hon. John Baird (Minister of Foreign Affairs):

The initial authorizations for funds to these unprecedented back-to-back summits was some $1.1 billion and we learned from the Auditor General today that they came in almost 40% under budget. The real lasting legacy of the G8 and G20 summits in Canada is the leadership of the Prime Minister. Canada has a lot to be proud of for the summit resulted in the launch of the maternal, child health initiative, a multi-year initiative plan that will literally save thousands and thousands of lives around the world thanks to the leadership of the Prime Minister.

(House of Commons Debates, 9 June 2011, p. 205)
(Débats de la Chambre des Communes, le 9 juin 2011, p. 205)

Mrs. Tilly O'Neill Gordon (Miramichi):

The G20 research group at the University of Toronto's Munk School of Global Affairs recently released its annual analysis of G20 commitments. The report tracks G8 and G20 members' progress in meeting their promises from the November 2010 Seoul summit until June 2011 [... What has been] Canada's progress [in this regard]?

Hon. Bev Oda (Minister of International Cooperation):

The Prime Minister has said that it is not enough to make pledges at conferences: it is important to pay what is pledged. Under his leadership, Canada met its 2009 food security commitment, and in fact was the first G8 country to do so. That is why he was asked to co-chair the UN commission for accountability in women's and children's health. The Munk School report says that Canada has fully complied with its official development assistance commitments. In fact, in meeting the G20 commitments, Canada ranked ahead of the U.K. [and] the U.S.A.

(House of Commons Debates, 4 October 2011, pp. 1841-42)
(Débats de la Chambre des Communes, le 4 octobre 2011, pp. 1841-42)

Iran

Mr. Joe Daniel (Don Valley East):

I was dismayed to learn last week some of the details surrounding the apparent plot by Iran to assassinate the Saudi Arabian ambassador to Washington [... Which] measures [is] Canada taking to respond to Iran's latest affront to international law?

Hon. John Baird (Minister of Foreign Affairs):

Canada finds Iran's actions absolutely and totally unacceptable. We condemn them without reservation. Last week I committed to working with our international partners in considering the consequences for such actions. Today, Canada is imposing sanctions on five additional Iranian nationals. Four are members of the Iranian national guard. These sanctions are on top of others already in place against Iran. As the Prime Minister said last week, this regime in Tehran represents probably the most significant threat to the world, to global peace and security, and I completely agree.

(House of Commons Debates, 18 October 2011, p. 2147)
(Débats de la Chambre des Communes, le 18 octobre 2011, pp. 2147)

Hon. Irwin Cotler (Mount Royal):

[T]he Iranian regime has accelerated its nuclear weaponization program, continued its state sponsorship of terrorism and genocidal incitement, and intensified its massive domestic repression. Will the government sanction the Central Bank of Iran, put the Islamic Revolutionary Guard Corps on the terrorist list, this epicenter of the Iranian threats, sanction the Iranian crude oil sector and those companies that trade with IRGC entities, and expand the orbit of sanctions against those entities and individuals engaged in the massive assault on human rights in Iran?

Hon. John Baird (Minister of Foreign Affairs):

Canada today has the toughest sanctions against the Iranian regime in the world. We are incredibly concerned by the IEA report on its nuclear weaponization program. We are tremendously concerned about the Saudi assassination plot. We are tremendously concerned by the abysmal and terrible record on human rights. We will continue to work with our allies to ensure that we continue to have the toughest sanctions on this despicable regime.

(House of Commons Debates, 16 November 2011, p. 3152)
(Débats de la Chambre des Communes, le 16 novembre 2011, pp. 3152)

Mr. Costas Menegakis (Richmond Hill):

This week's brazen attacks on the British Embassy in Tehran were extremely disturbing. Iranian authorities failed to uphold their responsibilities under the *Vienna Convention*, which specifically safeguard diplomatic missions. Following this outrageous act, the British have pulled their ambassador to Iran. [What is] the status and well-being of our diplomats in Tehran?

Hon. John Baird (Minister of Foreign Affairs):

The safety and security of our diplomatic staff in Tehran is a top concern when we hear about the outrageous attack on the British High Commission. We are in very close contact with the embassy in Tehran. We have had a limited engagement strategy for the last four years and we are following the situation very closely. I have asked my deputy minister to conduct a complete security review and we will do what is best for the Canadian officials who are doing the important work of Canada. We will ensure their safety if that requires evacuating them earlier.

(House of Commons Debates, 1 December 2011, p. 3870)
(Débats de la Chambre des Communes, le 1 décembre 2011, pp. 3870)

Japan / Japon

Mr. Richard Harris (Cariboo — Prince George):

On Christmas Day 70 years ago, the Allies had no choice but to surrender. During seventeen and a half days of heavy fighting, 290 Canadians were killed and 493 were wounded while trying to defend Hong Kong. Those who survived spent the duration of the war facing inhumane conditions in prisoner of war camps in Hong Kong and Japan. After 70 years, the Japanese government has now apologized to Canadian veterans. [What is] the importance of this apology?

Ms. Eve Adams (Parliamentary Secretary to the Minister of Veterans Affairs):

Earlier today, Canadian prisoners of war received an apology from the Government of Japan for the suffering they endured during World War II. For nearly four years, our prisoners of war endured systematic and continued abuse. They were frequently starved and they were forced into back-breaking labour. Of those who were able to return, many of them were disabled and many died prematurely. This apology is an important step in reconciliation and healing. It recognizes the suffering of our prisoners of war while honouring their courage and sacrifice.

(House of Commons Debates, 8 December 2011, p. 4204)
(Débats de la Chambre des Communes, le 8 décembre 2011, p. 4204)

Libya / Libye

Mr. Paul Dewar (Ottawa Centre):

Today's meeting with the Libya contact group brings together different ministers, top diplomats from around the world, including the United

Nations, the Arab League, the African Union and the Organization of the Islamic Conference ... Will the government commit to expanding regional diplomacy so we can see an end to the crisis in Libya?

Hon. John Baird (Minister of Foreign Affairs):

I certainly agree that Canada can play a robust role with the Libyan contact group. My cabinet colleague is representing Canada at that very important meeting today. Diplomatically we have to work with our partners in the United Nations, our Arab partners in the region, to not just effect a military mission but also to be diplomatically engaged on humanitarian and development efforts. Canada, as well as our allies, should have greater engagement with the transitional council in Benghazi.

(House of Commons Debates, 9 June 2011, pp. 202-3)
(Débats de la Chambre des Communes, le 9 juin 2011, pp. 202-3)

Palestine

Mr. John Carmichael (Don Valley West):

Later today, Palestinian President Mahmoud Abbas is due to address the United Nations General Assembly and perhaps table a resolution calling for full member status of a Palestinian state that does not yet exist. [What is] the long-standing position of the Government of Canada [in this regard]?

Mr. Deepak Obhrai (Parliamentary Secretary to the Minister of Foreign Affairs):

The long-standing position of the Government of Canada has not changed. The only route to peace in this conflict is a peace negotiated by both parties. One of the states must be a Jewish state and recognized as such, while the Palestinian state must be a non-militarized one. Any unilateral action is unhelpful to the situation. We urge both parties to get back to the table to undertake constructive, peaceful talks that may one day lead to an acceptable solution for both parties.

(House of Commons Debates, 23 September 2011, p. 1395)
(Débats de la Chambre des Communes, le 23 septembre 2011, p. 1395)

Mr. John Weston (West Vancouver — Sunshine Coast — Sea to Sky Country):

[L]'Autorité palestinienne cherche unilatéralement à devenir membre de l'Assemblée générale des Nations Unies ... The application is for full membership at the UN Educational, Scientific and Cultural Organization. It is only exacerbating the situation. [What is] the government's view on this problematic move by the Palestinian Authority?

Hon. John Baird (Minister of Foreign Affairs):

We are disappointed with the decision of UNESCO's executive body and urge all members of UNESCO to reject this unilateral action.

(House of Commons Debates, 6 October 2011, p. 1955)
(Débats de la Chambre des Communes, le 6 octobre 2011, p. 1955)

Poland / Pologne

Mr. Wladyslaw Lizon (Mississauga East — Cooksville):

Last week the *Globe and Mail* used the phrase, "Polish concentration camps" in reference to the Nazi German concentration and extermination camps in occupied Poland. Brave Polish citizens were the victims of Nazi occupiers and not the perpetrators of their evil crimes. The reference in the *Globe and Mail* article was an insult to thousands of Polish Righteous Among the Nations who risked their lives to save Jewish neighbours. [W]hat our government has done to correct the offensive misconception about the existence of Polish concentration camps?

Hon. Jason Kenney (Minister of Citizenship, Immigration and Multiculturalism):

[I]t is offensive to the memory of so many Poles who fought the Nazi occupation and invasion and who have been declared Righteous Among the Gentiles to refer to Nazi concentration camps as being Polish ones. That is why the Government of Canada has supported at UNESCO the official designation of the Nazi German concentration and extermination camps in occupied Poland. Let there be no mistake about this point in history. The Government of Canada certainly asks that all people be sensitive to the legitimate historic concerns of the Polish community in this regard.

(House of Commons Debates, 26 September 2011, pp. 1447-48)
(Débats de la Chambre des Communes, le 26 septembre 2011, pp. 1447-48)

Tunisia / Tunisie

Mme Hélène Laverdière (Laurier-Sainte-Marie):

Les Tunisiens vivant au Canada veulent voter lors de l'élection constituante tunisienne qui aura lieu bientôt. Or il semblerait qu'ils ne pourront pas voter parce que le gouvernement leur dit que le Canada ne peut pas être une circonscription électorale dans une assemblée étrangère. Le ministre sait-il que la France a des élus pour le Canada et les États-Unis dans son Assemblée nationale? Sait-il que la circonscription proposée par la Tunisie inclut le Canada et les États-Unis? Est-ce que le ministre va prendre les mesures nécessaires pour que les Tunisiens vivant au Canada puissent voter?

M. Chris Alexander (secrétaire parlementaire du ministre de la Défense nationale):

Nous comprenons très bien à quel point les Canadiens et les Canadiennes, surtout les néo-Canadiens, tiennent à exercer leur droit de vote, leur droit démocratique. Toutefois, notre gouvernement s'oppose à ce que le Canada soit utilisé comme circonscription électorale par n'importe quel autre pays à l'étranger. Néanmoins, nous sommes absolument d'accord pour appuyer la transition démocratique en Tunisie, et nous l'avons été dès le début.

(House of Commons Debates, 23 September 2011, p. 1396)
(Débats de la Chambre des Communes, le 23 septembre 2011, p. 1396)

Ukraine

Mr. Robert Sopuck (Dauphin — Swan River — Marquette):

Ukraine has undergone a considerable transformation since the beginning of the Orange Revolution. However, what originally seemed an unstoppable wave of democratic freedom has since gone sour with the news that former prime minister Yulia Tymoshenko is being politically persecuted. [What are] Canada's concerns with Ukraine's political situation?

Hon. John Baird (Minister of Foreign Affairs):

Our government has expressed to the Ukrainian government our serious concern about the apparent bias in the ongoing judicial proceedings against former prime minister Yulia Tymoshenko. Political persecution is completely unacceptable. The appearance of political bias in judicial proceedings undermines the rule of law. We urge, here today, the Ukrainian government to strengthen judiciary independence. We will continue to support efforts to build a peaceful, democratic and prosperous society in Ukraine.

(House of Commons Debates, 28 September 2011, p. 1572)
(Débats de la Chambre des Communes, le 28 septembre 2011, p. 1572)

United States / États-Unis

L'hon. Bob Rae (Toronto-Centre):

[L]e ministre des Finances vient de prononcer à New York, en plein milieu d'un grand débat politique aux États-Unis, un discours dans lequel il s'est rangé du côté des faucons républicains du Congrès américain [... D]epuis quand le gouvernement du Canada s'ingère-t-il dans les questions de politique intérieure des États-Unis, et depuis quand le gouvernement conservateur est-il devenu une filiale du mouvement républicain Tea Party aux États-Unis?

Le très hon. Stephen Harper (premier ministre):

Tout au long de la récession mondiale et de la reprise économique, les dirigeants des pays du G20 ont collaboré pour redresser la situation économique mondiale. Dans le contexte économique mondial actuel, les mesures que nous prenons dans nos pays respectifs ont des répercussions sur tous les autres. Bien entendu, nous travaillons ensemble pour assurer une forte reprise mondiale.

(House of Commons Debates, 15 June 2011, p. 391)
(Débats de la Chambre des Communes, le 15 juin 2011, p. 391)

HEALTH / SANTÉ

Food Inspection / Système d'inspection des aliments

M. Jean Rousseau (Compton — Stanstead):

Avec la crise de la bactérie E. coli qui frappe l'Europe, et en particulier l'Allemagne, les Canadiens ont raison d'être inquiets de la sécurité de leurs aliments. Cette crise survient malgré le fait que l'Allemagne ait un système d'inspection des aliments meilleur que celui du Canada. Le gouvernement peut-il assurer aux Canadiens que notre système d'inspection des aliments les protège de ce genre de danger?

Mr. Pierre Lemieux (Parliamentary Secretary to the Minister of Agriculture):

Food safety is of key importance to this government. We are taking measures to protect Canadians against what is happening in the European Union. CFIA is implementing enhanced border controls on vegetables from the European Union. If affected products are found, CFIA will facilitate recalls to keep Canadian families safe ... [A] report on OECD countries recognized that Canada's superior food safety system ranks us the best in the world on food recalls. Speaking of the budget, our recent budget includes an additional $100 million over five years to enhance food safety.

(House of Commons Debates, 7 June 2011, pp. 83-84)
(Débats de la Chambre des Communes, le 7 juin 2011, pp. 83-84)

HIV-AIDS / VIH-SIDA

Mme Anne Minh-Thu Quach (Beauharnois — Salaberry):

[C]e gouvernement est aussi fier de son bilan en matière de lutte contre le VIH-sida[.] [P]ourquoi refuse-t-il de participer au sommet de l'ONU, qui se déroule en ce moment à New York? ... Est-ce que la ministre peut nous dire quand elle entend faire preuve de leadership sur cette question?

Hon. Leona Aglukkaq (Minister of Health and Minister of the Canadian Northern Economic Development Agency):

I am proud of the work our government has accomplished in helping combat HIV-AIDS not only in Canada but also in the developing world. The Canadian HIV vaccine initiative, led by our government along with the Bill and Melinda Gates Foundation, highlights Canada's world-class HIV vaccine research expertise and this initiative will help our government advance the science for the development of a safe and effective HIV vaccine ... In addition, last year alone our government provided $42 million in HIV-AIDS research funding through the Canadian Institutes of Health Research, which partners not only with Canadian researchers but also the global community.

(House of Commons Debates, 9 June 2011, p. 204)
(Débats de la Chambre des Communes, le 9 juin 2011, p. 204)

World Health Organization / Organisation mondiale de la Santé

Mme Anne Minh-Thu Quach (Beauharnois — Salaberry):

Cette semaine, 118 pays se rencontrent au Brésil pour établir un plan d'action sur les déterminants sociaux de la santé.[8] Pourtant, ce gouvernement n'a pas cru bon y être représenté. Au Canada, 20 p. 100 des dépenses en santé sont attribuables aux enjeux sociaux tels que l'itinérance et le

8 Editor's note: World Conference on Social Determinants of Health / Déterminants sociaux de la santé, Rio de Janeiro, Brazil, 19-21 October 2011, online: <http://www.who.int/sdhconference/en/index.html>.

chômage. L'Organisation mondiale de la santé reconnaît que les inégalités sociales mènent à des iniquités en matière de santé. Les coûts sont astronomiques. La ministre de la Santé peut-elle nous expliquer pourquoi elle ne participe pas à cette importante rencontre internationale?

Hon. Leona Aglukkaq (Minister of Health and Minister of the Canadian Northern Economic Development Agency):

We do participate in a number of conferences internationally. Most recently, we were at a conference in New York, at the United Nations, on the declaration around poverty reduction initiatives across countries. Our government has worked hard to protect and promote the health and safety of all Canadians who make huge investments internationally, as well as in Canada.

(House of Commons Debates, 20 October 2011, p. 2287)
(Débats de la Chambre des Communes, le 20 octobre 2011, p. 2287)

Mrs. Tilly O'Neill Gordon (Miramichi):

At the request of the WHO, our Prime Minister agreed to co-chair the UN Commission on Information and Accountability for Women and Children's Health, which recently released a series of recommendations. Could the Minister of International Cooperation please update the House on progress being made?

Hon. Bev Oda (Minister of International Cooperation):

Canada continues its leadership on maternal, newborn and child health under the Prime Minister's leadership and the head of the WHO, who we are pleased to host here in Canada today, along with the top health experts in the field of maternal and child health. We are about accountability. We are about getting results. We are about better health for children and saving more lives. Canadians can be proud of our continued leadership to ensure that every MNCH dollar counts.

(House of Commons Debates, 21 November 2011, p. 3332)
(Débats de la Chambre des Communes, le 21 novembre 2011, p. 3332)

HUMAN RIGHTS / DROITS DE LA PERSONNE

Aboriginal Women / Femmes autochtones

Ms. Linda Duncan (Edmonton — Strathcona):

On November 1 National Chief Shawn Atleo called on the aboriginal affairs, justice and status of women committees to expedite joint action to address violence against indigenous women and children. [T]he ... government [has done] nothing. Now the UN has to step in to do the government's job. When will the government finally respond to the myriad of calls for a national inquiry into missing and murdered women and children?

Hon. Rona Ambrose (Minister of Public Works and Government Services and Minister for Status of Women):

First, to deal with the issue of the United Nations investigation, there is no United Nations investigation on this issue. I understand from the Department of Foreign Affairs that two civil society groups have made a request to a United Nations committee. The committee is looking into it and will be discussing it in February. In working with the United Nations in our response to that, we will ensure that it is aware that we have launched the murdered and missing aboriginal women's strategy that has a number of components that deal with all of the issues that we believe are necessary to deal with the systemic issues of not only racism but poverty affecting aboriginal women.

(House of Commons Debates, 13 December 2011, pp. 4390-1)
(Débats de la Chambre des Communes, le 13 décembre 2011, pp. 4390-1)

Anti-Semitism / Anti-sémitisme

Mr. Scott Reid (Lanark — Frontenac — Lennox and Addington):

[What] action is the government [...] taking to fight anti-Semitism?

Hon. Jason Kenney (Minister of Citizenship, Immigration and Multiculturalism):

This evening the Minister of Foreign Affairs and I will, on behalf of Canada, be the first government in the world to sign the Ottawa Protocol [on Combating Anti-Semitism], indicating that Canada will continue to take a leadership role in combating all forms of anti-Semitism, including the scourge of the new anti-Semitism, which seeks to target and vilify the collective Jews of the state of Israel. We stand in solidarity with the Jewish people and their democratic state.

(House of Commons Debates, 19 September 2011, p. 1149)
(Débats de la Chambre des Communes, le 19 septembre 2011, p. 1149)

Congo

Hon. Jim Karygiannis (Scarborough — Agincourt):

Since 1999 Canada's efforts in the Democratic Republic of Congo have included peacekeepers and millions of dollars in aid for rehabilitation and health care. Yet, when it came to the recent election in the DRC, Canada sent six international observers, despite requests from the community to send more. Why did the government abandon Canada's investment in the people of Congo during their recent election?

Hon. Bev Oda (Minister of International Cooperation):

Canada is very proud to always be involved in election observation where required and when asked to participate. In fact, we sent the maximum number of Canadians allowed by the EU commission. The election observers joined 46 long-term and 72 other observers as part of the EU mission. We are proud of Canada's participation.

(House of Commons Debates, 5 December 2011, p. 3975)
(Débats de la Chambre des Communes, le 5 décembre 2011, p. 3975)

Egypt / Égypte

Mr. Joe Daniel (Don Valley East):

The situation in Egypt continues to deteriorate for Coptic Christians. Copts, who make up 10% to 15% of the population in Egypt, are being targeted and persecuted for ethnic and religious reasons by hateful enemies. Countless murders of Copts have been reported in Cairo and across Egypt, and many others are going unreported ... What is our government doing to address this unprecedented violence toward the largest religious minority in the region?

Hon. Jason Kenney (Minister of Citizenship, Immigration and Multiculturalism):

Last Friday, the Minister of Foreign Affairs and I met with some 30 leaders of Canada's Coptic community to express Canada's solidarity with that community, particularly their loved ones in Egypt, to express once more this government's condemnation of the violence, particularly that by, apparently, members of the Egyptian military two weeks ago, killing innocent Coptic civilians. The Prime Minister led the inclusion of an expression of concern about vulnerable religious minorities in the Arab Spring declaration of the G8 at Deauville. We have called upon the United Nations Human Rights Council to investigate the most recent killings. We are creating an office for religious freedom to, in the words of the Prime Minister, make the promotion of religious freedom a key pillar of Canadian foreign policy.

We will always stand in solidarity with those who face this kind of persecution.

(House of Commons Debates, 24 October 2011, p. 2401)
(Débats de la Chambre des Communes, le 24 octobre 2011, p. 2401)

Mr. Ted Opitz (Etobicoke Centre):

The media has recently been reporting on clashes near Tahrir Square. Canadians are rightly concerned about the difficult transition from the Mubarak regime to a democratically elected and legitimate government of Egypt. [What are] the Canadian government's reactions to these most troubling media reports?

Hon. John Baird (Minister of Foreign Affairs):

We are outraged when we see the violence in Tahrir Square when people are seeking to peacefully protest. We are outraged when we see Coptic Christians in Egypt being targeted and many being killed. We are calling on all sides to work co-operatively toward the elections that are coming up this Monday and to ensure that democracy will outweigh the violence that we have seen in recent days.

(House of Commons Debates, 24 November 2011, p. 3553)
(Débats de la Chambre des Communes, le 24 novembre 2011, p. 3553)

Hon. Irwin Cotler (Mount Royal):

Egyptian blogger Maikel Nabil is one of the first political prisoners of the post-Mubarak era, convicted on trumped-up charges of insulting the Egyptian military. He had his conviction upheld yesterday at an oft-postponed hearing, after he earlier rejected an offer of freedom in exchange for a confession for "his alleged criminality." Given that Nabil is now in the 115th day of a hunger strike in protest both of the injustice of the Egyptian military tribunal and the injustice of his conviction, what measures are being undertaken by the Canadian government to help secure his immediate release?

Hon. John Baird (Minister of Foreign Affairs):

When the [issue was ...] brought to my attention, within a matter of hours we were in contact with the Egyptian ambassador. I met with him last week and expressed Canada's deep disappointment and real profound concern over the way this democracy activist had been treated. We demanded that this individual be let free and treated fairly in accordance with international standards of freedom and democracy. As of yet, we have not had a positive response, and we will continue to look to ensure that justice is done in this case.

(House of Commons Debates, 15 December 2011, p. 4509)
(Débats de la Chambre des Communes, le 15 décembre 2011, p. 4509)

Employment / Emploi

L'hon. Jack Layton (chef de l'opposition):

Il y a 300 000 personnes sans emploi de plus qu'avant la récession. Les emplois que le gouvernement se vante de créer sont temporaires, précaires et à temps partiel. Pourquoi le premier ministre refuse-t-il de constater l'échec de ses politiques en matière de création d'emplois dont les gens ont besoin dès maintenant?

Le très hon. Stephen Harper (premier ministre):

La création d'emplois reste une grande priorité pour ce gouvernement. Nous avons un des bilans les plus positifs à cet égard parmi les pays développés, et nous allons continuer en ce sens.

(House of Commons Debates, 7 June 2011, p. 81)
(Débats de la Chambre des Communes, le 7 juin 2011, p. 81)

Ms. Joyce Murray (Vancouver Quadra):

Immigrants admitted through the government's live-in caregivers stream [... have difficulties with gaining] access to permanent residency ... Will the minister stand up for these important immigrants?

Hon. Jason Kenney (Minister of Citizenship, Immigration and Multiculturalism):

This government has stood up for vulnerable caregivers ... We have, for example, eliminated the requirement for a second medical examination so that when caregivers get sick during their temporary period in Canada, they are not penalized ... We have moved the cost of recruitment fees, travel and health insurance from the caregivers to the employers. We have created a blacklist so we will deny work permits for caregivers to abusive employers.

(House of Commons Debates, 14 November 2011, p. 3031)
(Débats de la Chambre des Communes, le 14 novembre 2011, p. 3031)

M. Louis Plamondon (Bas-Richelieu — Nicolet — Bécancour):

Dans un rapport qui vient juste d'être publié, l'OCDE confirme noir sur blanc ce que les citoyens voient déjà: l'écart entre les riches et les pauvres s'accroît de plus en plus. [L]e Canada est parmi les derniers de classe en raison, notamment, de restrictions de plus en plus sévères à l'assurance-emploi. Résultat: malgré des appels répétés en faveur d'une réforme en profondeur, près de 60 p. 100 des chômeurs sont incapables de se qualifier à ce programme. Puisque ce gouvernement est insensible au sort des chômeurs, convient-il que la solution est de permettre au Québec de gérer le programme d'assurance-emploi, comme le demande le Conseil national des chômeurs et chômeuses?

L'hon. Diane Finley (ministre des Ressources humaines et du Développement des compétences):

Nous croyons que le meilleur moyen d'aider les chômeurs est de leur fournir de la formation pour qu'ils puissent trouver un emploi. C'est l'emploi qui va améliorer la situation, et c'est aussi l'avis de l'OCDE. C'est pourquoi, avec notre Plan d'action économique, nous avons fourni de la formation à plus de 1,2 million de Canadiens et de Canadiennes afin de les aider.

(House of Commons Debates, 5 December 2011, p. 3977)
(Débats de la Chambre des Communes, le 5 décembre 2011, p. 3977)

Health / Santé

Hon. Hedy Fry (Vancouver Centre):

Would the government ... ensure that women around the globe have access to evidence-based programs that include safe abortion and family planning services?

Hon. Bev Oda (Minister of International Cooperation):

It was reported last week at the United Nations that more progress is being made to reduce the rate of maternal mortality in the last year than over the past decade. Canada focused its Muskoka initiative on improving the health of mothers and children and taking real action, such as preventing malaria, better nutrition and training more midwives. We were clear on our criteria and we will fund projects.

(House of Commons Debates, 28 September 2011, p. 1570)
(Débats de la Chambre des Communes, le 28 septembre 2011, p. 1570)

Immigration

Deportation / Déportation

M. Justin Trudeau (Papineau):

Après avoir passé deux ans très difficiles en Albanie, Arjan Tabaj et sa famille sont finalement revenus au Canada. En effet, la Cour fédérale a reconnu que cette famille avait été déportée sans justification. Aujourd'hui, une autre famille se fait séparer par ce gouvernement. Mme Paola Ortiz est venue au Canada pour échapper à une vie d'abus physiques. Elle s'est mariée et elle a eu deux enfants. Or, à l'heure même où on se parle, elle est dans un avion qui la ramène au Mexique, où elle retrouvera sûrement le drame et la violence qu'elle fuyait. Pourquoi le ministre n'est-il pas intervenu pour éviter cette déchirure familiale?

Ms. Candice Hoeppner (Parliamentary Secretary to the Minister of Public Safety):

Part of CBSA's mandate is to investigate and remove persons who are in violation of Canada's immigration laws. Those individuals who are assessed to be in violation and do receive orders, do receive due process before the law. They are subject to various levels of appeal, including a preremoval risk assessment.

(House of Commons Debates, 23 September 2011, p. 1392)
(Débats de la Chambre des Communes, le 23 septembre 2011, p. 1392)

Mme Rosane Doré Lefebvre (Alfred-Pellan):

Si rien n'est fait d'ici demain, un homme de ma circonscription, Jean-Bernard Devilmé, sera expulsé vers Haïti. M. Devilmé réside au Canada depuis 25 ans. Il travaille comme charpentier et il contribue à la société. Même s'il a commis certaines infractions dans le passé, sa feuille de route est vierge depuis 2007. D'ailleurs, de nombreux organisms de suivi communautaire sont d'accord pour dire que cet homme, qui est père de quatre enfants, doit demeurer au pays. [Q]u'entend-[le ministre] faire pour venir en aide à M. Devilmé et sa famille?

Hon. Vic Toews (Minister of Public Safety):

The public record is clear: the person is not a permanent resident and is here illegally. He has been convicted of numerous criminal offences since coming to Canada. Numerous tribunals and courts have reviewed his status, and I am not prepared to interfere with the decisions of the judiciary in this matter.

(House of Commons Debates, 14 December 2011, p. 4437)
(Débats de la Chambre des Communes, le 14 décembre 2011, p. 4437)

Newcomers / Nouveaux arrivants

Mr. Dan Harris (Scarborough Southwest):

[Thirty-four] immigrant settlement agencies have lost their funding after $43 million was cut. It hits places like Toronto and Scarborough the hardest where 80,000 new Canadians are hurt by these service cuts ... Why is the government putting up barriers to the integration of immigrants into Canadian society and our economy?

Hon. Jason Kenney (Minister of Citizenship, Immigration and Multiculturalism):

[T]his government has more than tripled the federal investment in integration and settlement services for newcomers. It was $200 million five years ago. It is now over $600 million. It has increased in Ontario. It is true that there are now more newcomers settling in places like Atlantic Canada and western Canada than in Ontario, and the dollars are following them, because we have a responsibility to make sure that all newcomers get an equal chance to succeed in Canada.

(House of Commons Debates, 23 June 2011, p. 697)
(Débats de la Chambre des Communes, le 23 juin 2011, p. 697)

Permanent Residency / Résidence permanente

Mr. Don Davies (Vancouver Kingsway):

The Maeng family have put down firm roots since moving to Canada eight years ago. They have built their own business, and their eldest son is studying to become a dentist. However, despite having disclosed their younger son's health problems from the outset, they are now being told that his autism and epilepsy disqualify them from permanent residency. Will the minister commit to reviewing this troubling decision on humanitarian and compassionate grounds?

Hon. Jason Kenney (Minister of Citizenship, Immigration and Multiculturalism):

The minister cannot comment on particular cases because of the *Privacy Act.* Having said that, there is a very fair process, including access to applications for permanent residency for humanitarian and compassionate reasons by individuals. Those are not considered by elected officials but by highly trained public servants. I would point out that there is in our law provision for medical inadmissibility for those who the provinces deem would represent an undue burden to our tax-funded public health care system.

(House of Commons Debates, 7 June 2011, pp. 84-85)
(Débats de la Chambre des Communes, le 7 juin 2011, pp. 84-85)

Mr. Don Davies (Vancouver Kingsway):

The government's record of deporting refugees to torture is troubling. The Benhmuda family, including two Canadian-born children, lived in Canada for eight years. The family was deported into the hands of Moammar Gadhafi and the father was tortured for six months. The family was able to escape to Malta. They are not safe there, and the UN has asked the government to repatriate them. Will the minister bring these Canadian children and the family back to Canada, where they belong?

Hon. Jason Kenney (Minister of Citizenship, Immigration and Multiculturalism):

First, I have to take serious objection to the preamble of the hon. member's question. [N]o Canadian government of any political stripe deports people to torture. We have the fairest asylum system in the world. Any one who our courts, our IRB or decision makers determines could face risk overseas is not returned to face risk. Having said that, this is a particularly complicated case. I cannot comment on the details because of the *Privacy Act.* If we receive an application from that family, I can assure the member it will be given every humanitarian consideration and dealt with on an accelerated basis.

(House of Commons Debates, 23 June 2011, p. 696)
(Débats de la Chambre des Communes, le 23 juin 2011, p. 696)

Mme Sadia Groguhé (Saint-Lambert):

Le programme d'immigration spécial s'est terminé ce mois-ci, un programme qui devait permettre aux traducteurs afghans de vivre en sécurité au Canada ... Le ministre responsable peut-il nous expliquer pourquoi ce programme n'a pas été modifié pour atteindre son objectif?

L'hon. Jason Kenney (ministre de la Citoyenneté, de l'Immigration et du Multiculturalisme):

On n'a pas eu d'engagement face aux traducteurs qui ont travaillé avec les Forces canadiennes ni face à notre agence de développement international à Kandahar. C'était un programme discrétionnaire que nous avons introduit il y a trois ans avec, évidemment, certaines balises pour que les demandeurs soient qualifiés pour venir au Canada en tant que résidents permanents. L'estimation initiale était d'environ 400 à 500 personnes, et on va effectivement dépasser cet objectif en accueillant plus de 500 anciens traducteurs afghans ici au Canada.

(House of Commons Debates, 26 September 2011, p. 1450)
(Débats de la Chambre des Communes, le 26 septembre 2011, p. 1450)

Visitors' Visas / Visas de visiteurs

Mr. Kevin Lamoureux (Winnipeg North):

The ... government ... has put ... a two-year freeze [on sponsoring parents and grandparents]. The expectation of the super visa, on the other hand, was high, and it is turning into a super disappointment. Individuals are finding it too difficult to get the health care coverage necessary to get the super visa. Will the Minister of Citizenship, Immigration and Multiculturalism make the necessary modifications to enable the hundreds, if not thousands, of individuals to get their parents and grandparents to [Canada?]

Mr. Rick Dykstra (Parliamentary Secretary to the Minister of Citizenship and Immigration):

The super visa program for parents and grandparents from around the world who want to visit their children and grandchildren here in Canada was just undertaken on December 1. We have just begun the program. This is going to allow parents and grandparents to come to this country, visit their children and grandchildren, and enjoy quality time here with them.

(House of Commons Debates, 12 December 2011, pp. 4313-14)
(Débats de la Chambre des Communes, le 12 décembre 2011, pp. 4313-14)

Iran

Mr. Phil McColeman (Brant):

This week marks two years since Iranians went to the polls to express their democratic will. The regime in Tehran responded with repression. Could the Minister of Foreign Affairs please comment on this anniversary?

Hon. John Baird (Minister of Foreign Affairs):

We stand with our allies in condemning this regime and the crackdown that followed the election just two short years ago. It was absolutely brutal and totally uncalled for. Two years on, the repression continues, sadly, in Iran. Next door in Syria, Iranian officials are assisting the al-Assad regime's crackdown on the vulnerable people of Syria. We will work with the international community to increase pressure on these regimes. We stand with the people of Syria. We stand with the people of Iran who yearn to be free and to exercise their rights.

(House of Commons Debates, 16 June 2011, p. 448)
(Débats de la Chambre des Communes, le 16 juin 2011, p. 448)

Iraq / Irak

Mr. Scott Armstrong (Cumberland — Colchester — Musquodoboit Valley):

Camp Ashraf, in northern Iraq, is a makeshift home to political refugees ... Since the fall of Saddam Hussein, they have been protected by the U.S. and coalition forces. However, with the U.S. winding down its operations in Iraq, who is going to protect these people? Iraq has demanded the camp be closed by the end of the month. [What is the Minister's] opinion on what is going to happen at Camp Ashraf and of our action on this important file?

Hon. John Baird (Minister of Foreign Affairs):

Canada encourages the Iraqi government to extend the closure deadline to allow remaining residents sufficient time to take the required steps to seek asylum, and to allow the United Nations Human Rights Council to consider and process applications. We call on Iraq to meet its obligations under international law. We also want to ensure that Camp Ashraf residents are not forcibly transferred to another country where they could suffer.

(House of Commons Debates, 2 December 2011, p. 3925)
(Débats de la Chambre des Communes, le 2 décembre 2011, pp. 3925)

Persons with Disabilities / Personnes handicapées

Mme Manon Perreault (Montcalm):

Le Canada a signé la *Convention des Nations Unies relative aux droits des personnes handicapées* il y a plus de quatre ans ... Considérant qu'il y a plus de quatre millions de personnes au Canada vivant avec une incapacité, quand la ministre des Ressources humaines et du Développement des compétences entend-elle déposer un plan d'action pour instaurer la convention?

L'hon. Diane Finley (ministre des Ressources humaines et du Développement des compétences):

Nous avons fait beaucoup pour les handicapés au Canada. Nous avons introduit plusieurs programmes. For example, it was our government that launched the registered disability savings plan, one in which some 45,000 families are now perpetuating their ability to look after their disabled loved ones. Not only was it our government that signed the convention, but we also launched the enabling accessibility fund that has made over 600 new facilities across Canada accessible.

(House of Commons Debates, 23 June 2011, p. 694)
(Débats de la Chambre des Communes, le 23 juin 2011, p. 694)

Protecting Canadians Abroad / Protection des Canadiens à l'étranger

Mme Hélène Laverdière (Laurier-Sainte-Marie, NPD):

Depuis six ans, Nathalie Morin, une Canadienne de 27 ans, est retenue contre son gré par son mari en Arabie saoudite. Elle et ses trois enfants sont prisonniers dans leur maison, et selon la mère de Mme Morin, leurs droits et libertés sont brimés quotidiennement. Conformément à la motion adoptée à l'unanimité par l'Assemblée nationale du Québec vendredi dernier, est-ce que le gouvernement fédéral s'engage à prendre toutes les mesures nécessaires pour obtenir le rapatriement de Mme Morin et de ses enfants?

Hon. Diane Ablonczy (Minister of State of Foreign Affairs (Americas and Consular Affairs)):

We are aware of this case and have been in close touch with Ms. Morin on this issue. This is a complex family matter and there is no easy solution. Consular officials will continue to work with Ms. Morin and Saudi officials toward a positive resolution to the matter. I can also advise the House that this case has been raised by ministers in their meetings with Saudi officials ... However, [w]e are bound by both Saudi law and the *Hague Convention on the Civil Aspects of International Child Abduction*, under which the children cannot leave the country without the consent of both parents. We will continue to work on this case. We do hope for a positive resolution.

(House of Commons Debates, 13 June 2011, pp. 275, 276)
(Débats de la Chambre des Communes, le 13 juin 2011, pp. 275, 276)

Hon. Dominic LeBlanc (Beauséjour):

Henk Tepper, a New Brunswick potato farmer, has been in a Lebanese prison for almost three months following a commercial dispute ... When will the government intervene with Lebanese authorities, have Mr. Tepper released from the prison in Lebanon and brought back to Canada?

Hon. Diane Ablonczy (Minister of State of Foreign Affairs (Americas and Consular Affairs)):

In fact, Mr. Tepper and his family have been given substantial, vigorous and active assistance since the time he was arrested. There have been regular visits and there has been regular contact with Mr. Tepper, his family and his lawyers to give all possible assistance.

(House of Commons Debates, 14 June 2011, p. 352)
(Débats de la Chambre des Communes, le 14 juin 2011, p. 352)

Hon. Jim Karygiannis (Scarborough — Agincourt):

Majeed Uddin Ahmed, a Canadian citizen, together with his wife and their two Canadian children, ages five and one and a half, have been arrested and incarcerated in Saudi Arabia's notorious Dhaban prison for two weeks. One of the children is sick and requires medical care ... When will the minister order her officials to ... bring these kids home?

Hon. Diane Ablonczy (Minister of State of Foreign Affairs (Americas and Consular Affairs)):

We are in fact aware of reports of this family being detained in Saudi Arabia. Canadian officials have been working, and will continue to work, with local authorities to receive formal confirmation of the family's present situation. In addition, consular officials are seeking, if there is confirmation of the family's detention, to have consular access with the family. We are in constant daily contact with the family here in Canada and we will continue to work for the well-being of this family.

(House of Commons Debates, 6 October 2011, p. 1952)
(Débats de la Chambre des Communes, le 6 octobre 2011, p. 1952)

Ms. Jinny Jogindera Sims (Newton — North Delta):

The arrest of Mr. Al-Atar, an Edmonton imam, while participating in the hajj is part of a larger problem. Amnesty International has raised concerns about the ill treatment of Saudi prisoners and the country's continued use of the death penalty ... What is the minister doing to improve the treatment of Canadians detained in Saudi Arabia?

Hon. Diane Ablonczy (Minister of State of Foreign Affairs (Americas and Consular Affairs)):

Mr. Al-Atar was released from detention today, thanks to the good work of our consular officials and the co-operation of our partners in Saudi Arabia. [W]e are committed to providing the same level of assistance for all Canadians. However, each case is unique, and these cases are very often complex. We will continue to work with our partners to ensure due process and the well-being of Canadians in distress in Saudi Arabia, as we do for Canadians all over the world.

(House of Commons Debates, 31 October 2011, p. 2725)
(Débats de la Chambre des Communes, le 31 octobre 2011, p. 2725)

Hon. Irwin Cotler (Mount Royal, Liberal):

Naser Al-Raas, a Canadian citizen imprisoned in Bahrain for simply attending peaceful protests has been reportedly detained in solitary confinement, beaten, tortured and subjected to mock executions. Indeed, the Bahrain Independent Commission of Inquiry has itself decried the criminalization of peaceful protests and condemned such torture. Accordingly, will the Canadian government seek the immediate release of Mr. Al-Raas and the dropping of all charges, and ensure his safe return to Canada?

Hon. Diane Ablonczy (Minister of State of Foreign Affairs (Americas and Consular Affairs)):

The Government of Canada takes such allegations of mistreatment and torture very seriously, and we are seeking the Government of Bahrain's response concerning the events that transpired during Mr. Al-Raas' detention. Canada is also urging the Government of Bahrain to review the case in light of the recommendations of the Bahrain Independent Commission of Inquiry, as well as urging that Mr. Al-Raas' conviction be reviewed and his sentence commuted.

(House of Commons Debates, 14 December 2011, p. 4438)
(Débats de la Chambre des Communes, le 14 décembre 2011, p. 4438)

Religion

Mr. Merv Tweed (Brandon — Souris):

The right to one's religion and to practise that religion are fundamental human freedoms [... What are] Canada's efforts in this regard?

Hon. John Baird (Minister of Foreign Affairs):

Protecting and promoting religious freedom is an important part of Canada's principled foreign policy. We are speaking up around the world, at the United Nations, and every other corner of the world for religious freedoms. Whenever there are more religious freedoms, there are better human rights, and more freedoms which we strongly believe are important. I was pleased to see more than 100 people of different faiths come to Ottawa to offer their advice and suggestions on the establishment of an office of religious freedom, something we committed to do in the Speech from the Throne. We will listen and then we will act on a path to religious freedom.

(House of Commons Debates, 3 October 2011, p. 1762)
(Débats de la Chambre des Communes, le 3 octobre 2011, p. 1762)

Rights of Women / Droits des femmes

Mrs. Tilly O'Neill Gordon (Miramichi):

In a recent survey conducted by the American news outlet *Newsweek*, Canada was ranked among the top three best places in the world to be a woman. Canada was ranked a world leader on the key indicators of justice, health, education, economics and political involvement. [W]hat the government is doing to make Canada an even better place for women and the girls who will follow in their footsteps?

Hon. Rona Ambrose (Minister of Public Works and Government Services and Minister for Status of Women):

Our government has increased funding for women to its highest level ever, and we are working hard with women across the country to ensure they achieve their full potential. Women can count on our government to pursue measures that create jobs and growth, to end elder abuse, to protect our health care system, and of course to end violence against women and girls. We are very proud that Canada is ranked third-best place to be a woman in the world, third only to Iceland and Sweden.

(House of Commons Debates, 21 September 2011, pp. 1293-94)
(Débats de la Chambre des Communes, le 21 septembre 2011, pp. 1293-94)

Ms. Joyce Bateman (Winnipeg South Centre):

Despite progress, girls continue to face barriers that hamper their development. On March 24, the House unanimously passed a motion, brought forward by the Minister for Status of Women, calling on Canada to adopt a resolution proclaiming September 22 International Day of the Girl. [What are] Canada's efforts on this important initiative?

Hon. Rona Ambrose (Minister of Public Works and Government Services and Minister for Status of Women):

The International Day of the Girl will provide a key opportunity to consider girls' rights and raise awareness around the world. There are places in the world where girls are deprived of basic rights only because they were born girls. We are working successfully with countries around the world, as we submit our proposal to the United Nations in October, to shed light on the discrimination and injustice suffered by girls. Girls deserve to go to school and to have a full life. With Canada's leadership at the United Nations, we will support girls' rights all over the world.

(House of Commons Debates, 22 September 2011, p. 1346)
(Débats de la Chambre des Communes, le 22 septembre 2011, p. 1346)

Mrs. Nina Grewal (Fleetwood — Port Kells):

In Saudi Arabia a woman can face a punishment of 10 lashes for the simple act of driving a car, a routine act for most women in any democracy. Would the Minister of Foreign Affairs contemplate bringing issues such as this one to the attention of his counterparts around the world?

Hon. John Baird (Minister of Foreign Affairs):

Canada has enjoyed good diplomatic relations with the Kingdom of Saudi Arabia for many years, but reports of a Saudi woman being sentenced to 10 lashes for the crime of driving her own car are deeply disturbing. Although we have heard some positive signs of reform announced in recent weeks, [we] condemn, in the sharpest terms, this deeply offensive court decision.

(House of Commons Debates, 28 September 2011, p. 1569)
(Débats de la Chambre des Communes, le 28 septembre 2011, p. 1569)

Sexual Minorities / Minorités sexuelles

Mr. Randall Garrison (Esquimalt — Juan de Fuca):

The Commonwealth Eminent Persons Group has called on member states to address human rights directly and make it a priority at their upcoming meetings in Perth.

In 41 of 54 Commonwealth states being gay is still illegal, meaning people who are otherwise law-abiding could be arrested and prosecuted just for being gay. Would the Minister of Foreign Affairs commit to using Canada's prominent role in the Commonwealth to ensure that lesbian, gay, bisexual and transgender rights are a high priority at the Commonwealth heads of government meeting next week in Perth?

Hon. John Baird (Minister of Foreign Affairs):

Canada will be taking a very active role in Perth to ensure the issue of human rights is front and centre. There are substantial proposals that will be before Commonwealth leaders, including issues with respect to human rights, a Commonwealth charter, more democracy and more freedom. That certainly includes the rights of gays and lesbians ... Canada will continue to push human rights at the Commonwealth summit.

(House of Commons Debates, 19 October 2011, pp. 2214-15)
(Débats de la Chambre des Communes, le 19 octobre 2011, pp. 2214-15)

Sri Lanka

Hon. Jim Karygiannis (Scarborough — Agincourt):

During the last days of the civil war, the Government of Sri Lanka killed thousands of Tamil non-combatant refugees. International and United Nations human rights organizations have condemned the Sri Lankan government's cover-up ... Will the Prime Minister take steps today to urge the Commonwealth to revoke Sri Lanka's membership until it holds the perpetrators to account and they are judged in international courts? Will he support calls from the international community for action against the Sri Lankan government?

Hon. John Baird (Minister of Foreign Affairs):

I have certainly relayed the Government of Canada's position to both the high commissioner and directly to my counterpart, the minister of foreign affairs of Sri Lanka, to express our concerns on the lack of accountability for the serious allegations of war crimes, the lack of reconciliation with the Tamil community and with events that have taken place since the end of the civil war. Canada will continue to speak loudly and clearly on behalf of human rights around the world, especially in Sri Lanka ... [W]e did not sit idly by at the United Nations on Monday where I brought the plight of human rights violations to the floor of the General Assembly. The Prime Minister did not sit idly by when he expressed grave concern about attending a future summit of the Commonwealth in Colombo ... We will continue to stand up, do the right thing and fight for human rights around the world, especially in Sri Lanka.

(House of Commons Debates, 29 September 2011, pp. 1651, 1653)
(Débats de la Chambre des Communes, le 29 septembre 2011, pp. 1651, 1653)

Syria / Syrie

Mr. Kevin Sorenson (Crowfoot):

It is impossible to ignore the current unrest in Syria and the plight of its people. [What are] the ... government's latest steps to further support the Syrian people?

Hon. John Baird (Minister of Foreign Affairs):

[T]oday I have asked our Canadian delegation to the United Nations Human Rights Council to introduce and seek the support of like-minded nations to condemn the actions of the Assad regime in Syria as a gross violation of human rights. The Government of Canada, and I believe all parties in this place, calls on the Syrian regime to immediately end the killing, the arbitrary arrests, the torture and other acts of violence against its people. We also call on the Assad regime to stop trying to divert domestic and international attention from its brutal crackdown on peaceful, democratic demonstrations. The situation in Syria is completely unacceptable, and Canada will continue to show its support for people seeking freedom in Syria.

(House of Commons Debates, 15 June 2011, p. 395)
(Débats de la Chambre des Communes, le 15 juin 2011, p. 395)

Mr. Brad Trost (Saskatoon — Humboldt):

Yesterday the current Syrian president went on Syrian television to address the crisis. Rather than giving the Syrian people the real reforms they were seeking, he dealt in generalities and gave no real timeline for any reforms. Today the security forces killed even more people. [What is] Canada's position on this situation?

Hon. John Baird (Minister of Foreign Affairs):

Our government and I believe all Canadians strongly support the people of Syria in their peaceful efforts to realize democracy and human rights. Syrians have endured terrible crimes at the hands of this regime. Canada has joined several of our allies in saying that the president of Syria has a choice: he can reform or he can go. The status quo is no longer acceptable. While Canada does not have a Syrian ambassador posted in our country ... the government has summoned the chargé d'affaires on three occasions since the protests began, on April 29, June 3 and as recently as June 15.

(House of Commons Debates, 21 June 2011, p. 576)
(Débats de la Chambre des Communes, le 21 juin 2011, p. 576)

Ukraine

Hon. Ralph Goodale (Wascana):

As we recall the Holodomor genocide in Ukraine nearly 80 years ago, we are also concerned about the fragile state of Ukrainian democracy today. Interference in the legal system is used to stifle free political activity and now some mysterious illness seems to have befallen the leader of the opposition. Will the Canadian government press Ukrainian authorities to allow Ms. Tymoshenko independent medical treatment? Will Canada offer to provide that treatment if necessary and will Ukraine be warned that anything untoward happening to Ms. Tymoshenko would severely affect relations with Canada?

Hon. John Baird (Minister of Foreign Affairs):

We are tremendously concerned about the political prosecution of the former leader of the opposition there [... and] her well-being. I will certainly endeavour to follow up to ensure that Canada speaks strongly, that she gets the medical care that she needs. If necessary, we would certainly be prepared to offer her support here in Canada.

(House of Commons Debates, 25 November 2011, p. 3603)
(Débats de la Chambre des Communes, le 25 novembre 2011, p. 3603)

INTERNATIONAL CRIMINAL LAW / DROIT PÉNAL INTERNATIONAL

International Child Abduction / Enlèvements internationaux d'enfants

Ms. Jinny Jogindera Sims (Newton — North Delta):

In 2009 Stephen Watkins, from Newmarket, Ontario, awoke to his worst nightmare. His two sons, under his full custody, were abducted by their mother and flown to Poland, where they have been held ever since. The fate of these children rests with a Polish judge in a hearing set for this week. We have seen no action from the government for over two years. Why will the government not support the victims here? What is the government planning to do to bring these children back home for Christmas?

Hon. Diane Ablonczy (Minister of State of Foreign Affairs (Americas and Consular Affairs)):

Our government takes cases involving children especially seriously ... Since learning of the situation, our consular officials have been actively supporting Mr. Watkins both in Canada and in Poland. In addition, consular officials have been working with local authorities, the province and the police on this situation. [W]e will continue to be very active to resolve this case.

(House of Commons Debates, 13 December 2011, p. 4395)
(Débats de la Chambre des Communes, le 13 décembre 2011, p. 4395)

International Transfer of Offenders / Le transfèrement international des délinquants

Ms. Hélène Laverdière (Laurier-Sainte-Marie):

[The government] promised to bring [Omar Khadr] back this year to face justice in Canada. Now the government is ... saying it could take up to 18 months if the permit is returned at all. Why is the government misleading our allies and retreating on its commitments?

Hon. Vic Toews (Minister of Public Safety):

Mr. Khadr, in fact, did face justice. He pleaded guilty to very serious crimes, including the murder of an American medic. Decisions regarding the international transfer of offenders are made by me in my capacity as Minister of Public Safety, and at all times I put the safety of Canadians first. A decision will be made on this file, as on all applications, in due course.

(House of Commons Debates, 1 November 2011, p. 2803)
(Débats de la Chambre des Communes, le 1 novembre 2011, p. 2803)

Transportation of Dangerous Goods / Transport des marchandises dangereuses

Ms. Laurin Liu (Rivière-des-Mille-Îles):

The transportation of dangerous goods, like propane and acid, through our communities is a serious issue ... The government has known about these problems for years. Why has it not fixed them?

Hon. Denis Lebel (Minister of Transport, Infrastructure and Communities and Minister of the Economic Development Agency of Canada for the Regions of Quebec):

Transport Canada has accepted the recommendations of the Commissioner of the Environment and Sustainable Development. There are over 30 million shipments of dangerous goods every year in Canada. The program continues to be very successful in preventing incidents during the transportation of dangerous goods.

(House of Commons Debates, 13 December 2011, p. 4389)
(Débats de la Chambre des Communes, le 13 décembre 2011, p. 4389)

INTERNATIONAL HUMANITARIAN LAW / DROIT INTERNATIONAL HUMANITAIRE

Humanitarian Intervention and Aid / Aide et intervention humanitaire

Afghanistan

Mr. Paul Dewar (Ottawa Centre):

Today Canadians learned that our military trainers in Afghanistan were involved in active combat last week when a NATO compound in Kabul came under attack ... Will the government now acknowledge that there is no non-combat military role in a war?

Hon. Peter MacKay (Minister of National Defence):

The combat mission in Afghanistan has now come to an end. We have transitioned to training. That training is taking place in and around Kabul. However, I do not think the member is naive enough to suggest that Canadian Forces are not going to protect themselves when in a volatile city like Kabul. They will return fire and protect themselves. That is what happened in this instance ... Canadians would expect no less.

(House of Commons Debates, 23 September 2011, p. 1390)
(Débats de la Chambre des Communes, le 23 septembre 2011, p. 1390)

Africa / Afrique

Mr. John Carmichael (Don ValleyWest):

[W]hat [is] our government doing to help those affected by the humanitarian crisis in East Africa?

Hon. Bev Oda (Minister of International Cooperation):

Canada is doing its part to help the 13 million affected in East Africa. Canadians again have shown their compassion and generosity. Individual Canadians have donated over $70 million to Canadian organizations. As promised, the government will match their generosity through the African drought relief fund. This brings our government support to $142 million to provide needed food, medicine, nutrition and clean water.

(House of Commons Debates, 5 October 2011, p. 1881)
(Débats de la Chambre des Communes, le 5 octobre 2011, p. 1881)

Libya / Libye

Mr. Jack Harris (St. John's East):

Canada's contribution to the mission in Libya was authorized by Parliament within a clear United Nations mandate: to protect civilians, to enforce a no-fly zone and to obtain a ceasefire. [W]ill the government confirm that our mandate remains unchanged and that Canada's engagement does not include effecting regime change in Libya by force?

Hon. John Baird (Minister of Foreign Affairs):

I can confirm that the motion that the government will put forward next week will be to renew the current existing defence mandate, which will be to protect civilians. We will continue to work within the United Nations framework in that regard. We will continue with the current military mission that we sought approval for from Parliament.

Mr. Chris Alexander (Parliamentary Secretary to the Minister of National Defence):

Canada has indeed taken a leadership role in helping to protect innocent civilians in Libya from the Gadhafi regime that continues to attack them. [T]he cost to date, as of June 2 of the mission, was $26 million. The incremental costs associated with this mission in coming months will be approximately $10 million per month. We are extremely proud of the work of Canadian forces members who have been so courageous in reducing the ability of the Gadhafi regime to threaten its own people.

(House of Commons Debates, 9 June 2011, pp. 202, 204-5)
(Débats de la Chambre des Communes, le 9 juin 2011, pp. 202, 204-5)

L'hon. Jack Layton (chef de l'opposition):

[E]st-ce que l'objectif de la mission en Libye est toujours de protéger les civils, tel que demandé par la résolution de l'ONU?

L'hon. John Baird (ministre des Affaires étrangères):

Absolument. On travaille en Libye en vertu de la résolution de l'ONU. Notre mission militaire n'a pas changé. La résolution sur cette politique dont on va débattre demain visera à poursuivre la mission en cours pendant encore trois mois et demi.

(House of Commons Debates, 13 June 2011, p. 268)
(Débats de la Chambre des Communes, le 13 juin 2011, p. 268)

Mr. Peter Braid (Kitchener — Waterloo, CPC):

[What has been] the situation in Libya?

Mr. Deepak Obhrai (Parliamentary Secretary to the Minister of Foreign Affairs, CPC):

Today the Prime Minister attended the high-level meeting on Libya at the United Nations chaired by the Secretary-General. Canada has been at the forefront of the international effort to protect civilians in Libya against the oppressive Gadhafi regime. Canada stands ready to support the new Libyan government through the UN coordinated efforts committed to helping the people of Libya.

(House of Commons Debates, 20 September 2011, p. 1247)
(Débats de la Chambre des Communes, le 20 septembre 2011, p. 1247)

Pakistan

Mr. John Weston (West Vancouver — Sunshine Coast — Sea to Sky Country):

[H]ow [is] Canada responding to pleas for relief [in Pakistan]?

Hon. Bev Oda (Minister of International Cooperation):

Pakistan is once again suffering from a flood this year. Last year, when I visited Sindh province, I saw how floods can devastate families and children. Canada did its part last year and will do so again, with $11 million this year to help Pakistan. Canadians know that our government will ensure that victims get the food, clean water and health care they need.

(House of Commons Debates, 24 October 2011, pp. 2401-2)
(Débats de la Chambre des Communes, le 24 octobre 2011, pp. 2401-2)

Turkey / Turquie

Mr. John Carmichael (Don Valley West):

This past Sunday, a large earthquake struck eastern Turkey. Over 600 aftershocks followed the devastating earthquake and reports say that thousands of people have been left homeless.
[W]hat [has been] Canada's response to this recent disaster?

Ms. Lois Brown (Parliamentary Secretary to the Minister of International Cooperation):

This morning the Minister of International Cooperation announced Canada's response to this disaster. Canada stands by the people of Turkey, and we offer our support and sympathy to the families and loved ones affected by the tragic earthquake. We are sending 500 winterized tents to Turkey. The tents will ensure urgently needed emergency shelter for 500 families, and we will continue to monitor the situation there.

(House of Commons Debates, 28 October 2011, p. 2670)
(Débats de la Chambre des Communes, le 28 octobre 2011, p. 2670)

International Transfer of Detainees / Transfert international des détenus

Mr. Robert Sopuck (Dauphin — Swan River — Marquette):

Given that our Canadian Forces have left Kandahar, [h]ow is our government honouring its international obligations with regard to detainees in Afghanistan?

Hon. John Baird (Minister of Foreign Affairs):

With the combat mission in Afghanistan now complete ... our government has signed an arrangement with the Obama administration to facilitate the transfer of detainees, captured by Canadian Forces in Afghanistan, to U.S. custody at the detention facility in Parwan. The U.S. operates this facility with the full agreement of the Afghan government and detainees can be prosecuted under Afghan law. Canadian officials will continue to be present on the ground to monitor all Canadian transferred detainees until they are sentenced or released. From the onset of our engagement in Afghanistan, our government has consistently adapted processes for transferring detainees in Afghanistan to ensure that we met our international legal obligations.

(House of Commons Debates, 9 December 2011, p. 4261)
(Débats de la Chambre des Communes, le 9 décembre 2011, p. 4261)

Refugees / Réfugiés

Mrs. Nina Grewal (Fleetwood — Port Kells):

Canadians do not think human smugglers should be permitted to exploit vulnerable refugees. Every year thousands of people wait in line for a chance to come to Canada legally, but these criminals extort thousands of dollars in order to help people jump the queue. [… W]hat is our … government doing to put a stop to all of this?

Hon. Jason Kenney (Minister of Citizenship, Immigration and Multiculturalism):

Last year Canada welcomed the largest number of immigrants in six decades. We welcomed more refugees, resettled through the UN, than any other country in the world per capita. We have the fairest asylum system. What we will not accept are criminal gangs seeking to abuse this country's generosity and treating Canada like a doormat by facilitating the illegal and dangerous entry of people paying tens of thousands of dollars to smuggling syndicates. That is why later today the government will table our legislation to crack down on human smuggling, to stop those who would seek to abuse this country's immigration laws and undermine public confidence, and to support legitimate immigration and refugees.

(House of Commons Debates, 16 June 2011, p. 448)
(Débats de la Chambre des Communes, le 16 juin 2011, p. 448)

TRADE AND ECONOMY / COMMERCE ET ÉCONOMIE

Aerospace / Industrie aérospatiale

Hon. John McKay (Scarborough — Guildwood):

This week we witnessed the sorry spectacle of a Lockheed Martin representative on national television saying that the F-35 is only going to cost $65 million, engine included. Lockheed and the minister seem to be the only ones on earth who believe this. The congressional budget office and our own PBO have priced the figure at twice what the Lockheed Martin representative said. The U.K., Australia, Italy, Holland and Turkey are all considering getting out of this program. Why is the government the only true believer left?

Hon. Julian Fantino (Associate Minister of National Defence):

All reasonable people agree that Canada needs aircraft in order to defend Canadian sovereignty. The current CF-18s must be replaced and our budget for the purchase of F-35s remains on track ... We will ensure that our men and women in uniform have the best equipment to do the job they are required to do safely. As responsible citizens, responsible politicians and responsible government, we owe them no less.

(House of Commons Debates, 5 October 2011, p. 1882)
(Débats de la Chambre des Communes, le 5 octobre 2011, p. 1882)

Agriculture

Hon. Ralph Goodale (Wascana):

When the government kills the Canadian Wheat Board single desk, it could also kill Canada's brand in global grain markets. Private companies will no doubt try to gather up the Wheat Board's $6 billion in annual sales to enhance shareholder value for their owners, not for farmers. Then major foreign grain corporations are likely to come calling with takeover bids. Why does the government think farmers are better off with all key decisions about Canadian grain being made in Minneapolis, Chicago or Kansas City?

Hon. Gerry Ritz (Minister of Agriculture and Agri-Food and Minister for the Canadian Wheat Board):

If we accept the status quo and stay where we are, that is exactly what will happen, a doomsday scenario. What we are doing is moving ahead with marketing freedom for western Canadian farmers. They will now have the ability to choose whom they market through. They are the ones, the stewards of the land, who guarantee the quality and consistency of supply. They will continue to do that. The line companies, whether they are an American, British or European multinational or a Canadian multinational like Viterra, which is global in scope, will continue to market that top-quality grain produced by our farmers.

(House of Commons Debates, 24 October 2011, p. 2397)
(Débats de la Chambre des Communes, le 24 octobre 2011, p. 2397)

GMO / OGM

Mr. Malcolm Allen (Welland):

The ... government is trying to remove important safeguards that keep genetically modified crops separate from non-GMO crops. If the government has its way, the Canadian Food Inspection Agency will no longer test food and seeds that contain low level concentrations of GMOs, but even small traces of GMOs can compromise our trade with Europe and Asia. Why will the government not tell Canadians the truth about their food, and why is it willing to put our trade with our partners at risk?

Hon. Gerry Ritz (Minister of Agriculture and Agri-Food and Minister for the Canadian Wheat Board):

We are trying to protect our food, make sure that there are no trade actions taken when there is a low level presence, less than 1%. That is the right thing to do to enhance our trade and keep product moving.

(House of Commons Debates, 5 December 2011, p. 3974)
(Débats de la Chambre des Communes, le 5 décembre 2011, p. 3974)

Asia-Pacific Gateway / Porte d'entrée de l'Asie-Pacifique

Mr. Randall Garrison (Esquimalt — Juan de Fuca):

Last week, the president of the Asia Pacific Foundation advised the government that to be successful in expanding our trade, Canada needed to invest in human capacity building. This means investing in better language education, better training in cross-cultural communication and more support for international business education. Why [is the government] just shipping away Canadian raw materials and jobs instead of making the smart investments in Canadians that will build a foundation for expanding our trade with the region?

Mr. Gerald Keddy (Parliamentary Secretary to the Minister of International Trade, for the Atlantic Canada Opportunities Agency and for the Atlantic Gateway):

The Asia-Pacific gateway is critical to Canada's long-term economic prosperity. As the demand for Canadian exports to the Asia-Pacific markets continue to grow so do the opportunities for Canadian workers and companies. We are well-positioned to take advantage of the Asia-Pacific markets so we can create economic growth, more jobs and financial security for all Canadians.

(House of Commons Debates, 27 September 2011, p. 1523)
(Débats de la Chambre des Communes, le 27 septembre 2011, p. 1523)

Buy Local Policy / Politique d'achat locale

Hon. Bob Rae (Toronto Centre):

We now have just learned that President Obama's plan for reinvestment in the United States includes several buy American provisions that will cost Canada tens of thousands of jobs when it comes to infrastructure in North America. [H]ow could the government possibly have signed any kind of agreement or come to any kind of agreement with respect to perimeter security and at the same time allow the administration in the United States to carry on direct discrimination against our country?

Right Hon. Stephen Harper (Prime Minister):

[T]his is an important initiative to sustain, not just our security but obviously our access to the American market on which so many Canadian jobs are based. [W]e certainly do not support the protectionist measures that are included in the latest American bill as we have opposed those in the past and will continue to do so. When we do so on this side, we do so as the only party that has an unadulterated record of commitment to free trade.

(House of Commons Debates, 19 September 2011, pp. 1145-46)
(Débats de la Chambre des Communes, le 19 septembre 2011, pp. 1145-46)

Mr. Ron Cannan (Kelowna — Lake Country):

Last week, the U.S. administration proposed the inclusion of buy American provisions as part of their draft infrastructure funding proposal. Our government moved quickly on the matter, raising concerns with the American administration to defend Canadian workers and businesses ... Why is the government raising such strong concerns with the proposed legislation?

Hon. Ed Fast (Minister of International Trade and Minister for the Asia-Pacific Gateway):

I have raised our concerns regarding the draft buy American provisions with Ambassador Jacobson, as well as with Ambassador Kirk, and we have triggered formal consultations on the matter. I reminded the ambassadors that, if enacted, the proposed restrictions would send a negative signal to governments around the world that trade restrictions are an acceptable policy choice. They are not. Our government will continue to advocate opportunities for Canadian workers and businesses alike through free and open trade.

(House of Commons Debates, 20 September 2011, pp. 1249-50)
(Débats de la Chambre des Communes, le 20 septembre 2011, pp. 1249-50)

Canada-US Border / Frontière canado-américaine

Mr. Robert Chisholm (Dartmouth — Cole Harbour):

The government's ongoing incompetence in trade negotiations is once again on display. After failing to obtain an exemption to buy American rules and opening the door to Europe's big pharma ... we learn that ... Canadians will now be charged every time they cross the U.S. border. What is the government's explanation for its latest failure at the bargaining table?

Mr. Gerald Keddy (Parliamentary Secretary to the Minister of International Trade, for the Atlantic Canada Opportunities Agency and for the Atlantic Gateway):

The passage of the three new free trade agreements with the U.S., which include Colombia, Panama and Korea, is a clear recognition, which we applaud, by the U.S. lawmakers that free and open trade is the best way to create jobs and economic growth. We are, however, disappointed that the bill includes the removal of the $5.50 tax exemption on air and sea passengers, not on all passengers, arriving to the United States from Canada, Mexico and the Caribbean. We would hope the Americans recognize the error of their ways and that free and open trade is the way out of this economic depression, not into it.

(House of Commons Debates, 24 October 2011, p. 2398)
(Débats de la Chambre des Communes, le 24 octobre 2011, p. 2398)

Mr. Bryan Hayes (Sault Ste. Marie):

[What was] the announcement yesterday by the President of the United States and the Prime Minister?

Hon. John Baird (Minister of Foreign Affairs):

What we saw yesterday was the leadership of the Prime Minister and the leadership of the President of the United States doing everything they can to help create jobs and have more economic growth. Over recent years we have seen the border become thicker and thicker, and this has hurt Canadian competitiveness and cost Canadian jobs. Yesterday's announcement will make the job of an auto worker in Windsor more secure. Yesterday's announcement will make someone who works in a port in Montreal or on a railway in western Canada secure. This will lead to more jobs and more economic benefits for the Canadian economy. This is good news for the country and we should all be celebrating that.

(House of Commons Debates, 8 December 2011, p. 4201)
(Débats de la Chambre des Communes, le 8 décembre 2011, p. 4201)

Mr. Brian Masse (Windsor West):

Why did the government pretend the new Detroit-Windsor bridge was on track? When will it table its support and legislation to move the new bridge forward?

Hon. Denis Lebel (Minister of Transport, Infrastructure and Communities and Minister of the Economic Development Agency of Canada for the Regions of Quebec):

We remain fully committed to building the new publicly owned crossing between Windsor and Detroit. We will continue to work with the Governments of Michigan and the United States to examine options for delivering the new crossing. Already the Michigan governor, Mr. Snyder, has confirmed that this project remains a top priority for him. It is the same thing for our government.

(House of Commons Debates, 14 December 2011, p. 4436)
(Débats de la Chambre des Communes, le 14 décembre 2011, p. 4436)

Canada's Economy / Économie du Canada

Mr. Robert Chisholm (Dartmouth — Cole Harbour):

What is [the government's] plan for addressing Canada's serious trade imbalance? ... When will the government [... implement] targeted measures to boost exports and fix Canada's trade deficit?

Hon. Ed Fast (Minister of International Trade and Minister for the Asia-Pacific Gateway):

[T]rade is absolutely critical to building our economy ... to creating jobs ... to our long-term prosperity as a country ... T]he best way to boost exports is to expand our trading relationships around the world. Trade accounts for some 60% of our GDP.

(House of Commons Debates, 13 June 2011, pp. 270-71)
(Débats de la Chambre des Communes, le 13 juin 2011, pp. 270-71)

Hon. Michael Chong (Wellington — Halton Hills):

[W]ould the government update the House on its trade agenda?

Mr. Gerald Keddy (Parliamentary Secretary to the Minister of International Trade, for the Atlantic Canada Opportunities Agency and for the Atlantic Gateway):

Yesterday, the Minister of International Trade was, at his request, before committee discussing the enormous benefits of our job creating, pro-trade plan. Today, the minister will embark upon a trade mission to China, because we know that when Canadian businesses grow in this priority market, they create jobs and prosperity here at home [... W]e will continue to pursue our job creating a pro-trade, low-tax plan, a plan that created over 650,000 jobs since July 2009.

(House of Commons Debates, 7 October 2011, p. 2012)
(Débats de la Chambre des Communes, le 7 octobre 2011, p. 2012)

Mr. Randy Hoback (Prince Albert):

[H]ow our government is taking a leadership role on the world stage in response to today's global economic challenges?

Hon. Jim Flaherty (Minister of Finance):

We are representing Canada proudly ... by leading by example, including the strongest financial system in the world, the lowest debt to GDP ratio in the G7, the best job growth in the G7, the best place to invest in the G7. We are leading with the next phase of Canada's economic action plan and lowering taxes to create jobs. We are leading with a prudent plan to return to balanced budgets and surpluses. Now it is time for European leaders to act quickly with strong, decisive and united leadership.

(House of Commons Debates, 24 October 2011, p. 2399)
(Débats de la Chambre des Communes, le 24 octobre 2011, p. 2399)

Copyright / Droit d'auteur

M. André Bellavance (Richmond — Arthabaska):

Avec son projet de loi sur le droit d'auteur deposé aujourd'hui, le gouvernement fait plaisir aux multinationales et aux industries du logiciel, mais il fera perdre près de 75 millions de dollars par année aux artistes ... Le gouvernement est-il conscient que la Loi sur le droit d'auteur qu'il propose aura pour effet de nuire aux artistes et d'affaiblir la culture québécoise?

L'hon. James Moore (ministre du Patrimoine canadien et des Langues officielles):

On a mis sur la table un projet de loi équitable pour tout le monde, pour les créateurs, oui, mais aussi pour les consommateurs. Ce dont les artistes de partout au Canada ont besoin maintenant, dans un projet de loi sur le droit d'auteur, c'est de rendre le piratage illégal au Canada. Voilà ce que contient notre projet de loi C-11. Nous imposons également les Traités Internet de l'OMPI. Beaucoup d'éléments de ce projet de loi protègent les intérêts des artistes au pays et assurent que notre économie continue d'avancer, qu'on crée des emplois et des investissements ici, au Canada, pour tout le monde, incluant les créateurs.

(House of Commons Debates, 29 September 2011, p. 1653)
(Débats de la Chambre des Communes, le 29 septembre 2011, p. 1653)

Foreign Investment / Investissement étranger

Mr. Marc Garneau (Westmount — Ville-Marie):

Last year when the then minister of industry blocked the sale of a potash corporation to BHP Billiton, he said that there was clearly a need to upgrade to update the *Investment Canada Act*, particularly with respect to an extremely important evaluation criteria called net benefit. We have not heard a word for the past eight months ... Will the government give us that clarity for which we have been waiting for eight months?

Hon. Christian Paradis (Minister of Industry and Minister of State (Agriculture)):

Foreign investment is key to the growth of the Canadian economy and our government will continue to encourage it. That being said, significant investments will continue to be reviewable under the *Investment Canada Act*. [T]he House committee ... will continue ... to study the *Investment Canada Act* ... so we can look at ways to improve the act [to] work in the best interests of Canadians and our economy.

(House of Commons Debates, 13 June 2011, p. 271)
(Débats de la Chambre des Communes, le 13 juin 2011, p. 271)

Science and Technology / Sciences et la technologie

Mr. Peter Braid (Kitchener — Waterloo):

When it comes to supporting basic discovery-oriented university research, Canada is ranked number one among the G7 countries. [H]ow [has] our government helped to bring a world-leading facility to Canada [the Stephen Hawking Centre at the Perimeter Institute]?

Hon. Gary Goodyear (Minister of State (Science and Technology) (Federal Economic Development Agency for Southern Ontario):

This brand new federally funded facility will make the Perimeter Institute the largest theoretical physics research and academic organization [in] the world. This year we have invested more in the Perimeter Institute, showing our government's ongoing commitment to building a stronger economy, creating those job opportunities of the future and improving the standard of living for all Canadians through science and technology.

(House of Commons Debates, 21 September 2011, p. 1294)
(Débats de la Chambre des Communes, le 21 septembre 2011, p.1294)

Steel Industry / Industrie de l'acier

Mr. David Sweet (Ancaster — Dundas — Flamborough — Westdale):

In 2009, our government went to court to ensure U.S. Steel would meet commitments it made under the *Investment Canada Act* when it purchased Stelco. Could the Minister of Industry give the House an update on this important issue?

Hon. Christian Paradis (Minister of Industry and Minister of State (Agriculture)):

[O]ur top priorities are jobs and the economy. Today I am announcing that the government and U.S. Steel have come to an agreement that ends the court proceedings. Under this enhanced agreement, U.S. Steel has committed to continue operations in Canada until 2015, with $50 million in capital investments above its original undertaking of $200 million and a contribution of $3 million toward community programs in Hamilton and Nanticoke. When it comes to foreign investment and a company makes an undertaking, we will ensure it is respected.

(House of Commons Debates, 12 December 2011, p. 4312)
(Débats de la Chambre des Communes, le 12 décembre 2011, p. 4312)

Stock Markets / Bourses et les marchés de capitaux

M. Peter Julian (Burnaby — New Westminster):

La Bourse de Londres cherçhe à avaler les Bourses de Toronto et de Montréal pour prendre le contrôle des marchés de capitaux canadiens ... Pourquoi [le minister] refuse-t-il de tenir des audiences publiques sur ce sujet?

Mr. Mike Lake (Parliamentary Secretary to the Minister of Industry):

[We have] received an application for a review under the *Investment Canada Act* from the London Stock Exchange Group [... We] are conducting a thorough analysis of this proposed investment and will consult extensively, including with affected provinces and territories, to ensure that they have all of the information required to make the best decision. It should be noted that the minister will only approve applications where an investment demonstrates that it is likely to be of net benefit to Canadians.

(House of Commons Debates, 21 June 2011, p. 572)
(Débats de la Chambre des Communes, le 21 juin 2011, p. 572)

Tariffs / Tarifs

M. Mathieu Ravignat (Pontiac):

Les États-Unis envisagent, encore une fois, d'imposer un tarif special aux entreprises canadiennes. Cette fois, ce sont les cargos en provenance de la Colombie-Britannique qui devront payer une taxe de 140 $ le conteneur s'ils veulent accoster aux États-Unis ... Ce gouvernement se va-t-il se tenir debout face à son voisin américain et refuser cette nouvelle attaque à notre commerce?

Hon. Ed Fast (Minister of International Trade and Minister for the Asia-Pacific Gateway, CPC):

Any new tax is a bad idea as it raises costs on consumers. Canada's ports and railways are competing fairly. The Asia-Pacific gateway initiative that the member refers to is working as intended. We will defend Canada's competitive advantage wherever it is threatened. I have made this clear to FMC Commissioner Lidinsky as well as to my USTR counterpart Ambassador Kirk.

(House of Commons Debates, 5 October 2011, p. 1879)
(Débats de la Chambre des Communes, le 5 octobre 2011, p. 1879)

Taxation / Fiscalité

Mr. John Williamson (New Brunswick Southwest):

[W]hat steps [is] our government taking to protect Canadian taxpayers [in view of the new U.S. tax reporting requirements]?

Mrs. Shelly Glover (Parliamentary Secretary to the Minister of Finance):

We ... raised this issue directly with the U.S. government. We have also been very clear: any penalties imposed by the IRS under FBAR will not be collected by Canada. As such, we have called, and will continue to call, on the U.S. government to look upon them with leniency. We are also happy to report some progress as the IRS has released a statement that says [that] "The IRS recognizes that many Canadians face complex tax situations because of dual citizenship. Recent publicity about the issue has spotlighted a number of areas that the IRS will consider in our continuing effort to strike the right balance in administering the U.S. tax laws."

(House of Commons Debates, 3 October 2011, pp. 1761-62)
(Débats de la Chambre des Communes, le 3 octobre 2011, pp. 1761-62)

Telecommunications / Télécommunications

Mr. Glenn Thibeault (Sudbury):

[A]n OECD report ... shows that Canadians pay some of the highest cellphone fees in the world. In fact, our roaming rates are more than double the OECD average ... When will this minister act?

L'hon. Christian Paradis (ministre de l'Industrie et ministre d'État (Agriculture)):

Il est important de s'assurer qu'il y ait une bonne compétitivité au Canada. Des décisions seront prises correctement en temps et lieu, mais on veut que le service offert soit acceptable pour les consommateurs canadiens, et pour cela, une bonne compétitivité est nécessaire ... Down the road, we want consumers to have the choice to pick the cellphone they want. For this, we hope to have the support of the [House] to move forward on reforms to come.

(House of Commons Debates, 9 June 2011, p. 205)
(Débats de la Chambre des Communes, le 9 juin 2011, p. 205)

Trade Agreements / Accords commerciaux

Asia / Asie

Mr. Robert Chisholm (Dartmouth — Cole Harbour):

A new report from the Canadian Council of Chief Executives and the Canada China Business Council says that ... economic dealings with the region [are poor and] that Canada now has a bad reputation with Asia. How can [... the government] move Canada forward on trade [with the region]?

Hon. Ed Fast (Minister of International Trade and Minister for the Asia-Pacific Gateway):

Our government understands that closer and deeper economic ties between Canada and Asia will benefit both our countries by creating more jobs, opportunities and prosperity. The facts are this. I was in China last week demonstrating what Canada has to offer and to help expand our trade and investment relationship. Negotiations are moving forward on a FIPA with China. The week before I was in Indonesia and I signed Canada's first trade and investment framework agreement with Asia.

(House of Commons Debates, 19 October 2011, pp. 2212-13)
(Débats de la Chambre des Communes, le 19 octobre 2011, pp. 2212-13)

Mr. Ron Cannan (Kelowna — Lake Country):

[What have been] the recent achievements at the APEC summit?

Mr. Gerald Keddy (Parliamentary Secretary to the Minister of International Trade, for the Atlantic Canada Opportunities Agency and for the Atlantic Gateway):

We continue to strengthen our economic co-operation in the Asia-Pacific region. At the APEC summit, we signed a telecommunications agreement with Mexico and formally expressed our willingness to join the trans-Pacific partnership, which represents a potential market of more than 775 million people. At the same time, we will continue to defend and promote Canada's specific interests and every sector of our economy as part of our job-creating pro-trade plan.

(House of Commons Debates, 14 November 2011, p. 3031)
(Débats de la Chambre des Communes, le 14 novembre 2011, p. 3031)

Hon. Wayne Easter (Malpeque):

Why has the minister consistently failed to secure a trade agreement with South Korea?

Hon. Ed Fast (Minister of International Trade and Minister for the Asia-Pacific Gateway):

Our government is working hard to open up new doors for Canadian farmers, workers and businesses. We recently negotiated further steps toward opening up market access with South Korea on beef and are closely monitoring its domestic implementation process. We will only sign trade agreements that are actually in the best interests of Canadians, unlike the Liberals. In less than six years, we have concluded free trade agreements with nine countries. We continue to work on agreements with 50 more.

(House of Commons Debates, 2 December 2011, p. 3925)
(Débats de la Chambre des Communes, le 2 décembre 2011, p. 3925)

European Union / Union européenne

Hon. Wayne Easter (Malpeque):

What is the minister's specific position on the costs of drugs as it relates to the [Canada-EU trade] agreement[?]

Hon. Ed Fast (Minister of International Trade and Minister for the Asia-Pacific Gateway):

The European-Canada free trade negotiations are going to lead to a boost in trade for Canada in the order of $12 billion per year. We are talking about a dramatic increase in trade between our respective countries. With respect to the negotiations that are ongoing, there are many aspects of that agreement that still have to be negotiated ... We are standing up for Canadians. We will only sign an agreement that is in the best interests of Canadians.

(House of Commons Debates, 22 June 2011, pp. 612-13)
(Débats de la Chambre des Communes, le 22 juin 2011, pp. 612-13)

Mr. Robert Chisholm (Dartmouth — Cole Harbour):

Why do the Conservatives continue to negotiate bad trade deals that put Canadian jobs at risk?

Mr. Gerald Keddy (Parliamentary Secretary to the Minister of International Trade, for the Atlantic Canada Opportunities Agency and for the Atlantic Gateway):

Our trade negotiation with the European Union is Canada's most important trade initiative since the signing of the historic North American free trade agreement. A trade agreement with the EU will increase ... two-way trade by 20%[; it will create ...] 80,000 new jobs for Canadian workers; and $1,000 average extra income for Canadian families .... This is an ambitious free trade agreement.

(House of Commons Debates, 17-18 October 2011, pp. 2064-65, 2142)
(Débats de la Chambre des Communes, le 17-18 octobre 2011, pp. 2064-65, 2142)

Kuwait / Koweït

Mr. Devinder Shory (Calgary Northeast):

Today the Minister of International Trade signed a foreign investment promotion and protection agreement with Kuwait ... Could the ... Minister ... explain ... how Canadian workers and their families will benefit from [this] agreement?

Hon. Ed Fast (Minister of International Trade and Minister for the Asia-Pacific Gateway):

The agreement ... will encourage two-way trade and investment by providing certainty and predictability for investors. This will in turn create jobs and economic growth for Canadian workers and their families. Canadians intuitively understand that expanded trade is key to their long-term prosperity. We will continue to take measures that broaden and deepen our trading relationships.

(House of Commons Debates, 26 September 2011, p. 1450)
(Débats de la Chambre des Communes, le 26 septembre 2011, p. 1450)

Panama and Jordan / Panama et la Jordanie

Mr. Ed Holder (London West):

Today the Minister of International Trade tabled both the Canada-Jordan economic growth and prosperity act, as well as the Canada-Panama economic growth and prosperity act ... Would the minister please explain ...

why these pieces of legislation are critical to creating economic growth and prosperity in Canada?

Hon. Ed Fast (Minister of International Trade and Minister for the Asia-Pacific Gateway):

Free trade agreements with Jordan and Panama are a key part of our job-creating, pro-trade plan. I was proud to table this important legislation this morning. [O]ur government will continue to pursue our pro-trade plan because open markets create new opportunities for our farmers and small businesses[.]

(House of Commons Debates, 15 November 2011, pp. 3102-3)
(Débats de la Chambre des Communes, le 15 novembre 2011, pp. 3102-3)

Trans-Pacific Partnership / Partenariat transpacifique

Mrs. Nycole Turmel (Leader of the Opposition):

What will Canada give up in order to be allowed into the trans-Pacific partnership trade talks?

Hon. Peter MacKay (Minister of National Defence):

We have formally expressed an interest in our willingness to work with the trans-Pacific partnership. Having said that, all countries approach these negotiations with a view to protecting their interests, as Canada certainly will. Therefore, Canada's approach to the TPP will not be different with respect to the European Union free trade negotiations. Of course, this includes our interest in defending and promoting our specific interests in the economy, including supply management.

(House of Commons Debates, 14 November 2011, p. 3024)
(Débats de la Chambre des Communes, le 14 novembre 2011, p. 3024)

World Trade Organization (WTO) / Organisation Mondiale du Commerce (OMC)

Mrs. Joy Smith (Kildonan — St. Paul):

Today politicians of the European Union passed a motion calling on Canada to drop the World Trade Organization challenge against their unfair and improper ban on Canadian seal products. [Does] Canada intend … to back down on this challenge?

Mr. Gerald Keddy (Parliamentary Secretary to the Minister of International Trade, for the Atlantic Canada Opportunities Agency and for the Atlantic Gateway):

Canada's position on seals is a completely separate matter from ongoing negotiations with the European Union over our comprehensive economic trade agreement. Furthermore, the EU ban on virtually all Canadian seal products is inconsistent with the EU's international trade obligations. That is why the Canadian government has initiated the WTO dispute settlement process and we will be moving ahead with our WTO challenge.

(House of Commons Debates, 8 June 2011, p. 132)
(Débats de la Chambre des Communes, le 8 juin 2011, p. 132)

Mrs. Tilly O'Neill Gordon (Miramichi):

Today the WTO released the Canadian trade policy review. The report praises Canada's strong economic performance during the global recession and commends Canada's aggressive pro-trade plan. [... C]ould the minister explain why we will continue aggressively pursuing a free trade agenda?

Hon. Ed Fast (Minister of International Trade and Minister for the Asia-Pacific Gateway):

We recognize that one in five Canadian jobs is directly or indirectly related to trade and to exports. In order to protect and strengthen the financial security of hard-working Canadians, we will continue to pursue a low-tax free trade plan because we know it will create jobs. Canadians understand that this is a kitchen-table issue and we are pleased the World Trade Organization has acknowledged the merits of our job-creating pro-trade plan.

(House of Commons Debates, 20 June 2011, p. 502)
(Débats de la Chambre des Communes, le 20 juin 2011, p. 502)

Hon. Wayne Easter (Malpeque):

We have known for some time that Canada would win the WTO challenge against the United States protectionist country of origin labelling. We know that this action has cost Canadian livestock producers in excess of $5 billion and has forced some Canadian farmers out of business, yet with that leverage in hand, where are the ministers? [... H]as the government even entered negotiations with the United States to secure this victory for farmers?

Mr. Gerald Keddy (Parliamentary Secretary to the Minister of International Trade, for the Atlantic Canada Opportunities Agency and for the Atlantic Gateway):

Today the WTO panel released its final report which determined the country of origin labeling measures discriminated against foreign livestock and was inconsistent with U.S. WTO trade rules. [W]e will continue to work on behalf of Canadian producers to supply more Canadian jobs and more opportunity, whether that means going to the WTO or going directly to our trading partners.

(House of Commons Debates, 18 November 2011, p. 3271)
(Débats de la Chambre des Communes, le 18 novembre 2011, p. 3271)

LAW OF THE SEA / DROIT DE LA MER

Fisheries / Pêches

Mr. Fin Donnelly (New Westminster — Coquitlam):

After the discovery of infectious salmon anemia in two wild sockeye smolts, U.S. federal agencies are preparing an emergency research effort into this threat of their wild, hatchery and farmed salmon. [... W]hat emergency action ... will [Canada] take?

Hon. Keith Ashfield (Minister of Fisheries and Oceans and Minister for the Atlantic Gateway):

Stringent federal regulations are in place to protect Canada's aquatic species from disease. Infectious salmon anemia, ISA, has never been found in B.C. aquaculture salmon. Fisheries and Oceans Canada in the Pacific region has been testing wild sockeye salmon for ISA. In fact, 300 samples tested this year have all tested negative ... Fisheries and Oceans Canada will conduct testing in the national ISA reference laboratory.

(House of Commons Debates, 20 October 2011, p. 2282)
(Débats de la Chambre des Communes, le 20 octobre 2011, p. 2282)

Mr. Fin Donnelly (New Westminster — Coquitlam):

Toronto is the latest city to join others in Canada and across North America in banning the sale and use of shark fins. Up to 75 million sharks are finned and thrown away at sea every year, often while still alive. Will the government ... end this practice and ban the import of shark fins to Canada?

Hon. Keith Ashfield (Minister of Fisheries and Oceans and Minister for the Atlantic Gateway):

Shark finning is an offensive practice. It has been banned in Canada since the early 1990s.

(House of Commons Debates, 26 October 2011, p. 2524)
(Débats de la Chambre des Communes, le 26 octobre 2011, p. 2524)

Sustainability / Durabilité

Mr. Scott Armstrong (Cumberland — Colchester — Musquodoboit Valley):

Today marks World Oceans Day, a time when we recognize the importance of maintaining the health of a marine environment and its resources. [What has been] the recent progress to advance this effort?

Hon. Keith Ashfield (Minister of Fisheries and Oceans and Minister for the Atlantic Gateway):

Healthy oceans and their role in the economic and social life for our country are critically important. This is why earlier today I was pleased to announce three new candidate marine protected areas on the east coast and in the Gulf of St. Lawrence, as well as a strategy for protecting the important corals and sponge reefs on our Pacific coast. Today's announcements complement the eight marine areas which the government has protected since 2006, as well as our investments in science, the Coast Guard and sustainable fisheries.

(House of Commons Debates, 8 June 2011, p. 129)
(Débats de la Chambre des Communes, le 8 juin 2011, p. 129)

Mr. Fin Donnelly (New Westminster — Coquitlam):

Why has the government walked away from a plan to protect the economic, social and environmental health of our oceans?

Hon. Keith Ashfield (Minister of Fisheries and Oceans and Minister for the Atlantic Gateway):

This government remains fully committed to developing an integrated management plan for the Pacific north coast by December 2012. Our goal is to develop a plan that is relevant and effective for the specific area, using an approach that is consistent with similar large oceans management areas. It is our intention to continue to work closely with first nations and the province of British Columbia, which have been valuable partners in the planning process.

(House of Commons Debates, 5 October 2011, p. 1882)
(Débats de la Chambre des Communes, le 5 octobre 2011, p. 1882)

SPORTS

Mr. Chris Warkentin (Peace River):

Over the weekend, Team Canada travelled to Athens, Greece, where it will showcase the exceptional talent of our athletes and coaches at the Special Olympics World Summer Games. [W]hat [is] the government doing to support our Special Olympics athletes as they proudly represent us abroad?

Hon. Bal Gosal (Minister of State (Sport)):

Canada is home to some of the greatest athletes in the world. Last week, [the government] had the opportunity to send Team Canada on its journey of athletic excellence. Our government is proud to assist Special Olympics Canada by including regional funding in budget 2011 to provide opportunities for Canadian athletes with intellectual disabilities. This government congratulates Team Canada and wishes it great success at the World Summer Games.

(House of Commons Debates, 20 June 2011, p. 500)
(Débats de la Chambre des Communes, le 20 juin 2011, p. 500)

Mr. Kyle Seeback (Brampton West):

Over the next two weeks, athletes representing 44 countries will compete in the 2011 Pan American Games and later, the Parapan American Games in Guadalajara, Mexico. Among these athletes is our very own Team Canada. [...H]ow [is] Canada preparing to host the games in 2015?

Hon. Bal Gosal (Minister of State (Sport)):

Last week, I travelled to Guadalajara, Mexico to support our athletes at the 2011 Pan American Games. [S]o far Canada has won 33 medals. The government is proud to support Team Canada through funding to the Canadian Olympic and Paralympic committees and national sports organizations. As a proud supporter of the upcoming 2015 games in Toronto, we have committed funding to sports infrastructure, legacy and essential federal services. We look forward to welcoming these games to Canada.

(House of Commons Debates, 20 October 2011, p. 2287)
(Débats de la Chambre des Communes, le 20 octobre 2011, p. 2287)

Treaty Action Taken by Canada in 2010-11 / Mesures prises par le Canada en matière de traités en 2010-11

compiled by/ préparé par
SYLVIE CAMERON

BILATERAL

Bahamas
Agreement between Canada and the Commonwealth of the Bahamas for the Exchange of Information on Tax Matters. *Signed*: Nassau, 17 June 2010. *Entered into force*: 16 November 2011.

Barbados
Protocol Amending the Agreement between Canada and Barbados for the Avoidance of Double Taxation and the Prevention of Fiscal Evasion with Respect to Taxes on Income and on Capital, done at Bridgetown on 22 January 1980. *Signed*: Bridgetown, 8 November 2011.

Brazil
Framework Agreement between the Government of Canada and the Government of the Federative Republic of Brazil for Cooperation on Science, Technology and Innovation. *Signed*: Sao Paulo, 17 November 2008. *Entered into force*: 19 April 2010.

Agreement between the Government of Canada and the Government of the Federative Republic of Brazil on Air Transport. *Signed*: Brasilia, 8 August 2011.

Agreement on Social Security between Canada and the Federative Republic of Brazil. *Signed*: Brasilia, 8 August 2011.

Colombia
Free Trade Agreement between Canada and the Republic of Colombia. *Signed*: Lima, 21 November 2008. *Entered into force*: 15 August 2011.

Agreement on the Environment between Canada and the Republic of Colombia. *Signed*: Lima, 21 November 2008. *Entered into force*: 15 August 2011.

Agreement on Labour Cooperation between Canada and the Republic of Colombia. *Signed*: Lima, 21 November 2008. *Entered into force*: 15 August 2011.

Agreement Concerning Annual Reports on Human Rights and Free Trade

Sylvie Cameron is Treaty Custodian and Administrator in the Legal Affairs Bureau of the Department of Foreign Affairs and International Trade / Gardienne des traités et administratrice, Direction générale des affaires juridiques, Ministère des Affaires étrangères et du Commerce international. This list is based on the information available on 7 March 2012 / Liste à jour selon les renseignements disponibles au 7 mars 2012.

between Canada and the Republic of Colombia. *Signed*: Bogota, 27 May 2010. *Entered into force*: 15 August 2011.

Costa Rica
Agreement between the Government of Canada and the Government of the Republic of Costa Rica on Air Transport. *Signed*: San Jose, 11 August 2011.

Agreement between Canada and the Republic of Costa Rica for the Exchange of Information on Tax Matters. *Signed*: San Jose, 11 August 2011.

Dominica
Agreement between Canada and the Commonwealth of Dominica for the Exchange of Information with Respect to Tax Matters. *Signed*: Roseau, 29 June 2010.

European Community
Agreement on Civil Aviation Safety between Canada and the European Community. *Signed*: Prague, 6 May 2009. *Entered into force*: 26 July 2011.

Exchange of Letters Concerning the Amendment of Annex V to the Agreement between the European Community and the Government of Canada on Sanitary Measures to Protect Public and Animal Health in Respect of Trade in Live Animals and Animal Products. *Signed*: Brussels, 22 March and 16 April 2010.

European Space Agency
Cooperation Agreement between the Government of Canada and the European Space Agency. *Signed*: Paris, 15 December 2010.

Estonia
Agreement between the Government of Canada and the Government of the Republic of Estonia Concerning Youth Exchanges. *Signed*: Tallin, 14 December 2009. *Entered into force*: 1 August 2010.

France
Protocol Amending the Convention between the Government of Canada and the Government of the French Republic for the Avoidance of Double Taxation and the Prevention of Fiscal Evasion with Respect to Taxes on Income and on Capital signed on 2 May 1975, as amended by the Protocol signed on 16 January 1987 and as further amended by the Protocol signed 30 November 1995. *Signed*: Paris, 2 February 2010.

Greece
Exchange of Notes Recording an Agreement between Canada and Greece Providing for the Reciprocal Exemption from Income Tax of Earnings Derived from the Operation of Ships. *Signed*: London, 30 September 1929. *Entered into force*: 30 September 1929. *Terminated*: 16 December 2010.

Convention between Canada and the Hellenic Republic for the Avoidance of Double Taxation and the Prevention of Fiscal Evasion with Respect to Taxes on Income and on Capital. *Signed*: Athens, 29 June 2009. *Entered into force*: 16 December 2010.

Agreement between Canada and the Hellenic Republic concerning Youth Mobility. *Signed*: Athens, 28 May 2011.

Hungary
Agreement on Film and Video Relations between the Government of Canada and the Government of the Hungarian People's Republic. *Signed*: Budapest, 7 May 1987. *Entered into force*: 18 January 2010.

India
Agreement between the Government of Canada and the Government of the Republic of India for Co-operation in Peaceful Uses of Nuclear Energy. *Signed*: Toronto, 27 June 2010.

Israel
Agreement on Bilateral Cooperation in Industrial Research and Development between the Government of Canada and the Government of the State of Israel. *Signed*: Jerusalem, 10 July 2011. *Entered into force*: 21 February 2012.

Italy
Convention between the Government of Canada and the Government of the Italian Republic for the Avoidance of Double Taxation with Respect to Taxes on Income and the Prevention of Fiscal Evasion. *Signed*: Ottawa, 3 June 2002. *Entered into force*: 25 November 2011.

Treaty between the Government of Canada and the Government of the Italian Republic Concerning Extradition. *Signed*: Rome, 13 January 2005. *Entered into force*: 17 November 2010.

Kuwait
Agreement between Canada and the State of Kuwait for the Promotion and Protection of Investments. *Signed*: Ottawa, 26 September 2011.

Latvia
Agreement between the Government of Canada and the Government of the Republic of Latvia for the Promotion and Protection of Investments. *Signed*: Ottawa, 26 April 1995. *Entered into force*: 27 July 1995. *Terminated*: 24 November 2011.

Agreement between the Government of Canada and the Government of the Republic of Latvia for the Promotion and Protection of Investments. *Signed*: Riga, 5 May 2009. *Entered into force*: 24 November 2011.

Lithuania
Agreement between the Government of Canada and the Government of the Republic of Lithuania concerning Youth Exchanges. *Signed*: Vilnius, 19 November 2009. *Entered into force*: 1 October 2010.

Macedonia
Agreement on Social Security between Canada and the Republic of Macedonia. *Signed*: Ottawa, 26 August 2009. *Entered into force*: 1 November 2011.

Mexico
Protocol amending the Air Transport Agreement between the Government of Canada and the Government of the United Mexican States, done at Mexico City on 21 December 1961, as amended. *Signed*: Ottawa, 27 May 2010. *Entered into force*: 1 December 2011.

Mutual Recognition Agreement between the Government of Canada and the Government of the United Mexican States for Conformity Assessment of Telecommunications Equipment. *Signed*: Honolulu, 12 November 2011.

Morocco
Convention on Social Security between the Government of Canada and the Government of the Kingdom of Morocco. *Signed*: Rabat, 1 July 1998. *Entered into force*: 1 March 2010.

Namibia
Convention between Canada and the Republic of Namibia for the Avoidance of Double Taxation and the Prevention of Fiscal Evasion with Respect to Taxes on Income and on Capital. *Signed*: Windhoek, 25 March 2010.

Netherlands
Agreement between the Government of Canada and the Government of the Kingdom of the Netherlands on Mutual Administrative Assistance in Customs Matters. *Signed*: Ottawa, 14 August 2007. *Entered into force*: 1 September 2010.

Exchange of Notes Constituting an Amendment to the Agreement between the Government of Canada and the Government of the Kingdom of the Netherlands on Mutual Administrative Assistance in Customs Matters, done in Ottawa on 14 August 2007. *Signed*: Ottawa, 30 March 2009 and 28 April 2009. *Entered into force*: 1 December 2010.

Agreement between the Government of Canada and the Government of the Kingdom of the Netherlands in Respect of the Netherlands Antilles on Exchange of Information on Tax Matters. *Signed*: Vancouver, 29 August 2009. *Entered into force*: 1 January 2011.

Agreement between Canada and the Kingdom of the Netherlands in respect of Aruba for the Exchange of Information with respect to Tax Matters. *Signed*: Ottawa, 20 October 2011.

New Zealand

Agreement between the Government of Canada and the Government of New Zealand on Air Transport. *Signed*: Ottawa, 4 September 1985. *Entered into force*: 4 September 1985. *Terminated*: 18 October 2011.

Agreement between the Government of Canada and the Government of New Zealand on Air Transport. *Signed*: Singapore, 21 July 2009. *Entered into force*: 18 October 2011.

Panama

Agreement on the Environment between Canada and the Republic of Panama. *Signed*: Ottawa, 13 May 2010.

Agreement on Labour Cooperation between Canada and the Republic of Panama. *Signed*: Ottawa, 13 May 2010.

Free Trade Agreement between Canada and the Republic of Panama. *Signed*: Ottawa, 14 May 2010.

Romania

Agreement between the Government of Canada and the Government of the Republic of Romania for the Promotion and Reciprocal Protection of Investments. *Signed*: Bucharest, 17 April 1996. *Entered into force*: 11 February 1997. *Terminated*: 23 November 2011.

Agreement between the Government of Canada and the Government of Romania for the Promotion and Reciprocal Protection of Investments. *Signed*: Bucharest, 8 May 2009. *Entered into force*: 23 November 2011.

Agreement on Social Security between Canada and Romania. *Signed*: Ottawa, 19 November 2009. *Entered into force*: 1 November 2011.

Administrative Agreement between the Government of Canada and the Government of Romania for the Application of the Agreement on Social Security between Canada and Romania. *Signed*: Bucharest, 1 June 2010. *Entered into force*: 1 November 2011.

Agreement between Canada and Romania concerning Diplomatic Premises. *Signed*: Bucharest, 11 March 2011.

Saint Christopher and Nevis

Agreement between Canada and the Federation of Saint Christopher (St. Kitts) and Nevis for the Exchange of Information on Tax Matters. *Signed*: Basseterre, 14 June 2010. *Entered into force*: 21 November 2011.

Saint Lucia

Agreement between Canada and Saint Lucia for the Exchange of Information on Tax Matters. *Signed*: Castries, 18 June 2010.

Saint Vincent and the Grenadines

Agreement between Canada and St. Vincent and the Grenadines for the

Exchange of Information on Tax Matters. *Signed*: Kingstown, 22 June 2010. *Entered into force*: 4 October 2011.

San Marino
Agreement between Canada and the Republic of San Marino for the Exchange of Information on Tax Matters. *Signed*: San Marino, 27 October 2010. *Entered into force*: 20 October 2011.

Singapore
Protocol Amending the Convention between the Government of Canada and the Government of the Republic of Singapore for the Avoidance of Double Taxation and the Prevention of Fiscal Evasion with Respect to Taxes on Income, done in Singapore on 6 March 1976. *Signed*: Singapore, 29 November 2011.

Slovak Republic
Agreement between Canada and the Slovak Republic on Youth Mobility, *Signed*: Bratislava, 20 July 2010. *Entered into force*: 1 July 2011.

Agreement between Canada and the Slovak Republic for the Promotion and Protection of Investments. *Signed*: Bratislava, 20 July 2010. *Entered into force*: 14 March 2012.

Slovenia
Agreement between Canada and the Republic of Slovenia Concerning Youth Mobility. *Signed*: Ljubljana, 22 October 2009. *Entered into force*: 1 July 2010.

South Africa
Agreement between the Government of Canada and the Government of the Republic of South Africa Regarding Mutual Assistance between Their Customs Administrations. *Signed*: Johannesburg, 30 October 2009. *Entered into force*: 9 November 2010.

Switzerland
Agreement Concerning the Protocol Amending the Convention between the Government of Canada and the Swiss Federal Council for the Avoidance of Double Taxation with Respect to Taxes on Income and on Capital, done at Berne on 5 May 1997. *Signed*: Berne, 21 October 2010. *Entered into force*: 16 December 2011.

Protocol Amending the Convention between the Government of Canada and the Swiss Federal Council for the Avoidance of Double Taxation with Respect to Taxes on Income and on Capital, done at Berne on 5 May 1997. *Signed*: Berne, 22 October 2010. *Entered into force*: 16 December 2011.

Turkey
Agreement between Canada and the Republic of Turkey for the Avoidance of Double Taxation and the Prevention of Fiscal Evasion with Respect to Taxes on Income and on Capital. *Signed*: Ottawa, 14 July 2009. *Entered into force*: 4 May 2011.

United Kingdom of Great Britain and Northern Ireland
Agreement between the Government of Canada and the Government of Bermuda under Entrustment from the Government of the United Kingdom of Great Britain and Northern Ireland on the Exchange of Information with Respect to Taxes. *Signed*: Hamilton, Bermuda, 14 June 2010. *Entered into force*: 1 July 2011.

Agreement between the Government of Canada and the Government of the Turks and Caicos Islands under Entrustment from the Government of the United Kingdom of Great Britain and Northern Ireland for the Exchange of Information on Tax Matters. *Signed*: Cockburn Town, 22 June 2010. *Entered into force*: 6 October 2011.

Agreement between the Government of Canada and the Government of the Cayman Islands under Entrustment from the Government of the United Kingdom of Great Britain and Northern Ireland for the Exchange of Information on Tax Matters. *Signed*: George Town, 24 June 2010. *Entered into force*: 1 June 2011.

Agreement between the Government of Canada and the Government of Anguilla under Entrustment from the Government of the United Kingdom of Great Britain and Northern Ireland for the Exchange of Information with Respect to Tax Matters. *Signed*: Bridgetown, 28 October 2010. *Entered into force*: 12 October 2011.

Agreement between the Government of Canada and the Government of Jersey, under Entrustment from the Government of the United Kingdom of Great Britain and Northern Ireland, for the Exchange of Information Relating to Tax Matters. *Signed*: Saint Helier, 12 January 2011. *Entered into force*: 19 December 2011.

Agreement between the Government of Canada and the Government of the Isle of Man, under Entrustment from the Government of the United Kingdom of Great Britain and Northern Ireland, for the Exchange of Information on Tax Matters. *Signed*: Douglas, 17 January 2011. *Entered into force*: 19 December 2011.

Agreement between the Government of Canada and the States of Guernsey, under Entrustment from the Government of the United Kingdom of Great Britain and Northern Ireland, for the Exchange of Information on Tax Matters. *Signed*: Saint Peter Port, 19 January 2011. *Entered into force*: 18 January 2012.

United States

Exchange of Notes (26 and 30 June 1953) between Canada and the United States of America Regarding the Transfer to Canada of the Three Loran Stations at Port-aux-Basques, Battle Harbour and Bonavista in Newfoundland. *Signed*: Ottawa, 26 and 30 June 1953. *Entered into force*: 30 June 1953. *Terminated*: 24 September 2010.

Exchange of Notes (1 and 3 May 1954) between Canada and the United States of America regarding the Construction and Operation of a Loran Station by the United States Coast Guard at Cape Christian, Baffin Island. *Signed*: Ottawa, 1 and 3 May 1954. *Entered into force*: 3 May 1954. *Terminated*: 24 September 2010.

Exchange of Notes (7 and 8 June 1965) between the Government of Canada and the Government of the United States of America concerning the Loan by the United States of Certain Loran-A Equipment for Use in Canadian Loran-A Stations. *Signed*: Ottawa, 7 and 8 June 1965. *Entered into force*: 8 June 1965. *Terminated*: 24 September 2010.

Exchange of Notes (19 and 28 April 1966) between the Government of Canada and the Government of the United States of America concerning the Loan by the United States of Loran-A Equipment in Addition to that Loaned under the Agreement of 8 June 1965. *Signed*: Ottawa 19 April and 28 July 1966. *Entered into force*: 28 July 1966. *Terminated*: 24 September 2010.

Exchange of Notes (27 July and 25 October 1967) between the Government of Canada and the Government of the United States of America extending the Loan of Loran-A Equipment to Canadian Loran A Stations. *Signed*: Ottawa, 27 July and 25 October

1967. *Entered into force*: 25 October 1967. *Terminated* 24 September 2010.

Exchange of Notes between Canada and the United States of America relating to the Construction and Maintenance by Canada of a Loran-A Station at Gray Point, British Columbia. *Signed*: Ottawa, 8 April 1971. *Entered into force*: 8 April 1971. *Terminated*: 24 September 2010.

Exchange of Notes (28 May and 3 June 1976) between the Government of Canada and the Government of the United States of America Providing for the Establishment, Maintenance and Operation of a Loran-C Transmitting Station at Williams Lake, B.C. *Signed*: Ottawa, 28 May and 3 June 1976. *Entered into force*: 3 June 1976. *Terminated*: 24 September 2010.

Exchange of Notes between the Government of Canada and the Government of the United States of America Constituting an Agreement to Provide for the Establishment of an Experimental Loran-C Power Chain in the Vicinity of the St. Marys River in Ontario and Michigan. *Signed*: Washington, 29 March 1977. *Entered into force*: 29 March 1977. *Terminated*: 24 September 2010.

Exchange of Notes (19 and 29 March 1979) between the Government of Canada and the Government of the United States of America constituting an Agreement providing for the Establishment of a Loran-C Station in the vicinity of Port Hardy, Vancouver Island, B C. *Signed*: Ottawa, 19 and 29 March 1979. *Entered into force*: 29 March 1979. *Terminated*: 24 September 2010.

Exchange of Notes between the Government of Canada and the Government of the United States Constituting an Agreement renewing the Agreement of 29 March 1977 concerning the Establishment of Mini Loran-C Stations in the Vicinity of St. Mary's River in Ontario and Michigan. *Signed*: Ottawa, 28 October and 5 December 1980. *Entered into force*: 5 December 1980. *Terminated*: 24 September 2010.

Exchange of Notes between the Government of Canada and the Government of the United States of America Replacing the Agreement of 16 September 1964 regarding the Construction and Operation and Maintenance of a Loran-C Station in Newfoundland. *Signed*: Ottawa, 30 March and 3 May 1984. *Entered into force*: 3 May 1984. *Terminated*: 24 September 2010.

Exchange of Notes (3 and 8 May 1991) between the Government of Canada and the Government of the United States of America constituting an Agreement Amending the Agreement of 3 June 1976 Relating to the Construction, Operation and Maintenance of a Loran-C Station in the Vicinity of Williams Lake, BC. *Signed*: Washington, 3 and 8 May 1991. *Entered into force*: 8 May 1991. *Terminated*: 24 September 2010.

Exchange of Notes between the Government of Canada and the Government of the United States of America Concluding Amendments to the Treaty between the Government of Canada and the Government of the United States of America on Pacific Coast Albacore Tuna Vessels and Port Privileges. *Signed*: Washington, 12 June 2009. *Entered into force*: 8 March 2010.

Framework Agreement between the Government of Canada and the Government of the United States of America for Cooperation in the Exploration and Use of Outer Space for Peaceful Purposes. *Signed*: Washington, 9 September 2009. *Entered into force*: 11 May 2010.

Agreement between the Government of Canada and the Government of the United States of America on Government Procurement. *Signed*: Mississauga, and Washington, 11 and 12 February 2010. *Entered into force*: 16 February 2010.

Exchange of Notes between the Government of Canada and the Government of the United States of America Constituting an Agreement Extending the Agreement between the Government of Canada and the Government of the United States of America providing for Coordination of the Icebreaking Activities of Canada and the United States on the Great Lakes, done at Ottawa on 5 December 1980. *Signed*: Washington, 30 November and 2 December 2010. *Entered into force*: 2 December 2010.

Exchange of Notes between the Government of Canada and the Government of the United States of America Constituting an Agreement Amending Chapter 4 of Annex IV of the Treaty between the Government of Canada and the Government of the United States of America Concerning Pacific Salmon. *Signed*: Washington, 21 December 2010. *Entered into force*: 21 December 2010.

Vietnam
Agreement between the Government of Canada and the Government of the Socialist Republic of Vietnam on Air Transport. *Signed*: Montreal, 28 September 2004. *Entered into force*: 4 July 2011.

MULTILATERAL

Arctic
Agreement on Cooperation on Aeronautical and Maritime Search and Rescue in the Arctic, Nuuk, 12 May 2011. *Signed by Canada*: 12 May 2011.

Co-operation
Treaty of Amity and Cooperation in Southeast Asia, Denpasar, 24 February 1976. *Acceded to by Canada*: 23 July 2010. *Entry into force for Canada*: 23 July 2010.

Protocol Amending the Treaty of Amity and Cooperation in Southeast Asia, Manila, 15 December 1987. *Acceded to by Canada*: 23 July 2010. *Entry into force for Canada*: 23 July 2010.

Second Protocol Amending the Treaty of Amity and Cooperation in Southeast Asia, Manila, 25 July 1998. *Acceded to by Canada*: 23 July 2010. *Entry into force for Canada*: 23 July 2010.

Third Protocol Amending the Treaty of Amity and Cooperation in Southeast Asia, Hanoi, 23 July 2010. *Acceded to by Canada*: 23 July 2011.

Environment
Amendments to Annexes A, B, and C of the Stockholm Convention on Persistent Organic Pollutants, Geneva, 8 May 2009. *Accepted by Canada*: 4 January 2011. *Entry into force for Canada*: 4 April 2011.

Finance
Amendment of the Articles of Agreement of the International Monetary Fund to Enhance Voice and Participation in the International Monetary Fund, Washington, 28 April 2008. *Accepted by Canada*: 29 March 2010. *Entry into force for Canada*: 3 March 2011.

Amendment of the Articles of Agreement of the International Monetary Fund to Expand the Investment Authority of the International Monetary Fund, Washington, 5 May 2008. *Accepted by Canada*: 29 March 2010. *Entry into force for Canada*: 3 March 2011.

Fisheries
Convention for the Strengthening of the Inter-American Tropical Tuna Commission established by the 1949 Convention between the United States of America and the Republic of Costa Rica, Washington, 14 November 2003. *Signed by Canada*: 22 December 2004. *Ratified by Canada*: 3 June 2009. *Entry into force for Canada*: 27 August 2010.

Agreement on Port State Measures to Prevent, Deter and Eliminate Illegal, Unreported and Unregulated Fishing, Rome, 22 November 2009. *Signed by Canada*: 19 November 2010.

Human Rights
Convention on the Rights of Persons with Disabilities, New York, 13 December 2006. *Signed by Canada*: 30 March 2007. *Ratified by Canada*: 11 March 2010. *Entry into force for Canada*: 10 April 2010.

Labour
Maritime Labour Convention, 2006, Geneva, 23 February 2006. *Ratified by Canada*: 15 June 2010.

Convention Concerning Forced or Compulsory Labour (as modified by the Final Articles Revision Convention, 1946), Geneva, 28 June 1930. *Ratified by Canada*: 13 June 2011. *Entry into force for Canada*: 13 June 2012.

Convention Concerning Tripartite Consultations to Promote the Implementation of International Labour Standards, Geneva, 21 June 1976. *Ratified by Canada*: 13 June 2011.

Convention Concerning the Promotional Framework for Occupational Safety and Health, Geneva, 15 June 2006. *Ratified by Canada*: 13 June 2011. *Entry into force for Canada*: 13 June 2012.

Narcotics
Amendments to Annex I of the International Convention against Doping in Sport, Paris, 28 October 2009. *Entry into force for Canada*: 1 January 2010.

Amendments to Annex II of the International Convention against Doping in Sport, Paris, 29 January 2010. *Entry into force for Canada*: 15 March 2010.

Amendments to Annex I and Annex II of the International Convention against Doping in Sport, Paris, 17 November 2010. *Entry into force for Canada*: 1 January 2011.

Navigation
International Convention on Civil Liability for Bunker Oil Pollution Damage, 2001, London, 23 March 2001. *Signed by Canada*: 27 September 2002. *Acceded to by Canada*: 2 October 2009. *Entry into force for Canada*: 2 January 2010.

Protocol of 2003 to the International Convention on the Establishment of an International Fund for Compensation for Oil Pollution Damage, 1992, London, 16 May 2003. *Acceded to by Canada*: 2 October 2009. *Entry into force for Canada*: 2 January 2010.

Protocol of 1997 to amend the International Convention for the Prevention of Pollution from Ships, 1973, as Modified by the Protocol of 1978 relating thereto, London, 26 September 1997. *Acceded to by Canada*: 26 March 2010. *Entry into force for Canada*: 26 June 2010.

Annex IV (Regulations for the Prevention of Pollution by Sewage from Ships) and Annex V (Regulations for the Prevention of Pollution by Garbage from Ships) to the International Convention for the Prevention of Pollution from Ships, 1973, as modified by the Protocol of 1978 relating thereto, as amended (MARPOL 73/78). *Accepted by Canada*: 26 March 2010. *Entry into force for Canada*: 26 June 2010.

International Convention on the Control of Harmful Anti-Fouling Systems on Ships, 2001, London, 5 October 2001. *Acceded to by Canada*: 8 April 2010. *Entry into force for Canada*: 8 July 2010.

International Convention for the Control and Management of Ships' Ballast Water and Sediments, 2004, London, 13 February 2004. *Acceded to by Canada*: 8 April 2010.

Protocol of 1988 Relating to the International Convention on Load Lines, 1966, London, 11 November 1988. *Acceded to by Canada*: 8 April 2010. *Entry into force for Canada*: 8 July 2010.

Protocol of 1988 Relating to the International Convention for the Safety of Life at Sea, 1974, London, 11 November 1988. *Acceded to by Canada*: 8 April 2010. *Entry into force for Canada*: 8 July 2010.

International Convention on Standards of Training, Certification and Watchkeeping for Fishing Vessel Personnel 1995, London, 7 July 1995. *Acceded to by Canada*: 8 April 2010. *Entry into force for Canada*: 29 September 2012.

Protocol of 2010 to the International Convention on Liability and Compensation for Damage in Connection with the Carriage of Hazardous and Noxious Substances by Sea, 1996, London, 30 April 2010. *Signed by Canada*: 25 October 2011.

Pollution

Amendments to Annexes V and VII to the Protocol to the 1979 Convention on Long-Range Transboundary Air Pollution on Persistent Organic Pollutants, Aarhus, 24 June 1998. *Accepted by Canada*: 23 November 2011. *Entry into force for Canada*: 23 November 2011.

Post

Universal Postal Convention, Geneva, 12 August 2008. *Ratified by Canada*: 6 January 2010. *Entry into force for Canada*: 6 January 2010.

First Additional Protocol to the General Regulations of the Universal Postal Union, Geneva, 12 August 2008. *Ratified by Canada*: 6 January 2010. *Entry into force for Canada*: 6 January 2010.

Eighth Additional Protocol to the Constitution of the Universal Postal Union, Geneva, 12 August 2008. *Ratified by Canada*: 6 January 2010. *Entry into force for Canada*: 6 January 2010.

Final Protocol to the Universal Postal Convention, Geneva, 12 August 2008. *Ratified by Canada*: 6 January 2010. *Entry into force for Canada*: 6 January 2010.

Taxation

Protocol amending the Convention on Mutual Administrative Assistance in Tax Matters, Paris, 27 May 2010. *Signed by Canada*: 3 November 2011.

Telecommunications

Final Acts of the Plenipotentiary Conference of the International Telecommunication Union (Antalya, 2006), Antalya, 24 November 2006. *Signed by Canada*: 24 November 2006. *Acceded to by Canada*: 12 August 2010. *Entry into force for Canada*: 12 August 2010.

Final Acts of the World Radiocommunication Conference of the International Telecommunication Union – WRC-07, Geneva, 16 November 2007. *Signed by Canada*: 16 November 2007. *Acceded to by Canada*: 22 November 2011. *Entry into force for Canada*: 22 November 2011.

Amendments to the Convention on the International Mobile Satellite Organization adopted at the Twentieth Session of the Assembly, London, 3 October 2008. *Accepted by Canada*: 1 June 2010.

Final Acts of the Plenipotentiary Conference of the International Telecommunication Union, Guadalajara, 22 October 2010. *Signed by Canada*: 22 October 2010.

Trade
Modifications to Canada's Appendix I of the Agreement on Government Procurement, Geneva, 12 February 2010. *Signed by Canada*: 12 February 2010.

Modifications in the Schedule V of Canada to the General Agreement on Tariffs and Trade 1994, pursuant to Article XXVIII of that Agreement, of the Concessions Relating to Tariff Item 3504.00 Regarding Certain Milk Protein Concentrates, Geneva, 6 April 2011. *Entry into force for Canada*: 6 July 2011.

Anti-Counterfeiting Trade Agreement, Tokyo, 1 October 2011. *Signed by Canada*: 1 October 2011.

Tropical Timber
International Tropical Timber Agreement, 2006, Geneva, 27 January 2006. *Signed by Canada*: 2 March 2009. *Ratified by Canada*: 19 November 2009. *Entry into force for Canada*: 7 December 2011.

BILATÉRAL

Afrique du Sud
Accord entre le gouvernement du Canada et le gouvernement de la République d'Afrique du Sud concernant l'assistance mutuelle entre leurs administrations des douanes. *Signé*: Johannesburg, le 30 octobre 2009. *Entré en vigueur*: le 9 novembre 2010.

Agence spatiale européenne
Accord de coopération entre le gouvernement du Canada et l'Agence spatiale européenne. *Signé*: Paris, le 15 décembre 2010.

Bahamas
Accord entre le Canada et le Commonwealth des Bahamas sur l'échange de renseignements en matière fiscale. *Signé*: Nassau, le 17 juin 2010. *Entré en vigueur*: le 16 novembre 2011.

Barbade
Protocole amendant l'Accord entre le Canada et la Barbade tendant à éviter les doubles impositions et à prévenir l'évasion fiscale en matière d'impôts sur le revenu et sur la fortune, fait à Bridgetown le 22 janvier 1980. *Signé*: Bridgetown, le 8 novembre 2011.

Brésil
Accord cadre entre le gouvernement du Canada et le gouvernement de la République fédérative du Brésil sur la coopération en science, technologie et innovation. *Signé*: Sao Paulo, le 17 novembre 2008. *Entré en vigueur*: le 19 avril 2010.

Accord sur le transport aérien entre le gouvernement du Canada et le gouvernement de la République fédérative du Brésil. *Signé*: Brazilia, le 8 août 2011.

Accord sur la sécurité sociale entre le Canada et la République fédérative du Brésil. *Signé*: Brazilia, le 8 août 2011.

Colombie
Accord de libre-échange entre le Canada et la République de Colombie.

Signé: Lima, le 21 novembre 2008. *Entré en vigueur*: le 15 août 2011.

Accord sur l'environnement entre le Canada et la République de Colombie. *Signé*: Lima, le 21 novembre 2008. *Entré en vigueur*: le 15 août 2011.

Accord de coopération dans le domaine du travail entre le Canada et la République de Colombie. *Signé*: Lima, le 21 novembre 2008. *Entré en vigueur*: le 15 août 2011.

Accord concernant des rapports annuels sur les droits de l'homme et le libre-échange entre le Canada et la République de Colombie. *Signé*: Bogota, le 27 mai 2010. *Entré en vigueur*: le 15 août 2011.

Communauté européenne
Accord sur la sécurité de l'aviation civile entre le Canada et la Communauté européenne. *Signé*: Prague, le 6 mai 2009. *Entré en vigueur*: le 26 juillet 2011.

Échange de lettres concernant la modification de l'Annexe V de l'Accord entre la Communauté européenne et le gouvernement du Canada relatif aux mesures sanitaires de protection de la santé publique et animale applicables au commerce d'animaux vivants et de produits animaux. *Signé*: Bruxelles, les 22 mars et 16 avril 2010.

Costa Rica
Accord sur le transport aérien entre le gouvernement du Canada et le gouvernement de la République du Costa Rica. *Signé*: San Jose, le 11 août 2011.

Accord entre le Canada et la République du Costa Rica sur l'échange de renseignements en matière fiscale. *Signé*: San Jose, le 11 août 2011.

Dominique
Accord entre le Canada et le Commonwealth de la Dominique sur l'échange de renseignements en matière fiscale. *Signé*: Roseau, le 29 juin 2010.

Estonie
Accord entre le gouvernement du Canada et le gouvernement de la République d'Estonie relatif aux échanges jeunesse. *Signé*: Tallin, le 14 décembre 2009. *Entré en vigueur*: le 1er août 2010.

États-Unis
Échange de notes entre le Canada et les États-Unis d'Amérique concernant le transfert au Canada des trois stations de Loran de Port-aux-Basques, Battle Harbour et Bonavista (Terre-Neuve). *Signé*: Ottawa, les 26 et 30 juin 1953. *Entré en vigueur*: le 30 juin 1953. *Pris fin*: le 24 septembre 2010.

Échange de notes entre le Canada et les États-Unis d'Amérique concernant la construction et l'utilisation d'une station Loran par la garde côtière des États-Unis au Cap Christian, île de Baffin. *Signé*: Ottawa, les 1er et 3 mai 1954. *Entré en vigueur*: le 3 mai 1954. *Pris fin*: le 24 septembre 2010.

Échange de notes entre le gouvernement canadien et le gouvernement des États-Unis d'Amérique concernant le prêt, par les États-Unis, de matériel Loran-A destiné aux stations Loran-A canadiennes. *Signé*: Ottawa, les 7 et 8 juin 1965. *Entré en vigueur*: le 8 juin 1965. *Pris fin*: le 24 septembre 2010.

Échange de notes entre le gouvernement canadien et le gouvernement des États-Unis d'Amérique concernant le prêt par les États-Unis d'un matériel Loran-A s'ajoutant à celui prêté aux termes de l'Accord du 8 juin 1965.

Signé: Ottawa, les 19 avril et 28 juillet 1966. *Entré en vigueur*: le 28 juillet 1966. *Pris fin*: le 24 septembre 2010.

Échange de notes entre le gouvernement du Canada et le gouvernement des États-Unis prolongeant le prêt d'un matériel Loran-A aux stations Loran-A canadiennes. *Signé*: Ottawa, les 27 juillet et 25 octobre 1967. *Entré en vigueur*: le 25 octobre 1967. *Pris fin*: le 24 septembre 2010.

Échange de notes entre le Canada et les États-Unis d'Amérique relativement à la construction et l'entretien par le Canada d'une station Loran-A à Gray-Point (Colombie-Britannique). *Signé*: Ottawa, le 8 avril 1971. *Entré en vigueur*: le 8 avril 1971. *Pris fin*: le 24 septembre 2010.

Échange de notes entre le gouvernement du Canada et le gouvernement des États-Unis d'Amérique concernant l'établissement, l'entretien et l'exploitation d'une station d'émission Loran-C à Williams Lake (C.-B.). *Signé*: Ottawa, les 28 mai et 3 juin 1976. *Entré en vigueur*: le 3 juin 1976. *Pris fin*: le 24 septembre 2010.

Échange de notes entre le gouvernement du Canada et le gouvernement des États-Unis d'Amérique constituant un Accord prévoyant l'établissement d'une chaîne expérimentale Loran-C à proximité de la rivière Sainte-Marie, en Ontario et au Michigan. *Signé*: Washington, le 29 mars 1977. *Entré en vigueur*: le 29 mars 1977. *Pris fin*: le 24 septembre 2010.

Échange de notes entre le gouvernement du Canada et le gouvernement des États-Unis d'Amérique constituant un Accord prévoyant l'établissement d'une station Loran-C à proximité de Port Hardy sur l'île de Vancouver, C-B. *Signé*: Ottawa, les 19 et 29 mars 1979. *Entré en vigueur*: le 29 mars 1979. *Pris fin*: le 24 septembre 2010.

Échange de notes entre le gouvernement du Canada et le gouvernement des États-Unis d'Amérique constituant un Accord renouvelant l'Accord du 29 mars 1977 relatif à l'établissement de mini-stations Loran-C à proximité de la rivière Sainte-Marie en Ontario et au Michigan. *Signé*: Ottawa, les 28 octobre et 5 décembre 1980. *Entré en vigueur*: le 5 décembre 1980. *Pris fin*: le 24 septembre 2010.

Échange de notes entre le gouvernement du Canada et le gouvernement des États-Unis d'Amérique remplaçant l'Accord du 16 septembre 1964 concernant la construction, l'utilisation et l'entretien à Terre-Neuve d'une station Loran-C. *Signé*: Ottawa, les 30 mars et 3 mai 1984. *Entré en vigueur*: le 3 mai 1984. *Pris fin*: le 24 septembre 2010.

Échange de notes entre le gouvernement du Canada et le gouvernement des États-Unis d'Amérique constituant un Accord modifiant l'Accord du 3 juin 1976 concernant la construction, l'exploitation et l'entretien de la station Loran-C située près de Williams Lake. C.B. *Signé*: Washington, les 3 et 8 mai 1991. *Entré en vigueur*: le 8 mai 1991. *Pris fin*: le 24 septembre 2010.

Échange de notes entre le gouvernement du Canada et le gouvernement des États-Unis d'Amérique concluant les amendements au Traité entre le gouvernement du Canada et le gouvernement des États-Unis d'Amérique concernant les thoniers (thon blanc) du Pacifique et leurs privilèges portuaires. *Signé*: Washington, le 12 juin 2009. *Entré en vigueur*: le 8 mars 2010.

Accord cadre de coopération entre le gouvernement du Canada et le gouvernement des États-Unis d'Amérique relatif à l'exploration et à l'utilisation de l'espace extra-atmosphérique à des fins pacifiques. *Signé*: Washington, le 9 septembre 2009. *Entré en vigueur*: le 11 mai 2010.

Accord entre le gouvernement du Canada et le gouvernement des États-Unis d'Amérique en matière de marchés publics. *Signé*: Mississauga et Washington, les 11 et 12 février 2010. *Entré en vigueur*: le 16 février 2010.

Échange de notes entre le gouvernement du Canada et le gouvernement des États-Unis d'Amérique constituant un accord prolongeant l'Accord entre le gouvernement du Canada et le gouvernement des États-Unis d'Amérique prévoyant la coordination des activités canado-américaines de brisage des glaces dans les Grands Lacs, fait à Ottawa le 5 décembre 1980. *Signé*: Washington, les 30 novembre et 2 décembre 2010. *Entré en vigueur*: le 2 décembre 2010.

Échange de notes entre le gouvernement du Canada et le gouvernement des États-Unis d'Amérique constituant un accord amendant le chapitre 4 de l'Annexe IV du Traité entre le gouvernement du Canada et le gouvernement des États-Unis d'Amérique concernant le saumon du Pacifique. *Signé*: Washington, le 21 décembre 2010. *Entré en vigueur*: le 21 décembre 2010.

France

Avenant à la Convention entre le gouvernement du Canada et le gouvernement de la République française tendant à éviter les doubles impositions et à prévenir l'évasion fiscale en matière d'impôts sur le revenu et la fortune, signée le 2 mai 1975 et modifiée par l'avenant du 16 janvier 1987 puis par l'avenant du 30 novembre 1995. *Signé*: Paris, le 2 février 2010.

Grèce

Échange de notes comportant un Accord entre le Canada et la Grèce relatif à l'exemption réciproque de l'impôt sur le revenu en ce qui concerne les bénéfices réalisés dans les affaires d'armement maritime. *Signé*: Londres, le 30 septembre 1929. *Entré en vigueur*: le 30 septembre 1929. *Pris fin*: le 16 décembre 2010.

Convention entre le Canada et la République hellénique en vue d'éviter les doubles impositions et de prévenir l'évasion fiscale en matière d'impôts sur le revenu et sur la fortune. *Signée*: Athènes, le 29 juin 2009. *Entrée en vigueur*: le 16 décembre 2010.

Accord entre le Canada et la République hellénique concernant la mobilité des jeunes. *Signé*: Athènes, le 28 mai 2011.

Hongrie

Accord sur les relations cinématographiques et audiovisuelles entre le gouvernement du Canada et le gouvernement de la République populaire hongroise. *Signé*: Budapest, le 7 mai 1987. *Entré en vigueur*: le 18 janvier 2010.

Inde

Accord entre le gouvernement du Canada et le gouvernement de la République de l'Inde sur la coopération en matière d'utilisation de l'énergie nucléaire à des fins pacifiques. *Signé*: Toronto, le 27 juin 2010.

Israël

Accord sur la coopération bilatérale en recherche et développement industriels entre le gouvernement du

Canada et le gouvernement de l'État d'Israël. *Signé*: Jérusalem, le 10 juillet 2011. *Entré en vigueur*: le 21 février 2012.

Italie
Convention entre le gouvernement du Canada et le gouvernement de la République d'Italie en vue d'éviter les doubles impositions en matière d'impôts sur le revenu et de prévenir l'évasion fiscale. *Signée*: Ottawa, le 3 juin 2002. *Entrée en vigueur*: le 25 novembre 2011.

Traité d'extradition entre le gouvernement du Canada et le gouvernement de la République italienne. *Signé*: Rome, le 13 janvier 2005. *Entré en vigueur*: le 17 novembre 2010.

Koweït
Accord entre le Canada et l'État du Koweït concernant la promotion et la protection des investissements. *Signé*: Ottawa, le 26 septembre 2011.

Lettonie
Accord entre le gouvernement du Canada et le gouvernement de la République de la Lettonie pour l'encouragement et la protection des investissements. *Signé*: Ottawa, le 26 avril 1995. *Entré en vigueur*: le 27 juillet 1995. *Pris fin*: le 24 novembre 2011.

Accord entre le gouvernement du Canada et le gouvernement de la République de Lettonie concernant la promotion et la protection des investissements. *Signé*: Riga, le 5 mai 2009. *Entré en vigueur*: le 24 novembre 2011.

Lituanie
Accord entre le gouvernement du Canada et le gouvernement de la République de Lituanie relatif aux échanges jeunesse. *Signé*: Vilnius, le 19 novembre 2009. *Entré en vigueur*: le 1er octobre 2010.

Macédoine
Accord sur la sécurité sociale entre le Canada et la République de Macédoine. *Signé*: le 26 août 2009. *Entré en vigueur*: le 1er novembre 2011.

Maroc
Convention de sécurité sociale entre le gouvernement du Canada et le gouvernement du Royaume du Maroc. *Signée*: Ottawa, le 1er juillet 1998. *Entrée en vigueur*: le 1er mars 2010.

Mexique
Protocole amendant l'Accord relatif aux transports aériens entre le gouvernement du Canada et le gouvernement des États-Unis du Mexique, fait à Mexico le 21 décembre 1961, tel qu'amendé. *Signé*: Ottawa, le 27 mai 2010. *Entré en vigueur*: le 1er décembre 2011.

Accord de reconnaissance mutuelle entre le gouvernement du Canada et le gouvernement des États-Unis du Mexique concernant l'évaluation de la conformité de matériel de télécommunication. *Signé*: Honolulu, le 12 novembre 2011.

Namibie
Convention entre le Canada et la République de Namibie en vue d'éviter les doubles impositions et de prévenir l'évasion fiscale en matière d'impôts sur le revenu et sur la fortune. *Signé*: Windhoek, le 25 mars 2010.

Nouvelle-Zélande
Accord entre le gouvernement du Canada et le gouvernement de la Nouvelle-Zélande sur le transport aérien, tel qu'amendé par les échanges de notes signées le 4 septembre 1985 et le 27 juin 1995. *Signé*: Ottawa, le 4 septembre 1985. *Entré en vigueur*: le 4 septembre 1985. *Pris fin*: le 18 octobre 2011.

Accord sur le transport aérien entre le gouvernement du Canada et le gouvernement de la Nouvelle-Zélande. *Signé*: Singapour, le 21 juillet 2009. *Entré en vigueur*: le 18 octobre 2011.

Panama

Accord sur l'environnement entre le Canada et la République du Panama. *Signé*: Ottawa, le 13 mai 2010.

Accord de coopération dans le domaine du travail entre le Canada et la République du Panama. *Signé*: Ottawa, le 13 mai 2010.

Accord de libre-échange entre le Canada et la République du Panama. *Signé*: Ottawa, le 14 mai 2010.

Pays-Bas

Accord d'assistance mutuelle administrative en matière douanière entre le gouvernement du Canada et le gouvernement du Royaume des Pays-Bas. *Signé*: Ottawa, le 14 août 2007. *Entré en vigueur*: le 1er septembre 2010.

Échange de notes constituant un amendement à l'Accord d'assistance mutuelle administrative en matière douanière entre le gouvernement du Canada et le gouvernement du Royaume des Pays-Bas, fait à Ottawa le 14 août 2007. *Signé*: Ottawa, les 30 mars et 28 avril 2009. *Entré en vigueur*: le 1er décembre 2010.

Accord entre le gouvernement du Canada et le gouvernement du Royaume des Pays-Bas en ce qui concerne les Antilles néerlandaises sur l'échange de renseignements en matière fiscale. *Signé*: Vancouver, le 29 août 2009. *Entré en vigueur*: le 1er janvier 2011.

Accord entre le Canada et le Royaume des Pays-Bas en ce qui concerne Aruba sur l'échange de renseignements en matière fiscale. *Signé*: Ottawa, le 20 octobre 2011.

République slovaque

Accord entre le Canada et la République slovaque relatif à la mobilité des jeunes. *Signé*: Bratislava, le 20 juillet 2010. *Entré en vigueur*: le 1er juillet 2011.

Accord entre le Canada et la République slovaque concernant la promotion et la protection des investissements. *Signé*: Bratislava, le 20 juillet 2010. *Entré en vigueur*: le 14 mars 2012.

Roumanie

Accord entre le gouvernement du Canada et le gouvernement de la République de Roumanie pour l'encouragement et la protection des investissements. *Signé*: Bucarest, le 17 avril 1996. *Entré en vigueur*: le 11 février 1997. *Pris fin*: le 23 novembre 2011.

Accord entre le gouvernement du Canada et le gouvernement de Roumanie concernant la promotion et la protection réciproque des investissements. *Signé*: Bucarest, le 8 mai 2009. *Entré en vigueur*: le 23 novembre 2011.

Accord de sécurité sociale entre le Canada et la Roumanie. *Signé*: Ottawa, le 19 novembre 2009. *Entré en vigueur*: le 1er novembre 2011.

Accord administratif entre le gouvernement du Canada et le gouvernement de la Roumanie pour l'application de l'accord de sécurité sociale entre le Canada et la Roumanie. *Signé*: Bucarest, le 1er juin 2010. *Entré en vigueur*: le 1er novembre 2011.

Accord entre le Canada et la Roumanie concernant les locaux diplomatiques. *Signé*: Bucarest, le 11 mars 2011.

Royaume-Uni de Grande-Bretagne et d'Irlande du Nord
Accord entre le gouvernement du Canada et le gouvernement des Bermudes, agissant en vertu d'un mandat du gouvernement du Royaume-Uni de Grande-Bretagne et d'Irlande du Nord, sur l'échange de renseignements en matière fiscale. *Signé*: Hamilton, les îles Bermudes, le 14 juin 2010. *Entré en vigueur*: le 1er juillet 2011.

Accord entre le gouvernement du Canada et le gouvernement des îles Turks et Caicos, agissant en vertu d'un mandat du gouvernement du Royaume-Uni de Grande-Bretagne et d'Irlande du Nord, sur l'échange de renseignements en matière fiscale. *Signé*: Cockburn Town, le 22 juin 2010. *Entré en vigueur*: le 6 octobre 2011.

Accord entre le gouvernement du Canada et le gouvernement des îles Caïmans, agissant en vertu d'un mandat du gouvernement du Royaume-Uni de Grande-Bretagne et d'Irlande du Nord, sur l'échange de renseignements en matière fiscale. *Signé*: George Town, le 24 juin 2010. *Entré en vigueur*: le 1er juin 2011.

Accord entre le gouvernement du Canada et le gouvernement d'Anguilla, agissant en vertu d'un mandat du gouvernement du Royaume-Uni de Grande-Bretagne et d'Irlande du Nord, sur l'échange de renseignements en matière fiscale. *Signé*: Bridge Town, le 28 octobre 2010. *Entré en vigueur*: le 12 octobre 2011.

Accord entre le gouvernement du Canada et le gouvernement de Jersey, agissant en vertu d'un mandat du gouvernement du Royaume-Uni de Grande Bretagne et d'Irlande du Nord, sur l'échange de renseignements en matière fiscale. *Signé*: Saint Helier, le 12 janvier 2011. *Entré en vigueur*: le 19 décembre 2011.

Accord entre le gouvernement du Canada et le gouvernement de l'Île de Man, agissant en vertu d'un mandat du gouvernement du Royaume-Uni de Grande-Bretagne et d'Irlande du Nord, sur l'échange de renseignements en matière fiscale. *Signé*: Douglas, le 17 janvier 2011. *Entré en vigueur*: le 19 décembre 2011.

Accord entre le gouvernement du Canada et les États de Guernesey, agissant en vertu d'un mandat du gouvernement du Royaume-Uni de Grande Bretagne et d'Irlande du Nord, sur l'échange de renseignements en matière fiscale. *Signé*: Saint Peter Port, le 19 janvier 2011.

Sainte-Lucie
Accord entre le Canada et Sainte-Lucie sur l'échange de renseignements en matière fiscale. *Signé*: Castries, le 18 juin 2010.

Saint-Kitts-et-Nevis
Accord entre le Canada et la Fédération de Saint-Kitts-et-Nevis sur l'échange de renseignements en matière fiscale. *Signé*: Basseterre, le 14 juin 2010. *Entré en vigueur*: le 21 novembre 2011.

Saint-Marin
Accord entre le Canada et la République de Saint-Marin sur l'échange de renseignements en matière fiscale. *Signé*: San Marino, le 27 octobre 2010. *Entré en vigueur*: le 20 octobre 2011.

Saint-Vincent-et-les Grenadines
Accord entre le Canada et Saint-Vincent-et-les Grenadines sur l'échange de renseignements en matière fiscale. *Signé*: Kingstown, le 22 juin 2010. *Entré en vigueur*: le 4 octobre 2011.

Singapour
Protocole amendant la Convention entre le Canada et la République de Singapour, tendant à éviter les doubles impositions et à prévenir l'évasion fiscale en matière d'impôts sur le revenu, faite à Singapour le 6 mars 1976. *Signé*: Singapour, le 29 novembre 2011.

Slovénie
Accord entre le Canada et la République de Slovénie concernant la mobilité des jeunes. *Signé*: Ljubljana, le 22 octobre 2009. *Entré en vigueur*: le 1er juillet 2010.

Suisse
Accord concernant le Protocole amendant la Convention entre le Gouvernement du Canada et le Conseil fédéral suisse en vue d'éviter les doubles impositions en matière d'impôts sur le revenu et sur la fortune, faite à Berne le 5 mai 1997. *Signé*: Berne, le 21 octobre 2010. *Entré en vigueur*: le 16 décembre 2011.

Protocole amendant la Convention entre le Gouvernement du Canada et le Conseil fédéral suisse en vue d'éviter les doubles impositions en matière d'impôts sur le revenu et sur la fortune, faite à Berne le 5 mai 1997. *Signé*: Berne, le 22 octobre 2010. *Entré en vigueur*: le 16 décembre 2011.

Turquie
Accord entre le Canada et la République de Turquie en vue d'éviter les doubles impositions et de prévenir l'évasion fiscale en matière d'impôts sur le revenu et sur la fortune. *Signé*: Ottawa, le 14 juillet 2009. *Entré en vigueur*: le 4 mai 2011.

Vietnam
Accord sur le transport aérien entre le gouvernement du Canada et le gouvernement de la République socialiste du Vietnam. *Signé*: Montréal, le 28 septembre 2004. *Entré en vigueur*: le 4 juillet 2011.

MULTILATÉRAL

Arctique
Accord de coopération en matière de recherche et de sauvetage aéronautiques et maritimes dans l'Arctique, Nuuk, 12 mai 2011. *Signé par le Canada*: le 12 mai 2011.

Bois tropicaux
Accord international de 2006 sur les bois tropicaux, Genève, 27 janvier 2006. *Signé par le Canada*: le 2 mars 2009. *Ratifié par le Canada*: le 19 novembre 2009. *Entré en vigueur pour le Canada*: le 7 décembre 2011.

Commerce
Modifications de l'Appendice I concernant le Canada de l'Accord sur les marchés publics, Genève, 12 février 2010. *Signée par le Canada*: le 12 février 2010.

Modifications à la liste V du Canada de l'Accord général sur les tarifs douaniers et le commerce de 1994, en application de l'article XXVIII de cet Accord, des concessions se rapportant à la ligne tarifaire 3504.00 concernant certains concentrés de protéines laitières, Genève, 6 avril 2011. *Signée par le Canada*: le 6 avril 2011. *Entrées en vigueur pour le Canada*: le 6 juillet 2011.

Accord commercial anti-contrefaçon, Tokyo, 1er octobre 2011. *Signé par le Canada*: le 1er octobre 2011.

Co-opération
Traité d'amitié et de coopération en Asie du Sud-Est, Denpasar, 24 février 1976. *Adhéré par le Canada*: le 23 juillet 2010. *Entré en vigueur pour le Canada*: le 23 juillet 2010.

Protocole amendant le Traité d'amitié et de coopération en Asie du Sud-Est, Manille, 15 décembre 1987. *Adhéré par le Canada*: le 23 juillet 2010. *Entré en vigueur pour le Canada*: le 23 juillet 2010.

Second Protocole amendant le Traité d'amitié et de coopération en Asie du Sud-Est, Manille, 25 juillet 1998. *Adhéré par le Canada*: le 23 juillet 2010. *Entré en vigueur pour le Canada*: le 23 juillet 2010.

Troisième protocole amendant le Traité d'amitié et de coopération en Asie du Sud-Est, Hanoï, 23 juillet 2010. *Adhéré par le Canada*: le 23 juillet 2011.

Droits de la personne
Convention relative aux droits des personnes handicapées, New York, 13 décembre 2006. *Signée par le Canada*: le 30 mars 2007. *Ratifiée par le Canada*: le 11 mars 2010. *Entrée en vigueur pour le Canada*: le 10 avril 2010.

Environnement
Amendements aux annexes A, B, et C de la Convention de Stockholm sur les polluants organiques persistants, Genève, 8 mai 2009. *Acceptés par le Canada*: le 4 janvier 2011. *Entrés en vigueur pour le Canada*: le 4 avril 2011.

Finances
Amendement des Statuts du Fonds monétaire international visant à améliorer la représentation et la participation des États membres au sein du Fonds monétaire international, Washington, 28 avril 2008. *Accepté par le Canada*: le 29 mars 2010. *Entré en vigueur pour le Canada*: le 3 mars 2011.

Amendement des Statuts du Fonds monétaire international visant à étendre le pouvoir du Fonds monétaire international en matière d'investissement, Washington, 5 mai 2008. *Accepté par le Canada*: le 29 mars 2010. *Entré en vigueur pour le Canada*: le 3 mars 2011.

Imposition
Protocole d'amendement à la Convention concernant l'assistance administrative mutuelle en matière fiscale, Paris, 27 mai 2010. *Signé par le Canada*: le 3 novembre 2011.

Navigation
Convention internationale de 2001 sur la responsabilité civile pour les dommages dus à la pollution par les hydrocarbures de soute, Londres, 23 mars 2001. *Signée par le Canada*: le 27 septembre 2002. *Adhérée par le Canada*: le 2 octobre 2009. *Entrée en vigueur pour le Canada*: le 2 janvier 2010.

Protocole de 2003 à la Convention internationale de 1992 portant création d'un fonds international d'indemnisation pour les dommages dus à la pollution par les hydrocarbures, Londres, 16 mai 2003. *Adhéré par le Canada*: le 2 octobre 2009. *Entré en vigueur pour le Canada*: le 2 janvier 2010.

Protocole de 1997 modifiant la Convention internationale de 1973 pour la prévention de la pollution par les navires, telle que modifiée par le Protocole de 1978 y relatif, Londres, 26 septembre 1997. *Adhéré par le Canada*: le 26 mars 2010. *Entré en vigueur pour le Canada*: le 26 juin 2010.

Annexe IV (Règles relatives à la prévention de la pollution par les eaux usées des navires) et Annexe V (Règles relatives à la prévention de la pollution par les ordures des navires) à la Convention internationale de 1973 pour la prévention de la pollution par les navires modifiée par le Protocole de 1978 s'y rapportant (MARPOL 73/78). *Acceptées par le Canada*: le 26 mars 2010. *Entrées en vigueur pour le Canada*: le 26 mars 2010.

Convention internationale de 2001 sur le contrôle des systèmes antisalissure nuisibles sur les navires, Londres, 5 octobre 2001. *Adhérée par le Canada*: le 8 avril 2010. *Entre en vigueur pour le Canada*: le 8 juillet 2010.

Convention internationale de 2004 pour le contrôle et la gestion des eaux de ballast et sédiments des navires, Londres, 13 février 2004. *Adhérée par le Canada*: le 8 avril 2010. *Entrée en vigueur pour le Canada*: le 29 septembre 2012.

Protocole de 1988 relatif à la Convention internationale de 1966 sur les lignes de charge, Londres, 11 novembre 1988. *Adhéré par le Canada*: le 8 avril 2010. *Entré en vigueur pour le Canada*: le 8 juillet 2010.

Protocole de 1988 relatif à la Convention internationale de 1974 pour la sauvegarde de la vie humaine en mer, Londres, 11 novembre 1988. *Adhéré par le Canada*: le 8 avril 2010. *Entré en vigueur pour le Canada*: le 8 juillet 2010.

Convention internationale de 1995 sur les normes de formation du personnel des navires de pêche, de délivrance des brevets et de veille, Londres, 7 juillet 1995. *Adhérée par le Canada*: le 8 avril 2010.

Protocole de 2010 à la Convention internationale de 1996 sur la responsabilité et l'indemnisation pour les dommages liés au transport par mer de substances nocives et potentiellement dangereuses, Londres, 30 avril 2010. *Signé par le Canada*: le 25 octobre 2011.

Pêches

Convention relative au renforcement de la commission interaméricaine du thon tropical établie par la Convention de 1949 entre les États-Unis d'Amérique et la République du Costa Rica, Washington, 14 novembre 2003. *Signée par le Canada*: le 22 décembre 2004. *Ratifiée par le Canada*: le 3 juin 2009. *Entrée en vigueur pour le Canada*: le 27 août 2010.

Accord relatif aux mesures du ressort de l'État du port visant à prévenir, contrecarrer et éliminer la pêche illicite, non déclarée et non réglementée, Rome, 22 novembre 2009. *Signé par le Canada*: le 19 novembre 2010.

Pollution

Amendements aux Annexes V et VII du Protocole à la Convention sur la pollution atmosphérique transfrontière à longue distance, de 1979, relatif aux polluants organiques persistants, Aarhus, 24 juin 1998. *Acceptés par le Canada*: le 23 novembre 2011. *Entrés en vigueur pour le Canada*: le 23 novembre 2011.

Poste

Convention postale universelle, Genève, 12 août 2008. *Ratifiée par le Canada*: le 6 janvier 2010. *Entre en vigueur pour le Canada*: le 6 janvier 2010.

Premier Protocole additionnel au Règlement général de l'Union postale universelle, Genève, 12 août 2008. *Ratifié par le Canada*: le 6 janvier 2010. *Entré en vigueur pour le Canada*: le 6 janvier 2010.

Huitième Protocole additionnel à la Constitution de l'Union postale universelle, Genève, 12 août 2008. *Ratifié par le Canada*: le 6 janvier 2010. *Entré en vigueur pour le Canada*: le 6 janvier 2010.

Protocole final de la Convention postale universelle, Genève, 12 août 2008.

Ratifié par le Canada: le 6 janvier 2010. *Entré en vigueur pour le Canada*: le 6 janvier 2010.

Stupéfiants
Amendements à l'annexe I de la Convention internationale contre le dopage dans le sport, Paris, 28 octobre 2009. *Entré en vigueur pour le Canada*: le 1er janvier 2010.

Amendements à l'annexe II de la Convention internationale contre le dopage dans le sport, Paris, 29 janvier 2010. *Entré en vigueur pour le Canada*: le 15 mars 2010.

Amendements à l'annexe I et à l'annexe II de la Convention internationale contre le dopage dans le sport, Paris, 17 novembre 2010. *Entré en vigueur pour le Canada*: le 1er janvier 2011.

Télécommunications
Actes finals de la Conférence de plénipotentiaires de l'Union internationale des télécommunications, Antalya, 24 novembre 2006. *Signés par le Canada*: le 24 novembre 2006. *Adhérés par le Canada*: le 12 août 2010. *Entrés en vigueur pour le Canada*: le 12 août 2010.

Actes finals de la Conférence mondiale des radiocommunications de l'Union internationale des télécommunications - CMR-07, Genève, 16 novembre 2007. *Signés par le Canada*: le 16 novembre 2007. *Adhérés par le Canada*: le 22 novembre 2011. *Entrés en vigueur pour le Canada*: le 22 novembre 2011.

Amendements à la Convention portant création de l'Organisation internationale de télécommunications mobiles par satellites adoptés à la vingtième session de l'assemblée, Londres, 3 octobre 2008. *Acceptés par le Canada*: le 1er juin 2010.

Actes finals de la Conférence de plénipotentiaires de l'Union internationale des télécommunications, Guadalajara, 22 octobre 2010. *Signés par le Canada*: le 22 octobre 2010.

Travail
Convention du travail maritime, 2006, Genève, 23 février 2006. *Ratifiée par le Canada*: le 15 juin 2010.

Convention concernant le travail forcé ou obligatoire (telle qu'elle a été modifiée par la Convention portant révision des articles finals, 1946), Genève, 28 juin 1930. *Ratifiée par le Canada:* le 13 juin 2011.

Convention concernant les consultations tripartites destinées à promouvoir la mise en œuvre des normes internationales du travail, Genève, 21 juin 1976. *Ratifiée par le Canada*: le 13 juin 2011.

Convention concernant le cadre promotionnel pour la sécurité et la santé au travail, Genève, 15 juin 2006. *Ratifiée par le Canada*: le 13 juin 2011. *Entrée en vigueur pour le Canada*: le 13 juin 2012.

Cases / Jurisprudence

Canadian Cases in Public International Law in 2010-11 / Jurisprudence canadienne en matière de droit international public en 2010-11

compiled by / préparé par

GIB VAN ERT, GREG J. ALLEN, AND EILEEN PATEL

NOTE TO READERS: The following is a review of cases decided between 1er le July 2010 and 31 December 2011. Future issues will review cases decided in the calendar year.

AVIS AUX LECTEURS: Ce qui suit est un examen des arrêts rendus entre le 1er juillet 2010 et le 31 décembre 2011. Les prochains numéros examineront les arrêts rendus pendant à l'année civile.

Diplomatic relations — repatriation — Charter section 7

Khadr v Canada (Prime Minister), 2010 FC 715 (5 July 2010). Federal Court. *Khadr v Canada (Prime Minister)*, 2010 FCA 199 (22 July 2010) (Federal Court of Appeal). *Khadr v Canada (Prime Minister)*, 2011 FCA (19 March 2011) (Federal Court of Appeal).

These cases arose from an application for judicial review of two decisions of the federal government regarding the applicant, Omar Khadr. Mr. Khadr is a Canadian citizen who, at the time of writing, was being held in custody by the United States in Guantánamo Bay, Cuba. In 2003, Mr. Khadr was visited and questioned by Canadian officials. Information obtained by the Canadian officials in these visits was provided to the United States.

Since 2005, Mr. Khadr had repeatedly requested that the federal government ask the United States to repatriate him to Canada. In

Gib van Ert, Greg J. Allen, and Eileen Patel are of the British Columbia bar. They are associates with Hunter Litigation Chambers, Vancouver.

2008, Prime Minister Stephen Harper announced his decision not to request Mr. Khadr's repatriation. Mr. Khadr sought judicial review of this decision, and in January 2010 the Supreme Court of Canada held in a decision commonly referred to as "*Khadr* II" that the government's refusal to request Mr. Khadr's repatriation was a breach of his rights under section 7 of the *Charter*.[1] The Court did not grant Mr. Khadr a *Charter* remedy, due, in part, to deference to the constitutional obligation of the executive to make foreign policy decisions.[2] In the result, the Court held as follows:

> The prudent course at this point, respectful of the responsibilities of the executive and the courts, is for this Court to allow Mr. Khadr's application for judicial review in part and to grant him a declaration advising the government of its opinion on the records before it which, in turn, will provide the legal framework for the executive to exercise its functions and to consider what actions to take in respect of Mr. Khadr, in conformity with the *Charter*.[3]

Following *Khadr* II, the federal government announced that it had not changed its previous position and would not seek the repatriation of Mr. Khadr from the United States. In February 2010, the federal government sent a diplomatic note to the United States requesting that it not use any of the information obtained by Canadian officials in 2003 in its prosecution of Mr. Khadr.

Mr. Khadr sought judicial review of the actions taken by the federal government in response to *Khadr* II, namely requesting that information obtained by Canadian officials not be used in Mr. Khadr's prosecution but refusing to request Mr. Khadr's repatriation. Mr. Khadr argued that he had not been provided with adequate procedural fairness and natural justice with respect to the actions taken by the federal government. The federal government argued that its response to *Khadr* II was not justiciable, as it was a decision of the executive on broad grounds of public and foreign policy pursuant to its royal prerogative to act in those areas.[4]

In his reasons on the application for judicial review, Zinn J held that Mr. Khadr had a legitimate expectation that the federal government would craft a remedy that would cure the *Charter* breach.[5]

1 See *Khadr v Canada (Prime Minister)*, 2010 SCC 3 [*Khadr* II].

2 *Ibid* at para 39.

3 *Ibid* at para 47.

4 *Khadr v Canada (Prime Minister)*, 2010 FC 715 at para 57 [*Khadr* FC]

5 *Ibid* at para 65.

Zinn J held that this expectation was founded both in section 24 of the *Charter* and paragraph 47 of the Supreme Court of Canada's decision in *Khadr* II (reproduced earlier). In light of the finding in *Khadr* II that Canada had breached Mr. Khadr's rights, Zinn J held that Canada had a duty to intervene by diplomatic or other means to cure the breach. If the breach could not be cured, Canada nevertheless had a duty to take steps to ameliorate the breach.[6]

Zinn J held that if the federal government chose not to request Mr. Khadr's repatriation in accordance with his wishes, it owed him duties of natural justice and procedural fairness, including being given notice of the decision and being given the opportunity to make written submissions as to appropriate remedial solutions.[7]

Zinn J refused to make an order in the nature of *certiorari*, setting aside the federal government's decision to ask the United States not to use information gathered by Canadian agents in its prosecution of Mr. Khadr. As that note had already been sent, such an order would be ineffective.[8] Zinn J noted that the federal government's request had not been heeded, as evidence obtained by Canadian agents had been used in pre-trial motions in the course of Mr. Khadr's proceedings before a military commission at Guantánamo Bay.[9] As a result, the federal government's breach of Mr. Khadr's *Charter* rights had not been cured.

Zinn J held that if the federal government was required to cure or ameliorate a *Charter* breach, as it was in this case, and the only identifiable remedy involved an exercise of the royal prerogative, the court would nevertheless be required to order that the federal government provide the remedy.[10] In this case, however, Zinn J held that the parties deserved an opportunity to explore effective remedies that did not involve the federal government requesting Mr. Khadr's repatriation. He noted that Mr. Khadr's trial before the military commission was scheduled to commence on 10 August 2010 and ordered that the federal government was to advance at least one potential curative remedy prior to the commencement of Mr. Khadr's trial.[11] Zinn J held that the court must reserve the right to

6 *Ibid* at para 69.

7 *Ibid* at paras 71-76.

8 *Ibid* at para 82.

9 *Ibid* at paras 86-88.

10 *Ibid* at para 91.

11 *Ibid* at paras 94-95.

"oversee this explorative process, to amend the short time frame set out in the judgment for the steps that are to be taken, and to reserve the right to impose a remedy if none is forthcoming from that process."[12]

The federal government appealed the order of Zinn J and applied for a stay of execution of that order pending the outcome of the appeal.[13] The federal government argued, *inter alia*, that the order of Zinn J amounted to judicial supervision over any diplomatic action taken by the federal government with respect to Mr. Khadr. In his decision on the stay application, Blais CJ expressed surprise that Zinn J had assumed supervision over the *Charter* remedies to be afforded to Mr. Khadr in response to an application for judicial review on grounds of procedural fairness and natural justice.[14] Blais CJ also expressed skepticism that Zinn J had the power to impose a remedy on the federal government.[15]

In applying the accepted test for a stay of execution, Blais CJ held that the federal government would suffer irreparable harm if the stay were not granted, as the supervisory role envisioned by Zinn J would result in improper interference by the court in the conduct of foreign relations.[16] At paragraph 19 of his decision, Blais CJ commented as follows on the irreparable harm that could result from the order below:

> In my view, for a member of the judiciary to give himself the power to "supervise" the exercise of the Crown's prerogative in a context where the Supreme Court has recognized its limited role could be seen, in itself, as an affront to the division of powers that would cause irreparable harm. This is especially so when we consider that any action that could possibly cure the *Charter* breach would require the Appellants to take some kind of diplomatic action.[17]

Blais CJ then addressed the balance of convenience. He acknowledged that the prospect of Mr. Khadr's conviction on evidence partially obtained through unconstitutional means was a serious

[12] *Ibid* at para 94.

[13] *Khadr v Canada (Prime Minister)*, 2010 FCA 199.

[14] *Ibid* at para 13.

[15] *Ibid* at para 14.

[16] *Ibid* at para 20.

[17] *Ibid* at para 19.

matter but noted that the harm in question was not the overall harm caused to Mr. Khadr by his detention and prosecution but, rather, the harm visited upon him by the federal government's unconstitutional actions.[18] Blais CJ balanced this harm against the harm to the federal government caused by the order of Zinn J, which he held would be "unequivocal if the Crown's discretionary power in foreign affairs and national security were to be usurped by the judiciary."[19] He noted that the interplay between the judiciary and the executive in matters of foreign affairs and international diplomacy envisioned by the order of Zinn J did not accord with that envisioned by the Supreme Court of Canada in *Khadr* II.[20] Accordingly, he held that the balance of convenience favoured the federal government and stayed the order of Zinn J pending the outcome of the appeal.

Following the decision of Blais CJ on the stay application, Mr. Khadr pleaded guilty before the US military commission in Guantánamo Bay to five charges that had been brought against him. On 9 March 2011, the Federal Court of Appeal, per Noel JA, held that as a result of the guilty plea Mr. Khadr was no longer detained by reason of the breach of his *Charter* rights.[21] As the breach of his *Charter* rights formed the basis of the decision upon which Mr. Khadr had sought judicial review, the judgment of Zinn J had been rendered moot.[22] The federal government's appeal from the judgment of Zinn J was therefore dismissed for mootness.[23]

Reconnaissance de jugements étrangers — Loi sur l'immunité des États — exception de commercialité

Kuwait Airways Corporation c République d'Irak et Bombardier Aéronautique, 2010 CSC 40 (21 octobre 2010). Cour suprême du Canada.

Ce pourvoi s'agit d'une demande de reconnaissance judiciaire d'un jugement d'une cour du Royaume-Uni qui a condamné la République d'Irak à payer l'équivalent de 84 000 000 $C à l'appelante,

[18] *Ibid* at paras 26, 28.

[19] *Ibid* at para 29.

[20] *Ibid* at paras 31-32.

[21] *Khadr v Canada (Prime Minister),* 2011 FCA 92.

[22] *Ibid* at para 1.

[23] *Ibid* at para 3.

la société aérienne Kuwait Airways Corporation (KAC). Lors de l'invasion du Koweït en 1990, le gouvernement d'Irak ordonna à sa société d'État de transport aérien, Iraqi Airways Company (IAC), d'approprier des avions et de l'équipement de KAC. Suite à la libération du Koweït, KAC tenta de recouvrir sa propriété, mais elle ne parvint pas à le faire complètement. KAC prit action au Royaume-Uni contre IAC pour se faire indemniser, et obtint une condamnation de plus d'un milliard de dollars canadiens contre IAC. Ensuite KAC réclama contra l'Irak les dépens des actions qui avaient été intentées au Royaume-Uni, alléguant que l'Irak avait contrôlé, financé et surveillé la défense d'IAC tout au cours des procédures, procédures marquées de parjures et de manœuvres par IAC et l'Irak pour tromper les tribunaux britanniques. Le juge Steel de la High Court of Justice, Queen's Bench Division, Commercial Court, fit droit à la demande et condamna l'Irak à payer le montant réclamé. Selon le juge, les actes accomplis par l'Irak dans le contrôle de la défense d'IAC ne constituaient pas des actes de souveraineté, mais se situaient plutôt, pour l'application de la State Immunity Act 1978 (R.-U.), dans le cadre de l'exception commerciale au principe de l'immunité de juridiction des États.

En août 2008, KAC demanda la reconnaissance judiciaire de ce jugement devant la Cour supérieure du Québec. L'Irak, invoquant la Loi sur l'immunité des États (Can.) (la Loi), requit le rejet de la demande au motif que les actes qui lui étaient reprochés constituaient des actes de souveraineté et qu'elle bénéficiait en conséquence de l'immunité de juridiction reconnue par la loi canadienne. Cet argument fut accepté par la Cour supérieure et encore par la Cour d'appel. Selon ces tribunaux, la participation de l'Irak dans le procès engagé contre IAC en Angleterre demeurait un acte de souveraineté qui ne se situait pas dans le cadre de l'exception commerciale à l'immunité de juridiction établie dans la Loi.

Dans un jugement unanime rendu par le juge LeBel, la Cour suprême du Canada a accueilli le pourvoi. Au départ, le juge affirma que la Loi s'applique à une demande de reconnaissance judiciaire, même si une cour étrangère a déjà déterminé la question de l'immunité de juridiction. Selon le juge, l'art. 3076 CCQ spécifie que les dispositions du Code civil relatives au droit international privé, y compris celles qui portent sur la reconnaissance judiciaire des décisions étrangères, s'appliquent sous réserve des règles de droit en vigueur au Québec et dont l'application s'impose en raison de leur but particulier. Ces règles comprennent en l'espèce la législation fédérale sur l'immunité de juridiction des

États étrangers. Notamment, le juge ajoute que la Loi fut "[a]doptée par le Parlement du Canada dans l'exercice de la compétence fédérale sur les affaires étrangères," une compétence contestée et qui n'est pas prévue expressément par la Loi constitutionnelle de 1867. En réplique à la suggestion de l'appelante que la constitutionnalité de la Loi est douteuse car elle serait de nature procédurale puisqu'elle porte sur la reconnaissance des jugements, une matière qui, selon elle, relève de la compétence des provinces sur l'administration de la justice, le juge estime que la Loi n'a pas un caractère uniquement procédural. Pourtant le juge refuse d'examiner la question puisque la constitutionnalité de la loi n'a pas été attaquée dans les formes.[24]

Le juge LeBel explique que le Parlement du Canada a adopté la Loi pour "établir un cadre législatif destiné à mieux définir l'objet et le mode d'exercice de l'immunité coutumière de juridiction reconnue aux États souverains dans leurs rapports avec les autres membres de la société internationale par le droit international public contemporain." Bien que l'immunité était absolue à son origine, une forme d'immunité plus restreinte fut reconnue en droit international. Cette immunité restreinte "fait partie de la common law et du droit public en Angleterre et au Canada" et fut intégrée dans la législation fédérale quand le Parlement a adopté la Loi.[25] La Loi établit un principe d'immunité de juridiction en faveur des États étrangers, y inclus une immunité d'exécution. Pourtant, l'art. 5 reconnaît une exception à l'immunité quant aux activités commerciales, et l'art. 12(1)b) soustrait à l'immunité d'exécution les biens employés dans le cadre de ce type d'activités.[26]

Le juge LeBel (comme la Cour d'appel) rejette l'argument de l'appelante que la Loi ne s'applique pas à une demande de reconnaissance judiciaire d'un jugement étranger. Le juge cite avec approbation le raisonnement du juge en chef Robert: "Ce n'est que dans l'hypothèse où il existe une exception au principe général d'immunité que le tribunal pourra se prononcer sur le fond d'une demande visant un État étranger."[27] Bien que la Loi ne mentionne pas expressément une demande de reconnaissance d'un jugement étranger,

24 *Kuwait Airways Corporation c République d'Irak et Bombardier Aéronautique*, 2010 CSC 40 (21 octobre 2010) au para 12 [*Kuwait Airways*].

25 *Ibid* au para 14.

26 *Ibid* au para 17.

27 *Ibid* au para 19.

une telle demande est une "instance" au sens de l'art. 3 de la Loi, à la lumière des principes de droit international privé québécois.[28] La conclusion du juge sur ce point est renforcé, il note, par le fait qu'il est compatible avec la Loi sur la Convention Canada-Royaume-Uni relative aux jugements en matière civile et commerciale,[29] et la Convention qu'elle ratifie, bien qu'aucune de ces normes s'applique au Québec.[30]

Ayant déterminé que la Loi s'applique, le juge LeBel considère si les dispositions de cette Loi interdisent la reconnaissance du jugement anglais contre l'Irak. Ce dernier a droit à l'immunité sauf si KAC établit qu'elle peut invoquer une exception à cette immunité. Le juge souligne que "Cette question doit se décider sous le régime du droit canadien. En effet, même si le tribunal anglais a rendu sa propre décision sur la question, celle-ci n'a pas force de chose jugée, car, autrement, comme le rappelle le juge en chef Robert, la cour britannique et la loi du Royaume-Uni établiraient le contenu de la compétence des tribunaux québécois."[31] Cependant, le tribunal ne peut reprendre l'étude du fond de la décision. Selon le juge, "l'étude du problème de l'immunité de juridiction et des exceptions à celle-ci doit s'effectuer dans le cadre du droit applicable actuellement au Canada, y compris le droit international public, mais dans le respect des constatations de fait du juge Steel."[32]

Le juge passe ensuite à l'application de l'exception de l'activité commerciale. Il commence par l'observation intrigante qu'il n'est pas nécessaire de déterminer si la Loi "épuise le sujet et si l'évolution du droit international et celle de la common law font apparaître de nouvelles exceptions aux principes d'immunité de juridiction et d'exécution."[33] Revenant à la question devant lui, le juge constate que la conclusion de la Cour d'appel tend à reconnaître l'existence d'une catégorie d'actes de gestion qui, sans constituer des actes de souveraineté, bénéficieraient toujours de l'immunité de juridiction. Le juge LeBel rejette ce point de vue, en s'appuyant sur les jugements britanniques et américains sur la portée de la doctrine de

28 *Ibid* au para 20.

29 Loi sur la Convention Canada-Royaume-Uni relative aux jugements en matière civile et commerciale, LRC 1985, ch C-30.

30 *Kuwait Airways, supra* note 24 au para 21.

31 *Ibid* au para 22.

32 *Ibid* au para 23.

33 *Ibid* au para 24, citant François Larocque, "La Loi sur l'immunité des États canadienne et la torture" (2010) 55 RD McGill 81.

l'immunité des états. Selon le juge, "Il ne suffit ... pas de se demander si l'acte visé émanait d'une décision de l'État, et s'il a été accompli dans le but de protéger un intérêt étatique ou d'atteindre un objectif de politique publique. S'il en était ainsi, tous les actes d'un État, ou même d'un organisme qu'il contrôle, seraient assimilés à des actes de souveraineté."

En appliquant ces considérations à l'affaire portée devant lui, le juge examine la nature des actes en cause devant les tribunaux anglais. Pour ce faire, le juge LeBel juge nécessaire d'accepter les conclusions de fait "claires et éloquentes" du juge Steel.[34] L'Irak a contrôlé et financé la défense d'IAC devant les tribunaux anglais, une défense qui comprenait nombreux actes de fabrication de faux, de la dissimulation de preuves et de mensonges. Alors que l'appropriation originale des avions était un acte souverain, la rétention et la mise en service des avions par IAC étaient des actes de nature commerciale, comme l'étaient les interventions de l'Irak pour défendre IAC devant les tribunaux anglais. En conséquence, l'Irak ne pouvait pas s'appuyer sur l'immunité prévue à l'art. 3 de la Loi, et le moyen d'irrecevabilité présenté par l'intimée contre la demande de reconnaissance judiciaire aurait dû être rejeté.

Il est réconfortant de voir la Cour suprême du Canada renverser les décisions des tribunaux inférieurs et d'affirmer la responsabilité de l'Irak dans cette affaire. L'exception de l'activité commerciale à l'immunité des États ne doit pas être étendu afin de protéger un État qui choisit de patauger dans la poursuite d'une partie privée, en particulier là où il le fait par moyen de tromperies et de mépris des procédures judiciaires d'un autre État.

Extradition — non-refoulement — Roma

Németh v Canada (Justice), 2010 SCC 56 (25 November 2010). Supreme Court of Canada.

The appellants were Hungarian Roma (or Gypsies) who had been granted refugee status in Canada in 2001 following racially motivated attacks on them by Hungarian citizens between 1997 and 2001. Two years after their recognition as refugees in Canada, Hungary issued an international arrest warrant for them in respect of a charge of fraud concerning the sale of a right of lease worth approximately $2,700, which, it was alleged, they did not own. The minister of

34 *Kuwait Airways, supra* note 24 au para 34.

justice obtained a committal order from the Quebec Superior Court and then ordered the appellants' surrender. The appellants sought judicial review, contending that the principle of *non-refoulement* prevented their extradition to the very country from which they were granted refuge. The Quebec Court of Appeal upheld the minister's decision.

Cromwell J for the unanimous court identified two main issues: (1) does the minister have legal authority to surrender for extradition a refugee whose refugee status has not ceased or been revoked and (2) if so, did the minister exercise that authority reasonably? In addressing these questions, Cromwell J engaged in a remarkable, wide-ranging analysis of international refugee protection and its implementation in Canada by means of both the Immigration and Refugee Protection Act (IRPA) and the Extradition Act.

The starting point of Cromwell J's analysis is the principle of *non-refoulement* as embodied in Article 33 of the Refugee Convention.[35] Cromwell J identifies the IRPA as the "main" (but not the only) "vehicle for implementing Canada's refugee obligations," and identifies IRPA section 115 as "a statutory expression of the principle of *non-refoulement*" in Canadian law.[36] The appellants contended that section 115's requirement that a refugee "shall not be removed from Canada" prohibited their extradition to Hungary and that any other interpretation would breach Canada's obligations under the Refugee Convention. Cromwell J disagreed, accepting the Crown's submission that the removal contemplated in section 115 was a term of art applying only to removal orders made under the IRPA and its regulations and not to surrender orders made under the Extradition Act.[37] In response to the appellants' contention that section 115 must be interpreted consistently with Canada's international legal obligation of *non-refoulement*, Cromwell J agreed that, as a matter of international law, protection from *refoulement* applies to expulsions by extradition.[38] He also accepted "of course" that "where possible statutes should be interpreted in a way which makes their provisions consistent with Canada's international treaty obligations

35 Convention Relating to the Status of Refugees, [1969] Can TS, No 6; see also Protocol Relating to the Status of Refugees, [1969] Can TS, No 29.

36 *Németh v Canada (Justice)*, 2010 SCC 56 at paras 17-22 [*Németh*]. The learned judge notes in particular (at para 23) the "close correspondence" between s 115 and the relevant provisions of the Refugee Convention.

37 *Ibid* at paras 24-31.

38 *Ibid* at para 33.

and principles of international law."[39] He noted, however, that the presumption is rebuttable: "If the provisions [to be interpreted] are unambiguous, they must be given effect."[40] Cromwell J considered section 115 to be unambiguous. "Moreover," he added, "I do not accept that this interpretation of s. 115 results in Canadian domestic law failing to respect its *non-refoulement* obligations," which, in his view, "are fully satisfied by a correct interpretation and application of s. 44" of the Extradition Act.[41] In the learned judge's view, "the IRPA does not and was not intended to implement Canada's international obligations against *refoulement* in the context of expulsion by extradition. That role … is assigned to s. 44" of the Extradition Act.[42]

The appellants argued that, having been found to be refugees under the IRPA in 2001, this finding bound the minister in his determinations under the Extradition Act until such time as the appellants' refugee status ceased or was revoked as provided for by the IRPA. Cromwell J considered this argument in light of both the relevant IRPA and Extradition Act provisions and international legal principles. He described the rights of refugees under the convention as "temporal in the sense that they exist while the risk exists but end when the risk has ended."[43] The relevant time for assessment of risk, under the convention, is the time of the proposed removal — a point that argued against the submission that the appellants' refugee status in 2001 bound the minister today. Cromwell J added that,

> looking beyond the terms of the Refugee Convention, I have not found any international law norm to the effect that extradition may only be ordered if a previous finding that a person is a refugee has been formally set aside. So far as I have been able to determine, state practices on this point vary considerably.[44]

Cromwell J therefore concluded that the minister was not constrained by the IRPA not to extradite a person with refugee status.[45]

39 *Ibid* at para 34.

40 *Ibid* at para 35.

41 *Ibid* at para 35.

42 *Ibid* at para 41.

43 *Ibid* at para 50.

44 *Ibid* at para 52.

45 *Ibid* at para 55.

The learned judge next considered whether the minister had reasonably exercised his authority to surrender the appellants to Hungary. In answering this question, Cromwell J embarked upon a lengthy analysis of section 44(1) of the Extradition Act, which provides:

The Minister shall refuse to make a surrender order if the Minister is satisfied that

(a) the surrender would be unjust or oppressive having regard to all the relevant circumstances; or

(b) the request for extradition is made for the purpose of prosecuting or punishing the person by reason of their race, religion, nationality, ethnic origin, language, colour, political opinion, sex, sexual orientation, age, mental or physical disability or status or that the person's position may be prejudiced for any of those reasons.

Le ministre refuse l'extradition s'il est convaincu que :

a) soit l'extradition serait injuste ou tyrannique compte tenu de toutes les circonstances;

b) soit la demande d'extradition est présentée dans le but de poursuivre ou de punir l'intéressé pour des motifs fondés sur la race, la nationalité, l'origine ethnique, la langue, la couleur, la religion, les convictions politiques, le sexe, l'orientation sexuelle, l'âge, le handicap physique ou mental ou le statut de l'intéressé, ou il pourrait être porté atteinte à sa situation pour l'un de ces motifs.

Section 44(1)(a) and (b) set out the grounds on which the minister must refuse to surrender a person sought. Here, the minister considered only the first such ground, namely whether the surrender would be unjust or oppressive in all of the circumstances. Cromwell J concluded that the minister erred in law and acted unreasonably in failing to give sufficient weight to the scope of Canada's *non-refoulement* obligations, particularly as they relate to the second ground of impermissible surrender set out in section 44(1)(b).[46]

As the learned judge noted, previous case law has emphasized section 44(1)(a) over section 44(1)(b). Yet the ground for refusal of surrender set out in paragraph (b) is "Canada's primary legislative vehicle to give effect to Canada's *non-refoulement* obligations

46 *Ibid* at paras 56-58.

when a refugee is sought for extradition."[47] Cromwell J arrived at this conclusion by means of a detailed consideration of the legislative history of section 44(1) and its antecedents in the European Convention on Extradition 1957[48] and the UN Model Treaty on Extradition.[49] The international instruments indicate that section 44(1)(b) is concerned with both prosecution or punishment for a discriminatory purpose and more general discrimination that may prejudice a person's position. This latter branch of section 44(1)(b) is "directed to the same purpose as the comparable provision in the [European] Extradition Convention and the Model Treaty on Extradition: fulfilling *non-refoulement* obligations in the extradition context."[50] The legislative history of section 44(1) confirms its connection to the international instruments and its *non-refoulement* function. Cromwell J concluded that "domestic law aimed at implementing the Refugee Convention, such as s. 44(1)(b), must be interpreted in light of [the] human rights object and purpose" of the Refugee Convention.[51]

Returning to the minister's decision with respect to the appellants, Cromwell J concluded that the minister failed to address section 44(1)(b), wrongly imposed a burden on them to show continuing risk of persecution and applied a wrong and more onerous test than that prescribed by section 44(1)(b).[52] The learned judge allowed the appeal, set aside the judgment of the Court of Appeal and the minster's surrender decisions, and remitted the matter to the minister for reconsideration according to law.[53]

The profundity and subtlety of this decision are, with respect, greatly to be admired. Cromwell J's analysis displays at once a commitment to giving effect to Canada's international obligations and a respect for the means Parliament has chosen to do so. A simplistic application of the presumption of conformity to section 115 is rejected without doing violence either to Canada's international obligations

47 *Ibid* at para 77; see also para 102, describing "an important purpose of s. 44(1)(b)" as "to implement Canada's *non-refoulement* obligations in the extradition setting."

48 European Convention on Extradition, (1957) ETS no 24.

49 UNGA Res A/RES/45/116 (1990).

50 *Nemeth, supra* note 36 at para 81; see also paras 78-82 and paras 92-96.

51 *Ibid* at para 86.

52 *Ibid* at para 115.

53 Note that a companion case, *Gavrila v Canada (Justice)*, 2010 SCC 57, concerning extradition of a Roma refugee to Romania, was similarly disposed of.

or to a fundamental principle of the Canadian reception system. The court's treatment of the substantive international legal issues raised by the appeal is comprehensive, informed not only by analysis of the relevant treaties and commentary on them but also by decisions of other national courts.

Terrorism — international humanitarian law — "armed conflict" exception to terrorism offences

R v Khawaja, 2010 ONCA 862 (17 December 2010). Court of Appeal for Ontario.

This was an appeal of the accused's conviction and sentencing for terrorism-related offences under section 83.01(1) of the Criminal Code.[54] The accused was the first individual to be tried for terrorism-related offences in Ontario. At trial, the accused had been convicted of five terrorism-related offences and sentenced to ten years in prison. His convictions related to acts he carried out for the purpose of supporting violent "Jihad" around the world, including acts for the particular purpose of supporting the insurgency against coalition forces in Afghanistan.

At trial, the accused had argued that he had been engaged in legitimate armed conflict under international law, and the "armed conflict" exception in section 83.01(1) should apply to exclude his activities from the definition of terrorist activity. Section 83.01(1) excludes the following from the definition of terrorist activity:

[A]n act or omission that is committed during an armed conflict and that, at the time and in the place of its commission, is in accordance with customary international law or conventional international law applicable to the conflict.

[L]'acte — action ou omission — commis au cours d'un conflit armé et conforme, au moment et au lieu de la perpétration, au droit international coutumier ou au droit international conventionnel applicable au conflit.

The trial judge held that the exception could not apply, as there had been no armed conflict at the relevant times in Canada, Pakistan, or the United Kingdom, where the accused had carried out the acts for which he was charged.

54 Criminal Code, RSC 1985, c C-46, s 83.01(1).

On appeal, the accused argued, *inter alia*, that the trial judge had erred in failing to apply the exception. The court of appeal, in a decision attributed to the court as a whole, held that the construction applied by the trial judge was unnecessarily narrow. The court then outlined the proper construction of the exception:

> The availability of the exception does not require proof of an accused's physical presence in the area of armed conflict. Nor does it contemplate that an accused's impugned acts or omissions must be carried out within the territorial limits of an area of armed conflict. As we have already said, all that is required to trigger the exception is some evidence that (1) an accused's acts or omissions were committed "during" an armed conflict; and (2) those acts or omissions, at the time and place of their commission, accorded with international law applicable to the armed conflict at issue.[55]

In the result, the court held that there was no evidence that the accused had acted in accordance with international law or that the hostilities undertaken by insurgents in Afghanistan, in support of whom the accused had undertaken certain of the acts for which he was charged, were conducted in accordance with international law. As a result, the armed conflict exception could not apply.

The accused also argued on appeal that the trial judge had erred in taking judicial notice of the geopolitical situation in Afghanistan. The trial judge had relied on documents publicly available on the United Nations website,[56] including Security Council resolutions and a general background document produced by the United Nations, to take judicial notice of the following facts about the conflict in Afghanistan: (1) the Afghan government is supported by a coalition of western nations, including Canada, pursuant to various United Nations Security Council resolutions; (2) insurgents in Afghanistan are engaged in armed conflict against coalition forces, the local government and Afghan locals who support those two entities; (3) Canadian forces have been killed as a result of the insurgency; and (4) the purpose of the insurgency is to intimidate those conducting or supporting the peaceful reconstruction of Afghanistan and to compel those persons to stop their reconstruction efforts.[57]

55 *R v Khawaja*, 2010 ONCA 862 (17 December 2010) at para 165 [*Khawaja*].

56 Online: <http://www.un.org/documents>.

57 *Khawaja*, *supra* note 55 at para 172.

The court of appeal held that the trial judge did not err in taking notice of these "skeletal and obvious facts about the basic nature of the conflict in Afghanistan."[58] The court noted that these facts are notorious and beyond dispute among reasonable persons, using their recitation in numerous Security Council resolutions as the basis for their non-controversial nature. The court also noted that the accuracy of the facts judicially noticed by the trial judge had not been challenged on appeal.[59]

On 30 June 2011, the Supreme Court of Canada granted leave to appeal in this case.[60]

International labour law — freedom of association — collective bargaining

Ontario (Attorney General) v Fraser, 2011 SCC 20 (29 April 2011). Supreme Court of Canada.

In response to the Supreme Court of Canada's 2001 decision in *Dunmore v Ontario (Attorney General)*, the Ontario legislature enacted the Agricultural Employees Protection Act, 2002 (AEPA) — another attempt to establish a labour relations regime for the farming sector separate from that which applies generally in Ontario pursuant to the Labour Relations Act, 1995. The AEPA excludes farm workers from the general labour regime while creating a separate regime in which farm workers are granted certain associational rights and employers of farm workers are required to listen to or read representations made to them by farm worker associations. The AEPA also creates a tribunal to hear and decide disputes about its application.

The respondent farm workers and union challenged the constitutionality of the AEPA. In particular, they claimed that freedom of association as protected by section 2(d) of the Canadian Charter of Rights and Freedoms includes three specific requirements that the AEPA lacks: (1) statutory protection for majoritarian exclusivity (that is, recognition of the union selected by the majority of employees as sole and exclusive collective bargaining agent); (2) a statutory mechanism to resolve bargaining impasses and interpret collective agreements (as found in the Labour Relations Act, 1995);

58 *Ibid* at para 173.

59 *Ibid.*

60 *R v Khawaja*, [2011] SCCA No 80 (QL).

and (3) a statutory duty to bargain in good faith. (The respondents also challenged the AEPA under section 15 of the Charter, but that argument won no traction with any member of the court and will not be pursued here.)

The constitutional challenge was heard in chambers before Farley J prior to the Supreme Court of Canada's decision in *Health Services and Support — Facilities Subsector Bargaining Association v British Columbia*,[61] a decision that departed from precedent in holding that freedom of association under section 2(d) includes protection for collective bargaining. Farley J dismissed the application. The appeal from this decision was rendered after *Health Services.* Winkler CJO for the court reversed Farley J, holding that the AEPA substantially impaired the ability of agricultural workers to meaningfully exercise the right to bargain collectively contrary to Charter section 2(d). In particular, the AEPA did not provide what Winkler CJO regarded as the minimum statutory protections, namely a duty to bargain in good faith, majoritarian exclusivity, and a statutory mechanism for resolving bargaining impasses or disputes about collective agreements.

Eight of the nine justices of the Supreme Court of Canada agreed on allowing the appeal and restoring the first instance decision that the AEPA was not unconstitutional. Yet the court was split on the reasons for doing so. The majority reasons, written by McLachlin CJ and LeBel J with the concurrences of Binnie, Fish and Cromwell JJ affirmed and purported to apply *Health Services* to resolve the appeal. Rothstein J (Charron J concurring) attacked *Health Services* and called upon the court to reverse it. The conformity of section 2(d) with Canadian international labour law obligations was very much at issue in both judgments. (The reasons of Deschamps J, concurring in the result, and Abella J, dissenting, do not address the international law aspects of the problem and are disregarded here.)

The majority described the ultimate question before the court as "whether s. 2(d), properly understood and applied, requires the Ontario legislature to provide a particular form of collective bargaining rights to agricultural workers, in order to secure the effective exercise of their associational rights."[62] The court of appeal had effectively said yes and required the legislature to adopt for farm

61 *Health Services and Support — Facilities Subsector Bargaining Association v British Columbia,* 2007 SCC 27; reviewed in [2008] 46 CYIL 527 at 544ff.

62 *Ontario (Attorney General) v Fraser,* 2011 SCC 20 (29 April 2011) at para 18 [*Fraser*].

works the so-called Wagner Act model of labour relations that prevails in Canada and the United States. The majority disagreed, emphasizing that the majority of the court in *Health Services* "unequivocally stated that s. 2(d) does not guarantee a particular model of collective bargaining or a particular outcome."[63] The majority added that both *Health Services* and *Dunmore* were at odds with the view that section 2(d) protects a particular kind of collective bargaining. Rather, section 2(d) protects the right to associate to achieve collective goals.[64]

Much of the majority's reasons are given over to rebutting Rothstein J's assault on *Health Services.* It is in that context that Canada's international legal obligations arose. In *Health Services,* international law was cited as one of four reasons for overturning the court's previous jurisprudence on section 2(d) in the labour context (the so-called Labour Trilogy). In his reasons, Rothstein J questions the characterization of Canada's obligations in *Health Services.* He claims that the majority in *Health Services* conflated two distinct International Labour Organization conventions, namely Convention no. 87 Concerning Freedom of Association and Protection of the Right to Organise[65] (to which Canada is a party) and Convention no. 98 Concerning the Application of the Principles of the Right to Organise and Bargain Collectively[66] (to which Canada is not a party). Convention no. 87 does not specifically address collective bargaining. Convention no. 98 does, but Canada has no obligations under that treaty, having not ratified it. Thus, the court's interpretation of the scope of Canada's international obligations in *Health Services* is flawed.[67] Rothstein J goes further, saying that even if Convention no. 98 were applicable to Canada the majority in *Health Services* would still have erred in relying on it "to constitutionalize a version of collective bargaining that includes a duty to bargain in good faith" because that treaty conceives of collective bargaining as a process of voluntary negotiation "fundamentally distinct from the model of collective bargaining incorporated in the Wagner

[63] *Ibid* at para 45.

[64] *Ibid* at para 46.

[65] Convention no. 87 Concerning Freedom of Association and Protection of the Right to Organise, [1973] Can TS No 14.

[66] Convention no. 98 Concerning the Application of the Principles of the Right to Organise and Bargain Collectively, 96 UNTS 257.

[67] *Fraser, supra* note 62 at para 248.

model."[68] In particular, Convention no. 98 does not contemplate the imposition of a duty on parties to bargain in good faith.

Against this, the majority invokes a decision rendered by the ILO Committee on Freedom of Association (CFA) arising from the same facts as those that produced *Health Services.* The majority notes that the CFA in that case concluded that the BC government's action in cancelling collective agreements by law violated the health service employees' rights to freedom of association. The CFA reached this conclusion after noting that Canada was a party to Convention no. 87 but not Convention no. 98.[69] The majority continues, in response to Rothstein J, that while voluntariness is "a component of the international model of collective bargaining ... the ILO Committee of Experts has not found compulsory collective bargaining to be contrary to international norms."[70] On this basis, the majority is, it seems, satisfied that "Canada's international obligations support the view that collective bargaining is constitutionally protected in the minimal sense discussed in *Health Services*"[71] — a turn of phrase that is surely weaker than Dickson CJ's formulation, cited in *Health Services*, that "the Charter should be presumed to provide at least as great a level of protection as is found in the international human rights documents that Canada has ratified." Similarly, the majority declares, "Charter rights *must* be interpreted in light of Canadian values and Canada's international and human rights commitments."[72] Like so many other Supreme Court of Canada pronouncements on the relationship between international law and the Charter, this phrase is emphatic about international law having a role in Charter interpretation but non-committal about the interpretive weight to be given to it. The majority went on to conclude that the AEPA does not infringe section 2(d) of the Charter and that the appeal should be allowed.

Labour law academics and practitioners may debate whether the majority or Rothstein J have better appreciated Canada's obligations under international labour law. The issue of what interpretive weight ought properly to be given to decisions of the CFA in interpreting ILO conventions appears to me crucial to that determination. That

68 *Ibid* at para 249.

69 *Ibid* at para 94.

70 *Ibid* at para 95.

71 *Ibid* at para 93.

72 *Ibid* at para 92 [emphasis in the original].

the court has split on this point is deeply regrettable, as it may tend to foster an all-too-easy belief that international legal obligations are amorphous or inscrutable and, therefore, lawyers and judges may be excused from paying them close attention. The more likely explanations for this divergence of judicial opinion, I suspect, are a failure of the parties (in this case and *Health Services*) to adequately brief the international aspects of the issue for the benefit of the court and too great a willingness by the judges to take on international legal problems without the assistance of full submissions from counsel. The result is a decision that does not shed much light on the requirements of international labour law.

There is, however, a positive note to be sounded here. The dispute between the majority and Rothstein J was not in any way about the propriety of considering international law in the first place or even the propriety of giving it significant (if still uncertain) weight. The dispute between the two camps was about what international law requires of Canada — not about whether the court should turn its mind to such requirements. Now that the relevance of international law in Charter interpretation is (it seems) uncontroversial, let us hope courts and counsel begin directing their efforts more fully to its substantive requirements.

Extradition — abuse of process — torture

United States of America v Khadr, 2011 ONCA 358 (6 May 2011). Court of Appeal for Ontario.

The Attorney General of Canada, on behalf of the United States, appealed from an order staying extradition proceedings against Abdullah Khadr. The extradition judge stayed proceedings in response to Mr. Khadr's treatment at the hands of US and Pakistani authorities while in detention in Pakistan.

Abdullah Khadr, a Canadian citizen, was apprehended by the Pakistani Inter-Services Intelligence Directorate (ISI) at the request of the United States and on payment of a $500,000 bounty. He was detained for fourteen months. Mr. Khadr was subject to beatings by the ISI, who interrogated him for the purpose of obtaining intelligence information, but who refused to charge him or bring him before the Pakistani courts. US officials discouraged access by the Canadian Security Intelligence Service to Mr. Khadr.[73] It was held

[73] *United States of America v Khadr*, 2011 ONCA 358 at paras 8-9 [*Khadr* ONCA].

at the extradition hearing that Mr. Khadr's detention was illegal under Pakistani law.[74] The final six months of Mr. Khadr's detention in Pakistan, after his usefulness as a source of information had been exhausted, was at the request of the United States, to permit it to start a criminal investigation and to pursue the rendition of Mr. Khadr to the United States. Mr. Khadr was repatriated to Canada in December 2005.

Upon his arrival in Canada, Mr. Khadr was questioned by both RCMP and FBI officers. Criminal charges in relation to terrorism offences were filed against Mr. Khadr in Massachusetts, the United States sought his extradition, and a request for extradition was made in February 2006. The minister of justice issued an authority to proceed the following month, and the Attorney General proceeded with an application for an order of committal for extradition.

At the hearing, the extradition judge heard the application for committal, a voluntariness *voir dire* relating to the statements given to RCMP and FBI officers, and an application for a stay of proceedings based on abuse of process. The statement given to the FBI was excluded, as it had its foundation in statements made in interviews with Mr. Khadr in Pakistan. The proceedings were stayed for abuse of process.

The Attorney General of Canada appealed to the Ontario Court of Appeal on the grounds that (1) the extradition judge had no jurisdiction to order a stay once the minister of justice had exercised his discretion to issue an authority to proceed, and (2) even if the judge had the jurisdiction, this was not "the clearest of cases" in which a stay is available. The Ontario Court of Appeal dismissed the appeal and upheld the extradition judge's decision to issue a stay of proceedings. The court's reasons are remarkable both for the condemnation of the requesting state's conduct and for the court's clear statement of its inherent ability to defend the integrity of its process in the light of egregious human rights violations.

On the first point, the extradition judge's jurisdiction, Sharpe JA, writing for the court, held that there was nothing in the legislation or in the case law suggesting that the court's inherent jurisdiction to control its own process had been limited. He held that "recognizing the extradition judge's residual power to stay proceedings for an abuse of process also coincides with the deeply embedded common law principle that, absent express legislation to the contrary,

74 *United States of America v Khadr* (2010), 258 CCC (3d) 231 at para 124 (Ont Sup Ct) [Khadr Sup Ct].

the courts must not surrender the authority to protect their own integrity to the executive."[75]

On the second ground of appeal, that the extradition judge had erred in his determination that this was one of those clearest of cases in which a stay could be ordered, absent any trial unfairness, the Court of Appeal was equally unyielding. Sharpe JA found no reason to interfere in the extradition judge's determination that the conduct of the requesting state had been egregious and that the remedy of a stay in this instance would have the effect of dissociating the court from the requesting state's conduct and would also serve as a specific deterrent to such conduct in the future.[76] The learned judge also rejected arguments that the extradition judge was not entitled to consider foreign law in coming to his determination that Mr. Khadr had been illegally detained or even to take into account the behaviour of the Pakistani or American authorities while in Pakistan.

The final argument of the Attorney General was that the extradition judge was required to conduct a meaningful balancing of the benefit to be derived from committing an alleged terrorist for extradition against the gravity of the requesting state's conduct. This argument was rejected first as not accurately stating the law — a trial judge considering a stay must only perform a balancing exercise in borderline cases where it is unclear whether the abuse is sufficient to warrant a stay.[77] On the trial judge's findings of egregious violations of Mr. Khadr's rights, this was not a borderline case.

Sharpe JA rejected Canada's position. Drawing on several decisions of foreign courts, he approved and expanded on the extradition judge's statement that "[i]n civilized democracies, the rule of law must prevail over intelligence objectives."[78] Sharpe JA stated:

> These eminent jurists make a fundamental point: the rule of law must prevail even in the face of the dreadful threat of terrorism. We must adhere to our democratic and legal values, even if that adherence serves in the short term to benefit those who oppose and seek to destroy those values. For if we do not, in the longer term, the enemies of democracy and the

[75] Khadr ONCA, *supra* note 73.

[76] *Ibid* at para 57.

[77] *Ibid* at para 69, citing from *Canada (Minister of Citizenship and Immigration) v Tobiass,* [1997] 3 SCR 391 at para 92 and *R v Regan,* [2002] 1 SCR 297, 2002 SCC 12 at para 57.

[78] *Khadr* ONCA, *supra* note 73 at para 72, citing Khadr Sup Ct, *supra* note 74 at para 150.

rule of law will have succeeded. They will have demonstrated that our faith in our legal order is unable to withstand their threats. In my view, the extradition judge did not err in law or in principle by giving primacy to adherence to the rule of law.[79]

Hague Convention — non-refoulement — federal paramountcy

AMRI v KER, 2011 ONCA 417 (2 June 2011). Court of Appeal for Ontario.

In this case, a father appealed the lower court's decision that his fourteen-year-old daughter should be returned to the custody of her mother in Mexico pursuant to the Convention on the Civil Aspects of International Child Abduction 1980 (Hague Convention),[80] to which Canada is a party. The child had originally visited her father in Toronto in 2008, with her mother's consent. During that visit, the child revealed to her father that she had been abused by her mother. The child did not return to Mexico, staying in Canada with her father and later her paternal aunt (after her father was denied refugee status in Canada and moved to Norway). In May 2010, the child was found to be a refugee in Canada by reason of the abuse she had suffered from her mother.

In July 2010, the mother brought an application under the Hague Convention, as implemented into the law of Ontario by the Children's Law Reform Act (CLRA),[81] to have the child returned to Mexico. The application judge held that the child was being wrongfully retained in Ontario and ordered that she be returned to her mother's custody in Mexico. The father appealed that decision.

Article 12 of the Hague Convention requires the mandatory return of children who have been wrongfully removed or retained, so long as less than one year has elapsed. Section 46(2) of the CLRA states that the provisions of the Hague Convention are law in Ontario.

Canada is, of course, a party to the Convention Relating to the Status of Refugees 1951 and its protocol (Refugee Convention).[82] Article 33 of the Refugee Convention enshrines the principle of *non-refoulement*, which prohibits contracting states from returning

[79] *Ibid* at para 76.

[80] Convention on the Civil Aspects of International Child Abduction, [1983] Can TS No 35 [Hague Convention].

[81] Children's Law Reform Act, RSO 1990, c C.12.

[82] Convention Relating to the Status of Refugees, [1969] Can TS No 6 [Refugee Convention].

refugees to states where there is a risk that the refugee will be subjected to human rights violations. The principle of *non-refoulement* from Article 33 of the Refugee Convention has been received in the laws of Canada through section 115 of the Immigration and Refugee Protection Act (IRPA).[83]

On this appeal, the father argued that section 46(2) of the CLRA conflicted with section 115 of the IRPA, as the CLRA would mandate the child's return while the IRPA would prevent it. As a result of this conflict, the father argued that section 46(2) of the CLRA was rendered inoperable by operation of federal paramountcy. The court of appeal rejected this argument, holding that there was no conflict between the two provisions. Citing *Nemeth v Canada (Justice),*[84] the court noted that the prohibition on removal of refugees who face persecution, torture, cruel treatment, or cruel punishment in section 115 of the *IRPA* did not apply to removals effected under different statutory schemes.

The court also held that section 46 of the CLRA does not frustrate the purpose of Canada's *non-refoulement* obligations as set out in section 115 of the IRPA. At para 67, the court held that the principle of *non-refoulement* is directly implicated when an application is made for the return of a refugee child under the Hague Convention.[85] The court held that the Hague Convention contemplates respect for, and fulfillment of, Canada's *non-refoulement* obligations, noting that Article 13(b) of the Hague Convention allows a state to refuse to return a child if "there is a grave risk that his or her return would expose the child to physical or psychological harm or otherwise place the child in an intolerable situation."[86]

The court also noted that Article 20 of the Hague Convention allowed a state to refuse to return a child if the return of the child would be impermissible "by the fundamental principles of the requested state relating to the protection of human rights and fundamental freedoms."[87] The court held that the *refoulement* of convention refugees would be a violation of section 115 of the IRPA and a breach of Canada's international human rights obligations, and therefore Article 20 of the Hague Convention was engaged.[88]

[83] Immigration and Refugee Protection Act, SC 2011, c 27.

[84] *Németh v Canada (Justice),* 2010 SCC 56.

[85] *AMRI v KER,* 2011 ONCA 417 (2 June 2011) at para 67 [*AMRI*].

[86] Hague Convention, *supra* note 80, Article 13(b).

[87] *Ibid,* Article 20.

[88] *AMRI, supra* note 85 at para 71.

Finally, the court noted that under the Vienna Convention on the Law of Treaties 1969,[89] a treaty is to be interpreted in accordance with any applicable rules of international law. As the Refugee Convention came into force prior to the Hague Convention, the tenets of the Refugee Convention were applicable rules of international law at the time the Hague Convention came into force. Accordingly, section 46(2) of the CLRA must be interpreted consonant with Canada's obligations under the Refugee Convention.

The Immigration and Refugee Board must be satisfied that a refugee claimant faces a reasonable chance of persecution in his or her country of habitual residence prior to granting a claim for refugee status. In light of this, the court held that when a child has been recognized as a convention refugee, there arises a rebuttable presumption that the child will face a risk of the harm contemplated in Article 13(b) if a return is ordered. The child therefore has a *prima facie* entitlement to protection against *refoulement*. On an application for the return of the child under the Hague Convention, there is no burden placed on the child to prove that the circumstances giving rise to his or her refugee status have not changed.[90]

The court noted that the *prima facie* entitlement to protection against *refoulement* was also in accordance with Canada's obligations under the Convention on the Rights of the Child 1989,[91] which states at Article 3 that the best interests of the child are a primary consideration in all actions concerning children.[92] In the result, the court held that the application judge had erred by failing to properly consider the child's refugee status and her entitlement to protection from *refoulement*. A new hearing was ordered.

Refugee protection — admissibility — complicity in crimes against humanity

Ezokola v Canada (Minister of Citizenship and Immigration), 2011 FCA 224 (15 July 2011). Federal Court of Appeal.

The respondent was a government employee and diplomat for the Democratic Republic of Congo (DRC). Following the election of Joseph Kabila, whom the respondent did not support, as president

[89] Vienna Convention on the Law of Treaties, [1989] Can TS No 37.

[90] *AMRI, supra* note 85 at paras 77-78.

[91] Convention on the Rights of the Child, [1992] Can TS No 3.

[92] *AMRI, supra* note 85 at para 82.

of the DRC, the respondent resigned his position and fled to Canada. He claimed refugee status under the Refugee Convention.[93] His claim of refugee status was rejected, with the Immigration and Refugee Board (IRB) finding that there were serious reasons to believe that he had been complicit in crimes against humanity and, therefore, that he fell within the ambit of Article 1F(a) of the Refugee Convention:

> F. The provisions of this Convention shall not apply to any person with respect to whom there are serious reasons for considering that:
>
> (a) he has committed a crime against peace, a war crime, or a crime against humanity, as defined in the international instruments drawn up to make provision in respect of such crimes.[94]

The IRB found that the respondent had not personally committed any of the crimes listed in Article 1F(a) of the Refugee Convention, but it was sufficient to establish complicity by association that the respondent had "personal and knowing awareness" of the crimes and enabled his government to perpetuate itself and perpetuate crimes against humanity while doing nothing to disassociate himself from the government.[95]

On judicial review, the application judge reversed the decision of the IRB. The application judge accepted the IRB's findings that the DRC government had committed crimes against humanity and that the respondent had personal awareness of these crimes. However, the application judge held that there must be a personal nexus between the refugee claimant and the crimes alleged in order to establish complicity by association, and no such nexus existed on the evidence before him.[96] This constituted a departure from existing jurisprudence, which had applied the test of whether the refugee claimant had "personal and knowing participation" in the alleged crimes.[97]

93 Convention Relating to the Status of Refugees 1951 and Protocol 1967, [1969] Can TS No 6.

94 *Ibid*, Article 1(F)(a).

95 *Ezokola v Canada (Minister of Citizenship and Immigration)*, 2011 FCA 224 (15 July 2011) at paras 17, 74-75 [*Ezokola*].

96 *Ibid* at para 21.

97 *Ibid* at para 52.

In reaching this decision, the application judge read the provisions of the Rome Statute of the International Criminal Court (Rome Statute)[98] as establishing that criminal responsibility for crimes against humanity requires either personal participation in the alleged crime or personal control over the events that led to the crime.[99] The application judge used this approach to criminal responsibility in the Rome Statute to inform the Canadian case law on complicity by association under Article 1F(a) of the Refugee Convention, ultimately holding that complicity by association requires either personal participation or personal facilitation of the alleged crimes.

On appeal from the decision of the application judge, Noel JA examined Articles 25 and 30 of the Rome Statute, which had been relied upon by the application judge. Noel JA noted that Article 25(3) of the Rome Statute was worded broadly, applying to individuals who assisted or "[i]n any other way" contributed to the commission of an alleged crime.[100]

Noel JA held that the wording of the Rome Statute did not limit criminal responsibility to situations of personal participation or personal facilitation. He held that the test of "personal and knowing participation," which was first applied to Article 1F(a) of the Refugee Convention by the Federal Court of Appeal in *Ramirez v Canada (Minister of Employment and Immigration)*,[101] was harmonious with the wording of the Rome Statute and remained the appropriate test. He held that the IRB had erred in applying a standard of "personal and knowing awareness," which was a lesser standard than personal and knowing participation in a crime.[102]

Noel JA held that the term "complicity by association" was misleading, as it suggested that mere association with the perpetrators of an alleged crime was sufficient to fit within the ambit of Article 1F(a) of the Refugee Convention. In fact, liability for international crimes is generated by personal and knowing participation in the crimes, not mere association. Noel JA suggested that the term "complicity by association" be dropped in favour of "complicity."[103]

98 Statute of the International Criminal Court, [2002] Can TS No 13.

99 *Ezokola, supra* note 95 at para 61.

100 *Ibid* at para 64.

101 *Ramirez v Canada (Minister of Employment and Immigration)*, [1992] 2 FC 306 (CA).

102 *Ezokola, supra* note 95 at paras 68, 75.

103 *Ibid* at para 58.

Finally, Noel JA rejected the application judge's suggestion that complicity must be understood as a presumption. Noel JA clarified that a presumption of complicity only arises as a result of participation in an organization pursuing a limited, brutal purpose. If the organization is not pursuing such a purpose, participation with the organization does not raise such a presumption, and it is for the minister to establish the refugee claimant's personal and knowing participation in the organization's crimes. In this case, the DRC government was not pursuing a limited and brutal purpose, and no presumption of complicity arose.[104]

In the result, Noel JA remitted the issue for a *de novo* hearing before the IRB.

International organizations — immunity — wrongful dismissal claim

Northwest Atlantic Fisheries Organization v Amaratunga, 2011 NSCA 73 (23 August 2011). Nova Scotia Court of Appeal. (Leave to appeal sought 24 October 2011.)

The respondent Tissa Amaratunga was deputy executive secretary of the Northwest Atlantic Fisheries Organization (NAFO) for seventeen years until his summary dismissal in 2005. NAFO's headquarters are in Dartmouth, Nova Scotia. Amaratunga commenced an action in the Supreme Court of Nova Scotia for damages for wrongful dismissal. Against the claim, NAFO alleged that it enjoyed immunity and the court was without jurisdiction. NAFO asserted this immunity as a matter of customary international law as well as by virtue of a federal order-in-council[105] granting it the privileges and immunities set forth in Articles II and III of the Convention on the Privileges and Immunities of the United Nations 1946[106] "to such extent as may be required for the performance of its functions."

The Supreme Court of Canada heard evidence from two professors of international law on the immunities of international organizations in customary international law. NAFO's expert, Professor

104 *Ibid* at para 71.

105 Northwest Atlantic Fisheries Organization Privileges and Immunities Order, SOR/80-64, made pursuant to the Foreign Missions and International Organizations Act, SC 1991, c 41.

106 Convention on the Privileges and Immunities of the United Nations, [1948] Can TS No 2, reproduced as Schedule III to the Foreign Missions and International Organizations Act, *supra* note 105.

Morgan, was of the opinion that international organizations such as NAFO were entitled to complete immunity from civil actions as a matter of customary international law. Wright J rejected that opinion, preferring Professor Saunders' view that there is no such customary international rule and that the sole source of NAFO's immunity was the order-in-council. The court also agreed with Professor Saunders that the level of immunity "required for the performance of [NAFO's] functions" should be determined consistently with Canada's obligations under Article 14(1) of the International Covenant on Civil and Political Rights 1966 (ICCPR)[107] to grant everyone a fair and public hearing by a competent, independent and impartial tribunal established by law in the determination of his rights and obligations in a suit at law. The court held that NAFO had not established that immunity from Amaratunga's damages claim was required for the performance of its functions and that he was at liberty to proceed with his action on the merits.

NAFO successfully appealed to the Nova Scotia Court of Appeal. MacDonald CJ for the court noted that NAFO had abandoned its reliance on customary international law on appeal,[108] leaving only two questions for the court: (1) did the judge below err in his interpretation of the phrase "required for the performance of its functions" in section 3(1) of the order-in-council and (2) did the judge err in finding that immunity was not required in this case?[109]

MacDonald CJ considered the judge below to have interpreted the phrase "required for the performance of its functions" too demandingly. Quoting the lower court's observation that "there is very little factual evidence to sustain the argument that it would be an impermissible intrusion into NAFO's internal management for the court to take jurisdiction," the learned chief justice worried that this approach was overly restrictive.[110] In the absence of direct precedent on the degree of immunity to be accorded to an international organization in such circumstances, MacDonald CJ took guidance from the decision of the Supreme Court of Canada in *Canada (House of Commons) v Vaid*,[111] a case concerning parliamentary privilege and

107 International Covenant on Civil and Political Rights, [1976] Can TS No 47.

108 *Northwest Atlantic Fisheries Organization v Amaratunga*, 2011 NSCA 73 (23 August 2011) at para 23 [*Amaratunga*].

109 *Ibid* at para 24.

110 *Ibid* at paras 28-32.

111 *Canada (House of Commons) v Vaid*, 2005 SCC 30.

the immunity from legal process flowing from it. The touchstone in *Vaid* was necessity — immunity should exist only to the extent necessary to ensure the proper functioning of Parliament. MacDonald CJ considered the qualification set out section 3(1) of the order-in-council as importing the same consideration: what was "required" — that is, necessary, for the performance of NAFO's functions? Necessity was to be read broadly with a view to preserving the organization's autonomy to carry out its functions.[112] MacDonald CJ invoked — unconsciously? — a fishing metaphor, declaring that NAFO "should not get caught in the net of Canadian/Nova Scotia domestic law simply because it chose to set up shop here."[113]

Having established functional necessity as the applicable standard, MacDonald CJ considered whether immunity from Amaratunga's claim was necessary for NAFO on the facts. In the chief justice's view, wrongful dismissal actions by their nature "represent critical exposés of the employer/employee relationship," particularly in a case such as this involving a senior employee with over fifteen years experience.[114] Amaratunga's claim "would inevitably put NAFO's core operations under a microscope,"[115] particularly given his claim for punitive damages. MacDonald CJ concluded that this action would interfere with NAFO's operations and was therefore the sort of claim from which NAFO enjoyed immunity under section 3(1) of the order-in-council. In response to the lower court's invocation of the ICCPR, MacDonald CJ observed that Wright J had "quite properly acknowledged that Canada's international treaty obligations in this regard should inform the required analysis,"[116] but he added that "it is one thing to interpret legislation in a manner that reflects the values and principles of international treaties" but "quite another to deny immunity in circumstances where, by legislation, it clearly exists."[117]

112 *Amaratunga*, *supra* note 108 at paras 35-42.

113 *Ibid* at para 44.

114 *Ibid* at para 57.

115 *Ibid* at para 58.

116 *Ibid* at para 72.

117 *Ibid* at para 73. The learned chief justice might have added that reliance on the ICCPR, Article 14(1) was question-begging: whether there in fact existed "a suit at law" in which Amaratunga must be granted "a fair and public hearing by a competent, independent and impartial tribunal established by law" was the question Wright J had before him.

If one proceeds from the plain meaning of section 3(1), it is hard to see how NAFO "required" immunity from a wrongful dismissal claim for the performance of its functions. The NAFO website describes the organization as "an intergovernmental fisheries science and management body" with an objective "to contribute through consultation and cooperation to the optimum utilization, rational management and conservation of the fishery resources" in the northwest Atlantic ocean.[118] No doubt Amaratunga's claim would be an unwelcome distraction from NAFO's work, especially given the allegations of misconduct meriting an award of punitive damages, but it remains difficult to see how these considerations justify a finding of immunity even on a broad interpretation of the concept of necessity.

This case is yet another in recent years to look to professors of international law, called as expert witnesses, to elucidate international legal principles for the benefit of the court. I have criticized this approach and doubted the admissibility of such evidence, in previous editions of the *Yearbook* and elsewhere.[119] The objection ought to have been stronger still in this case, as both witnesses opined not only on questions of public international law but also on the meaning and application of section 3(1) of the order-in-council — a pure question of domestic law and the very question the court was being asked to determine. In this instance, both professors were also members of the bar. Their "opinions," which were no doubt of some assistance to both the court below and the appeal court, ought to have been expressed as legal submissions, either by the parties' chosen counsel or by the professors themselves acting as co-counsel.

International arbitration — NAFTA Chapter 11 — standard of review

United Mexican States v Cargill, Inc, 2011 ONCA 622 (4 October 2011). Court of Appeal for Ontario.

This appeal arose out of arbitration proceedings brought by Cargill, Incorporated and its Mexican subsidiary against Mexico under Chapter 11 of the North American Free Trade Agreement

118 Online: <http://www.nafo.int>.

119 See, eg, G van Ert, *Using International Law in Canadian Courts*, 2nd edition (Toronto: Irwin Law, 2008) at 41-56.

(NAFTA).[120] Mexico had imposed trade barriers to prevent the importation of high fructose corn syrup by Cargill and other manufacturers in an attempt to protect its cane sugar industry. Prior to the imposition of the trade barriers, Cargill had established a division of its Mexican subsidiary to sell high fructose corn syrup in Mexico. Cargill claimed that the trade barriers constituted a breach of various provisions of NAFTA's Chapter 11. Cargill sought damages for both the direct losses suffered by its Mexican subsidiary (characterized as "down-stream losses") and for the losses suffered by Cargill itself as a result of its inability to sell high fructose corn syrup to its Mexican subsidiary (characterized as "up-stream losses").

The arbitration tribunal held that both down-stream and up-stream losses were compensable. With respect to up-stream losses, the tribunal noted that Chapter 11 of NAFTA only applies to trade measures relating to investments that are within the territory of the state party enacting the trade measures. However, the tribunal held that supplying high fructose corn syrup to the Mexican subsidiary was an inextricable part of Cargill's investment in Mexico, and, therefore, losses resulting from Cargill's inability to supply its Mexican subsidiary were compensable under Chapter 11.[121]

Mexico applied to the Ontario Superior Court of Justice to have the arbitration award set aside. The parties had executed a consent to arbitration under NAFTA Chapter 11, which set Toronto, Ontario, as the place of arbitration. This gave the Ontario Superior Court of Justice the jurisdiction to review the award under the International Commercial Arbitration Act.[122]

Mexico argued that the award should be set aside on the basis of Article 34(2)(a)(iii) of the UNCITRAL Model Law on International Commercial Arbitration (Model Law),[123] which is incorporated as a schedule to the International Commercial Arbitration Act. Article 34(2)(a)(iii) of the Model Law reads as follows:

Article 34. Application for setting aside as exclusive recourse against arbitral award

(2) An arbitral award may be set aside by the court specified in article 6 only if:

120 North American Free Trade Agreement, [1994] Can TS no 2.

121 *United Mexican States v Cargill, Inc*, 2011 ONCA 622 (4 October 2011) at para 13 [*Cargill*].

122 International Commercial Arbitration Act, RSO 1990, c I.o.

123 United Nations Commission on International Trade Law, 21 June 1985, UN Doc A/40/17, Annex 1.

(a) the party making the application furnishes proof that: …

(iii) the award deals with a dispute not contemplated by or not falling within the terms of the submission to arbitration, or contains decisions on matters beyond the scope of the submission to arbitration, provided that, if the decisions on matters submitted to arbitration can be separated from those not so submitted, only that part of the award which contains decisions on matters not submitted to arbitration may be set aside.[124]

Mexico argued that the tribunal had no jurisdiction to award the up-stream losses, as those losses were not suffered in connection with Cargill's investment in Mexico and were therefore not compensable under Chapter 11 of NAFTA. The application judge held that the standard of review to be applied to the tribunal's decision was reasonableness.[125] She noted that no provision of NAFTA required that damages be suffered solely in the territory of the investment in order to be compensable. In the result, she held that Mexico had not raised a jurisdictional issue but, rather, sought to attack the merits of the tribunal's decision. As this was beyond the scope of permissible review by the court, the application judge dismissed the application.[126]

The court of appeal, per Feldman JA, addressed the proper standard of review to be applied by a court reviewing a decision of a Chapter 11 NAFTA tribunal under Article 34(2)(a)(iii) of the Model Law. At para 30 of his reasons, Feldman JA stated that importing domestic concepts of standard of review, both from the administrative and appellate contexts, was unhelpful in this analysis.[127]

Feldman JA addressed the specific wording of Article 34(2) of the Model Law, noting that an award can only be set aside if the moving party furnished proof that one of a delineated set of deficiencies had taken place. None of the delineated deficiencies allow a reviewing court to review the merits of the tribunal's decision. Feldman JA noted that reviewing courts have consistently stated that courts should afford a high degree of deference to international arbitration tribunals, but also cited the decision of Lord Mance for the

124 UNCITRAL Model Law on International Commercial Arbitration, UN Doc A/40/17, Annex 1 (1985), Article 34(2)(a)(iii).

125 *Cargill, supra* note 121 at para 19.

126 *Ibid* at para 23.

127 *Ibid* at para 30.

United Kingdom Supreme Court in *Dallah Real Estate and Tourism Holding Co. v Ministry of Religious Affairs of the Government of Pakistan*[128] for the proposition that an arbitration tribunal's view of its own jurisdiction has no legal or evidentiary value.[129] Ultimately, Feldman JA held that there was nothing in the Model Law that detracts from the normal rule that on questions of jurisdiction a tribunal could not act beyond its jurisdiction. Accordingly, the tribunal had to be correct in making its decision within the scope of the submission to arbitration and the provisions of NAFTA.[130]

Feldman JA held that reviewing courts are obligated to narrowly define the scope of any jurisdictional question and strenuously avoid straying into the merits of the issue before the tribunal. Having defined the scope of the reviewing court's obligations, Feldman JA assessed the merits of Mexico's argument on jurisdiction as follows:

> Clearly there is an argument as to whether lost capacity in Cargill's U.S. plants constitutes damages by reason of, or arising out of, Mexico's breaches to the extent that those breaches affected [the Mexican subsidiary]. However, this is a quintessential question for the expertise of the tribunal, rather than an issue of jurisdiction. Had there been language in the Chapter 11 provisions that prohibited awarding any damages that were suffered by the investor in its home business operation, even if those damages related to and were integrated with the Mexican investment, that would have been a jurisdictional limitation that would have precluded the arbitration panel from awarding such damages, even if in its view, they otherwise flowed from the breaches. But there is not such limiting language …
>
> The only issue is whether the tribunal was correct in its determination that it had jurisdiction to decide the scope of damages suffered by Cargill by applying the criteria set out in the relevant articles of Chapter 11, and that there is no language in Chapter 11, or as agreed by the NAFTA Parties, that imposes a territorial limitation on those damages. Once the court concludes that the tribunal made no error in its assumption of jurisdiction, the court does not go on to review the entire analysis to decide if the result was reasonable. As I have determined that the tribunal acted within its jurisdiction, there is no review of the merits of the decision.[131]

128 *Dallah Real Estate and Tourism Holding Co. v Ministry of Religious Affairs of the Government of Pakistan,* [2010] UKSC 46.

129 *Cargill, supra* note 121 at paras 33, 36.

130 *Ibid* at para 42.

131 *Ibid* at paras 72, 74.

Finally, Mexico (along with the United States and Canada, who intervened in the appeal) argued that the state parties to NAFTA had agreed subsequent to NAFTA coming into force that an investor could only claim damages suffered in the territory of its investment and not in the territory of its home business operation. The NAFTA parties relied on Article 31(3)(b) of the Vienna Convention on the Law of Treaties 1969,[132] which states that treaties should be interpreted with reference to "any subsequent practice in the application of the treaty which establishes the agreement of the parties regarding its interpretation."

Feldman JA accepted that if the NAFTA parties had come to a clear and agreed-upon position that an investor could not be compensated for damages suffered in the territory of its home business operation, it would have been an error of jurisdiction for the tribunal to award the up-stream losses to Cargill. However, Feldman JA held that no such agreement had been reached, as the general agreement reached by the NAFTA parties simply repeated the proposition (set out in the text of NAFTA) that in order to be compensable, losses must be suffered by an investor in its capacity as an investor. The parties had not reached an agreement as to a territorial limit to be placed on compensable losses.[133]

Human rights — polygamy — Charter interpretation

Reference re Criminal Code of Canada, 2011 BCSC 1588 (23 November 2011). British Columbia Supreme Court.

This case was a reference to the court by the Government of British Columbia regarding the constitutionality of section 293 of the Criminal Code,[134] which prohibits the practice of polygamy. At the hearing, the Attorney General of Canada and several interveners argued that Canada's international obligations as well as customary international law justified a prohibition on polygamy and, therefore, rendered any infringement of Charter rights justifiable under section 1 of the Charter.

The Attorney General of Canada identified four international treaties to which Canada was a state party that in his submission, were relevant to the issue of polygamy:

132 Vienna Convention on the Law of Treaties, [1989] Can TS no 37.

133 *Cargill, supra* note 121 at para 84.

134 Criminal Code, RSC 1985, c C-46.

- International Covenant on Civil and Political Rights 1966 (ICCPR);[135]
- International Covenant on Economic, Social and Cultural Rights 1966 (ICESCR);[136]
- Convention on the Rights of the Child 1989 (CRC);[137] and
- Convention on the Elimination of All Forms of Discrimination against Women 1979 (CEDAW).[138]

None of the aforementioned treaties specifically reference polygamy. Therefore, in examining the extent and character of Canada's obligations under these treaties, Bauman CJSC looked to the views expressed by each treaty body on polygamy. He noted that each of the treaty bodies conceptualize the harm caused by polygamy in two ways, described as the "inherent wrong" of polygamy and its "associated harms."[139] By way of example, Bauman CJSC referred to the following statement from the CEDAW Committee's General Recommendation no. 21 on Equality in Marriage and Family Relations:[140]

> States parties' reports also disclose that polygamy is practised in a number of countries. Polygamous marriage contravenes a woman's right to equality with men, and can have such serious emotional and financial consequences for her and her dependents that such marriages ought to be discouraged and prohibited. The Committee notes with concern that some States parties, whose constitutions guarantee equal rights, permit polygamous marriage in accordance with personal or customary law. This violates the constitutional rights of women, and breaches provisions of article 5(a) of the Convention.[141]

Bauman CJSC held that the consensus of the treaty bodies under the aforementioned four treaties is that the practice of polygamy

135 ICCPR, *supra* note 107.

136 International Covenant on Economic, Social and Cultural Rights, [1976] Can TS No 46.

137 Convention on the Rights of the Child, *supra* note 91.

138 Convention on the Elimination of All Forms of Discrimination against Women, [1982] Can TS No 31.

139 *Reference re Criminal Code of Canada,* 2011 BCSC 1588 (23 November 2011) at para 805.

140 UN CEDAWOR, 13th Sess, (1994), UN Doc A/49/38 at para 14.

141 *Reference re Criminal Code of Canada, supra* note 139 at para 815.

violates various provisions of each treaty. Bauman CJSC acknowledged that the treaties also contain protections for freedom of religion but noted that he had been presented with no authority or statements from a treaty body suggesting that polygamy was protected by any of the treaties. Bauman CJSC held that as a state party to these treaties, Canada has an obligation to take all appropriate measures to eliminate polygamy, including an obligation to prevent private actors from violating the treaties through the practice of polygamy. Criminalization is one such measure.[142]

Bauman CJSC rejected the argument that restriction or prohibition of polygamy was a rule of customary international law, noting that polygamy is still widely practised in many countries worldwide, particularly in Africa and the Middle East. Bauman CJSC held that there was not sufficient evidence before him to establish a distinct trend in state practice towards the restriction or prohibition of polygamy.[143]

In the result, Bauman CJSC held that section 293 of the Criminal Code infringed sections 2(a) and 7 of the Charter. However, he held that these infringements were largely justified under section 1. Within the section 1 analysis, Bauman CJSC held that the prohibition of polygamy was a pressing and substantial objective for the federal government, in part due to Canada's aforementioned treaty obligations.

Briefly Noted / Sommaire en bref

Convention on the Rights of the Child — child's right to be heard — custody and access

B.J.G. v D.L.G, 2010 YKSC 44 (26 August 2010). Supreme Court of Yukon.

Haberman v Haberman, 2011 SKQB 415 (2 November 2011). Saskatchewan Court of Queen's Bench (Family Law Division).

Briefly noted are two remarkable cases in which courts endeavoured to give effect to Article 12 of the Convention on the Rights of the Child 1989[144] by means of out-of-court, face-to-face meetings between the child and the judge. Article 12 provides:

142 *Ibid* at paras 838-40.

143 *Ibid* at paras 843, 850.

144 Convention on the Rights of the Child, *supra* note 91.

1. States Parties shall assure to the child who is capable of forming his or her own views the right to express those views freely in all matters affecting the child, the views of the child being given due weight in accordance with the age and maturity of the child.
2. For this purpose, the child shall in particular be provided the opportunity to be heard in any judicial and administrative proceedings affecting the child, either directly, or through a representative or an appropriate body, in a manner consistent with the procedural rules of national law.

In *B.J.G. v D.L.G.* the parties, parents of a twelve-year-old boy, applied to vary an existing custody and child support order under the Divorce Act.[145] Martinson J noted that there was no evidence of the child's views or whether he wished to express them. She therefore raised the issue herself and heard submissions. The resulting judgment is a detailed exposition of Article 12 and the legal effect of the convention as a whole for Canada both internationally and in domestic law. Concerning the implementation status of the convention in domestic law, Martinson J explained:

> Canada has not directly incorporated the Convention into domestic law. It takes the position that it is not necessary to do because it has complied with its international obligations under the Convention by determining that existing domestic laws, including provincial and territorial laws, comply with the Convention …
>
> Before this Convention was ratified, the federal government consulted with the provinces and territories to determine whether their laws complied. The government of Canada advised the Senate Committee that it does not ratify a Convention until all jurisdictions indicate they support ratification and are in compliance with the obligations contained in it. In the case of this Convention, though it was signed in May 1990, it was not ratified until December 1991, when all the provinces and territories sent letters of support to the federal government.
>
> The federal government and the provinces and territories continue to say that Canadian domestic law complies with the Convention in their periodic reports to the United Nations Committee on the Rights of the Child.[146]

Concerning the role of the judge in ascertaining a child's views, Martinson J observed:

[145] Divorce Act, RSC 1985 c 3 (2nd Supp) s 16.

[146] *BJG. v DLG,* 2010 YKSC 44 (26 August 2010) at paras 34-6.

> Giving children the opportunity to speak directly to the judge who will be making a decision that could profoundly affect their lives provides meaningful participation, consistent with the values and principles found in the Convention. Judges who have to make decisions that have such a significant impact on a child's life should have the benefit of spending the time necessary to get to know that child.[147]

Applying Article 12 to the case at bar, Martinson J noted that counsel for both parties thought it would be inappropriate to involve the child in the hearing. Even without his participation, there was evidence before the court as to his views, for the current custody arrangements dated from a 2009 request by the child to spend alternating weeks with each parent. Martinson J was satisfied that she knew the child's views and that the child did not want be drawn into his parents' legal dispute. She concluded that it was in the child's best interests to keep in place the existing residency arrangement on an alternating week basis, with the mother continuing to have sole custody and both parents sharing guardianship.[148]

The *Haberman* case was again about a twelve-year-old boy whose parents were disputing his custody and guardianship. The child had lived with his father since the parents' separation in 2006 with very limited access to his mother. The mother alleged that the father had alienated the child from her, while the father alleged that the mother's abuse was the reason for the child's disaffection. A custody and access report was in evidence, as was a "Voices Report" by a social worker that included an interview with the child. Immediately following the trial, Sandomirsky J informed counsel for the parties that he intended to meet with the child at his school. He noted that this was the first time he had taken this step in a custody case and that he did not wish to interview or question the child but to "put a face to the name ... and to observe the child's demeanour and maturity."[149] The learned judge added, as his last reason for meeting with the child, his own reading on the rights of children and youth in legal proceedings as set out in the Convention on the Rights of the Child. He quoted Articles 12 and 3(1) and cited *B.J.G. v D.L.G.*[150]

Sandomirsky J met with the child at his school in the presence of a local registrar. He explained to the child that he would be making

147 *Ibid* at para 56.

148 *Ibid* at paras 64-8; see also 2010 YKSC 33.

149 *BJG v BLG, supra* note 146 at para 162; see also paras 159-61.

150 *Ibid* at paras 165-69.

some important decisions that would affect his life and that it was therefore important that the two should meet. He informed the child that "12 year olds have a right to be recognized by the court and that he was free to ask me any questions about the trial process and how judges do our work."[151] The child explained why he resisted spending time with his mother and told the judge that he would do what the judge told him to do.[152]

The learned judge held that the father had alienated the child from his mother and ordered joint custody and guardianship with the child residing with the father but visiting the mother twice a week and on holidays. The judge also wrote an open letter to the child, appended to the judgment, explaining his order and asking him to obey it.

These two cases are instances of courts departing from orthodox rules of evidence and civil procedure with a view to fulfilling Canada's obligation under Article 12 of the convention to assure children the right to express their views and the opportunity to be heard in proceedings affecting them. Notably, the judges in these cases did not feel obliged to wait for legislative authorization to take these steps. It is too soon to opine on the wisdom and implications of such judicial innovation. The most that can be ventured at present is that the impact of the Convention on the Rights of the Child on Canadian law may be more far-reaching than traditional notions of treaty implementation allow.

151 *Ibid* at para 88.

152 *Ibid* at paras 87-92.

Canadian Cases in Private International Law in 2011 / Jurisprudence canadienne en matière de droit international privé en 2011

compiled by / préparé par

JOOST BLOM

JURISDICTION / COMPÉTENCE DES TRIBUNAUX

Common Law and Federal

Jurisdiction *in personam*

Non-resident defendant — attornment to the jurisdiction

Note. See *Wolfe v Pickar*,[1] noted below under Foreign Judgments; *Common Law and Federal*; Recognition as *res judicata*; *Foreign decision on limitations statute — whether issue estoppel.*

Non-resident defendant — claim essentially financial — jurisdiction simpliciter *found to exist — jurisdiction not declined*

Laxton v Jurem Anstalt, 2011 BCCA 212, 334 DLR (4th) 76

Laxton and her ex-husband, Coglon, had been in litigation for eight years about the division of family assets pursuant to their 2003 divorce. When the initial division was made, Coglon failed to disclose assets he held through two British Columbia companies, one of which had lent some $2.5 million to a real estate developer. When the development in which the funds had been used was sold and the lender company was repaid that amount, Laxton applied for an order to freeze those funds. Before that order was granted, the lender company transferred the whole of that sum electronically to Jurem, an entity under the law of Liechtenstein. This was done on orders from Juricon, another Liechtenstein entity. Both of these

Joost Blom is in the Faculty of Law at the University of British Columbia.

[1] *Wolfe v Pickar*, 2011 ONCA 347, 332 DLR (4th) 157 (*sub nom. Wolfe v Wyeth*).

entities were under the direction of a man, Mechnig, who was also the operating mind of one of Coglon's British Columbia companies. Laxton pursued her action against these companies and obtained a declaration from the court that she was the beneficial owner of the whole of the $2.5 million, and an order that the funds held by Jurem were held on constructive trust for her benefit.

Eighteen months after that, Laxton brought this proceeding against Jurem and Juricon to recover the funds, arguing that the transfer to them amounted to theft and conversion or, alternatively, a breach of trust. She also claimed that Jurem was unjustly enriched by the receipt of the trust funds. She claimed a right in equity to trace or follow the funds into any asset remaining in the Liechtenstein entities' hands. Neither Jurem nor Juricon, both of which functioned to provide various business services, had a registered office, address, agent, or place of business in British Columbia. All of their activities were conducted according to the laws of Liechtenstein. They applied for an order that Laxton's action be dismissed or, alternatively, stayed because the British Columbia courts lacked jurisdiction over them or should decline to exercise jurisdiction.

The BC Court of Appeal affirmed the chamber judge's dismissal of the application. The court had territorial competence in respect of the claims against the two entities under the Court Jurisdiction and Proceedings Transfer Act (CJPTA),[2] because there was a real and substantial connection between the province and the facts giving rise to the proceeding (section 3(e)). The claim in conversion had a presumed real and substantial connection with the province under section 10(g) of the act since it was arguable that the tort was committed in British Columbia. The funds were said to have been transferred from there with the apparent knowledge of Mechnig, who knew of Laxton's claims against the transferor company. Even if the equitable wrongs of knowing receipt of trust funds and knowing assistance of a breach of trust were not "tort" claims within section 10(g), they were restitutionary claims that arose in British Columbia, giving rise to a presumed real and substantial connection pursuant to section 10(f). The presumptions of a real and substantial connection had not been rebutted. In the course of this finding, the court expressly disapproved[3] of the use of the "*Muscutt* factors," by which the Ontario courts assess jurisdiction

[2] Court Jurisdiction and Proceedings Transfer Act, SBC 2003, c 28 [CJPTA (BC)].

[3] *Laxton v Jurem Anstalt*, 2011 BCCA 212, 334 DLR (4th) 76 at para. 42.

simpliciter,[4] to rebut the presumptions in section 10 or to prove affirmatively that a real and substantial connection exists for the purposes of section 3(e) in a case when there is no presumption.

The court also affirmed the chamber judge's decision, applying the discretion in section 11 of the act, not to stay the proceeding on the round of *forum non conveniens.* Liechtenstein had not been shown to be clearly a more appropriate forum for the litigation. In their appeal, the defendants relied on the factors that Liechtenstein law would be applicable to their conduct in that country and that any agreement between them and the British Columbia transferor of the funds was governed by the law of that country and concerned services to be performed in that country. Essentially, this amounted to arguing that the judge had over-weighted the first factor in section 11, that of expense and inconvenience to the parties. It was a discretionary decision, and the judge had committed no error of principle.

Note. On the reception of the *Muscutt* factors outside Ontario, see also *Fewer v Ellis*, noted below under *Non-resident defendant — claim arising out of personal injury or damage to property or reputation — jurisdiction* simpliciter *found to exist on basis of real and substantial connection — jurisdiction not declined.*

Tucows.com Co. v Lojas Renner S.A., 2011 ONCA 548, 336 DLR (4th) 443

Tucows, a Nova Scotia company with its principal office in Ontario, had acquired from a company called Mailbank the rights to various Internet domain names, including "renner.com." Tucows' right to use "renner.com" was challenged by Renner, which operated department stores in Brazil and had registered the trademark "Renner" in that and other countries. Renner commenced a proceeding against Tucows under the World Intellectual Property Organization's (WIPO) Uniform Domain Name Dispute Resolution Policy (UDRP). Tucows brought the present proceeding for a declaration that it had rights in, or legitimate interests in respect of, the "renner.com" domain name. Renner, which had no presence in Ontario, applied

4 *Muscutt v Courcelles* (2002), 213 DLR (4th) 577 (Ont CA) [*Muscutt*]. The factors were revised in *Van Breda v Village Resorts Ltd.*, 2010 ONCA 84, 316 DLR (4th) 201, noted at (2010) 48 CYIL 529 and since aff'd, *Club Resorts Ltd. v Van Breda*, 2012 SCC 17.

to set aside service *ex juris* on it of the statement of claim or to stay the action for want of jurisdiction or because Ontario was *forum non conveniens.* The motion judge dismissed the application.

The Ontario Court of Appeal affirmed the refusal of a stay. On jurisdiction *simpliciter,* the court applied its decision in *Van Breda v Village Resorts Ltd.,*[5] which held that a real and substantial connection with Ontario should be presumed to exist if the claim was one in which the plaintiff was entitled to serve the defendant *ex juris* without leave under the rules of court.[6] Service *ex juris* without leave was authorized in this case. The action for a declaration was a "proceeding [that] consists of a claim ... in respect of ... personal property in Ontario" under Rule 17.02(a). Although there was little jurisprudence in Canada on the issue, the dominant view from cases and commentary elsewhere was that domain names were a new type of intangible property. Given the bundle of rights inherent in a domain name, it was appropriate to characterize it as a form of personal property. And it could be considered to be located in Ontario because it was a business asset of Tucows and had its maximum contacts with Ontario. Those contacts included the presence of the registrar in Ontario. The presumption of a real and substantial connection with Ontario, flowing from Rule 17.02(a), had not been rebutted.

The court considered whether to decline jurisdiction in favour of the WIPO Administative Panel. It held that to entertain Tucows' action did not undermine the UDRP because that policy explicitly allowed parties to choose to go to court even if a mandatory dispute resolution proceeding had already been commenced, and it gave the panel discretion on whether to terminate or stay its proceedings if a party did so. The panel in this case had decided to terminate the proceeding brought by Renner. Part of its reason for doing so was that this dispute was one of several arising from Tucows' acquisition of Mailbank's portfolio of domain names that had been brought before WIPO's tribunals, with inconsistent results, and it was appropriate in the light of this background that the parties litigate the dispute in court.

[5] *Van Breda v Village Resorts Ltd.*, 2010 ONCA 84, 316 DLR (4th) 201 [*Van Breda*], noted at (2010) 48 CYIL 529, aff'd, *Club Resorts Ltd. v Van Breda*, 2012 SCC 17.

[6] *Rules of Civil Procedure,* RRO 1990, Reg. 194, r. 17.02. Two of the grounds for service *ex juris,* those relating to damage suffered in Ontario (subrule (h)) and a necessary or proper party to a proceeding against a person in Ontario (subrule (o)), were held not to give rise to such a presumption.

Note. The presumption of a real and substantial connection was applied in three other jurisdiction *simpliciter* cases in the same court. In *Dundee Precious Metals Inc. v Marsland*, 2011 ONCA 594, 341 DLR (4th) 515, an Ontario employer's breach of fiduciary duty claim against an executive who worked for it in Australia was a claim based on a contract governed by Ontario law, and so it fell within one of the classes of claim for which service *ex juris* was available without leave (Rule 17.02(f)(ii)). In *Cannon v Funds for Canada Foundation*, 2011 ONCA 185, an action against a trustee of a Bermuda trust for having made, or allowing others to make, improper investments in Ontario was held to be a claim in respect of a tort committed in Ontario (Rule 17.02(g)). And *Brisbin v Lunev*, 2011 ONCA 15, applied the presumptions based on a contract having been made in Ontario (Rule 17.02(f)(i)), and a tort having been committed in Ontario (Rule 17.02(g)). In none of these cases were the presumptions rebutted.

Obégi Chemicals LLC v Kilani, 2011 ONSC 1636

In late 2010, the Ontario Superior Court made orders for a worldwide freeze of the assets (*Mareva* injunctions) belonging to the Kilanis, a family who formerly lived in the United Arab Emirates but now lived in Nova Scotia. Mr. Kilani was formerly employed by Obégi, a Luxembourg-based chemicals company, in senior management positions in Saudi Arabia and Dubai. Obégi had brought actions against the Kilanis in the United Arab Emirates and in Jordan to recover a large amount of money that Mr. Kilani had allegedly embezzled from the company. It had also obtained *ex parte*, in Ontario, a *Mareva* injunction to freeze the Kilanis' assets anywhere in the world and a local freezing order as well. In the present proceeding, the court refused the Kilanis' application to set aside and permanently stay the freezing orders on jurisdictional grounds. There was a real and substantial connection with Ontario to support the court's jurisdiction, namely the presence in Ontario of a bank account belonging to the Kilanis and the rationale of injunctive relief in aid of foreign proceedings. If this decision was wrong and there was no real and substantial connection with Ontario, the court should nevertheless take jurisdiction on the basis of necessity, a ground affirmed by *Van Breda v Village Resorts Ltd.*[7] The jurisdiction to grant injunctive relief did not extend to jurisdiction over Obégi's

7 *Van Breda, supra* note 5.

claims based on a settlement agreement Mr. Kilani had signed — those claims would be adjudicated elsewhere pursuant to a forum selection clause.

Non-resident defendant — claim essentially financial — jurisdiction simpliciter *found not to exist*

AECOM Canada Ltd. v Fisher, 2011 BCSC 860, 335 DLR (4th) 410

The plaintiffs, engineering firms with offices in British Columbia and Saskatchewan, sued their primary insurer, which was ordinarily resident in British Columbia because it had an office there, and a firm of Saskatchewan lawyers for having negligently settled claims against the engineers for an amount over the primary liability policy limit. The excess insurers were also plaintiffs. All of the agreements out of which the subject claims arose were governed by the law of Saskatchewan. The court held that under the CJPTA[8] it lacked territorial competence over the claims against the lawyers because those claims had no real and substantial connection with British Columbia. The fact that negligent advice was said to have been received in British Columbia was not enough. There was territorial competence in respect of the claims against the insurer because that defendant was ordinarily resident in British Columbia, but the claims were more appopriately heard together with the claims against the lawyers. The entire proceeding was therefore ordered transferred under the act to the Court of Queen's Bench in Saskatchewan.

Jafarzadehahmadsargoorabi v Sabet, 2011 ONSC 5827

An Iranian entertainer commenced an action in Ontario against his Quebec-resident manager for having mishandled and failed to promote his appearances at various venues in the United States and in Montreal and Vancouver in Canada. Two months later, the manager began a counter-action in Quebec against the plaintiff. The manager now sought a stay of the Ontario action for want of jurisdiction. The court granted the stay. The plaintiff had already tried to persuade the Quebec court to decline jurisdiction in favour of Ontario, and the Quebec court had held against him, so the jurisdictional questions were covered by issue estoppel. In any event, the Ontario court lacked jurisdiction *simpliciter*. Applying the *Van*

[8] CJPTA (BC), *supra* note 2.

Breda case,[9] there was a presumed real and substantial connection with Ontario because service *ex juris* without leave could be made under Rule 17.02(f)(i),[10] but the presumption was rebutted. Neither the plaintiff's claim nor the defendant's activities had a real and substantial connection with Ontario.

Note. Jurisdiction *simpliciter* was also found not to exist in *Galaxy Dragon Ltd. v Topwater Exclusive Fund IV LLC*, 2011 ONSC 6818, an action by a Hong Kong investor against an American investment fund and American brokers in which the only connection with Ontario was that, when the funds were invested, they had been routed through the plaintiff's business office in Toronto.

Non-resident defendant — claim arising out of personal injury or damage to property or reputation — jurisdiction simpliciter *found to exist on basis of real and substantial connection — jurisdiction not declined*

Cougar Helicopters Inc. v Sikorsky Aircraft Corp., 2011 NLCA 49, 335 DLR (4th) 203

Cougar, a Newfoundland helicopter operator, brought a tort action in the Newfoundland Supreme Court against Sikorsky, the Connecticut-based manufacturer of a helicopter that crashed in the sea off Newfoundland while ferrying workers to an oil rig platform. The court, affirming the applications judge, held there was jurisdiction *simpliciter*. The court followed its decision in *Fewer v Ellis*, noted below under *Non-resident defendant — claim arising out of personal injury or damage to property or reputation — jurisdiction simpliciter found not to exist*, in rejecting the relevance of fairness to the issue of jurisdiction *simpliciter* and eschewing the use of presumptions. The defendant, Sikorsky, had little connection with the province, but Cougar's claim had a real and substantial connection. So far as negligent manufacture and design were concerned, Sikorsky knew or reasonably should have known that its helicopters were being operated in Newfoundland to service the offshore oil industry. So far as the claims based on negligent and fraudulent misrepresentation and failure to warn were concerned, the alleged wrongs had an impact on Cougar's conduct in Newfoundland and so also satisfied the real and substantial connection requirement. Connecticut had not been shown to be a more appropriate forum. In addition,

9 *Van Breda*, *supra* note 5.

10 *Rules of Civil Procedure* (Ontario), *supra* note 6.

just before the hearing of the appeal, the Connecticut court had decided to decline jurisdiction in a parallel action that Sikorsky had brought in that state against Cougar.

Paulsson v Cooper, 2011 ONCA 150, 332 DLR (4th) 558

The court, reversing the decision of the motions judge, held that the Ontario courts had jurisdiction *simpliciter* over an Ontario-resident scholar's libel action against an American journal of Slavic studies, for a book review written by an Australian resident. Libel is committed where the defamatory material is published, and so the plaintiff's claim was for a tort committed in Ontario and, thus, was presumed to have a real and substantial connection with Ontario under the *Van Breda* principle that any claim for which service *ex juris* was available without leave (with two exceptions) raised such a presumption.[11] The presumption had not been rebutted because the plaintiff's home was in Ontario and his reputation was centred there. As for the discretion to decline jurisdiction, the defendants had not shown that Illinois or Australia would be more appropriate forums than Ontario.

Non-resident defendant — claim arising out of personal injury or damage to property or reputation — jurisdiction simpliciter *found not to exist*

Fewer v Ellis, 2011 NLCA 17, 305 Nfld & PEIR 39

Fewer, a resident of Newfoundland and Labrador, had been principal of a school in Manitoba, where he was injured in an encounter with Ellis. He brought this action against Ellis for assault and against the operators of the school for failing to take care of his (Fewer's) safety. The applications judge dismissed Fewer's actions on the ground that the Newfoundland and Labrador court lacked jurisdiction *simpliciter* over the claims. The Newfoundland Court of Appeal affirmed this decision. The court disagreed with the approach the Ontario courts had taken to jurisdiction *simpliciter*, in two respects. First, the *Muscutt* approach,[12] with its highlighting of the relevance of fairness as an element in determining whether there is a real and substantial connection, brought the jurisdiction *simpliciter* test too close to that of *forum non conveniens*. Second, *Van Breda*[13] went too

[11] See *Van Breda, supra* note 5 and accompanying text.

[12] See *Muscutt, supra* note 4 and accompanying text.

[13] *Van Breda, supra* note 5.

far in attaching presumptions of a real and substantial connection to the grounds for service *ex juris*. The fact that a case fell within one of those grounds was just an important indicator that jurisdiction *simpliciter* exists. On the facts, the court held that neither the tort nor the contract claims had the requisite connection with Newfoundland and Labrador. The fact that the defendants could foresee that Fewer might well return home if he was injured was insufficient to create such a connection. Given there was no jurisdiction *simpliciter*, the proper remedy was a dismissal, not a stay, of the action.

Note. A similar result was reached in *Dembroski v Rhainds*,[14] an action in British Columbia by a local resident against Alberta-resident defendants for injuries received in a motor vehicle accident in Alberta. The plaintiff's residence in the province, and his having suffered damages there, were not enough of a connection to found territorial competence under the CJPTA.[15] Jurisdiction was also held not to exist in a locally resident truck driver's claim in Ontario for injuries received in an accident in Illinois: *Jennings v Haas*.[16] In *Moore v Vancouver Port Authority*,[17] an Ontario Provincial Police officer who was injured at the harbour in Vancouver, British Columbia, while on security duty for the 2010 Winter Olympics was held unable to sue the Vancouver Port Authority because his claim lacked a real and substantial connection with Ontario. *Wielgomas v Anglocom Inc.*[18] held that an Ontario resident's claim, for injuries suffered when he was struck by ice that fell from the roof while he was using a bank machine in Quebec, had no real and substantial connection with Ontario. And *Export Packers Co. Ltd. v SPI International Transportation*[19] held there was no jurisdiction *simpliciter* in respect of a third party claim against a Quebec cold storage company in respect of the theft from its facility of a consignment of frozen pork ribs. The cargo owner was suing the shipper in Ontario for loss of the cargo.

14 *Dembroski v Rhainds*, 2011 BCCA 185, 333 DLR (4th) 437.

15 CJPTA (BC), *supra* note 2 at s 3(e) (real and substantial connection with the province).

16 *Jennings v Haas*, 2011 ONSC 2872, 335 DLR (4th) 225.

17 *Moore v Vancouver Port Authority*, 2011 ONSC 3692.

18 *Wielgomas v Anglocom Inc.*, 2010 ONSC 6289, aff'd 2011 ONCA 490, 335 DLR (4th) 741.

19 *Export Packers Co. Ltd. v SPI International Transportation*, 2011 ONSC 5907.

Elfarnawani v International Olympic Committee, 2011 ONSC 6784

The plaintiff was an Ontario-resident consultant of Egyptian origin who had advised cities that were bidding to host the Olympic Games. As a consequence of allegations made against him in a British Broadcasting Corporation (BBC) program, for which he had been interviewed in Cairo, he was declared *persona non grata* by the International Olympic Committee (IOC) in Switzerland, which posted information to this effect on its website. He brought this action in Ontario against the IOC for defamation and other torts. The court held there was no jurisdiction *simpliciter*. The plaintiff had produced no evidence that anyone in Ontario had viewed the allegedly defamatory material on the Internet. The court rejected the plaintiff's argument that proof of publication in Ontario was a matter for trial and ought to be presumed for the purposes of a motion concerning jurisdiction. The plaintiff's being a Canadian resident was not mentioned on the BBC program, nor was there any allegation or evidence that the IOC had "targeted" Ontario in its posting of the information.

Declining Jurisdiction *in personam*

Non-resident defendant — claim essentially financial — related proceedings in foreign court

Perfect 10 Inc. v Google Inc., 2011 FC 348, 91 CPR (4th) 444

Perfect 10 Inc., a California company in the business of posting "adult" images of women on the Internet, sued Google US in an American court for infringement of its American copyright and sued Google US and Google Canada, a Nova Scotia corporation, in the Federal Court of Canada for infringement of its Canadian copyright. The alleged infringement in each country consisted of the same Internet postings. The defendants sought to have the Canadian action stayed on the ground that the United States court was a more appropriate forum, but their motion was dismissed. A Canadian court has jurisdiction over infringements of intellectual property rights that take place in Canada and should not defer to a foreign court in respect of them. It was not forum shopping to assert Canadian rights in Canadian courts and United States rights in United States courts.

Note. Another case involving litigation in the United States and Canada concerning intellectual property rights, specifically confidential information, was *Wolfe v Pickar*,[20] noted below under Foreign Judgments; *Common Law and Federal*; Recognition as *res judicata*; *Foreign decision on limitations statute — whether issue estoppel.* Jurisdiction was not declined because the American action had concluded without resolving the merits. In *Cheng v Yu*,[21] an action on a guarantee executed in China was stayed because the BC Court of Appeal was advised that a court in China had heard a claim putting in issue the validity of the guarantee and was poised to deliver judgment.

Consbec Inc. v Walker, 2011 ONSC 2944

An Ontario company brought an action in Ontario against a former employee and his British Columbia-based companies for having, in breach of duty, gone into competition with the plaintiff. Eight years later, the plaintiff brought a British Columbia action on the same claims. The defendants were able to have the Ontario action stayed because British Columbia was the more appropriate forum. The only argument against a stay was the fact that the Ontario proceeding had been under way for so long, but, under the circumstances, which included the fact that none of the parties had been particularly active in moving the Ontario case along, it still made sense to decline jurisdiction in favour of the British Columbia proceeding.

Jurisdiction *in personam* — Class Actions

Certification — jurisdiction simpliciter *found to exist in respect of the claim*

Microcell Communications Inc. v Frey, 2011 SKCA 136, 377 Sask R 156

A class action was brought in Saskatchewan on behalf of customers of six wireless telephone companies, claiming the defendants had been unjustly enriched by access fees they had improperly charged. One defendant, Bell Aliant, was not ordinarily resident in the province within the meaning of sections 4(d) and 6 of the Saskatchewan Court Jurisdiction and Proceedings Transfer Act[22] and argued that the court lacked jurisdiction *simpliciter* over any claims against it. It had no customers in Saskatchewan and, therefore, according to this argument, all claims against it lacked a real and substantial

20 *Wolfe v Pickar*, 2011 ONCA 347, 332 DLR (4th) 157 (*sub nom. Wolfe v Wyeth*).

21 *Cheng v Yu*, 2011 BCCA 62.

22 Court Jurisdiction and Proceedings Transfer Act, SS 1997, c C-41.1 [CJPTA (Sask.)].

connection with Saskatchewan under section 4(3) of the act, the only other ground of territorial competence that could apply. The Saskatchewan Court of Appeal held that the necessary connection with Saskatchewan was supplied by the facts that all six defendants charged for their wireless services under a common regulatory scheme, the other five defendants were all resident in Saskatchewan (as well as other provinces), Bell Aliant was alleged to have charged similar fees in a similar manner to the others under similar contractual provisions, and the resolution of the common issues applied equally to Bell Aliant as it did to the other defendants.

Certification — whether it can be delayed pending outcome of application in other jurisdiction

Turon v Abbott Laboratories Ltd., 2011 ONSC 4343, 340 DLR (4th) 510

Class action proceedings had been commenced in British Columbia, Quebec, and Ontario on behalf of consumers of Abbott's weight-loss drug, Meridia. The plaintiffs in the Ontario action applied for a stay, pending the outcome of the certification application being made by the same law firm in British Columbia. Plaintiffs' counsel had advised that if certification were to be refused in British Columbia the Ontario action would be discontinued, but they did not say what the plaintiffs would do if the British Columbia court certified the proceeding there and gave Ontario residents the opportunity to "opt in" to that proceeding. The Ontario action had been commenced, it was said, to protect the plaintiffs against the expiry of the limitation period in that province.

The Ontario court held that class action litigation, which necessarily involves common issues and facts, engages different considerations from ordinary civil actions. A multiplicity of proceedings might be a necessary and acceptable result of our federal system. That did not mean, however, that parties could commence national class actions in several different provinces and, against the wishes of the defendant, leave some of those actions in limbo while one or more other actions proceeded. To do so was an abuse of the class action procedure because it left defendants, potential class members, and the court up in the air about the plaintiffs' intentions. The plaintiffs were ordered to deliver their certification motion record by a certain date, failing which their class action would be permanently stayed.

Effect of arbitration clause

Seidel v Telus Communications Inc., 2011 SCC 15, [2011] 1 SCR 531, 329 DLR (4th) 577

The question in this case was whether a class proceeding ought to be stayed on the ground that the plaintiffs, who were customers of the defendant Telus's wireless telephone services, had agreed that any dispute in relation to their contract with Telus was to be resolved by private and confidential mediation and arbitration and had agreed to waive any right to participate in or commence a class action. The plaintiffs claimed that Telus had misrepresented to its customers how it calculated air time for billing purposes. This was said to give rise to various claims, including claims under section 172 of the Business Practices and Consumer Protection Act (BPCPA).[23] This provision can be invoked by anyone, irrespective of whether they have an interest in the transactions in question, and it empowers the British Columbia Supreme Court to grant a declaration that a supplier's act or practice contravenes the act or the regulations made under it and to grant an interim or permanent injunction against the contravention. The BC Court of Appeal had stayed the certification proceeding. The issue whether any of the plaintiffs' claims, including those under section 172, were beyond the arbitrators' jurisdiction was, according to the competence-competence principle embodied in the provinces' arbitration legislation,[24] a matter for the arbitral tribunal to decide in the first instance.

The Supreme Court of Canada, by a narrow majority, reversed that decision in part, holding that, on the proper construction of the BPCPA, the right to seek a remedy under section 172 was a "right, benefit or protection" under the act that, according to section 3 of the act, could not be waived. The consumer protection purpose of the legislation militated in favour of the non-waivability of the right to seek the section 172 remedies. The plaintiff's other claims, however, were rightly stayed. The fact that the plaintiffs' claims were in

23 Business Practices and Consumer Protection Act, SBC 2004, c 1.

24 Commercial Arbitration Act, RSBC 1996, c 55, s. 22, makes applicable the Domestic Arbitration Rules of the British Columbia International Commercial Arbitration Centre (BCICAC), s 20(1), which provides that the "arbitration tribunal may rule on its own jurisdiction."

the form of a class action under the Class Proceedings Act[25] did not render them non-arbitrable. The act provided an alternative procedure for asserting claims but did not alter the principle, adopted by the legislature, that court proceedings must be stayed unless the arbitration agreement is void, inoperative, or incapable of being performed.[26] By contrast, section 172 of the BPCPA fell outside the competence-competence principle because the arbitrators' jurisdiction to adjudicate claims under that provision, in the face of the explicit right to seek relief from the Court, was a question of law to be determined on undisputed facts. The dissenting judges thought that section 172 did not fall outside the arbitration agreement because British Columbia law, as they construed it, permitted an arbitrator, as well as the Supreme Court of Canada, to grant the declaratory and injunctive relief contemplated by that provision.[27]

Subject Matter Jurisdiction

Arbitration agreement — appointment of arbitrator

Canada Life Assurance Co. v Holidair Insurance Services Ltd., 2011 SKQB 194, 97 CCLI (4th) 192, aff'd, 2011 SKCA 140, 377 Sask R 234

The parties to a reinsurance contract were Holidair, a British Columbia travel insurer, and a reinsurer that at the time of the contract, in 1986, was headquartered in Saskatchewan but had since been taken over by Canada Life, which was based in Ontaro. The contract was expressly governed by Saskatchewan law and contained an arbitration clause. A dispute arose that fell within the clause. The parties agreed in 2004, as found by the chambers judge, that the arbitration should proceed in Ontario, and the parties each appointed an arbitrator resident in Ontario but were unable to agree on the joint appointment of a chair. One party applied to the Saskatchewan Queen's Bench for an order under the Saskatchewan

25 Class Proceedings Act, RSBC 1996, c 50.

26 Commercial Arbitration Act, *supra* note 24 at s 15(2). The effectiveness of arbitration agreements to pre-empt judicial jurisdiction in consumer cases, absent legislation to the contrary, was upheld in *Dell Computer Corp. v Union des consommateurs*, 2007 SCC 34, [2007] 2 S.C.R. 801.

27 The judges cited, *inter alia*, s 29(1)(k) of the BCICAC Domestic Arbitration Rules, *supra* note 24, which expressly gives arbitrators the power to grant any equitable remedies.

arbitration legislation,[28] that the arbitration proceed and that the two arbitrators choose a third. The court rejected Canada Life's contention that it was *forum non conveniens* for the application. The arbitration agreement was governed by Saskatchewan law, and the court's jurisdiction to make the order stemmed from the agreement. The court's powers under the act were not limited to arbitration proceedings to be conducted in the province. To hear the application in Ontario would be more convenient for Canada Life but not for Holidair.

Bankruptcy and insolvency — tort claim against trustee

Title v Canadian Asset Based Lending Enterprise (CABLE) Inc., 2011 ONCA 715, 108 OR (3d) 71

Title, an Ontario resident, sought to bring an action in that province against two brothers resident in Quebec; Sistek and Premier, two federal corporations based in Quebec; CABLE, a secured creditor of Sistek; and a trustee in bankruptcy for Sistek and Premier appointed by the Quebec Superior Court. Title alleged the defendants had conspired to bring fraudulent bankruptcy proceedings in Quebec in order to defeat an Ontario breach of contract and shareholder oppression proceeding that Title, a shareholder and officer of Sistek, had commenced against Sistek and Premier and the two brothers, who were shareholders in the two companies. The defendants argued this proceeding was a collateral attack on a bankruptcy proceeding and so was barred by the Bankruptcy and Insolvency Act (BIA).[29]

The Onatrio Court of Appeal affirmed the motion judge's decision that the Ontario court had jurisdiction *simpliciter* in respect of Title's claims and should not decline jurisdiction on *forum non conveniens* grounds. The plaintiff's claims had ample connections with Ontario, since they related to an alleged conspiracy to deprive him of rights arising out of his employment in Ontario and to interfere with his Ontario legal proceedings. The defendants' activities in question were, by the same token, substantially connected with Ontario. The plaintiff's claims were not an attempt to nullify or set aside the Quebec bankruptcy proceeding but, rather, sought to obtain redress for the consequences of that proceeding. However, the claim against the trustee in bankruptcy did have to be stayed

28 Arbitration Act, 1992, SS 1992, c A-24.1, s 7.

29 Bankruptcy and Insolvency Act, RSC 1985, c B-3.

because, contrary to what the motion judge held, section 215 of the BIA bars any claim against a trustee in bankruptcy without leave of the bankruptcy court, which in this case was the court in Quebec.

Securities and corporations legislation — statutory relief

Note. Three cases involved the territorial ambit of provincial legislation on securities regulation and shareholder rights. In *Abdula v Canadian Solar Inc.*,[30] the Ontario court held it had jurisdiction under Ontario securities law[31] to grant a civil remedy in respect of misrepresentations by a federally incorporated company that had an executive office in Ontario and carried on business there, although the bulk of its business was in China and its shares were traded only on the NASDAQ exchange in the United States. Since it was an issuer of shares that were publicly traded, and because it had a real and substantial connection with Ontario, it was a "responsible issuer" as defined in the act,[32] and the court had jurisdiction.

The British Columbia Securities Commission was held, in *Torudag v British Columbia (Securities Commission)*,[33] to have jurisdiction in respect of an insider trading claim made against an Ontario company. The basis for that jurisdiction was the real and substantial connection with British Columbia stemming from the fact that the shares in question were traded on the TSX Venture Exchange in Alberta. The exchange had many British Columbia issuers, and the commission had, along with its Alberta counterpart, regulatory responsibility for activities on the exchange.

In *Ironrod Investments Inc. v Enquest Energy Services Corp.*,[34] by contrast, the Ontario court lacked jurisdiction to grant relief to an Ontario-resident shareholder for oppression stemming from misrepresentations made in the course of an amalgamation of two Alberta companies. Although the Ontario corporations legislation included an oppression remedy in terms similar to the Alberta legislation, it was only the Alberta court that had jurisdiction to grant such relief in respect of Alberta corporations.[35]

[30] *Abdula v Canadian Solar Inc.*, 2011 ONSC 5105, aff'd 2012 ONCA 211.

[31] Securities Act, RSO 1990, c S.5, s 138.3(1).

[32] *Ibid* at s 138.1.

[33] *Torudag v British Columbia (Securities Commission)*, 2011 BCCA 458.

[34] *Ironrod Investments Inc. v Enquest Energy Services Corp.*, 2011 ONSC 308.

[35] Business Corporations Act, RSA 2000, c B-9, s 1(m), defining the "court" as the Court of Queen's Bench of Alberta.

Administration and Succession

Jurisdiction to vary a will — domicile

Note. See *Foote v Foote Estate*,[36] noted below under Choice of Law; *Common Law and Federal*; Connecting Factors; *Domicile.*

Matrimonial Causes

Nullity of marriage

Note. See *Sahibalzubaidi v Bahjat*,[37] noted below under Choice of Law; *Common Law and Federal*; Matrimonial Causes; *Marriage — essential validity — non-consummation.*

Child support obligations — inter-jurisdictional enforcement of support orders

Sun v Guilfoile, 2011 ONSC 1685, 105 OR (3d) 439

The applicant Sun had been married to the respondent Guilfoile, a United States citizen who was born in Japan. The parties were divorced in Japan, where they had been living. Both parties participated in the Japanese proceedings, and the court ordered Guilfoile to pay Sun child support of $1,200 a month for the two children. Sun moved with the children to Hong Kong, where they still lived. Guilfoile moved frequently in his work and was now living for a year or two in Ontario. Sun applied to the Ontario Superior Court for an order for child support under section 33 of the Family Law Act.[38] Guilfoile had complied and continued to comply with the Japanese child support order. Japan was not a reciprocating state for the purposes of the Interjurisdictional Support Orders Act,[39] and so the Ontario court could not entertain an application to vary the Japanese order under that act. This fact, however, did not mean that a valid support order from a Japanese court could be avoided simply by making a new support order in the respondent's current home. Where a valid and subsisting foreign court order provided for support, there was no jurisdiction in Ontario to proceed with

36 *Foote v Foote Estate*, 2011 ABCA 1, 328 DLR (4th) 695, leave to appeal to SCC refused, 8 July 2011.

37 *Sahibalzubaidi v Bahjat*, 2011 ONSC 4075, 339 DLR (4th) 166.

38 Family Law Act, RSO 1990, c F.3.

39 Interjurisdictional Support Orders Act, 2002, SO 2002, c 13.

an originating application for support under section 33. Such an application was nothing more than a disguised variation application. The court also held that, even if it had jurisdiction, Ontario was *forum non conveniens* for Sun's application because Hong Kong was clearly a more appropriate forum. Sun's action was stayed so long as Guilfoile participated in, and responded to, proceedings brought by her in a court of competent jurisdiction to vary the order of the Japanese court and complied with the Japanese support order unless and until it was varied in such proceedings.

Infants and Children

Custody — jurisdiction

Note. The basic rule for jurisdiction to make a custody order under the Children's Law Reform Act[40] is that the child must be habitually resident in Ontario. *Riley v Wildhaber*[41] held that the children in that case were habitually resident both in Ontario and Quebec since they spent time in both provinces. However, the court declined custody jurisdiction on *forum non conveniens* grounds because the parties had previously litigated their family law disputes in Quebec and the court in that province was therefore the more appropriate forum for the application. In *Kaur v Guraya*,[42] the Ontario court held it had jurisdiction under the act, based on the children's habitual residence in the province, to supersede a custody and access order made in the state of Washington, provided that the applicant could show there had been a material change in circumstances that affected the best interests of the children.[43]

Child support obligations — extraprovincial order to take out life insurance policy

Stewart v Stewart, 2011 BCSC 774

After his father died, the plaintiff, who was left nothing in the father's will, claimed to be entitled to a constructive trust against the estate on the basis that his father had never complied with a 1992 order of a Mississippi court, made in proceedings for the

40 Children's Law Reform Act, RSO 1990, c C.12, s. 22(2)(b).

41 *Riley v Wildhaber*, 2011 ONSC 3456, 336 DLR (4th) 604.

42 *Kaur v Guraya*, 2011 ONSC 2853, 4 RFL (7th) 346.

43 Children's Law Reform Act, *supra* note 40 at s 42.

father's divorce from the plaintiff's mother, that the father maintain a $100,000 life insurance policy for the plaintiff's benefit. The court held, based on evidence of Mississippi law, that this obligation had ceased when the plaintiff reached the age of majority in 1997. Even if the obligation had continued, there was no basis for asserting a constructive trust against the estate, since the estate had not been unjustly enriched and the father had committed no breach of fiduciary duty.

Québec

Règles générales de compétence juridictionnelle

Forum non conveniens — *article 3135 CcQ*

Dalnoki c SSQ Life Insurance Company Inc, 2011 QCCS 2763

La demanderesse est résidente de l'Ontario. Dans le cadre de son travail, elle adhère à un contrat d'assurance collective interne entre son employeur et SSQ, dont le siège social est au Québec. Victime d'un accident de travail, la demanderesse adresse à SSQ en 2007 une demande de prestations d'invalidité longue durée. Cette demande est adressée à Toronto, endroit où SSQ possède une établissement. SSQ a décidé en août 2007 de ne pas verser les prestations à la demanderesse. La demanderesse a adressé le présent recours en juillet 2010 en contestation de la décision de SSQ. SSQ a présenté une requête que la Cour décline compétence au motif de *forum non conveniens*, selon l'article 3137 CcQ.

La Cour a refusé la requête de SSQ. Selon la *Loi des assurances de l'Ontario*[44] les règles de cette loi s'appliquent aux droits et obligations de la personne couverte par l'assurance, si elle résidait en Ontario au moment où elle s'est assurée. Or, le droit de l'Ontario pourrait s'appliquer en l'espèce. Mais l'Ontario n'était pas mieux à même de trancher le litige, comme requiert l' article 3135 CcQ, compte tenu de l'intérêt de la justice. Lors de la présentation d'un moyen déclinatoire par SSQ, cette dernière, bien qu'ayant réservé ses droits de présenter la présente requête concernant le *forum non conveniens*, a demandé le transfert du dossier du district judiciaire de Hull au district judiciaire de Québec. Aux yeux du tribunal, SSQ a fait son lit à compter de ce moment. La présente demande du *forum non conveniens* aurait pour effet de mettre fin au litige entre les parties

44 Loi des assurances de l'Ontario, LRO 1990, chap I-8, article 292.

dans la province de Québec, et obligerait la demanderesse à initier un autre recours dans l'Ontario. Il s'agit d'un rapport de force inéquitable faisant ainsi obstacle à la recherche d'équilibre. Pour la demanderesse, il s'agit de coûts exorbitants qu'une étape supplémentaire, inutile dans les circonstances, engendrera pour la partie demanderesse. En outre, imposer à la demanderesse d'intenter un nouveau recours dans l'Ontario implique pour la demanderesse qu'elle risque de se voir imposer la prescription du recours en Ontario. Cette situation pourrait lui faire perdre ses droits de recevoir une pleine et entière compensation en vertu de son contrat de travail.

Litispendance — article 3137 CcQ — action en recours collectif

Lebrasseur c Hoffmann-La Roche Ltée, 2011 QCCS 5457

Lebrasseur a déposé le 15 juillet 2010 une requête en autorisation d'exercer un recours collectif contre Hoffmann-La Roche au nom de personnes ayant consommé un produit pour le traitement de l'acné, connu sous le nom "Accutane." Hoffmann-La Roche demande la suspension de la requête pour cause de litispendance internationale, selon l'article 3137 CcQ. Le groupe qui Lebrasseur souhaite représenter comprend "toutes les personnes au Canada, ou subsidiairement au Québec, ayant consommé le médicament Accutane" et ayant souffert des maladies intestinales inflammatoires ou d'autres effets secondaires. Entre les 17 février et 13 juin 2005, soit antérieurement à la Requête en autorisation, sept requêtes en autorisation d'exercer un recours collectif sont déposées contre Hoffmann-La Roche dans autant de provinces canadiennes. Trois d'entre elles, dont celle déposée le 24 février 2005 par Patkus devant la Cour supérieure de justice de l'Ontario, demandent la permission d'exercer un recours collectif pour représenter toutes les personnes au Canada ayant consommé le médicament Accutane et souffert de problèmes de santé. La Cour supérieure a refusé la requête de Hoffmann-La Roche de suspendre la requête de Lebrasseur en autorisation d'exercer un recours collectif, au motif de litispendance.

Les conditions de l'article 3137 sont remplies. L'identité des parties est établie. La jurisprudence ne requiert pas l'identité physique des requérants, mais leur identité juridique puisqu'à cette étape, ils n'ont toujours pas obtenu le statut de représentant; c'est en leur qualité de membre du groupe recherché qu'ils déposent leur requête. Le groupe que cherche à représenter Lebrasseur au Québec, et celui que cherche à représenter Patkus en Ontario, est le même groupe national. L'identité des faits à laquelle réfère l'article 3137 est également établie. L'objet des requêtes est également le même: l'autorisation de procéder par voie collective en vue de l'indemnisation des personnes ayant souffert de problèmes de santé à la suite de la consommation d'Accutane. Quant aux quatrième et cinquième conditions requises en vertu de l'article 3137 CcQ, la Requête Patkus est antérieure à la Requête Lebrasseur et elle est également susceptible de donner lieu à une décision pouvant être reconnue au Québec selon l'article 3155 CcQ.

Bien que les conditions énoncées à l'article 3137 CcQ soient remplies, la Cour a décidé qu'elle ne doit pas exercer sa compétence de suspendre la procédure. En l'absence d'ententes à l'échelle nationale entre les entités judiciaires, politiques et administratives pertinentes et en l'absence de disposition législative propre aux recours collectifs, le Tribunal doit exercer sa discrétion aux termes de l'article 3137 CcQ en fonction des critères de la doctrine du *forum non conveniens*, parmi lesquels on retrouve notamment le progrès déjà effectué dans la poursuite de l'action étrangère, l'intérêt de la justice et l'intérêt des parties. En l'instance, plus de six ans séparent le dépôt des deux requêtes et le tribunal ne peut conclure que la Requête Patkus progresse dans les délais auxquels les membres potentiels du groupe sont en droit de s'attendre. En refusant le sursis en l'instance, le tribunal n'endosse pas pour autant la multiplicité des procédures. Il dresse plutôt le constat, à la lumière des faits dont il est saisi, que le recours en Ontario ne semble pas progresser. Dans un tel contexte, la saine administration de justice ne milite pas en faveur d'un tel sursis pour une période indéterminée. Bien que les membres du groupe visé par la Requête en autorisation soient également visés par la Requête Patkus, leur accès à la justice en serait indûment retardé. De plus, Hoffmann-La Roche a des activités tant au Québec, qu'en Ontario. Le dossier ne permet pas de conclure que les facteurs de rattachement sont plus importants dans une province que dans l'autre. Par ailleurs, Lebrasseur, qui réside au Québec, est certainement dans une meilleure position pour représenter les intérêts des membres du Québec, notamment visés par le groupe recherché.

Note. Veuillez voir aussi *Fastwing Investment Holdings Ltd. c Bombardier inc.*[45]

[45] *Fastwing Investment Holdings Ltd. c Bombardier inc.*, 2011 QCCA 432.

Actions personnelles à caractère patrimonial

Décliner compétence — clause d'élection de for

General Motors du Canada Ltée c 178018 Canada inc, 2011 QCCA 1461

En mai 2009, GM écrit à Saillant, le principal actionnaire de l'intimée 178018 Canada inc., et l'informe que la conjoncture économique sans précédent qui touche alors les États-Unis et le Canada l'oblige à restructurer en profondeur l'entreprise et ses activités. Dans le cadre de cette restructuration, GM a décidé de ne pas renouveler un contrat de concession de vente et de service après-vente entre l'intimée et GM qui est conclu en avril 2009. GM invite l'intimée à signer, après avoir obtenu un avis juridique indépendant, une Convention de retrait progressif (CRP). Saillant signe la CRP au nom de l'intimée. En juillet 2010, après avoir reçu la totalité de la compensation financière visée par la CRP, l'intimée, Saillant et quelques autres intentent une action contre GM visant à la résolution de la CRP au motif que GM a contrevenu au contrat de franchise en décidant d'y mettre fin sans renouvellement possible et sans formuler aucun reproche à l'intimée. De plus, selon les intimés, c'est de mauvaise foi et par dol que GM leur a forcé la main pour signer la CRP. En conséquence, le consentement de l'intimée à la signature de la CRP a été vicié avec le résultat que cette entente est nulle. L'intimée réclame, au titre des dommages, les profits qu'elle a manqués en raison de l'interruption fautive et prématurée de sa relation d'affaires avec GM. Les autres intimés, les trois administrateurs de l'intimée, réclament personnellement au titre du préjudice psychologique et de leur perte de temps. L'appellante GM a présenté une requête en irrecevabilité. Elle plaide que, en vertu de l'article 19 de la CRP, la Cour supérieure du Québec n'a pas compétence pour entendre le litige, selon l'article 3148, alinéa 2 CcQ: "les autorités québécoises ne sont pas compétentes lorsque les parties ont choisi, par convention, de soumettre les litiges nés ou à naître entre elles, à propos d'un rapport juridique déterminé, à une autorité étrangère ou à un arbitre, à moins que le défendeur n'ait reconnu la compétence des autorités québécoises." L'article 19 de la CRP se lise, "Les parties reconnaissent que les réclamations ou litiges entre les parties aux présentes au sujet du présent contrat relèvent de la compétence exclusive des tribunaux de la province de l'Ontario."

La juge de première instance a rejeté la requête en irrecevabilité, mais la Cour d'appel a accueilli la requête. Tant dans le contrat de concession et que dans la CRP, les parties ont convenu que le contrat est régi par les lois de l'Ontario. De plus, à la clause 19 de la CRP, elles reconnaissent que les litiges entre elles "au sujet du présent contrat" relèvent de la compétence exclusive des tribunaux ontariens. C'est une "véritable clause d'élection de for" parce qu'elle "en termes clairs, oblige impérativement et irrévocablement les parties ... à intenter tous ses recours devant un tribunal précisément désigné et exclusivement devant ce tribunal."[46] Or, dans leur action en nullité de la CRP, les intimés invoquent de la part de GM "une violation flagrante d'une part de ses obligations générales de bonne foi résultant du *Code civil du Québec*." Ils demandent donc d'appliquer le droit québécois des contrats pour évaluer la validité de la CRP alors que les parties l'ont expressément exclu. Il y a lieu de donner plein effet à la clause d'élection de for contenue à la CRP qui doit recevoir application même à l'égard d'une action demandant l'annulation au motif de dol de la convention dans laquelle cette clause est stipulée. La demande de nullité est un litige "au sujet du présent contrat" selon le libellé de la clause d'élection de for.

PROCEDURE / PROCÉDURE

Common Law and Federal

Evidence Obtained Locally for Use in Foreign Proceedings

Evidence given on discovery in Ontario proceeding — application to use in foreign proceeding

The Gap Inc. v G.A.P. Adventures Inc (2011), 336 DLR (4th) 745, 95 CPR (4th) 377 (FC (Prothonotary))

The applicant was engaged in parallel trademark infringement actions in the United States and in Canada and applied to the Federal Court for an order that it could use discovery evidence given by a witness for the purpose of the proceeding in that court in order to impeach the same witness's testimony given in the American proceeding. The prothonotary granted the application. The applicant was bound by the implied undertaking not to use discovery evidence for any purpose other than the proceeding for which it was obtained. However, the court had a discretion to relieve from the rule if the evidence was sought to be used in another proceeding between the

46 La Cour cite (au para 29) *St Microelectronics inc c Matrox Graphics inc*, 2007 QCCA 1784, [2008] RJQ 73, au para. 84.

same or similar parties and the prejudice to the examinee was virtually non-existent.

Letters rogatory

Note. An order to enforce letters rogatory from a United States District Court in Pennsylvania, and order a Canadian party to produce evidence and give testimony for the purpose of a class action certification proceeding in the American court, was upheld in *Treat America Ltd v Nestlé Canada Inc.*[47] The court rejected arguments that the motion judge had failed to make his own assessment of the basis for the American court's request.

FOREIGN JUDGMENTS / JUGEMENTS ÉTRANGERS

Common Law and Federal

Conditions for Recognition or Enforcement

Jurisdiction of the original court — attornment

Note. Applying to set aside a British Columbia default judgment was held in *Canada (Minister of National Revenue) v Glazer*[48] to constitute attornment to the jurisdiction, and qualified as submission "during the proceedings" for the purposes of the Reciprocal Enforcement of Judgments Act.[49]

Jurisdiction of the originating court — default judgment against non-resident of originating country — real and substantial connection

CIMA Plastics Corp v Sandid Enterprises Ltd, 2011 ONCA 589, 341 DLR (4th) 442

Sandid was the Ontario sales agent for an Illinois company, Pro Tech. It obtained a judgment against Pro Tech in Ontario for unpaid sales commissions and, in execution of the judgment, garnished a debt owing to Pro Tech by an Ontario customer. Sandid was sued

47 *Treat America Ltd v Nestlé Canada Inc*, 2011 ONCA 560, 340 DLR (4th) 707.

48 *Canada (Minister of National Revenue) v Glazer*, 2011 ABQB 559.

49 Reciprocal Enforcement of Judgments Act, RSA 2000, c R-6, s 2(6)(b), which provides that a judgment must not be registered if the judgment debtor was neither carrying on business nor ordinarily resident in the originating state and "did not voluntarily appear or otherwise submit during the proceedings."

in Illinois by Cemi, an Illinois-based creditor of Pro Tech, which had taken an assignment of Pro Tech's receivables before Sandid obtained its Ontario judgment. Cemi contended that Sandid, by garnishing a debt it knew belonged to Cemi rather than Pro Tech, was liable for interference with an existing business and for abuse of process. Sandid decided not to appear in the Illinois proceeding, and a judgment was given against it in default for $89,000, representing the legal fees and finance charges Cemi had incurred as a consequence of Sandid's garnishment. Cemi now brought an action on the Illinois judgment against Sandid. The Ontario Court of Appeal upheld summary judgment against Sandid, on the basis that Cemi's claim had a real and substantial connection with Illinois. An Illinois company had sought redress for interference with payment of an account receivable purchased from another Illinois company. The account receivable arose from business at least partly carried on in Illinois, and the damages were suffered in Illinois. The fact that Sandid did no business in Illinois and had no relationship with Cemi did not alter the fact that the claim against it was substantially connected to Illinois.

Defences to Recognition or Enforcement

Lack of natural justice

SHN Grundstuecksverwaltungsgesellschaft mbH v Hanne, 2011 ABCA 185, 336 DLR (4th) 723

The Alberta Court of Appeal upheld the granting of a summary trial in an action for enforcement of a German judgment holding the debtor liable for breach of trust. The debtor had not made out any relevant defences. There was no breach of natural justice in the fact that the plaintiff's lawyer, whose affidavit was the basis of the action, was also the plaintiff's managing director and had acted as counsel in the original proceeding. The debtor had also opposed a summary trial on the basis that the German lawyer had failed to accept a number of undertakings to produce documentary evidence relating to the German proceeding and a related German criminal prosecution of the debtor. These undertakings were held irrelevant to any available defence to enforcement. The information sought related to the merits of the German civil action, which were not reviewable in the Alberta enforcement action, and to a criminal proceeding that was unrelated to the enforceability of the judgment.

Note. A United States District Court default judgment from Florida for US $67 million, including treble damages for violations of the Racketeer Influenced and Corrupt Organizations Act (RICO), 18 U.S.C. § 1961, was held enforceable in Ontario in *Bank of Mongolia v Taskin.*[50] There was no violation of natural justice because the debtor had been fully informed of the proceedings at all times. Enforcement was, however, stayed pending the outcome of the debtor's application to the Florida court for relief from the judgment despite the expiry of the appeal period.

Means of Enforcement

Canadian Judgments Act (NB) — *excluded judgment*

Note. The New Brunswick Canadian Judgments Act,[51] unlike the uniform registration statutes in most provinces, is a complete code with respect to enforcement. Section 6(2) precludes the registration of a judgment against an individual resident in New Brunswick if it arose out of a proceeding to enforce "a contract for the supply of consumer goods or services within New Brunswick." This was held, in *Mowery v 2063010 Ontario Inc,*[52] not to encompass a judgment for debts owing by a number of individual real estate agents in New Brunswick to an Ontario real estate commission discounter. The exclusion was not meant to apply to judgments in business-to-business relationships.

Recognition of judgment as res judicata

Note. An abuse of process was found when a party sought to relitigate in Ontario issues that had been decided against it in an action in New York: *Contacare inc v CIBA Vision Corp.*[53]

Foreign decision on limitations statute — whether issue estoppel

Wolfe v Pickar, 2011 ONCA 347, 332 DLR (4th) 157 (*sub nom. Wolfe v Wyeth*)

Wolfe claimed to have invented a particular medical therapy while working at a university in Ontario. He disclosed confidential

50 *Bank of Mongolia v Taskin,* 2011 ONSC 6083, 285 OAC 263 (Div'l Ct.).

51 Canadian Judgments Act, RSNB 2011, c 123.

52 *Mowery v 2063010 Ontario Inc,* 2011 NBCA 32, 335 DLR (4th) 493.

53 *Contacare Inc v CIBA Vision Corp,* 2011 ONSC 4276.

information about the therapy to Wyeth pursuant to an agreement with them. Wyeth subsequently applied to patent a similar therapy in Canada, on the basis that it was different from Wolfe's and had been invented by Pickar, a senior Wyeth employee. Wolfe began proceedings in the Federal Court of Canada for an order that Wyeth's application list him as sole inventor. On the same day, Wolfe and a company he owned began the present proceeding against Wyeth and Pickar for breach of contract, breach of confidence, and breach of fiduciary duty. The statement of claim was served on Wyeth and Pickar in Pennsylvania. Some months later, the latter began proceedings in that state against Wolfe, for a declaration that any claims Wolfe had against them were statute-barred and, in any event, lacked merit. Wolfe's application to the Pennsylvania court for a stay, based on lack of jurisdiction over him, was dismissed. The Pennsylvania court subsequently granted Wyeth's motion for judgment on the pleadings on the issue of the statute of limitations, but declined to do so on the merits of Wyeth's action. Wyeth and Pickar then brought the present motion in the Ontario proceeding to dismiss or stay Wolfe's action because it was barred by the Pennsylvania judgment by way of issue estoppel, or because the Ontario court lacked jurisdiction, or because Ontario was *forum non conveniens*.

On appeal from the motion judge's dismissal of this motion, the Ontario Court of Appeal held that the Pennsylvania judgment did not give rise to an issue estoppel with respect to the limitation question. All the Pennsylvania judgment decided was that, if Wolfe's claims were litigated in Pennsylvania, they would be time-barred. It did not decide that Pennsylvania law should apply to Wolfe's claims brought in Ontario. This view was consistent with the ends of justice because the choice of law question was fact-dependent and might depend on the cause of action and so should be decided on a full record at trial. As for lack of jurisdiction, Wyeth and Pickar had voluntarily appeared in the Ontario proceeding by making the argument about issue estoppel and so had given the court jurisdiction by consent. In any event, Wolfe's claims had a real and substantial connection with Ontario so as to give the court jurisdiction *simpliciter* on that basis. The negotiations between the parties had taken place in Ontario, Wolfe suffered his losses in Ontario, and Wyeth had carried on business in Ontario by concluding its arrangements with Wolfe. As for *forum non conveniens*, Wyeth had not shown that Pennsylvania was a more appropriate forum for the litigation than Ontario.

Support Orders

Uniform Interjurisdictional Support Orders Act

Note. A court, in deciding whether to confirm a provisional order made in a foreign country that is a reciprocating jurisdiction under the act,[54] effectively decided the merits of the support application. In *Arcinas v Stanley*,[55] the British Columbia court refused to confirm an English court's provisional order reducing arrears and future support under an existing support order, because the respondent's failure to pay was wilful, and it had not been shown that the respondent's circumstances had changed.

Arbitral Awards

United Nations Convention on the Recognition and Enforcement of Foreign Arbitral Awards (New York Convention) — defence of public policy

Subway Franchise Systems of Canada Ltd v Laich, 2011 SKQB 249, 380 Sask R 54.

In an arbitration in the United States between an American franchisor and a Saksatchewan franchisee, the arbitrator had decided that the franchise agreement was terminated and awarded the franchisor damages. Since the award was made, however, the franchisee had continued to operate the franchise, and the franchisor had accepted its share of the ongoing profits from the franchisee. The franchisor now sought to register the award under the New York Convention.[56] The court held that to do so would be contrary to public policy within the meaning of Article 36(1)(b)(ii) of the convention. The franchisor had waived the arbitrator's termination decision and was seeking double recovery since it would receive both the monetary award that was based on the termination and its share of the profits from the continuing operation of the franchise.

[54] The British Columbia version is the Interjurisdictional Support Orders Act, SBC 2002, c 29.

[55] *Arcinas v Stanley*, 2011 BCSC 1094.

[56] United Nations Convention on the Recognition and Enforcement of Foreign Arbitral Awards, implemented by the Enforcement of Foreign Arbitral Awards Act, 1996, SS 1996, c E-9.12.

Québec

Conditions nécessaires à l'*exequatur*

Compétence de l'autorité étrangère — article 3155, alinéa 1 et article 3168 CcQ — litispendance — article 3155, alinéa 4 CcQ

Stonecroft Resources inc c Marble Point Energy Ltd, 2011 QCCA 141

Marble Point a présenté une requête en reconnaissance et exécution de divers jugements rendus dans les Îles vierges britanniques (IVB). La Cour des IVB a statué sur des "proprietary claims" ou "constructive trusts" contre deux compagnies et a condamné ces compagnies à payer à Marble Point des sommes d'argent appartenant à celle-ci. Ces sommes lui ont été remises. La Cour des IVB a aussi condamné les deux individus appelants, les âmes dirigeantes des compagnies, de payer "non-party costs," soit l'équivalent des dépens, par une procédure postérieure au jugement rendu sur l'action principale, comme le permet le droit interne des IVB. La présente requête en reconnaissance et exécution concerne les jugements ordonnant le paiement de ces "non-party costs." La juge a accueilli la requête de Marble Point et la Cour d'appel a affirmé ce jugement.

Les individus appelants plaident que les tribunaux des IVB n'étaient pas compétents à leur égard, n'étant ni domiciliés aux IVB, ni parties aux procédures principales. Selon cet argument, le recours dirigé contre eux constitue une action personnelle à caractère patrimonial et la compétence des IVB à leur égard ne pouvait pas être reconnue par le tribunal québécois, selon les principes édictés à l'article 3168 CcQ. La Cour a rejeté ce moyen d'appel. Certes, ces individus appelants sont résidents au Québec. Toutefois, ils ont choisi librement de constituer leur société respective précisément là où une partie importante des fonds réclamés se sont retrouvés. Tous les appelants reconnaissent que les tribunaux des IVB étaient compétents à l'égard des sociétés appelantes et que les jugements qui y sont rendus contre elles sont exécutoires. Il est acquis au débat que les individus appelants sont respectivement l'âme dirigeante de ces sociétés et c'était comme tels qu'ils sont condamnés à payer les "non-party costs."

Un autre moyen d'appel s'agit de l'exception de litispendance. Marble Point a intenté une procédure au Québec deux jours avant que les procédures dans les IVB sont intentées. La Cour a partagé l'opinion de la juge de première instance qu'il n'y a pas identité d'objet puisque les procédures au Québec constituent essentiellement un recours en dommages résultant de ce que Marble Point allègue être de fraude. Le juge a noté que les tribunaux des IVB ont refusé d'entendre toute réclamation sur cette base et ont uniquement statué sur le "proprietary claim" ou "constructive trust." Quant à l'argument des appelants concernant le risque d'une double condamnation pour le même montant, le tribunal québécois sera à même de réduire corrélativement les dommages.

CHOICE OF LAW (INCLUDING STATUS OF PERSONS) / CONFLITS DE LOIS (Y COMPRIS STATUT PERSONNEL)

Common Law and Federal

Exclusion of Foreign Law

Public policy

Sangi v Sangi, 2011 BCSC 523, 2 RFL (7th) 59

The court rejected the public policy defence, which was raised against the enforcement of the support provisions of a separation agreement governed by the law of Iran. The evidence indicated that Iranian law had no concept of unconscionable bargain, such as the Canadian common law applies to contracts between spouses, but the lack of such a doctrine did not offend against fundamental notions of Canadian justice. In any event, the agreement, though it gave the wife less than she would have been awarded in a British Columbia court, would not have been unconscionable under British Columbia law.

Connecting Factors

Domicile — loss of domicile of choice

Foote v Foote Estate, 2011 ABCA 1, 328 DLR (4th) 695, leave to appeal to SCC refused, 8 July 2011

Eldon Foote was originally from Alberta but, for the thirty years before his death, had made his home in Norfolk Island, a self-governing territory of Australia. Foote had made a fortune in the marketing of cleaning products and left a large estate. He had a widow, who was his third wife, and six children. He had made three wills dealing respectively with the assets in Canada, the British Virgin Islands, and Norfolk Island. Bentley, a friend of Foote's and a resident of Alberta, was appointed executor under each will. Foote left almost all of his $120 million estate, not to his family, but to two charities, one in Australia and the other in Alberta. The widow, who still lived in Norfolk Island, and the children applied to the Alberta Court of Queen's Bench for advice and directions on certain issues relating to Foote's estate. One was the law that would govern the validity of the wills, which depended on where Foote was domiciled when he died. The widow and children wanted the court to say that Foote had died domiciled either in Alberta or British Columbia, because they intended to apply for variation of the wills under the law of those jurisdictions, the widow contending for Alberta and the children for British Columbia.

There was little doubt, and the trial judge found, that Foote had acquired a domicile of choice in Norfolk Island when he established his home there in 1972. The question was whether he had lost that domicile of choice and, if so, whether his domicile of origin in Alberta revived, as the widow argued, or whether he had acquired a new domicile of choice in British Columbia, which was the children's position. The evidence was that in 1999 he and his wife had bought a condominium property under construction in Victoria, British Columbia. The building was completed in 2001, and that year and the two following years they spent the summer in Victoria, living the rest of the time mainly in Norfolk Island. They made plans to sell their Norfolk Island property but had taken no steps to do so when, early in 2004, Foote became ill and travelled to Australia, where he was diagnosed with cancer. He then went to Edmonton, Alberta, for treatment and died there in May of that year.

The trial judge held that, notwithstanding the decision to leave Norfolk Island, Foote had not lost his domicile of choice there because, when he died, he had not yet moved his home from the island. The Alberta Court of Appeal upheld that finding. Domicile being a question of mixed fact and law, the standard of review was palpable and overriding error, and the judge had made no such error. The loss of a domicile of choice involves two elements, an intention to cease to reside in a place, coupled with acts that end the residence there. The judge had found that by 2002 Foote had formed the intention to re-establish his primary residence in British Columbia, but his intention was, in certain senses, provisional and under-developed. No steps had been taken to sell the Norfolk Island home, nor to ascertain the tax consequences of the move, which would have been important to him. The judge had been right to find, under those circumstances, that the intention to abandon the domicile of choice had not been established. There was also no error in the judge's finding that the act of ceasing to reside had not been proven. Foote's house in Norfolk Island was still his principal residence when he died. The judge had also been right to reject the widow's argument that, upon leaving Norfolk Island for medical treatment, and even though he had not yet acquired a new domicile of choice in British Columbia, Foote had lost his Norfolk Island domicile of choice and his Alberta domicile of origin had revived. This argument, too, rested upon Foote's having abandoned his domicile in Norfolk Island, which on the facts he had not done.

Contracts

Particular classes of contract — marriage contract — dowry

Aziz v Al-Masri, 2011 BCSC 985

The petitioner brought this action to enforce her husband's obligation to pay a dowry, as promised in a marriage contract entered into in 1997 at the time of the parties' wedding in Jordan, where the parties then lived. Part of the dowry had been paid, but part remained unpaid. The wife's application for an order for payment was dismissed. If British Columbia law applied to the contract, it was unclear whether the wife was a party to the contract or even whether she was the intended recipient of the dowry since the marriage contract, although it was signed by her, recited that the two parties to it were the husband and the wife's uncle, and payment of the dowry was to be made to the uncle. If Jordanian law gave her a right to enforce the obligation for payment, that law had not been proven.

Note. See also *Sangi v Sangi*, noted above under Exclusion of Foreign Law; *Public Policy*.

Particular classes of contract — insurance — automobile — statutory rules

Moldovan v Republic Western Insurance Co, 2011 BCCA 418, 24 BCLR (5th) 251

This case concerned the effect of an out-of-province insurer's liability when the insured suffers a loss due to an accident in the province. The differences between compulsory automobile insurance coverage throughout North America are regulated by requiring an insurer to file a power of attorney and undertaking (PAU) with the relevant public official in each jurisdiction to which the insured's coverage is to extend. The PAU requires the insurer to respond to any action in the jurisdiction arising out of an accident there. It also obliges the insurer to quote the language of the British Columbia legislation,[57] "not to set up any defence to any claim, action or proceeding, under a motor vehicle liability policy issued by it, that might not be set up if the policy has been issued in British Columbia in accordance with the law of British Columbia relating to motor vehicle liability policies." The plaintiff in the case was injured in British Columbia as a passenger in a rental truck insured under a policy issued in Arizona. The plaintiff claimed no-fault benefits that, under the BC legislation, were required to be paid by the Insurance Corporation of British Columbia, subject to a two-year limitation period for making the claim.[58] The Arizona insurer, which was responsible for paying the no-fault benefits as a result of the PAU, claimed the benefit of the two-year limitation period.

The chambers judge had held that the two-year provision was legislation in respect of a British Columbia contract of insurance and should not be given extraterritorial effect by applying it to a contract governed by foreign law. The BC Court of Appeal disagreed. The provision was not an imputed contractual term but, rather, a rule that applied to anyone claiming no-fault benefits pursuant to the legislation. The plaintiff was claiming benefits as defined by the British Columbia statute and so was subject to that limitation period. No question of extraterritoriality arose. On the facts, however, the two-year limitation period was overridden by a longer period provided in the general limitations law.[59]

Property

Tangible movables — vessel — maritime lien

World Fuel Services Corp v Nordems (The), 2011 FCA 73, 415 NR 100

World Fuel, a Singapore company, or its parent, a Florida company (together the "plaintiff"), had supplied bunker fuel in South Africa to the *Nordems*, a vessel owned and managed by German entities

[57] Insurance Act, RSBC 1996, c 226, s 134(9)(b)(iii), since repealed and replaced by the Financial Institutions Act, RSBC 1996, c 141, s 92.1, the relevant wording of which is identical.

[58] Insurance (Vehicle) Regulation, BC Reg 447/83, Part 7. The limitation provision is s 130.

[59] Limitation Act, RSBC 1996, c 266, s 4.1(d), which deals with adding parties to an action already brought. The plaintiff had sued the Insurance Corporation of British Columbia within two years.

and registered in Cyprus.[60] The plaintiff had the *Nordems* arrested in Baie Comeau, Quebec, and claimed a maritime lien against the vessel on the basis that the applicable law for determining whether a lien arose was the maritime law of the United States, since the fuel was supplied under a contract expressly governed by American law. The purchaser under the contract was the vessel's South Korean sub-charterer at the time, which had subsequently gone bankrupt.

The Federal Court of Appeal, affirming the decision of the Federal Court, held that the plaintiff had no lien against the vessel because the issue was governed by the law, not of the United States, but of Canada. Earlier decisions of the court, dealing with maritime liens claimed by suppliers of necessaries to the vessel, had attached weight to the law governing the contract of supply. However, that was because, in those cases, the contract had been made by an agent entitled to bind the vessel's owners. It was appropriate in such a case that the choice of law question, namely, which law governed the non-contractual relationship between the supplier of necessaries and the ship, should be decided by giving preponderant weight to the law that governed the contract of supply. However, the choice of law issue depended on all of the circumstances surrounding the relationship between the supplier and the ship. Where, as here, the buyer of the necessaries did not — as the trial judge correctly found on the facts — have authority to bind the owners, a choice of law clause in the contract made by the buyer was of no weight. In this case, the law of the United States had no real and substantial connection with the issue whether the supplier, whether Singaporean or American, acquired a lien against the Cyprus-registered, German-owned vessel as a result of a supply of necessaries in South Africa. Since neither South African law nor any other relevant law had been proved, Canadian law must be applied.

Succession — wills — essential validity

Davies v Collins, 2011 NSCA 79, 341 DLR (4th) 237

Davies was originally from the United Kingdom and married Pamela Davies there in 1971. They moved to Nova Scotia in 1975. They lived in Nova Scotia until they separated in 1993 and were divorced there in 2001. In 1999, Davies had moved to Trinidad, and the following year he began a relationship with Jennifer Collins. He became

60 Which of the two entities was the actual supplier was unclear on the materials before the court.

terminally ill in 2007 and, two days before he died in Trinidad on 29 July 2007, he married Collins. His estate included immovables in Trinidad and Wales, and movables in Canada, the United Kingdom, Ireland, and Trinidad. Davies had made a will in 1989, naming Pamela as executrix and principal beneficiary. Collins obtained a grant of administration in Trinidad in April 2008. Pamela brought proceedings there to revoke the grant, but the court dismissed her application without a hearing in December 2009. Pamela subsequently tried to have the will probated in Nova Scotia, but the court refused to do so because of the grant of administration in Trinidad. Pamela then applied to the Nova Scotia Supreme Court for a declaration that Davies' marriage to Collins did not revoke the 1989 will. Under Nova Scotia law, marriage revokes a will, but Pamela argued that the law of Trinidad and Tobago distinguished between a regular marriage, which does revoke a will, and a marriage *in extremis* or deathbed marriage, which does not have that effect. She contended that Davies' marriage to Collins was a marriage *in extremis* and so, according to the law of Trinidad and Tobago, did not revoke the will. Both sides agreed that Davies' domicile at the time of his death was still Nova Scotia.

The trial judge held that the question, which system of law governs the issue whether a marriage revokes a will, is a choice of law question distinct from the validity of a will generally.[61] It should be decided according to the law of the testator's domicile, not at his death, but at the time of the marriage. Since it was agreed that at the time of his marriage to Collins Davies was still domiciled in Nova Scotia, the Nova Scotia rule applied that a "marriage" revokes a will. The only issue was whether the deathbed marriage, in light of the law of Trinidad and Tobago, qualified as a "marriage" for the purpose of this rule. The trial judge held that it did, and his decision was affirmed on appeal.

It was argued for Pamela that the question was better characterized as one of matrimonial law than as one of succession and that, accordingly, the choice of law rule should refer to the "matrimonial domicile," a concept different from that of Davies' personal domicile at the time of the marriage. In this case, it was said, the matrimonial domicile for the second marriage was Trinidad and Tobago. The Nova Scotia Court of Appeal held this argument was unsupported by the authorities, which applied the law of the testator's own domicile at the time of the marriage, not some independent concept of

[61] The trial decision is noted at (2010) 48 CYIL 568.

a matrimonial domicile. Nor did the concept of "comity" provide grounds for applying Trinidad and Tobago law here. The Nova Scotia Court of Appeal further agreed with the trial judge that the rule — the law of the testator's domicile at the time of the marriage applies to the issue of revocation — should extend to the immovables as well as to the movables in the estate.

Note. See also *Foote v Foote Estate,* noted above under Connecting Factors; *Domicile — loss of domicile of choice.*

Matrimonial Causes

Marriage — essential validity — non-consummation

Sahibalzubaidi v Bahjar, 2011 ONSC 4075, 339 DLR (4th) 166

The wife, who was domiciled in Canada, married the husband, who was domiciled in Iraq, in a ceremony in Malaysia, where they had met when they were both students there. The ceremony was the civil portion of the Islamic tradition. A religious celebration of the marriage was to follow in Canada. The wife sponsored her husband's immigration to Canada, but he acted abusively towards her and they never lived together. She sought a decree of nullity of marriage on the ground that the ceremony was invalid, that the marriage was induced by fraud, or that the marriage had not been consummated. The judge rejected the first two arguments but accepted the third. Authority supported the application of the law of the domicile of the incapable party at the time of the marriage, but it also supported the proposition that even if a marriage is valid by the law of the ante-nuptial domicile, it can nevertheless by annulled if it was voidable for non-consummation by Canadian law as the *lex fori.* Canadian law regarded a marriage as voidable if one party regarded consummation as impossible. In this case, the wife would not contemplate sexual relations with the husband until after the religious marriage ceremony, which never took place.

Marriage — essential validity — consent

Grewal v Kaur, 2011 ONSC 1812, 94 RFL (6th) 322

The husband sought a nullity decree on the basis that the wife, who was then domiciled in India, had fraudulently persuaded the husband, domiciled in Canada, to marry her in order to be able to emigrate to Canada. The court applied the law of Ontario, as the law of the domicile of the partly allegedly lacking consent. Since by that law the marriage was valid, the proper relief was to grant a divorce.

Divorce — recognition of foreign decree — public policy

Marzara v Marzara, 2011 BCSC 408

The husband and wife married in Iran, their native country, in 1980, and their eldest child was born there in 1981. Their second child was born in Germany in 1985, during a protracted process of emigration to Canada. After a brief return to Iran, they moved to British Columbia in 1986. Their youngest child was born there in 1989. The husband established a very successful business that exported pulp and paper from Canada to Iran and neighbouring countries. The parties separated in March 2006, and in May 2006 the wife commenced divorce proceedings in British Columbia. The husband filed a statement of defence and counter-claim. However, in May 2007, the husband obtained an order for divorce in Iran. Both parties had maintained their Iranian passports, and both still owned property in Iran. The order of the Iranian court ordered the husband to pay the equivalent of US $30,000 as a division of assets and US $1,500 as lump sum support.

The court held that the Iranian court had jurisdiction to grant the divorce according to Canadian common law conflicts rules because there was still a real and substantial connection between the parties and Iran.[62] However, the divorce was refused recognition on the ground of public policy. The parties had chosen to immigrate to Canada and continued to live here. Given that the matrimonial assets exceeded a million dollars, the very low amounts awarded by the Iranian court in respect of division of property and support were starkly in contrast with the policy reflected in the Canadian legislation and jurisprudence. The wife had commenced divorce proceedings in British Columbia, and the husband had responded to that proceeding before he took steps to obtain a divorce in Iran. His purpose in getting the Iranian divorce was to ensure that the British Columbia court would not make orders concerning spousal support and division of assets. In other words, he was seeking to

62 The main statutory recognition rule in s 22(1) of the Divorce Act, RSBC 1985 (2nd Supp), c 3, is based on one year's ordinary residence of either party in the country granting the divorce. It did not apply because both parties continued to live in Canada. Common law recognition rules are, however, preserved by s 22(3) of the act.

avoid his legal responsibilities to the wife. The court proceeded to grant a decree of divorce and made orders for the division of assets and support.

Note. A case on contrasting facts, also involving an Iranian divorce, is *Sangi v Sangi*, noted above under Exclusion of Foreign Law; *Public Policy*.

Québec

Statut personnel

Adoption étrangère — reconnaissance — articles 574 et 3092 CcQ

Adoption – 11356, 2011 QCCA 2353, [2012] RJQ 33

En juin 2006, la mère biologique, résidant en Haïti, consent par acte notarié à l'adoption de son fils, âgé de seize ans, par l'appelante, la tante paternelle de l'enfant, qui résidait au Québec. En octobre 2006, le tribunal de première instance de Port-de-Paix, Haïti, homologue le procès-verbal de consentement à l'adoption et prononce l'acte d'adoption. En novembre 2008, l'appelante dépose une requête en reconnaissance d'un jugement d'adoption rendu hors du Québec. En septembre 2009, la mère biologique souscrit à nouveau un consentement, cette fois sur le formulaire intitulé *Consentement général à l'adoption d'un enfant domicilié hors du Québec par une personne domiciliée au Québec*. La requête en reconnaissance du jugement d'adoption prononcé en octobre 2006 est rejetée par le juge de la Cour du Québec. Il a décidé que les lois du Québec n'autorisent pas une conversion d'une adoption simple à une adoption plénière pour les pays non membres à la Convention sur la protection des enfants et la co-opération en matière d'adoption internationale.[63] L'article 574, alinéa 1 CcQ requiert que le tribunal appelé à reconnaître une décision d'adoption rendue hors du Québec s'assure que "les règles concernant le consentement à l'adoption et l'admissibilité à l'adoption de l'enfant ont été respectées et que les consentements ont été donnés en vue d'une adoption qui a pour effet de rompre le lien préexistant de filiation entre l'enfant et sa famille d'origine." Selon le droit haïtien l'adoption ne rompt pas le lien de filiation et, par conséquent, un consentement donné par une mère Haïtienne en Haïti ne satisfait pas la deuxième exigence de l'article 574 CcQ.

[63] Convention sur la protection des enfants et la coopération en matière d'adoption internationale, 29 mai 1993, 1870 RTNU 167 (entrée en vigueur: le 1er mai 1995).

La Cour d'appel a infirmé le jugement et accueilli la requête en reconnaissance du jugement d'adoption. Le juge ayant prononcé, en octobre 2006, en Haïti le jugement d'adoption connaissait l'origine de l'adoptante et le projet qu'elle nourrissait pour l'enfant adopté, soit de vivre au Québec. Ce jugement atteste également que le juge a vérifié le consentement de la mère à l'adoption de son enfant. Ces constats suffisent à conclure que les règles internes du pays d'origine concernant le consentement à l'adoption et l'admissibilité à l'adoption de l'enfant ont été respectées, ce qui satisfait la première exigence de l'article 574 CcQ. Le tribunal québécois n'a pas à s'investir davantage pour vérifier la conformité du consentement avec les lois du pays d'origine de l'enfant, dès lors qu'il est en mesure de constater que l'exercice a été dûment fait pair le juge d'adoption. En outre, le caractère libre et éclairé du consentement de la mère biologique à l'adoption de son enfant ne fait aucun doute en l'espèce.

Si les règles concernant le consentement et l'admissibilité à l'adoption sont celles du pays d'origine, les effets du jugement de reconnaissance d'un jugement étranger d'adoption sont, comme le précise le deuxième alinéa de l'article 3092 CcQ, soumis à la loi du domicile de l'adoptant(e). La rupture du lien de filiation est un des effets de l'adoption, comme l'énonce l'article 577 CcQ. L'article 581 CcQ précise que "La reconnaissance d'une décision d'adoption produit les mêmes effets qu'un jugement d'adoption rendu au Québec à compter du prononcé de la décision d'adoption rendue hors du Québec."

Note. Veuillez voir aussi *Adoption – 1117*.[64]

Statut réel

Successions — article 3098 CcQ — immeubles et meubles à l'étranger

Nicolas (Succession de), 2011 QCCS 6803

Rosalie Nicolas était domiciliée au Québec et y est décédée en 2005. Elle avait la double nationalité française et canadienne. Selon son testament olographe, signé en 2002, ses biens devaient être partagés entre son employé et ami, Soltermann, et ses quatre petits-enfants. Ses deux enfants, Yolande et Jean-Paul Guillemot, ne recevaient rien en vertu de ce testament. Le liquidateur de la succession a

[64] *Adoption – 1117*, 2011 QCCA 1129, [2011] RJQ 1239.

demandé au tribunal d'homologuer le plan de distribution finale qu'il a préparé en 2010. Certains des mis en cause contestent le contenu de ce plan et expriment des réserves en regard de son homologation. Une des points controversés concerne le partage des biens situés en France et la question de la réserve héréditaire en droit français. Au moment de son décès, Rosalie Nicolas avait des biens meubles et immeubles en France. Le liquidateur considère que les sommes d'argent déposées dans des comptes de banque en France sont des biens meubles qui sont assujettis à la loi successorale québécoise, et qu'elles doivent être partagées entre Soltermann et les petits-enfants conformément aux dispositions du testament olographe. Jean-Paul Guillemot plaide que ces sommes proviennent de revenus locatifs générés par un immeuble à Larmor-Plage, en France, avant 2005. Il soutient qu'en vertu du droit français, ces revenus doivent être assimilés à des biens immeubles et que leur dévolution successorale doit être décidée par les autorités françaises selon le droit français dans le respect des droits des héritiers réservataires.

La Cour a décidé que les enfants, Yolande et Jean-Paul, bénéficient de la réserve héréditaire sur l'immeuble de Larmor-Plage, parce que les successions immobilières sont régies par la loi de leur situation. De plus, en vertu de la loi successorale française, les héritiers réservataires de nationalité française peuvent revendiquer l'application d'un droit de prélèvement sur les biens mobiliers et immobiliers situés en France afin de compenser la part dont ils sont privés dans les actifs dont la dévolution est réglée par une loi étrangère. Dans l'espèce, le droit français a donc pour conséquence de constituer les enfants Guillemot héritiers de la succession de Rosalie Nicolas en raison de l'application de la réserve héréditaire et, par le droit de prélèvement, de leur attribuer la propriété des biens meubles et immeubles situés en France. C'est sur cette base que devraient être déterminés leurs droits et obligations dans la succession. Les revenus de location de l'immeuble de Larmor-Plage sont assimilés à des immeubles en droit français. Ils sont sujets à la réserve héréditaire et peuvent faire l'objet d'un droit de prélèvement.

Book Reviews / Recensions de livres

Redirecting Human Rights: Facing the Challenge of Corporate Legal Humanity. By Anna Grear. Hampshire, UK: Palgrave Macmillan, 2010. 256 pages.

The long-standing global debate on the relationship between corporations and human rights has been primarily concerned with the impunity of transnational corporate actors with respect to violations or their complicity in violations of the human rights of individuals and communities in host states. This discourse has resulted in an abundant literature and, among other things, the appointment of a UN special representative on business and human rights, a set of UN Guiding Principles on Business and Human Rights, and, most recently, a Working Group on Business and Human Rights.

A less trammelled aspect of the debate on the corporate-human rights relationship is the concern raised by Upendra Baxi, among others, that human rights discourse is being appropriated in support of business interests and, further, that corporate actors have themselves been able to claim certain human rights protections under both domestic and international law. Anna Grear has written a sophisticated and groundbreaking book in which she explores the conceptual developments that have facilitated this corporate colonization of human rights. In this book, she puts forward a theory to reorient international human rights law towards the exclusive protection of the human person. Drawing on the literature on embodiment from cognitive science and philosophy, Grear calls for a reconceptualization of human rights, based on embodied vulnerability, which she argues would establish "an ethically important space … between the corporation and the human being for the purposes of human rights attribution."[1]

1 Anna Grear, *Redirecting Human Rights: Facing the Challenge of Corporate Legal Humanity* (Hampshire, UK: Palgrave Macmillan, 2010) at 32.

The first chapter examines the neo-liberal globalization challenge to human rights. Grear demonstrates that the already weak, state-centred international human rights system is even further threatened by the ascendency of transnational corporations and the global constitutionalization of corporate rights through international economic law and the policies and practices of international financial institutions. Grear argues that within this context, human rights discourse is being appropriated to serve the interests of global capital. This is exemplified in the rhetoric found in certain World Trade Organization and international investment treaties as well as in the use of human rights discourse in corporate domestic law suits to protect corporate interests and suppress public dissent to economic development.

In Chapter 2, Grear examines the link between the European Convention on Human Rights and liberal capitalism and the ease with which the European Court of Human Rights has allowed business actors to claim protection as victims of human rights abuses under the convention. The author highlights the court's failure to consider the conceptual implications of allowing corporations to claim international human rights protections. She compares this "lack of judicial contestation" with the landmark nineteenth-century decision of the Supreme Court of the United States in *Santa Clara County v Southern Pacific Railroad Co.*, in which the court, "without argumentative justification" allowed corporations protection under the 14th Amendment, a constitutional amendment enacted to ensure that former slaves were recognized as persons before the law.[2]

For Grear, the colonization of human rights language and protections by powerful corporate actors represents perhaps the most concerning, yet not the only, example of the "danger in stretching the semantic structure of human rights to the point where they become a meaningless, all-embracing reference for anything thought to have ethical importance or a claim for inclusion within the legal community of concern."[3] She makes it clear that she is not suggesting that corporations, animals, or the environment should not benefit from legal protection, but only that rhetorical and protective power human rights should be reserved for embodied human beings.

With the aim of determining how the language of human rights and international human rights law became vulnerable to such

2 *Ibid* at 28. *Santa Clara County v Southern Pacific Railroad Co.*, 118 US 394 (1866).

3 Grear, *supra* note 1 at 47.

appropriation, Grear engages in a masterful exploration of the entangled conceptual history of liberal law's person and the liberal subject of rights. In Chapter 3, she excavates the notions of the legal person and corporate personality as well as the links between liberal legal personality and property. Her central finding is that the dominant notion of law's person (P3), which emerged from liberal enlightenment theory, does not reflect the embodied vulnerable human being. Rather, it emerges as an abstraction, a quasi-disembodied, rational, possessive, gendered entity with male morphology, a concept into which the notion of the corporation could easily fit.[4]

In Chapter 4, Grear explores and critiques the theoretical construction of the liberal subject of rights in Western thought and, in particular, the important influence of the social contract theories of Jean-Jacques Rousseau, Thomas Hobbes, and John Locke. She dissects the former's enmeshment with emergent liberal capitalism and the eventual personification of the corporation by UK and US courts. The liberal subject of rights — despite the revolutionary potential of the idea of natural rights — emerged in the form of the abstract, disembodied male property owner. Grear argues that the corporation, an entity created to pursue wealth, emerges as the archetypal legal person, being both structurally and ideologically better suited than the human person to fill this concept of the liberal subject of rights.

Having examined these complex theoretical developments, Grear goes on in Chapter 5 to consider the conceptual history of disembodiment in relation to international human rights law. She notes that the subject of international human rights law suffers from the same closures as the subject of natural rights that emerged in the eighteenth century. Although the embodied human person and empathy were fundamental to the emergence of both of these concepts of legal subjectivity, liberal law also had a significant influence on the development of the concept of human rights and "the dominant philosophical conception of the universal bearer of rights was quasi-disembodied and rationalistic."[5] Grear identifies two ways in which disembodiment creates exclusions or "closures" in international human rights law. First, the universal subject of human rights is an abstraction. In other words, the concept of the universal subject of rights in liberal thought was "constructed around a figure

4 *Ibid* at 45.

5 *Ibid* at 102.

fully consistent with the exclusory interests of an identifiable socio-economic group."[6] Second, when the idea of human rights is transposed into law, and, thus, the human person is transposed into a legal person, she becomes "enmeshed in a discourse in which the human person is conceptualized, particularly in liberal law … as the quasi-disembodied legal subject."[7] Grear concludes that these two features of international human rights law continue to exclude those human individuals who do not correspond to this prototype, such as women, racialized individuals, sexual minorities, and others. In order to address these closures, which represent the gap between the legal subject and the human person, Grear argues that a reconceptualization of human rights is necessary. Such a reimagining of human rights, she contends, must capture the notion of the universal, "the embodied complexity and vulnerability of human beings … in a way that is capable of being genuinely inclusive."[8]

While her arguments up to this point are an important contribution to the literature on human rights and the corporate-human rights relationship, it is in Chapter 6 that Grear establishes herself among some of the leading human rights scholars. She draws on the phenomenological philosophy of Maurice Merleau-Ponty and his concept of "'intercorporeality' — the idea that 'all being is interbeing, intertwining — and such interrelating is intrinsic to the very structure of subjectivity and lived reality.'"[9] She also draws on the findings of cognitive science that show that law and a sense of justice have roots in human biology and that rationality is shaped by the human body. Applying these ideas to law, she comes to the conclusion that "a disembodied view of reason is not only impossible, but also — and profoundly ironically — *irrational*."[10] Grear argues that the universal subject of human rights should be reconceptualized as a vulnerable embodied human being who represents the universal human condition — "an ontic reality that unites all human beings in a community of living flesh."[11] Grear's concept of vulnerability is broader than a notion of vulnerability to pain and suffering and includes the capacity for well-being, joy, empathy, and

6 *Ibid* at 99.

7 *Ibid* at 97.

8 *Ibid* at 113.

9 *Ibid* at 118.

10 *Ibid* at 136.

11 *Ibid* at 131.

intimacy. This broader concept, she contends, can encompass the variation in vulnerability that exists between human beings.

In Chapter 7, Grear considers whether the rights contained in the Universal Declaration of Human Rights, the International Covenant on Civil and Political Rights, and the International Covenant on Economic, Social and Cultural Rights can support her concept of embodied vulnerability. She concludes that these instruments "simply make *no conceptual sense without pre-supposing a vulnerable living body*."[12] Even rights such as the right to a legal personality are aimed at protecting embodied human beings. In Chapter 8, Grear applies the concept of embodied vulnerability to an examination of the nature of property and proposes a reconceptualization of property and property rights in order to demonstrate "the global salience of vulnerability as an overarching theoretical construct" and its capacity for "linking human rights and environmental concerns, and property rights and the notion of the commons, in a common theoretical framework."[13]

Grear's reconceptualization of human rights law and theory, based on her concept of embodied vulnerability, has broad-reaching implications, which she herself identifies. It not only addresses the concern of corporate appropriation of human rights by excluding the corporation as a subject of international human rights law but also has implications for, among other things, international and domestic human rights law in terms of addressing the closures inherent in the current conceptualization of the subject of human rights and the more general notion of law's person.

It is difficult to do justice to the complex and rich arguments put forth in this seminal piece of scholarship. *Redirecting Human Rights: Facing the Challenge of Corporate Legal Humanity* is meticulously and compellingly argued. It is written in an engaging and accessible style. Grear provides vital insights into the complex conceptual limitations of human rights both as a discourse and as law as well as providing an understanding of the problematic nature of our current notions of legal subjectivity and corporate legal personality. Her book is a "must-read" not only for those engaged in addressing the corporate-human rights relationship but also for human rights and social justice scholars and practitioners.

Penelope Simons
Associate Professor, Faculty of Law, University of Ottawa

12 *Ibid* at 161.

13 *Ibid* at 200.

The Islamic Law of War: Justifications and Regulations. By Ahmed Al-Dawoody. New York: Palgrave Macmillan, 2011. 338 pages.

In the aftermath of the events of 11 September 2001, the laws and principles of Islam have been abruptly thrust into the spotlight in the West, often being misrepresented and misinterpreted. The United States' "war on terror," which is explicitly associated with what the US National Commission on Terrorist Attacks labels "Islamist terrorism," has created a pervasive sentiment of fear and suspicion throughout many Western states of all that is Islam.[1] Islam has also become the world's focus since 2011, as a wildfire of protests, uprisings, and revolts spread across much of the predominantly Muslim Arab regions in a matter of months. As a consequence, Islam has become inescapably linked to an array of armed conflicts. In the midst of this turbulent context, permeated with contradiction and confusion, Ahmed Al-Dawoody attempts to provide some much-needed clarity on Islamic law in his extensively researched publication entitled *The Islamic Law of War: Justifications and Regulations.*

In his first book-length publication, Al-Dawoody, a lecturer at the Al-Azhar University in Cairo, offers rarely found insights into the Islamic law of war from an "insider's" perspective — that is, the perspective of an Arab-speaking Muslim legal scholar. Having undertaken a large part of his studies in the United Kingdom and in the Netherlands, he is able to offer an extensively researched, yet accessible, insight into Islamic law for the non-Islamic world. As a result, Al-Dawoody's book should be seriously considered as core reading for anyone interested in gaining a detailed understanding of the Islamic law of war.

Despite noting that classical Muslim jurists focused on *jus in bello* to regulate the conduct of conflict in a time where war was the default state in international relations, the first three chapters of Al-Dawoody's book concentrate on *jus ad bellum* — that is, the legality of waging war in Islamic law.[2] The fourth chapter alone is devoted to the examination of *jus in bello* in Islamic law, while the fifth and final chapter addresses both the legality and conduct of internal armed conflicts, rebellions, and terrorism. The distinction between *jus ad bellum* and *jus in bello* is not always clear in Islamic law as it is in international humanitarian law, as the former is far less codified

1 National Commission on Terrorist Attacks of the United States, *The 9/11 Commission Report* (New York: W&W Norton and Company, 2002).

2 Ahmed Al-Dawoody, *The Islamic Law of War: Justifications and Regulations* (New York: Palgrave Macmillan, 2011) at 141.

and, therefore, open to interpretation. Nevertheless, Al-Dawoody makes a rather successful attempt at separating and elaborating on both *jus in bello* and *jus ad bellum* independently of one another.

Al-Dawoody thus dedicates the first three chapters of his book to examining the Islamic justifications for the use of force in international conflicts or, as seen from an Islamic perspective, "going to war against non-Muslims."[3] He begins by delving into one of the fundamental constituents of Islamic law: the acts and words of the Prophet. In doing so, Al-Dawoody relies primarily on the work of early biographers of the Prophet, which, according to the author, are widely recognized by scholars throughout the Muslim world.[4] He also examines the writings of another category of Islamic scholars known as *muhaddithūn* or specialists in the sayings and actions of Muhammad and his companions. Many of these Islamic sources would be unfamiliar or difficult to access for non-Islamic scholars. Al-Dawoody's presentation of such texts is therefore one of the many valuable contributions of this book.

In examining the Prophet's conduct in relation to armed conflict, Al-Dawoody makes his intended audience clear as he addresses what he perceives to be a significant misperception of Islamic law on the part of many Western scholars. Al-Dawoody dedicates a significant part of the first chapter to elucidating the meaning of *ghazawāt*, generally translated as military raids in non-Arab literature. By exploring a variety of *ghazawāt* in which the Prophet was involved, and many of which did not involve any occurrence of violent conflict, Al-Dawoody asserts that this term may represent expeditions of many sorts, thereby undermining the conclusions of several other authors on the willingness of the Prophet to engage in war.[5]

While the point is relevant and well argued, Al-Dawoody's desire to contradict what he sees as misperceptions of Islamic law may lead him to make broad assertions that do not always seem to be fully supported. For instance, at one point he asks: "[W]ould there have been any outbreaks of hostility in early Islam if the Prophet and the Muslims had not been persecuted?"[6] Indeed, in Al-Dawoody's opinion, the Prophet and the Muslims who lived alongside him were always victims rather than aggressors, and any act of armed violence

3 *Ibid* at 5.

4 *Ibid* at 12.

5 Reuven Firestone is just one of many authors identified and addressed by Al-Dawoody throughout the first chapter of his book.

6 Al-Dawoody, *supra* note 2 at 37.

was thus simply a defence of their person and their religion from the persecution of those who would suppress them. It is therefore not surprising that Al-Dawoody states that his "book thus finds that the Muslims' engagements in *all* these hostilities during the Prophet's lifetime were defensive."[7]

Such an unequivocal assertion of the victimization of Muslims can certainly be questioned. In fact, Al-Dawoody explicitly acknowledges this point as he discusses and refutes various other interpretations. Nonetheless, he is categorical about his conclusion, despite historical facts that may contradict his view. Muhammad's conquest of the city of Mecca, from whence he had been driven eight years prior, with an overwhelming force of ten or twelve thousand men, for example, is particularly hard to justify as being purely a defensive act.[8] Al-Dawoody's view that early Islamic conflicts were all defensive actions is likely emphasized to support his overall objective of reconciling the Islamic law of war with contemporary international rules on the use of force that retain a right to self-defence. Nevertheless, this objective may have led to a certain level of selectivity in Al-Dawoody's interpretation of historical events.

The second chapter is similar to the first in its arguments. However, there is a shift in focus to the contents of the Qur'ān, as opposed to the life of the Prophet. Accordingly, Al-Dawoody examines whether the Qur'ānic *casus belli* allows for offensive wars or solely defensive ones. Given the significant ambiguity of many Qur'ānic verses, as well as the panoply of interpretations made by Muslim jurists on such verses, Al-Dawoody is faced with the ambitious task of providing an account of the state of disagreement and contradiction around the justifications for war contained in the Qur'ān. To Al-Dawoody's credit, he shows himself to be up to the task. Not only are several contrasting perspectives depicted in equal detail, his overview is done in a way that provides remarkable clarity to a largely confounding debate, particularly to Western "outsider" readers. While acknowledging the lack of consensus among scholars, Al-Dawoody adamantly argues that "unbelief" is never a reason in and of itself for armed conflict under Islamic law. He concludes that "apart from defence against military aggression, the religious persecution of Muslims and the need to secure freedom of religion, there is no text in the Qur'ān that supports force of arms, let alone for the purpose

7 *Ibid* at 39 [emphasis added].

8 *Ibid* at 28.

of compelling others to accept Islam."[9] His argument is compelling and appears to reconcile Islamic law with international law. However, while his argument may appease those who believe that Islam has an aggressive view on the use of force, it is important to consider that Al-Dawoody is putting forth an argument that does not attract consensus among other Islamic scholars and jurists.

Al-Dawoody begins his third chapter with an informative and accessible clarification of the difference, in Islamic law, between *Sharī'ah* and *Fiqh*. While *Sharī'ah* and *Fiqh* together make up Islamic law, Al-Dawoody highlights that only the first of these two is divine and, thus, unchangeable — a significant fact largely ignored by "outside" scholars who often view Islamic law as unchangeable. Since Al-Dawoody argues for the reconciliation of Islamic law with international legal regimes, the tremendous importance of this distinction is evident. Any contradictions between Islamic law and international law can be overcome as Islamic law is open to revision.

The remainder of Al-Dawoody's third chapter is dedicated to analyzing the works of classical Muslim jurists in four prominent schools of legal thought found in Sunnite literature: the Hanafī, Mālikī, Shāfi'ī, and Hanbalī schools. The author's choice to solely consider these schools of thought is largely unjustified, giving the impression that the reasoning behind such a choice should be self-evident. A reader with limited knowledge of Islamic law will not be able to determine if the decision to limit the analysis to these schools of legal thought may limit the scope of the conclusions. This decision may certainly represent an important limitation in the eyes of other Muslim scholars, as Shia literature, the second largest branch of Islam after Sunni, is given no attention whatsoever.

Based on these four schools of Sunnite legal thought, Al-Dawoody sheds light on the misrepresented concept of jihād, a term generally understood to mean "war." Al-Dawoody quite convincingly explains that a more accurate translation of this concept would be: a "great effort ... to achieve a laudable goal, either by doing something good or by abstaining from doing something bad."[10] When attempting to explain the justifications to resort to *violent* jihād, however, Al-Dawoody must once again resign himself to depicting a state of disagreement between the principal schools of thought in Sunnite classical legal thought. While three of the four schools support the

[9] *Ibid* at 68.

[10] *Ibid* at 76.

author's view that Qu'rānic *casus belli* is restricted to acts of defence, the Shāfi'ī school promotes the view that jihād may take the form of a war on "unbelievers" (a term used by Al-Dawoody) for their disbelief.[11] Al-Dawoody emphasizes that the majority of Muslim scholars disagree with such an interpretation of Islamic *jus ad bellum*, critically noting that "[t]he stereotypical portrayal of the Islamic theory of international law as a doctrine of offensive war, that is, jihād against the *dār al-ḥarb*, or the so-called infidels, is imported to interpret current events in order to justify holding Islam responsible for the so-called clash with the West's values of democracy and liberalism."[12]

The fourth chapter shifts the reader's focus towards an area of Islamic law that is somewhat more codified, namely the rules of *jus in bello* in international armed conflicts. Al-Dawoody explains how "[c]lassical Muslim jurists focused on the Islamic *jus in bello* because they wanted to regulate the conduct of Muslims during a period in history when war was the normal state of international relations unless a peace treaty was concluded between its members."[13] Al-Dawoody analyzes numerous aspects of Islamic *jus in bello*, including non-combatant immunity, safe conduct, prisoners of war, destruction of property, and various types of weapons that may be prohibited. Throughout this analysis, Al-Dawoody makes repeated comparisons with international humanitarian law (IHL), highlighting areas in which the two coincide. The comparative analysis provides an important tool for scholars of both legal regimes who seek to bridge perceived differences.

The analysis of the Islamic *jus in bello* rules leads Al-Dawoody to outline his most forceful recommendation: the need to codify Islamic rules of warfare. Indeed, despite concluding that "the [Islamic] position is clear: there is no justification for warfare directed intentionally against noncombatants in *jihad*," Al-Dawoody argues that a lack of clarity in relation to many other issues justifies the codification of Islamic law.[14] In this way, the author argues for a codification process similar to the one that has long governed IHL.

The fifth and final chapter seeks to explain the rules that would permit both Islamic state authorities and its citizens to resort to war

11 *Ibid* at 81.

12 *Ibid* at 101.

13 *Ibid* at 141.

14 *Ibid* at 116, citing James Turner Johnson, *Morality and Contemporary Warfare* (New Haven, CT: Yale University Press, 1999) at 272.

against one another. Al-Dawoody identifies various types of internal hostilities recognized in Islamic law. Fighting against *al-bughāh* — that is, rebels or secessionists — is the object of a significant degree of legal elaboration. Similarly (though not identically) to the threshold for internal armed conflicts set out in the second 1977 Additional Protocol to the Geneva Conventions, Al-Dawoody identifies three conditions that must exist for an insurgent group to be treated as rebels under Islamic law. First, their cause must be just. Under Islamic law, this means that they must have *shawkahl man'ahlfay'ah* (just cause). Second, the group must possess a degree of power or force, and, third, the rebels must be well organized. Al-Dawoody argues that there is a surprising degree of leniency in the Islamic treatment of rebels. Indeed, the author explains that "full recognition of the rulings of the rebels and their judges ... proves that the rebels are not treated under Islamic law as criminals or terrorists."[15] A reader with a basic knowledge of IHL will likely realize how significant this lower threshold for the recognition and legal treatment of rebels is when compared to the minimal protections available in internal armed conflicts under IHL.

A second category of internal strife — fighting against *quṭṭā' al-ṭarīq / al-muḥāribūn* or bandits / highway robbers / pirates — is shown to correspond strikingly to modern-day terrorism. Interestingly, this is also the category of crime that is most severely punished under Islamic law. Indeed, Al-Dawoody makes a very strong case for the universal use of the Islamic definition of criminal terrorist activity. He argues that there is no consensus in the West on the proper definition of terrorism. Most definitions are limited by the inclusion of a motive (political being the most common).[16] Islamic law, on the other hand, focuses on the impact of the criminal actions of terrorists (damage to life / property, spread of terror, and so on).

Overall, one of the greatest strengths of Al-Dawoody's text is his ability to present a wealth of often contradictory interpretations of Islamic law in a clear and accessible way for all readers, regardless of their previous knowledge of Arab legal traditions, Islamic law, or IHL. Readers will gain a solid understanding of the scope and content of Islamic laws of war and will certainly be challenged to confront any misperceptions that may have previously clouded their understanding of Islamic law.

15 Al-Dawoody, *supra* note 2 at 166.

16 *Ibid* at 190-91.

The book does, however, have some shortcomings. As mentioned previously, Al-Dawoody can, at times, rely on broad generalizations, both in interpreting aspects of Islamic law and in depicting the views of the "West." There is certainly some truth to Al-Dawoody's argument that Islamic law is poorly perceived and misunderstood in much of the Western academic and political world. However, Al-Dawoody bases some of his generalizations on a very limited amount of material actually written by Western scholars. The Western academic publications and newspaper articles referred to by Al-Dawoody are substantive in content, but the limited number of these sources does not seem to justify many of the generalizations made, and this threatens to undermine the strength of Al-Dawoody's valuable conclusions. Nevertheless, Al-Dawoody's *The Islamic Law of War: Justifications and Regulations* is a coherently structured account of the many conflicting interpretations of the Islamic laws of war. He convincingly illustrates the relevance of this body of law to international law and current events. In this way, Al-Dawoody provides an essential and scholarly treatment of the Islamic law of war that any reader, Muslim or not, will find interesting and valuable.

Nathan Reyes
Human Rights Officer, UN Joint Human Rights Office,
Office of the High Commissioner for Human Rights
and the UN Stabilization Mission in Congo

Conflits de lois en droit maritime. Par Sergio M. Carbone. Leiden, Pays-Bas/Boston, MA: Martinus Nijhoff Publishers, 2010. 308 pages.

Le droit maritime est une branche de droit qui a connu très tôt le besoin d'être assujetti aux règles internationales. Le présent ouvrage fait valoir l'importance de ces règles pour le droit maritime en présence de conflits de lois.

Le livre est rédigé par Sergio M. Carbone, professeur à la faculté de droit de l'Université de Gênes en Italie et auteur de nombreux livres et articles de droit maritime, droit international privé, droit de la mer, droit du transport, droit commercial international, droit comparé, et droit européen. Son expertise en matière de droit maritime et de droit international privé est attestée par ses publications savantes, mais aussi par son travail au niveaux national et international. En effet, Carbone est membre titulaire du Comité maritime international (CMI), de l'Institut international pour l'Unification du Droit privé (UNIDROIT), ainsi que de nombreuses institutions nationales et internationales et de commissions gouvernementales qui traitent des sujets faisant l'objet de la présente publication. Il est, par conséquent, bien placé pour familiariser les lecteurs et lectrices avec les questions des conflits de lois qui surgissent en droit maritime.

L'ouvrage est divisé en cinq chapitres. Chapitre I commente le caractère international et la spécificité du droit maritime, ses origines, et l'uniformité des règles qui marque cette matière en insistant sur les caractéristiques de cette dernière et l'élaboration du droit maritime uniforme. Les Chapitres II, III, IV et, en partie, V, identifient les critères qui déterminent la loi applicable à certains rapports contractuels et extracontractuels en droit maritime en présence de conflits de lois. Les chapitres II et III portent sur la détermination de la loi applicable aux contrats de transport maritime des marchandises (chartes-parties et connaissements) et le contrat de travail maritime, respectivement. Le Chapitre IV a pour thème central l'identification de la loi applicable en matière de responsabilité extracontractuelle en droit maritime. Le dernier chapitre, Chapitre V, conclue sur l'analyse des chapitres précédents en insistant sur le caractère international des critères utilisés en cas des conflits de lois en droit maritime, le rôle résiduel, mais présent de la loi du pavillon et l'importance de l'autonomie privée comme précurseur des solutions uniformes adoptées au niveau international.

La contribution de ce livre dans le domaine de droit maritime n'est pas négligeable. Comparé à d'autres branches de droit, comme le droit commercial international ou le droit pénal international, le droit maritime n'a pas fait l'objet d'une prolifération d'ouvrages. Des publications de qualité dans ce domaine sont, par conséquent, bienvenues. Le présent livre constitue une publication de qualité dans la catégorie de livre de poche à cause de son contenu compréhensif. En effet, Carbone réussit à faire ressortir l'importance des règles internationales pour résoudre les conflits de lois en droit maritime en s'aventurant dans des secteurs particulièrement diversifiés, comme le transport maritime des marchandises, le travail maritime, et la responsabilité extracontractuelle. Dans tous ces domaines, l'auteur détaille les règles applicables, leurs nuances, et les exceptions applicables sur la base de situations tangibles, utilisant un langage clair et facile à comprendre. Le lecteur peut, par conséquent, tirer avantage de la richesse des connaissances que l'auteur possède dans cette matière. Le fait que Carbone est membre de différentes organisations internationales et nationales qui s'intéressent aux sujets en question permet au lecteur d'avoir une expérience de première main des règles applicables, ainsi que des enjeux auxquels les professionnels œuvrant dans le domaine de droit maritime font face en traitant des questions des conflits de lois.

À cet égard, l'étude comparée des solutions adoptées par les pays de droit civil au niveau européen et par la common law anglaise, américaine ou canadienne en cas de conflits de lois en droit maritime ajoute une grande valeur à l'analyse et sera d'un intérêt particulier, non seulement pour les experts en droit maritime, mais aussi pour les adeptes du droit comparé. On ne peut que mentionner, à ce sujet, l'étude comparée intéressante du droit américain, italien, et français que l'auteur entreprend concernant les critères de rattachement utilisés pour déterminer la loi applicable dans le cadre du contrat de travail maritime.[1] Carbone n'a aussi pas peur de critiquer les solutions adoptées dans des cas précis ou, en plus, de suggérer comment le droit pourra évoluer à l'avenir.[2] Les lecteurs et lectrices peuvent ainsi tirer profit d'un raisonnement critique des règles applicables et d'une analyse qui prête à réflexion.

La variété des sources de droit utilisées par l'auteur est aussi remarquable. Les documents des organisations internationales, des institutions de l'Union européenne, ainsi que des lois et de la jurisprudence des différents pays maritimes de l'Union européenne, des lois et de la jurisprudence des États-Unis et du Canada, et de la doctrine régionale (par exemple, celle des pays de l'Union européenne) et internationale forment la base de l'étude du présent ouvrage. Les sources utilisées sont d'actualité, certaines d'entre elles, très récentes.

Il y a, pourtant, des aspects relatifs à la forme de l'analyse qui, selon nous, devraient être considérés plus attentivement par l'auteur et la maison d'édition. Il s'agit de petites erreurs d'expression[3] et

[1] Sergio M Carbone, *Conflits de lois en droit maritime*, Leiden, Pays-Bas, Martinus Nijhoff, 2010 aux pp 153-75.

[2] Voir, par exemple, l'opinion de l'auteur sur l'adoption des critères de rattachement en matière d'abordage: "Selon moi, en revanche, la règlementation de la responsabilité extracontractuelle dans le secteur maritime, et en particulier celle découlant d'abordages entre navires, doit être confiée le plus unitairement possible à la loi régulatrice de l'abordage, selon les tendances normatives exprimées à cet égard, plus en général, à propos de la détermination de la loi applicable aux obligations extracontractuelles et, par ailleurs, codifiées à l'article 15 du Règlement Rome II." *Ibid* à la p 240. Pour un autre exemple, voir *ibid* à la p 238.

[3] Les mots en italique marquent les termes à considérer. Exemple 1: "D'ailleurs, *et en revanche*, en la matière ne manquent pas des indications favorables, même

de la présence des phrases longues qui peuvent prêter à la confusion.[4] Aussi, pour un ouvrage écrit en français, on s'est lamenté de l'usage fréquent des termes et expressions anglais. Par exemple, les termes comme "civil law" et "charter-party," qui sont très souvent utilisés par l'auteur, ont des correspondants en français qui pourraient facilement faire partie de l'étude.[5]

Malgré ces critiques, la qualité supérieure de l'ouvrage ne fait aucun doute. Celui-ci peut servir de référence aux professionnels (juristes, professeurs de droit, avocats, et autres praticiens) œuvrant dans les domaines du droit maritime, du droit international privé, du droit comparé, et du droit commercial international. De plus, les étudiants qui suivent des cours reliés à ces matières pourront puiser la richesse de son contenu. Il mérite, par conséquent, une place dans les bibliothèques de droit de tous les pays du monde.

Marel Katsivela
Professeure adjointe, Faculté de droit, Université d'Ottawa

---

en présence de la nationalité commune des navires, à l'application de la lex fori." *Ibid* à la p 231. Exemple 2: "D'autre part, cette interprétation 'autonome,' comme nous l'avons mentionné à plusieurs reprises, ne doit pas s'achever *compte tenu* du seul instrument normatif d'origine internationale, au sein duquel doit être précisé le contenu d'une règle spécifique." *Ibid* à la p 62. Exemple 3: "Et sous ce profil également, *donc*, la fonction des travaux préparatoires aux fins de l'interprétation est tout à fait marginale." *Ibid* à la p 64. Exemple 4 porte sur l'utilisation du terme "spécialité" du droit maritime au lieu du terme 'spécificité' ou 'particularisme' de cette branche de droit. Exemple: "Dans le contexte de cette évolution, il semble donc que l'internationalité est la caractéristique et la justification la plus importante de ladite 'spécialité' ou dudit 'particularisme' du droit maritime." *Ibid* à la p 23. Ce qui est indiqué comme exemple aux notes de bas de page du présent paragraphe ne constitue pas une liste exhaustive.

4 Par exemple: "Mais, il est tout aussi vrai encore que, souvent, ces modèles contractuels prévoient le choix entre des clauses alternatives qui en compromettent le caractère unitaire, en tout cas mis en discussion par les interférences qui peuvent survenir à la suite de la présence de règles et/ou de principes difformes, voire conflictuels, dans les systèmes étatiques intéressés à leur exécution et dans le cadre desquels, de toute façon, les rapports contractuels doivent être encadrés et/ou dans lesquels doivent être décidés les différends y relatifs." *Ibid* aux pp 81-82.

5 *Ibid* aux pp 87, 91, 104, 208, 216, 220, 280, parmi d'autres. Voir aussi, à titre indicatif, des phrases qui reproduisent des expressions anglaises: "Et, selon cette approche, on comprend la raison pour laquelle on a jugé de préciser que, au contraire, les "preventive measures to prevent or minimize such damage" rentrent aussi dans sa sphère d'application, même si, "wherever taken." *Ibid* à la p 51.

The Public International Law Regime Governing International Investment. By José E. Alvarez. Hague Academy of International Law, 2011. 502 pages.

The international investment law regime has been experiencing significant changes in recent decades, making it timely to explore them from a new perspective. José Alvarez's monograph offers a fresh look at the difficult challenges currently faced by the international investment law regime and puts forth a broad range of points relevant to the relationship between international investment law and public international law.

José Enrique Alvarez is a distinguished and well-known author and editor of books and articles on international investment law, public international law, and international criminal law. This book is the product of a series of lectures that were recently given by Alvarez at The Hague Academy of International Law. The book is composed of five chapters covering topics ranging from general features of the international investment law regime to a range of contentious issues the field is experiencing at present. The book also presents various proposals for perfecting the regime in the future.

Chapter 1 provides an overview of basic principles and characteristics of the international investment regime. Alvarez begins by pointing out the high volume of transborder capital flows in the form of foreign direct investments as a result of globalization. He then illustrates the nature and content of international investment treaties by using the example of the 1987 US bilateral investment treaty (BIT) model. Alvarez uses a comparative approach in a masterful way to highlight how international investment treaties are similar yet distinguishable from other regimes, such as the trading system under the World Trade Organization (WTO) and the regimes administered by the International Court of Justice and the European Court of Human Rights. He identifies party control of the dispute resolution process, the remedies available for injuries, and the impact on state sovereignty as the main criteria for comparing both the merits and disadvantages of these regimes. These criteria allow Alvarez to provide a succinct and clear presentation of the particular and distinctive attributes of the international investment law regime.

Besides identifying the advantages of the international investment law regime, the author outlines the ways in which it has been criticized as illegitimate, categorizing the existing critiques as vertical, horizontal, ideological, and legal perspectives. The investment regime's established top-down form of regulation on states is regarded as illegitimate by proponents of the vertical perspective. It is argued that there is a vertical disconnect between the supranational law that is produced under the investment regime and the law that is created by a country's elected representatives. Alvarez argues that "vertical" deficits are primarily driven by perceptions that a substantial part of delegated international "law making" is occurring in the course of deciding investor-state disputes and the establishment of arbitral case law that other investor-state arbitrations attempt to follow. The substantive decisions issued by investor-state arbitrations are viewed as intruding on fundamental questions of sovereignty. Vertical concerns are especially aggravated by a clash between the requirements of investment treaties and those imposed by national law, which elevate the public nature of investor-state disputes. Therefore, unlike the WTO regime, bringing claims of public interest against states by private parties is stressed as a noticeable vertical deficit of the investment regime. This deficit was increasingly discussed in recent years as the volume of foreign investments (particularly Chinese) in the United States has grown significantly, leading to concerns about the difficulties that this may pose for the United States in accomplishing its treaty commitments as a host state. Alvarez notes that investment obligations might put the US government in a critical situation during an economic crisis when states may have more difficulty in fulfilling their treaty commitments to foreign investors.

The investment regime is also criticized for its imbalance in failing to take into account developing countries' interests in BITs. The author describes this "horizontal critique" as follows:

> [D]eveloping countries concluded BITs because they were caught in a prisoner's dilemma from which they could not individually defect; they concluded treaties that 'hurt them' because they were individually pressured to do so, in some cases because they were under the barrel of the IMF gun to demonstrate their commitment to the free market principles that such institutions demanded in exchange for their financial assistance.[1]

Within this critique, investment arbitration under the auspices of the World Bank is also ironically characterized as a forum of "gunboat arbitration" replacing the predecessor "gunboat diplomacy"

1 José E Alvarez, *The Public International Law Regime Governing International Investment* (Leiden: Martinus Nijhoff, 2011) at 86.

for its bias not only towards the claimants but also towards more powerful governments.

Under ideological critiques, which are conceptually distinct from other critiques, the international investment law regime is viewed as structurally biased in favour of the free market, privatization, and other elements related to the "Washington consensus." The author points out that besides their association with traditional North/South divides, these ideological concerns also extend to elements of civil society located within developed countries.

As for legal critiques, the alleged imperfections of the investment regime are criticized from a rule of law perspective. First, Alvarez discusses Gus Van Harten's argument that international arbitration is a fundamentally inapposite mechanism for deciding contested and politically loaded issues of public policy. According to this view, in order to reach a politically acceptable result, such issues need to be resolved before constitutionally accountable national courts or by a permanent body of international judges. The author then gives an overview of other rule of law concerns such as forum-shopping by foreign investors; confidentiality of the arbitral process; and inconsistency of investment arbitration decisions. He notes that the failure of investor-state arbitrators to produce consistent decisions is not only making the investor-state mechanism unstable and unpredictable but also contributing to the overall fragmentation of international law, which, as a result, undermines its efficacy.

In Chapter 2, Alvarez sheds light on the object and purpose of investment treaties, again using the example of the 1987 US BIT model. He presents a detailed analysis of the main goals of investment treaties from the perspective of foreign investors' interests. By focusing on the interpretation of each word in the preamble of the 1987 US BIT model and its main peculiar characteristics, the author is able to unveil the essence of the meaning of encouraging and protecting investments. Subsequently, the author discusses the content of BITs in light of the imbalance that they represent between the host state and foreign investors' interests. He also explores the reasons that push the least developed countries (LDCs) to sign BITs with unequal terms. In this regard, the author addresses the "prisoner's dilemma" posited by Andrew Guzman who describes the economic factors that drive countries to sign BITs.[2] According to Guzman,

2 AT Guzman, "Why LDCs Sign Treaties That Hurt Them: Explaining the Popularity of Bilateral Investment Treaties" (1998) 38 Va J Int'l L 639.

> as a group, developing states had a common interest in toppling the Hull Rule and other rules of customary international law that sought to protect alien investors. They successfully did so through their General Assembly efforts but they were unable to sustain a united front; instead, as individual prisoners they defected from the NIEO and concluded BITs with wealthier nations for purely economic reasons, that is, to try to get a leg up on their neighbors by attracting foreign investors to their own shores first.[3]

Along with presenting Guzman's opinions, Alvarez argues that the economic rationale for concluding BITs by LDCs does not necessarily undercut the potential for BITs to affirm, or otherwise affect, customary international law. In contrast to Guzman's view, the author believes that economic self-interest is one reason states may express support for a rule of custom.

A noteworthy feature of this chapter is that it identifies the advantages of the contemporary international investment law regime as compared to its predecessor. The author outlines the main benefits of the 2004 US BIT model over the previous model of 1987. Besides listing the differing features of the former, the author also touches upon current tendencies in the US Congress to revise the imbalanced 2004 US BIT model, which encompasses the deletion of investor-state arbitration; greater clarifications to narrow the scope of indirect takings; and greater scope for governments to protect themselves from financial instability. However, in his discussion of narrowing foreign investors' rights in BITs, Alvarez does not elaborate on possible ramifications of revised BITs for foreign investors, which in my view is one of the weaknesses of the chapter. If, in commenting on the changes that BITs have undergone, the author had adopted a more critical approach, he would have presented a more balanced analysis of both parties' interests in the contemporary investment regime.

Chapter 3 presents a thorough overview of current issues concerning the interpretation of the fair and equitable treatment obligation (FET) by investment arbitration tribunals. The author focuses mainly on their interplay with similar protections in customary international law, offering the reader a solid comparative analysis of treaty and non-treaty sources of law. The author makes a significant effort to assess the approaches taken by arbitral tribunals in the interpretation of FET clauses by covering relevant arbitral cases that had a great influence on the evolving norms of customary

[3] Alvarez, *supra* note 1 at 120.

international law. By discussing various interpretations of the difference between treaty-based FET and the minimum standard of treatment in customary international law, the author identifies the relative advantages of a treaty-based standard, which opens the avenue for academic debate on the possibility of displacement of outdated and vague protections of customary international law by treaty protections.

Alongside elaborating on the interrelation of FET with the minimum standard treatment, Alvarez also analyzes the interpretation of full protection and security clauses, which sometimes accompany FETs in the same investment treaties. He does so through the lens of customary international law. It is worth noting that by comparing the approaches the arbitral tribunals have taken in interpreting FET clauses, the author identifies what he sees as their common fault in the interpretation process. He points out that arbitral tribunals have looked for common general interpretation principles instead of emphasizing textual differences between FET clauses that could justify different results.

Chapter 4 presents a remarkable overview of all controversial investment dispute cases that have arisen as a result of the Argentine financial crisis in the early 2000s. The distinguishing feature of this chapter is that the author provides a fresh look at the necessity defence by thoroughly analyzing the recent annulment decisions that reached inconsistent results.[4] Alvarez analyzes differing features of the tribunals' decisions by using various demonstrative tables that are very helpful to the reader. The chapter focuses mainly on questions related to invoking and interpreting the necessity defence in both security clauses in BITs and customary international law. In this regard, it gives an analytical overview of the contentious issues that the arbitral tribunals have tackled, such as whether the security clause in the US-Argentina BIT is "self-judging," whether BIT security clauses and customary international law necessity are distinct defences, and whether Argentina had contributed to the crisis.

Moreover, in this chapter, the author touches upon the issues related to using the General Agreement on Tariffs and Trade (GATT) and WTO case law in interpreting the notion of "necessity" in investment arbitral practice. By comparing Article XI of the US-Argentina

[4] *Sempra Energy International v Argentine Republic,* ICSID Case no. ARB/02/16, Decision on Annulment (29 June 2010); *Enron Creditors Recovery Corp. Ponderosa Assets. LP v Argentine Republic,* ICSID Case no. ARB/01/3, Decision on Annulment (30 July 2010).

BIT to Article XX of GATT and analyzing the main points of the only Argentinean case in which such an approach was taken, the author argues that using trade law by an investment tribunal is illogical.[5] He further makes critical arguments regarding points that the tribunal failed to address, which in my view is a valuable contribution in the field of investor-state arbitration.

In Chapter 5, all of the main issues outlined in the previous chapters of the book are synthesized in order to analyze the nature of the regime's deficits and its efficiency. In particular, the problems of inconsistent investment arbitral awards, the regime's possible threats to sovereignty, and its perceived "bias" in favour of foreign investors are re-examined. Furthermore, certain system reform proposals, such as the creation of an appellate facility in the International Centre for the Settlement of Investment Disputes similar to the WTO appellate body and establishing a Permanent International Investment Court, are analyzed in terms of their viability and efficiency. This chapter also presents a detailed overview of ten points of intersection between the international investment law regime and public international law: treatification and other positivist sources; fragmentation; the impact of non-state parties; globalization and its discontents; the profession of international law; the move to judicialization; hegemonic international law; global administrative law; constitutionalization; and humanity's law.

Overall, with its fresh look on contentious issues related to the international investment law regime, this book undoubtedly makes a valuable academic contribution and provides essential guidance for legal academics and researchers who are interested in the recent updates in this field. There can also be no doubt that this book will broaden avenues for further discussion, debate, and analysis of the many developments that the international investment law regime is presently experiencing.

Otabek Ismailov
Ph.D. candidate, Faculty of Law, University of Ottawa

5 *Continental Casualty Co v Argentine Republic,* ICSID Case no. ARB/03/9, Award (5 September 2008).

The Fog of Law: Pragmatism, Security, and International Law. By Michael J. Glennon. Stanford, CA: Stanford University Press, 2010. 224 pages.

How I wish the late Oscar Schachter were alive to review Michael Glennon's *The Fog of Law: Pragmatism, Security and International Law.* Schachter's brilliant general course on public international law, delivered to the Hague Academy in 1982 and later published as *International Law in Theory and Practice,* is an important rejoinder to Glennon's creative, well-documented, and multidisciplinary, but ultimately confusing, championship of the dangerous US doctrine of pragmatism.[1] Glennon, an established professor of international law at the Fletcher School of Law and Diplomacy and a former legal counsel to the US Senate Foreign Relations Committee, instructs that

> the pragmatist approach counsels skepticism toward doctrine, reservations about theory, insistence upon hard evidence, concentration on efficacy, tolerance of competing visions of the good life, suspicion about assertions of causation, aversion to moralism, preference for practicality, and predilection to doubt ... [T]he best that can be done by international law is to minimize the consequences of human differences, so that we can muddle through as best we can.[2]

In this vein, pragmatism is to public international law what situational ethics is to philosophy, an often slippery slope, which leads to fog rather than sunlight or illumination. Whether subject to moral suasion at one end of the spectrum or coercion at the other, fixed, enforceable obligations do not seem to be part of the pragmatist's lexicon. It seems that Schachter and other scholars of his extraordinary calibre did not see fog, as described by Glennon in his recent book, but, rather, illumination when they scrutinized the progressive developments of public international law.

Analyzing obligation and consent under the 1969 Vienna Convention on the Law of Treaties, Glennon makes concrete his departure from mainstream public international lawyers, whom he divides into "positivist" and "naturalist" camps. In his view, Article 26 of the convention, which codifies the time-honoured international

[1] Oscar Schachter, *International Law in Theory and Practice* (Boston: Martinus Nijhoff, 1991).

[2] Michael J Glennon, *The Fog of Law: Pragmatism, Security and International Law* (Stanford, CA: Stanford University Press, 2010) at 2.

legal principle of *pacta sunt servanda,* is neither infallible nor dependent upon explicit or implicit state consent. He writes in his introductory chapter that "[t]he likelihood of a state's complying with a given rule varies with the circumstances of a state's history, culture, relative military and economic power, political leadership, allies, security status, and myriad other factors."[3] This theme is further developed in Chapters 2 and 3. The pragmatist's "prism" does not countenance the morality of law, either as it derives from "natural" or "higher" legal principles or from positive or customary legal concepts. International legal principles of justice, rule of law, due process, prohibitions of torture and aggression, and essential human dignity are not part of the calculus Glennon's pragmatists adopt for regulating relations among nations.

At the October 2010 launch of his book at the Woodrow Wilson Center in Washington, DC, Glennon was asked how the pragmatist would analyze the "religion of international human rights." Glennon thoughtfully reflected upon the "hard case" of torture and the ticking time bomb. It is, however, in "easy," everyday matters of respect for human dignity, especially by public authorities, that the worth of the pragmatists' contribution to international law development can be questioned, particularly absent a more substantive philosophical debate of principles of justice and morality. One might take issue with Glennon's conclusion in Chapter 1 that "[i]t is the province of moral philosophy, not law, to determine whether the violation of law is moral. No legal system, unless it imports notions of morality, can judge whether its violation is morally permissible, and to the extent that it does so it ceases to be a legal system."[4] He extends this notion further in Chapter 6 by stating that "[n]atural law concepts, such as universal human rights and the notion of a just cause to fight a just war, are intellectually incoherent."[5] Yet in critiquing the International Criminal Court, he references Article 21(3) of its 1998 Statute of the International Criminal Court (Rome Statute), which requires that the application and interpretation of the treaty be "consistent with internationally recognized human rights," including the prohibitions of retroactivity and guarantees of the principle of legality. There are additional seemingly contradictory references to universal civil and political rights embodied in international criminal law in Chapter 9 and in the conclusion.

3 *Ibid* at 18.

4 *Ibid* at 35.

5 *Ibid* at 125.

Distinguishing international from domestic law, Glennon offers reflections in Chapter 2 on the concept of desuetude, which "occurs only when a sufficient number of states join in breaching a rule, so that a new custom emerges."[6] The problem is not only determining which and when arcane or ignored rules have become extinct and non-binding. More importantly, "[w]hether states are obligated to adhere to a ['neutral and reciprocal'] principle [not derived from state consent] is … not a legal question, but a moral one, which international law cannot resolve."[7]

In his third chapter on "Why Some International Legal Rules Are Obeyed," Glennon paraphrases H.L.A. Hart to conclude: "If a given norm is a rule of international law, it is by definition obligatory. The question is rather, what *makes* a norm obligatory? … It is legally obligatory because the costs of violation outweigh the benefits for nearly all states nearly all of the time, and violations are therefore rare?"[8] Without mentioning Hart's distinction between primary and secondary rules ("rules about rules"), Glennon posits that norms (which he inadequately defines at p. 53, n. 11), as opposed to legal rules, "derive from many sources" and "have evolved over centuries and have been reinforced through multiple levels of interstate contact."[9] According to Glennon, quoting Richard Falk:

> The decline of normative restraint can be seen in the broadening of the definition of self-defense and in the increasing resort to unilateral force by sovereign states … The conclusion is that the legal effort to regulate recourse to force in international relations has virtually collapsed in state-to-state relations.[10]

This is not to say that so-called "non-law" has no effects: "Foreign policy decision-makers are affected by sublegal norms, just as they are affected by legal norms; the difference is only a matter of degree."[11]

In Chapter 4, entitled "Objections to the Doctrine of Desuetude — And the Pragmatist Reply," Glennon illustrates his case that UN

6 *Ibid* at 40.

7 *Ibid* at 42.

8 *Ibid* at 54.

9 *Ibid* at 56-57.

10 *Ibid* at 62.

11 *Ibid* at 64.

Charter Article 2(4) has been abandoned. He provides a well-footnoted, but unconvincing, analysis of what he judges to be inapposite doctrines of naturalist *jus cogens* ("peremptory nonsense") and positivist persistent objector or "persistent gibberish." *Opinio juris* and self-interest are only two motivators in what Glennon describes as "largely epiphenomenal [international law]. International legal rules are, in varying degrees, derived from the same forces that are often responsible for state behavior that looks like compliance. In part, this 'compliance illusion' stems from shortcomings in our vocabulary — in particular, in facile use of the concept of causation."[12] He rejects as sophomoric the application of a "common threshold critique" to cases of widespread law-breaking which do not extinguish the duty to comply, citing the obvious "prohibitory rules" against rape, robbery, and murder (one should add and contrast torture, illegal drug prohibitions, and tax evasion). In Glennon's view, the key distinction between domestic and international desuetude is that compliance in the former is governed by coercion, while compliance in the latter is dependent upon state consent.

In Chapters 5, 6, and 7, Glennon argues that actual state practice is the measure and definition of international law. In his view, the present "decaying de jure catechism is overly schematized and scholastic, disconnected from state behavior and unrealistic in its aspirations for state conduct."[13] State responsibility, proportionality, and "anticipatory" self-defence do not lead to an improved international framework for security. Rather, such developments depend upon unspecified "propitious conditions," citing Robert Ellickson's warning that "lawmakers who are unappreciative of the social conditions that foster informal cooperation are likely to create a world in which there is both more law and less order."[14]

A pessimistic Chapter 8, entitled "A Pragmatist View of the United Nations," suggests that the UN system is built on the "burnt embers" of the League of Nations and that "[t]he harsh reality is that the old order of the United Nations cannot be resurrected — not because of any particular design flaw but because the conditions needed to make its use-of-force regime work are not present in the world today and likely will not be present any time soon."[15]

12 *Ibid* at 82.

13 *Ibid* at 110.

14 *Ibid* at 127.

15 *Ibid* at 166.

The blame for this devolution is shared by the "security consumers" of the UN General Assembly and the Security Council, which "cannot prevent unwanted uses of force, and the likelihood is that nothing useful can be put in its place."[16]

Glennon bolsters his condemnation of the UN system in an admirably exhaustive and self-contained Chapter 9: "The Proposed [and Ill-Advised] Crime of Aggression." He warns against proposals to "includ[e] the political roulette wheel that is the UN Security Council in the decision to prosecute," at the same time admitting that such a safeguard could protect U.S. interests, even if it continues to refuse to adopt the ICC Statute.[17] Glennon concludes his penultimate chapter with this statement:

> [The Rome Statute's states parties'] decision will determine, in the end, not only whether the United States can become a party, but the likely future of the ICC itself. For the United States will not be the only state to reject the ICC if the nations behind it turn their back upon the cornerstone of the rule of law, the principle of legality — and the assurance set out in its own statute that it will act "consistent with internationally recognized human rights."[18]

This admonition seems to be an odd twist on his abhorrence of naturalist principles.

It is in the final chapter on "Pragmatism versus Moralism" that Glennon most disappoints. He seems to misappropriate Hans Morgenthau's teachings on political morality and legal realism in order to support his own new "religion" of chaotic pragmatism:

> One type [of political morality] takes its standard from subjective preference masquerading as universal law; the other recognizes the inescapability of relativity, contingency, situationality, and incommensurability. One views legal rules as unaffected by power, the other recognizes that legal rules are created by power. One contends that obligation should precede experience, the other that obligation must flow from experience. One marches to the beat of presupposition, ideology, and dogma; the other takes its cue from the possible, the practical, and the pragmatic. One proceeds from certainty and faith, the other from doubt and skepticism.[19]

16 *Ibid* at 167.

17 *Ibid* at 171.

18 *Ibid* at 221.

19 *Ibid* at 234.

As suggested in Chapter 8, Glennon is looking for yet another "new world order" based on "painstaking research by social sciences that are now in their relative infancy, guided by policymakers and diplomats who know the difference between wishful thinking and real-world possibility."[20] The problem is that the pragmatist's unpredictable, situational approach is long on talk and short on concrete "new rules" to be negotiated, adopted, and implemented. Glennon's alternative to an evolving international rule of law is simply too uncertain and ultimately destructive for traditional public international lawyers to countenance.

MARY DOMINICK
Member, District of Columbia Bar

Making the Law of the Sea: A Study in the Development of International Law. Par James Harrison. Cambridge: Cambridge University Press, 2011. 340 pages.

Dans l'ouvrage *Making the Law of the Sea: A Study in the Development of International Law,* James Harrison décrit le processus d'élaboration du droit de la mer et s'attèle à démontrer comment ce droit a contribué au développement non seulement du droit de la mer moderne, mais plus particulièrement à l'évolution du droit international. Harrison fait l'historique de la codification de cette branche du droit international et du processus de négociation ayant conduit à son adoption; il examine ses procédures d'amendement et de révision; et présente ses accords de mise en œuvre. Encore plus important est le regard que l'auteur jette sur les rôles institutionnels que comblent le Secrétariat général de l'ONU et ses institutions spécialisées, notamment l'Organisation des Nations Unies pour l'alimentation et l'agriculture (FAO), l'Organisation maritime internationale (OMI), et l'Autorité internationale des fonds marins, dans l'élaboration des normes et règles régissant les affaires maritimes. Pour être efficace, selon l'auteur, ces institutions sont appelées à coopérer et à coordonner leurs efforts et activités en vue de résoudre de potentiels ou réels conflits de juridiction ou de compétence. Essentiellement, l'auteur analyse l'impact de la Convention des Nations Unies sur le droit de la mer (la Convention), en mettant

20 *Ibid* at 168-69.

en relief, sinon en reprenant la formule d'un auteur qui considère ce droit comme "a shining example of international cooperation, diplomacy and the role of international law in the regulation of international affairs and is considered to be one of the most complex and ultimately successful international diplomatic negotiations that took place in the twentieth century."[1]

Le chapitre 1 de l'ouvrage se veut une introduction générale du sujet. Ce chapitre décrit les défis et avancés de la Convention sur le droit de la mer, tout en expliquant dans quelle mesure les principales sources du droit international, à savoir les traités et le droit coutumier, ont contribué au développement du droit de la mer. Le chapitre 2 trace l'évolution de la codification du droit de la mer en décrivant ses grandes étapes, de son origine jusqu'au régime conventionnel des temps modernes, c'est à dire celui marqué par l'adoption et l'entrée en vigueur de la Convention des Nations Unies sur le droit de la mer de 1982. Cette convention, faut-il le rappeler, a eu le mérite de légiférer sur la quasi-totalité des questions liées aux océans et aux affaires maritimes internationales. En tant que convention de compromis, la technique pour ne pas porter atteinte à son intégrité a été de la considérer comme un "package deal," c'est à dire comme un tout auquel les États sont tenus d'y adhérer sans égard aux gains ou aux pertes que ces derniers pouvaient obtenir ou subir sur tel ou tel aspect de la Convention. Dans le chapitre 3, l'auteur démontre comment les diverses procédures de modification de la Convention, ainsi que les réunions des États parties à cette Convention, ont contribué au développement progressif de ce droit. L'auteur insiste sur la pertinence de la Réunion des États parties eu égard d'une part aux pouvoirs qu'elle détient pour prendre des décisions à même de modifier les dispositions de la Convention et d'autre part en prenant en considération sa capacité à conclure des traités liant les États parties.

La Convention sur le droit de la mer étant perçu comme une convention-cadre, c'est-à-dire une convention établissant des règles de référence, il est évident qu'elle n'a pas vocation ou la prétention à régler dans les moindres détails, et avec la précision voulue, toutes les questions juridiques relevant des affaires maritimes internationales. D'où la prévoyance par la Convention de l'obligation pour les États membres de poursuivre leurs relations à travers la conclusion de traités subséquents. Les deux principaux accords de mise

1 James Harrison, *Making the Law of the Sea: A Study in the Development of International Law,* (Cambridge, UK: Cambridge University Press, 2011 à la p 60).

en œuvre de la Convention sont l'Accord de 1994 portant sur la mise en œuvre de la Partie XI (Accord sur la Partie XI) et de l'Accord de 1995 relatif à la conservation et la gestion des stocks de poisons chevauchants et des stocks de poissons hautement migrateurs. Après avoir fait l'historique des négociations de ces deux accords d'application, Harrison analyse dans le chapitre 4 les rapports juridiques entre lesdits accords et la Convention. En ce qui a trait à l'Accord sur la partie XI, ce rapport juridique est bien établi en vertu d'articles qui disposent qu'en cas de conflit entre la Partie XI de la Convention et de l'Accord de 1994, ce dernier l'emporte, modifiant ainsi le régime juridique prévu par la Convention. L'auteur s'est par ailleurs penché sur les implications juridiques découlant de ces deux accords d'application pour les États, que ceux-ci soient parties ou non-parties aux dits accords.

Le régime minier et minéral des grands fonds marins fait l'objet d'examen dans le chapitre 5. Ce régime est régi par la Convention en sa Partie XI qui dispose que la zone au-delà des espaces sous juridictions nationales des États est réputée "Patrimoine commun de l'humanité" et doit être géré par la Communauté internationale à travers une organisation internationale appelée l'Autorité internationale des fonds marins. L'auteur décrit en détail les pouvoirs de cette Autorité, qui vont de l'adoption des règles et règlements, aux procédures de prise de décision impliquant les différents organes de l'Autorité que sont la Commission juridique et technique, le Conseil et l'Assemblée, en faisant remarquer que ce processus décisionnel n'est pas l'affaire des seuls États membres de l'Autorité, mais d'autres États et acteurs non étatiques. L'Autorité des fonds marins a apporté sans aucun doute une contribution majeure au développement progressif du droit de la mer à travers les règles et règlements pris dans le domaine de la prospection, de l'exploration et de l'exploitation des nodules polymétalliques, des sulfures polymétalliques, ainsi que des croutes riches en cobalt. Plus remarquable encore, est l'instauration en vertu de la Partie XI de la Convention d'un mécanisme spécial de règlement des différends pour résoudre les conflits se rapportant au régime d'exploration et d'exploitation des ressources des grands fonds marins.

On retiendra pour l'essentiel que l'Autorité internationale des fonds marins aura contribué au développement progressif du droit de la mer, dans la mesure où elle se pose comme une institution créatrice de normes, de règles et règlements applicables aux États parties ou non à la Convention, ainsi qu'aux autres acteurs non étatiques participant aux activités minières des grands fonds marins.

Il est à noter que les procédures de prise de décisions ont pour objectif de s'assurer que les règles et règlements adoptés par l'Autorité sont acceptés par tous les grands groupes d'intérêts siégeant au Conseil, en vue de maintenir le consensus sur la Partie XI. Harrison soutient, à juste raison d'ailleurs, que sans cette mesure de sauvegarde, c'est-à-dire ce consensus, l'acceptation par une grande majorité des États du régime juridique applicable à la zone serait menacée. La sauvegarde d'un tel consensus est un facteur qui contribue au développement progressif du régime des fonds marins, en faisant baisser les tensions et les vives controverses ayant caractérisé ce régime pendant plusieurs décennies.

L'Organisation maritime internationale est une agence spécialisée des Nations Unies responsable du transport maritime international et ses questions connexes. En tant qu'organisation intergouvernementale, elle accomplit ses fonctions dans le cadre de son statut, mais surtout dans le cadre juridique établi par la Convention sur le droit de la mer. Dans le chapitre 6, l'auteur décrit les diverses fonctions de l'OMI en lien avec la réglementation de la navigation, ainsi que le champ de ses compétences en matière d'adoption des règles et des règlements. Par exemple, l'OMI adopte des standards internationaux dans le domaine du transport maritime, lesquels standards tiennent compte des règles de référence adoptées par la Convention. L'organisation peut également établir des mesures portant sur la navigation dans les différentes zones maritimes, établissant ainsi l'équilibre entre les intérêts des États côtiers et ceux des États du pavillon, c'est-à-dire ceux qui prennent la qualité de transporteurs maritimes. Le rôle significatif joué par l'OMI dans le développement progressif du droit de la mer s'observe à plusieurs niveaux: la préparation, l'adoption, la révision et l'amendement des traités établissant les standards techniques en matière de navigation, à savoir l'architecture et la construction navale, ainsi que la navigabilité des navires; et l'intégration des traités établissant des standards techniques à la Convention sur le droit de la mer grâce aux règles de référence prévues par cette Convention.

On note que le rôle de l'OMI ne se limite pas à l'adoption des mesures techniques se rapportant exclusivement aux navires. Il va plus loin pour s'intéresser à la réglementation en matière de navigation dans les zones maritimes particulières ou très sensibles. Ainsi, l'OMI a adopté des mesures sur la séparation du trafic et des zones, sur les lignes maritimes, sur le trafic côtier, sur les routes à deux voies, sur les routes recommandées, les routes aux eaux profondes et les zones maritimes à éviter. Plus précisément, elle a adopté des mesures en matière de navigation dans les détroits internationaux, dans les eaux archipélagiques et dans les zones économiques exclusives (ZEE). L'auteur décrit comment l'OMI s'y prend, dans son rôle de créateur de normes, pour adopter des mesures innovatrices dans le domaine de la navigation maritime, notamment dans les zones maritimes sensibles.

Dans le chapitre 7, Harrison examine de plus près comment la FAO, en tant qu'agence spécialisée des Nations-Unies dans les domaines de l'alimentation et de l'agriculture, a contribué au développement des pêcheries maritimes par la production de normes en vue de la conservation et de la gestion des ressources biologiques marines. De fait, la FAO possède une fonction normative, ou législative, en vertu de l'article 14 de son statut qui lui permet de soumettre aux États membres des conventions dans le domaine de l'alimentation et de l'agriculture. Elle dispose même de la compétence pour adopter des conventions ou des accords, comme c'est le cas pour certains traités établissant des instruments régionaux de pêche. Plusieurs instruments juridiques en matière de pêche ont justement été adoptés sous l'égide de la FAO. Il s'agit notamment de : l'Accord de 1993 relatif à la mise en œuvre des mesures internationales de conservation et de gestion; du Code de conduite de pêches responsables de 1995; et de l'Accord de 2009 sur les mesures du ressort de l'État du port en vue de prévenir, de réduire et d'éliminer les pêcheries illégales, non rapportées et non réglementées.

À ces trois instruments juridiques précités, s'ajoute la Convention sur le droit de la mer qui a prévu des dispositions particulières en matière de pêcherie, notamment les obligations des États côtiers et celles des États du pavillon en matière de conservation et de gestion des stocks de poissons se trouvant dans les espaces sous compétence nationale. En tant que convention-cadre, la Convention sur le droit de la mer n'a fait qu'adopter des règles de référence qui sont d'une trop grande généralité pour produire l'efficacité recherchée. En effet, cette lacune ou faiblesse a conduit plus tard à l'adoption d'un accord plus contraignant pour les États parties, soit l'Accord de 1995 sur les stocks de poissons chevauchants. Cet Accord a eu pour effet utile de faire du Code de bonne conduite, ainsi que d'autres instruments juridiques de pêche adoptés par la FAO, des instruments contraignants pour les États parties dans la mesure où il requiert de ces derniers qu'ils prennent en compte les principes définis par le Code de bonne conduite.

Cependant, selon Harrison, il est de plus en plus évident que tous les instruments juridiques adoptés par la FAO ne peuvent être efficaces et effectifs que s'ils prennent leur ancrage dans les cadres régionaux, à travers précisément des conventions régionales et sous-régionales de pêche en vue d'une meilleure évaluation des mesures de conservation et de gestion des stocks de poissons chevauchants et stocks grands migrateurs. Ceci explique la nécessité d'une coopération accrue entre la FAO et les organisations régionales de pêche afin d'assurer le développement progressif du droit des pêcheries maritimes, notamment par la surveillance des activités de toutes les organisations régionales et sous-régionales de pêche; par la coordination des politiques de pêche; et par la promotion des meilleures pratiques de pêche entre les États. On retient que dans ses relations avec les organisations régionales de pêche, la FAO joue un rôle d'animateur et de facilitateur des échanges et discussions sur les bonnes pratiques en matière de conservation et de gestion des stocks de poissons. Elle n'entretient pas avec ces organisations des rapports d'autorité, mais des rapports de coordination en vue d'une meilleure coopération.

Plusieurs autres institutions contribuent au développement du droit de la mer, chacune dans ses domaines de compétences. Ceci pose la problématique de la fragmentation des dites institutions ou organisations, en soulevant aussi celle des conflits de compétence. Harrison relève la controverse doctrinale au sujet de cette fragmentation dans le chapitre 8. Si pour les uns la fragmentation se veut une réponse à l'expansion même du droit international et donc à une tendance naturelle à une plus grande spécialisation, pour d'autres au contraire cette fragmentation ne peut qu'engendrer des conflits de compétence, et instaurer une sorte de concurrence entre les institutions concernées. En droit de la mer, l'auteur estime que cette fragmentation se pose avec beaucoup plus d'acuité au regard du trop grand nombre d'institutions impliquées dans les activités maritimes. Il donne l'exemple de la qualification et de la formation des membres de l'équipage des navires où deux agences spécialisées des Nations Unies ont toutes deux compétence en la matière. Il s'agit de l'OMI et de l'Organisation internationale du travail (OIT), chacune ayant adopté des conventions relatives aux droits des marins et à leur formation. Bien que ces deux institutions aient le même objectif, de conflits potentiels ou réels peuvent survenir, d'autant plus que ces deux organisations internationales peuvent avoir des approches différentes dans le traitement de cette question.

Pour l'auteur, la coordination et la coopération sont des moyens pour résoudre la problématique de la fragmentation des institutions du droit de la mer. Il précise la double nature juridique de cette coordination à travers ce qu'il qualifie de coordination verticale et horizontale des activités maritimes. S'agissant de la coordination verticale des activités, elle se rapporte aux activités menées sous l'égide des Nations Unies, c'est-à-dire celles qui découlent de la Charte de l'ONU et les accords y afférents. S'y ajoute la coordination par la Convention sur le droit de la mer à travers, d'une part, le rapport du Secrétaire général sur les océans et le droit de la mer, et d'autre part, les résolutions de l'Assemblée générale de l'ONU, ainsi que les travaux du Processus consultatif officieux sur le droit de la mer. Pour ce qui est de la coordination horizontale, selon l'auteur, la coordination des activités de production des normes s'effectue lorsqu'elle intéresse diverses institutions. Dans le cas du droit de la mer, la coordination horizontale peut être illustrée par les relations entre l'OMI et l'OIT. En effet, bien que ces deux organisations aient des mandats différents qui portent respectivement sur la navigation et les conditions de travail de marins, l'on peut relever les possibilités de chevauchement entre ces mandats, sans pour autant aboutir à la conclusion que ces deux institutions n'entretiennent aucune relation. Bien au contraire, elles coopèrent et coordonnent leurs activités grâce à des accords de coopération lorsqu'il s'agit de résoudre des questions d'intérêts communs. De telles questions sont en général réglées à travers des échanges d'informations, de documentation et la mise en place des comités mixtes. À ce propos, on peut citer d'une part l'exemple du groupe de travail mixte sur la responsabilité et l'indemnisation en matière de réclamation pour décès, dommages corporels et abandon de marins et d'autre part l'exemple du groupe de travail mixte sur le démantèlement des navires. Ici l'OMI et l'OIT entretiennent une étroite coopération pour résoudre les questions liées au démantèlement des navires et ses conséquences sur la protection de l'environnement marin, la sécurité et la santé.

Après avoir démontré comment les institutions peuvent diverger dans leurs mandats, tout en étant tenues par l'obligation de coopérer, Harrison a analysé le problème du règlement des différends au sujet du droit applicable. Dans le cas spécifique du droit de la mer, il fait savoir que le conflit du droit applicable peut être réglé par une clause qui prévoit le droit applicable en cas de conflit. Il soutient pour terminer que les conflits entre les institutions internationales, plus précisément entre celles qui régulent les activités ou les affaires maritimes, ne peuvent être résolus que par la coopération et la coordination. Le développement progressif du droit de la mer est appelé à se poursuivre au niveau institutionnel, tout en favorisant la participation de tous les acteurs concernés par les négociations et l'adoption des normes par le biais de la recherche du consensus, afin d'assurer la cohérence d'ensemble du droit de la mer.

En conclusion, on retient pour l'essentiel que l'excellente étude de Harrison aurait été complète si l'auteur avait consacré quelques pages à une revue générale de la jurisprudence du Tribunal international du droit de la mer qui se développe et se densifie progressivement, ainsi qu'aux travaux de la Commission des limites du plateau continental au-delà des 200 milles marins des côtes.

Yacouba Cissé
Barreau de Côte d'Ivoire et Enseignant-chercheur,
Université de Bouaké-La Neuve, Côte d'Ivoire

National Courts and the International Rule of Law. By André Nollkaemper. Oxford: Oxford University Press, 2011. 337 pages.

The practice of domestic courts considering, and even applying, rules of public international law in the course of their deliberations is not new. However, the frequency with which this practice occurs has increased in recent decades. The increased interest shown lately by domestic courts in international law is roughly parallelled by international law's own greater interest, since the end of the Second World War, in matters formerly regarded as the preserve of domestic laws and courts. Both legal orders are converging, not by the imposition of one upon the other but, rather, by a seemingly mutual interest in meeting in the middle. In his book *National Courts and the International Rule of Law,* André Nollkaemper attempts to describe how the confluence and compromise of international and domestic law is occurring in state judicial practice, drawing chiefly on cases decided in the last ten years. The author also considers the significance and consequences of such domestic judicial activity for the coherence of the international legal system.

In principle, there are two ways in which a domestic court might engage with an international legal norm: either by considering its application to the home state or, alternatively, to a foreign state. In practice, however, instances of domestic courts determining the rights and obligations of foreign states under international law are rare to non-existent, due to the principles of state immunity and other related doctrines. Rather, a domestic court's interest in international law is almost always directed at its application to the court's own state. In a national legal system where judicial independence is strongly protected, the anomaly (seen from the international perspective) of a state sitting in judgment of itself is, one hopes, greatly mitigated. Domestic courts are routinely called upon to control government action in light of applicable legal norms and routinely discharge that responsibility. Generally, it should not matter whether the applicable norm is domestic or international in origin. Yet even in jurisdictions where judicial review of government action by an independent judiciary is common, there is a risk that such a review will be conducted less objectively, less enthusiastically, or less capably where the controlling norm is of an international character. The predictable reaction of international lawyers, and maybe even states themselves, is skepticism about the capacity of domestic courts to play a significant international law role. As Nollkaemper writes, "[p]erhaps the greatest barrier against acceptance of national courts as an institutional force in the protection of the international rule of law is that these courts are organs of the very entities that they are to control."[1]

Nollkaemper's study amply illustrates that such skepticism is usually misplaced. Domestic courts around the world accept, in principle, the relevance and potential applicability of public international legal norms in their jurisdictions. The author identifies three techniques that enable national courts to give effect to international obligations when their states' political actors have failed to do so. Using the first technique, direct effect, the court treats the international norm at issue as directly effective in domestic law without the need for an intervening legislative step. In the author's view, direct effect is the most reliable means of ensuring that international law controls the exercise of the public power of the state.[2] Yet whether an international norm is directly effective (or "self-executing") is a matter of domestic law. General international law does not require states to allow their courts to apply international law directly, a fact that the author considers as "perhaps the single greatest limitation of the role of national courts as a systemic force in the protection of the international rule of law."[3]

1 André Nollkaemper, *National Courts and the International Rule of Law* (Oxford: Oxford University Press, 2011) at 47.

2 *Ibid* at 123.

3 *Ibid* at 126.

The author's second judicial technique is consistent interpretation or the interpretation of domestic law in conformity with international obligations. While consistent interpretation is theoretically entirely distinct from direct effect, the author observes from the outset of his discussion of the former that its results may look similar to those of the latter to such a point that, in European Community law at least, the concepts are barely distinguishable.[4] This observation is reminiscent of Hersch Lauterpacht's provocative conclusion in 1939 that "[t]he presumption that Parliament did not intend to commit a breach of the law of nations has been a powerful weapon wielded with a determination which on occasions has come near to a denial of the supremacy of Parliament."[5] Also unlike direct effect, which is constitutionally impermissible in some states, consistent interpretation appears to be permitted and (to varying degrees) practised in domestic courts around the world.

Nollkaemper's third judicial technique, reparation, strikes the book's only false note. Unlike the two preceding techniques, for which the author is able to marshal extensive judicial authority, there appears to be only limited judicial practice to support the author's suggestion that domestic courts recognize themselves as having a role to play in discharging their states' obligations under the law of international responsibility. Nollkaemper acknowledges that domestic courts "rarely make explicit findings on the international responsibility of the state"[6] and characterizes any existing decisions as signifying an "emerging judicial practice," which it hopefully is, although it is difficult to prove such a claim.[7] Overall, the author's discussion of reparation reads more like a compelling argument for what domestic courts ought to do rather than a description of what they in fact do.

Having thus surveyed state judicial practice, the author turns to consider the consequences of internationally informed domestic adjudication for the integrity and development of public international law. His first concern is fragmentation, a concept that "is mostly used to refer to horizontal fragmentation between institutions and functional regimes within the international legal order"

4 *Ibid* at 140.

5 H Lauterpacht, "Is International Law a Part of the Law of England?" (1940) 51 Transactions of the Grotius Society 51 at 58-59.

6 Nollkaemper, *supra* note 1 at 169.

7 *Ibid* at 178.

but which need not be confined in this way.[8] Vertical fragmentation may also occur if domestic and international tribunals adopt diverging interpretations of international norms. The author's discussion of fragmentation — specifically, why it is a risk and why forces in both international and domestic law will tend to counteract it — is one of the most stimulating aspects of the book. Nollkaemper next considers the authority that domestic judicial decisions on matters of international law have, or should have, on the international plane. The author convincingly argues that the orthodox approach to this question, whereby domestic decisions on matters of international law are merely instances of state conduct to be weighed by international tribunals against the requirements of international law, may be too simplistic. Instead, there are instances in which domestic courts may, by their decisions, contribute to the development of international law.

A central proposition of Nollkaemper's book is that domestic courts are, at least potentially, a force in the protection of the international rule of law. Where such courts enjoy institutional independence from government and employ the techniques of direct effect, consistent interpretation, and reparation in applicable and compelling ways, the rule of international law may be advanced. In support of his arguments, the author cites a perhaps unparallelled variety of domestic decisions, many drawn from the *Oxford Reports on International Law in Domestic Courts,* of which he is editor-in-chief. Inevitably, perhaps, there is an overrepresentation of the European and Anglo-American legal traditions in these sources when viewed on a representation-by-population basis. Also unavoidable is the high level of generality with which the author makes references to specific domestic legal systems. However, I offer these as characteristics of the book rather than as criticisms of it. From these materials and by these means, Nollkaemper advances a compelling vision of an international legal system composed not merely of a handful of international tribunals but also of national judiciaries, working together — although in their respective spheres — to apply the rule of law to international affairs.

GIB VAN ERT
Associate, Hunter Litigation Chambers

8 *Ibid* at 221.

Analytical Index / Index analytique

THE CANADIAN YEARBOOK OF INTERNATIONAL LAW

2011

ANNUAIRE CANADIEN DE DROIT INTERNATIONAL

(A) Articles; (NC) Notes and Comments; (Ch) Digest; (P) Practice; (C) Cases; (BR) Book Reviews

(A) Articles; (NC) Notes et commentaires; (Ch) Chronique; (P) Pratique; (C) Jurisprudence; (BR) Recensions de livres

acquisition of title by succession, 188-92

Additional Protocol 1, and severe damage to the environment, 216-21, 228-29, 232, 235

agent international, la notion d', 244

agents ou fonctionnaires internationaux, 243-62; et l'étendue de leur immunité de juridiction pénale, 244-48; et la répression des infractions imputables, 248-57; et le cas particulier des opérations de maintien de la paix, 257

Al-Dawoody, Ahmed, *The Islamic Law of War: Justifications and Regulations,* book review by Nathan Reyes (BR), 604-9

Allen, Greg J., Gib van Ert, and Eileen Patel, *Canadian Cases in Public International Law in 2010-11 / Jurisprudence canadienne en matière de droit international public en 2010-11* (C), 519-58

Alvarez-Jimenez, Alberto, *Private Rights, the Use of Maps, State Responsibility, and Other Issues in the International Court of Justice's Boundary Jurisprudence: 2000-10* (A), 177-211

Alvarez, José E., *The Public International Law Regime Governing International Investment,* book review by Otabek Ismailov (BR), 614-19

Andean Indian Programme, 119

animal welfare, and general principle of international law, 3-47; and criteria of legality, 41-43; in European law, 32-35;in global domestic law, 29-32; initiatives focusing on, 25-27; in international law and policy, 21-35; and practice of legality, 43-46; and shared understanding, 35-41

animals, as other nations, 7-10

annulation de sentences arbitrales, l'approche des tribunaux canadiens, 370-79

arbitrage investisseur-état, la diversité des approches, 357-70

Arctic environment, 223-39; as a civilian object, 235-38; and industrial development, 225; and widespread, long-term, and severe damage, 225-39

The Arctic Environment and International Humanitarian Law, by Ashley Barnes and Christopher Waters (A), 213-41

Arctic Monitoring and Assessment Programme, 228
Arctic, and international humanitarian law, 213-39; and militarization, 214-16; and UN Convention on the Law of the Sea, 213, 238

Barnes, Ashley, and Christopher Waters, *The Arctic Environment and International Humanitarian Law* (A), 213-41
bilateral investment treaty, and international investment, 614-19
Bill C-300, An Act Respecting Corporate Accountability for Mining, Oil and Gas Corporations in Developing Countries, 66-75, 84
Blom, Joost, *Canadian Cases in Private International Law in 2011 / Jurisprudence canadienne en matière de droit international privé en 2011* (C), 559-98
boundary jurisprudence, and the ICJ, 177-210; acquisition of title by succession, 188-92; impermissible modes of acquisition, 192-94; recognition and protection of private rights, 184-88; territory that cannot be appropriated, 179-84; unilateral donations of territory, 192; use of maps, 195-204
Brunnée, Jutta, and Stephen Toope, interactional international law, 10-47
Building the Canadian Advantage: A Corporate Social Responsibility Strategy for the Canadian International Extractive Sector, 52, 75-115
Business and Human Rights in Conflict-Affected Regions, 110

Cameron, Sylvie, *Treaty Action Taken by Canada in 2010-11 / Mesures prises par le Canada en matière de traités en 2010-11* (P), 497-517
Canadian Cases in Private International Law in 2011, Joost Blom (C), 559-98
Canadian Cases in Public International Law in 2010-11, Gib van Ert, Greg J. Allen, and Eileen Patel (C), 519-58
Canadian Extractive Sector Advisory Group, 60
Canadian Mining Internationally and the UN Guiding Principles for Business and Human Rights, by Sara L. Seck (A), 51-116
Canadian mining, and guiding principles for business and human rights, 51-115
Canadian Network on Corporate Accountability, 69
Canadian Practice in International Law: At the Department of Foreign Affairs and International Trade in 2010-11, Alan H. Kessel (P), 381-418
Canadian Practice in International Law: Parliamentary Declarations in 2011, Alexandra Logvin (P), 419-95
Canadian Practice in International Law: Treaty Action Taken by Canada in 2010-11, Sylvie Cameron (P), 497-517
Carbone, Sergio M., *Conflits de lois en droit maritime,* recension par Marel Katsivela (BR), 610-13
Charles B. Bourne (1921-2012), in memory, by Donald M. McRae, 293-94
Chronique de droit international économique en 2010-11: Commerce, Richard Ouellet et Hervé A. Prince (Ch), 295-334
Chronique de droit international économique en 2010-11: Investissement, Céline Lévesque (Ch), 353-79
Chronique de droit international économique en 2010-11: Le Canada et le système financier international en 2010-11, Bernard Colas (Ch), 335-52
Cissé, Yacouba, recension de *Making the Law of the Sea: A Study in the Development of International Law,* par James Harrison (BR), 625-32
civilian object, the environment as a, 235-38
Colas, Bernard, *Chronique de droit international économique en 2010-11: Le Canada et le système financier international en 2010-11* (Ch), 335-52
Comité de bâle sur le contrôle bancaire, et droit international économique, 344-48
commerce canadien, 295-334; et les développements dans le système

commercial multilatéral en 2010-2011, 307-12; et les différends devant l'Organisation mondiale du commerce impliquant le Canada, 312-34; et les différends lies à l'ALÉNA impliquant le Canada, 306-07; et le groupe d'action financière, 349-50; et l'intégration économique à l'échelle planétaire, 298-306; et le joint forum, 350-51; et l'Organisation mondiale du commerce, 307-34; et les organismes de contrôle des établissements financiers, 344-49

Common Commercial Policy, EU's exclusive competence over, 279-82

competition law, and the Lisbon Treaty, 284-85

Conflits de lois en droit maritime, par Sergio M. Carbone, book review by Marel Katsivela (BR), 610-13

Constitutional Court of Colombia, 169-70

Constitutional Court of Guatemala, 170

consultation, co-operation, and participation, in regard to indigenous peoples, 141-46

Convention no. 169 Concerning Indigenous and Tribal Peoples in Independent Countries, 128-75; from assimilation to preservation of indigenous cultures, 129-36; consultation, co-operation, and participation, 141-46; educational and linguistic rights, 154-59; influence, 163-75; land and resource rights, 146-54; from "populations" to "peoples," 136-40; and self-identification, 134-35;

corporate power, and international law, 105-15; and *Guiding Principles on Business and Human Rights*, 106

corporate social responsibility, 51-115; Counsellor of, 81-112; rules of procedure, 80-85; voluntary, 86

criteria of legality, within interactional international law, 14-16, 19, 41-43

Czech Republic, refusal to ratify Lisbon Treaty, 273-74

déclarations en réponse aux questions, 439-95; sur affaires étrangères, 443-50; sur commerce et économie, 476-92; sur droit international humanitaire, 472-76; sur droit de la mer, 492-94; droit pénal international, 470-72; sur droits de la personne, 452-70; sur l'environnement, 439-43; sur santé, 450-52; sur sports, 494-95

déclarations parlementaires en 2011, 419-95; et déclarations sur l'introduction de la législation, 422-39; et déclarations en réponse aux questions, 439-95

déclarations sur l'introduction de la législation, 422-39; et Loi C-3, 422-23; et Loi C-4, 424-25; et Loi C-10, 426-28; et Loi C-13, 428-31; et Loi C-18, 431-33; et Loi C-23, 433-36; et Loi C-24, 437-39

democratic reform of institutions, and Lisbon Treaty, 286

Department of Foreign Affairs and International Trade in 2010-11, 381-418; and air and space law, 381-86; and international criminal law, 386-87; and international economic law, 387-91; and international environmental law, 391-93; and international human rights law, 393-95; and law of the sea, 417-18; and international law of treaties, 395-403; and international trade law, 403-17

Dominick, Mary, book review of *The Fog of Law: Pragmatism, Security, and International Law,* by Michael J. Glennon (BR), 620-25

droit international économique, 295-379; et commerce, 295-334; et investissement, 353-79; et le système financier international, 335-52

droit international privé, jurisprudence canadienne en 2011, 559-98; actions personnelles à caractère patrimonial, 580-81; conditions nécessaires à l'*exequatur,* 587-88; litispendance, 578-80; règles générales de compétence juridictionnelle, 577-78; statut personnel, 596-97; statut réel, 597-98

droit international public, jurisprudence canadienne en 2010-11,

519-58; reconnaissance de jugements étrangers, 523-27
droit maritime, et conflits de lois, 610-13
due regard, and severe damage to the environment, 221-23

educational and linguistic rights, in regard to indigenous peoples, 154-59
The Entry into Force of the Lisbon Treaty: The European Union in Retrospect and Prospect, by Avinash Sharma (A), 265-90
Equator Principles, 69, 76, 79
EU Charter of Fundamental Rights, 285-86
European External Action Service, 265
European Union, and the Lisbon Treaty, 265-89; and the distribution of exclusive, shared, and supportive competences, 276-77; as a legal entity under public international law, 275-76
exclusive, shared, and supportive competences between the European Union and its member states, 276-77

fair and equitable treatment obligation, 617-19
Federal German Constitutional Court, and approval of the Lisbon Treaty, 272-73
The Fog of Law: Pragmatism, Security, and International Law, by Michael J. Glennon, book review by Mary Dominick (BR), 620-25
Fond monétaire international, et droit international économique, 338-42
Fuller's criteria of legality, as relevant to interactional international law, 14-16, 19; and congruence, 43-46

Glennon, Michael J., *The Fog of Law: Pragmatism, Security, and International Law,* book review by Mary Dominick (BR), 620-25
Global Reporting Initiative, 57-58, 60, 77, 82, 102, 104-5
Grear, Anna, *Redirecting Human Rights: Facing the Challenge of Corporate Legal Humanity,* book review by Penelope Simons (BR), 599-603
Groupe d'action financière, et droit international économique, 349-50
Groupe de la Banque mondiale, et droit international économique, 342-44
Groupe des 20, et droit international économique, 335-38
Guiding Principles on Business and Human Rights: Implementing the United Nations "Protect, Respect and Remedy" Framework, 52-53, 87-115

Harrison, James, *Making the Law of the Sea: A Study in the Development of International Law,* recension par Yacouba Cissé (BR), 625-32
High Court of Kenya, 173-74
high representative for foreign affairs and security policy, 278-79, 281-82
human rights, and business, 599-603; and the exclusive protection of the human person, 599-603
humanitarian law, international, and the Arctic environment, 213-39; and the International Court of Justice, 232-33; and potential damage to the environment, 223-39; and the prohibition of serious damage to the environment, 216-232; and proportionality, 232-35

IFC Performance Standards on Social and Environmental Sustainability, 76, 82
ILO Convention no. 107 Concerning the Protection and Integration of Indigenous and Other Tribal and Semi-Tribal Populations in Independent Countries, 120-28; assessment of, 125-28; philosophy of, 120-23; and its protection framework, 123-25
impermissible modes of acquisition of territory, 192-94; geographic proximity, 194; historical consolidation, 193-94
Indigenous Peoples: Living and Working Conditions of Aboriginal Populations in Independent Countries, 120
indigenous peoples, rights of, 117-75; and ILO Convention no. 169, 128-75; and the ILO's supervisory system, 160-62

Inter-American Court of Human Rights, 164-68
interactional international law, 10-47; applying its framework, 35-46; and formal law, 16-17; and general principles of law, 17-21, 46-47; and its three elements, 11-16, 35-46
International Court of Justice, and boundary jurisprudence, 177-210; assurances of non-repetition, 205-6; awards of damages, 204-5; and state responsibility, 204-10; use of maps, 197-204
international humanitarian law, and the Arctic environment, 213-39; environment as a civilian object, 235-38; and the International Court of Justice, 232; and potential damage to the environment, 223-39; and the prohibition of serious damage to the environment, 216-39; and proportionality, 232-35
international investment, and public international law, 614-19
International Labour Organization, 117-75; and indigenous peoples, 118-75; structure of, 117-18; supervisory system of, in regard to indigenous peoples, 160-62
The International Labour Organization and Its Contribution to the Protection of the Rights of Indigenous Peoples, by Athanasios Yupsanis (A), 117-76
international rule of law, and national courts, 632-35
Inuit, and environmental damage to the Arctic, 231, 237
Irish Referendum, in regard to the Lisbon Treaty, 271-72
Islamic law of war, 604-9
The Islamic Law of War: Justifications and Regulations, by Ahmed Al-Dawoody, book review by Nathan Reyes (BR), 604-9
Ismailov, Otabek, book review of *The Public International Law Regime Governing International Investment,* by José E. Alvarez (BR), 614-19

Joint forum, et droit international économique, 350-51
Jurisprudence canadienne en matière de droit international public en 2010-11 / Canadian Cases in Public International Law in 2010-11, Gib van Ert, Greg J. Allen, and Eileen Patel (C), 519-58

Katsivela, Marel, recension de *Conflits de lois en droit maritime,* par Sergio M. Carbone (BR), 610-13
Kessel, Alan H., *Canadian Practice in International Law: At the Department of Foreign Affairs and International Trade in 2010-11 / Pratique canadienne en matière de droit international: Au ministère des Affaires étrangères et du Commerce international en 2010-11* (P), 381-418

Laeken Declaration on the Future of the European Union, 267
land and resource rights, in regard to indigenous peoples, 146-54
law of the sea, and the development of international law, 625-32
Leslie C. Green (1920-2011), in memory, 291-92
Lévesque, Céline, *Chronique de droit international économique en 2010-11: Investissement* (Ch), 353-79
Logvin, Alexandra, *Canadian Practice in International Law: Parliamentary Declarations in 2011 / Pratique canadienne en matière de droit international: Déclarations parlementaires en 2011* (P), 419-95

Making the Law of the Sea: A Study in the Development of International Law, par James Harrison, recension par Yacouba Cissé (BR), 625-32
maps, use of in boundary jurisprudence, 195-204; with disclaimers, 204; as expression of the will of the parties, 198-201; that are not the expression of the will of the parties, 201-4
McRae, Donald M., *Charles B. Bourne (1921-2012),* in memory, 293-94
mesures prises par le Canada en matière de traités en 2010-11, 497-517; bilatéral, 507-14; multilatéral, 514-17
Mining in Developing Countries — Corporate Social Responsibility: The Government's Response to the Report of the Standing Committee on Foreign

Affairs and International Trade, government report, 52-54
Mining in Developing Countries, SCFAIT report, 51-115
mining, Canadian, and guiding principles for business and human rights, 51-115
ministère des Affaires étrangères et du Commerce international en 2010-11, 381-418; and air and space law, 381-86; and international criminal law, 386-87; and international economic law, 387-91; and international environmental law, 391-93; and international human rights law, 393-95; and international law of treaties, 395-403; and international trade law, 403-17; and the law of the sea, 417-18

Namountougou, Matthieu Aldjima, *Responsabilité pénale des agents ou fonctionnaires internationaux et immunité de juridiction* (A), 243-63
National Courts and the International Rule of Law, by André Nollkaemper, book review by Gib van Ert (BR), 632-33
National Roundtables on Corporate Social Responsibility and the Extractive Sector in Developing Countries, 59
"Nations Like Unto Yourselves": An Inquiry into the Status of a General Principle of International Law on Animal Welfare, by Katie Sykes (A), 3-49
Nollkaemper, André, *National Courts and the International Rule of Law,* book review by Gib van Ert (BR), 632-33
Norms on the Responsibilities of Transnational Corporations and Other Business Enterprises with regard to Human Rights, 87-88

OECD Guidelines for Multinational Enterprises, 56-57, 65, 82, 91, 104
Office of the Extractive Sector CSR Counsellor, 63, 75-115
opérations de maintien de la paix, aspects rétrospectifs, 257-58; aspects prospectifs, 258-60
Organisation internationale des commissions des valeurs, et droit international économique, 348-49
Organisation mondiale du commerce, et commerce canadien, 307-34
Ouellet, Richard, et Hervé A. Prince, *Chronique de droit international économique en 2010-11: Commerce* (Ch), 295-334

parliamentary declarations in 2011, 419-95; and statements made on the introduction of legislation, 372-406; and statements in response to questions, 407-95
Patel, Eileen, Gib van Ert, and Greg J. Allen, *Canadian Cases in Public International Law in 2010-11 / Jurisprudence canadienne en matière de droit international public en 2010-11* (C), 519-58
practice in international law, Canadian, 381-517; at the Department of Foreign Affairs and International Trade in 2010-11, 381-418; parliamentary declarations in 2011, 419-95; treaty action in 2010-11, 497-517
practice of legality, within interactional international law, 16, 19, 43-46
pragmatism, and international law, 620-25
pratique canadienne en matière de droit international, 381-517; déclarations parlementaires en 2010-11, 419-95; mesures prises en matière de traités en 2010-11, 497-517; au Ministère des Affaires étrangères et du Commerce international en 2010-11, 381-418
president of the European Council, 278
private international law, Canadian cases in 2011, 559-98; administration and succession, 575; arbitral awards, 586-87; conditions for recognition or enforcement, 582-83; connecting factors, 588-90; contracts, 590-91; declining jurisdiction *in personam,* 568-69; defences to recognition or enforcement, 583-84; evidence obtained locally for use in foreign

proceedings, 581-82; exclusion of foreign law, 588; infants and children, 576-77; jurisdiction *in personam*, 559-68, 569-72; matrimonial causes, 575-76, 594-96; means of enforcement, 584-85; property, 591-94; subject matter jurisdiction, 572-75; support orders, 586

private rights, recognition and protection of in boundary jurisprudence, 184-88

Private Rights, the Use of Maps, State Responsibility, and Other Issues in the International Court of Justice's Boundary Jurisprudence: 2000-10, by Alberto Alvarez-Jimenez (A), 177-211

proportionality, and international humanitarian law in the Arctic environment, 232-35

Protect, Respect and Remedy Framework for Business and Human Rights, 52-115

public international law, Canadian cases in 2010-11, 519-58; Convention on the Rights of the Child, 555-58; diplomatic relations, 519-23; extradition, 527-32, 538-41; Hague Convention, 541-43; human rights, 553-55; international arbitration, 549-53; international labour law, 534-38; international organizations, 546-49; refugee protection, 543-46; terrorism, 532-34

The Public International Law Regime Governing International Investment, by José E. Alvarez, book review by Otabek Ismailov (BR), 614-19

qualified majority voting, and Lisbon Treaty, 287

radioactive fallout in the Artic, 227-28

Redirecting Human Rights: Facing the Challenge of Corporate Legal Humanity, by Anna Grear, book review by Penelope Simons (BR), 599-603

répression des infractions imputables aux agents ou fonctionnaires internationaux, 248-62; de droit interne, 248-50; de droit international, 251-57

Responsabilité pénale des agents ou fonctionnaires internationaux et immunité de juridiction, par Matthieu Aldjima Namountougou (A), 243-63

Responsabilité pénale, des agents ou fonctionnaires internationaux et immunité de jurisdiction, 243-62

Reyes, Nathan, book review of *The Islamic Law of War: Justifications and Regulations*, by Ahmed Al-Dawoody (BR), 604-09

San Remo Manual on International Law Applicable to Armed Conflict at Sea, 221, 229, 232

Seck, Sara L., *Canadian Mining Internationally and the UN Guiding Principles for Business and Human Rights* (A), 51-116

security, and international law, 620-25

self-identification of indigenous peoples, 134-35; from "populations" to "peoples," 136-40

shared understandings, within interactional international law, 11-14, 19, 35-41

Sharma, Avinash, *The Entry into Force of the Lisbon Treaty: The European Union in Retrospect and Prospect* (A), 265-90

Simons, Penelope, book review of *Redirecting Human Rights: Facing the Challenge of Corporate Legal Humanity*, by Anna Grear (BR), 599-603

Special Representative to the UN Secretary-General on Business and Human Rights, 51-115

state responsibility, and boundary jurisprudence, 204-10; assurances of non-repetition, 205-6; awards of damages, 204-5

state succession, 188-92

statements in response to questions, 439-495; on the environment, 439-43; on foreign affairs, 443-50; on health, 450-52; on human rights, 452-70; on international criminal law, 470-72; on international humanitarian law, 472-76;

on law of the sea, 492-94; on trade and economy, 476-92; on sports, 494-95
statements made on the introduction of legislation, 422-39; on Bill C-3, 422-23; on Bill C-4, 424-25; on Bill C-10, 426-58; on Bill C-13, 428-31; on Bill C-18, 431-33; on Bill C-23, 433-36; on Bill C-24, 437-39
Supreme Court of Chile, 168-69
Sykes, Katie, *"Nations Like Unto Yourselves": An Inquiry into the Status of a General Principle of International Law on Animal Welfare* (A), 3-49

terra nullius, 179-84
Toope, Stephen, and Jutta Brunnée, interactional international law, 10-47
trade and investment laws, EU's expansion, 282-84
treaty action taken by Canada in 2010-11, 497-517; bilateral treaty action, 497-504; multilateral treaty action, 504-7
Treaty Establishing a Constitution for Europe, 269-70
Treaty of Lisbon Amending the Treaty on European Union and the Treaty Establishing the European Community (Lisbon Treaty), 265-89; background, 266-70; and the changes it introduced, 274-89; and Common Commercial Policy, 279-82; and competition law, 284-85; and Czech Republic, 273-74; and democratic reform of institutions, 286-87; and EU Charter of Fundamental Rights, 285-86; and exclusive, shared, and supportive competences, 276-77; and Federal German Constitutional Court, 272-73; and Irish Referendum, 271-72; and qualified majority voting, 287; ratification process, 270-74; and trade and investment law, 282-84
Treaty on European Union, 274-75, 284-85
Treaty on the Functioning of the European Union, 274-75, 278, 285

UN Declaration on the Rights of Indigenous Peoples, 231-32
unilateral donations of territory, 192
Universal Declaration on Animal Welfare, 26-27

van Ert, Gib, book review of *National Courts and the International Rule of Law*, by André Nollkaemper (BR), 632-33
van Ert, Gib, Greg J. Allen, and Eileen Patel, *Canadian Cases in Public International Law in 2010-11 / Jurisprudence canadienne en matière de droit international public en 2010-11* (C), 519-58
Voluntary Principles on Security and Human Rights, 60, 67, 76, 82, 102

Waters, Christopher, and Ashley Barnes, *The Arctic Environment and International Humanitarian Law* (A), 213-41
wide-spread, long-term, and severe damage to the environment, 216-21; environment as a civilian object, 235-38
wildlife law, international, 22-25
Working Group on Protection for the Arctic Marine Environment, 228
World Organisation for Animal Health, 27-29

Yupsanis, Athanasios, *The International Labour Organization and Its Contribution to the Protection of the Rights of Indigenous Peoples* (A), 117-76

Index of Cases / Index de la jurisprudence

114957 Canada Ltée (Spraytech, Société d'arrosage) v Hudson (Ville), 21, n 96

Abdula v Canadian Solar Inc, 574
Abitibi Bowater c Canada, 356
Adoption – 1117, 597
Adoption – 11356, 596-97
AECOM Canada Ltd v Fisher, 564
Affaire relative au personnel diplomatique et consulaire des États-Unis à Téhéran (États-Unis d'Amérique c Iran), 246, n 18
Affaire des frontières colombo-vénézuéliennes (Colombie c Vénézuéla), 182, n 18
Al Adsani c Royaume-Uni, 252
Alasdair Ross Anderson et al c Costa Rica, 354
Alejandro Papic Dominguez Con Comunidad Indigena Aymara Chusmiza v Usmagama, 168
AMRI v KER, 541-43
Anvil Mining v Association canadienne contre l'impunité (ACCI), 65, n 66
Archer Daniels Midland Company and Tate & Lyle Ingredients Americas, Inc c Mexico, 371, n 94
Arcinas v Stanley, 586
Association canadienne contre l'impunité (ACCI) v Anvil Mining Ltd, 65, n 66
Aziz v Al-Masri, 590

BJG v DLG, 555-57
Bank of Mongolia v Taskin, 584
Barrick Gold Corp c Éditions écosociété inc, 87, n 174
Bayview Irrigation District #11 et al c United Mexican States, 370, n 91
BCE Inc v 1976 Debentureholders, 101, n 252
Biwater Gauff (Tanzania) Ltd c United Republic of Tanzania, 367, n 76
Brésil – Pneus rechapés, 326
Brisbin v Lunev, 563

Cal v Attorney General, 172
Canada – Certain Measures Affecting the Renewable Energy Sector, 413
Canada – Certaines mesures affectant le secteur de la production d'énergie renouvelable, 331-33
Canada – Mesures relatives au programme de tarifs de rachat garantis, 333-34
Canada (Attorney General) c S.D. Myers Inc, 370, n 92
Canada (House of Commons) v Vaid, 547
Canada (Minister of Citizenship and Immigration) v Tobiass, 540, n 77
Canada (Minister of National Revenue) v Glazer, 582
Canada Life Assurance Co v Holidair Insurance Services Ltd, 572-73
Cannon v Funds for Canada Foundation, 563
Cargill c Mexico, 354
Case Concerning Pulp Mills on the River Uruguay (Argentina v Uruguay), 18
Case Concerning the Gabčíkovo-Nagymaros Project (Hungary v Slovakia), 18, 47, 395, 400
Case Concerning the Temple of Preah Vihear (Cambodia v Thailand), 196
Case of the Mayagna (Sumo) Awas Tingni Community (Nicaragua), 163-64
Case of the Moiwana Community (Suriname), 147, n 159
Case of the Sawhoyamaxa Indigenous Community (Paraguay), 166
Case of the Yakye Axa Indigenous Community (Paraguay), 164
CE – Sardines et Canada – Brevets pour les produits pharmaceutiques, 326
Chemtura Corporation c Canada, 354
Cheng v Yu, 569
China – Auto Parts, 411

China – Measures Related to the Exportation of Various Raw Materials, 408, 410
Choc v Hudbay Minerals Inc, 65, n 66
CIMA Plastics Corp v Sandid Enterprises Ltd, 582-83
Club Resorts Ltd v Van Breda, 561, n 4
Commission v Austria, 284, n 76
Communautés européennes – Certaines mesures prohibant l'importation et la commercialisation de produits dérivés du phoque, 314-15
Communautés européennes – Mesures concernant les viandes et produits carnés (hormones), 312-14
Communautés européennes – Mesures prohibant l'importation et la commercialisation de produits dérivés du phoque (Plaignant: Canada), 330-31
Consbec Inc v Walker, 569
Contacare Inc v CIBA Vision Corp, 584
Continental Casualty Co v Argentine Republic, 619, n 5
Corée – Viande de boeuf, 324
Corn Products International, Inc c Mexico, 371, n 94
Cougar Helicopters Inc v Sikorsky Aircraft Corp, 565-66
Council Decision of 1 December 2009 Adopting the Council's Rules of Procedure, 281, n 65
Cristiani c Italian Latin-American Institute, 255, n 64

Dallah Real Estate and Tourism Holding Co. c Ministry of Religious Affairs of the Government of Pakistan, 374, n 113, 552
Dalnoki c SSQ Life Insurance Company Inc, 577-78
Davies v Collins, 592-94
Decision Regarding Delimitation of the Border between the State of Eritrea and the Federal Democratic Republic of Ethiopia, 202
Dell Computer Corp v Union des consommateurs, 572, n 26
Dembroski v Rhainds, 567
Dispute Regarding Navigational and Related Rights (Costa Rica v Nicaragua), 185, 205-7, 210
Dow Agrosciences LLC c Canada, 356, n 16
Dragon Ltd v Topwater Exclusive Fund IV LLC, 565
Dundee Precious Metals Inc v Marsland, 563
Dunmore v Ontario (Attorney General), 534

EC – Customs Matters, 415
Eckhardt v European Organization for the Safety of Air Navigation (Eurocontrol), 255, n 63
Elfarnawani v International Olympic Committee, 568
États-Unis d'Amérique – Certaines prescriptions en matière d'étiquetage indiquant le pays d'origine, 315-29
Ethyl Corporation c Canada, 356
Europemballage Corporation and Continental Can Company v Commission, 285
Export Packers Co Ltd v SPI International Transportation, 567
Ezokola v Canada (Minister of Citizenship and Immigration), 543-46

FAO v INPDAI, 255, 64
Fastwing Investment Holdings Ltd c Bombardier Inc, 579
Fewer v Ellis, 561, 565-67
Fisheries (United Kingdom v Norway), 193
Foote v Foote Estate, 575, 588-90, 594
Frontier Dispute (Benin v Niger), 179, n 4, 187, 197, 201, 207
Frontier Dispute (Burkina Faso v Republic of Mali), 196

The Gap Inc v G.A.P. Adventures Inc, 581-82
Gavrila v Canada (Justice), 531, n 53
General Motors du Canada Ltée c 178018 Canada Inc, 580-81
Grand River Enterprises et al c United States, 354
Grewal v Kaur, 594-95

Haberman v Haberman, 555-58
Health Services and Support — Facilities Subsector Bargaining Association v British Columbia, 535
Honduras Borders (Guatemala v Honduras), 197, n 94

India – Additional Import Duties, 412

International Status of South-West Africa, 18
Iran-United States Claims Tribunal v AS, 255, n 63
Ironrod Investments Inc v Enquest Energy Services Corp, 574
Island of Palmas Case (Netherlands v United States of America), 194, n 73

Jafarzadehahmadsargoorabi v Sabet, 564-65
Jennings v Haas, 567

Kaur v Guraya, 576
Khadr v Canada (Prime Minister), 519-23
Kuwait Airways Corporation c République d'Irak et Bombardier Aéronautique, 523-27

LaGrand (Germany v United States of America), 206
Land and Maritime Boundary between Cameroon and Nigeria (Cameroon v Nigeria: Equatorial Guinea intervening), 186, 189, 192-193, 198, 204-5, 207, 209-10
Land, Island and Maritime Frontier Dispute (El Salvador v Honduras), 178, n 3, 181, n 15
Laxton v Jurem Anstalt, 559-61
Lebrasseur c Hoffmann-La Roche Ltée, 578-79
Legal Status of Eastern Greenland, 179, n 5
Legality of the Threat or Use of Nuclear Weapons, 232
Lemeiguran v Attorney General, 173
Lisbon Decision, 273, n 27
Loewen Group, Inc. and Raymond L Loewen c United States, 367, n 72

Maastricht Decision, 273, n 26
Mandat d'arrêt du 11 avril 2000 (République démocratique du Congo c Belgique), 252, n 44
Maritime Delimitation and Territorial Questions between Qatar and Bahrain, 179, 207, 210
Marzara v Marzara, 595-96
Merrill & Ring Forestry L.P. c Canada, 354
Methanex Corporation c United States, 367, n 72
Microcell Communications Inc v Frey, 569
The Minquiers and Ecrehos Case (France v United Kingdom), 181, n 15, 196, n 83
Moldovan v Republic Western Insurance Co, 590-91
Moore v Vancouver Port Authority, 567
Mowery v 2063010 Ontario Inc, 584
Muscutt v Courcelles, 561, n 4

Németh v Canada (Justice), 527-32, 542
Nicolas (Succession de), 597-98
Northwest Atlantic Fisheries Organization v Amaratunga, 546-49
Nova Scotia Power Incorporated (NSPI) c Venezuela, 355, n 9
NS v Secretary of State for the Home Department, C-411/10; ME v Refugee Applications Commissioner, 274, n 31

Obégi Chemicals LLC v Kilani, 563-64
Ontario (Attorney General) v Fraser, 534-38
Opinion 1/08 – Opinion Pursuant to Article 300(6) EC – General Agreement on Trade in Services (GATS), 278, n 46

Paulsson v Cooper, 566
Perfect 10 Inc v Google Inc, 568-69
Piedra v Copper Mesa Mining Corp, 65, n 64 and n 65
Presbyterian Church of Sudan v Talisman Energy Inc, 64, n 63
Prosecutor v Anto Furundzija, 252, n 57
Provincial Gov't of Marinduque v Placer Dome Inc, 64, n 63
Pushpanathan c Canada, 372

R v Khawaja, 532-34, 533, n 55
R v Ménard, 41, n 194
R v Regan, 540, n 77
Ramirez v Canada (Minister of Employment and Immigration), 545
Recherches Internationales Québec v Cambior Inc, 58, n 29
Reference re Criminal Code of Canada, 553-55
Reparation for Injuries Suffered in the Service of the United Nations, 275-76
République de Corée – Mesures visant l'importation de viande bovine et de

produits à base de viande bovine en provenance du Canada, 329-30
Riley v Wildhaber, 576

Sahibalzubaidi v Bahjar, 575, 594
Sangi v Sangi, 588, 590, 596
Santa Clara County v Southern Pacific Railroad Co, 600
Seidel v Telus Communications Inc, 571-72
SHN Grundstuecksverwaltungsgesellschaft mbH v Hanne, 583-84
Sovereignty over Pedra Branca/Pulau Batu Puteh, Middle Rocks and South Ledge (Malaysia/Singapore), 181, n 15, 182, 188, 191-92, 194, 202-4, 207-8
Sovereignty over Pulau Ligitan and Pulau Sipadan (Indonesia/Malaysia), 183-84, 191-92, 197-99, 203, 207-8
St Microelectronics inc c Matrox Graphics inc, 581, n 46
Stewart v Stewart, 576-77
Stichting Greenpeace Nederland v Euratom, 255, n 63
Stonecroft Resources inc c Marble Point Energy Ltd, 587-88
Subway Franchise Systems of Canada Ltd v Laich, 586
Sun v Guilfoile, 575-76

Territorial and Maritime Dispute (Nicaragua v Colombia), 201
Territorial and Maritime Dispute between Nicaragua and Honduras in the Caribbean Sea, 179, n 5, 181, 184, 197, 201-2, 204, 207
Title v Canadian Asset Based Lending Enterprise (CABLE) Inc, 573-74
Torudag v British Columbia (Securities Commission), 574
Treat America Ltd. v Nestlé Canada Inc, 582
Tucows.com Co v Lojas Renner S.A., 561-62
Turner c Secretary General of the United Nations, 244, n 4
Turon v Abbott Laboratories Ltd, 570

United Mexican States c Feldman Karpa, 370, n 91
United Mexican States c Metalclad Corporation, 370, n 90, 373, n 105
United Mexican States v Cargill Inc, 549-53
United States – Anti-Dumping and Countervailing Duties (China), 416
United States – Certain Country of Origin Labelling (COOL) Requirements, 404-5
United States – Measures Concerning the Importation, Marketing and Sale of Tuna and Tuna Products, 403
The United States of America v Canada, 306, n 48, 307, n 49 and n 51
United States of America v Khadr, 538-41

Van Breda v Village Resorts Ltd, 561, n 4, 562-63, 566-67

Wielgomas v Anglocom Inc, 567
Wolfe v Pickar, 559, 569, 584-85
World Fuel Services Corp v Nordems (The), 591-92